CQ Press, an imprint of SAGE, is the leading publisher of books, periodicals, and electronic products on American government and international affairs. CQ Press consistently ranks among the top commercial publishers in terms of quality, as evidenced by the numerous awards its products have won over the years. CQ Press owes its existence to Nelson Poynter, former publisher of the *St. Petersburg Times,* and his wife Henrietta, with whom he founded Congressional Quarterly in 1945. Poynter established CQ with the mission of promoting democracy through education and in 1975 founded the Modern Media Institute, renamed The Poynter Institute for Media Studies after his death. The Poynter Institute (*www.poynter.org*) is a nonprofit organization dedicated to training journalists and media leaders.

In 2008, CQ Press was acquired by SAGE, a leading international publisher of journals, books, and electronic media for academic, educational, and professional markets. Since 1965, SAGE has helped inform and educate a global community of scholars, practitioners, researchers, and students spanning a wide range of subject areas, including business, humanities, social sciences, and science, technology, and medicine. A privately owned corporation, SAGE has offices in Los Angeles, London, New Delhi, and Singapore, in addition to the Washington DC office of CQ Press.

SECOND EDITION

CONTROVERSIES
IN
GLOBALIZATION

CONTENDING APPROACHES
TO INTERNATIONAL RELATIONS

Edited by

Peter M. Haas
University of Massachusetts Amherst

John A. Hird
University of Massachusetts Amherst

Los Angeles | London | New Delhi
Singapore | Washington DC

Los Angeles | London | New Delhi
Singapore | Washington DC

FOR INFORMATION:

CQ Press

An Imprint of SAGE Publications, Inc.

2455 Teller Road

Thousand Oaks, California 91320

E-mail: order@sagepub.com

SAGE Publications Ltd.

1 Oliver's Yard

55 City Road

London EC1Y 1SP

United Kingdom

SAGE Publications India Pvt. Ltd.

B 1/I 1 Mohan Cooperative Industrial Area

Mathura Road, New Delhi 110 044

India

SAGE Publications Asia-Pacific Pte. Ltd.

3 Church Street

#10-04 Samsung Hub

Singapore 049483

Acquisitions Editor: Elise Frasier

Associate Editor: Nancy Loh

Production Editor: Laureen Gleason

Copy Editor: Erin Livingston

Typesetter: C&M Digitals (P) Ltd.

Proofreader: Jen Grubba

Indexer: Will Ragsdale

Cover Designer: Glenn Vogel

Marketing Manager: Jonathan Mason

Permissions Editor: Adele Hutchinson

Printed in the United States of America

Library of Congress Cataloging-in-Publication Data

Controversies in globalization : contending approaches to international relations / edited by Peter M. Haas, John A. Hird, University of Massachusetts, Amherst.—Second edition.

page cm

Includes bibliographical references and index.

ISBN 978-1-60871-795-8 (pbk. : alk. paper)

1. Globalization. I. Haas, Peter M. II. Hird, John A.
JZ1318.C6577 2013
327—dc23   2012037214

This book is printed on acid-free paper.

SUSTAINABLE FORESTRY INITIATIVE

Certified Chain of Custody
Promoting Sustainable Forestry
www.sfiprogram.org
SFI-01268

SFI label applies to text stock

12 13 14 15 16 10 9 8 7 6 5 4 3 2 1

CONTENTS

CONTRIBUTORS

ABOUT THE EDITORS

Peter M. Haas is Professor of Political Science at the University of Massachusetts Amherst. He is coeditor of the MIT Press series on *Politics, Science, and the Environment*. Haas's books include *International Environmental Governance* (2008); *Global Environmental Governance* (with Gus Speth, 2006); *Emerging Forces in Environmental Governance* (with Norichika Kanie, 2004); *The International Environment in the New Global Economy* (2003); *Knowledge, Power, and International Policy Coordination* (1997); *Institutions for the Earth* (with Robert O. Keohane and Marc A. Levy, 1993); and *Saving the Mediterranean* (1990).

John A. Hird is Professor of Political Science and Public Policy and Senior Associate Dean in the College of Social and Behavioral Sciences at the University of Massachusetts Amherst. His areas of interest and expertise include policy advising, regulatory policy, the use of science and technical knowledge in policymaking, and policy analysis. Prior to coming to Amherst, he served at the Brookings Institution, Resources for the Future, and the President's Council of Economic Advisers. His books include *Power, Knowledge, and Politics: Policy Analysis in the States; Controversies in American Public Policy;* and *Superfund: The Political Economy of Environmental Risk;* and he has published articles in the *American Political Science Review, Journal of Policy Analysis and Management, Yale Journal on Regulation, Social Science Quarterly,* and other professional journals

ABOUT THE CONTRIBUTORS

Kenneth Anderson is professor of law at Washington College of Law, American University, and a fellow of the Hoover Institution at Stanford University. He was formerly general counsel to the Open Society Institute and was founding director of the Human Rights Watch Arms Division. He has written widely in scholarly and policy journals, is a member of the editorial board of the *Journal of Terrorism and Political Violence,* and was legal editor of *Crimes of War* (1999).

Kwame Anthony Appiah is Laurance S. Rockefeller University Professor of Philosophy at the Center for Human Values at Princeton University. His books include two monographs in the philosophy of language as well as *In My Father's*

House: Africa in the Philosophy of Culture (1992), *Color Conscious: The Political Morality of Race* (with Amy Gutmann, 1996), and *Cosmopolitanism: Ethics in a World of Strangers* (2006). He has also edited or coedited many books, including *Africana: The Encyclopedia of the African and African-American Experience* (with Henry Louis Gates Jr., 1996). His most recent book is *The Honor Code: How Moral Revolutions Happen* (2011).

George B. N. Ayittey, a native of Ghana, is Distinguished Economist at American University and president of the Free Africa Foundation. He was nominated for the Africa Prize for Leadership by *The Times of London*; was a National Fellow at the Hoover Institution, Stanford University; and was a Bradley Scholar at the Heritage Foundation. In 1993, he started the Free Africa Foundation to serve as a catalyst for reform in Africa. An internationally renowned authority on Africa, Ayittey has written several books, including *Africa Betrayed* (1992), which won the H.L. Mencken Award for "Best Book for 1992." His latest book is *Defeating Dictators: Fighting Tyranny in Africa and Around the World* (2011). A frequent contributor to the *Wall Street Journal* and the *Los Angeles Times,* he has written numerous book chapters and articles on Africa. He has also appeared on several radio talk shows and television programs and has testified before many U.S. congressional committees.

Doug Bandow is a senior fellow at the Cato Institute and a former special assistant to President Ronald Reagan. He writes a weekly column for *Forbes* online and has been widely published in such periodicals as *Foreign Policy, Orbis, National Interest, Time, Newsweek,* and *Fortune* as well as leading newspapers including *The New York Times,* the *Wall Street Journal,* and *Washington Post.* He has written several books, including *Foreign Follies: America's New Global Empire* (Xulon Press), *Tripwire: Korea and U.S. Foreign Policy in a Changed World* (Cato Institute), and *The Politics of Plunder: Misgovernment in Washington* (Transaction). He received his BS in economics from Florida State University in 1976 and his JD from Stanford University in 1979.

Jagdish Bhagwati is a university professor at Columbia University and a senior fellow in International Economics at the Council on Foreign Relations. He has been economic policy adviser to Arthur Dunkel, director general of GATT (1991–1993), special adviser to the UN on globalization, and external adviser to the World Trade Organization (WTO). He has served on the Expert Group appointed by the Director General of the WTO on the Future of the WTO and on the Advisory Committee to Secretary-General Kofi Annan on the New Economic Partnership for African Development (NEPAD) process in Africa; he was also a member of the Eminent Persons Group under the chairmanship of President Fernando Henrique Cardoso on the future of UNCTAD. Five volumes of his scientific writings and two of his public policy essays have been published by MIT Press. The recipient of six festschrifts in his honor, he has also received several prizes and honorary degrees, including awards from the governments of India (Padma Vibhushan) and Japan (Order of the Rising Sun, Gold and Silver Star). Professor Bhagwati's latest book, *In Defense of Globalization*, was published by Oxford University Press in 2004 to worldwide acclaim.

Nancy Birdsall is the founding president of the Center for Global Development. Previously, she served for three years as senior associate and director of the Economic Reform Project at the Carnegie Endowment for International Peace, where her work focused on issues of globalization and inequality as well as on the reform of the international financial institutions. From 1993 to 1998, Birdsall was executive vice president of the Inter-American Development Bank. Prior to that, she spent fourteen years in research, policy, and management positions at the World Bank, most recently as director of the Policy Research Department. Birdsall is the author, coauthor, or editor of more than a dozen books and over 100 articles in scholarly journals and monographs published in English and Spanish. Shorter pieces of her writing have appeared in dozens of U.S. and Latin American newspapers and periodicals. She holds a PhD in economics from Yale University.

Isobel Coleman is senior fellow for U.S. foreign policy at the Council on Foreign Relations and director of its Women and Foreign Policy program. Her areas of expertise include economic and political development in the Middle East, regional gender issues, educational reform, and microfinance. In 2006, she coauthored (with A. Lawrence Chickering, P. Edward Haley, and Emily Vargas-Baron) *Strategic Foreign Assistance: Civil Society in International Security.* Her book, *Paradise beneath Her Feet: Women and Reform in the Middle East,* was published in 2009. Prior to joining the Council, Coleman was CEO of a health care services company and a partner with McKinsey & Company in New York. She was formerly a research fellow at the Brookings Institution and an adjunct professor at American University, where she taught political economy. A Marshall Scholar, she holds a DPhil and an MPhil in international relations from Oxford University and a BA in public policy and East Asian studies from Princeton University.

John F. Copper is the Stanley J. Buckman Distinguished Professor of International Studies (Emeritus) at Rhodes College in Memphis, Tennessee.

He is the author of more than twenty-five books on China, Taiwan, and Asian Affairs. Professor Copper's most recent books include *Taiwan: Nation-State or Province?* (sixth edition, 2012); *The KMT Returns to Power: Elections in Taiwan 2008 to 2012* (2012); *Taiwan's Democracy on Trial: Political Change During the Chen Shui-bian Era and Beyond* (2010); *The A to Z of Taiwan (Republic of China)* (2010); and *Playing with Fire: The Looming War with China over Taiwan* (2006). One of Professor Copper's early books, *China's Global Role*, won the Clarence Day Award for Outstanding Research. In 1997, Professor Copper was recipient of the International Communications Award.

David Dollar works for the U.S. Treasury Department. Previously, he was World Bank country director for China and Mongolia, based in Beijing. He speaks and writes frequently on economic, environmental, and social issues in China. Prior to moving to China, Dollar spent eight years in the research department of the World Bank. He was the World Bank country economist for Vietnam from 1989 to 1995, a period of intense reform and structural adjustment. Before joining the Bank, Dollar taught in the economics department at University of California, Los Angeles (UCLA) and spent the spring semester of 1986 on a Ford Foundation program teaching economics at the Chinese Academy of Social Sciences in Beijing. He has a PhD in economics from New York University and a BA in Chinese language and history from Dartmouth College. He has published a wide range of studies on issues of globalization, trade and growth, investment climate, and growth and poverty.

Jack Donnelly is the Andrew Mellon Professor at the Joseph Korbel School of International Studies, University of Denver. The author of three books and over sixty articles and book chapters on the theory and practice of human rights, including *Universal Human Rights in Theory and Practice* (3rd ed., 2012), he is best known for his work on the concept of human rights, cultural relativism, development and human rights, international human rights regimes, and human rights and foreign policy. He has also published in the area of international relations theory, including *Realism and International Relations* (2000). He is currently working on two major projects: a book on politics in Homeric Greece—a prelude to a planned study of ancient Greek international society—and a series of articles leading to a book on rethinking the nature of structural theory in international relations.

Charles Duelfer is special advisor to the CEO of Omnis, Inc. He was the special advisor to the Director of Central Intelligence for Iraq weapons of mass destruction (WMD). He led the Iraq Survey Group (ISG) investigation in Iraq, which conducted the investigation of Iraq's WMD programs. The ISG was a unique intelligence organization of over 1,600 military and civilian staff that investigated Iraq WMD programs. It used all possible collection and analytic capabilities in a hostile environment. The Duelfer Report (2004) is the definitive work on the relationship of the Saddam Regime to WMD. Previously, Duelfer was the Deputy Executive Chairman of the UN Special Commission on Iraq (UNSCOM) from 1993 until its termination in 2000. For the last several months of its existence, he was the acting chairman. Duelfer also served in the Political-Military Bureau of the State Department for several years in a variety of capacities, including directing regional security programs in Africa (including Somalia, Sudan, and Chad), Latin America, and the Middle East. He also participated in the policy development for nuclear weapons and arms control subjects. From 2006 to 2008, Duelfer was chairman and CEO of Transformational Space Corporation, a small entrepreneurial company developing a launch system for transportation to low earth orbit. He is the author of numerous articles on security and intelligence and the book *Hide and Seek: The Search for Truth in Iraq* (Public Affairs Books, 2009).

Christopher Flavin is president of the Worldwatch Institute, an international research organization that focuses on innovative solutions to global environmental problems. Flavin is a leading voice on the potential for new energy options and strategies to replace fossil fuels, thereby increasing energy security and avoiding dangerous climate change. He is coauthor of three books on energy, including *Power Surge: Guide to the Coming Energy Revolution* (with Nicholas Lenssen, 1994), which anticipated many of the changes now underway in world energy markets. Flavin is a founding member of the board of directors of the Business Council for Sustainable Energy and serves as a board member of the Climate Institute. He is on the advisory boards of the American Council on Renewable Energy and the Environmental and Energy Study Institute. He is also a member of the Greentech Innovation Network, an initiative of the venture capital firm, Kleiner Perkins Caufield & Byers.

Francis Fukuyama is a senior fellow at the Center on Democracy, Development, and the Rule of Law at Stanford University. He is also chairman of the editorial board of *The American Interest*. His book, *The End of History and the Last Man* (1992), has appeared in over twenty foreign editions and made the best-seller lists in the United States, France, Japan, and Chile; it has been awarded the *Los Angeles Times*'s Book Critics Award in the Current Interest category as well as the Premio Capri for the Italian edition. Fukuyama is the author of several other books, including *State-Building: Governance and World Order in the 21st Century* (2004), *America at the Crossroads: Democracy, Power, and the Neoconservative Legacy* (2006), and *Falling Behind: Explaining the Development Gap between Latin America and the United States* (2008).

Marlies Glasius is a lecturer in international relations at the School for Social and Behavioral Sciences at the University of Amsterdam and a visiting fellow at the Centre for the Study of Global Governance, London School of Economics and Political Science. She is the author of *The International Criminal Court: A Global Civil Society Achievement* (2006) and a founding editor of the *Global Civil Society Yearbook.*

Joshua S. Goldstein is Professor Emeritus of International Relations at American University and Research Scholar at the University of Massachusetts Amherst. He has a PhD from MIT (1986) and a BA from Stanford (1981). Goldstein is an interdisciplinary scholar of war whose most recent book is *Winning the War on War: The Decline of Armed Conflict Worldwide* (Penguin, 2011). His other books include the textbook *International Relations* (with Jon C. Pevehouse); the International Studies Association's "Book of the Decade" *War and Gender: How Gender Shapes the War System and Vice Versa* (Cambridge, 2001); *The Real Price of War* (NYU, 2004); *Three-Way Street: Strategic Reciprocity in World Politics* (Chicago, 1990; with John R. Freeman); and *Long Cycles: Prosperity and War in the Modern Age* (Yale, 1988). Goldstein has published articles in *The American Political Science Review, Journal of Conflict Resolution,* and *International Studies Quarterly,* among others, and op-ed pieces in *The New York Times* and elsewhere. Goldstein has won a MacArthur Foundation Individual Research and Writing Grant, the International Studies Association's Karl Deutsch Award for research, and the American Political Science Association's Victoria Schuck Award, among others.

Marcia E. Greenberg is an independent gender mainstreaming consultant, and a former adjunct professor of law at the Cornell Law School, where she taught courses on international perspectives on law and social change as well as international women's rights. She received her JD from Northwestern University School of Law and a Master's of Law and Diplomacy from the Fletcher School of Law and Diplomacy at Tufts University. Her law-related work has included litigation on labor and employment cases and human rights work for the Reebok Corporation and the Robert F. Kennedy Center for Human Rights. For more than a decade, she has focused on gender mainstreaming in relation to democracy programs, post-conflict reconstruction, community development, youth development, and food security. She has worked with women's groups in Eastern Europe on the five-year review of the Beijing Platform for Action, undertaken gender assessments of U.S. programs in Eastern Europe and Africa, and evaluated gender mainstreaming for the United Nations Development Programme and the World Food Programme.

Mark Heywood is executive director of the AIDS Law Project (ALP) and an executive member of the Treatment Action Campaign (TAC); he has worked for the ALP since 1994 and was one of the founders of the TAC. He is an editor of *HIV/AIDS and the Law: Resource Manual* (3rd ed., 2003) as well as a coeditor of *Health and Democracy: A Guide to Health, Law and Policy in Post-Apartheid South Africa* (2007) and *The National Health Act, a Guide* (2008). He has published more than 100 articles on legal, ethical, and human rights questions linked to HIV/AIDS and health.

James F. Hollifield is professor and director of the Tower Center for Political Studies at Southern Methodist University. He is a member of the Council on Foreign Relations; has worked as a consultant on trade, migration, and development for the UN, the World Bank, and OECD; and has published widely on these issues, including *Immigrants, Markets, and States* (1992), *L'immigration et l'État Nation* (1997), *Controlling Immigration* (2nd ed., 2004), *Migration Theory: Talking across Disciplines* (2nd ed., 2008), and *International Political Economy: History, Theory, and Policy* (forthcoming).

Philip I. Levy teaches at Columbia University School of International and Public Affairs. His research focuses on international trade policy, political economy, economic development, and international finance. Levy serves as resident scholar at the American Enterprise Institute. He previously handled international economic issues for the U.S. Secretary of State's policy planning staff (2005–2006) and served as senior economist for trade for the President's Council of Economic Advisers (2003–2005). Prior to that, Levy served on the economics faculty at Yale University, where he was a member of the Economic Growth Center. He also served one year as academic director of the Yale Center for the Study of Globalization. Levy received a PhD in economics from Stanford University and an AB in economics from the University of Michigan in Ann Arbor. Levy's scholarly work has appeared in journals such as the *American Economic Review*, the *Journal of International Economics*, and *Economic Journal*. He is a regular contributor to *Foreign Policy* and has published in the *Wall Street Journal, Investor's Business Daily*, and *American.com*, among other outlets.

Michael Lynch is president of Strategic Energy and Economic Research. He has combined Bachelor of Science and master's degrees in political science from the Massachusetts Institute of Technology (MIT), and he has performed a variety of studies related to international energy matters, including forecasting of the world oil market, energy and security, and corporate strategy in the energy industries as well as analysis of oil and gas supply. He is a former Chief Energy Economist at DRI-WEFA, Inc., a leading economic consulting firm, and a past-president and senior fellow of the United States Association for Energy Economics. His publications have appeared in eight languages, and he serves on several editorial boards, including those of the journals *Energy Policy* and *Geopolitics of Energy*.

Edward D. Mansfield is Hum Rosen Professor of Political Science and director of the Christopher H. Browne Center for International Politics at the University of Pennsylvania. His research focuses on international security and international political economy. He is the author of *Power, Trade, and War* (1994) and the coauthor of *Electing to Fight: Why Emerging Democracies Go to War* (with Jack Snyder, 2005). He has edited ten books and has published over seventy articles in various journals and books. The recipient of the 2000 Karl W. Deutsch Award in International Relations and Peace Research, Mansfield has been a National Fellow at the Hoover Institution. He is coeditor of the University of Michigan Press Series on international political economy and an associate editor of the journal *International Organization*.

Philip Martin is a labor economist in the Department of Agricultural and Resource Economics at the University of California, Davis (UCD). After graduating from the University of Wisconsin–Madison, he worked at the Brookings Institution and the White House on labor and immigration issues. He has worked for the World Bank, IMF, and UN agencies such as the ILO and UNDP in countries around the world, and he is the author of numerous articles and books on labor and immigration issues. Martin's research focuses on farm labor and rural poverty, labor migration and economic development, and immigration policy and guest worker issues; he has testified before Congress and state and local agencies numerous times on these issues. Martin is the editor of *Migration News* and *Rural Migration News,* and he received UCD's Distinguished Public Service award in 1994.

Michael McFaul is a U.S. Ambassador to Russia. He was senior director for Russian affairs at the National Security Council since 2009. Previously, he served as the director of the Center on Democracy, Development, and Rule of Law at

Freeman Spogli Institute for International Studies at Stanford University and as the Peter and Helen Bing Senior Fellow at the Hoover Institution, where he codirected the Iran Democracy Project. He is the author of several books and monographs, most recently, *Advancing Democracy Abroad: Why We Should and How We Can* (2009). McFaul's current research interests include democracy promotion, comparative democratization, and the relationship between political and economic reform in the postcommunist world.

Scott McKenzie received his Bachelor of Arts degree in environmental studies, philosophy, and American studies from the University of Kansas in 2004 and a Juris Doctorate from the University of Iowa in 2011. Currently, McKenzie serves as fellow at the World Affairs Council in New Orleans and is a blogger for *Global Policy*. His research and writing focuses on international environmental law. He is interested in questions of global resource use, particularly water, in Africa and the Middle East. His work often focuses on the intersection of human rights and economic development. Before law school, McKenzie worked as an environmental education development agent for the United States Peace Corps in Morocco. He lived in a small village and worked with community groups on projects, creating the town's first municipal garbage program. He also worked at the Cairo office of the Near East Foundation, where he researched the impacts of climate change on the Nile Delta.

John Mueller holds the Woody Hayes Chair of National Security Studies, Mershon Center and is professor of political science at Ohio State University, where he teaches courses in international relations. His most recent book is *Terror, Security and Money: Balancing the Risks, Benefits and Costs of Homeland Security* (2011). Among his other books are *Overblown* (2006), *The Remnants of War* (2004), *Retreat from Doomsday* (1996), and *War, Presidents and Public Opinion* (1973).

Karl T. Muth is a lecturer in economics and public policy at Northwestern University. While a postgraduate research student at the London School of Economics and Political Science, he lived in East Africa for extended periods on fieldwork. Muth also holds a graduate degree in law and a master's degree with a concentration in economics, the latter from the University of Chicago. His positions on issues ranging from financial regulation to urban gentrification have been featured in academic journals and mainstream media, including *The Journal of International Business and Law, The Journal of Private Equity,* and *The Oprah Winfrey Show*. Muth is particularly interested in the economic aspects of risk, negotiation, privatization, and altruism; he is a co-author of a forthcoming book on charity and philanthropy.

Mead Over is a senior fellow at the Center for Global Development, researching economics of efficient, effective, and cost-effective health interventions in developing countries. His most recent book is *Achieving an AIDS Transition: Preventing Infections to Sustain Treatment* (2011), in which he offers options for donors, recipients, activists and other participants in the fight against HIV to reverse the trend in the epidemic through better prevention. His previous publications include *The Economics of Effective AIDS Treatment: Evaluating Policy Options for Thailand* (2006). In addition to his numerous research projects at the Center, Over currently serves as a member of PEPFAR's (President's Emergency Plan for AIDS Relief) Scientific Advisory Board and as a member of the Steering Committee of the HIV/AIDS modeling consortium funded by the Bill & Melinda Gates Foundation.

Reid Pauly is a social science research assistant at the Center for International Security and Cooperation at Stanford University. He graduated magna cum laude from Cornell University in 2010, with a BA in history and government. His thesis, "Containing the Atom: Paul Nitze and the Tradition of Non-Use of Nuclear Weapons," was awarded the Janice N. and Milton J. Esman Prize for Outstanding Undergraduate Scholarship at Cornell and also won prizes from the Center for Strategic and International Studies and the Virginia Military Institute.

Brent Ranalli practices environmental policy consulting at The Cadmus Group, Inc., an employee-owned firm, and is a Prince Edward Senior Fellow with the MIT International Development Initiative. Ranalli co-edits *Environment: An Interdisciplinary Anthology* for Yale University Press, and is the author of numerous scholarly and popular articles. Ranalli holds a BA in the history of science from Harvard University and a MSc in environmental science and policy from the Central European University.

Jeffrey D. Sachs is director of the Earth Institute, Quetelet Professor of Sustainable Development, and professor of health policy and management at the Earth Institute at Columbia University. He is also special advisor to UN Secretary-General Ban Ki-moon. From 2002 to 2006, he was director of the UN Millennium Project and special advisor to UN Secretary-General Kofi Annan on the Millennium Development Goals. Sachs is also president and cofounder of Millennium Promise Alliance, a nonprofit organization aimed at ending extreme global poverty. For more than twenty years, Sachs has been in the forefront of the challenges of economic development, poverty alleviation, and enlightened globalization, promoting policies to help all parts of the world to benefit from expanding economic opportunities and well-being. He is the author of hundreds of scholarly articles and many books, including the *New York Times* best-sellers *Common Wealth: Economics for a Crowded Planet* (2008) and *The End of Poverty* (2005).

Scott D. Sagan is the Caroline S.G. Munro Professor of Political Science at Stanford University, and a Senior Fellow at the Center for International Security and Cooperation and the Freeman Spogli Institute. He is also the co-chair of the American Academy of Arts and Sciences' Global Nuclear Future Initiative. He has served as a special assistant to the director of the Organization of the Joint Chiefs of Staff in the Pentagon and as a consultant to the office of the Secretary of Defense, the National Intelligence Council, Sandia National Laboratory, and Los Alamos National Laboratory. He is the author of *Moving Targets: Nuclear Strategy and National Security* (1989), *The Limits of Safety: Organizations, Accidents, and Nuclear Weapons* (1993), and with co-author Kenneth N. Waltz, *The Spread of Nuclear Weapons: An Enduring Debate* (2012).

Todd S. Sechser is assistant professor of politics at the University of Virginia. His publications include articles about nuclear weapons safety, civil–military relations, and European–American relations, and he is currently writing a book about the effectiveness of coercive threats. Sechser holds a PhD in political science from Stanford University and a BA in economics, political science, and international relations from Drake University.

Jack Snyder is the Robert and Renée Belfer Professor of International Relations in the political science department and the Saltzman Institute of War and Peace Studies at Columbia University. His books include *Electing to Fight: Why Emerging Democracies Go to War* (with Edward D. Mansfield, 2005); *From Voting to Violence: Democratization and Nationalist Conflict* (2000); and *Myths of Empire: Domestic Politics and International Ambition* (1991). His articles have appeared in *Foreign Affairs, Foreign Policy,* and academic journals. He is a fellow of the American Academy of Arts and Sciences.

Elsa Stamatopoulou is chief of the Secretariat of the UN Permanent Forum on Indigenous Issues. She has worked for more than twenty years in the human rights field at the UN, publishing and lecturing extensively. In recent years, a major focus of her efforts has been on integrating indigenous peoples' issues and human rights in development and peace processes as well as development with culture. She is the founder and member of human rights and other nongovernmental organizations (NGOs) and has been recognized by various awards. She obtained her law degree from the University of Athens Law School and entered the Athens Bar Association. She completed her master's studies in the administration of criminal justice at Northeastern University in Boston and her doctoral studies in political science with specialization in international law at the University Institute of Graduate International Studies, University of Geneva as well as additional graduate training at the University of Vienna. In 2007, she published *Cultural Rights in International Law.*

Samuel Thernstrom is senior climate policy advisor to the Clean Air Task Force (CATF). Prior to coming to CATF, Thernstrom was a resident fellow at the American Enterprise Institute (AEI) for Public Policy in Washington, DC, where he served as the codirector of a program exploring the policy implications of geoengineering. Previously, Thernstrom was director of communications for the White House Council on Environmental Quality, a speechwriter for New York governor George E. Pataki, a press secretary for the New York State Department of Environmental Conservation, and chief speechwriter at the U.S. Department of Labor. Thernstrom is a frequent guest on radio and television, commenting on climate policy for National Public Radio, BBC News, ABC News, CNN, Fox News, and *The News Hour with Jim Lehrer* on PBS. He was educated at Harvard University.

Kate Vyborny was a program coordinator for Nancy Birdsall, president of the Center for Global Development. She was previously a junior fellow for trade, equity, and development at the Carnegie Endowment for International Peace. She is currently a Rhodes Scholar and a graduate student in economics at the University of Oxford.

Robert H. Wade is professor of political economy at the London School of Economics and Political Science and winner of the Leontief Prize in Economics for 2008. His research and writing have taken him from Italy to South Korea (*Irrigation and Agricultural Politics in South Korea,* 1982), India (*Village Republics,* 1988, 2007), East Asia more generally (*Governing the Market,* 1990, 2004), and the World Bank ("Greening the Bank," in *The World Bank,* vol. 2, ed. D. Kapur et al., 1997) as he examines the world economy and global governance ("Globalization, Growth, Poverty, Inequality, Resentment and Imperialism," in *Global Political Economy,* ed. J. Ravenhill, 2008) and financial crises ("Financial Regime Change?" *New Left Review,* September–October 2008).

L. Alan Winters is professor of economics at the University of Sussex. He is a research fellow and former program director of the Centre for Economic Policy

Research in London and fellow of the Institute for the Study of Labor in Munich. From 2004 to 2007, he was director of the Development Research Group of the World Bank, where he had previously been division chief and research manager (1994–1999) and economist (1983–1985). He has been editor of the *World Bank Economic Review* and associate editor of the *Economic Journal*, and he is currently editor of *The World Trade Review*. He has also advised, inter alia, the Organization for Economic Cooperation and Development, the U.K. Department for International Development, the Commonwealth Secretariat, the European Commission, the European Parliament, the United Nations Conference on Trade and Development, the World Trade Organization, and the Inter-American Development Bank.

PREFACE

Globalization is variously viewed as the solution to national economic problems, the scourge of the developing world, the source of job dislocations and economic stratification in the wealthy West, the means to more interesting culture and food, the path to lower consumer prices, and just about anything else reflecting the increasingly international character of society, politics, and economics. It is said—theoretically and with a touch of hyperbole—that a butterfly's movements can bring about a hurricane half a world away. While this metaphor exaggerates the extent of life's global interconnections, it is clear that they are a prominent feature of the lives of the world's citizens and environment. How we understand, adapt, and act toward trends in globalization will condition the impacts they have on the world's human and natural environment. Because the term *globalization* is both vague and ubiquitous, it offers a convenient catchall for what we like and dislike about the past and future integration of our economies, politics, and cultures.

There are plenty of books on globalization available, and yet we believe that an important gap remains, because many fail to fully appreciate the various dimensions of and perspectives on the subject. This gap derives in part from the polemical nature of much that has been written about globalization and in part from the simplistic assertions and beliefs that too often prevail as a result. This book seeks to acknowledge that the most important issues involving globalization—whether they involve trade, security, the environment, the role of women in development, or a host of other crucial matters—are best understood and addressed by recognizing the different perspectives (or discourses) through which they are viewed. We seek to illuminate *some* of these perspectives here, and we hope that the recognition that reasonable people can and do disagree on important matters will spur our readers to seek additional views, both complementary and competing, than just those elucidated here.

It is no secret that many view globalization warily: a BBC worldwide poll showed that half of respondents believed that economic globalization and trade were growing too quickly, while only a third felt that such growth was moving too slowly. In **Group of 8 [G8]** countries, fully 57 percent said that globalization was moving too quickly. Nonetheless, according to the Pew Global Attitudes survey, vast majorities of the world's population believe that trade is beneficial, and even **multinational corporations** are generally viewed favorably. According to the Pew poll, free markets are widely accepted in much of the world, although Americans and Western Europeans are less receptive to globalization than they were five years ago, particularly in the United States, Italy, France, and Great Britain.

Interestingly, the generally supportive view of economic globalization does not translate to immigration, which many people worldwide believe should be restricted. For example, fully three-quarters of U.S. respondents—as well as 87 percent of Italians, 89 percent of South Africans, and large percentages elsewhere—support further restrictions and controls on immigration. Of forty-seven countries surveyed, in only three (South Korea, the Palestinian territories, and Japan) did a majority of the public favor more immigration, while majorities in all forty-seven had favorable views of international trade. (The United States had the least support for **free trade** among these countries, with just 59 percent.) Thus, even in polls conducted prior to the economic deterioration that became apparent in late 2008, the world's citizens clearly had mixed views on how far and in which directions globalization should go.

We hope that this book will be of interest to students as well as to a more general audience of readers who seek to expand their understanding of globalization by examining the opposing perspectives of scholars and practitioners engaged in thoughtful debate.

HOW THE BOOK IS ORGANIZED

This book is geared toward courses in international relations, world or global politics, and other topics that cover globalization more generally. The controversies format is intended to highlight important issues involved in contemporary globalization and to expose readers to the intellectual underpinning of the debates. Instructors should remind students that for each controversy, these are but two of the possible perspectives. Students should be encouraged to read further to understand other views and to begin to develop their own.

The book is organized around a series of seventeen issues that we believe are among the most important in the globalization debate. For each general topic, we provide a brief introductory overview and some frames of reference as well as a few discussion questions that are intended to stimulate dialogue in class. Each chapter then offers original articles crafted by some of the world's leading scholars in response to a question that highlights a specific issue. Through these articles, we seek to promote the recognition that debates about globalization are not simply about self-interest but involve the clash of values and ideas.

Students should remain aware of several points about this book's depiction of globalization. First, although each chapter's controversy is treated separately, there are important relationships between these controversies that instructors should explore and discuss in class. For example, what is the relationship between globalization's impacts on economic growth and democracy or on the role of women in society? Second, we have isolated seventeen topics that we believe are central to an understanding of globalization, but instructors and students may choose to concentrate instead on their interconnections—such as the relationship of immigration to national security or economic growth—as well as on other areas not covered in this volume. Finally, and perhaps most importantly, there are many other perspectives on globalization to be explored and developed. The two perspectives presented in each chapter here should be only the beginning of an exploration of alternative views that extends far beyond this book. The glossary at the end of the book defines many of the more technical terms and deciphers acronyms presented throughout.

ACKNOWLEDGMENTS

We are indebted to many for their help in developing this book. We would like to thank our families for indulging our curious pursuit of the meaning of globalization. This book emerged, in part, from the ongoing hiring initiative on contemporary political change in the University of Massachusetts Amherst, Department of Political Science, which is organized around cross-field themes: global forces; governance and institutions; and democracy, participation, and citizenship. We continue to benefit from the lively intellectual atmosphere in the department. We would like to thank the editors and staff at CQ Press, who have been a joy to work with, and in particular, Charisse Kiino, Elise Frasier, and Nancy Loh for helping us to bring this book to fruition. Laureen Gleason and Erin Livingston were everything we could ask for in helping to move the book through production. We received valuable feedback from Charli Carpenter (of University of Massachusetts Amherst), Craig Murphy (of Wellesley College), and seven reviewers enlisted by CQ Press: Abdallah Battah, Minnesota State University–Mankato; Iva Bozovic, University of Southern California; Alison Brysk, University of California, Santa Barbara; John Doces, Bucknell University; Andrea Haupt, Santa Barbara City College; Yi Edward Yang, James Madison University; and Jeremy Youde, University of Minnesota–Duluth. We also had superb research assistance along the way from Rachel Jackson and Sorin Dan. We would like to thank for their financial support the Dean of the College of Social and Behavioral Sciences as well as the Center for Public Policy and Administration at University of Massachusetts Amherst. Finally, the Dirty Truth in Northampton, Massachusetts, served as an excellent venue for hashing out many of the ideas in this volume, sustaining our efforts with great food and an outstanding beer selection that reflects one of the benefits of a globalized world.

UNDERSTANDING GLOBALIZATION

> We have witnessed three economic transformations in the past century. First came the Industrial Revolution, then the technology revolution, then our modern era of globalization.
>
> UN Secretary-General Ban Ki-moon,
> *Washington Post,* December 3, 2007

> Globalization is a reality, not a choice or a policy. But how we respond to it is a matter of choice and of policy.
>
> Richard N. Haass, director, Office of the Policy Planning Staff, "Remarks to the National Defense University," September 21, 2001

Globalization has become the political lodestone of contemporary international relations. Political positions and political identities are defined in light of their orientation to it. Yet definitions of globalization abound, and the consequences of globalization are deeply contested—as are the available techniques for altering the distribution of its costs and benefits. At the heart of globalization is an array of multiple transboundary forces and processes that reduce national control over what happens within national boundaries and enable a set of new political actors to project social, economic, and political influence over long distances. Globalization includes a host of problems or issues that do not respect national boundaries—they are, as some have written, "problems without passports." Since national governments remain the primary legal authorities at the international and national levels, this transnational impact represents a considerable challenge to governance and to the international political system.

It is no wonder that globalization is controversial. The term itself is subject to multiple interpretations as well as measurements, chronologies, and explanations. As a result, any fixed definition of globalization remains elusive, and the multiple definitions that exist tend to highlight whatever features its proponents (or opponents) want to emphasize. Contending understandings of international relations provide alternative interpretations of the consequences of globalization and, indeed, of the desirability and even the possibility of effectively guiding such an unwieldy set of global forces. The consequences of globalization are also significant. Just as Charles Lindblom defined politics as a matter of who gets what, when, how, and why, globalization forces influence the systematic distribution of who gets what, when, how, and why.

Groups that are inconvenienced by some set of social, cultural, economic, or political setbacks now have a vocabulary and a frame for assigning meaning and blame to their misfortune: globalization did it. Yet, because it is so widely contested a term, who and what one reads on globalization can color its meaning for those seeking to understand their own experiences and how to change them. *Globalization* may become a proxy for opposition to the Iraq War, for **xenophobia**, for worries about one's own job security, for fears of cultural **hegemony**, or for fears about the ecological health of the planet.

In order to frame the debate on this elusive topic, we review here, first, the core elements of globalization; next, the history of globalization; then, some contending perspectives on globalization; and, finally, the various implications or effects of globalization on citizens' lives and on the major political processes that influence citizens' lives worldwide. In this introduction, we focus on the sets of forces that characterize globalization rather than presuming the effects to which those forces may contribute or be associated, such as the end of space and spatial divisions, as meaningful categories in international politics (see Held and McGrew 1999; Scholte 2000; and Rosenau 2003). We do, however, discuss some of the possible effects of globalization itself, from alternative perspectives.

WHAT'S NEW ABOUT GLOBALIZATION?

Scholars dispute the origins of globalization. Some historians claim that aspects of globalization have been present always—or at least since the Industrial Revolution. International economic interdependence was high from the 1880s through World War I, during which period, proportions of national reliance on foreign sources of trade for markets, and capital markets for investment, were similar to current levels. Migration flows were significant—indeed, the American transcontinental railroads would not have been built without the cheap labor of Chinese immigrants.

So what is new about globalization? Observers in the late nineteenth and early twentieth centuries painted a similar picture, reflecting unprecedented volumes of international commerce—trade, financial exchanges—and flows of people. Indeed, the most extreme drops in the cost of transportation and communication occurred in the late nineteenth century. Pandemics were also global—the influenza epidemic of 1918 killed millions of people across Europe and the United States. Possibly, it was only the incomplete global nature of telecommunications that impaired our understanding of widespread health conditions in the developing world.

John Maynard Keynes wrote the following in 1919:

> The inhabitant of London could order by telephone, sipping his morning tea in bed, the various products of the whole earth, in such quantity as he

might see fit, and reasonably expect their early delivery upon his doorstep; he could at the same moment and by the same means adventure his wealth in the natural resources and new enterprises of any quarter of the world, and share, without exertion or even trouble, in their prospective fruits and advantages; or he could decide to couple the security of his fortunes with the good faith of the townspeople of any substantial municipality in any continent that fancy or information might recommend. He could secure forthwith, if he wished it, cheap and comfortable means of transit to any country or climate without passport or other formality, could dispatch his servant to the neighboring office of a bank for such supply of the precious metals as might seem convenient, and could proceed abroad to foreign quarters, without knowledge of their religion, language, or customs, being coined wealth [*sic*] upon his person, and would consider himself greatly aggrieved and much surprised at the least interference. But, most important of all, he regarded this state of affairs as normal, certain, and permanent, except in the direction of further improvement, and any deviation from it as aberrant, scandalous, and avoidable. (quoted in Frieden 2006, 28)

The possible effects of globalization during this early period were depicted in hyperbolic terms, similar to those employed in the contemporary era. Norman Angell argued that high levels of economic interdependence would lead to the end of war, because the cost of severing valued economic ties would simply be too great. As with many of the grandiloquent claims for the effects of globalization in the current era, these projections were proved painfully false by the outbreak of World Wars I and II.

Still, there are several new key developments in the current era of globalization. The spread of political actors—in numbers and types—is new. Foreign investment has shifted from portfolio to equity investment and, more recently, to global production lines. The increasingly universal acceptance of democratic and liberal values appears to be another distinguishing feature of our contemporary era of globalization. Environmental globalization is also increasingly important: global resource depredation and ecosystem collapse may be irreversible.

The most important aspect of contemporary globalization may be the pace of individual globalization processes—what we have amounts to a synchronicity of acceleration (Crutzen 2002; Schellnhuber and Crutzen et al. 2004). Whereas in the past, globalization was primarily economic and demographic, over the past forty years, the scope of global forces has increased to include environmental and political globalization. Although rates of technological change themselves may not have changed, the speed of globalization has accelerated, making the elapsed time between a decision taken in one part of the world and its effects elsewhere far shorter than it has been in the past.

With synchronicity has come a transformation in the nature of international relations. As the world has become more complex and uncertain, surprises such as the recent pace of climate change and the 2008 global financial meltdown are more likely to occur frequently. New forms of threats to national security have also received attention.

Thomas Pickering, a U.S. diplomat, identified three major foreign threats to U.S. security: financial crisis, accidental nuclear exchange, and environmental dangers. None are geographic, but all are global functional threats. Ernesto Zedillo, a former president of Mexico, concurs, listing the following prospects as potentially destabilizing threats from globalization: financial crises triggered by persistent U.S. balance-of-payments imbalances; tariff wars; public health pandemics; nuclear exchanges; and climate change (Zedillo 2008, 10–11).

Another aspect of acceleration is the declining longevity of power concentrations internationally. The Roman Empire lasted roughly five hundred years, and the Ottoman Empire nearly seven hundred years. Spain, France, and England each prevailed as superpowers for periods between one hundred and one hundred and fifty years. U.S. dominance lasted perhaps sixty years. To the extent that the United States was deemed "imperial" following the collapse of the Soviet Union in 1991, the American empire had to be one of the shortest on record, having dissipated by 2004, when its imperial overstretch in Iraq undermined its ability to claim legitimacy for its efforts to lead the international community (Brzezinski 2007, 3).

There is a "chicken or the egg" dimension to understanding that globalization is driven both by physical forces such as technology and trade (which reduce the costs of long-distance transactions and make them more attractive to citizens in individual countries) and by social forces (which create and reinforce the physical forces themselves). Groups that benefit from economic globalization—such as those that specialize in the production of tradable goods (agricultural or manufactured) and foreign investment—become political supporters of globalization and seek to promote policies that will cement its forces in place. For example, lower flying costs spur greater international air travel by the general public, which in turn creates political and cultural demands for its continuation. Similarly, lower costs of trade stimulate more trade and also create coalitions in participating nations in support of additional trade.

Globalization is most commonly experienced through a variety of more tangible social pressures. Among the many international forces commonly identified as the drivers of globalization are these:

- technological innovation

- economic interdependence/expansion

- demographic dispersion

- political diversification

- environmental degradation/concern

- ideational convergence (aspirations and doctrines of management)

TECHNOLOGICAL INNOVATION

At its heart, globalization occurs by means of advancing technology. Starting with the Industrial Revolution, developments in communication and transportation greatly facilitated contact and commerce over long distances, while the use of **fossil fuels** allowed for far greater industrial productivity. Transport over long distances was eased by the invention of the steamship, the building of railroads, the opening of canals (Suez in 1869, Panama in 1914), and the introduction of refrigeration (which allowed more products to travel long distances, such as beef exported from Argentina to England and the United States). Communications advances included the telegraph (whose reach was greatly extended in 1850 by the first Atlantic cable linking the United States and England) and the telephone; by the 1870s, both technologies had spread broadly. Historian Tim Blanning (2008) estimates that until the late nineteenth century, most information and goods flowed at the pace of walking on rutted tracks—perhaps 2 to 2.5 miles per hour—while horse livery might go as fast as 20 mph. Today, goods travel greater distances and far faster, and the pace of information flows is nearly instantaneous in much of the world.

Technological change continued apace throughout the twentieth century, as containerization, airplanes, fiber optics, and satellite telecommunications further drove down the cost of long-distance transport and communication. The average cost of freight and port charges fell from $90 per ton in 1920 to roughly $25 in 1980 and $30 in 1990. The cost of a three-minute telephone call between London and New York fell from $250 in 1930 to $31 in 1970 to $3 in 1990 (in real, inflation-adjusted, terms)—the precipitous rate of reduction contributing to a doubling of phone traffic between 1988 and 1993.

The pace of innovation and dissemination of new technologies has accelerated as new generations of technologies are brought online. It took thirty-eight years from the inception of radio to its adoption by 50 million users, but similar transitions required only sixteen years for the personal computer, thirteen years for television, and four years for the Internet. In real terms, the cost per mile of air passenger travel today is less than one-tenth the amount required in the mid-1920s. In each case, the upshot of these forces was to create new proximities: people were in closer contact with another—physically through travel and symbolically through access to each other's goods, music, Internet sites, and movies.

GLOBALIZATION IN ACTION
CULTURE-CROSSING MUSIC AND FOOD

Globalization, as popularized in the mass media and scholarly press since the late twentieth century, has come to refer to the integration of international trade. The intended exchange of goods is invariably accompanied by integration of cultural elements as well. In music, this exchange has resulted in hybrid forms and ensembles. It is not rare in contemporary music to hear an electric sitar featured on a Brazilian pop record or raga rhythms employed by a jazz composer. As these eclectic ensembles and compositional approaches evolve, their development is accompanied by controversy between the adherents of purism and those who advocate cultural mixing as an inevitable and desirable part of artistic advancement. Does such integration diminish the purity of the traditional musical cultures that gave birth to the current generation of hybrids?

However, while the concept of globalization may be a modern one when used in a purely economic context, the concept of culture accompanying the international exchange of goods is as old as the human urge to travel. Eleventh-century trouvères brought North African musical influences with them to France and Spain, and ancient trade routes likewise encircled the Sahara desert for centuries, leaving an enduring cultural legacy as well as the intended (though arguably more temporary) economic one. And what well-known musical form could be said to have more cross-cultural roots than the blues? Taken in this larger context of human history, was Duke Ellington's 1966 "Far East Suite" (or its subsequent remake by Anthony Brown employing indigenous Asian instruments) really a product of a different impulse?

In addition to hybrid forms of music, globalization has spawned entirely new cuisines. The proximity of peoples triggered by migration has given rise to a variety of fusion cuisines now popular in the United States and Europe, including French-Asian, pan-Asian, and Cuban-Chinese restaurants and dishes. Consequently, a diverse array of fresh and processed international foods are now available in Western supermarkets, expanding the parameters of the American diet and creating more jobs in agriculture in the developing world.

An interesting related phenomenon is the spread of American fast-food restaurants to foreign countries, where they have had to adjust their menus and presentations to accommodate local tastes and cultures. For instance, KFC tried to expand to India but found the Hindu market resistant to chicken cooked in lard; ultimately, the Colonel learned to serve curries. Similarly, McDonald's alters its condiments and offerings to reflect local tastes. Despite such efforts to adapt to foreign markets, there remains widespread concern, in terms of health, economics, and cultural identity, about the spread of American fast food worldwide.

Source: Andrew W. Jaffe, Lyell B. Clay Artist-in-Residence in Jazz and Director of Jazz Performance, Williams College.

But such technical forces are not the only driving forces behind globalization, which is reinforced as well by social institutions that governments have created to accelerate globalization and to stimulate technological change. For instance, the gold standard in the nineteenth century and the Bretton Woods set of international institutions in the twentieth century greatly accelerated the spread of economic globalization by providing incentives for firms to conduct business across long distances. Similar institutional support encouraged the flow of people, although to a lesser extent.

EXPANDED ECONOMIC INTERDEPENDENCE

Economic globalization involves growing interdependence among national economies across various forms of commercial exchange: trade, finance and investment, and flows of people.

Trade

National economies have become increasingly reliant on one another. Volumes of international trade have grown dramatically since World War II, at nearly three times the rate of national economic growth, on average. Figure 1 (p. xxxiv) shows this increase in international trade contrasted with growth in **gross domestic product (GDP)**. Tariffs also dropped during this period, showing the intent of governments to reduce **barriers to trade**.

Trade has grown across the board as a share of GDP. Consequently, individual countries are increasingly reliant on other countries to purchase their goods, thus providing the demand for goods that stimulates jobs and economic growth. Figure 2 (p. xxxv) shows the increasing share that trade has played in the U.S. economy. The United States is more subject to foreign influence than it was in the past but is still less vulnerable than are most other countries. By the late 1990s, commerce with other countries accounted for nearly 25 percent of U.S. national income (measured as **gross national product [GNP]**). By international standards, this is a relatively low reliance on other countries, thus insulating the United States to some extent from decisions taken abroad. On the other hand, the share of foreign influence over the U.S. economy has grown dramatically since World War II, reducing the ability of U.S. politicians to make decisions independently of their colleagues abroad. Economic policies made by U.S. trading partners may influence the demand for U.S. products as well as employment in the related sectors of the U.S. economy. Conversely, because the impact of trade on the

Figure 1

Growth in Real World Exports and GDP after World War II

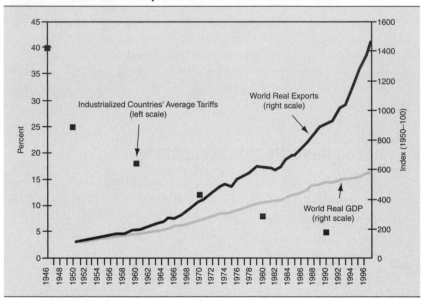

Source: Joseph Grieco, "The International Political Economy since World War II," prepared for the CIAO Curriculum Case Study Project, October 2000, exhibit 1.
Note: The squares denote industrialized countries' average tariffs (left scale). Tariff reduction is part of **trade liberalization**, promoting growth in exports.

United States is still relatively low, its leaders may feel freer than those of other countries to use instruments of trade policy (such as tariffs, quotas, embargoes, and subsidies).

The nature of international trade and production has changed over the past five decades. A vast proportion of what is recorded as trade is actually intrafirm transfers between affiliates within a corporation. For example, General Motors may import computer technology for its automobiles from Southeast Asia into Mexico for assembly there before selling the finished product in the United States. Beyond such internal transfers, much of the sale of goods between countries consists of partnerships and supply chains, wherein a company sells a partially finished product or component to a foreign company with which it has a long-standing contractual relationship. Consequently, trade may actually be a set of international relationships, in which the partners have long-standing commitments to one another and learn about markets and production from one another.

Considered in this light, trade is a social relationship that can contribute to forms of social learning as well as to simple commercial exchange. As we will see in the substantive chapters of this volume, different interpretations are available

Figure 2

U.S. Trade as a Percentage of GNP

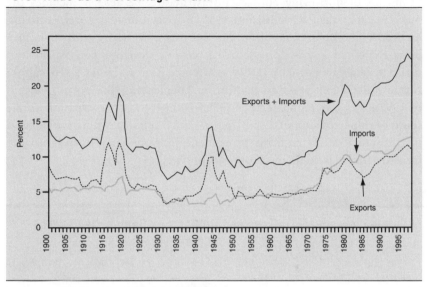

Source: Joseph Grieco, "The International Political Economy since World War II," prepared for the CIAO Curriculum Case Study Project, October 2000, exhibit 2.

as well. Such supply chains can be seen as exploitative, when those at the bottom end have no choice but to continually cut costs, trim their labor force, reduce wages, and otherwise make sacrifices to keep their partners happy. This negative view of supply chains has been termed the "Wal-Mart Effect" (Fishman 2006).

Investment

Another aspect of economic globalization is the growing ability of countries to borrow abroad. Since banking deregulation in the 1960s—and especially since 1995—capital flows worldwide have grown dramatically. The **International Monetary Fund (IMF)** records that gross global capital flows rose from $1.5 trillion in 1995 (about 3 percent of world GDP) to $12 trillion in 2005 (15 percent of world GDP).[1] Capital flows encompass foreign investment by companies as well as public and private purchases of government securities. To a large extent, the United States has been able to sustain government deficits by selling its debt and treasury bonds to other governments, sovereign wealth funds, and private firms. By 1994, capital inflows accounted for about 9 percent of U.S. GNP—well above the historical average, as can be seen in Figure 3 (p. xxxvi).

More generally, firms and governments have been able to pay for fixed capital formation (basically the money to pay for building infrastructure) by means of borrowing abroad. Infrastructure, because it includes the physical apparatus for production and transportation—airports, railroads, highways, power plants, mobile phone networks, electricity grids, and fiber-optic cables—is key to long-term sustainable development. Worldwide, **direct foreign investment (DFI)** as a percentage of **gross fixed capital formation (GFCF)** grew from a little over 2 percent in 1980 to over 7 percent by 1997 for all geographic regions. GFCF is the total of construction, so the share of imported capital to pay for all construction projects provides an insight into how foreign firms' investment decisions can influence broader infrastructure development in other countries.

Figure 3

Direct Foreign Investment: Inflows and Outflows by Region, 1970–2010

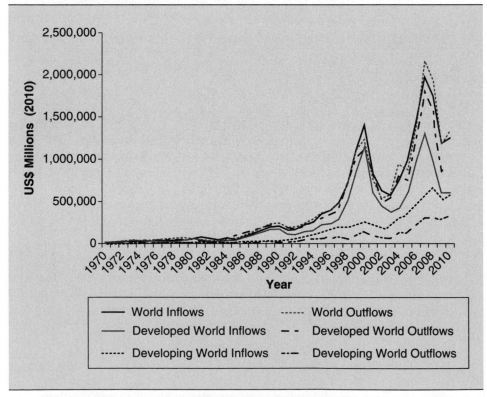

Source: United Nations Conference on Trade and Development (UNCTAD) Database, "Inward and Outward Foreign Direct Investment flows, annual, 1970–2010," accessed February 18, 2012.

GLOBALIZATION IN ACTION
CAMPAIGNING FOR THE ENVIRONMENT ON THE GLOBAL STAGE

The diffusion of global media and institutions allows **nongovernmental organizations (NGOs)** to deftly apply political pressure and effect change, especially in the environmental realm. In 1995, Shell Oil decided to dispose of the aged Brent Spar oil-storage buoy on the seabed of the North Sea. **Greenpeace International** believed that this decision was environmentally destructive and that disposal was better done on land. Unable to secure any political influence over Shell in England, where the government supported Shell's decision, Greenpeace quickly shifted the target of its campaign and launched a consumer boycott against Shell Oil in Germany, where the company had a substantial market share and consumers were environmentally aware. Fearful of losing significant profits in Germany, Shell reversed its position within weeks and chose to dispose of the Brent Spar onshore, where it was soon being dismantled. A few years later, the governments of nations in the northern Atlantic region imposed a ban on seabed disposal of oil platforms in the North Sea. By leveraging its international presence and refocusing its campaign in Germany, Greenpeace International effectively swayed both a global corporation and an international regulating body to achieve its environmental goal.

When NGOs are unable to exercise direct influence in one locale, they can apply their influence in other venues and over other political actors who may be able to influence their target. Political scientists Margaret Keck and Katharine Sikkink (1998) have dubbed this tactic the "boomerang effect." One example is the effort in the late 1980s by the U.S.-based Environmental Defense Fund (EDF) to reverse policies of the Brazilian government that were encouraging rapid deforestation of the Amazonian rain forest, often with loans from the **World Bank**. Unable to gain any direct political purchase within Brazil, the EDF instead successfully lobbied the U.S. Congress to threaten to withhold U.S. contributions to World Bank-funded projects that had environmentally destructive effects.

In turn, the World Bank adopted a number of internal reforms to make its own lending practices more environmentally friendly, including withholding money that had been targeted for the construction of a key road project in Brazil's program for opening up the Amazon to economic development. Thus, similar to Greenpeace's boycott of Shell Oil, EDF's strategy took advantage of the interrelatedness of institutions on the global stage, following a serpentine route in influencing a previously unresponsive government and thus accomplishing policy change.

Source: Bruce Rich, *Mortgaging the Earth* (Boston: Beacon Press, 1995).

Internationally, DFI has grown from around $100 billion[2] in 1970 to $1.5 trillion in 2000, followed by a dip and growth back by 2007 (see Figure 3). A booming Chinese economy is increasingly attracting DFI. But DFI is no longer exclusively the purview of the industrialized countries. Tata Industries, India's largest manufacturing company (and one of the world's largest), is, according to its executive director, "surfing the tsunami of globalization." From 2002 to 2009, Tata spent $18 billion buying thirty-seven companies in other countries.

DEMOGRAPHIC DISPERSION

Many patterns of social movement contribute to globalization. Larger numbers of people are mobile across national borders than ever before. Total tourist flows worldwide have risen from around 180 million in 1970 to 650 million in 1999.

Immigration is a major factor contributing to globalization. The 1990–1999 decade saw the largest number of people (some 10 million) moving internationally, exceeding the previous highest-migration decade—8 million people between 1900 and 1909—by about 25 percent. Most migrants move in order to search for better employment opportunities, and the majority of them come to live in the United States, as is seen in Figure 4 (p. xxxix).

Migrants also transform the identity of the country that welcomes them. Figure 5 (p. xl) indicates the high percentages of foreign-born residents (not all are citizens) in the populations of many countries.

Refugees, who move for political reasons, tend to concentrate in far fewer places, because they are placed in refugee camps and so lack the ability to travel freely. Some 11.4 million refugees were forced to leave their home countries in 2007, up from 9.9 million in 2006. Some 26 million were displaced within their own countries. Overall, some 37.4 million people are involuntarily uprooted from their place of origin.

Increased flows of people increase the ease of transmission of communicable diseases. In part because of the increase in numbers of business travelers worldwide, diseases can be easily and rapidly transmitted through human contact and in the air of airplanes. Concerns about the rapid spread of Severe Acute Respiratory Syndrome (SARS) from Asia in 2003 led to the introduction of significant limits on travel, which reduced the rate of economic growth in the region for 2004. China, fearing the bad publicity that might follow from reporting on SARS, then suppressed its published data, making it more difficult for the international public health community to contain the disease. Advances in transportation thus mean that new diseases can spread worldwide much more rapidly, when in the past, they would have been contained geographically.

Figure 4

Number of Migrants per Country

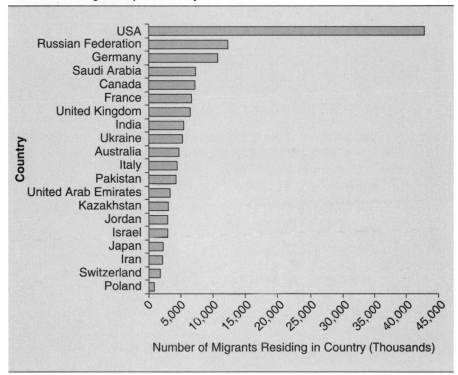

Number of Migrants Residing in Country (Thousands)

Source: United Nations, Department of Economic and Social Affairs, Population Division (2009). Trends in International Migrant Stock: The 2008 Revision (United Nations database, POP/DB/MIG/Stock/Rev.2008).

POLITICAL DIVERSIFICATION

The key political actor in international affairs remains the nation state. Only nation states are allowed to be members of the **United Nations** or to make foreign policy with respect to other governments. Nation states enjoy the legal convention of national **sovereignty**, which gives them the right to make policy within their own territory and to represent that territory to other nation states.

The number of nation states has grown nearly geometrically since 1900, particularly since the decolonization movement of the 1950s and 1960s. In 1900, there were fewer than 25 independent states, a number that had grown to over 190 by 2008. The United Nations had an original membership of 51 states in 1945; it included 192 members by 2008. With the independence of

Figure 5

Percentage of Migrants per Country

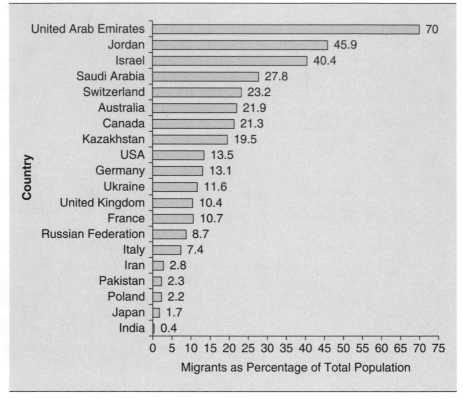

Source: United Nations, Department of Economic and Social Affairs, Population Division (2009). Trends in International Migrant Stock: The 2008 Revision (United Nations database, POP/DB/MIG/Stock/Rev.2008).

former colonies throughout the Third World, the political balance within the United Nations shifted: there are now more developing country members than industrialized country members.

The number of international organizations has also grown dramatically. In 1900, there were roughly 50 international organizations, according to the *Yearbook of International Organizations.*[3] By 2005, there were over 250, although the number had fallen since 1985, with the elimination of many alliances and organizations left over from the **Cold War** era. The functional focus of international organizations has also expanded dramatically, growing from their original military and diplomatic roles to address human rights, food, public health, environment, and economic issues.

Accompanying the spread of functional international organizations—bodies responsible for administering or coordinating policies in a specific functional domain such as public health, economic relations, food supply, environmental quality, and so on—has come growth in international law. Two trends are remarkable in this area: over 90 percent of the multilateral treaties negotiated since 1648 have been concluded since 1951, and the post–World War II years have seen a dramatic increase in attention paid to economic and environmental concerns, at the expense of the more traditional political/diplomatic and military focus of international law (Chasek 1995).

NGOs grew at a similarly exponential pace over the twentieth century. Whereas there were only 176 NGOs worldwide in 1909, by 1951, there were 832; the number had increased to 3,318 by 1968, to 9,521 by 1978, and to 40,306 by 1997. NGOs work with social movements to educate populations and to hold governments and private firms accountable for their commitments. They often coordinate strategies and campaigns in multiple countries, and others work as gadflies, publicizing various aspects of globalization.

Multinational corporations (MNCs)—also called transnational corporations (TNCs)—have also become important global actors. Firms first started siting production facilities in multiple countries, run from headquarters that were typically located in the United States or the United Kingdom, in the late nineteenth century. Previously, companies had been involved in long-distance trade of raw materials, but few had ownership or joint ownership over factories abroad. Thus foreign investment by MNCs came to provide the technological and skill-based foundation for global economic development. The UN and other sources estimate the current number of MNCs at about 60,000 parent firms, which direct the operations of some 500,000 affiliates around the world. Figure 6 (p. xlii) depicts the global distribution of MNCs in 1997. As it shows, the majority of MNCs are headquartered in the industrialized world—what is known as the "triad" of the United States, Europe, and Japan.

When the revenues of the largest MNCs are compared to the national income of states, the singular economic power of MNCs becomes evident. Figure 7 (p. xliii) shows some of the largest MNCs and states, contrasting countries' annual GNP with annual corporate earnings.

Scientific networks have also proliferated. Loose organizations of scientists who are experts in various aspects of global concern have become increasingly important in the governance of globalization as collective rules are developed to deal with aspects of globalization. As political actors find the need to cope with the increasingly complex and technical aspects of globalization, they look to professionals—engineers, scientists, economists—both in their own countries and abroad.

Many groups of political actors or stakeholders organize themselves through issue-specific policy networks. Groups drawn from many sets of actors who share a common interest in a specific issue meet regularly to identify interests and develop common policies to deal with globalization.

Figure 6

Corporations and Foreign Affiliates

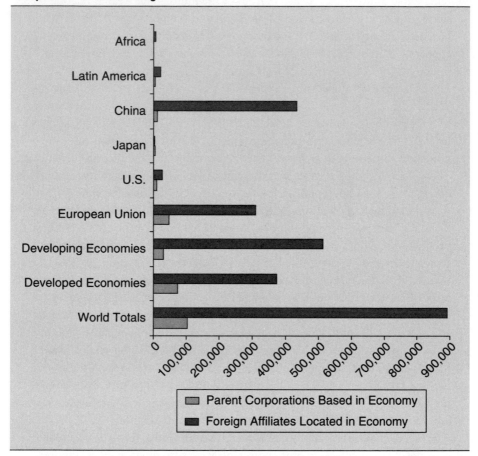

Source: United Nations Conference on Trade and Development (UNCTAD). 2011. *World Investment Report 2011.* Annex Table 34—Number of parent corporations and foreign affiliates, by region and economy, latest available year. New York and Geneva: UNCTAD. http://www.unctad.org/sections/dite_dir/docs/WIR11_web%20tab%2034.pdf.

One of the most important political actors of the twentieth century, of course, was the United States. To some extent, globalization has consisted of the projection of the U.S. military presence worldwide by means of military bases and foreign deployments. Just since the end of the Cold War, U.S. military operations have occurred in the following locales:

- Panama (1989)
- Colombia (military advisers, 1989)
- Iraq (1991)

Figure 7

The World's Largest Corporations and the GDP of Selected Countries, 2011

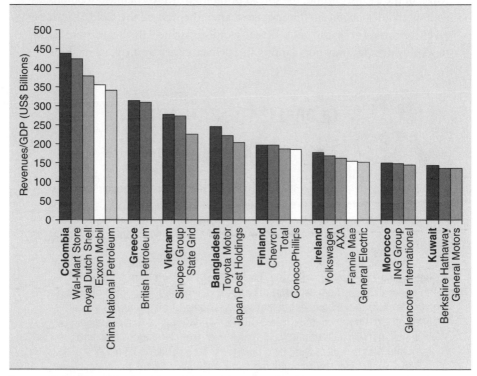

Sources: World Bank, World Development Indicators Database. *CNN Money, 2011 Global 500 List,* http://money .cnn.com/magazines/fortune/globa1500/2011/full_list/index.html (accessed February 18, 2012).

- Somalia (1992)
- Haiti (1994)
- Bosnia (1995)
- Kosovo (1999)
- Afghanistan (2001)
- Iraq (2003)

Changes in military technology have increased the ability of nonstate actors to deploy force at long distances. Before the twentieth century, for instance, terrorists tended to operate locally, but two sets of global forces have since contributed to the globalization of security concerns. One has to do with the emergence of new groups—criminals and political terrorists—with antipathy toward the West and a wish to apply force against their enemy. The spread of such formal political networks facilitates the diffusion of military technology, as seen by the sale of nuclear weapon technology by the Pakistan-based A.G. Khan in the 1990s. Second, the spread of biological and chemical weapons, as well as the dispersion of "loose-nukes" after the end of the Cold War, have given terrorists access to more lethal weapons, which they can more easily deploy against faraway populations and deliver either by airplane or ship.

GLOBALIZATION IN ACTION

THE WORLDWIDE MARKETPLACE

Especially since the rise of the Internet, globalization has greatly facilitated consumers' access to inexpensive items from abroad by virtually bringing together consumers and sellers who would not otherwise interact in person. One of this book's authors recalls two personal experiences that capture this phenomenon.

Shortly after 9/11, he made plans to fly out of his local airport, and, unheeding the new security rule, brought with him his favorite Swiss Army knife—which was then seized at the airport. Upon returning from his trip, he tried to replace the knife but discovered that sale of his preferred model had been discontinued in the United States. Using the online service eBay, however, he was able to purchase that model from a vendor in Poland, new, for about 40 percent of what he'd paid for the confiscated knife.

Some years later, he was looking for a birthday present for his son, who liked Peruvian music. While searching online, he found a professional model of a Peruvian panpipe (a "semi-toyo") that was available from a vendor in Bolivia. The panpipe was made by hand and shipped to the United States within a month. Third World artisans are able to make a living selling goods internationally as well as having their cultures recognized and supported through such small-scale, personal international trade.

While the Internet allows information to travel instantaneously and at nearly zero cost, in some instances the cost of shipping goods impedes further globalization. For example, in 2008 Tesla Motors, the California-based electric car maker, planned to manufacture 1,000-pound battery packs in Thailand, ship them to the United Kingdom for installation, and then import the nearly-assembled cars to the United States. But the shipping costs were found to be prohibitive, forcing the company to manufacture the batteries in California. While an integrated global economy contributes to the bulk of the goods we consume, from the coffee we drink to the cars we drive, globalization still faces obstacles—such as high oil prices—that may hinder its continued spread.

Source: Larry Rother, "Shipping Costs Start to Crimp Globalization," *New York Times*, August 3, 2008.

ENVIRONMENTAL DEGRADATION (AND CONCERN)

Globalization has given rise to a whole new class of environmental threats. Humanity has always influenced the natural environment in which it lived. But since the nineteenth century, modern industrial societies have generated contaminants that have the potential to degrade the global ecosystems on which human survival depends. The shift to fossil fuels during the Industrial Revolution led to widespread emissions of carbon dioxide and sulfur dioxide, contributing respectively to global warming and acid rain. As countries have emulated the economic model of England and the early industrializers, the ecological footprint of the world's population is growing increasingly heavy. And estimates of per capita consumption at current rates suggest that satisfying the material needs of the world's aspiring consumers would require four or five Earths.

Other dimensions of globalization have generated and augmented environmental threats around the world. Because of the reliance on national sovereignty as the organizing political principle for global governance, accumulated wastes concentrate in parts of the world that are beyond the political jurisdiction of the world's authorities: "tragedies of the commons" occur in the atmosphere, in open oceans, and in tropical rainforests. Concern about global environmental threats was initially sparked in the late 1960s, when residues of the pesticide DDT were discovered in Antarctica, far from its original application. Most of the world's fisheries are overused, because there is no effective enforcement of fishery quotas on the open oceans. Acid rain and the 1986 Chernobyl nuclear disaster made it clear that environmental destruction does not stop at national boundaries.

Long-distance trade contributes to environmental degradation and loss of biodiversity. For instance, tropical hardwoods are pillaged in Malaysia, Burma, and Brazil in order to supply furniture for consumers in the West. Low stumpage fees charged to the forestry companies by the government increase the incentive to overcut the forests.

Also, long-distance trade often physically interferes with local ecosystems. Invasive species are transmitted by freighters, introducing them to parts of the world where there are no natural predators, and so they proliferate. For example, the Black Sea fisheries have collapsed due to the new presence of jellyfish, while underwater exhaust vents from nuclear power plants on the Great Lakes are being clogged by the profusion of various species of nonnative mussels.

Many of the human stresses on the global environment began with the Industrial Revolution, but they have accelerated unabated since the 1950s. World production of sulfur dioxide and carbon dioxide, pesticide use, toxic-waste emissions, production of synthetic chemicals, and numbers of vehicles all continue to grow, causing potentially devastating effects on the integrity of global ecosystems (Kates et al. 1990; Ponting 1993; Speth 2008).

Globalization, and the attendant concentration of production and employment in cities, has led to worldwide urbanization. Over 50 percent of the world's population now lives in cities rather than in the countryside (see Figure 8, this page). Consequently, basic commodities must be transported to where people live, requiring greater consumption of energy for their transport and greater amount of emissions of **greenhouse gases**.

Figure 8

Percentages of Population Living in Cities, Figures and Estimates, 1950–2050

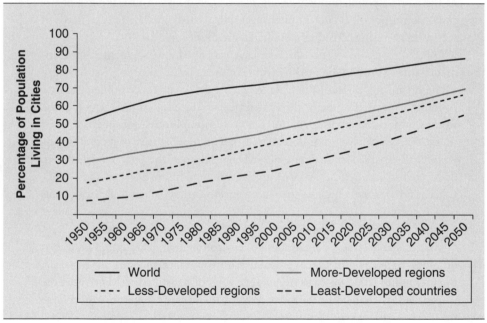

Source: United Nations, Department of Economic and Social Affairs, Population Division (2010). *World Urbanization Prospects: The 2009 Revision.* http://esa.un.org/unpd/wup/Analytical-Figures/Fig_10.htm.

IDEATIONAL CONVERGENCE

At the global level, a number of ideas or beliefs inform popular and elite attitudes about the world—affecting both legitimate aspirations and calculations about who is likely to be viewed favorably as an ally and to whom resources should be extended on favorable terms.

Many ideas have competed historically for dominance, at least in terms of hemispheric scale. From the fifteenth through the seventeenth centuries, Spanish Catholicism competed with the British Reformation for the hearts and minds of people in Europe and Latin America. The consequence of this ideational struggle, the German sociologist Max Weber argued, was the consolidation of the cultural institutions, which located the Industrial Revolution and early economic innovation and development in the United Kingdom and Protestant Europe.

More recently, some other ideas have attracted almost universal acclaim. By the 1980s, most economists had agreed on a loose set of principles about how states should manage their economies, dubbed the **Washington Consensus**. Such a blueprint, often administered by the IMF but widely endorsed by international cohorts of economists, laid out a common set of policy guidelines, primarily for developing-country governments:

- fiscal discipline by the state
- tax reform
- financial liberalization
- unified and competitive exchange rates
- trade liberalization
- openness to foreign direct investment
- privatization
- deregulation
- secure property rights

This list was never meant to be universally applied or categorical. By the turn of the new century, as the importance of national and international institutions was increasingly recognized, Harvard economist Dani Rodrik (2001, 51) notes that the original list had been augmented to include these further guidelines:

- legal/political reform
- regulatory institutions
- anti-corruption regulations
- labor market flexibility
- **World Trade Organization** (WTO) agreements
- financial codes and standards
- "prudent" capital-account opening
- non-intermediate exchange rate regimes
- social safety nets
- independent central banks and targeting inflation
- targeted poverty reduction[4]

Governments have embraced a core set of aspirational goals to be pursued by the international community. The eight **Millennium Development Goals** (MDGs) adopted by the UN General Assembly in 2000 call for fighting poverty, improving gender equality, improving public health, and increasing environmental protection.[5] The MDGs, which set specific targets that are to be reached by 2015 from a 2000 baseline, are discussed at greater length by Jeffrey Sachs in Chapter 3 of this book and include the following:

- halve the proportion of people living on less than a dollar a day

- ensure that all children complete primary school

- educate boys and girls equally

- reduce the mortality rate among children under five by two-thirds

- reduce the maternal mortality rate by three-quarters

- halt and begin to reverse the spread of HIV/AIDs, malaria, and other major diseases

- halve the proportion of people without access to safe water and sanitation

- increase aid and improve governance

By 2012, good progress had been made on achieving these goals in all areas other than Africa, and procedures are afoot at the UN to introduce a new set of MDGs in 2015, possibly augmented with sustainability targets.

New economic development doctrines have also been gaining currency. The idea of sustainable development and belief in the inseparable nature of economic development, democracy, peace, and environmental quality have become solidly entrenched on the international agenda since it was first popularized in the 1987 *Our Common Future* report by the World Commission on Sustainable Development. Decision makers worldwide are increasingly recognizing the complexity of the global policy environment—and the need to heed the connections between policy domains when making choices (Clark and Munn 1986; Haq 1995).

Democracy has gained currency as an idea about how to politically organize domestic society. In 1850 there were, at best, three democracies in the world—the United States, the United Kingdom, and France. One of the biggest surges in democratization occurred in the 1990s, and by 1998, about 45 percent of the world's countries could be regarded as democratic, according to standard basic political science measures of democracy (Huntington 1991; Simmons et al. 2006, 913). World public opinion polls administered in 2008 by Gallup and by WorldPublicOpinion. org confirmed that, on average, 85 percent of respondents across the world agreed that "the will of the people should be the basis for the authority of government" and stated that they favored democratic governance in their country, even if many expressed discontent with the way that such democracy might operate in practice (Gilani 2008, 15–20). At a deeper level, globalization itself has been gaining currency as a shared belief in how the world should be organized (Biersteker 2000). While many people worldwide report in response to surveys that they favor increased trade liberalization between countries, they are concerned about the possible negative side effects of globalization, such as threats to their culture, damage to the environment, and challenges posed by immigration (Knowlton 2007).

GLOBALIZATION IN ACTION
THE NEW FACE OF OUTSOURCING

One feature of globalization is the increased ease of **outsourcing**—subcontracting services to a third party, which often involves moving jobs overseas. Idaho-based Nighthawk Radiology hires radiologists in India to interpret x-rays for hospitals in the United States and elsewhere. X-rays are sent via the Internet from U.S. laboratories to Indian laboratories for interpretation. The Indian doctors' findings are promptly relayed back to the United States and other countries using the service. Given the scarcity of medical specialists in the United States and the relatively low wages of Indian workers, such practices bring down U.S. medical costs while creating technical infrastructure in India and, because of the time zone differences involved, may even speed the interpretation of medical tests.

Outsourcing was once thought to involve the U.S. and Western European countries sending jobs to India and other economically developing nations. But in some cases, outsourcing itself is being outsourced. Infosys, the Indian technological giant based in Mysore, trains thousands of workers from dozens of countries in six-month stints and then sends them overseas to work in its overseas operations. Indian technology companies are opening offices in Uruguay, Mexico, Canada, Portugal, Romania, Thailand, China, and parts of the United States. In one office alone, more than a dozen languages are spoken.

As an Infosys vice president puts it, in the new world of outsourcing, the effort is "to take the work from any part of the world and do it in any part of the world." In one example, a U.S. bank wanted to market to Hispanic customers, so it contracted with a Monterrey, Mexico, office of Infosys to provide the services. This new form of outsourcing supports rising Indian wages and currency as well as increased competition from other up-and-coming countries (such as China, Morocco, and Mexico) on the ever-changing terrain of the global economy.

Source: Anand Giridharadas, "Outsourcing Works, So India Is Exporting Jobs," *New York Times*, September 25, 2007.

GLOBALIZATION'S EFFECTS

In this section, we review some of the major claims about the effects of globalization. Who benefits? Who suffers? In large part, these debates presume that globalization itself is responsible for many of the outcomes that are to be either celebrated or lamented. But far more research is needed to tease out the interaction between global forces and the role played by domestic factors and policy choices in the effects that are so widely discussed.

Much progress in the quality of individual livelihood has been documented over the past fifty years. Infant mortality has fallen, and life expectancy has increased for most of the world. Only some countries in Eastern Europe, Central Asia, and sub-Saharan Africa have failed to see these improvements (World Bank 2004, 10–11, 22–23). But to what extent are these observed differences attributable to globalization itself? That is, in the absence of globalization, would things be any different? Or might these changes actually be due to one or more other factors? A long-standing puzzle that captures this question is the differential development trajectory of South Korea and Ghana: Ghana is rich in natural resources, and South Korea lacks them. In the 1950s, Ghana's per capita GDP was higher, yet today, South Korea is no longer a Third World country, while conditions have not significantly changed in Ghana.

Another factor to be considered in this debate is to what extent the benefits of globalization are regionally concentrated. The IMF reports that annual average GDP growth in sub-Saharan Africa has lagged behind world rates since the 1970s. The much discussed "digital divide"—reflecting unequal access to computers and the Internet—is another instance of how many of the benefits of globalization have accrued to the countries of the North (the industrialized countries in North America, Australia, New Zealand, Japan, and Western Europe).

Figures 9 and 10 demonstrate the unequal distribution of income. Figure 9 (p. li) presents income per head as a percentage of the North, indicating a decline outside of Asia—in this table, primarily Japan, Malaysia, Thailand, Taiwan, Singapore, and Hong Kong—and China since 1950. Figure 10 (p. lii) shows regional percentages of world GDP over time: the world's richest countries (the Group of 8 [G8], consisting of the United States, the United Kingdom, France, Canada, Italy, Germany, Russia, and Japan) controlled 30 percent of world GDP in 1820, 55 percent in 1975, and around 45 percent in 2004.

In the early 1970s, Harvard economist Richard Cooper (1972) realized that economics textbooks had to be rewritten to accommodate globalization. Economic management could no longer occur in isolation of what was going on in other countries. Indeed, the role of foreign trade for such countries as the United States, which historically has remained relatively insulated from the world economy, has been growing—making it (and other vulnerable countries)

Figure 9

Gross National Income per Capita, 1975–2010

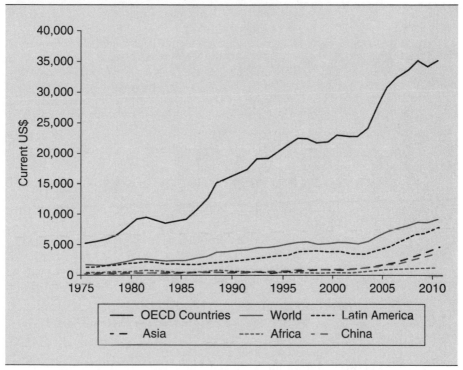

Source: World Bank Development Indicators, "GNI per Capita, Atlas Method (current US$)" [database]. Accessed February 22, 2012.

increasingly sensitive to economic turmoil from abroad. For instance, a recession in a major trading partner would reduce demand for U.S. goods. As Cooper argued originally, central bank policies must be coordinated, or unilateral efforts at economic management will be counterproductive.

Many economists suggest that globalization should lead to convergence of economic conditions across countries. However, Benjamin Cohen (1998) finds that exchange rates have not yet fully converged. Geoffrey Garrett (1998) shows that left-leaning governments are able to preserve higher labor standards and stronger social support policies in the face of global pressures. Peter Katzenstein (1985) demonstrates that small, politically liberal social democracies are able to work with labor and quickly adjust to international economic conditions without facing extensive domestic economic cuts.

One of the most widely contested aspects of economic globalization involves economic equality. Does globalization accentuate or reduce economic

Figure 10

Percentage of World GDP by Region, 1820–2004

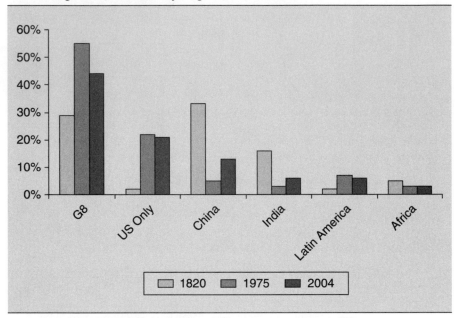

Source: Global Policy Forum, http://www.globalpolicy.org/component/content/article/104/46589.html.
Note: The North includes North America, Australia, New Zealand, Japan, and Western Europe.

inequalities between and within countries? The evidence is mixed, and much depends on the chosen tools of statistical interpretation.

The World Bank estimates that economic inequality between countries has decreased since 1950, although economic inequality within countries has increased during that period. However, there are a variety of ways of calculating economic inequality within countries. One common technique is to look at the percentage or numbers of the population living on less than $1 or $2 a day. The percentage of people living in poverty appears to have fallen between 1970 and 1998, although different analysts offer widely diverging estimates of the number of people in absolute poverty. Much of the change has to do with the growing size of the Chinese middle class, which has elevated between 250 and 400 million people out of absolute poverty.

Until the 1970s, economic growth rates in the industrialized countries far exceeded that of the developing world, leading to a deep divide in GDP per-capita figures worldwide. However, over the past twenty-five years or so, the "Asian Tigers" have outpaced the West. Despite a 1997 setback from the financial meltdowns in Southeast Asia, Taiwan, South Korea,

Singapore, Thailand, Malaysia, and China have had exceptionally high rates of economic growth, nearly doubling that of the West from 1973 to 2001 (Maddison 2007, 337, 379–382).

Another way of estimating inequality within countries is by looking at the ratio of incomes of the richest fifth of the population to the incomes of the poorest fifth. Estimates of wealth rather than income would be a better indicator of such inequality, but rich people have to disclose only their income for tax purposes, some assets are difficult to value, and cross-national estimates of individual wealth are difficult to come by. Worldwide, income inequality grew much worse from 1960 to 2000. The UNDP Human Development Index reports that the ratio of income of the richest to that of the poorest fifth of the world's population spread from 30 percent to nearly 75 percent over that period.[6]

Power Shifts

The nature and distribution of political influence is also changing as a consequence (or a cause) of globalization. Many analysts either observe or predict profound changes in the nature of diplomacy and international relations.

National sovereignty, the bedrock of international relations, is being transformed. Diplomats and international lawyers have regarded states as the paramount legal authorities in international politics since the Treaty of Westphalia in 1648. States are responsible for formulating foreign policy; only representatives of states may legally commit their countries to any obligations at international meetings (one of the first actions that newly independent countries take is to seek recognition by the United Nations); and national governments are the national authorities responsible for maintaining control (security and economic prosperity) within their national boundaries.

The influence of new political actors is posing increasing challenges to the state's national sovereignty. Exercising control domestically is virtually impossible without close consultation with MNCs and NGOs. Economic and environmental conditions are often the consequence of decisions taken by firms and individuals, not by the state. Foreign policy is increasingly subject to direct influence by MNCs, NGOs, scientists, and even international organizations.

This diffusion of power makes it even more difficult for states to impose policies. Effective policy implementation requires consensus, and states must feel that their interests are represented if they are to willingly accept meaningful international obligations and enforce them at home. Legitimacy is thus based on process for small powers (were they heard and able to participate?), recourse to broader underlying principles by leaders, and representation (for an increasing number of nonstate actors). There is a paradox here about participatory legitimacy, though, as nonstate actors require some measure of participation if they are to consider an international decision to be legitimate, whereas traditional state actors may base their assessment of legitimacy on whether the states were able to dominate the process and so ensure that the principle of sovereignty persists.

States face a dilemma in justifying their policies. Domestically, they must demonstrate that the policies they support represent the interests of their population. In the international arena, though, they have to justify their positions against those of many other actors, whose interests may not be regarded as legitimate in the eyes of domestic constituencies. Consider the difficulties that the United States encounters at the United Nations: although the UN does not enjoy widespread legitimacy (at least in the U.S. Congress) Europeans and other international partners regard decisions taken outside the UN as highly suspect. Ulrich Beck, a German sociologist, writes that "globalization denotes the processes through which sovereign nation states are crisscrossed and undermined by transnational actors" (Beck 1992, 11).

The conduct of diplomacy is changing with globalization as well. Many more political partners must be consulted when formulating policies. It was striking that Colin Powell, then the U.S. secretary of state, would greet by name not just journalists (as was the practice of his predecessors) but also NGO representatives at meetings.

The nature of diplomacy is also changing. With the growth of new political issues and the increased salience of perceived legitimacy based both on the articulation of domestic interests and the process by which policies are created, the tools of diplomacy have to be modified. Pure force is no longer the solution to most problems—and it may often be counterproductive. Joseph Nye, a Harvard political scientist with an acute foreign policy eye, has written persuasively of the need for "soft power": leading by example and relying on multilateralism and close consultation with other political actors worldwide. In terms of the tools of statecraft, soft power emerges from the attractiveness of a country's culture and from consistency between its policies and uniformly accepted **norms**, such as democracy and human rights (Nye 2002, 127; Brzezinski 2007).

As Table 1 (p. lv) indicates, there are multiple measures of power and of a country's ability to project influence at a great distance. The United States still enjoys preeminence in terms of the size of its economy, nuclear warheads, and aircraft carriers—and, thus, its ability to quickly project airpower abroad. While other countries may have large traditional militaries, they lack the capacity to project military force at a great distance, and the size of their economies still do not measure up to that of the United States.

Table 1

Measures of Power and Ability to Project Influence at a Great Distance, 2009–2010

	Population (% of world) 2010	GDP (% of world) 2010	Active Armed Forces 2010	Nuclear Warheads 2009	Aircraft Carriers in Service 2010
U.S.	4.5	23.1	1.4 million	3575	11
China	19.5	9.3	2.3 million	>125	0
France	0.9	4.1	0.4 million	300	1
India	17.8	2.7	1.3 million	~50	1
Russia	2.1	2.3	1.0 million	3113	1
U.K.	0.9	3.6	.2 million	~160	1
Germany	1.2	5.2	.3 million	N/A	0

Sources: UN Data (http://data.un.org/Default.aspx), "Total population, both sexes combined (thousands)," "GDP (Current US$)" databases; Hackett, James (ed.), International Institute for Strategic Studies, *The Military Balance 2010* (London: Routledge); The Carnegie Endowment for International Peace, *World Nuclear Arsenals 2009*, http://www.carnegieendowment.org/2009/02/03/world-nuclear-arsenals-2009/fr5.

Still, the ability to exercise economic leverage over other countries—one of the major sources of diplomatic statecraft—may be shifting away from the United States to China and India. A forecast of GDP in 2020 in terms of **purchasing power parity** (a measure of how much can be bought with a particular currency) has China first (at approximately $30 trillion), the United States second (at slightly less), and India third (at around $12 trillion). By 2050, China may have a GDP of $75 trillion, with the United States and India tied at $40 trillion.[7]

Shifting Political Identities

As exposure to the rest of the world grows and people become more mobile, identity shifts occur as well. In Europe, public opinion polls reveal that an increasing number of citizens regard themselves as European, rather than (or in addition to) being citizens of a particular country. Diasporic communities often associate themselves with their country of origin, where they may hope to retire and where many of their relatives continue to reside. In addition to the economic remittances they send back to their country of origin—which in some instances accounts for a significant proportion of the national income of the country of origin (Philippines, Pakistan, Egypt)—migrants acquire new attitudes, for good and ill.

Many political consequences are associated with globalization as well. Many critics express concern about the "Americanization" of the world—a homogenization of culture that is a consequence of the dissemination of

American styles and values (through the deliberate exercise of soft power) and the spread of U.S. multinationals. Smaller languages become extinct. Traditional lifestyles are endangered. And other cultures feel swamped by the American juggernaut, leading to **protectionism** (as promoted by the French film industry) or political backlash (as embodied in Moslem fundamentalism).

It is possible that this view of the overarching power of U.S. mass culture to project its cultural shadow abroad, unchallenged, is overdrawn. Indigenous cultures are robust. One example is beer. There was long a concern that the large breweries were generating a uniformly boring product that was overwhelming the market; similar arguments were made about coffee. Yet, currently, the United States is awash in microbreweries offering innovative and distinctive flavors of beer, while local coffee roasters and cafés compete with Dunkin' Donuts and Starbucks.

The United States also projects a disproportionately large ecological footprint. If other countries fully emulate the American consumer model, the globe will suffer. Estimates from 2003 indicated that satisfying the demands of one American required 9.6 hectares (about 2.5 acres) while individuals in Europe required 4.2 hectares; those in the Middle East and Central Asia, 2.2 hectares; Latin America, 2.0 hectares; Asia Pacific, 1.3 hectares; and those in Africa, 1.1 hectares (Burman 2007, 16–17). In the aggregate, satisfying individuals worldwide at the American level of consumption (or even less) will deplete the world's total resource base and deplete its ecosystemic foundations. The global projection of U.S. consumer habits through movies and advertising reinforces these pressures.

Complexity of Decision Making

The growing agenda of political participants makes the entire enterprise of diplomacy and international relations more complex than ever before (Jervis 1997; La Porte 1975; Perrow 1999; Simon 1981).

More political actors mean that there are simply more possible political connections to track. The number of binary connections follows from the simple formula $n*(n-1)/2$. For instance: a world of 81 states requires 2,140 embassies and foreign ministry desks simply to maintain bilateral ties; a world of 167 states requires 7,762 embassies and foreign ministry desks. While most governments find shortcuts to deal with such complexity, such as regional representation and bargaining through blocs, the proliferation of other actors makes things even messier.

Many issues on the international agenda are poorly understood or are interconnected with other issues in ways that are often not fully recognized.

Some contemporary analysts refer to these global issues as *networked problems*. Such issues make it much more difficult for decision makers to accurately understand their own interests (as well as others' interests) or to identify clear policies that may be widely acceptable. Decision makers operate under conditions of uncertainty—they are subject to frequent unanticipated consequences, surprises, and crises as the interconnection between issues transmits policy effects geographically and functionally. Consequently, states increasingly value political actors who may promise to attenuate such uncertainty by clarifying the nature of the international system, helping actors to identify their interests, and helping to establish useful policies and the likely consequences of alternate policies.

An example of unanticipated consequences is U.S. reliance on biofuel substitutes for petroleum. The U.S. government has encouraged its farmers to convert agricultural crops to corn in order to generate feedstocks for substitute energy sources. Yet the effect of this policy has been to drive up the price of grain while producing a fuel that may require more energy to produce than it generates. (Brazilian ethanol comes from sugar beets rather than corn and thus requires far fewer energy inputs to produce it.) Consequently, the United States, by trying to protect national security, contributes to food scarcity and to energy inefficiency. Policies that may make good political sense for the American Midwest generate policy effects that are globally detrimental.

This new global policy environment creates the need for new approaches to policymaking. Organization theorist Donald Chisholm notes that "central coordinating schemes work well when the task environment is known and unchanging, and can be treated as a closed system" (cited in Scott 1998, 82). Globalization challenges all these assumptions about the policy environment. Effective responses to globalization call for international cooperation and governance—including agreement on common rules, norms, participatory arrangements, and enforcement provisions.

PERSPECTIVES ON GLOBALIZATION

A variety of clear perspectives on globalization have been identified. David Held and Anthony McGrew (2007) find three general normative orientations and six analytic or policy views, while James Rosenau (2003, 78) has five views on multilevel governance and democracy, and Jan Aart Scholte (2000) has four.

For our purposes, there are five dominant perspectives on globalization, as shown in Table 2 (p. lviii). Each perspective, or worldview, varies in how the key political driving forces are defined, who are identified as the principal actors,

Table 2

Dominant Perspectives on Globalization

	Political Realism	Market Liberalism	Skepticism/ Political Liberalism	Radicalism	Transformationalism/ Cosmopolitanism
Key proponents	Brzezinski, Kissinger, Rice	Friedman, Wolf	Keohane, Krugman, Nye, Rodrik, Slaughter, Stiglitz	Bello, Khor, Klein, Roy, Shiva	Castells, Giddens, Held, Ruggie, Khagram, Sikkink,
Key actors	States	MNCs	All	MNCs	Nonstate actors
Major forces	Military, economic	Economic	Military, economic, cultural	Markets, culture	Networks
General assessment	Mixed	Positive	Mixed	Overwhelmingly negative	Hopeful
Guidance techniques	Reassertion of strong state leadership	Market liberalization, rule of law	Multilateralism	Constant challenges, regional cooperation, national self-reliance, citizen mobilization	Network formation

what is the assessment of costs and benefits to the majority of the world's population, and what specific policy agenda is recommended to better steer globalization forces. Each perspective has its proponents, whose publications (provided in the bibliography at the end of this chapter) can be read in order to follow the perspective in greater detail.

Political Realism: L'état Eternel

Political realism is a long-standing perspective on international relations that emphasizes the key role of the nation state in international politics. According to realists such as Henry Kissinger, Condoleezza Rice, Brent Scowcroft, Zbigniew Brzezinski, Robert Kagan, and Richard Haass, global forces operate according to the wishes of powerful states. All states are obsessed with protecting their national security and wealth, and all states construct international rules and allow international flows of goods, people, and ideas within these parameters. Globalization, according to this perspective, is largely an artifact of British hegemony in the nineteenth century and U.S. hegemony in the twentieth century. The dominant political powers—the hegemons—set the rules by which their own interests can be served through global actions.

Realists thus take a highly pragmatic view of globalization. For them, globalization is not a seamless whole but rather a set of highly controlled and discrete sets of activities. Realists believe that certain forces of globalization—such as international trade liberalization—are allowed to proliferate, because it is seen in the United States as benefiting the U.S. economy. Conversely, other forces of globalization—such as migration—are suppressed if they are seen to undermine long-term U.S. interests.

GLOBALIZATION IN ACTION
GLOBAL CRIME

Globalization makes corporate crime possible on a large scale. Two recent examples can be found in the scandals involving financier Bernard L. Madoff and the German firm, Siemens. Madoff is the con artist who swindled $50 billion from investors by constructing a "Ponzi scheme"—in effect, gathering funds from new investors to pay off current ones. To be successful, one needs many potential investors, but even the world was not big enough to handle Madoff's enterprise, which was called the world's first global Ponzi scheme. Starting with an "exclusive" set of friends and clients in New York and in Florida, Madoff expanded his scope to Europe and eventually starting hawking his products in China and elsewhere in Asia. But feeding such a large number of investors requires attracting ever more new investors, which cannot go on forever, even in a globalized world. However, such a scheme now can grow larger and last longer because the con artist's reach is vastly extended through globalization.

A second example of the global scale of corruption is the recent multibillion-dollar fine charged to the German engineering conglomerate, Siemens, by agencies of the U.S. and German governments. Reportedly, Siemens ran a bribery operation on the scale of $30 to $40 million per year, paying off government officials and companies in Russia, Argentina, China, and around the world.

Bribery is hardly new, yet Siemens' operations were brazen and transparent, setting up "cash desks" where employees could fill suitcases with up to one million euros in cash for the purpose of bribing foreign officials to grant them telecommunications contracts. Moreover, Siemens claimed tax deductions for these bribes—called "useful expenditures"—which was legal in Germany until 1999. From 2001 through 2007, Siemens paid foreign officials over $800 million to help them win contracts. On December 15, 2008, Siemens pleaded guilty in U.S. court and agreed to pay fines of $800 million in the United States and $540 million in Germany.

Globalization, it seems, fosters both multinational trade and multinational graft.

Sources: "Madoff Scheme Kept Rippling Outward, Across Borders," *New York Times*, December 19, 2008; "At Siemens, Bribery Was Just a Line Item," *New York Times*, December 20, 2008; and "Bavarian Baksheesh," *The Economist*, December 20, 2008, 112.

Too much globalization, from a realist perspective, is a bad thing, because it erodes the power of dominant players. A wider balance of power internationally is seen as detrimental to political order at the international level, because there is no clear source of leadership or enforcement for collective commitments. Deeper influence of nonstate actors further undermines the ability of dominant states to provide the clear leadership on which systemic order relies.

However, many realists realize that some aspects of globalization may be moving beyond simple control by powerful states. This is a terrifying prospect, as it raises doubts about the stability of the international system and the political calculus that they have held to be universal and eternal.

Market Liberalism: Swords into Stock Shares

Market liberals believe that free markets provide universal benefits. All good liberal values go together: free trade reinforces democratization and human prosperity as well as the rule of law, human rights, and the welfare of women. Market liberals—most notably economist Milton Friedman and the journalist Thomas Friedman (no relation)—advance the long-standing argument for capitalism that if human competitive urges are channeled into commerce, there will be less violence, and individuals everywhere will press for a strong respect for the rule of law and transparent democratic principles so that they can be confident in making contracts and engaging in long-distance commerce (Friedman 2000). They believe that if economic markets are allowed to prevail in most areas of human endeavor, then MNCs will spread their operations worldwide, providing employment, prosperity, and Western values.

Globalization, for market liberals, is a decidedly good thing that is to be embraced and promoted in almost all forms, since it expands the reach of free markets. However, market liberals would still advocate the use of force against groups that violently challenge globalization, such as political regimes or nonstate actors that could interfere with the easy flow of energy supplies.

Skepticism: Accentuate the Positive and Adjust the Negative

Political liberals tend to be skeptical about globalization. They see much to like about its creative possibilities—such as the potential for mutual economic benefit and for political identity formation beyond the nation state (thus serving as a bulwark against nationalism and warfare)—but they are concerned about globalization's potential for forging connections between opponents of liberal ideals and generating backlash against the forces that may be beneficial.

Liberals are aware of possible contradictions in the short term between democracy building in new states and other goals, such as peace and economic vitality. Political scientist Ronald Parris argues that economic growth in many emerging economies may be best accomplished by deferring democratization. Others have noted that supporting democratization, particularly in the Middle East, may entail supporting political parties that oppose the West.

Basically, despite their skepticism, liberals believe in the potential for what the economist Jagdish Bhagwati calls "globalization with a human face" (Bhagwati 2008). They believe that states can and should intervene to temper the excesses of globalization, such as widespread financial crises or environmental degradation. Environmental regulations and labor standards should be adopted to counter the tendencies toward a race to the bottom from pure, market-based globalization.

Liberals are also aware of the possibility that globalization may foster a backlash that undermines any potential gains. Thus they seek to promote globalization cautiously (in domains that are least likely to galvanize opposition), to offer carefully qualified defenses of globalizing forces, and to educate people about their benefits, hoping to diffuse challenges based on emotional response to radical change.

Radicalism: Challenge the Dominant Paradigm

Radicals believe that globalization is primarily a set of economic and social forces that consolidate political control in the hands of northern multinational corporations (Bello 2004; Cavanagh 1995; Ling and Khor 2001; Roy 2001; Shiva 2005). They are outraged by the unequal distribution of benefits from globalization. Since the demonstrations against the WTO in Seattle in 1999, many radical critiques have been launched that seek to document growing inequities—claiming, for instance, that during the period of highest global engagement in the United States, the share of total income accruing to the wealthiest 1 percent of Americans grew from about 7.5 percent throughout the 1970s to nearly 18 percent in 2006.[8]

Globalization, in this view, is merely imperialism by another name, for it has the effect of projecting unsustainable and inappropriate modes of production to the majority of the world by facilitating free trade, foreign investment, and exposure to foreign mass-consumption culture. The resulting economic integration brings with it a race to the bottom: lowered labor standards, environmental degradation, exacerbated economic inequality, and the consolidation of political power in the hands of a plutocratic few. Radicals advocate a constant campaign of challenging globalization through public demonstrations and public education. They support viable alternatives to globalization, such as national self-reliance, more radical forms of democratic participation at all levels of governance, and greater cooperation among countries and groups in the global South.

Cosmopolitan Transformationalism: Jazz and Constant Improvisation

Globalization has given rise to a distinctive new set of perspectives that are associated with cosmopolitanism at the international level. These authors, such as Kwame Anthony Appiah (whose essay on culture and diversity is included here) and British sociologist David Held, believe in the transformative potential of globalization, the salient feature of which—from their perspective—is the proliferation of networks of new political actors. These networks, driven by rapid technological innovation, facilitate the prompt flow of information between major state and nonstate actors. According to the adherents of this perspective, globalization may be seen metaphorically as jazz, full of improvisation and change, unlike the more bombastic military marches of the realists or the carefully orchestrated classical symphonies of the liberals. These globalized networks create the potential for widespread learning as well as decentralized mechanisms of oversight and information that can facilitate international cooperation.

Cosmopolitans recognize the geographic and regional disparities that may inhibit the spread of these networks. China and Russia still actively suppress nonstate claimants to political legitimacy. Still, many cosmopolitans believe that there is a great potential for inducing political change in such staunch statist opponents through opening up global channels to China and Russia and promoting civil society within those countries. Elsewhere, endemic poverty can be a serious limit to the spread of virtual networks, and economic policies and foreign aid may provide the infrastructure from which networks may continue to grow in Latin America and Africa.

CONCLUSION

Globalization is a contested concept. Views differ on the prospects it presents for humanity. The essays in this volume seek to span some of the perspectives on globalization, presenting arguments about the degree to which its positive potential may be realized. At a high level of abstraction, one could ask, to what extent does globalization further the development and transmission of new useful new ideas for better policy? To what extent does it consolidate ossified political structures that inhibit progress? To what extent is political change possible to promote reform and change?

The essays and debates that follow in this volume focus less abstractly on applied policy debates that are associated with globalization. Authors engage one another on questions of what interventions are politically and technically likely to improve basic human conditions under conditions of globalization: how and when can human rights be promoted, poverty alleviated, ecological sustainability assured, and individuals protected from threats of violence?

Discussion Questions

1. How can different political actors deal with the uncertainty created by globalization?
2. What does globalization mean for identity?
3. Should globalization be made more equitable? How can the distribution of benefits from globalization be made more egalitarian?
4. Which features of globalization appear to be most important? Why?

NOTES

1. "Global Capital Flows," *Finance & Development,* March 2007, 14.
2. Dollar amounts are in US dollars.
3. See http://www.uia.be/yearbook
4 See also Held and McGrew 2007, 187–189.
5. See http://www.mdgmonitor.org
6. See http://hdr.undp.org/en/
7. *The Economist,* June 30, 2007, 31.
8. *The Economist,* July 26, 2008, 34.

TECHNOLOGICAL INNOVATIONS

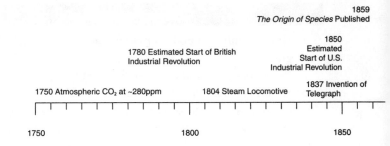

1859
The Origin of Species Published

1850
Estimated
Start of U.S.
Industrial Revolution

1780 Estimated Start of British
Industrial Revolution

1750 Atmospheric CO₂ at ~280ppm

1804 Steam Locomotive

1837 Invention of
Telegraph

1750   1800   1850

POLITICAL DEVELOPMENTS

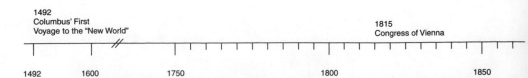

1602
Dutch East
India Company
Established

1599
British East India
Company Established

1494
Treaty of Tordesillas

1492
Columbus' First
Voyage to the "New World"

1815
Congress of Vienna

1492   1600   1750   1800   1850

Top timeline

2012 Atmospheric CO_2 at 392ppm

2011 Third ofWorld's Population Has Internet Access

2003 Human Genome Project Completed

1965 Moore's Law - Computer Transistor Capacity Doubles Yearly

2001 Advent of "Space Tourism"

2011 Fukushima Nuclear Disaster

1961 Soviet Union Launches First Manned Space Flight

1990 World Wide Web created

1957 Soviet Union Launches Sputnik

1986 Chernobyl Disaster

1985 Discovery of "Ozone Hole"

1914 Opening of Panama Canal

1945 Atomic Bomb

1952 Commercial Air Traffic

1951 Nuclear Power Plants

2009 Estimated 4.1 Billion Mobile Phone Subscriptions

1912 Sinking of the *Titanic*

1920 Radio Broadcasting

1980 Mobile Phones

1919 First Transatlantic Flight

1959 Atmospheric CO_2 at 315ppm

1869 Opening of the Suez Canal

1908 Ford Model T

1905 Einstein's Special Theory of Relativity

1969 ARPANet (Precursor to Modern Internet)

1903 Wright Brothers' First Manned Flight

1969 U.S. Moon Landing

2003 Prevalence of Social/Digital Media

1882 First Commercial Power Station in U.S.

1928 Television Broadcasting

1973 Gene Splicing

1973 Personal Computers

1876 First Telephone Call is Made

1928 Discovery of Antibiotics

1972 Modern Satellite Imagery

1900   1950   2000   2020

Bottom timeline

2012 Rio Conference on Sustainable Development

2002 Formation of the International Criminal Court

2003 U.S. Invasion of Iraq

2002 Johannesburg World Summit on Sustainable Development

1995 World Trade Organization Replaces General Agreement on Tariffs and Trade

2001 U.S. Invasion of Afghanistan

1991 Fall of Soviet Union/End of Cold War

1949 Mao Tse-Tung Proclaims People's Republic of China

2001 9/11 Terrorist Attacks

1989 Fall of Berlin Wall

1992 UN Conference on Environment and Development

1949 NATO Established

1989 "Washington Consensus"

1992 U.S., Canada, and Mexico Sign NAFTA

1948 UN Universal Declaration of Human Rights

1980 Democracies & Free Markets in South America

2011 Death of Osama bin Laden

1945 United Nations

1975 First Meeting of G6 countries (later G8)

1896 First Modern Olympic Games

1939 Start of WWII

1973 First Oil Shock

2008 Global Financial Crisis

1919 League of Nations

1972 UN Conference on the Human Environment

1918 End of WWI

1947 Start of Cold War

1971 Bretton Woods System of Monetary Management Ends

1917 Russian Revolution

2011 UN Sanctions Military Intervention in Libya

1965 U.S. Combat Units Deployed to Vietnam

1945 End of WWII

1962 Cuban Missile Crisis

1914 Start of WWI

1960 European Free Trade Area Association

1944 Bretton Woods Agreement

1957 European Economic Community

1884 Berlin Conference

1956 Suez Crisis

2011 Arab Spring

1993 Maastricht Treaty

1900   1950   2000   2020

trade liberalization and economic growth

Does Trade Liberalization Contribute to Economic Prosperity?

YES: David Dollar, *U.S. Treasury Department*

NO: Robert H. Wade, *London School of Economics and Political Science*

The economic underpinnings of arguments for freer trade (trade liberalization) stem from the belief that the voluntary exchange of goods and services between individuals increases the well-being of both the buyer and the seller. This belief, which has served as the foundation of modern economics since Adam Smith wrote *The Wealth of Nations* in 1776, was originally a highly subversive idea: that not only would trade liberalization lead to mutual benefits but also that increased trade and interconnections would contribute to international peace. Writ large, the argument goes that the accumulation of individual voluntary economic exchanges benefits nations as a whole, for the benefits of exchange aggregate within and transcend political boundaries.

While it is well understood that rapidly increasing communications technologies have facilitated nearly instantaneous long-distance exchanges involving many more actors (whether news or financial markets) than in the past, at a more prosaic level, so too have reduced transportation costs facilitated international trade. Thus, the costs of trade—both financial and temporal—have been significantly reduced, thereby facilitating trade's rapid expansion. Coupled with **neoclassical economic thinking** and, in particular, the notion of **comparative advantage**—that more specialization and trade expands economic growth, even for nations facing absolute trade disadvantages compared with more productive counterparts—the reduced costs of trade should directly translate to more trade and, therefore, to more aggregate prosperity.

While the theory is well-understood, the question is whether trade liberalization has led empirically to greater prosperity.

Yet it is also clear to some observers that the stylized version of free trade championed by many—the win-win promise of free exchange—fails to live up to the realities of international trade. Global institutions that have been pushing trade liberalization, such as the International Monetary Fund (IMF) and the World Trade Organization (WTO), have been buffeted by political protest as a result. While Chapter 2 takes up the impact of trade on inequality, the initial consideration here is the impact of trade on overall economic prosperity. While the vast majority of economists believe that free trade promotes aggregate economic expansion, the policy choices required typically involve not binary choices between trade and no trade but more complex decisions over expansion or contraction of relatively modest tariffs and export subsidies and who is likely to benefit in the short term from trade liberalization.

Aside from aggregate trade levels, an important policy issue involves the **trade deficit** (total exports minus imports) for any particular nation. For many years, the United States enjoyed positive trade balances, meaning that it exported a greater value of goods than it imported. However, beginning with the sudden onset of elevated petroleum prices in the late 1970s, the nation began running trade deficits, and it has done so ever since. Recent increases in oil prices have exacerbated the situation to the point that, by 2010, trade deficits were hovering around $42 billion per month (or over $500 billion annually), despite a relatively weak dollar (which favors U.S. exports by enabling foreign buyers to purchase U.S. products with relatively inexpensive dollars). The political and economic concern is that consistent and increasing trade imbalances mean that the U.S. economy is, in effect, borrowing from the rest of the world to sustain its current consumption. Figure 1 (p. 3) shows the value of U.S. imports and exports since 1980, while Figure 2 (p. 3) portrays the difference between them—exports minus imports— thus reflecting the recent large and growing trade deficits.

Trade is, of course, more than a product of economics; it involves overt political and policy considerations as well. A general, global political preference for market liberalization, as well as efforts by the WTO, have had the effect of reducing import duties and other barriers to trade worldwide. The **General Agreement on Tariffs and Trade (GATT)** of 1947, along with other subsequent treaties, has reduced tariffs around the world. Many argue that reducing tariffs and diminishing other barriers to trade have increased levels of economic growth. While trade barriers tend to be lower in the wealthier nations of the **Organization for Economic Cooperation and Development (OECD)**, the costs of trade have been reduced overall by lowering both economic and political costs. Figures 3 and 4 (pp. 4 and 5) detail the broad reduction in

Figure 1

U.S. Exports and Imports in Goods and Services, 1978–2010

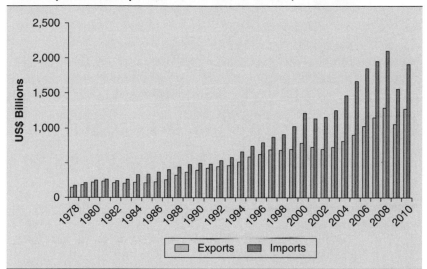

Source: U.S. Department of Commerce, Bureau of Economic Analysis, International Transactions database, http://www.bea.gov/iTable/iTable.cfm?ReqID=6&step=1 (accessed October 12, 2011).
Note: Data prior to 1978 not available from Bureau of Economic Analysis.

Figure 2

U.S. Trade Balance, 1960–2010

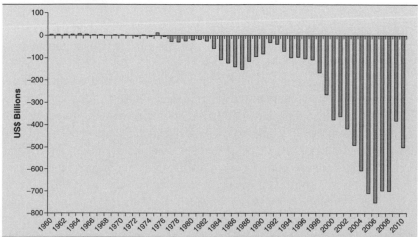

Source: U.S. Department of Commerce, Bureau of Economic Analysis, International Transactions database, http://www.bea.gov/iTable/iTable.cfm?ReqID=6&step=1 (accessed October 12, 2011).

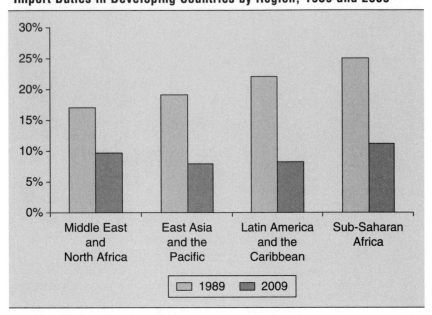

Figure 3

Import Duties in Developing Countries by Region, 1989 and 2009

Sources: United Nations Development Programme, *Human Development Report 2005* (New York: Oxford University Press, 2005), 116; World Bank, "Tariff Rate, Applied, Simple Mean, All Products (%)," (database), http://data.worldbank.org/indicator/TM.TAX.MANF.SM.AR.ZS/countries/XQ-XJ-ZF-4E-XS?display=graph (accessed October 12, 2011).

import duties from 1989 to 2009. In addition, increased transportation costs—particularly the cost of the petroleum that fuels most transportation—may affect overall levels of international trade.

The question raised here—whether tariff reductions and other trade liberalization policies contribute to economic prosperity—inevitably leads to discussion of whether these measures are preferable to some kind of industrial or strategic trade policy (such as export subsidies or tariffs on imported goods) that is intended to benefit domestic firms. Contemporary trade theory casts doubt on the simple notion that more trade equals more prosperity, in part because of increasing returns to scale (that is, the cost per unit produced decreases as more of it is produced), which suggests that free markets may lead to dominance by one or a few producers. Also, the benefits from expanded trade may not be evenly distributed within societies. For example, if sugar tariffs were reduced in the United States, domestic producers would be hurt while foreign producers would gain, as would U.S. taxpayers and

Figure 4

Import Duties in Developed and Developing Countries, 1989 and 2009

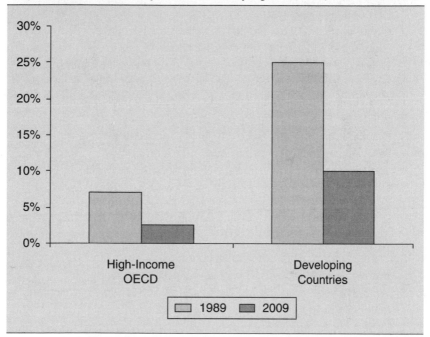

Sources: United Nations Development Programme, *Human Development Report 2005* (New York: Oxford University Press, 2005), 116; World Bank, "Tariff Rate, Applied, Simple Mean, All Products (%)," (database), http://data.worldbank.org/indicator/TM.TAX.MANF.SM.AR.ZS/countries/XQ-XJ-ZF-4E-XS?display=graph (accessed October 12, 2011).

consumers, who would pay slightly lower prices for sugar. Thus, even if aggregate prosperity increases, the benefits may be highly concentrated in the firms or sectors that are most competitive internationally and the costs imposed on those least internationally competitive. Furthermore, the empirical evidence linking trade and prosperity is mixed. For all the rhetoric surrounding economists' belief that free trade leads to greater prosperity, there are also other means of addressing problems associated with trade liberalization, such as economic assistance and retraining programs for workers who lose jobs as a result of the heightened competition.

The following two articles detail opposing viewpoints by two prominent economists: David Dollar and Robert Wade. Wade favors a nuanced approach to international trade policy rather than grand free trade agreements while Dollar argues that trade liberalization explains the economic resurgence of several developing economies.

Discussion Questions

1. Trade liberalization has made the world economy more highly integrated than ever before. Are there risks to such a highly integrated global economy? What are they? Do the benefits outweigh the risks?

2. Global trade liberalization has reduced tariffs and barriers to trade. One impact of this is cheaper imports. As a result, the United States has run a trade deficit for the past three decades. What are the risks of running a trade deficit instead of a trade surplus? What are the benefits?

3. China has emerged as one of the largest economies in the world, but its integration into the global economy and its move toward trade liberalization have not occurred without controversy or concern. What have the concerns been about, and who has expressed them? Consider such issues as jobs, quality standards of goods, foreign policy, democratization, and human rights. Are these concerns valid? Why or why not?

4. Is trade liberalization good for all countries? Why or why not? In what situations would a country reject liberalization as a trade policy?

5. What evidence does David Dollar cite to link trade liberalization and economic prosperity? Is his evidence convincing?

6. Robert Wade argues that trade liberalization is not a necessary condition for economic growth. What evidence does he use to argue his point? What would Dollar say in regard to Wade's claims? Who do you think is right?

YES: David Dollar, *U.S. Treasury Department*[1]

Trade liberalization is one of the controversial issues in the debates about the benefits and costs of globalization. There is no doubt that trade liberalization increases economic prosperity. Trade enables a country to sell more of the things it produces relatively efficiently and to purchase in return things that it produces not at all or less efficiently. The notion that this exchange is a "win-win" situation for both countries involved was developed as the theory of comparative advantage by David Ricardo. These benefits, however, are "static" in the sense that they represent a one-time increase in real income, rather than leading to continual increases in income (that is, economic growth).

A more interesting and controversial question is whether in general there are "dynamic" benefits to trade liberalization that lead to faster growth and hence much larger cumulative benefits. To address this question, it is useful to begin with what one would expect from economic theory. As Paul Romer (1986) has suggested, traditional theories about growth and differences in income levels among countries focused on accumulation and the "object gap" between poor countries and rich ones:

> To keep track of the wide range of explanations that are offered for persistent poverty in developing nations, it helps to keep two extreme views in mind. The first is based on an object gap: Nations are poor because they lack valuable objects like factories, roads, and raw materials. The second view invokes an idea gap: Nations are poor because their citizens do not have access to the ideas that are used in industrial nations to generate economic value....
>
> Each gap imparts a distinctive thrust to the analysis of development policy. The notion of an object gap highlights saving and accumulation. The notion of an idea gap directs attention to the patterns of interaction and communication between a developing country and the rest of the world.

If the preferred way to grow income is just to increase the number of factories and workplaces, then it does not matter if this increase is accomplished in a closed environment or a state-dominated environment. That model was followed in the extreme by China and the Soviet Union, and, to a lesser extent, by most developing countries, which followed import-substituting industrialization strategies throughout the 1960s and 1970s. It was the disappointing results from this development approach that led to new thinking both from policymakers in developing countries and from economists studying growth.

Romer was one of the pioneers of the new growth theory that put more emphasis on how innovation occurs and is spread and on the role of technological advance in improving the standard of living. According to this theory, trade liberalization—by allowing specialization, economies of scale, and purchase of the latest equipment and technology—can potentially help to overcome the "idea gap" that separates poor and rich nations. The straightforward approach, then, is to write down a growth model in which access to a large world market will accelerate growth, at least for some period of time. The debate over whether trade liberalization actually leads to faster growth is not going to be settled by theory, however, for this is inherently an empirical question.

In order to shed light on this question, we need to briefly review the history of trade liberalization, noting that the developed countries of Western Europe, North America, and Japan went through a postwar period of multilateral trade liberalization, while developing nations mostly sat on the sidelines. Starting around 1978, however, more and more developing economies chose to undertake unilateral trade liberalization. At about the same time, the aggregate growth rate of the developing world accelerated, and the world entered a remarkable period of poverty reduction.

Next, we will need to consider whether or not one can make a convincing empirical link from trade liberalization to faster growth. Case studies, cross-country statistical evidence, and micro evidence from firms all support the view that trade liberalization accelerates growth in an underdeveloped economy.

GROWING INTEGRATION BETWEEN NORTH AND SOUTH

Global economic integration has been going on for a long time; in that sense, globalization is nothing new. What is new in this most recent wave of globalization is the way in which developing countries are integrating with rich countries. As in previous waves of integration, this change is driven partly by technological advances in transport and communications, and partly by deliberate policy changes.

The first great era of modern globalization ran from about 1870 to 1914, spurred by the development of steam shipping and by an Anglo–French trade agreement. In this period, the world reached levels of economic integration comparable in many ways to those of today. Global integration took a big step backward, however, during the period of the two world wars and the Great Depression. Some discussions of globalization today assume that it is inevitable, but this painful episode is a powerful reminder that restrictive policies can halt and reverse integration. By the end of this dark era, both trade and foreign asset ownership were back down nearly to their levels of 1870—the protectionist period had undone fifty years of integration.

In the period from the end of World War II to about 1980, the industrial countries restored much of the integration that had existed among them. They negotiated a series of mutual trade liberalizations under the auspices of the General Agreement on Tariffs and Trade (GATT). In this second wave of modern globalization, many developing countries chose to sit on the sidelines. Most developing countries in Asia, Africa, and Latin America followed import-substituting industrialization strategies—that is, they kept their levels of import protection far higher than those in the industrial countries in order to encourage domestic production of manufactures, and they usually restricted foreign investment by multinational firms as well in order to encourage the growth of domestic firms. While limiting direct investment, quite a few developing countries turned to the practice of international bank borrowing that was expanding in the 1970s and thereby took on significant amounts of foreign debt.

The most recent wave of globalization began in 1978 with the initiation of China's economic reform and opening to the outside world. China's opening coincided roughly with the second oil shock, which contributed to external debt crises throughout Latin America and elsewhere in the developing world. In a growing number of countries—from Mexico to Brazil to India to sub-Saharan Africa—political and intellectual leaders began to fundamentally rethink their development strategies. What is distinctive, then, about this latest wave of globalization is that the majority of the developing world (measured in terms of population) has shifted from an inward-focused strategy to a more outward-oriented one.

Some measure of this policy trend can be seen in average import tariff rates for the developing world. Average tariffs have declined sharply in South Asia, Latin America, and East Asia—mostly the result of decisions to unilaterally liberalize trade—while in Africa and the Middle East there has been much less tariff-cutting (see Figure 1, p. 10). These reported average tariffs, however, capture only a small amount of what is happening with trade policy.

Often the most pernicious impediments are nontariff barriers: quotas, licensing schemes, restrictions on purchasing foreign exchange for imports. In China's case, reducing such nontariff impediments starting in 1979 led to a dramatic surge in trade (see Figure 2, p. 10). Whereas in 1978 external trade had been monopolized by a single government ministry, in the following year China began to shift to a policy of "free trade." (That phrase refers to a situation in which trade is not monopolized by the government, but rather is permitted to private firms and citizens as well.) The specific measures adopted in China included allowing a growing number of firms, including private ones, to trade directly and opening a foreign exchange market to facilitate this trade.

Figure 1

Average Unweighted Tariff Rates by Region, 1980–1998

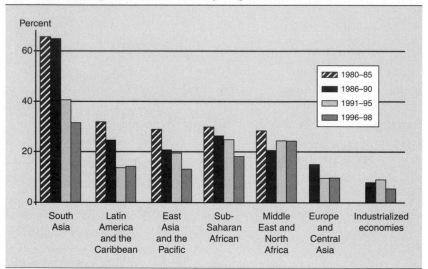

Source: Berg, Andrew and Anne Krueger, 2003. "Trade, Growth, and Poverty: A Selective Survey." IMF Working Paper, WP/03/30, p. 16.

Figure 2

Trade Reforms and Trade Volumes in China, 1978–2000

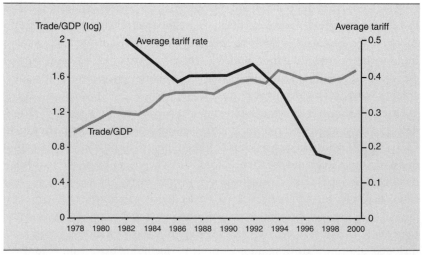

Source: Dollar, David and Aart Kraay. 2003. "Institutions, Trade, and Growth," *Journal of Monetary Economics* 50 (133–162), p. 151.

The immediate result of this altered strategy can be seen in the huge increases in trade integration of developing countries over the last two decades of the twentieth century. China's ratio of trade to national income more than doubled in that period, and countries such as Mexico, Bangladesh, Thailand, and India saw large increases as well (see Figure 3, this page). It was also the case, however, that quite a few developing countries traded less of their income over those two decades. Some of these countries engaged in relatively little formal trade liberalization, while in others, such as Kenya, formal trade liberalization was not complemented by efforts to improve customs and ports, with the result that the country traded less of its income in 1997 than it had done twenty years before.

The change was reflected not just in the *amount*, but also in the *nature of what was traded*. Prior to 1980, nearly 80 percent of developing countries' merchandise exports were primary products—the stereotype of poor countries exporting tin or bananas had a large element of truth. The big increase in merchandise exports over the next two decades, however, consisted of manufactured products, so that, by the century's end, 80 percent of merchandise exports from the low-income countries of the South were manufactures (see Figure 4, p. 12). Garments from Bangladesh, refrigerators from Mexico, computer peripherals from Thailand, CD players from China—this had become the modern face of developing country exports. Service exports from the developing world had

Figure 3

Change in Trade/GDP, 1977–1997 (Selected Countries)

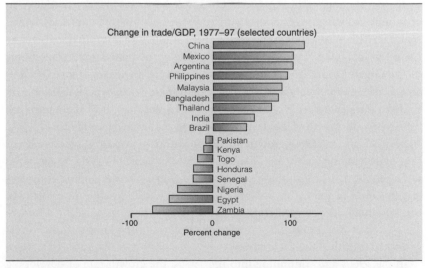

Source: Dollar, David. 2004. "Globalization, Poverty, and Inequality since 1980." World Bank Policy Research Working Paper, No. 3333, p. 7.

Figure 4

Developing Country Exports, 1965–1998

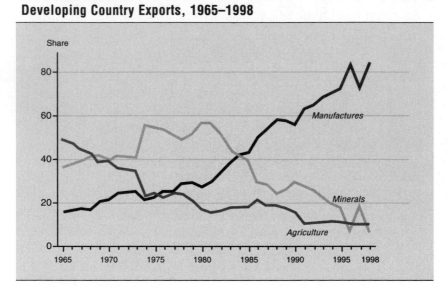

Source: Dollar, David. 2004. "Globalization, Poverty, and Inequality since 1980." World Bank Policy Research Working Paper, No. 3333, p. 8.

also increased enormously, both traditional services such as tourism and more distinctively modern ones, such as software from Bangalore, India.

At the same time as trade was being liberalized, the aggregate growth rate of the developing world was accelerating. We have reasonably good data on economic growth going back to 1960 for about one hundred countries, which make up the vast majority of the world's population, summarized in the Penn World Tables. If you aggregate all of the industrial countries (members of the Organization for Economic Cooperation and Development [OECD]) and all of the developing countries for which there are data back to 1960, you find that, in general, rich country growth rates declined until the end of the century, while growth of the developing world accelerated (see Figure 5, p. 13). In particular, in the 1960s growth of OECD countries was about twice as fast as that of developing countries. This was a period in which the OECD countries were benefiting from mutual trade liberalization while developing countries largely chose to follow inward-oriented strategies. The rich country growth then gradually decelerated from about 4 percent per capita in the 1960s to 1.7 percent in the 1990s. The latter figure is close to the long-term historical growth rate of the OECD countries.

In the 1960s and continuing into the 1970s, the growth rate of developing countries in the aggregate was well below that of rich countries—a paradox

Figure 5

Growth Rates of Per Capita GDP, 1960s–1990s

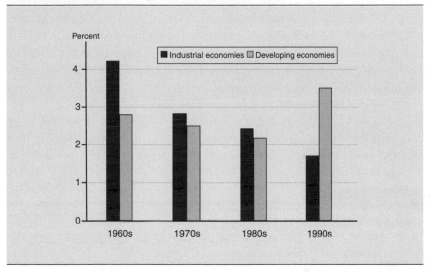

Source: Dollar, David. 2004. "Globalization, Poverty, and Inequality since 1980." World Bank Policy Research Working Paper, No. 3333, p. 13.

whose origin has been long debated in the economics profession. The slower growth of backward economies in that period appeared to contradict the dominant neoclassical growth theory, which suggested that, other things being equal, poor countries should grow faster. This expected pattern finally emerged in the 1990s, when per capita growth in developing countries reached about 3.5 percent, more than twice the rate of rich countries. Since 2000, developing country growth has been even faster.

Poverty reduction in low-income countries is very closely related to the GDP growth rate. Hence, the accelerated growth of low-income countries has led to unprecedented poverty reduction. (By *poverty,* we mean subsisting below some absolute threshold. In global discussions, one often sees reference to an international poverty line of $1 per day, calculated at purchasing power parity.) Shenhua Chen and Martin Ravallion (2004) have used household survey data to estimate the number of individuals classified as poor worldwide based on the $1 poverty line, back to 1981. They find that the incidence of extreme poverty (consuming less than $1 per day) was basically cut in half over a twenty-year period, from 40.3 percent of the developing world's population in 1981 to 21.3 percent in 2001. In 1981 extreme poverty was concentrated in East and South Asia, and these were the regions that grew especially well over the next two decades, dramatically reducing extreme poverty.

Poverty incidence has been gradually declining throughout modern history, but in general population growth has outstripped the decline in incidence, so that the total number of poor people was actually rising. Even in the 1960–1980 period, which was reasonably good for developing countries, the number of poor continued to rise (see Figure 6, this page).[2] What is really striking about the two decades that followed—indeed, it was unprecedented in human history—is that the number of extreme poor declined by 375 million, while at the same time the world's population rose by 1.6 billion. While this overall decline in global poverty is encouraging, it should be noted that there has been very different performance across regions. While East and South Asia grew well and reduced poverty, sub-Saharan Africa had negative growth between 1981 and 2001 and a rise in poverty.

Figure 6

World Poverty, 1820–2001

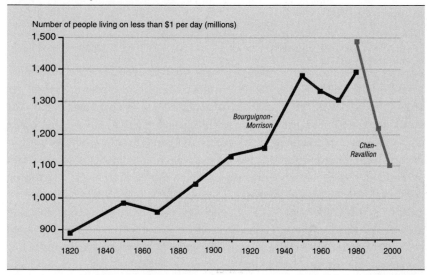

Source: Dollar, David. 2004. "Globalization, Poverty, and Inequality since 1980." World Bank Policy Research Working Paper, No. 3333, p. 18.

THE LINK FROM INTEGRATION TO GROWTH

Developing countries became more integrated with the global economy over the last two decades of the twentieth century, while growth and poverty reduction accelerated. A natural question to ask is whether there was a link between these two phenomena. In other words, could countries such as Bangladesh, China, India, and Vietnam have grown as rapidly as they did, had they remained as closed to foreign trade and investment as they were in 1980? This is not the kind of question that can be answered with scientific certainty, but there are several different types of evidence that we can bring to bear on it.

First, a large number of case studies show how this process can work in particular countries. Among the countries that were very poor in 1980, China, India, Vietnam, and Uganda provide an interesting range of examples.

China

China's initial reforms in the late 1970s focused on the agricultural sector and emphasized strengthening property rights, liberalizing prices, and creating internal markets. As indicated in Figure 2 (p. 10), liberalizing foreign trade and investment was also part of the initial reform program and played an increasingly important role in growth as the 1980s proceeded.

The role of international linkages is described in a case study by Richard Eckaus (1997):

> After the success of the Communist revolution and the founding of the People's Republic of China, the nation's international economic policies were dominated for at least thirty years by the goal of self-reliance.... China's foreign trade began to expand rapidly as the turmoil created by the **Cultural Revolution** dissipated and new leaders came to power. Though it was not done without controversy, the argument that opening of the economy to foreign trade was necessary to obtain new capital equipment and new technology was made official policy.

At the same time, Eckaus notes, international transactions outside the state planning system were growing. Enterprises created by foreign investors were exempted from the foreign trade planning and control mechanisms, and substantial amounts of other types of trade, particularly that between township and village enterprises and private firms, were made relatively free. "The expansion of China's participation in international trade since the beginning of the reform movement in 1978 has been one of the most remarkable features of its remarkable transformation," says Eckaus. "While GNP [gross national product] was growing at 9 percent from 1978 to 1994, exports grew at about 14 percent and imports at an average of 13 percent per year."

India

India pursued an inward-oriented strategy into the 1980s and got disappointing results in terms of growth and poverty reduction. Jagdish Bhagwati (1992) crisply defines the main problems and failures of the strategy:

> I would divide them into three major groups: extensive bureaucratic controls over production, investment and trade; inward-looking trade and foreign investment policies; and a substantial public sector, going well beyond the conventional confines of public utilities and infrastructure.
>
> The former two adversely affected the private sector's efficiency. The last, with the inefficient functioning of public sector enterprises, impaired additionally the public sector enterprises' contribution to the economy. Together, the three sets of policy decisions broadly set strict limits to what India could get out of its investment.

Under this policy regime, India's growth in the 1960s (1.4% per annum) and the 1970s (−0.3%) was disappointing. The country's economic performance improved during the 1980s, but this surge was fueled by deficit spending and borrowing from abroad that was unsustainable. In fact, the spending spree led to a fiscal and **balance of payments** crisis that brought a new, reform government to power in 1991. Key aspects of its program of reform were an initial devaluation of the rupee and subsequent market determination of its exchange rate, abolition of import licensing (with some important exceptions), convertibility of the rupee on current account, reduction in the number of tariff lines as well as tariff rates, and an easing of entry requirements for direct foreign investment.

In general, India has gotten good results from its reform program, as per capita income growth remained above 4 percent per annum in the 1990s and then accelerated to around 6 percent after 2000. This pattern reinforces the conclusion that growth and poverty reduction have been particularly strong in states that have made the most progress in liberalizing their economies.

Vietnam

Another interesting case is Vietnam—a country that went from basket-case status in the mid-1980s to that of a dynamic exporter and darling of international investors twenty years later. In a case study of that startling turn-around, Dollar and Ljunggren (1997) reflect on its proximate causes:

> That Vietnam was able to grow throughout its adjustment period can be attributed to the fact that the economy was being increasingly opened to the international market. As part of its overall effort to stabilize the

economy, the government unified its various controlled exchange rates in 1989 and devalued the unified rate to the level prevailing in the parallel market. This was tantamount to a 73 percent *real* devaluation; combined with relaxed administrative procedures for imports and exports, this sharply increased the profitability of exporting.

According to these authors' analysis, this policy produced strong incentives for export throughout most of the 1989–1994 period, during which real export growth averaged more than 25 percent per annum. Exports—mainly of rice at first, but later of a wide range of exports, including processed primary products (for example, rubber, cashews, and coffee), labor-intensive manufactures, and tourist services—were a leading sector spurring the expansion of the economy.

While the country's current account deficit declined from more than 10 percent of GDP [gross domestic product] in 1988 to zero in 1992, Vietnam's export growth was sufficient to ensure that imports could continue to grow, rather than being cut back, as might have been expected. Noting that investment increased sharply between 1988 and 1992, while foreign aid [from the Soviet Union] was drying up, Dollar and Ljunggren explain: "In response to stabilization, strengthened property rights, and greater openness to foreign trade, domestic savings increased by twenty percentage points of GDP, from negative levels in the mid-1980s to 16 percent of GDP in 1992."

Uganda

Uganda was one of the most successful reformers in Africa during this recent wave of globalization, and its experience has interesting parallels with Vietnam's. It, too, was a country that was quite isolated economically and politically in the early 1980s.

According to Paul Collier and Ritva Reinikka (2001, 30–39), trade liberalization was central to Uganda's structural reform program:

> During the 1970s, export taxation and quantitative restrictions on imports characterized trade policy in Uganda. Exports were taxed, directly and implicitly at very high rates. All exports except for coffee collapsed under this taxation.
>
> Part of the export taxation was achieved through overvaluation of the exchange rate, which was propelled by intense foreign exchange rationing, but mitigated by an active illegal market. Manufacturing based on **import substitution** collapsed along with the export sector as a result of shortages, volatility, and rationing of import licenses and foreign exchange.

The NRM [National Resistance Movement] government that came to power in 1986 thus inherited a trade regime that included extensive nontariff barriers, biased government purchasing, and high export taxes, coupled with considerable smuggling. The nontariff barriers were gradually removed after the introduction in 1991 of automatic licensing under an import certification scheme. During the latter half of the 1990s, the government implemented a major tariff reduction program, and, as a result, "by 1999 the tariff system had been substantially rationalized and liberalized, which gave Uganda one of the lowest tariff structures in Africa." The maximum tariff was set at 15 percent on consumer goods, zero for capital goods, and 7 percent for intermediate imports.

Collier and Reinikka summarize the results of this reform effort:

> The country's average real GDP growth rate was 6.3 percent per year over the entire recovery period (1986–1999) and 6.9 percent in the 1990s. The liberalization of trade has had a marked effect on export performance. In the 1990s export volumes grew (at constant prices) at an annualized rate of 15 percent, and import volumes grew at 13 percent. The value of noncoffee exports increased fivefold between 1992 and 1999.

CONCLUSION

These cases provide persuasive evidence that openness to foreign trade and investment—coupled with complementary reforms—can lead to faster growth in developing countries. All of them also illustrate the earlier failure of import-substitution strategies based on protecting the domestic market. However, individual cases always beg the question, how general are these results? Does the typical developing country that liberalizes foreign trade and investment get good results?

Cross-country statistical analysis is useful for looking at the general patterns in the data, and such studies generally find a correlation between trade and growth. As reflected in the case studies reviewed above, some developing countries have had large increases in trade integration (measured as the ratio of trade to national income), while others have had small increases or even declines. In general, the countries that have had large increases in trade integration have also seen accelerations in growth. This relationship between trade and growth persists after controlling for reverse causality from growth to trade and for changes in other institutions and policies (Dollar and Kraay 2002).

A third type of evidence about integration and growth comes from firm-level studies and links us back to Paul Romer's theories about trade liberalization and innovation, quoted earlier. Developing countries often have large productivity dispersion across firms making similar things: high productivity and low productivity firms coexist, and in small markets there is often insufficient competition to spur innovation. A consistent finding of firm-level studies is that openness leads to lower productivity dispersion—the less efficient, high-cost producers exit the market as prices fall. While the destruction and creation of new firms is a normal part of a well-functioning economy, attention is too often paid only to the destruction of firms, missing half of the picture. In a more open economy, there are more firm start-ups, a prime source of jobs and productivity growth. The higher turnover of firms is thus an important source of the dynamic benefit of openness. In general, dying firms have falling productivity, and new ones tend to increase productivity.

While these studies shed some light on why open economies are more innovative and dynamic, they also remind us why integration is controversial. There will be more dislocation in an open, dynamic economy, as some firms close and others start up. If workers have good social protection and opportunities for developing new skills, everyone can benefit. But without such policies, there can be some big losers.

The economic historians Peter Lindert and Jeffrey Williamson (2001, 29–30) make a nice point about the different pieces of evidence linking integration to growth: "The doubts that one can retain about each individual study threaten to block our view of the overall forest of evidence. Even though no one study can establish that openness to trade has unambiguously helped the representative Third World economy, the preponderance of evidence supports this conclusion." Going on to note the "empty set" of "countries that chose to be less open to trade and factor flows in the 1990s than in the 1960s and rose in the global living-standard ranks at the same time," they conclude: "As far as we can tell, there are no anti-global victories to report for the postwar Third World. We infer that this is because freer trade stimulates growth in Third World economies today, regardless of its effects before 1940."

NOTES

1. Views expressed are those of the author and do not necessarily represent official views of the U.S. Treasury Department.
2. It is difficult to take the survey-based estimates of poverty back before 1980. Bourguignon and Morrison (2002) combine what survey data are available with national accounts data to provide rough estimates of poverty back to 1820. The broad trend is clear: The number of poor in the world kept rising up to about 1980.

NO: Robert H. Wade, *London School of Economics and Political Science*

There is nothing that economists agree about more than the virtues of free or almost-free trade.[1] Nicholas Stern, former chief economist at the World Bank, declared in 2008, "95 percent of the arguments for protection are rubbish, and the other 5 percent don't work in practice."[2] Jagdish Bhagwati, a distinguished trade economist, claimed that belief in the superiority of the free or near-free trade strategy over the "import substitution" strategy is all but universal among economists, "insofar as any kind of consensus can ever be found in our tribe."[3] A survey of economists' opinions elicited responses to twenty-seven propositions about the economy from about 1,000 economists in five industrialized countries, using terms of "generally agree," "agree with provisos," and "generally disagree." Of the twenty-seven, "tariffs and import controls lower economic welfare" elicited the most agreement. Fifty-seven percent of the whole sample "generally agreed" with it, including 79 percent of the American economists but only 27 percent of the French economists.[4]

The free trade consensus has justified the World Bank's emphasis on trade liberalization as not just one policy reform among many but as the queen of reforms. Its Structural Adjustment Loans over the 1980s and 1990s carried more trade liberalization conditions than those in any other policy domain.[5] Moreover, the Bank's Country Policy and Institutional Assessment (CPIA) formula—by which it scores each of its developing country members each year on more than a dozen dimensions of policy and institutions—requires a country to have a virtually completely free trade regime in order to get the top score for "trade policy." The same neoliberal thrust is expressed in the other economic components of the formula; under "labor market institution," for example, a country gets the top score only if it is free of trade union "rigidities" like collective bargaining.

To see how these ideas shape country policy today, take the case of Mongolia. The government that took power as communism ended in 1991 swung to the noncommunist extreme and embarked on fast, unstrategic economic liberalization. It was hailed as a star pupil of the Washington Consensus. But the industrial sector collapsed, urban unemployment soared, people retreated into pastoralism, pastoral yields collapsed, and social indicators fell (having been high relative to per capita income in the bad old communist days).[6]

However, the government did want to retain one primitive industrial policy: a tax on the export of unprocessed wool (an instrument the English government had used to develop the wool industry in competition with already-established competitors on the Continent in the fifteenth century). The Asia Development Bank offered the government a big loan (roughly $200 million)—on condition that the government drop the export tax. The government obliged, removed the export tax, and Mongolia's wool came to be processed in China and Italy. Good for China and Italy, bad for Mongolia, which continued to struggle with high unemployment, overpopulation in the pastoral economy, and a large current-account deficit. Mongolia's experience illustrates that the alternative to an "inefficient" industrial sector, measured in world market prices, may be not an "efficient" one, but none.

Fast forward to 2002, when a German Development Bank mission arrived in Ulan Bator to help with the country's World Trade Organization (WTO) accession. The mission discussed Mongolia's situation with the World Bank country director and floated the idea of restoring an export tax on unprocessed wool. The World Bank country director put his foot down, declaring, "That would be going backwards. We don't want the government to intervene in the economy. We want the government to stick to free trade."[7] In the Mongolia story, we see the **Asian Development Bank**, the World Bank, and the postcommunist Mongolian government giving a high priority to free trade policy, as if there were no sensible alternative.

The idea that trade has almost magical developmental effects is frequently reiterated from authoritative positions in the international development community, as in World Bank president Paul Wolfowitz's declaration that, "It is trade that will allow poor countries to generate growth. . . . It is trade that has helped 400 million Chinese escape poverty in the past 20 years and the same can happen elsewhere." Fudging the important distinction between "trade policy" and "trade quantities and values," such statements assume that freer trade policy reliably generates more trade and that more trade reliably improves indicators of economic development.

In the same vein, most commentators in the West agree that the early 2007 collapse of the WTO's Doha Round trade negotiations—aimed at intensifying the Uruguay Round's multilateral liberalization of trade and investment (while retaining tough protection of intellectual property)—was a bad thing for everyone except some special interest groups. They paint a post-Doha scenario of crumbling multilateral trade arrangements, proliferating bilateral or regional trade agreements ("stumbling blocks" rather than "building blocks"), and trade quarrels seemingly immune to the WTO's Dispute Settlement Mechanism. They also say that developing countries are the big losers, because various aid-for-trade and trade facilitation measures written into Doha will be suspended while agricultural support in the United States, the **European Union,** and Japan will continue, making it more difficult for developing countries both to sustain their own agricultures in the face of cheap food imports and to export agricultural products to the developed countries' markets—thus assuming that they should specialize more in agriculture, their "comparative advantage."

The Financial Times rebuked Japan in 2009 for attempting to hang on to a large manufacturing sector, on grounds that manufacturing is no longer in Japan's comparative advantage. "[I]t no longer makes sense to deploy [the] ability [of companies like Sony, Canon and Panasonic] in Japan. Instead, they need to complete the shift of their manufacturing offshore, whether it is outsourced or kept in-house." At home, Japanese companies should concentrate on research and on "telling others what to make." *The Financial Times* kept silent on the obvious question: will concentrating on research and telling others what to make provide sufficient employment and sufficient exports with which to import the now-outsourced manufactured goods? [8]

The larger normative vision is of a "globalized" world where "the market"—the institution of "efficiency," "freedom," "democracy," and of "ordinary people versus elites"—has maximum scope, conversely, where national borders have little economic significance (except perhaps to restrain labor migration). As Martin Wolf of *The Financial Times* says, "It cannot make sense to fragment the world economy more than it already is but *rather to make the world economy work as if it were the United States*"— that is, with national borders having no more economic significance than the borders between U.S. states.[9] The normative vision is articulated in the global policy paradigm known as the "Washington Consensus" about what is good for developing countries. It prescribes as its central thrusts privatization of state enterprises, liberalization of markets, and macroeconomic stability, with the end point being an integrated global free trade zone, free of government restrictions on the movement of goods and services, and an integrated global free production zone, free of government restrictions on foreign direct investment and the movement of company ownership from place to place.[10]

Yet one need look no further than the Latin America–China comparison to see that something is amiss with the free trade consensus and the larger Washington Consensus. Twenty years ago, Latin America was the champion liberalizer, while China not only retained high barriers to trade and foreign investment and capital flows but also allowed its government to continue to steer the economy, including through state-owned banks. Latin America was expected to ascend to the First World while China would languish in the Third World. Twenty years on, however, China is the great success story; it is now a major world economic power, and many fewer of its people are living in poverty. Latin America, meanwhile, experienced an export boom, from $100 billion in 1981 to $750 billion in 2007; but the export boom was driven by rising demand for commodities with low value added per capita more than by rising industrial investment. Latin America's growth now depends heavily on China's; the industrial sector has been eroded (most of Brazil's Carnevale costumes are now made in China, and Brazil's steel exporters have lost out to Chinese steel exporters in third markets, whose steel is made with Brazilian iron ore); and its poverty headcount (number of people living on less than $2 a day) soared from 140 million in 1980 to 210 million in 2005. Between 2007 and 2011, the East Asian region increased gross domestic product (GDP) by some 60 percent, compared to Brazil's 16 percent (and developed countries' 3 percent).

An equally telling piece of evidence comes from the comparison of Latin America's productivity growth in 1960–1975, the period of "bad" import-substituting industrialization (with planning, trade and capital protection, and subsidies to new industries), and in 1990–2005, the period of "good" Washington Consensus policies. Labor productivity under import-substituting industrialization policies grew *twice* as fast as in the Washington Consensus period. Virtually all the faster rate of growth in the earlier period was due to structural change, as labor moved from sectors of lower productivity to those of higher productivity. This structural change almost stopped during the Washington Consensus era.[11] To this day, Latin American countries depend dangerously on external sources of growth, mainly exports of commodities and inflows of foreign capital.

This essay argues that both theoretical developments and new empirical evidence call for a rethinking of the free trade consensus. Indeed, it shows that the consensus does not now hold among the subset of economists working directly on trade and trade policy. Economists in general, political leaders, business leaders, and concerned citizens should pay attention to the shifting ground of theory and evidence, taking a questioning approach to the claim that trade liberalization is a necessary condition for economic progress and even more so to the claim that it is an almost sufficient condition for economic progress.[12]

GIVENS

To clear the ground, we can take the following propositions as given.

- Some trade is better than no trade (no one champions **autarky**, not even North Korea).

- Trade can expand markets, lower costs, intensify competition, disseminate knowledge of tastes and technology, and raise productivity.

- Countries that have sustained fast growth have generally experienced a rising share of trade in GDP.

- In these cases, the broad direction of change in trade barriers has been downward.

- Very high average tariffs (say 40 percent or more) and large variations in effective tariffs between one sector and another reflecting not national strategy but inertia or interest-group pressures constitute a "bad" trade regime. As between this bad regime and free trade, free trade wins hands down.

But this last is a phony choice. The policy question generally is, "Should the government now give high priority to *further and across-the-board* trade liberalization?" as distinct from all the other things that compete for the government's attention. Part of the answer should rest on the answer to the question, "Is trade liberalization reliably associated with subsequent higher growth and lower poverty?"

FREE TRADE THEORY

If the residents of London and Manchester both gain by trading with one another, why not equally the residents of England and Portugal? What difference does a national border make? If two autarchic economies start trading with each other, both will gain as each moves to specialize in its "comparative advantage." Therefore, according to free trade theory, trade is good and more trade is better. If an economy currently has tariffs or restrictions on imports, it can almost always gain (improve efficiency) by lowering or removing them, regardless of starting level, even if other countries maintain protection. In the words of a *Financial Times* editorial, "The case for trade liberalisation is simple: it is not wise to throw rocks into your own harbours. Liberalisation has run aground [in the failure of the Doha Round of trade negotiations] because its defenders have failed to make that simple argument."[13]

The core proposition of this popular theory is that fully employed resources will be utilized more efficiently in the absence of barriers to trade.[14] It assumes that fuller exposure to international competition does not cause higher unemployment, so the efficiency gains from lifting trade barriers are not measured against the various kinds of costs associated with higher unemployment. Where, as is common in developing countries, the economy's main problem is failure to fully utilize its resources rather than failure to direct them into the most efficient uses, this assumption is problematic.

Evidence for Free Trade

An impressive amount of evidence seems to support the free trade argument. Since the late 1960s, a dozen major studies have examined the impact of trade regimes on economic growth, income distribution, poverty, and other development indicators.[15] These studies confirm that free or almost-free trade produces the best economic results (with some small exceptions) and that countries with freer, less distorted trade regimes have better development performance than countries with less open, more distorted ones. In the words of one such study, "The best evidence available shows ... [that] the current wave of globalization, which started around 1980, has actually promoted economic equality and reduced poverty."[16]

The implications of this finding go well beyond trade policy. Import tariffs and import controls are only a subset of the ways in which governments try to alter the composition of economic activity. The neoclassical mainstream says that most such interventions are a mistake—not just one mistake among many, but a mistake so big as to constitute one of the main reasons for the slow progress of most developing countries. As a cause of poor development performance, bad government intervention dwarfs other domestic factors such as location, lack of natural resources and "inherent" market failures (those not caused by government) and also external factors such as falling terms of trade, volatility in exchange rates between the major currencies, and rich country trade regimes rigged against exports from developing countries.[17]

The free market argument is derived from classical liberalism, which sees "the state" as artificial and "the market" as natural and the two in fundamental tension. The proposition that real-world states are even more imperfect than real-world markets has not been subject to testing in any direct way, but the many studies of trade policy do constitute the most systematic testing of propositions derived from it. Through their support for free (or always freer) trade, they also support the meta-belief that imperfect markets are generally better than imperfect states and therefore that states should withdraw from directly influencing resource allocation in directly productive activities. And so these studies of trade regimes also support the allergy in neoclassical economics toward anything called "industrial policy," which involves the state protecting or giving preferential resources to certain sectors, such as infant industry protection.[18] They affirm the truth of the core neoliberal belief, succinctly expressed by Garry Kasperov, "The free market is what works—and having the state help it is usually a contradiction in terms."[19]

NEW TRADE THEORY

However, the foundational ideas of free trade advocates—the line of theory associated with Smith-Ricardo-Heckscher-Ohlin-Samuelson—deal with the static efficiency gains from trade, as in the reallocation of *existing* resources due to the switch from no-trade to trade, causing a one-time increase in the level of GDP per capita. This is quite separate from the proposition that a rise in the trade-to-GDP ratio causes higher *growth* rates (faster expansion of available resources) and also from the separate proposition that trade policy liberalization (cutting tariffs and nontariff barriers) causes higher growth rates.

Also, the foundational ideas assume that: (1) international trade is inter-industry trade (English cloth for Portuguese wine, for example); (2) firms are "homogeneous" (hence the unit is a "representative" producer); (3) the free international market will "automatically" shunt every national economy into its comparative advantage specialization by the same "invisible hand" mechanism that operates in the domestic economy; (4) countries have no spatial structure between them or within them—no clustering or agglomeration; (5) diminishing returns to economic activities prevail over increasing returns; and (6) production factors (capital, labor) are mobile within countries but immobile between them. On this wobbly pyramid of assumptions and factoids economists' confidence in free trade is substantially based.

In the mid- to late 1980s, "the deep slumber of a decided opinion" (to use J. S. Mill's phrase) suddenly stirred to life. A number of younger economists—including Paul Krugman, Elhanan Helpman, Gene Grossman, and Paul Romer—tried to develop theory capable of explaining two glaring facts not explainable by standard theory:

(a) very large spatial disparities in income and wealth persist over decades and centuries, even within well-functioning market economies (northern and southern Italy, for example), and still more between countries at different levels of development that are engaged in international trade; and

(b) most trade is of the kind that earlier trade theory conveniently assumed away: intra-industry trade (Italian shoes to India, Indian shoes to Italy).[20]

The resulting stream of literature came to be known as "new trade theory." It incorporated more "realistic" assumptions, such as imperfect competition, increasing returns to scale; and it allowed for different products (grain, apparel, machine tools) having different intensities of these characteristics and so having different potential for further growth and diversification.

New New Trade Theory

New trade theory retained the earlier assumption of no differences between firms—the assumption of a "representative" firm for each product category. By the early 2000s, however, large-scale data on firm-level participation in international trade became available, making it clear that differences among firms matter for understanding international trade. Most firms, even in traded-goods sectors such as manufacturing, agriculture, and mining, do not export: in the United States in 2000, only 15 percent of firms in these sectors exported. Also, among exporting firms, exports are highly concentrated: the top 10 percent of U.S. exporting firms account for 96 percent of aggregate U.S. exports. These stylized facts about firm differences prompted a new wave of literature—known, clunkily, as "new new trade theory"—that was developed by Marc Melitz, Stephen Redding, Richard Baldwin, and others.[21]

Pinelopi Goldberg and Nina Pavcnik spell out the significance of the new data. "In recent years, it has become increasingly apparent that trade is more than the flow of goods between countries as traditionally modeled in international trade theory. Trade represents exchange between firms that are located in different countries. . . . Accordingly, questions, such as what types of firms produce what goods and for which markets, which firms export and which ones produce for the domestic market, what are the characteristics of workers employed by different types of firms, etc., are becoming more prominent in the literature."[22] Richard Baldwin and Frederic Robert-Nicoud present a model of trade with heterogeneous firms that concludes that a rise in a country's trade "openness" (a fall in the transaction costs of trade, including tariffs and quantitative restrictions) may have growth-depressing effects as well as growth-enhancing effects, and the balance of the two effects is ambiguous.[23]

The policy implications of this theoretical upheaval have hardly begun to be developed, but it is clear that they seriously complicate the old verities. Still, even those who have done the most to develop the new theories—and to show theoretical mechanisms by which countries might gain from managed trade—tend to row back toward free trade as the best *practical* policy, as in Paul Krugman's dictum, "Free trade rules are best for a world whose politics are as imperfect as its markets."[24] They justify the retreat to free trade by reference to the danger that more strategic policy would be "hijacked" by special interests. Yet they make no analysis of this claim, in contrast to the sophistication they bring to the arguments against free trade. As for the operational economists in organizations such as the World Bank, they don't pay much attention to the new theory. They have strong career incentives to prescribe with certainty—"I know what country X should do even before I get out of the airplane"—and they can be more certain if they believe in a single broad policy package for all countries, whether it be Mongolia, Sri Lanka, or Brazil. The commitment of operational economists to this orthodoxy limits the diffusion of the new ideas, because the World Bank has a strong "cowbell" effect, a disproportionate weight in shaping others' beliefs about what is true or not true.

Theories of Increasing Returns, Multiple Equilibria, and Spatial Structure

The most profound challenge to the theory of comparative advantage comes from beyond the new and newer trade theories—from a broader, less trade-specific economics of "multiple equilibria" and spatial structure, which sometimes goes under the name of "new economic geography."[25] Ralph Gomery, William Baumol, Paul Krugman, Anthony Venables, Dani Rodrik, and Anthony Thirlwall are leading thinkers in this stream.[26]

The empirical starting point for this approach is the finding that the location of a given industry in one country or another is often not a matter of comparative advantage but of accident and path-dependence. There is no reason of comparative advantage to explain why Switzerland has long dominated the watch industry, why Taiwan dominated the production of laptops (but not their branding), why Pakistan specializes in soccer balls and Bangladesh specializes in hats rather than the other way around, or why Liechtenstein's big companies specialize in, respectively, power tools, microwave meals, and false teeth.[27] It turns out that industries have different "retainability" scores in the sense that some industries, once established, are sheltered from the blast of full competition and can earn "super-normal" returns, because would-be competitors find it difficult to break in.

The new stream of theory shows how, in a world of increasing returns (rather than constant or diminishing, as in standard models), the existing market equilibrium may not be optimal. The existing allocation of industries across countries is (a) fragile and (b) not necessarily "globally" optimal (*globally* in the sense of better than any feasible alternative, not in the geographical sense). But the market lacks a mechanism for getting to a global optimum. The theory suggests that trade liberalization would not necessarily shunt the economy into a more desirable position than it could have reached with more activist trade and industrial policy, contrary to Ricardian trade theory. The theory of comparative advantage, being concerned with how an economy can best exploit its *present* stock of resources, can hardly tackle the trade-off between acting today to maximize short-term efficiency and acting today to accelerate the economy's shift of tomorrow's comparative advantage into higher value-added, higher return products.[28]

One of the key analytical mechanisms is the link from spatial proximity to productivity, a link which is often characterized by increasing returns ("proximity promotes productivity"). Denser spatial configurations of economic activity—more firms and more skilled people in the same space—promote productivity more than looser ones, up to some point of diminishing returns due to congestion and other costs. This kind of market "externality" underlies the importance of clustered networks of supporting industries for the growth of any one industry, as in Silicon Valley and the east coast of China.

The networks can also operate across a national space. For example, U.S. military procurement is a giant industrial policy protecting whole chains of high-tech supplier industries across the United States under the justification of "national security," which allows the U.S. government to give protection to firms producing in the United States while demanding that other countries give up protecting their own.[29] The U.S. government paid for 50–70 percent of total R&D expenditures in the United States from the 1950s to the mid-1990s, mostly under cover of the defense umbrella. But the opposite tendencies are also in evidence. As Boeing switches component suppliers to China, U.S.-based component suppliers stop producing in the United States; U.S. supply networks fragment, causing knock-on costs to other industries; and Chinese firms buy U.S. component-making technology, the better to supply companies such as Boeing from China.

INDUSTRIAL POLICY AND INTER-STATE COMPETITION

The "new economic geography" suggests a new rationale for "infant indus-try protection," a long-but-grudgingly accepted partial exception to the prescription of free trade. In conventional trade theory, the infant indus-try exception is presumed to apply—if at all—only to newly-industrializing countries trying to lay down basic industries. But multiple equilibria theory suggests that the continuous technological evolution of the world economy means that parts of many industries are "infants" at any one time, even in the most technologically advanced economies. The task of governments, even in advanced economies, is to capture "high retainability" industries for their jurisdiction, using trade and other industrial policy instruments—even at the cost of short-term inefficiency. The new thinking suggests how strate-gic industrial policy (including trade as well as technology, infrastructure, and education policies) can help in securing the economy's place in higher-potential industries with higher "retainability" scores. But as a general rule, the intervention should be temporary so that the market eventually supports the better equilibrium unaided. Of course, all governments—not just that of the United States—try to disguise what they are doing, so as to get others to do what they *say*: "we must all embrace free trade." The strategy could be called "optimal obfuscation."

In these terms, we can make sense of the observed intense rivalry between nations as they jockey for industrial advantage—a far cry from the harmonious world of comparative advantage theory (whose assumption of mutual rather than conflicting interests is one of its strongest selling points for the international development community). Developed nations are silently implementing mercantilist industrial policy not mainly with trade instruments, such as tariffs, but with more subtle, less noticeable behind-the-border instruments, such as anti-dumping legislation, antitrust, rules of origin, health standards, and especially government procurement; and, as suggested earlier, these nations often invoke national security to justify support that cannot be concealed. This international rivalry helps to explain why the business school myth of multinational corporations as free-floating, cosmopolitan entities owing allegiance to nowhere is just that—a myth. State support tends to be geared toward high-tech firms regarded as "nationals" of the same state: the United States channels its support more toward American firms than to foreign firms operating within its borders, as do the other two centers, Europe and Japan–China.

In these terms, we can also make sense of the Doha trade talks agenda, which was shaped by U.S. and European Union (EU) governments with one eye on "holding back" developing countries from advancing into industrial and service areas now dominated by the developed countries.[30] For the theory shows that productivity growth in the less-productive trading partners of an advanced country is not necessarily in the interests of the bulk of the citizens of the latter. None other than the celebrated Paul Samuelson recently developed an argument along these lines, showing that as China, for example, catches up in the production of goods that had been produced in the United States (whether through outsourcing or through domestic innovation), U.S. export prices fall, worsening the U.S. terms of trade. The United States still benefits from trade (relative to "no trade") but less so than before.[31]

All this new thinking remains within the tradition of trade theory insofar as it assumes away unemployment, foreign direct investment, speculative financial flows across borders, financial instability, systematic mispricing of foreign exchange, and persistent trade deficits and trade surpluses. When these noticeable facts are factored in, the case for strategic industrial and trade policy—for not letting some markets work freely—becomes stronger. The objective of strategic policy is to enable resources to be combined and employed in a national economy when those resources would not be employed—or would be employed less productively—if the economy were fully exposed to efficiency criteria derived from world market prices, especially when those prices are moved up and down by essentially speculative financial flows. However, the assistance must be delivered in such a way that learning-by-doing takes place so that, after a time, the strategic policy support can be redirected to other resource combinations.[32]

EVIDENCE

In short, new and newer trade theory no longer supports the old truth about free trade being, with only partial exceptions, best in theory. The case for free trade has been further undermined by (a) exposure of the serious defects in the major studies referred to earlier, which purport to find that freer trade is generally better in the real world, (b) evidence of chronic balance of payments problems following trade liberalization, (c) evidence on structural changes during development, (d) evidence suggesting that more trade openness can generate more income inequality in developing countries, and (e) evidence from the development trajectories of the pre- and post-Second World War industrializers.

Constraints on space prevent more than a bald summary. It turns out that the impressive evidence supporting a high priority to further trade liberalization is not impressive when the methods, data, and conclusions are subject to unbiased scrutiny. For example, following a large-scale review of the existing literature on the relationships between trade liberalization, growth, inequality, and poverty, a set of economists concludes that "the results are weak."[33] Another review says that "the evidence on the causal link between trade openness and growth has been controversial and inconclusive to date."[34] Dani Rodrik, Ricardo Hausmann, and Lant Pritchett find that spells of accelerated (national) growth often occur spontaneously, without preceding "reforms," or only marginal ones, whether in trade or anything else. They identify more than eighty episodes since 1950 in which a country's growth rate increased by at least 2 percentage points for at least seven years—almost all of them without preceding liberalization or opening.[35]

Advocates of trade liberalization stress the benefits of faster export growth but tend to overlook the surge of imports which often results, resulting in balance of payments problems. This applies particularly to the typical developing country, whose exports have a low income elasticity of demand and whose imports have a high income elasticity of demand.

Again, the evidence suggests that the dominant process in development is not increasing specialization in line with comparative advantage (rising **Gini coefficient** of sectoral shares in production), but *diversification* of production and employment,[36] not just the familiar diversification from agriculture to manufacturing and on to services but also diversification within manufacturing. As poor countries get richer, sectoral production and employment within manufacturing become more diversified among sectors. Diversification dominates specialization right up to a per capita level at the lower end of the "old" OECD countries (such as Portugal in the early 1990s)— above which, specialization dominates diversification. And as suggested by the Gomery-Baumol-Krugman-Venables work, the pattern of diversification in each country seems to have a large element of arbitrariness or randomness in the sense that it reflects "self-discovery" of export opportunities and cost structures by a small number of entrepreneurs whom others then copy.

This evidence confirms the intuition that a central process of development is mastery over an expanding range of activities, rather than specialization in "what one does best today." Since diversification is central, the question becomes whether "the market" can be relied on to promote diversification—learning to master an expanding range of activities—sufficient to sustain catch-up growth; and if not, what the state can do to accelerate the process. The market may encourage diversification into "nearby" products (those with similar inputs) but with much the same value added. Diversification to more distant products with increasing returns and higher income elasticity of demand and higher potential for further diversification (from radios to steel, in the Korean case) may well require a push from the state. This kind of state push into products distant from present ones (requiring the supply of new private and public inputs) might be called "leading the market." State help for diversification to products in between "nearby" and "distant" might be called "following the market"—helping to support private entrepreneurs to do (some of) what they would want to do anyway.[37]

As for the effects of trade liberalization on inequality, a survey of the evidence reports that the large majority of developing countries have experienced contemporaneous increases in trade openness and inequality over the past three decades, contrary to the expectations of traditional trade theory. While acknowledging that the causality is unclear, the survey concludes, "it seems fair to say that the evidence has provided little support for the conventional wisdom that trade openness in developing countries would favor the less fortunate (at least in relative terms)."[38]

Finally, the historical evidence from development trajectories gives little support for the proposition that trade liberalization reliably generates higher economic growth and lower poverty. Almost all the now-developed countries used substantial trade protection during their rapid development stage.

The newly industrialized East Asian countries (Japan, Taiwan, and South Korea) managed their trade as part of a larger industrial policy for the best part of forty years, such that industries to be nurtured to international competitiveness initially received substantial protection that was conditional on performance—especially on movement toward international prices and quality standards; as they became internationally competitive, protection was scaled back—as it was also scaled back if they continued not to be competitive. Hence, at any one time, the East Asian countries showed fairly high dispersion of effective protection rates across industrial sectors, quite contrary to the "low dispersion" prescription of neoclassical trade policy.[39] Of course, some of the supported industries "failed" in the sense of not becoming internationally competitive. But as Thomas Watson, the founder of IBM, is reputed to have said, "If you want to be more successful, double your failure rate."

The East Asian countries provide concrete examples of how protection can be combined with competition, of how "inward orientation" can be combined with "export orientation." It takes fundamentalist liberal faith to argue that these countries, which have demonstrated the fastest development in history (recent China aside), would have done *even better* had they practiced free market economics.[40] As for China, it maintained average tariffs of more than 30 percent for decades up to the mid-1990s, when it was already growing and diversifying very fast. Recall the contrast between China and Latin America made earlier. . . .

In short, the empirical evidence in favor of trade liberalization is not as clear as champions of free trade claim. This is also the view of an independent panel of economists tasked with evaluating World Bank research on development policies, which said the following of the big-bank-sponsored cross-country studies allegedly showing that free market policies are best:

> We see a serious failure in the checks and balances within the system that has led the Bank to repeatedly trumpet these early empirical results without recognizing their fragile and tentative nature. . . . [O]nce the evidence is chosen selectively without supporting argument, and empirical skepticism selectively suspended, the credibility and utility of the Bank's research is threatened.[41]

OPTIMAL TRADE POLICY

No one argues that a strongly inward-oriented trade regime—with high, uniform, and unconditional import protection plus export taxes—is better than a liberal trade regime. The point is that trade liberalization has been oversold and does not deserve the priority it receives in the international development community.[42] Further openness is not always in every country's national interest (not least because it may lock a developing country into specialization in export products with low income elasticity of demand); and a prescription of freer trade and freer investment (through the World Bank, International Monetary Fund [IMF], WTO, or bilateral trade agreements) is not generally in the global interest—though it may be in the collective *advanced country firms*' interest, given that such global rules make it more difficult for developing countries to diversify and upgrade into more technologically sophisticated products other than as subcontractors of advanced country firms. That is, the prescription supports the collective "primacy" project of the United States, European Union, and Japan to keep other countries and firms asymmetrically dependent on them.[43]

Trade policy will be an even more controversial subject going forward than it has been in the recent past, especially because of China. First, the ability of China's manufacturing agglomerations to produce a wide range of manufactured goods at 50 percent of the cost of other producers poses the acute question of how manufacturing can flourish elsewhere. (Chinese door makers are even able to ship doors to landlocked Mali and outcompete local carpenters.) Increased specialization in (diminishing returns) commodities and raw materials is bad news for the people of Africa and Latin America and bad news for the prospects of a wider global diffusion of the material benefits of growth. It is a recipe for specialization in poverty, except for those lucky enough to produce commodities with high income elasticity of demand (such as fish from Iceland). Getting the "proximity-productivity" dynamic to work in these economies has to involve some kinds of protection, even though not only the West but now also China will insist otherwise.

Second, trade policy will also be involved in the West's strategy for curbing China's ability to develop its own world-beating firms. The West is anxious that China not be allowed to follow Japan and Korea with their Toyotas and Samsungs; rather, Chinese firms should be accommodated as junior partners to Western firms. Getting China to lift restrictions on trade, foreign investment, and capital flows and eschew a "developmental state"—in other words, getting China to behave "responsibly"—is a key part of the strategy.[44]

The policy implications of this argument—at both national (developing country) and multilateral level—are anything but straightforward. Within broad limits, beyond which everyone would agree that a policy is crazy, there is no one-policy-fits-all for strategic trade policy akin to the universal free trade policy of neoclassical economics. Like other powerful policy instruments, trade protection can be used well and it can be used badly. The fact that it has often been used badly does not mean that it cannot be used well, and the gains from using it well are high compared to possible substitute instruments such as targeted subsidies, which tend to be more difficult for developing country states to implement. Sensible policy prescription starts from this pragmatic state of mind.

The next step is to discard the neoclassical distinction between "inward-oriented" trade regimes and "outward-oriented" ones, or at least to qualify it to recognize that a given trade regime—such as Japan's in 1950–1980, South Korea's in 1955–1990—can be both, in the sense of including policy-based incentives for both import substitution and export promotion but in different sectors at any one time.

Then, one has to recognize that import substitution is the mother of most (not all) new exports for the good reason that learning to produce for the domestic market—given that the demand already exists—is easier than producing for export sales. Further, import substitution policies do not necessarily give rise to cozy monopolies. Protection and competition can go together, even though, historically, protection has often been designed in such a way that it does cut competition, whether intentionally or not. Protection can coexist not only with domestic competition but also with (buffered) international competition. For example, governments can use the price and quality gap between domestic and internationally available versions of the same product to calibrate protection— as in, "you have two years to bring your price and quality to within X percent of the imported price, and you can get access to several kinds of publicly supported facilities in order to do so; but after Y years we will phase out the protection."[45]

Finally, one has to see trade policy as a subset of a larger strategic development policy designed to build on increasing returns and the proximity-productivity mechanism rather than seeing trade policy as the queen and industrial policy as a subset. As suggested earlier, both new theory and new evidence suggest that a low and uniform level of trade restrictions and tariffs is neither a necessary nor a sufficient condition for a successful growth strategy. On the other hand, rising trade/GDP and foreign investment/GDP are indeed likely outcomes of a successful growth strategy, and if these ratios are prevented from rising— perhaps by advanced countries' rigging their trade regimes against sophisticated exports from developing countries—the strategy may not remain successful.

For neoclassical economists brought up to believe the classic liberal postulate of "natural" markets versus "artificial" government, this line of argument is upsetting. For others, the challenge is to develop guidelines for strategic trade policy which correspond with empirical evidence from the successful developing countries, which have some foundation in theoretical mechanisms and which are not wide open to hijacking by vested interests. Then they have to translate these guidelines into revisions of WTO treaties, World Bank prescriptions, U.S. and EU preferential trade agreements, and other components of the Western primacy project.

CONCLUSION

"Does trade liberalization contribute to economic progress?" The best short answer is "it depends." My main point is that the substantial "yes" consensus among economists is challenged by recent theoretical and empirical research.

Given that the arguments in favor of always freer trade for all are highly questionable, we should give up on the ambition of reaching another Big Global Trade and Investment Deal that all must sign. Progress is more likely to be made by asking, "What are the ten key challenges that the world must act on in the next ten years, and what changes should be made to the multilateral (and bilateral/regional) trade regime to address them?"

One of those challenges is particularly pressing at the time of writing (early 2012). Countries of the eurozone running large current account deficits have only two broad options: one is to comply with the demands of creditors that their governments inflict savage austerity on the population; the second is to exit from the eurozone, adopt a devalued national currency, and use a variety of industrial policies, including trade controls, to boost investment, boost exports, and replace some imports with domestic production. Insofar as governments adopt the latter, they will not only cause crises in creditor-debtor relationships far beyond their immediate creditors, they will also challenge the basic premise of the international economic order—that movement should always be toward freer trade.

NOTES

1. I thank Fadi Hassan, Diana Weinhold, Brian Hindley, Razeen Sally, and Manfred Bienefeld for their helpful discussions.
2. Seminar at London School of Economics, April 30, 2008.
3. Jagdish Bhagwati, "Rethinking Trade Strategy," in *Development Strategies Reconsidered*, ed. J. Lewis and V. Kallab (New Brunswick, NJ: Transaction Books, 1986), 93. In "The Free Trade Consensus Lives On" (*Financial Times*, October 10, 2007), Bhagwati reiterated the point: "Turn to the leading U.S. newspapers these days and you will read the . . . 'loss of faith' in free trade by economists. . . . The truth of the matter is that free trade is alive and well among economists."

4. Bruno Frey, W. Pommerehne, F. Schneider, and G. Gilbert, "Consensus and Dissensus among Economists: An Empirical Inquiry," *American Economic Review* 74 (1984): 986–994.

5. World Bank, "Strengthening Trade Policy Reform" (Washington, DC: World Bank, November 13, 1989).

6. Erik Reinert, "Globalisation in the Periphery as a Morgenthau Plan: The Underdevelopment of Mongolia in the 1990s," in *Globalization, Economic Development and Inequality: An Alternative Perspective*, ed. Erik Reinert (Cheltenham, U.K.: Edward Elgar, 2004).

7. From a participant who requested anonymity.

8. "The Malady of Manufacturing," *Financial Times*, May 25, 2009.

9. Martin Wolf, *Why Globalization Works* (New Haven: Yale University Press, 2004), 4, emphasis added.

10. Robert Wade, "The Washington Consensus," in *International Encyclopedia of the Social Sciences*, ed. William A. Darity Jr., 2nd edition, vol. 9 (Detroit: Macmillan Reference USA, 2008) pp. 38–40.

11. Inter-American Development Bank, *The Age of Productivity* (Washington DC: author, 2010).

12. For an idiosyncratic and entertaining discussion of some of the issues of the trade policy debate, see Edward Leamer, "A Flat World, a Level Playing Field, and Small World after All, or None of the Above? A Review of Thomas L. Friedman's *The World Is Flat*," *Journal of Economic Literature* 45 (March 2007): 83–126. For a World Bank argument substantially more nuanced than anything the Bank has said about trade policy for decades, see World Bank, *Economic Growth in the 1990s* (Washington DC, 2005), chap. 5.

13. "Free Trade's Best Defense is the Truth," *Financial Times*, editorial, July 25, 2006.

14. Many advocates of free trade, including Montesquieu, Smith, J. S. Mill, and Lionel Robbins, also argue that free trade brings peace at the same time as it enhances national economic strength in readiness for war.

15. For example, I. Little et al., *Industry and Trade in Some Developing Countries* (London: Oxford University Press, 1970); A. Kreuger, *Foreign Trade Regimes and Economic Development: Liberalization Attempts and Consequences* (Cambridge: Ballinger, 1978); J. Bhagwati, *Foreign Trade Regimes and Economic Development: Anatomy and Consequences of Exchange Control Regimes* (Cambridge: Ballinger, 1978); B. Balassa and Associates, *Development Strategies in Semi-Industrial Economies* (Baltimore: Johns Hopkins University Press, for the World Bank, 1982); World Bank, *World Development Report 1987* (Washington, DC: World Bank, 1987), chap. 5; Armeane Choksi, Michael Michaely, and Demetris Papageorgiou, *Liberalizing Foreign Trade* (Oxford: Blackwell, 1989), vols. 1 and 7; World Bank, *Best Practices in Trade Policy Reform* (New York: Oxford University Press, 1991); World Bank, *World Development Report 1991* (Washington, DC: World Bank, 1991), chap. 5; J. Sachs and A. Warner, "Economic reforms and the process of global integration," *Brookings Papers on Economic Activity* (Washington, DC: Brookings

Institution, 1995), 1–118; World Bank, *Globalization, Growth, and Poverty: Building an Inclusive World Economy* (Washington, DC: World Bank, 2002).

16. World Bank, Globalization, Growth, and Poverty: Building an Inclusive World Economy (Washington, DC: World Bank, 2002), 50.

17. See Ian Little, *Economic Development: Theory, Policy and International Relations* (New York: Basic Books, 1982). For counterarguments, see Robert Wade, *Governing the Market: Economic Theory and the Role of Government in East Asian Industrialization* (Princeton: Princeton University Press, 2004) chap. 12.

18. See contributions by Adrian Wood, John Roberts, Robert Wade, Sanjaya Lall, "Symposium on Infant Industries," *Oxford Economic Papers* 31, no. 1 (2003): 3–20.

19. Garry Kasperov, "If I Ruled the World," *Prospect*, February 2012, p. 6.

20. E. Helpman and P. Krugman, *Market Structure and Trade* (Cambridge: MIT Press, 1985); G. Grossman and E. Helpman, *Innovation and Growth in the World Economy* (Cambridge: MIT Press, 1991); P. Romer, "Endogenous Technological Change," *Journal of Political Economy* 98 (1990): 71–102.

21. Marc Melitz, "The Impact of Trade on Intra-Industry Reallocations and Aggregate Industry Productivity," *Econometrica* 71 (2003): 1695–1725.

22. Pinelopi Goldberg and Nina Pavcnik, "Distributional Effects of Globalization in Developing Countries," *Journal of Economic Literature* 45, no. 1 (2007): 39–82, p.78.

23. Richard Baldwin and Frederic Robert-Nicoud, "Trade and Growth with Heterogeneous Firms," *Journal of International Economics* 74 (2008): 21–34.

24. Paul Krugman, "Is Free Trade Passé?" *Journal of Economic Perspectives* 1 (1987): 143.

25. Alan Goodacre, "What Would Post-Autistic Trade Policy Be?" *Post-Autistic Economics Review* 41 (March 2007), 2–8; Thomas Palley, "Rethinking Trade and Trade Policy: Gomery, Baumol and Samuelson on Comparative Advantage," *Levy Economics Institute*, Public Policy Brief 86, 2006.

26. Ralph Gomery and William Baumol, *Global Trade and Conflicting National Interests* (Cambridge: MIT Press, 2000); Paul Krugman and Anthony Venables, "Globalisation and the Inequality of Nations," *Quarterly Journal of Economics* 110 (1995): 857–880; A. Thrilwall and P. Pacheco-Lopez, *Trade Liberalisation and the Poverty of Nations* (Cheltenham, U.K.: Edward Elgar, 2008).

27. On Liechtenstein, see Eric Pfanner, "Liechtenstein Works to Move beyond Tax Feud," *New York Times*, February 23, 2008.

28. For a nontechnical discussion of this argument, see Ha-Joon Chang, *Bad Samaritans* (London: Random House, 2007), chap. 3.

29. Gregory Hook, "The Rise of the Pentagon and U.S. State Building: The Defense Program as Industrial Policy," *American Journal of Sociology* 96, no. 2 (1990): 358–404.

30. Robert Wade, "Goodbye Doha, Hello New Trade Round," *Challenge*, November–December 2006, 14–19.

31. Paul Samuelson, "Where Ricardo and Mill Rebut and Confirm Arguments of Mainstream Economists Supporting Globalization," *Journal of Economic Perspectives* 18 (2004).

32. Robert Wade, *Governing the Market* (Princeton: Princeton University Press, 2004).

33. Jennifer Mbabzi, Oliver Morissey, and Chris Milner, "The Fragility of Empirical Links between Inequality, Trade Liberalization, Growth and Poverty," in *Perspectives on Growth and Poverty*, ed. Rolph van der Hoeven and Anthony Shorrocks (Tokyo: United Nations University Press, 2003), 113, 137.

34. Pinelopi Goldberg and Nina Pavcnik, 2007, 41.

35. R. Hausmann, L. Pritchett, and D. Rodrik, "Growth Accelerations," *Journal of Economic Growth* 10 (2005): 303–329; Charles Sabel, "Bootstrapping Development: Rethinking the Role of Public Intervention in Promoting Growth," Columbia University Law School, November 2005.

36. J. Imbs and R. Wacziarg, "Stages of Diversification," *American Economic Review* 93, no. 1 (March 2003): 63–86; discussed in Dani Rodrik, "Industrial Policy for the Twenty-First Century," Kennedy School of Government, Harvard University, September 2004. See also Jane Jacobs, *Cities and the Wealth of Nations* (New York: Viking, 1984).

37. Robert Wade, "Industrial Policy in East Asia: Does It Lead or Follow the Market?" in *Manufacturing Miracles: Paths of Industrialization in Latin America and East Asia*, ed. Gary Gereffi and Donald Wyman (Princeton: Princeton University Press, 1990).

38. Pinelopi Goldberg and Nina Pavcnik, "Distributional Effects of Globalization in Developing Countries," *Journal of Economic Literature* 45, no. 1 (2007): 39–82, p.77.

39. Robert Wade, "Managing Trade," *Comparative Politics* 25, no. 2 (1993); Robert Wade, *Governing the Market* (Princeton: Princeton University Press, 2004), chap. 5; Alice Amsden, *Asia's Next Giant* (Oxford: Oxford University Press, 1989); Ha-Joon Chang, *Kicking Away the Ladder* (London: Anthem Press, 2002).

40. See Albert Fishlow, Catherine Gwin, Stephan Haggard, Dani Rodrik, and Robert Wade, *Miracle or Design? Lessons from the East Asian Experience* (Washington, DC: Overseas Development Council, 1994).

41. Abhijit Banerjee, Angus Deaton, Nora Lustig, and Ken Rogoff, *An Evaluation of World Bank Research, 1998–2005*. World Bank: 2006, 53–56. Available at www.tinyurl.com/yck7wc

42. See further, United Nations Development Program (UNDP), *Making Global Trade Work for People*, Earthscan, 2003; Amit Bhaduri, "Toward the Optimum Degree of Openness," in *Putting Development First*, ed. Kevin Gallagher (London: Zed, 2005).

43. On the economic institutions of primacy, see Robert Wade, "Globalization as the Institutionalization of Neoliberalism: Commodification, Financialization, and the Anchorless Economy," in *Institutions and Market Economies: The Political Economy of Growth and Development*, ed. William Garside (Basingstoke, UK: Palgrave, 2007); Robert Wade, "The Invisible Hand of the American Empire," *Ethics and International Affairs* 17, no. 2 (2003).

44. See Kuen Lee, John Mathews, and Robert Wade, "Rethinking Development Policy: From Washington Consensus to Beijing–Seoul–Tokyo Consensus," *Financial Times*, October 19, 2007.

45. Robert Wade, *Governing the Market* (Princeton: Princeton University Press, 2004) chaps. 5, 6, 9; Richard Luedde-Neurath, *Import Controls and Export-Oriented Development: A Reassessment of the South Korean Case* (Boulder: Westview, 1986).

2

trade and equality

Does Free Trade Promote Economic Equality?

YES: L. Alan Winters, *University of Sussex*

NO: Kate Vyborny and Nancy Birdsall, *Center for Global Development*

Chapter 1 addressed the issue of whether trade liberalization promotes economic prosperity. This chapter tackles a problem that is even knottier—the effects of trade on economic equality—both because the impacts of international trade are difficult to assess and because definitions of equality vary significantly. When you imagine a society of economic equality, what do you consider? That every individual earns approximately the same income? That basic needs are met for everyone? (And what is a need?) That every individual has access to conditions (such as education) that would enable him or her to earn a living? That minimal government regulations and interference allow individuals to achieve to the extent possible? Among the many competing definitions of what economic equality might mean, the Millennium Development Goal targets (discussed in Chapter 3) are one means of setting minimum international goals for equality.

Layered on top of the conceptual issues entailed in defining economic equality is the problem of choosing the unit of analysis along which to gauge its extent within a given context. For example, if (in)equality is to be measured internationally, using states as units of analysis, the process will involve taking the mean income (or some other aggregate statistic, such as median individual or household income, or a Gini coefficient, explained below) for a given country and comparing that statistic cross-nationally. Another form of inequality can be measured at the intra-national level: how much income inequality exists within different states? Yet another means of measuring inequality focuses on the purely individual level, without respect to national boundaries.

Of course, each of these varying levels of analysis will provide different perspectives on how equal or unequal economic *outcomes* are without regard to how people attained their income or how it compares with that of others in the society.

In measuring economic inequalities, a common measure is the Gini coefficient, which represents the ratio of the cumulative share of individuals (represented on the horizontal axis in Figure 1, this page) to their cumulative share of income (the vertical axis). A society with an equal distribution of income will be represented as the 45-degree line connecting endpoints of the two axes, while societies with more unequal distributions will be represented with steeply sloped curved lines. The larger the Gini coefficient—the ratio of shaded area in the figure compared with the entire triangle—the more unequal the distribution of economic outcomes.

There are multiple ways of measuring Gini coefficients, and the results vary depending on whether they are aggregated at the individual, national, or international levels. Measured this way, the Gini coefficient of world income inequality increased between 1970 and 2000, as represented in Figure 2 (p. 42). And income disparities are particularly pronounced in some nations, such as those in the developing countries of Latin America and Africa (see Figure 3, p. 43). Another factor complicating these calculations is whether

Figure 1

The Gini Coefficient

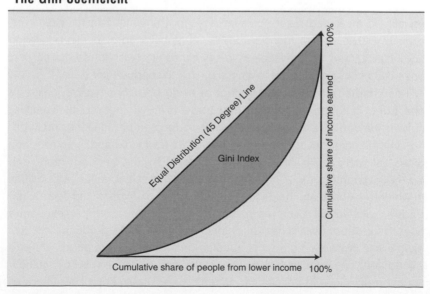

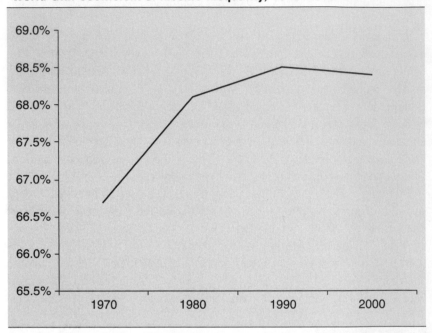

Figure 2

World Gini Coefficient of Income Inequality, 1970–2000

Source: Yuri Dikhanov, "Trends in Global Income Distribution, 1970–2000 and Scenarios for 2015," United Nations Development Programme, Human Development Report Office, New York, 2005, 37–43.

equality is measured before or after any governmental transfer payments, such as public welfare, pension payments, subsidized or public education and housing, and so on. Needless to say, those who wish to make a political point can choose among competing statistics to support their views.

This chapter questions the impact of trade on economic inequality. At one level, it is natural to think that trade is advantageous to wealthier nations that are able to capitalize on more educated populations and superior technologies. But these advantages in trade expand income gaps cross-nationally while intra-nationally widening gaps between high- and low-skilled workers. On the other hand, trade brings economic possibilities to workers globally and helps to lower prices for all. What some see as free trade is viewed by others as exploitative when the economic exchange occurs between vastly unequal actors. Because trade produces not just exchanges of finished products but also changes in *where* goods are produced, tensions arise involving manufacturing facilities owned by multinational corporations in developing nations, particularly those characterized

Figure 3

Gini Coefficient of Income Inequality by Region, 1970–2000

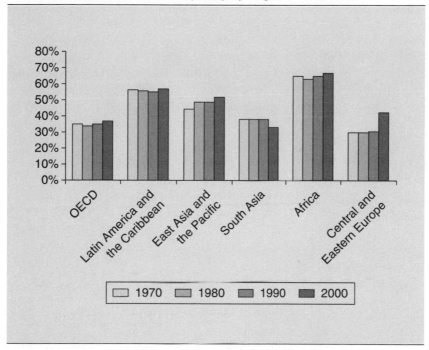

1970 ■ 1980 ■ 1990 ■ 2000

Source: Yuri Dikhanov, "Trends in Global Income Distribution, 1970–2000 and Scenarios for 2015," United Nations Development Programme, Human Development Report Office, New York, 2005, 37–43.

by substandard labor practices. Yet, despite conditions that many in the West would abhor, even some social liberals—such as *New York Times* columnist Nicholas Kristof[1]—view the possibilities of jobs at sweatshops as a net improvement in living conditions.

The mobility of both goods and means of production contributes to a complicated relationship between trade and immigration, which also complicates policy responses. For example, policies that would restrict immigration may serve to increase pressures to send manufacturing facilities overseas and vice versa. This effect, in turn, complicates domestic political responses to outsourcing and immigration policy. Those actors (such as organized labor) who favor policies to protect U.S. workers thus face a trade-off between wanting to restrict immigration (for fear of losing jobs to immigrants) and encouraging outsourcing.

Trade policy is also influenced in important ways by domestic political constituencies, perhaps none so strong and enduring as the political sway held by farmers in wealthy nations. Subsidized farmers in the United

Figure 4

Support to Agriculture in High-Income Countries, 1986–1988 and 2007–2009

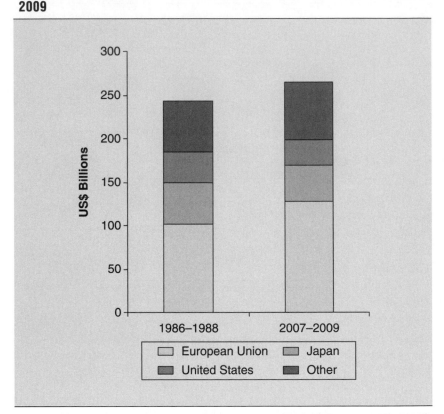

Source: United Nations Development Programme, *Human Development Report 2005* (New York: Oxford University Press, 2005), 129; OECD, "Producer and Consumer Support Estimates: Producer Support Estimate and Related Indicators by Country 2010," *OECD Agriculture Statistics* (database), accessed December 13, 2011.

States, the European Union, Japan, and elsewhere produce and sell crops at below-market rates at the expense of farmers (or prospective farmers) in some developing nations that could compete were it not for these agricultural subsidies, export controls, tariffs, and so on. And yet, as Figure 4 (this page) indicates, agricultural support has grown in the developed nations in recent years.

The impact of trade on economic equality is one of the most politically potent and economically compelling issues raised by globalization. Owing to the complexities involved, the two articles that follow are not diametrically opposed in their views on this issue but nonetheless represent different perspectives on the likely impacts of free trade. Kate Vyborny and Nancy Birdsall argue that trade tends to increase inequalities, while Alan Winters suggests that overall inequalities will be dampened by freer trade.

Discussion Questions

1. How do you measure equality—by income? By standard of living? Between whom do you measure it—between countries? Between individuals within a country? Between all individuals in the world? What is most fair?

2. Is economic equality a desirable goal? An achievable goal? Why or why not? Aside from moral reasons, why is equality important?

3. Opponents of globalization and free trade often cite the poor working conditions and low wages of sweatshops and factories set up in developing nations by wealthy multinational companies as evidence that free trade does not promote equality. Proponents of free trade say that the jobs and wages provided at these factories are better than the local alternatives, allowing those workers to achieve a higher standard of living. Which argument do you agree with? Why?

4. What challenges does Alan Winters cite before considering whether free trade promotes economic equality? How does he address these challenges?

5. How do Kate Vyborny and Nancy Birdsall propose to address the inequality brought on by trade liberalization? What specific policies do they recommend? Do you agree with their policy proposals?

NOTE

1. Nicholas D. Kristof, "In Praise of the Maligned Sweatshop," *New York Times,* June 6, 2006.

YES: L. Alan Winters, *University of Sussex*

U nfortunately, the question "Does free trade promote economic equality?"
doesn't admit an easy answer. It depends on what you mean by "economic
equality" and by "free trade"—and even then it depends on the specific circumstances of the case. I will argue that free trade is likely to promote equality
overall, but that there are clearly some senses and circumstances in which it
may not do so. A closely related question that, indeed, is sometimes confused
with the title question is "Does freeing international trade reduce poverty?" I
have done a good deal of research on the latter question over the past decade
and, while explicitly recognizing the existence of exceptions, I would answer,
"Almost always yes."[1]

GROUND CLEARING

So what do we mean by "economic inequality"? There are many significant
dimensions to inequality and poverty—such as access to power, cultural fulfillment, freedom from violence—but I shall focus just on the economic variables
of real income and consumption. The latter typically tracks very closely with
wealth, however, so I will not even deal with wealth explicitly. When I deal with
poverty, I will refer to people with incomes below the (very low) poverty line
that is often fixed, for international comparisons, at $1 a day per head at 1985
international prices.

The principal question in regard to inequality is "Between whom?" There are
three obvious alternatives: between countries, between individuals (or households) within a country, and between all the individuals in the world. The last
of these alternatives combines elements of the first two, allowing, so far as the
data permit, for the fact that some Indians are richer than some Americans, but
there is no simple mathematical formula for the combination.

The definitive discussion and measurement of these different concepts is the
brilliant book by Branko Milanovic (2005a), which shows that about 80 percent
of world income inequality is due to differences in mean income between countries, while only about 20 percent is due to differences within countries. The
former statistic has increased significantly since around 1980, and the latter a
little; overall inequality has also increased a little, but not dramatically.[2]

The remaining concept to define is "free trade." Strictly, there is no such thing—
all trade costs effort to conduct—but we could imagine international trade free
from all interferences by government. Even this limited sort of freedom is relatively rare, however: many imports pay no tariff but still face inspection for, say,

conformity to local safety standards. Hence we need to be rather pragmatic about the definition and hold to a notion of trade that is *relatively* free from official frictions and conducted with *relatively* efficient logistics and physical infrastructure. Precise measurement of the degree of trade friction poses serious challenges (as we shall see), although we can often identify changes in the "freedom of trade"— that is, trade liberalizations—easily enough.

TRADE AND INTER-COUNTRY INEQUALITY

Trade liberalization may affect inter-country inequality in two ways: either all countries free their trade but the consequences for national income per head differ by country, or only some countries do so, which will affect distribution even if all economies respond to liberalization the same way. Remember that inequality will be reduced if the poor experience strong growth relative to the rich. If all countries achieve the same growth rate, inequality—which is almost always measured as a relative magnitude—will be unchanged.[3]

Obviously, the experience of different countries will vary in detail, but some scholars have argued in theory that trade between rich and poor countries systematically benefits the rich countries and harms the poor ones (see Winters 2008 for a brief account). There is no hard evidence at all to support this theory. Over any given period, some countries will do relatively badly, by definition, and will get relatively poorer, but this outcome is not systematically related to their initial levels of income or their economic structures. In fact, the evidence suggests that, once we make allowance for the fact that policies are generally better in rich than in poor countries, poorer countries tend to grow a bit faster— that is, they catch up, reducing inequality, albeit slowly. As examples, think of Botswana, Chile, Korea, and Mauritius, which have all grown from very low levels of income and have all opened up their economies pretty strongly, too.

To make the discussion more concrete and more policy-relevant, let us narrow the question a little. Suppose that we have a set of rich and largely open economies—those of the OECD [Organization of Economic Cooperation and Development]—which show steady growth: will developing countries improve their chances of catching up with them by opening up their economies strongly? That is, does openness boost developing countries' incomes?[4]

Economic theory offers many reasons to expect a country's own trade liberalization to stimulate its economic growth, at least for a period:

- specializing in goods for which world prices exceed those that would be available at home

- reaping economies of scale

- improving performance in the face of new competition, and

- benefiting from better inputs and technologies available from abroad

None of these effects is guaranteed, though, so whether trade does stimulate developing countries' incomes is ultimately an empirical matter. Over the 1990s, several highly visible global cross-country studies argued that openness is good for income levels, but at the decade's end, these studies were subjected to a searching criticism and reworking by Francisco Rodriguez and Dani Rodrik (2001). These authors showed that the earlier studies' measures of openness were not appropriate to the theories they propounded, that their results were sensitive to particular but extraneous features of the data, and that the econometric methods they used failed adequately to identify causation running from trade liberalization to growth. Rodriguez and Rodrik also found it hard to replicate some of the results reported in the literature, raising some concern about their accuracy.

The difficulty of establishing an empirical link between liberal trade and income arises from at least four sources (Winters 2004). First, apart from extreme cases such as North Korea (closed) or Hong Kong (open), it is difficult to measure a country's trade stance accurately: for example, tariffs need to be aggregated across goods, quantitative restrictions assessed and then aggregated, and the levels of predictability and enforcement of trade policies measured. Second, causation is difficult to establish, for actual openness, which is usually measured by the ratio of international trade to national income, is almost certainly the result of growth as well as a possible cause of it. But there is also concern that even policy-based measures, such as average tariffs, could face the same problem, because growing countries might be more willing to liberalize. There are technical fixes for this analytical problem, but they leave at least some doubt.

The third challenge is that, while liberal trade policies are likely to be somewhat beneficial under any circumstances (because they enlarge the set of opportunities for economic agents), a lasting effect almost certainly requires combination with other good policies and sound institutions as well. This necessary combination makes it difficult to isolate the individual effects of trade reform—indeed, it raises the question of whether it is even worth trying to do so if policies always come in packages. It also raises the issue of "which other policies"—that is, when is trade liberalization most effective? This situation becomes even more complex if, fourth, openness could *cause* improvements in other policies and institutions. For example, countries with simple, open trade regimes appear to be less corrupt, and open economies have less inflation. Both outcomes could be associated with higher incomes.

Since 2001, further work has re-established to most economists' satisfaction that openness does generally enhance income—at least conditionally. Researchers have worked hard to establish causation by isolating those parts of international trade that are genuinely not caused by income (such as economic size and distance between trading partners) and asking if they, in turn, cause higher incomes; it turns out that they do (see Noguer and Siscart 2005). Researchers have also determined that at least a minimal degree of labor market flexibility, firm entry flexibility, financial access, and human capital investment are appropriate complementary policies if liberalization is to have strong effects (Chang, Kaltani, and Loayza 2005).

Further scrutiny of the connection between openness and income examines possible causal links between openness and growth separately. Many studies associate openness with faster accumulation (that is, investment) and have observed that policies that hinder investment will reduce the benefits of trade liberalization. A second key linkage is between openness and productivity. Everyone agrees that improved productivity is necessary for sustained economic growth and development, and that it is the only secure basis for higher incomes at the level of the individual worker. The evidence from country, sectoral, and firm-level studies suggests very strongly that opening up international trade stimulates productivity. Part of the way in which it does so is by allowing more efficient (exporting) firms to grow faster than less efficient ones, and allowing import competition to pick off weaker domestic firms. Such rationalization effects may lead to short-term poverty concerns, for failing firms can easily harm their workers and owners. But equally clearly, long-term progress requires adaptation and adjustment, so that higher productivity can become the norm and generate higher incomes throughout a sector. One such case is the Chilean experience—in which firms were allowed to disappear during the trade liberalizations of the 1970s and 1980s, and the economy eventually emerged much stronger and richer.

Despite the econometric difficulties of establishing beyond all doubt that openness enhances income, the weight of experience and evidence seems to lean strongly in that direction. Thus, by boosting growth among countries, trade liberalization can narrow the gap between wealthy, industrialized nations and poor, developing ones—an important component of global inequality. Liberalizers have to undertake other reforms as well, but to a fair extent we know what these are: for example, reasonably flexible labor markets, capital markets, and corporate regulations that allow new firms to emerge, and decent port facilities and administration to allow goods to get in and out.

Moreover, even the critics (Rodriguez and Rodrik 2001) concede that there is no coherent evidence that openness adversely affects income. One might think of parallels with the debate on smoking. There was a long period during which the weight of evidence was sufficient to convince most rational people that smoking was harmful to health, although proof conclusive by either scientific or judicial standards had not been achieved. And during this period, just as in today's openness and growth debate, the hold-outs often cited specific counter-examples as if they overturned the general presumption.

TRADE AND INTRA-COUNTRY INEQUALITY

Let us now turn to whether international trade raises or lowers inequality within countries—and the related question of whether it causes or cures poverty. The baseline facts are that liberalizing international trade certainly affects people's incomes, that it can affect overall inequality either way, that there is a *little* evidence that it widens inequality in poor countries, and that, although it can drive some individuals into poverty, it tends to reduce poverty overall. I shall consider the arguments in two steps. First, as we have seen, trade liberalization tends to increase growth, so we need to ask how growth affects inequality. Second, we can move inside the aggregates to ask how trade affects individual incomes and then infer poverty/inequality effects from this perspective.

Economists have long argued that economic growth tends, overall, to reduce poverty (see Fields 1989). David Dollar and Aart Kraay (2002) recently quantified this assertion by relating the mean income of the poor—the bottom 20 percent of the income distribution—to overall mean income plus some of the additional variables that economists associate with influencing the rate of economic growth and that are often argued to affect the distribution of income. Among these variables, they found that, while inflation appeared to have an adverse effect on the poor on top of its growth-reducing effects, factors such as government consumption, the rule of law, democracy, social expenditure, primary school enrollment, and two measures of openness had no effects other than their effects on economic growth. While there were some instances in which growth was associated with rising poverty, Dollar and Kray's results suggest that, on average, these instances were balanced by those in which growth disproportionately benefited the poor.

An overview of the growth and inequality literature by Martin Ravallion (2001) reviews the data and their shortcomings and reminds us that even if rich and poor receive proportionately equal increases in income, the rich still receive several times more absolutely. Ravallion also discusses the role of initial income inequalities in determining the effect of growth on the number of poor—the concept known as "poverty-elasticity." The greater the inequality, the lower is the share of aggregate growth that accrues to the poor and, hence, the smaller the number of those who are likely to be pulled out of poverty by any given growth increment.[5] Ravallion concludes that all these aggregate approaches to poverty lose information by ignoring differences between individuals: one needs, as the title of his article suggests, to look beyond the averages. If this advice is important for estimating the effects of growth on poverty and inequality, it is doubly so for estimating the effects of trade and trade reform, for these effects will typically be far less evenly spread over individuals, sectors, or regions than will "regular" growth.

Two more recent contributions shed further light on the issue. First, Kraay (2006) revisits the Dollar and Kraay exercise with better data and methods, but finds the basic results unchanged. For longer periods—above, say, six or seven years—by far the largest determinant of whether a country has reduced poverty is whether it has grown. Changes in income distribution do occur, but they account for only about 6 to 8 times less of the change in poverty than does growth.

Second, Milanovic (2005b) uses a similar dataset to explore the effects of growth and openness on the whole of the distribution of income by looking at the share of total income accruing to individuals with incomes in each decile of the distribution, allowing the openness effect to vary with the level of average income. He finds that, for poorer countries (below around $8,000 per annum at international prices), openness is unequalizing—that is, higher incomes grow by more than lower ones—presumably because the richer members of society are better placed or better equipped to take advantage of the opportunities it offers. Above the ($8,000 yearly) threshold, openness is apparently equalizing, perhaps because its ability to curb market power is more important where incomes are higher.

The conclusion from all this scholarly analysis is that there is not much evidence that growth worsens inequality, even when it is caused by openness, although one study has suggested that it might do so in low-income economies. There is no evidence that growth or, in the long run, openness, is bad for the poor. Figure 1 (p. 52) offers a useful summary view. It reflects growth and inequality over 117 periods since 1970 for which we have reasonably good and comparable household surveys for two years for the same developing country; about 70 countries are covered, so some countries contribute more than one period to this exercise. When income is rising, there is no clear tendency in inequality (see the right hand column); when income

| Figure 1 |

Growth, Inequality, and Poverty

		What is happening to average household income between the surveys?	
		Falling	Rising
What is happening to relative inequality?*	Rising	**16% of spells** Poverty is *rising* at a median rate of 14.3% per year	**30% of spells** Poverty is *falling* at a median rate of 1.3% per year
	Falling	**26% of spells** Poverty is *rising* at a median rate of 1.7% per year	**27% of spells** Poverty is *falling* at a median rate of 9.6% per year

Source: Martin Ravallion, "Globalization and Poor People: The Debate and Evidence," Max Corden Lecture, University of Melbourne, 2005.

falls (see the left hand column), there is some tendency for inequality to do so, too. Notice, however, the entries on poverty: where incomes rise, poverty falls (on average) and vice versa.

INTRA-COUNTRY INEQUALITY: THE DIRECT EFFECTS ON HOUSEHOLDS

Finally, let us turn to the direct effects of trade liberalization on households. After all, even if inequality/poverty doesn't change in aggregate, there may be a great deal of what economists call "churning," whereby households change places in the income distribution. Treating the household as the basic unit for which income is defined, household fortunes depend on how the price changes generated by liberalization affect their consumption and sources of income. I distinguish three channels of causation: the prices of goods and services, the market for labor, and the role of the taxation and government expenditure.

Taxation

The role of taxation and government expenditure is important but not sophisticated analytically. Critics of trade liberalization frequently argue that it reduces government revenue. The share of total revenue provided by trade taxes is higher for poorer countries than for rich ones, so this is potentially a major issue at low levels of economic development. But, in fact, there is no simple link between trade reform and tariff revenue. In many cases, as tariff rates are reduced, total collections actually increase because, at lower rates of tax, fewer exemptions are sought or granted, it is less worthwhile to engage in tax evasion, and the volume of trade—the tax base—increases.

Of course, as the tariff rate falls to zero, tariff revenue must also eventually fall to zero—a zero tax raises zero revenue no matter how large the tax base. But whether the revenue loss affects services for the poor is essentially a political decision, albeit one constrained by a country's administrative capacity, and so, too, is the choice of alternative taxes to replace revenue losses. That is, there is no law of physics requiring that losses of government revenue must hurt the poor—that is a decision taken by governments, which often prefer to hit the poor rather than other constituencies.

Prices and Markets

A more interesting link is that between trade policy and the prices of the goods that poor households consume and produce. The bulk of the world's poor are self-employed in either low-level agriculture or the informal sector of the economy.[6] Thus their incomes are directly affected by price changes induced by international trade. An increase in the price of something that the household sells (labor, good, or service) increases its real income, while a decrease reduces it. Equally important, prices also matter to households as consumers, just as they do to individuals who earn wages, salaries, or rents.

Whether trade-policy changes on the border get transmitted into price changes for poor or nearly-poor households depends on factors such as transport costs and other costs of distribution, the structure of markets, and domestic taxes and regulations. Some impediments, such as transport costs, are unavoidable, although they may be increased by policy decisions such as the levying of fuel taxes or provision of inadequate infrastructure. But some other impediments represent direct economic inefficiency, such as permitting marketing monopsonies (where there is only one buyer for a product or service) or monopolies (only one seller).

Price transmission is likely to be particularly ineffective for poor people living in remote rural areas, possibly preventing families from making market transactions almost completely. Such isolation saves the poor from any negative shocks emanating from the international economy, but it also prevents them from experiencing positive shocks or the secular benefits from openness that were the subject of the previous section. Their problem is too little globalization, not too much. Thus the policy conclusion of most of this literature is that governments should pursue complementary reforms such as enhanced infrastructure or human capital accumulation to try to connect poor households to the market and thence to the border, while at the same time remaining aware of the possible adverse consequences for subsets of these newly connected populations.

There may also be extreme price changes—either to zero as existing export trades are destroyed, or to infinity if imports disappear. These drastic changes can cause dramatic losses of income, which may be very painful but nonetheless illustrate the gains that emanated from trade in the first place.

A household's ability to adjust to a trade shock—say, by switching production toward goods whose prices have risen—clearly affects the size of any impact it suffers. For many of the poor, a major constraint on improving agricultural productivity following an external liberalization, by making such an adjustment, has been shown to be the absence of key productive assets (draft animals, implements), capital, credit, or information. These demonstrations again highlight the importance of complementary policies targeted at small farmers to enable them to benefit fully from new trading opportunities—for example, fostering asset accumulation, improving access to credit, and providing good-quality extension services.

Adjustment is also the mechanism by which shocks in one market spill over into another, as consumers substitute from expensive to cheaper goods and producers substitute from lower-priced to higher-priced goods. If these spillovers are concentrated onto just a few products or regions, they can be significant locally. A major attraction of liberalizing small-scale agriculture is, arguably, that the direct beneficiaries (farmers) spend much of their extra income on goods and services—such as construction, personal service, and simple manufactures—that are provided locally by other poor people.

Factor Markets

For the self-employed, the main determinant of income is the difference between the prices commanded by their output and those paid for their inputs, but for employees it is factor prices (wages) or employment opportunities. Obtaining employment is one of the surest ways out of poverty, while the loss of a job is probably the most common reason for the precipitate declines into poverty that attract most public attention. The structure of the labor market is critical to how trade liberalization gets translated into wage and employment changes. If wages rise, many wage-earners will typically benefit. If, on the other hand, wages are somehow fixed and adjustment occurs through employment, the smaller number of lucky individuals who get the new jobs created by a trade liberalization are likely to win big increases in income. Thus, who gets the jobs becomes an important issue. Sometimes the lucky ones will be the poor, but at other times the jobs go to additional workers from households that already hold formal employment or to more skilled workers.

Where unskilled labor is abundant, the goods it produces will be plentiful and hence relatively cheap in the absence of international trade. But these are the goods that will be exported when trade is opened up, and hence trade liberalization will generally relieve poverty. However, not all developing countries fall into this class. For example, many Latin American and African countries enjoy very strong endowments of natural resources, and so liberalization will stimulate these sectors rather than labor-intensive ones. In these cases, an active redistribution policy—including helping the poor to obtain access to land, skills, markets, and so on—may be required to spread the benefits of openness.

One of the features of the past twenty years has been the growing skills gap—the excess of skilled wages over unskilled wages—even in developing countries. This effect is unexpected, given the analysis of the previous paragraph, but some authors attribute the widening gap to openness. Various reasons are given for this surprising development.

- The arrival of China on the world scene may have fixed the level of unskilled wages very low.

- When countries liberalize, they import new capital equipment, which tends to need more skilled than unskilled labor to work.

- The business of exporting requires skilled labor or calls for quality that only skilled workers can provide.

- The tasks that relocate from developed to developing countries as trade opens up are unskilled in the former but skilled relative to existing jobs in the latter—hence their transfer raises the relative demand for skills.

The increasing skill gap generally raises inequality.

The arguments in this section are almost bound to vary a good deal from case to case. Detailed research has not thrown up any universal regularities for these direct effects of trade on poverty or inequality. It has, on the other hand, shown that, with sufficient information, we can predict some of the effects—which is useful for designing policies to support a trade liberalization. It has also shown that the key issue to consider is how trade (or any other) reform affects the way people earn their living. This consideration is not just a matter of looking at the labor market, however, because the poor are frequently self-employed. Instead, it arises because while most households consume large number of goods and services, and in fairly similar proportions, they have very many different and much more specialized ways of earning their incomes. Thus, for identifying differences across households (inequalities), we need to focus on the income-generating component.

CONCLUSION

The conclusion of this survey is simultaneously simple and complex. Simply, the evidence suggests strongly that openness to trade tends to boost average incomes over the medium term. This growth has relatively little systematic effect on inequality, and so liberalizing trade tends to be poverty-reducing overall. There will be some exceptions, but the broad tendencies are well-established.

At a more complex level, the direct effects of liberalizing international trade on the real incomes of households will often be small and, where they are not, may be either positive or negative. It is often possible to predict these effects when the household's characteristics are known, but in the absence of detailed information, no general tendencies or results can be relied upon. Thus, while the "average" trade liberalization may well hurt some households, its growth effects are very likely to reduce overall poverty significantly.

NOTES

1. For example, see McCulloch, Winters, and Cirera 2001; Winters 2002; and Winters, McCulloch, and McKay 2004, on all of which I draw freely. Winters 2006 offers an accessible account of the field, and Winters 2007 provides a collection of economic readings on the subject.
2. Milanovic also shows that our view of the degree of inequality and changes in it over time depend strongly on the following: the index of inequality that we use (that is, how we value one income against another); the prices we use to value different elements of consumption (haircuts and piano lessons are cheap in China but not in the United States); and the source of our income data—household surveys (Milanovic's preference) or national income accounts (as, for example, in Bhalla 2005). I shall not discuss these issues here, but when considering contributions to the debate, they must be taken into account.
3. A simple example helps. Two countries have incomes per head of $1,000 and $10,000, respectively, so that the max/min ratio (one measure of inequality) is 10. If both grow by 50 percent to $1,500 and $15,000, the ratio remains 10. Note, however, that the absolute gap has increased from $9,000 to $13,500. Such absolute inequality almost always increases with income growth, but it is not the concept we commonly use.

4. This question is often expressed as "Is openness good for growth?" but growth is the change in income, not the level. The evidence suggests that openness raises the level of income but does not boost growth permanently, although, of course, increasing openness (liberalization) will lead to increasing income (growth) as the economy converges to the higher level of income commensurate with its greater openness; see Winters 2004.

5. If income is very unequally distributed, there will be only a relatively small proportion of households whose income is, say, 5 percent below the poverty line. Thus, if growth increases everyone's income by 5 percent, only a relatively small number of these households are pulled up over the line. If, on the other hand, income distribution is very concentrated, but the average is still low enough to reflect significant poverty, a large share of households will be just below the line and thus will be pulled above it by an increase in all incomes. Imagine two economies, each with one hundred households whose incomes are spread evenly over a range. The unequal society might have a range of $50 to $150—basically one household for every dollar of the distribution. If the poverty line is $100, there are only five households with incomes between $95 and $100, which would be pulled above $100 by 5 percent growth. The more equal society might have all its households in the range of $90 to $115—four households per dollar, or twenty in the range $95 to $100. Here, 5 percent growth will pull twenty households over the poverty line.

6. The informal sector is, loosely speaking, that part of the economy that is not registered, pays no tax, and provides no benefits for workers apart from wages. It is typically comprised of single-person or very small enterprises, such as selling cigarettes on the sidewalk.

NO: Kate Vyborny and Nancy Birdsall, *Center for Global Development*

F ree trade has increased global income as well as the total income of countries that have opened up to it. However, when trade opens up, different groups within countries see differential increases in their income, and some groups may lose income in absolute terms. In the past in some countries—such as those for which trade leads to big increases in agricultural exports—the poor have, initially, gained more than the rich. But over the past three decades, the tendency in most countries has been in the other direction. The globalization of markets for goods and services has tended to benefit the relatively rich more, and so has tended to increase income inequality.

Because trade is beneficial in itself as well as a catalyst for other changes that are needed for countries to grow and reduce poverty, efforts to block trade and globalization have almost always ended with countries losing out. Instead of closing off borders to trade, therefore, the best solution is to find fair, sustainable ways to compensate the losses and ease the transition of those who lose out from major economic shifts such as trade liberalization, and to open up opportunities for the poor and middle classes to take advantage of new economic opportunities. These policies are important for maintaining political support for trade liberalization, as well as for protecting the losers from disastrous declines in consumption. Such policies are needed at both the national and international levels.

FREE TRADE INCREASES INCOME

We know that trade allows countries to specialize in what they produce most efficiently, increasing global income, and then exchange it for the products of others, making all countries better off—even those that are not "best" at producing anything, where producers can compete only by paying lower wages. The basic insight of David Ricardo into how trade can unlock a country's comparative advantage is well summarized in Paul Krugman and Maurice Obstfeld's textbook (1999), which offers the example of two countries, Home and Foreign. Home produces cheese at the rate of one hour of labor per pound, while Foreign produces cheese at six hours per pound; Home produces wine at two hours of labor per gallon, while Foreign produces wine at three hours of labor per gallon. In other words, *Home has higher labor productivity in both industries.* But, as Krugman and Obstfeld note,

> [A]n hour of Home labor produces only 1/2 gallon of wine. The same hour could be used to produce 1 pound of cheese, which can then be traded for 1 gallon of wine. Clearly, Home does gain from trade. Similarly, Foreign could use 1 hour of labor to produce 1/6 pound of cheese; if, however, it uses the hour to produce 1/3 gallon of wine it could then trade the 1/3 gallon of wine for 1/3 pound of cheese. This is twice as much as the 1/6 pound of cheese it gets using the hour to produce the cheese directly. In this example, each country can use labor twice as efficiently to trade for what it needs instead of producing its imports for itself . . . (1999, 4–21).

Trade also stimulates investment. For example, when clothing can be exported with lower tariffs from a country, more foreign companies invest in clothing factories there. Open trade can also encourage the transfer of technology to developing countries—a U.S.-based company is more likely to invest and share technology with overseas suppliers in order to increase the quality and reliability of its own goods, and this enhanced technical capability may eventually spill over to the suppliers' domestic industries (see Saggi 2002).

Of course, the real world is more complicated than these examples may suggest. But the basic principle that trade increases the income of trading countries is one of the best verified findings in economics (Sachs and Warner 1995; Edwards 1993). (There are two exceptions to this principle, which we discuss later.)

THE ROLE OF RELATIVE INEQUALITY

So we know that trade increases total income. But does it matter how trade affects the distribution of income? Does inequality matter, too?

A thought experiment: if you could choose to make one change to your society, which of the following options would you choose?

1. Everyone has at least a minimum standard level of income, but the richest 5 percent have one thousand times that standard.

2. The poorest 5 percent have at least one-tenth the income of the richest 5 percent.

If you considered option 2, why did you do so? What is the inherent virtue of a more equal society? While absolute income is clearly important, it turns out that relative income is also important for a number of reasons.

First, relative income plays a major role in how content we are. Adam Smith, the first economist, noted that in one society a man may need enough income to buy a linen shirt in order to retain his dignity, while in another that expenditure may be seen as a luxury (Hirschman 1973). Surveys of people's relative happiness reveal that individuals report being happier when their own absolute income is higher, but also when their income is higher than that of others in their reference group (Easterlin 1995). This concern for relative well-being becomes important only above a low threshold—in abject poverty, people are primarily concerned about meeting their basic needs (Ravallion and Lokshin 2005). (As globalization has broadened people's access to information about the broader world, they may be comparing their income to a broader reference group as well—see Box 1.)

Box 1	

Inequality among Whom?

In the thought experiment just introduced, what did you have in mind when asked which change you would rather make to your society? Was it your neighborhood, your city, your state, country, or the whole world?

One effect of globalization has been to expand people's frame of reference, as travel becomes more accessible and mass communication expands. People living not just in Johannesburg or Phnom Penh, but even in rural villages in South Africa or Cambodia are now more likely to be able to compare their lifestyle with that of Americans or Europeans as shown on television shows or described by migrant relatives. This expanded perspective has an effect on how people perceive their relative income. So globalization has made global inequality more relevant for people's lives.

Besides measuring and considering the inequality within a single country, there are three ways to consider global inequality. The first is to compare average incomes country by country. But this method effectively weighs the well-being of a citizen of Palau in the South Pacific (population 20,000) as 65,000 times more important than that of a citizen of China (population 1.3 billion). Alternatively, we can weigh the incomes by population. But that method still completely ignores the inequality within countries. A third measure of global inequality is to compare all individuals globally as if we were measuring the inequality in a single country, thus taking into account inequality both within and between countries (Milanovic 2005). The sole disadvantage of this method is that it abstracts from the inequality within a country.

As globalization progresses, these measures become more important. We touch on the effects of trade on these global measures of inequality in this chapter, but we are dealing primarily with inequality within countries—which people care about because it is most immediate, and which affects country politics and policy.

Second, inequality may actually affect economic growth, the driver of any improvements in absolute income. Attempting to force perfect equality is counterproductive, for some level of inequality provides an incentive for people to work hard and innovate. But beyond that level, inequality can also become counterproductive. Such "destructive inequality" reflects inefficient privileges for the rich, a kind of social and economic discrimination that reduces incentives for effort, investment, and innovation, and in general cuts the potential for productive contributions by the poor (see Birdsall 2007b). This destructive potential is more of a problem in poor countries, where, for example, capital markets are less developed, and so those without collateral have little access to credit. Evidence suggests that growth has been lower in the past several decades than would have been expected in countries below a certain income level (about US$3,200), where income inequality is relatively high (described by a Gini coefficient higher than .45—see Box 2).[1]

Box 2

How Do We Measure Inequality?

How does the income of the richest 1 percent of Americans compare to that of the other 99 percent? The income of the top 20 percent to that of the bottom 80 percent? Or is it more important to pay attention to the position of the bottom 10 or 20 percent?

These comparisons differ in the picture they draw. If the richest man in the country doubled his income this year, and everyone else's income stayed the same, that disparity would be much more noticeable in the first measure.

One measure of inequality along the entire income distribution is the Gini coefficient. To calculate the Gini coefficient, we draw a graph with a "Lorenz curve" that shows for each segment of the population what portion of total income that group commands. (The same measure can be applied to total income, disposable income, wealth, and so on.)

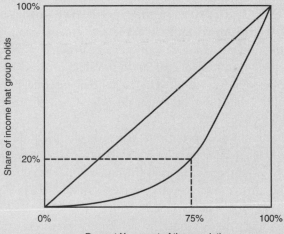

Poorest X percent of the population

In this graph, the poorest 75 percent of the population receives only 20 percent of the income—and so the top 25 percent receives the other 80 percent of the income. Each point on the curve represents such a ratio. The 45-degree diagonal line represents perfect equality, because 20 percent of the people have 20 percent of the income, and so on. The Gini coefficient measures the area between the straight line and the curved line.

So the higher the Gini, the more unequal the society. A society where everyone has exactly the same income would have a Gini coefficient of zero. A society where one person has all the income and the others have no income would have a Gini coefficient of one. The United States has a Gini coefficient of income inequality about .45 (UN WIDER 2008). Northern European countries such as Sweden, on the other hand, have Gini coefficients around .30. Brazil is consistently among the most unequal countries in the world by this measure, with a Gini around .55.

Third, high levels of inequality can have a range of negative social and political effects. Because the size and economic power of the middle class, in particular, is thought to play a major role in democratic accountability, the "missing middle" may be one of the reasons some states have such weak institutions and poor public services: the poor have too little clout and access to information and are too consumed with the day-to-day challenges of survival to exert much pressure on the government, and the rich are able to compensate for the poor quality of government services by using connections, offering bribes, or just paying for private schools or clinics instead (see Birdsall 2005, 2008).

So, if inequality is important in and of itself, how does free trade affect it? The real world is, of course, much more complex than the basic examples just discussed. As it turns out, opening up to trade affects different people's incomes in different ways. The losers—even when they lose only relatively to others—are often more vocal than the winners in this process, and they are more likely to attribute the change to trade than are the winners. As one manufacturer says, "When **NAFTA [North American Free Trade Agreement]** came into force, we closed a factory in Canada, where four hundred people lost their jobs, and replaced it by opening another one in South Carolina, where we hired eight hundred people. Now the four hundred in Canada hate free trade, and the eight hundred in South Carolina think they got the job because they are qualified, and don't care about free trade."

The gains also tend to be spread out—cheaper clothes, food, and appliances affect everyone's budgets, especially those of the poor, but people tend not to be aware of these benefits as the result of free trade, and they are unlikely to lobby for free trade because of them. And where the (potential) losers are well-organized, wealthy, or influential, their voices are heard more loudly—as with some wealthy farmers in rich countries who reap millions of dollars in agricultural subsidies at the expense of the poor abroad who could otherwise export crops such as sugar (Elliott 2005). So we must take reports of losses from trade in context.

ECONOMIC THEORY AND ECONOMIC REALITIES

Let us take a closer look at the theory and evidence of the effects of trade liberalization on inequality across and within countries.

Economic theory suggests that developing countries entering the global trading system in the most recent, post–World War II period of globalization were likely to gain more from this liberalization than richer countries because they were less integrated into the global economy at the start and so had more to gain—and because, from a lower initial income, those income gains could be more rapid (Lindert and Williamson 2001). (Of course, to the extent that some have liberalized less than industrialized countries, they should, in theory, have gained less, and so would not have converged or caught up with richer countries.)

What about inequality within countries? Economic theory predicts that freer trade will redistribute income in a country away from the factors of production (land, capital, skilled or unskilled labor) that are scarce and toward those that are more abundant, compared to the proportions available in the world as a whole.[2] Thus, in rich, industrialized countries, which have an abundance of capital and skilled labor, the wages of unskilled labor should go down, while in poor countries, which have an abundance of unskilled labor, those wages should go up.

So, what has actually happened? First, has free trade reduced inequality across countries?

Across developing countries, trade should, theoretically, increase the income of all those that participate, and especially of those that begin more closed and so can more fully exploit an opening. In reality, however, some—such as China—have grown rapidly while trading more, closing the income gap with the rich world, but many others—particularly in Africa and Latin America— have not. There seem to be two exceptions to the expected income benefits of trade for developing countries.

The first exception is where there are unusual pre-existing trade distortions benefiting some countries over others, such as free trade areas (such as NAFTA) or preferential trade agreements (that is, special trade privileges for the poorest countries, such as the Africa Growth and Opportunity Act). When other countries then open up, this special access gives the previous beneficiaries less of an edge, and they can lose income (see Vyborny 2005). In this case, compensation may be required to ease the transition—these proposed transfers of "aid for trade" for the poorest countries were the subject of much discussion in the (now dormant) Doha Round of global trade negotiations.

The second and more important exception is that in a global market, countries producing goods, such as primary commodities, may lack the people, financing, or access to broader markets that would encourage diversification, especially into manufacturing or new services—the kinds of production that would drive the development of technology and change the countries' comparative advantage over time. This inability to diversify tends to reduce economic growth in the long run (Lindert and Williamson 2001). Concern about this possibility has led many countries to try to nurture "infant industries" by closing themselves off to trade. But this approach has consistently failed, as trying to opt out of globalization has led to those countries' losing out. This pattern leaves countries with a strong comparative advantage in production of primary commodities in a bind—how best to develop a manufacturing base? It seems that many ingredients are needed: investing in education and health to develop a productive workforce, improving infrastructure, reducing corruption and streamlining regulatory processes to reduce costs to businesses, ensuring a functioning justice system that businesses can rely on to resolve disputes, and maintaining a stable macroeconomic environment. As it turns out, some have done better than others in managing these other factors and in diversifying their production to include manufacturing and services as well as primary commodities. Those countries have grown more rapidly and reduced the gap between their average income and the average income in rich countries (Birdsall 2007a).

What about inequality within countries: has trade increased inequality in rich countries and reduced it in poor countries, as theory predicted?

It is critical to understand that trade is not always the key factor—and it is never the sole factor—in bringing about changes in the economy, including those affecting inequality. And it is particularly difficult to tease out the effects that trade liberalization has had; while a country liberalizes, many other changes may be occurring, so simply looking at the changes in the level of inequality over that time is not enough to establish a relationship. For instance, technological change, which affects the types of jobs that are available, is a major driver of inequality—and it has tended to accompany trade liberalization. Also, some studies have found that the proportion of young people in a society is a major determinant of overall inequality, so a baby boom might affect income distribution independent of changes in trade (Higgins and Williamson 1999).

Countries that are more open to free trade are likely to share many other characteristics in addition, so simply comparing income distribution between countries that have and have not opened up is insufficient as well. This is part of the reason that any single study is insufficient to prove the answer one way or another. To establish a causal link requires careful quantitative analysis controlling for these other factors. The evidence that trade increases overall income is well established; but its effects on inequality have been less fully explored. Later, we sometimes refer simply to changes in trade coinciding with changes in inequality, without implying any necessary causal link.

In today's rich countries, as expected, there has been an increase in inequality coinciding with broad-based trade liberalization since the 1980s (Lindert and Williamson 2001). In fact, only a relatively small part of this increase is due to trade; the evidence suggests that at least half has been driven by other factors—most importantly, improvements in technology (see Lawrence and Slaughter

1993; Sachs and Shatz 1994; Wood 1994, 1995). More sophisticated equipment and computing power have made many jobs obsolete, reducing demand for unskilled labor, and so wages for unskilled labor have gone down relative to those for skilled labor.

But in some poor countries—in particular, those in Latin America—free trade has not brought the expected declines in inequality.[3] Why not?

Some of the increases in inequality in liberalizing developing countries have likely occurred because of other factors occurring at the same time as liberalization. The liberalization of Latin American countries in the 1970s and 1980s coincided with the entry into the world market of more competitive countries, including China and other Asian exporters (Lindert and Williamson 2001). Mexico was a higher-wage country than its new competitors— in this case Mexico was the richer country in the dynamics of trade liberalization described earlier, and so we would expect its inequality to increase. Liberalization in some countries, including Chile and Mexico, coincided with removal of policies that had favored less skilled workers, such as powerful unions in Chile and protection of low-wage industries in Mexico. So unskilled, low-wage workers saw their relative wages fall compared to their more skilled counterparts.

But some of the increases in inequality have happened because the world differs from the simplifying assumptions of the textbook. For example, in the real world, there are more than two countries and two goods. In the real world, a worker who has completed high school—and so is considered "skilled" in Bangladesh—is counted as comparatively "unskilled" in the United States (without a college degree or English language skills). Let us now consider in detail some of the ways in which the real world becomes more complicated than the theory, allowing free trade to have some disequalizing effects.

Adjustment Costs

First, there are short-term costs of adjustment to changed patterns of production— for example, low-skilled jobs in garment factories may be lost, while low-skilled jobs in toy factories are generated. The same individuals may move from the garment to the toy factories, but they incur costs in searching for and training for their new jobs. These costs are difficult to measure, but are likely regressive, simply because hurdles such as searching for employment are more costly for the poor (Fernandez de Cordoba, Laird, and Serena, n.d.). And the effects of unemployment and bankruptcy may be permanent for the poor, so repeated shocks can increase inequality (Diwan 2001). During periods without work, the poor may be forced to sell off productive assets (such as farm equipment, a milk cow, or a sewing machine); their children may drop out of school and never return (Székely 1999).

Advantages for Countries with Most Productive Assets

The inequality implications of trade theory outlined earlier build on the assumption that the main difference between countries in determining what they produce and trade is the difference between their endowments—one country may have more unskilled labor and land, the other more skilled labor and capital. But this assumption leaves out the major productivity differences between countries—producing the same good or service may require more of the total inputs in developing countries than in developed countries (Easterly 2004). In other words, everything else being equal, a hundred workers may be able to produce more widgets per hour in the United States than in Nigeria—because of frequent power cuts in the Nigerian widget plant, higher costs to ship widget inputs and the finished widgets to and from the factory because of poor roads, higher operating costs from licenses and export procedures with a less efficient or corrupt government, and so on. Such differences in productivity help to explain why 80 percent of all foreign investment occurs among the industrialized countries, while just 0.1 percent of U.S. foreign investment goes to sub-Saharan Africa (UNCTAD [UN Conference on Trade and Development] 2001).

Recall that the gains from trade by Home and Foreign (discussed at the beginning of this chapter) demonstrated that lower- and higher-productivity countries still gain from trade in aggregate income, even when a country can compete only by offering lower wages. But what do these differences mean for inequality? For inequality within countries, Easterly argues that these productivity differences effectively make skilled labor and capital more scarce in higher-productivity rich countries, so they would benefit more from trade liberalization. But the effect on inter-country inequality also depends on how freer trade affects productivity differences. Trade can lead to technology transfer, which increases productivity. So the effects of trade may depend on the extent of this effect. And if trade increases investment, that may also change factor endowments by making labor more scarce compared to capital. For inequality between countries might suggest that industrialized, higher productivity countries could experience a greater benefit than lower productivity countries because a larger share of the investment that trade helps to stimulate would flow to them.

In addition to these productivity differences, the change in global demand for goods and services has increased the demand for skilled labor, due to technological change and the resulting global growth in sectors with more complex inputs. Demand for skills has risen faster than the supply of skilled workers everywhere, despite the fact that more and more people are going to a university, including across the developing world (Levy 1999; Duryea and Székely 1998; Terrell 2000). The earnings of those with a higher education relative to those without have therefore continued to rise. Because in many countries education is reinforcing initial advantages instead of compensating for initial handicaps, the resulting tendency is growing income inequality.[4]

Costs of Market Failures on the Poor

The classic example of a market failure is that of pollution, as the polluter captures the benefits of polluting without paying the full costs. Because free trade makes global production chains possible—allowing firms to shift production or switch suppliers between countries—the costs of market failures such as pollution often shift to the poor citizens of poor countries with the weakest institutions to control them. And global integration allows firms to shift greenhouse gas-generating production to countries with the weakest controls, making it harder to combat climate change, which disproportionately affects the poor (Cline 2007).

Bias against the Poor in Global Economic Rules

It is better to have a rules-based system—such as the World Trade Organization—than no system at all; such a system helps to level the playing field compared to the default to anarchy in international affairs, in which the most powerful countries simply determine the outcome. But the richer and more powerful countries are also able to influence the design and implementation of global rules to their own advantage, at the expense of the developing countries. And within those developing countries, the rules are slanted in particular against the poor, who have little voice in their government and even less voice at the negotiating table with trading partners.

The effort to reduce rich country agricultural subsidies and tariffs that discriminate against poor countries is a good example. Domestic agricultural lobbies in industrialized countries matter more at the negotiating table than unequal opportunities for cotton farmers in West Africa do. Developing countries are at a disadvantage in global trade and other negotiations, and the smallest and poorest countries need transfers of aid from rich countries simply to participate effectively—to command the legal and economic expertise to negotiate and analyze the potential effects for them of different outcomes of the negotiations. For example, about one-half of legal cases brought in the WTO against the trade violation known as "dumping" are initiated against developing country producers, who account for 8 percent of all exports (Birdsall 2005).

SOLUTION: COMPLEMENTARY "FAIR GROWTH" POLICIES

Despite the disequalizing tendencies they can have, trying to block trade and globalization has almost without exception caused whole countries to lose out economically (Lindert and Williamson 2001). As we stressed at the beginning of the chapter, the benefits of trade are significant, and staying on the sidelines is not the answer.

Instead, the best solution is to find fair, sustainable ways to compensate the losses and ease the transition of those who lose out from trade liberalization and other major economic shifts, as well as to open up opportunities for the poor and middle classes to become upwardly mobile by taking advantage of new economic opportunities. These policies are important to maintain political support for trade liberalization, as well as for equity where the losers from trade are poor.

Even where trade makes some people worse off and so increases inequality, it is still possible—and desirable—for everyone to gain if the "winners" from trade compensate the "losers" with a portion of their increased income. Since total income in a country will increase with trade liberalization, such partial transfers would still leave everyone better off than they started (Dixit and Norman 1980; Corden 1974). This sort of compensation is particularly important for poor people in poor countries, because they have the fewest assets to fall back on and less access to information about opportunities in other sectors (for example) and so are the least well-equipped to deal with the transitions that trade can bring (Bannister and Thugge 2001). The less diversified economies in many low-income countries also mean that a larger proportion of workers may lose their livelihoods at once, making it more difficult for all of them to find new sources of income.

But it turns out in practice that such compensatory policies often do not come through for these people, for a number of reasons. First, there is a strategic problem—governments and voters do not usually face a choice of a package of free trade plus compensation, so it is difficult for the poor to demand that trade liberalization take place if and only if they are adequately compensated. Government revenue also takes a hit when tariffs are cut, particularly in some of the poorest countries which rely heavily on tariffs for revenue, making boosting transfer programs unattractive. Finally, because the poor tend to be less organized and less politically effective, redistributive programs may never take place, and when they do, they often respond to more vocal entrenched interests, transforming these initiatives into a regressive tax rather than a safety net. For example, Senegal's program to cushion the effects of its economic reforms channeled state money to privileged groups within the system (civil servants and university graduates), while doing nothing to protect the urban and rural poor from rising consumer prices and unemployment. Often, even those subsidies originally meant for the poor are quickly captured by the middle class and the rich.

It is also logistically difficult for governments to make lump-sum transfers to the "losers" from trade, for there is a major challenge in identifying who has lost from trade, especially in poor countries where large segments of the population work in agriculture or the informal sector (Bannister and Thugge 2001; Winters 2000; Ravallion 1999). It is also difficult to justify paying those who have lost because of trade and not because of other economic shifts such as advancing technology making their jobs obsolete. (This identification problem has been an issue with the U.S. federal program to assist those who have lost jobs because of trade—the Trade Adjustment Assistance, or TAA program [GAO (Government Accountability Office) 2007].)

So what can be done to compensate the losers? Strengthening general social safety net policies such as food vouchers and adult job training programs is likely the fairest and most sustainable way to compensate the losers. The design and implementation of these programs still requires attention to ensure that they reach those who need them most. A broader set of "fair growth" policies that will empower the poor and the middle class to take advantage of new and existing economic opportunities—such as social investments in education and health, and fairer application of tax systems and regulatory changes to help small businesses formalize and grow—is also needed.[5]

A Global Social Contract

Some policies to address the equity effects of trade, such as strong social safety net programs, can be made at the national level. But because of the political and economic challenges just outlined, the only way they are likely to become a reality is with at least some international support. The (now dormant) Doha Round of international trade negotiations has incorporated discussions on "aid for trade," including funds to compensate countries for adjustment costs to liberalization and/or to help countries better take advantage of new trading opportunities (Hoekman and Prowse 2005). But so far, these commitments have been problematic because they may not be binding and the aid may not be additional. And there has been almost no discussion of funding to ease the adjustment costs of the poor within countries, or to underwrite what may be a longer-term need for support for social safety net programs. These transfer payments are in the interest of rich as well as poor countries: fairer compensation can help to build broader support for trade liberalization that allows economic expansion and opportunity in the industrialized world as well.

There is also a need for compensatory policies that fall into the global arena, which cannot be addressed on the national level. Global regulatory arrangements and rules are needed to manage global market failures, such as climate change, and to discourage corruption and other anticompetitive processes (a global antitrust agency, for example).[6] These global programs are particularly important for the poor, but they would benefit everyone in both rich and poor countries. In principle, they could be financed internationally by some mechanism that mimics taxes within national economies, such as a levy on international aviation or on carbon emissions.

Free trade does not always—and cannot by itself—increase economic equality at the national or global levels. But in combination with these proposed policies at country and international levels, it can be a powerful instrument to increase wealth and welfare equitably.

NOTES

1. Barro 2000. Also, Cornia, Addison, and Kiistki (2004) report a positive effect on growth as the Gini coefficient increases from very low levels (from the .15 typical of subsistence economies and of the former socialist economies to .30) and a negative effect as the Gini coefficient rises from .45 (typical in Latin America and sub-Saharan Africa) to higher levels. The $3,200 is in purchasing power parity terms, in 2005.
2. This result is known as the Stolper-Samuelsen theorem.
3. Easterly 2004. Also see, among many others, Milanovic and Squire 2005; Lindert and Williamson 2001; Stiglitz 2002; and Wade 2004.
4. Cuba, China, and Kerala in India are exceptions; see Birdsall 2005.
5. For a menu of fair growth policies and their application in Latin America, see Birdsall, de la Torre, and Menezes 2007.
6. Birdsall (2005) refers to Bardhan 2004 on this idea.

poverty

Can Foreign Aid Reduce Poverty?

YES: Jeffrey D. Sachs, *The Earth Institute at Columbia University*

NO: George B. N. Ayittey, *American University*

More than 3 billion people—nearly half the world—live on less than $2 a day. Tens of thousands of children die every day from conditions associated with poverty, more than 1 million each year from diarrhea alone. Millions lack access to lifesaving immunizations that are routine in the West. More than 1 billion lack access to adequate water supplies. Figure 1 (p. 72) details the geographic distribution of the poor worldwide, indicating that while progress was made in most of the world—including significant improvements made in East Asia—over a recent twenty-year period, the percentage of those living in extreme poverty decreased only modestly in sub-Saharan Africa. Statistics such as these are both appalling and overwhelming: how can material excess and deprivation exist side-by-side in our globalized world, and how can the relatively privileged provide assistance to the bottom billion?

The **United Nations Development Programme** (the principal development network within the UN), the World Bank (International Bank for Reconstruction and Development), and the International Monetary Fund (IMF) are the principal multilateral institutions for economic development and debt relief. After the **Marshall Plan** of 1947 helped to rebuild nations in Europe following World War II, President Harry Truman instituted bilateral foreign aid as a feature of U.S. foreign policy. In the 1960s, President John F. Kennedy established the U.S. Agency for International Development (USAID), which provides development assistance as well as humanitarian aid, and the Peace Corps, which sends people to live and serve in developing nations. The **Camp David accords** of 1979 catapulted Israel and Egypt to the top of nations receiving U.S. foreign aid, although recently they have been supplanted by development assistance to Iraq. The 1980s and 1990s saw reductions in U.S. foreign aid, but in the wake of the terrorist attacks on September 11, 2001, aid began to be seen as a potential impediment to

Figure 1

Percentage of Total Population in Each Region Living on Less than $1.25/Day, 1981–2005

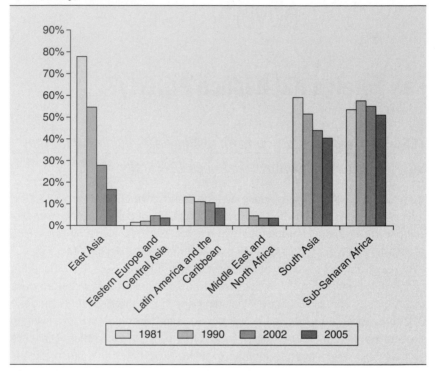

Source: The World Bank, World Development Indicators Database. http://data.worldbank.org/indicator/SI.POV
.DDAY/countries/8S-ZF-XQ-XJ-7E-4E?display=graph. Accessed December 14, 2011.
Note: Population below $1.25 a day is the percentage of the population living on less than $1.25 a day at 2005
international prices.

terrorism, and it has increased since then, particularly in Iraq and Afghanistan. Figure 2 (p. 73) shows substantial increases in foreign aid contributions by the Organization of Economic Cooperation and Development's (OECD) Development Assistance Committee (DAC) since 1960.

In response to extreme world poverty, the United Nations, in its Millennium Summit in 2000, agreed upon a set of Millennium Development Goals (MDGs) to be reached by year 2015 as a way of guiding future efforts to address poverty. (See Table 1 in Jeffrey Sachs's contribution [p. 77] for a brief listing of these goals.) One of the important commitments required to meet the MDGs was for wealthy nations to increase their aid to 0.7 percent of gross national income, a target that had been in place since the mid-1960s. However, most

Figure 2

Net Official Development Assistance Disbursed by OECD Development Assistance Committee, 1960–2010 (in constant 2011 US Dollars)

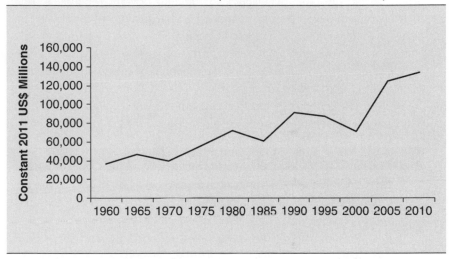

Source: OECD-DAC, *Total net official development assistance*, updated April 2011, available at http://www.oecd.org/doc ument/11/0,3746,en_2649_34447_1894347_1_1_1_1,00.html (accessed December 14, 2011).
Note: Figures include total assistance disbursed by countries that are members of the OECD Development Assistance Committee (OECD-DAC).

of these nations remain far short of that goal. The United States contributes more than any other nation in raw figures—more than $30 billion in 2010—yet it sits near the bottom of the list in terms of its aid donations as a proportion of gross national income (GNI), of which it gives just 0.21 percent. Only five nations—Norway, Sweden, Luxembourg, Denmark, and the Netherlands— have reached the UN target of 0.7 percent of GNI, and the average for the OECD's Development Assistance Committee is just 0.32 percent.

Some forms of aid are motivated more by internal politics and support for strong domestic constituencies in the developed nations than by recognition of the need for improving conditions elsewhere, and they may in turn harm developing nations. For example, food aid in the form of export subsidies in developed nations and delivery of heavily-subsidized or free food to develop- ing nations is often a political effort to support domestic farmers (either in the United States or in Europe) and may serve to artificially depress food export prices and, therefore, extinguish food production possibilities in developing nations. Furthermore, the farm policies of the developed world all serve to stimulate production, thereby further depressing world food prices and stunt- ing farm production in the developing world.

Three principal disagreements shape debates about foreign aid: (1) the extent to which it is simply an instrument of foreign policy and therefore not intended to actually improve the lives of those most in need; (2) which types of foreign aid are most beneficial in combating poverty, regardless of the motivation; and (3) the relative importance of foreign aid compared with other forms of economic activity—such as international trade—in raising living standards. The two articles that follow present varying perspectives on the prospects for foreign aid influencing international development by reducing poverty. Dr. George Ayittey argues that a free press and independent judiciary are important ingredients to development, while Jeffery Sachs advocates large increases in development aid along the lines of the Marshall Plan.

Discussion Questions

1. Do wealthy nations have an obligation to provide aid to poor nations? In what ways can foreign aid be used as a foreign policy tool by wealthy nations? Does it matter what donor nations' motives are when they provide aid? Why or why not?

2. The **Monterrey Consensus** is an agreement among the world's wealthy nations that recognizes the importance of trade in reducing poverty in poor nations. It affirms the *aid for trade* concept, whereby foreign aid is given to poor nations in order to improve the infrastructure needed for trade. Do you agree with this concept? Is this the best way to reduce poverty? In what other ways can foreign aid be used?

3. What recommendations does Jeffrey Sachs make for combating poverty? What justifications does he cite? Do you agree with his proposals?

4. What does George Ayittey cite as the biggest reason for foreign aid's failure to reduce poverty in Africa? He proposes *smart aid* as an alternative. What is smart aid? What are its key components?

YES: Jeffrey D. Sachs, *The Earth Institute at Columbia University*

In the broadest terms, national and international efforts to promote economic development around the world during the past fifty years have been highly successful, with the notable exception of large parts of sub-Saharan Africa, which remain trapped in extreme poverty. The biggest development successes have come in Asia, a vast region with more than half the world's population. Economic growth in China, India, Korea, and many other countries—along with public investments in health, education, and infrastructure—have powered the most rapid improvement in living standards in world history. Aid has played an enormous role in those gains. The fact that Asia can feed itself is due in no small part to the **Green Revolution** that began in the 1960s, heavily supported by the U.S. public and philanthropic sectors. The fact that disease burdens have come down sharply is due in important part to global aid successes such as smallpox eradication, widespread immunization coverage, malaria control (outside of Africa), and the uptake of oral rehydration to fight death from diarrhea. The fact that population growth has slowed markedly is a success of aid-supported family planning efforts, which the United States has helped to initiate since the 1960s. The fact that countries such as Korea, Malaysia, and Thailand became manufacturing successes grew out of U.S. and Japanese aid for core infrastructure and technological upgrading.

DEVELOPMENT ASSISTANCE AS A TOOL IN PROMOTING ECONOMIC DEVELOPMENT

There are now sixty years of experience in deploying development assistance as a tool in promoting economic development in low-income settings. Development aid has long been a mix of public and private contributions. When aid is from the public sector, it is known as **Official Development Assistance (ODA)**. Both ODA and private assistance have played an important and successful role in development. Many of the greatest successes in development assistance in the past six decades have come through Public-Private Partnerships (PPPs), which

---

This article, which is based on excerpts from the HELP Commission Minority Report, "Revamping U.S. Foreign Assistance," by Jeffrey Sachs, Leo Hindery Jr., and Gayle E. Smith (2007), was prepared in August 2008 and does not take into account developments since the 2008 U.S. presidential election.

typically link ODA with private-sector and philanthropic leadership of various kinds. The Green Revolution in India was spurred by such a partnership. The campaign against polio, which is on the verge of eradicating that dreaded disease, is a partnership of several public and private institutions, including the **World Health Organization** and **Rotary International.**

Of course, aid has worked in conjunction with powerful market forces, most importantly international trade and investment—the forces of globalization have helped to spread the benefits of advanced technologies to all corners of the world. Aid should certainly be seen not as a substitute for market-led development, but rather as a complementary component of market forces, especially for impoverished countries that lack sufficient infrastructure, income, and creditworthiness to mobilize needed investments on their own behalf via market forces and domestic budget revenues.

The special role for ODA as one of several complementary forces of economic development was well described in the Monterrey Consensus, a 2002 agreement among the world's nations, which the United States strongly supports and repeatedly backs. That agreement is notable in recognizing the interconnections among private capital flows, international trade, and ODA— all of which are vital to economic development of the poor countries. Rather than pitting trade against aid, the Monterrey Consensus explains why they are both vital and complementary, and, indeed, why aid is vital to supporting trade competitiveness of the poorest countries. The Monterrey Consensus has therefore contributed to the new concept of "aid for trade," in which ODA is used to help poor countries to improve their international trade, mainly by building the infrastructure (roads, ports, power) needed to support trade.

U.S. Commitments to Economic Development and Poverty Reduction

The United States has long recognized that it cannot and should not carry the world's development financing burden on its own. Support for economic development in the poorest countries must be a shared global effort, based on agreed targets. The United States and partner countries have therefore pursued shared global goals for several decades, achieving great successes in disease control, increased food production, the spread of literacy and numeracy, increased school enrollments, improved infrastructure, and many other core development objectives. By far the most important of the shared development objectives today are the Millennium Development Goals (see Table 1, p. 77) adopted by all nations in the Millennium Declaration of the year 2000 and reconfirmed regularly since then, including at the G8 summits.

Table 1

Millennium Development Goals

Goal 1: Eradicate extreme poverty and hunger	Target 1: Halve, between 1990 and 2015, the proportion of people whose income is less than $1 per day
	Target 2: Halve, between 1990 and 2015, the proportion of people who suffer from hunger
Goal 2: Achieve universal primary education	Target 3: Ensure that, by 2015, children everywhere, boys and girls alike, will be able to complete a full course of primary schooling
Goal 3: Promote gender equality and empower women	Target 4: Eliminate gender disparity in primary and secondary education, preferably by 2005, and in all levels of education by 2015
Goal 4: Reduce child mortality	Target 5: Reduce by two-thirds, between 1990 and 2015, the under-five mortality rate
Goal 5: Improve maternal health	Target 6: Reduce by three-quarters, between 1990 and 2015, the maternal mortality ratio
Goal 6: Combat HIV/ AIDS, malaria, and other diseases	Target 7: Have halted by 2015 and begun to reverse the spread of HIV/AIDS
	Target 8: Have halted by 2015 and begun to reverse the incidence of malaria and other major diseases
Goal 7: Ensure environmental sustainability	Target 9: Integrate the principles of sustainable development into country policies and programs, and reverse the loss of environmental resources
	Target 10: Halve, by 2015, the proportion of people without sustainable access to safe drinking water and basic sanitation
	Target 11: By 2020, to have achieved a significant improvement in the lives of at least 100 million slum-dwellers
Goal 8: Develop a global partnership for development	Target 12: Develop further an open, rule-based, predictable, non-discriminatory trading (includes a commitment to good governance, development, and poverty reduction—both nationally and internationally)
	Target 13: Address the special needs of the Least Developed Countries (includes tariff- and quota-free access for their exports; enhanced program of debt relief for heavily indebted poor countries [HIPC]; and cancellation of official bilateral debt; and more generous official development assistance for countries committed to poverty reduction)
	Target 14: Address the special needs of landlocked developing countries and small island developing states
	Target 15: Deal comprehensively with the debt problems of developing countries through national and international measures in order to make debt sustainable in the long term
	Target 16: In cooperation with pharmaceutical companies, provide access to affordable drugs in developing countries
	Target 17: In cooperation with the private sector, make available the benefits of new technologies, especially information and communications technologies

The Millennium Development Goals (MDGs) constitute a very important instrument for effective U.S. development assistance for the following reasons:

- The world has agreed to the goals and reconfirmed that support each year since 2000.

- The world has agreed to a trade and financing framework in the Monterrey Consensus.

- The MDGs address extreme poverty in all its interconnected dimensions: income, hunger, disease, deprivation.

- The MDGs promote long-term economic growth and wealth creation by encouraging countries to focus on productive investments to end the poverty trap.

- The MDGs are ambitious and yet achievable.

- The MDGs are quantitative and time-bound, therefore offering objective indicators of success and accountability.

Current Levels of U.S. Official Development Assistance in Comparative Perspective

Although development, defense, and diplomacy are the three pillars of U.S. national security, the current investments in national security are almost entirely in the direction of defense spending. In 2007 defense spending was $611 billion, while spending for diplomacy could be estimated at around $9 billion and that for development assistance at $22.7 billion. The allocation of official development assistance is equally important. U.S. aid is divided between **"bilateral" aid**, given by the U.S. government directly to other countries, and **multilateral aid**, given by the U.S. government to international organizations such as the World Bank, the African Development Bank, and the Global Fund to Fight AIDS, TB, and Malaria. Distressingly, only around one-quarter of overall bilateral aid is spent on development directed at long-term poverty reduction and disease control. The vast bulk of aid is devoted to emergencies and U.S. political aims, rather than to the objectives that are most effectively served by official development assistance: long-term economic development.

The United States is the largest aid donor in terms of absolute amount, as shown in Figure 1a (p. 79), but this fact is hardly surprising since it is also by far the most populous donor country, with a 2006 population of 299 million, compared with 128 million in Japan, 83 million in Germany, 60 million in the United Kingdom, 63 million in France, 9 million in Sweden, and 5 million in

Figure 1a

Net ODA in 2007—amounts

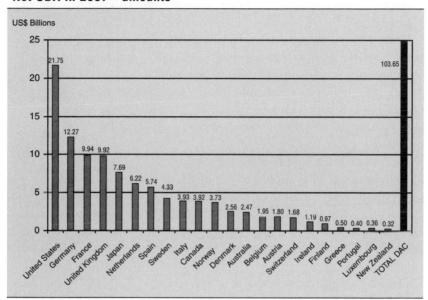

Figure 1b

Net ODA in 2007—as a Percentage of GNI

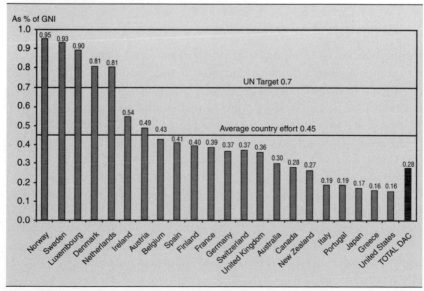

Source: OECD [Organization of Economic Cooperation and Development], April 4, 2008.

Norway. In per capita terms, however, Norwegians average $629 per person in aid, while Americans average only $76 per person. As a share of national income, U.S. aid is actually the lowest among donor countries, as shown in Figure 1b (p. 79).

Since 1970, most donor countries have pledged to achieve the target of 0.7 percent of GNP [gross national product] as ODA (following a recommendation of an International Commission headed by Lester Pearson), and reiterated that pledge many times, most recently in the Monterrey Consensus.[1] Only five countries—Denmark, Luxembourg, the Netherlands, Norway, and Sweden—have consistently achieved or exceeded that goal. All of the other seventeen donors in the OECD's Development Assistance Committee (DAC) have fallen short, despite their adoption of the target.

Following the 2002 Monterrey Conference, most donor countries set a specific timetable to achieve the 0.7 percent target. Donors in the (pre-enlargement) European Union agreed to contribute at least 0.51 percent of GNP as ODA by 2010, and 0.7 percent by 2015. The United States, despite its strong and repeated support for the Monterrey Consensus, has not yet made concrete efforts to achieve the target of 0.7 percent of GNP. The current U.S. level of ODA, alas, remains stuck at 0.16 percent of GNP (2007)—the lowest level among all twenty-two donors in the Development Assistance Committee. Unlike the European Union, the United States has established no timetable or political consensus to reach that goal, despite its pledge at Monterrey to make concrete efforts to do so.

Private Development Assistance

During the 1960s, the idea took hold in various forums that the rich countries should support the poor countries with an annual transfer of 1 percent of national income. This transfer, in turn, was to be divided between ODA, targeted at 0.7 percent, and aid from private donors, targeted at 0.3 percent. While a few donor governments have achieved the 0.7 target, however, no donor country's private sector has come close to reaching the 0.3 percent of GNP target for private development assistance.

Meanwhile, it is often said that development assistance is passé, since private financial flows of all kinds (development assistance, foreign direct investment, foreign portfolio investments, and so on) now swamp official flows. Still, this fact does not make ODA obsolete, because the private capital flows are heavily concentrated in middle-income countries and in low-income countries with high-value natural resources such as hydrocarbons, minerals, or precious metals. Private capital flows bypass the world's poorest countries, which lack the basic infrastructure—roads, power, ports, clinics, and schools—that is needed to attract private investments in the first place. ODA is complementary to private capital flows, and it must generally *precede* private flows into impoverished regions. We should therefore think about using ODA to create the base—in infrastructure, health, skills, and other necessary conditions—to attract private capital.

Similar points can be made about trade. An open trading system is essential for economic development, including among the poorest countries. Developing countries need to import technology from abroad and must pay for that technology through their own exports. For this basic reason, export-led growth has been vital for economic success in recent decades. To achieve export-led growth, poor countries need to maintain relatively open trading systems (featuring low to moderate tariffs and convertible currencies), while rich countries, including the United States, have to keep their own borders open to the exports of the poor countries. However, even trade reforms such as these cannot substitute for official development aid.

WHAT WORKS AND WHAT DOESN'T WORK WITH ODA

The discussion on aid effectiveness is clouded by confusions, prejudices, and simple misunderstandings. Many studies try to find a correlation between overall aid and economic growth; when they find little positive correlation, they declare aid to be a failure. But the low correlation does not prove that aid is failing, since much of the aid is directed to countries in violence, famine, or deep economic crisis. It ought not to be a surprise, therefore, that aid often correlates with "economic failure"—not because aid has caused the failure, but rather because aid has responded to it.

There has been vast development success internationally, including stunning increases in average incomes, life expectancy, child survival, literacy, school completion rates, and other gains, in most parts of the world. When we look at ODA success stories, however, we find that aid is most successful when it is indeed used for development assistance. In other words, the ODA tool truly is a *development* tool.

Here are several great success stories of development assistance:

- **The Asian Green Revolution.** During the 1950s and 1960s, the Rockefeller Foundation and other donors spurred the development of high-yield seed varieties and new techniques for modernized farming. The U.S. Agency for International Development (USAID) helped to finance the rapid uptake of these new technologies, including the improved seeds, fertilizer, and irrigation. Dramatic successes were achieved in the 1960s in India and Pakistan, and later in China, Southeast Asia, and other parts of the developing world.

- **Smallpox Eradication.** In 1967 the World Health Organization (WHO) established the Smallpox Eradication Unit and launched a donor-supported worldwide campaign to eradicate the disease. By 1980, WHO was able to declare the world free of smallpox.

- **Family Planning.** During the 1960s, the U.S. government and various organizations (including the Ford Foundation and the Population Council) launched a global effort to spread access to modern contraception, based on individual voluntary choices. The uptake of these contraceptive methods, supported by international and U.S. funding, has been widespread (though still largely bypassing sub-Saharan Africa). As a result of these actions, together with declining child mortality rates, spreading literacy, and broader economic trends, fertility rates and population growth rates have declined sharply throughout most of the developing world.

- **The Campaign for Child Survival.** In 1982 the **United Nations Children's Fund (UNICEF)** launched a campaign to promote child survival, based on the powerful combination known as GOBI: growth monitoring of children, oral rehydration therapy, breastfeeding for nutrition and immunity to infectious diseases, and immunizations against childhood killers. Backed by development assistance, the package enjoyed a remarkably rapid uptake, enabling many of the poorest countries to reach at least 80 percent immunization coverage.

- **Treatment for AIDS, TB, and Malaria.** After years of international neglect and underfinancing, international donors agreed to step up their actions to fight three killer pandemic diseases: AIDS, tuberculosis (TB), and malaria. At the urging of the then UN secretary-general Kofi Annan, they formed a new Global Fund to Fight AIDS, TB, and Malaria, as a means to pool their resources and invite countries to formulate national strategies that would be backed by development aid. In a period of only five years, the Global Fund successfully financed the access of more than 1 million HIV-infected individuals to antiretroviral medicines; the distribution of more than 30 million bed nets (protective against mosquitoes), mainly in Africa; and the treatment of more than 2 million individuals for TB. At the same time, the United States launched the **PEPFAR (President's Emergency Plan for AIDS Relief)** program to extend AIDS prevention and treatment programs in low-income countries.

There are six crucial lessons in these development success stories:

- First, the interventions are based on a powerful, low-cost technology. Given that the main underlying force of economic development is technological advance, it is not surprising that successful development assistance typically involves the diffusion of a powerful technology, such as high-yield seeds, immunizations, modern contraception, or Internet connectivity.

- Second, the interventions are relatively easy to deliver, based on standardized protocols and local ownership. Modern technologies are embodied in systems. Vaccinations, for example, are delivered on a specific timetable for young children, and high-yielding seeds are deployed in specific packages of farm inputs (such as combinations of seed, fertilizer, irrigation, and agricultural extension). The key to success is to deploy the technology in a system that is evidence-based, scientifically sound, administratively feasible, and tailored to local conditions.

- Third, the interventions are applied at the scale needed to solve the underlying problem. The key to success in the examples cited earlier was not the demonstration of the underlying technology, but rather the deployment of the technology at a scale in which it could make a difference. Typically, once the technology is known, and once the expert system has been identified, rapid scale-up is possible, building on global strategies and local adaptation and support.

- Fourth, the interventions are reliably funded. All of the success stories involve budget outlays over a period of many years, so that participating countries can be confident of sustained financing, and therefore can establish institutional systems and provide training and capacity-building.

- Fifth, the interventions are multilateral, drawing support from many governments and international agencies. The greatest development challenges—extreme poverty, hunger, disease, lack of infrastructure—are beyond the financing capacity of any single donor country. Moreover, a unified effort is more efficient than a congeries of small and disparate projects, at least once the technologies and delivery mechanisms have been developed.

- Sixth, the interventions have specific inputs, goals, and strategies, so that success rates can be assessed. All of the success stories involve clear strategies, such as coverage rates of immunizations, hectares planted with high-yield seeds, and timely isolation of smallpox outbreaks. They do not directly aim for excessively broad and overarching goals—such as "economic growth," or "rule of law," or "democracy," or "end of terror"— though broad goals such as these were among the indirect and long-term objectives that motivated the programs in the first place. Instead, the programs work on much more specific objectives, which can be measured, audited, evaluated, and reassessed as needed.

These six specific points all come down to one overarching lesson: be practical when deploying development aid—understand the targeted inputs, the outputs, the financing, and the objectives.

MODERNIZING U.S. DEVELOPMENT ASSISTANCE IN THE TWENTY-FIRST CENTURY

Development goals must be made clear and appropriate, the technologies must be identified, the systems for delivery must be assessed, and the multilateral financing must be assured. In this section, I consider each of these aspects of U.S. governmental efforts to provide Official Development Assistance.

The Goals

The priorities for U.S. development assistance should be based mainly on the development commitments that the United States and the rest of the world have made in recent years, after considerable diplomatic and scientific discussions and negotiations. At the core of the effort should be the Millennium Development Goals [MDGs], which are already the central organizing tool for most development agencies and multilateral development institutions around the world. The MDGs have the profound advantage not only of specifying explicit and quantitative targets, but also of automatically aligning U.S. efforts with those of partner countries, thereby massively leveraging American resources and expertise. The focus of the development challenge is in those regions still trapped in extreme poverty, or those places suffering extremely high burdens of hunger, disease, or lack of infrastructure. This means that U.S. efforts should be mainly directed toward sub-Saharan Africa, Central Asia, the Andean region, Haiti, and the remaining pockets of extreme poverty in South Asia. Development aid for middle-income countries (such as China, Brazil, and Mexico) should be scaled back accordingly, since these regions can generally finance their own investment needs.

The Technologies

For each of the MDGs, there is a set of core interventions, based on proven low-cost technologies that can spur rapid advances toward the goals. The UN Millennium Project, among other studies, has identified the powerful tools at our disposal in each of the key areas of need. While much can be said about each area, the following recommended interventions should be noted:

- **Income poverty:** microfinance; electricity generation (off-grid and on-grid); all-weather roads; access to cell phones and Internet; improved population health (see below)

- **Hunger:** improved food production through the extension of "Green Revolution" technologies (high-yield seeds, fertilizer, small-scale irrigation, agricultural extension services); micronutrient supplementation for Vitamin A, iodine, zinc, and iron; nutrition interventions for low-weight children; school feeding programs, with take-home rations for pre-school-aged children

- **Universal school completion:** construction of schools; training of teachers; wireless Internet connectivity for (solar-charged) computers at schools; separate hygienic facilities for girls and boys; mid-day feeding programs

- **Gender equality:** time-saving infrastructure for rural women (water, power, mills, and clinics, within reach of villages); micro-finance for women's groups; improved inheritance and property rights

- **Reduced maternal mortality:** emergency obstetrical theatres in all sub-district hospitals; training of assistant medical officers (AMOs) to perform emergency procedures; use of wireless phone systems to create emergency-response units for ambulance services

- **Reduced child mortality:** integrated management of childhood illnesses (IMCI), including diarrhea, malaria, acute lower respiratory infection (ALRI), vaccine-preventable diseases, parasitic infections (worms), micronutrient deficiencies, and expert systems for neonatal care; increased use of community health workers, supported by mobile phone and Internet connectivity

- **Control of AIDS, TB, and malaria:** packages of preventative and curative health services, such as access to medicines and universal protection by insecticide-treated bed nets in the case of malaria

- **Universal access to family planning and contraceptive services:** logistics and supply chain management for contraceptive availability;

community-worker outreach to ensure access to family planning services and contraception on a voluntary basis

- **Safe drinking water and sanitation:** application of modern hydrological tools to identify sustainable water sources, based on seasonal and annual runoff, rainwater harvesting, sustainable use of groundwater, and improved year-round water storage; investments in sanitation systems, including septic tanks and recycling of human and animal wastes in rural areas, and piped wastewater treatment in urban areas

While there is much debate about "development assistance" in the abstract, there is near consensus on the use of aid to expand access of the poor to vital and proven technologies. Aid-skeptic William Easterly, for example, endorses this approach:

> Put the focus back where it belongs: get the poorest people in the world such obvious goods as the vaccines, the antibiotics, the food supplements, the improved seeds, the fertilizer, the roads, the boreholes, the water pipes, the textbooks, and the nurses. This is not making the poor dependent on handouts; it is giving the poorest people the health, nutrition, education, and other inputs that raise the payoff to their own efforts to better their lives.[2]

The Delivery Systems

Much is made of the difficulty of delivering such technologies to the poor—focusing on perceived high risks of corruption, mismanagement, and other delivery failures. Yet such fears have been shown time and again to be misplaced as long as the aid is practical, subject to monitoring, adapted to local circumstances, endorsed by local communities, and embedded in a sensible delivery system with audits and evaluation. In recent years, enormous successes have been achieved in the mass distribution of anti-malaria bed nets, the mass scale-up of new vaccines (through the Global Alliance for Vaccines and Immunizations), the mass treatment of children for worm infections, the mass increase in primary-school enrollments and completion rates by eliminating school fees, and the mass access of farmers to high-yield inputs through voucher systems. In all of these cases, success has resulted from transparency, specificity, accountability, and auditing of delivery systems.

The Financing

The basic principles of financing are clear. First, donor aid should be directed at communities and regions that cannot fund their own development efforts. As the

Monterrey Consensus rightly noted, this means an emphasis on the least developed countries, particularly on sub-Saharan Africa as a major focus for financing. Second, aid should avoid program designs that aim to have the poorest of the poor pay for vital services. Attempts to sell bed nets or health insurance or medicines to the poor have inevitably led to the exclusion of large parts of the population (especially in rural areas) from coverage. Third, donor aid should be a mix of bilateral and multilateral initiatives, divided roughly half-and-half. The United States will not, and should not, aim to fund the delivery of services on its own; such efforts should reflect a pooling of bilateral (that is, governmental) donors, international organizations, the private sector, and private philanthropy (including foundations and individuals). In some cases, such financing mechanisms already exist, but in other cases they need to be created. Here is a quick rundown.

- **Health financing.** The Global Fund to Fight AIDS, TB, and Malaria (GFATM) has become the most effective instrument for multilateral financing. The United States should increase its contributions to the GFATM, in conjunction with increases by other donor partners. There are currently three "windows" at the Global Fund (for the three diseases). At least two new funding windows should be opened: one for "health systems" (nurses, community health workers, clinic construction and facilities) and one for other readily controllable "neglected tropical diseases" (soil-transmitted helminthes, lymphatic filariasis, trachoma, onchocerciasis, and schistosomiasis).

- **Education financing.** The Education-for-All (EFA) initiative of the Millennium Development Goals is backed by a Fast Track Initiative (FTI) that is largely funded by the United Kingdom. The United States should join the U.K. and other donors in ensuring full financing for EFA-FTI.

- **Agriculture financing.** There is an urgent need for increased multilateral financing for improved agricultural productivity and food production of smallholder subsistence farmers in sub-Saharan Africa and other hunger hotspots. The Gates and Rockefeller Foundations have recently established an Alliance for a Green Revolution in Africa (AGRA), with initial financing of $500 million. The World Bank and the International Fund for African Development (IFAD) are prepared to channel increased assistance to smallholder agriculture, but so far they lack the requisite backing of donors to do so at the needed scale.

- **Infrastructure financing.** Some infrastructure, notably telecommunications and Internet connectivity, is being expanded rapidly on the basis of private-sector investments. Other infrastructure, including roads, power, ports, and large-scale urban water and sanitation systems, will require very substantial public financing. Currently, infrastructure financing is provided in a somewhat haphazard way by a variety of donors, including bilateral donors, the concessionary financing window of the World Bank (the International Development Association, IDA), the regional development banks, the European Investment Bank, and others. There is no overall coordination to ensure that total financing is in line with total needs. What is needed, therefore, is a new pooled financing system for critical infrastructure, especially for sub-Saharan Africa—and the United States should play an important role in developing that system.

THE STRUCTURE OF U.S. DEVELOPMENT ASSISTANCE

There is a strong case for moving U.S. development assistance to a new, separate, cabinet-level Department for International Sustainable Development (DfISD). The new department would house the existing USAID, PEPFAR, the President's Malaria Initiative, the Millennium Challenge Corporation, and emerging initiatives in climate change, especially vis-à-vis the developing countries. The case for a separate department rests on the following principles:

- The need to upgrade U.S. development assistance as a pillar of U.S. national security.

- The need to improve U.S. government management and expertise in public health, climate change, agronomy, demography, environmental engineering, and economic development.

- The need to work effectively with similar cabinet-level departments and ministries in partner countries.

- The need to depoliticize development assistance, so that it can be directed at the long-term investments that are critical in the fight against poverty, hunger, disease, and deprivation.

- The need for coherence of U.S. policies that impact international sustainable development, including ODA, trade relations with low-income countries, efforts on climate-change adaptation and mitigation, and efforts on global public health and disease control.

The current system, in which USAID is a part of the Department of State, is failing. U.S. aid is excessively politicized by connecting aid with short-term foreign policy exigencies (such as the war in Iraq and the Israel–Palestine crisis). It would be very useful to *insulate* development aid from such short-term diplomatic pressures. Moreover, USAID has been gutted of much key talent and staffing, and the U.S. government is currently unable to attract the best young experts in development fields—and it will remain unable to do so until the status of sustainable development within the government is improved. The organizational upgrade in the United Kingdom from a mere subcabinet development agency (the Overseas Development Administration) to a cabinet-level department (the Department for International Development, DfID) has dramatically increased that nation's standing, reputation, and expertise in the area of international development. DfID is far ahead of USAID as a global thought-leader in development policy, and DfID's departmental rank is playing a key role in that success.

The new U.S. cabinet-level department would have several specific tasks in its start-up years, in addition to the development challenges already described. DfISD would bring together countless aid programs now strewn in a disconnected way across the U.S. government. It would bolster technical competence (in health, agronomy, engineering, climate, hydrology, finance, and other areas related to sustainable development), and it would fix the procurement and contracting systems, widely regarded to be broken. It would promote results-based aid delivery, with monitoring, accountability, and audits. DfISD would be much better placed than USAID to work with counterpart Ministries of International Development and to coordinate multilateral efforts. DfISD would promote partnerships with civil society and the private sector. Businesses, especially, would be encouraged to utilize their technologies (in sectors such as health, agriculture, energy, logistics, finance, and ICT [information and communication technology]) in partnership with the U.S. government and multilateral agencies.

THE FINANCING OF U.S. DEVELOPMENT ASSISTANCE IN THE NEXT ADMINISTRATION

The current level of worldwide official development assistance—roughly $100 billion per year, of which roughly $25 billion is directed to sub-Saharan Africa—is widely and repeatedly acknowledged—by the United Nations, the G8, and the donor countries in the OECD Development Assistance Committee—to be inadequate to support the achievement of the Millennium Development Goals. This is a very important point for U.S. political leaders and the broader public to recognize. The global community, including the U.S. and other governments, have repeatedly acknowledged the need for much more aid and promised significant increases. Yet the administration and Congress have not yet delivered on those promises, most importantly the commitments made in Monterrey, Mexico, in 2002 to support the MDGs:

> We recognize that a substantial increase in ODA and other resources will be required if developing countries are to achieve the internationally agreed development goals and objectives, including those contained in the Millennium Declaration.[3]

It was in that context that the countries agreed to make concrete efforts to meet the 0.7 percent target. The recognition that much more aid is needed has since been reiterated on several occasions—at the G8 summits, the UN World Summit in September 2005, and several follow-up UN General Assembly sessions and special meetings on the MDGs. Many significant studies, including those of the UN Millennium Project and the Africa Commission (launched by Britain's then prime minister Tony Blair), outlined bottom-up estimates of the costs of achieving the MDGs. The UN Millennium Project found that the OECD-DAC donors would need to contribute around 0.54 percent of GNP as of 2015 in order to co-finance the MDGs on a global basis. Since ODA will be needed for other purposes as well—such as disaster relief or post-reconstruction financing—the UN Millennium Project recommended that donor countries honor their commitment of 0.7 percent of GNP, in order both to enable success in the MDGs and to meet other challenges that will surely arise.

The overwhelming problem is that, until now, these repeated pledges have not been fulfilled. Real cash flows of ODA have hardly risen since 2004, especially taking into account global inflation and exchange-rate movements. While President George W. Bush promised in 2002 that the Millennium Challenge Account would be funded at the level of $5 billion per year by fiscal year 2006, in fact the funding has been under $2 billion per year. Poor countries, unsure whether the promises will ever be fulfilled, are therefore not able to plan for the future, and they are certainly not able to rely on pledges to make multiyear investment decisions, including investments in capacity and training.

The United States should now join the European Union in setting a specific timetable for increasing aid through the period to 2015. The United States should commit to reach 0.5 percent of GNP no later than 2012, and 0.7 percent of GNP by the year 2015. Such a guaranteed schedule of aid would underpin global success in achieving the Millennium Development Goals by 2015, and would put the world on a trajectory to achieve the end of extreme poverty by the year 2025 (as I have described in *The End of Poverty*[4]). Of the total aid package, roughly half the U.S. aid should be allocated through multilateral channels (such as IDA; the Global Fund to Fight AIDS, TB, and Malaria; and a new Global Fund for African Agriculture), and roughly half should be allocated through U.S. bilateral initiatives (such as PEPFAR, the President's Malaria Initiative, and other effective programs).

In closing, it is well to remember the words of General George Marshall in 1947 in launching the concepts of the world-changing Marshall Plan—words that can help us to find a way to a renewed motivation and success in U.S. foreign policy. The rationale of the Marshall Plan, one of the most successful U.S. foreign policy initiatives in history, resonates today:

> It is logical that the United States should do whatever it is able to do to assist in the return of normal economic health in the world, without which there can be no political stability and no assured peace. Our policy is directed not against any country or doctrine but against hunger, poverty, desperation and chaos. Its purpose should be the revival of a working economy in the world so as to permit the emergence of political and social conditions in which free institutions can exist. Such assistance, I am convinced, must not be on a piecemeal basis as various crises develop. Any assistance that this Government may render in the future should provide a cure rather than a mere palliative.[5]

NOTES

1. The Monterrey Consensus of the International Conference on Financing for Development, http://www.un.org/esa/sustdev/documents/Monterrey_Consensus.htm.
2. William Easterly, *The White Man's Burden* (New York: Penguin, 2006), 368–369.
3. Paragraph 41 in Monterrey Consensus.
4. Jeffrey Sachs, *The End of Poverty* (New York: Penguin, 2005).
5. General George Marshall, speech at Harvard University, June 5, 1947.

NO: George B. N. Ayittey, *American University*

A frica remains a paradox: immense economic potential and, yet, faltering economic progress. Despite signs of recent progress, Africa's development prospects remain bleak. Former UN Secretary-General Kofi Annan warned at the January 2005 African Union summit in Abuja, Nigeria, that Africa was failing to meet its Millennium Development Goals (MDGs). This warning was echoed two years later by the United Nations' African Development director, Gilbert Houngbo, in Congo-Brazzaville: "The

[African] continent will fail to reach the goal of slashing poverty in half by 2015."[1] In recent years, however, the international community has mobilized to come to Africa's aid.

In a 2005 meeting in Gleneagles, Scotland, G8 leaders pledged to write off $40 billion of poor nations' debts and to double aid to Africa (to $50 billion) by 2010. Two years later, at the G8 summit in Heiligendamm, Germany, Chancellor Angela Merkel again placed debt relief and more aid to Africa at the top of the agenda. Elsewhere, a cacophonous galaxy of rock stars, antipoverty activists, and African heads of state are demanding more: total cancellation of Africa's crippling $350 billion foreign debt and fulfillment of the promises made in Gleneagles to double aid to Africa. (By June 2007, only 10 percent of those promises had been realized.) Also, China declared 2007 to be the "year for Africa."

A cynic might note that all this concern for Africa's plight appears to follow a ten-year attention-deficit cycle. Every decade or so, rock concerts are held to whip up international compassion for Africa's woes (starvation, war, refugees, and disease); mega-plans are drawn up, but acrimonious wrangling over financing modalities ensues; years slip by, and the campaign fizzles. A decade later, another grand Africa initiative is unveiled. Back in 1985, there was "Live Aid" and a "Special Session on Africa" held by the United Nations to boost aid to Africa. Then, in March 1996, the UN launched a $25 billion "Special Initiative for Africa." With clockwork precision, the plight of Africa again took center stage at a UN conference in September 2005. Expect another major initiative in 2015.

The "more aid for Africa" campaign has become so steeped in emotionalism, overt racial sensitivity, and guilt (over colonial iniquities) that pragmatism, rationality, and efficiency have been sacrificed. So many Western governments, development agencies, and individuals have tried to help a continent and its people that they do not understand. More than $450 billion in foreign aid— the equivalent of six Marshall Plans—has been pumped into Africa since 1960, with negligible results. Helping Africa is a noble exercise that has become a theater of the absurd, in which the blind are leading the clueless.

It may sound uncaring, but the truth is that Africa really doesn't need foreign aid. In fact, the resources it desperately needs can be found in Africa itself. Providing more aid to Africa is akin to pouring more water into a bucket that leaks horribly—obviously, plugging the leaks ought to be the first order of business. But even then, the provision of more foreign aid will make little difference unless it is coupled with meaningful reform. So far, African leaders have shown little interest in reforming their abominable political and economic systems.

AFRICA'S LEAKY BEGGING BOWL

Africa has the resources it needs to launch self-sustaining growth and prosperity. Unfortunately, the problem has been a leadership that is programmed to look only outside Africa—principally to the West—for such resources. The result has been hopeless dependency on foreign aid. When the African Union unveiled the **New Economic Partnership for African Development (NEPAD)** in 2000, it was trumpeted as "Africa's own initiative," "Africa's Plan," "African-crafted," and, therefore, "African-owned." NEPAD talked of "self-reliance" and argued forcefully that Africans must be "masters of their own destiny." Still, it sought $64 billion in investments from the West. The partnership's fate was sealed when, seven years after its launch, Senegalese President Abdoulaye Wade—one of the architects of NEPAD—dismissed it as "a waste of time [and] of money, which had failed to produce concrete results."[2]

At a workshop organized for the Parliamentary Sub-Committee on Foreign Affairs at Ho, Ghana, Dr. Yaw Dzobe Gebe, a fellow at the Legon Center for International Affairs at the University of Ghana, stressed the need for the African Union to look within the continent for capital formation to build a viable continental union with less dependency on foreign aid: "With an accumulated foreign debt of nearly $350 billion and estimated capital requirement of more than $50 billion annually for capacity building, it is time Africa begins to look within for capital formation. Experience in the last 40 years or more of independence and association with Europe and America should alert African leaders of the fact that there are very limited benefits to be derived from benevolence of the development partners."[3]

An irate Namibian, Alexactus T. Kaure, weighed in:

> What I want to talk about is the uncritical belief—especially by African leaders—that somehow Africa's salvation and development will come from outside. This state of affairs has in turn led to the development of a number of industries in Europe and North America to reinforce and sustain that belief.... You would always hear of a conference on Africa, for Africans *but not by Africans,* to discuss this or that issue, being held in places like Paris, London, Stockholm, Washington, Toronto and, of course, Brussels. And as you are reading this piece now, there is one going on in Brussels—termed EU–Africa Week. This conference will discuss a range of issues such as (good) governance, social rights, corruption, inequalities and vulnerable groups and the role of the media in development among others.

Now most of these issues don't need a rocket scientist to actualize them and thus there is no need for these endless conferences. To make things even worse, the very same people who are supposed to implement most of the good practices in their countries and who are either unable or unwilling to, are the ones frequenting these conference halls. For them, of course, it's just another short holiday and opportunity for shopping and a bit of extra cash . . . (per diem).[4]

Africa's investment process may be compared to that leaky bucket. The level of the water therein—GNP [gross national product] per capita—is determined by inflows of foreign aid, investment, and export earnings relative to outflows or leakages of imports (food, luxury consumer items), corruption, and civil wars. In 2005 Africa's balance of payment situation showed a payment deficit of $21.7 billion. This deficit had to be financed by new borrowing, which would increase Africa's foreign debt, or by the use of reserves, which were nonexistent for most African countries. This number, however, does not tell the full story. Hidden from view was a much grimmer story—the other, more serious leakages.

According to one UN estimate, "$200 billion or 90 percent of the sub-Saharan part of the continent's gross domestic product (much of it illicitly earned), was shipped to foreign banks in 1991 alone."[5] Capital flight out of Africa is at least $20 billion annually. Part of this capital flight represents wealth created legitimately by business owners who have little faith in keeping it in Africa. The rest represents loot stolen by corrupt African leaders and politicians. Former Nigerian President Olusegun Obasanjo charged that corrupt African leaders have stolen at least $140 billion (£95 billion) from their people in the decades since independence.[6]

Foreign aid has not been spared, either. Said *The Economist*: "For every dollar that foolish northerners lent Africa between 1970 and 1996, 80 cents flowed out as capital flight in the same year, typically into Swiss bank accounts or to buy mansions on the Cote d'Azur."[7] At the Commonwealth Summit in Abuja, Nigeria, on December 3, 2003, former British secretary of state for international development, Rt. Hon. Lynda Chalker, revealed that 40 percent of wealth created in Africa is invested outside the continent. Chalker said African economies would have fared better if the wealth created on the continent were retained within: "If you can get your kith and kin to bring the funds back and have it invested in infrastructure, the economies of African countries would be much better than what there are today," she said.[8]

On October 13, 2003, Laolu Akande, a veteran Nigerian freelance journalist, wrote:

Nigeria's foreign debt profile is now in the region of $25–$30 billion, but the president of the Institute of Chartered Accountants of Nigeria,

ICAN, Chief Jaiye K. Randle, himself an eminent accountant and social
commentator, has now revealed that individual Nigerians are currently
lodging far more than Nigeria owes in foreign banks. With an estimate he
put at $170 billion it becomes immediately clear why the quest for debt
forgiveness would remain a far-fetched dream.[9]

In August 2004, an African Union report claimed that Africa loses an
estimated $148 billion annually to corrupt practices—a figure that represents
25 percent of the continent's Gross Domestic Product (GDP). "Mr. Babatunde
Olugboji, Chairman, Independent Advocacy Project, made this revelation in
Lagos while addressing the press on the survey scheduled to be embarked upon
by the body to determine the level of corruption in the country even though
Transparency International has rated Nigeria as the second most corrupt
nation in the world."[10] The pillage in Nigeria has been massive.

Mallam Nuhu Ribadu, the chairman of the Economic and Financial Crimes
Commission, set up three years ago, said that £220 billion ($412 billion) was
"squandered" between independence from Britain in 1960 and the return of
civilian rule in 1999. "We cannot be accurate down to the last figure but that
is our projection," said Osita Nwajah, a commission spokesman.[11] The stolen
fortune tallies almost exactly with the £220 billion of Western aid given to
Africa between 1960 and 1997—a sum that amounted to six times the U.S. help
given to postwar Europe under the Marshall Plan.

To be fair, upon assuming office, former President Obasanjo vowed to recover
the funding looted by former head of state, General Sani Abacha. Obasanjo
established the Corruption Practices and Other Related Offences Commission,
and much public fanfare accompanied the announcement that the sum of
about $709 million and another $144 million had been recovered from the
late Abacha's family and his henchmen. But, apparently, this recovered loot
was itself quickly relooted, for the Senate Public Accounts Committee found
only $6.8 million and $2.8 million of the recovered booty in the Central Bank
of Nigeria (CBN).[12] Uti Akpan, a textiles trader in Lagos was not impressed:
"What baffles me is that even the money recovered from Abacha has been
stolen. If you recover money from a thief and you go back and steal the money,
it means you are worse than the thief."[13]

Back in the late 1980s, Sammy Kum Buo, director of the UN Center for Peace
and Disarmament, lamented that "Africa spends about $12 billion a year on the
purchase of arms and the maintenance of the armed forces, an amount which
is equal to what Africa was requesting in financial aid over the next 5 years."[14]
Since then, this amount has increased for all of Africa: "Excluding South Africa,
spending on arms in sub-Saharan Africa totaled nearly $11 billion in 1998,
if military assistance and funding of opposition groups and mercenaries are
taken into account. This was an annual increase of about 14 percent at a time

when the region's economic growth rose by less than 1 percent in real terms."[15] Total expenditures on arms and militaries exceed $15 billion annually.

Civil wars continue to wreak devastation on African economies. They cost Africa at least $15 billion annually in lost output, wreckage of infrastructure, and refugee crises. The crisis in Zimbabwe, for example, has cost Africa dearly. Foreign investors have fled the region and the South African *rand* has lost 25 percent of its value since 2000. More than 4 million Zimbabwean refugees have fled to settle in South Africa and the neighboring countries, and the South African government is preparing a military base at Messina to house as many as 70,000 refugees. Since 2000, almost 60,000 physicians and other professionals have left Zimbabwe.[16] According to the *London Observer*, Zimbabwe's economic collapse caused $37 billion worth of damage to South Africa and other neighboring countries.[17] South Africa has been worst affected, while Botswana, Malawi, Mozambique, and Zambia have also suffered severely.

Finally, the neglect of peasant agriculture, the uprooting of farmers by civil wars, devastated infrastructure, and misguided agricultural policies have made it difficult for Africa to feed itself. Therefore, Africa must resort to food imports, spending $15 billion in 1998. By 2000, food imports had reached $18.7 billion, slightly more than donor assistance of $18.6 billion to Africa in 2000.[18]

Table 1 (this page) offers a breakdown of how Africa loses money (and how much). As the table shows, the amount of leakage grossly overshadows the $64 billion NEPAD sought in investments from the West. It is apparent that if Africa could feed itself, if the senseless wars raging on the continent would cease, if the elites would invest their wealth—legitimate or ill-gotten—in Africa, and if expenditures on arms and the military were reduced, Africa could find within itself the resources it needs for investment. In fact, more resources could be found if corrupt leaders would disgorge the loot they have stashed abroad. This dual perspective suggests a new way to approach the investment issue: plug the leakages and repatriate the booty that has been hoarded abroad.

Table 1

How Africa Loses Money

Cause	Amount
Corruption	$148 billion
Capital flight	$20 billion
Food imports	$18 billion
Expenditures on arms and the military	$15 billion
Civil war damage	$15 billion
Total other leakages	$216 billion

Source: George B. N. Ayittey, *Africa Unchained* (New York: Palgrave/Macmillan, 2005), 326.

MONUMENTAL LEADERSHIP FAILURE

The entire foreign aid business has become a massive fraud, a huge scandal, and a charade. The donors are being duped—and, in many instances, they know it. As Patricia Adams of Probe International, a Toronto-based environmental group, charged, "In most cases, Western governments knew that substantial portions of their loans, up to 30 percent, says the World Bank, went directly into the pockets of corrupt officials for their personal use."[19] Donors pretend that they are helping Africa in order to atone for the sins of colonialism and soothe their own conscience, and African leaders pretend that they are helping the people.

Monumental leadership failure remains the primary obstacle to Africa's development. After independence in the 1960s, the leadership, with few exceptions, established defective economic and political systems that set the stage for the ruination of postcolonial Africa. The economic system of statism (or *dirigisme*), with its plethora of state controls, created chronic commodity shortages and black markets and spawned a culture of bribery and corruption, virtually destroying Africa's productive base. The political system of one-party states and military dictatorships degenerated into tyranny, as these systems, concentrating enormous economic and political power in the state, evolved into "vampire states." Government, thus, has ceased to exist as an institution—its power having been hijacked instead by a phalanx of unrepentant bandits and thugs, who use the state machinery to enrich themselves, their cronies, and their tribes. Those who do not belong to this charmed circle of relatives, cronies, or tribesmen are excluded from the gravy train. The richest persons in Africa are heads of state and their ministers, and, quite often, the chief bandit is the head of state himself.

Eventually the "vampire state" metastasizes into what Africans call a "coconut republic" and implodes when politically-excluded groups rise up in rebellion: Somalia (1993), Rwanda (1994), Burundi (1995), Zaire (1996), Sierra Leone (1998), Liberia (1999), Ivory Coast (2000), and Togo (2005). Only reform—intellectual, economic, political, and institutional—will save Africa, but the leadership is not interested.

In 2005 Africa's case for more aid and debt relief was not helped by President Obasanjo of Nigeria, which has, arguably, the most mismanaged economy in Africa. Even as he was pleading for more aid at the World Economic Forum in Davos, Switzerland, in February 2005, four of his state governors were being probed by London police for money laundering. The most galling case was that of the Plateau State governor, Chief Joshua Dariye, who was accused of diverting N1.1 billion (over $90 million) into his private bank accounts. Dariye was dragged to the Federal High Court in Kaduna by the Economic and Financial Crimes Commission (EFCC), but Justice Abdullahi Liman ruled on December 16, 2004, that although Dariye was a principal actor in the case, Section 308 of the Nigerian Constitution protected sitting governors from criminal prosecution. Imagine.

And would the police apprehend such a thief if he had no "constitutional immunity"? In February 2005, Nigeria's police chief himself, Inspector General Tafa Balogun, was forced into early retirement—after being on the job for only two years—when investigators probing money-laundering allegations found $52 million hidden in a network of fifteen bank accounts. Balogun was eventually prosecuted and sentenced to a mere six-month jail term—a slap on the wrist.

The Governor of the oil-rich Nigerian state of Bayelsa, Chief Diepreye Alamieseigha, was arrested at London Heathrow Airport on September 15, 2005, for money laundering in Britain. Appearing in a U.K. court a few days later, he was charged with laundering £1.8 million ($3.2 million) found in cash and in bank accounts. Seven London bank accounts have been traced to him.

Nigeria's Economic and Financial Crimes Commission has overwhelming evidence on most of the alleged corrupt government officials—especially state governors. The commission's chairman, Mallam Nuhu Ribadu, has described the case the Bayelsa State governor as just the tip of the iceberg. In fact, an allegation of corruption has been leveled against President Olusegun Obasanjo himself by the governor of Abia State, Orji Uzor Kalu.

Many Nigerians scoffed at Obasanjo's anticorruption campaign as an elaborate form of public relations to win concessions from lenders and burnish the president's reputation as a world leader. Critics noted that he waited so long—over four years—before cracking down on corruption, and even then, no major figures were brought to justice and few went to jail. One such figure, General Ibrahim Babangida, an ex-military dictator, thumbs his nose at his people by refusing even to testify before the anticorruption commission. When senior government officials are caught, punishment often amounts to a mere dismissal.

ACROBATICS ON REFORM

Efforts to stem corruption in Nigeria began making headlines in August 2004, when Nasir Ahmad el-Rufa'i, who had just been named to a ministerial post overseeing the Abuja capital region, announced that two senators had asked him for bribes to facilitate his confirmation. El-Rufa'i estimated that at least three out of every four lawmakers, and more than half of the nation's governors and many of its civil servants, are corrupt. "If a few more ministers go to jail, if a few more members of the National Assembly go to jail, believe me, people will line up and do the right thing," el-Rufa'i said.[20]

Until then, outright debt relief and massive inflow of aid without any conditions, safeguards, or monitoring mechanisms—as well as substantial reform—would be absurd. Budgets have careened out of control in Africa. Dysfunctional state bureaucracies, riddled with inefficiency and graft, have swollen, packed with political supporters. Corruption is rampant. Without reform, new debts will simply replace canceled old debts. But, with few exceptions, the leadership is just not interested in reform, period.

Ask these leaders to develop their countries, and they will develop their pockets. Ask them to seek foreign investment, and they will seek a foreign country in which to invest their booty. Ask them to cut bloated state bureaucracies or government spending, and they will set up a "Ministry of Less Government Spending." Ask them to establish better systems of governance, and they will set up a "Ministry of Good Governance" (Tanzania). Ask them to curb corruption, and they will set up an "Anti-Corruption Commission" with no teeth and then sack the commissioner if he gets too close to the fat cats (Kenya). Ask them to establish democracy, and they will impanel a coterie of fawning sycophants to write the electoral rules, hold fraudulent elections while opposition leaders are either disqualified or in jail, and return themselves to power (Ivory Coast, Rwanda).

Ask them to privatize inefficient state-owned enterprises, and they will sell them off at fire-sale prices to their cronies. In 1992, in accordance with World Bank loan conditions, the Government of Uganda began a privatization effort to sell off 142 of its state-owned enterprises. In 1998, however, the process was halted twice by Uganda's own parliament because, according to the chair of a parliamentary select committee, Tom Omongole, it had been "derailed by corruption," implicating three senior ministers who had "political responsibility."[21] The sale of these 142 enterprises was initially projected to generate 900 billion Ugandan shillings or $500 million. However, by the autumn of 1999, the revenue balance was only 3.7 billion Ushs.

The reform process has stalled through vexatious chicanery, willful deception, and vaunted acrobatics—all sound and fury but no action. Only sixteen of the fifty-four African countries are democratic; fewer than eight are "economic success stories"; and only eight have free and independent media. Without genuine political reform, more African countries will implode. The continent is stuck in a political cul-de-sac.

BETTER WAYS OF HELPING AFRICA

Smart aid would be that which empowers African civil society and community-based groups to monitor aid money and to instigate reform from within. Empowerment requires arming these entities with information and with the freedom and the institutional means to unchain themselves from the vicious grip of repression, corruption, and poverty. The true agents of reform are found outside government, not in "reformist partnerships" with crooked governments.

Africa already has its own Charter of Human and Peoples' Rights (the 1981 Banjul Charter), which recognizes each individual's right to liberty and to the security of his person (Article 6); to receive information, to express and disseminate his opinions (Article 9); to free association (Article 10); and to assemble freely with others (Article 11). Though the Charter enjoins African governments to recognize these rights, few do.

The institutional tools the African people need are these: free and independent media (to ensure free flow of information); an independent judiciary (for the rule of law); an independent electoral commission; an independent central bank (to assure monetary stability and stanch capital flight); an efficient, professional civil service; and a neutral, professional armed security force. Events in Ukraine, Ghana, Zimbabwe, Lebanon, and Togo in 2004 and 2005 unerringly underscore the critical importance of these institutions. Elections alone do not make a country democratic; nor are democracies nurtured in a vacuum. What is needed is a "political space" in which the people can air their opinions, petition their government without being fired on by security forces, and choose who should rule them in elections that are not rigged by electoral commissions packed with government cronies. This "space" does not exist in much of Africa.

The institutions just listed could help to create this political space, and their establishment would solve the majority of Africa's woes. For example, the two effective antidotes to corruption are independent media and an independent judiciary. But only eight African countries have free media in 2003, according to Freedom House. These institutions cannot be established by the leaders or the ruling elites (because of conflict of interest); they must be established by the civil society. Each professional body has a "code of ethics," which should be rewritten by the members themselves to eschew politics and uphold professionalism. Start with the "military code," and then the "legal code," the "civil service code," and so on. The military code should debar soldiers from intervening in politics, mandating that they be court-marshaled for doing so. The legal code should decertify corrupt judges who do not uphold the rule of law, and the civil service code should sack public servants who do not uphold professionalism. Assistance to the Bar Association or the Civil Service Association to enforce their respective codes would be useful.

On May 13, 2006, thousands of Egyptian judges, frustrated by government control over the judiciary, threatened to thwart their country's September presidential elections by refusing to oversee polling unless they were granted full independence from the executive in their oversight of the process. "The institutions are presenting Mr. Mubarak with an unexpected challenge from within, one that will be difficult to dismiss. The fact is, major changes in this country are going to come out of those institutions, not from the streets," said Abdel Monem Said, director of the Ahram Center for Strategic Studies, a government-backed research and policy organization.[22] Government-backed newspapers, long the official mouthpiece, have lately published articles deemed unfavorable to the government, says Hussein Amin, professor of journalism and mass communications at the American University in Cairo.

The seeming mutiny by the Egyptian judges presents an altogether different and, in many ways, more serious challenge to a corrupt status quo than does the opposition movement. This is where smart aid would put its money. The situation is dicey, however, as direct assistance to Egyptian judges may constitute an "interference in the internal affairs of a sovereign nation." Funneling aid through Western-based NGOs is an option—about 36 percent of Canadian aid is so channeled—but those organizations can be expelled if they incur the displeasure of an African government. They can be accused of "spying" or engaging in subversive activities—charges that were leveled by Russia against Freedom House, a human rights group, in Ukraine and Kyrgyzstan.

But if, alas, direct assistance to Egyptian judges proves impossible, both third and fourth alternatives exist: the Bar Association in Egypt can be a conduit, or, if that is not feasible, Egyptians or Africans residing abroad could be the next best alternative. Many Africans in the diaspora are professionals, human rights activists, and reformers in exile. They understand conditions in their home countries better than do the Western-based NGOs. Funneling covert aid through their organizations may yield great results. After all, such was the case with Soviet dissidents during the Cold War.

The distinction between African governments and the people is important. Naïve EU officials think handing aid money to governments in Africa necessarily helps the people—a model they did not follow when dealing with the former Soviet Union. There the West did not hand over money to communist regimes, nor simply cajole them to reform. Instead, assistance to such groups as Solidarity in Poland and the establishment of Radio Free Europe accelerated the demise of the former Soviet Union. Why treat Africa differently? And how about Radio Free Africa?

The entire Western foreign aid program needs to be critically evaluated— not by Western or African government officials, but by people outside government—before more money is wasted.

NOTES

1. *Washington Times,* April 26, 2007, A14.
2. *London Mail and Guardian,* June 29, 2007.
3. *Daily Graphic,* July 24, 2004, 16.
4. *The Namibian,* November 24, 2006; http://www.namibian.com.na.
5. *New York Times,* February 4, 1996, A4.
6. *London Independent,* June 14, 2002; www. independent.co.uk.
7. *The Economist,* survey, January 17, 2004, 12.
8. *This Day* [Lagos], December 4, 2003.
9. http://nigeriaworld.com/columnist/laoluakande/articles.html.
10. *Vanguard* [Lagos], August 6, 2004; www.allafrica.com.
11. *London Telegraph,* June 25, 2005.
12. *Post Express,* July 10, 2000.
13. *New York Times,* August 30, 2000, A10.
14. *West Africa,* May 11, 1987, 912.
15. *Washington Times,* November 8, 1999, A16.
16. *Washington Post,* March 3, 2002, A20.
17. *London Observer,* September 30, 2001.
18. *Africa Recovery,* January 2004, 16.
19. *Financial Post,* May 10, 1999.
20. *Washington Post,* May 1, 2005, A18.
21. *The East African,* June 14, 1999.
22. *Washington Post,* June 6, 2008, A20.

4

financial crises

Will Preventing Future Financial Crises Require Concerted International Rulemaking?

YES: Jagdish N. Bhagwati, *Columbia University*

NO: Philip I. Levy, *Columbia University School of International and Public Affairs*

International financial crises and national defaults are not new—England defaulted on external debt in 1340, and the speculative bubble on tulips in the Netherlands was recorded in 1637—yet modern instantaneous international transactions mean that problems—and solutions—can spread rapidly. The most recent financial crisis in 2008 is considered the worst financial crisis since the Great Depression of the 1930s and resulted in downturns in stock markets and economies around the world, the collapse of financial institutions, taxpayer-funded bailouts of financial and other institutions such as the automobile industry in the U.S., government-funded stimulus packages in the U.S. and abroad, and severe declines in economic activity globally. The origins of these problems are many, yet there remains considerable controversy about the causes, not to mention possible solutions. These problems quickly spread to and implicated markets globally, and while commentators disagree on the principal causes of the crisis and their relative severity, several factors are generally acknowledged to be important contributors.

One set of causes involves domestic political influences. The **Glass-Steagall Act** of 1933 had, on the heels of that depression, separated the activities of commercial banks and securities firms. The Gramm-Leach-Bliley Act of 1999 repealed Glass-Steagall, which allowed investment banks to invest—some would say gamble with—depositor holdings in commercial banks. These massive and newly merged "too big to fail" institutions took on riskier investments without capitalization requirements normally assigned to commercial banks. The subsequent deregulation of financial institutions meant relatively little oversight of these financial institutions, leading to significant risk in the event of a downturn. Credit-rating agencies also played a role, with incentives pushing them to inflate ratings (i.e., understate risks) for bundled securities. Borrowers happily complied by signing up for variable rate mortgages, with banks offering low "teaser rates" to lure buyers unlikely to afford the inevitable upward adjustments. And the Federal Reserve kept interest rates low, creating added incentives to speculate on real estate investments with relatively inexpensive money. Nearly everyone bet on continued steep increases in U.S. real estate prices.

The burst **housing bubble** in the U.S. was a triggering event whose reach was extensive due to the size and pervasiveness of the problem. The complexity of financial instruments, such as **credit default swaps**, meant that risk could not reasonably be assigned to bundled instruments and, therefore, could not be appropriately priced. Subprime lending created unsustainable housing speculation and building, and its collapse shook financial institutions worldwide that had purchased mortgage-backed securities in the market. Investment banks sometimes sold bad investments to their clients. Stock markets worldwide plummeted in value; the Dow Jones Industrial Average dropped from a peak just over 14,000 in 2007 to approximately 6,500 in March 2009, while U.S. and Europeans banks lost trillions of dollars on toxic assets. Lehman Brothers failed, U.S. automakers received large bailouts from the federal government, and financial markets around the world were shaken.

Economic factors also helped trigger broader problems in the U.S. securitization, where banks convert volumes of mortgage loans into securities they can sell to investors, an important innovation in financial markets that spread the risk broadly. As a result, when the housing market bubble burst and homeowners were unable to repay their mortgages—in some instances, the value of the mortgage suddenly outstripped the value of the house itself—the bundled mortgage assets plummeted in value and affected financial institutions around the world. What once had seemed a safe investment in mortgage-backed securities—after all, housing prices seemed to rise inexorably—suddenly saddled financial institutions with near-worthless assets. This was exacerbated by overaggressive mortgage sellers who were luring homebuyers into mortgages beyond their means, as everyone expected housing prices to continue to rise. (The U.S. government has for years, subsidized owner-occupied housing with generous tax deductions for mortgage interest payments.) Also, bundled securities generate substantial fees for banks and mortgage brokers, which provided additional incentives to generate and sell more loans. Finally, individual incentives to investment bank traders—reaching tens of millions of dollars per trader per year—meant risk taking was rewarded regardless of economic conditions. Insurance conglomerate AIG, for example, was paying multimillion dollar bonuses in 2008 after losing tens of billions of dollars and receiving an investment from the federal government amounting to $180 billion.

Because banks rely on each other so heavily, the subprime mortgage crisis in the U.S. implicated other banks quickly and globally. When borrowers could not afford to repay mortgages, banks tried to sell off the securities at sharply reduced prices but could not refinance because banks stopped lending to each other, creating a credit crunch. Financial institutions worldwide began to collapse, and the effects would have been catastrophic were it not for substantial bank bailouts worldwide. Economic slowdowns and bank bailouts in the U.S. and EU caused several Eurozone members, particularly Ireland, Greece, and Portugal, to face substantial deficits and long-term debts that were judged unsustainable. Austerity measures required by the EU were coupled with bailouts of all three countries, though most of the attention was focused on Greece. National failures are now felt globally.

While the most recent financial crisis in the U.S. reached global status quickly, that does not imply that international coordination necessarily is essential to containing and reversing financial crises. Two Columbia University economists take opposing views on this question. Jagdish Bhagwati, in articles published before and after the 2008 financial crisis, cautions against nationalistic retrenchment and urges determined leadership to maintain global trade and coordination. Philip I. Levy, who is also Resident Scholar at the American Enterprise Institute, argues that international financial coordination is both difficult to achieve and potentially deleterious to the international financial system.

Discussion Questions

1. What changes in national policies are required to avert a financial crisis like the one that engulfed the U.S.? Should other nations without such protections be required to follow suit?
2. Which constituencies lost the most during the financial crisis? Which suffered least?
3. Widespread outrage in the U.S. and Europe followed reports of large bonuses paid to bankers and investment bankers who had been bailed out by national governments. Why were such bonuses permitted to continue?

4. What role can regulatory agencies play in containing future financial crises?
5. Why were the impacts of the financial crisis felt so acutely in the U.S. automobile industry?
6. What role has China played throughout the crisis?
7. What lessons can be learned from the global financial crisis?

YES: Jagdish N. Bhagwati, *Columbia University*

THE PERILS OF GUNG-HO INTERNATIONAL FINANCIAL CAPITALISM

Starting in Thailand in the summer of 1997, the Asian financial crisis swept through Indonesia, Malaysia, and South Korea, turning the region's economic miracle into a debacle. Capital, which had been flowing in, flew out in huge amounts. Where these four economies and the Philippines had attracted inflows of over $65 billion in 1996, the annual outflows during 1997 and 1998 were almost $20 billion, amounting to an annual resource crunch of over $85 billion—a staggering amount indeed! This caused currencies to collapse, stock prices to crash, and economies to go into a tailspin. This was not all. The fear of ruination by contagion sent shock waves worldwide. The Russian ruble went into turmoil in August 1998; the Brazilian real did so in January 1999.

Per capita incomes tumbled to almost one-third their 1996 level in Indonesia, with the other crisis-stricken Asian countries showing declines ranging from a quarter to nearly half of the 1996 levels. The devastation was reminiscent of the Great Crash of 1929, a searing experience that ushered in the New Deal in the United States and led to competitive escalation of tariffs worldwide. Writing about this crisis that had spread ruin within almost a hundred days, I thought of Octavio Paz's famous lines from "Happiness in Herat":

> I met the wind of the hundred days.

> It covered all the nights with sand.

> Badgered my forehead, scorched my lids.

This crisis, precipitated by panic-fueled outflows of capital, was a product of hasty and imprudent financial liberalization, almost always under foreign pressure, allowing free international flows of short-term capital without adequate attention to the potentially potent downside of such globalization. There has been no shortage of excuses and strained explanations scapegoating the victims, suggesting they committed hara-kiri instead of being slaughtered. It is hard not to conclude that the motivation underlying these specious

Source: Reprinted from *In Defense of Globalization* by Jagdish Bhagwati (2004), Chp. 13, "The Perils of Gung-ho International Financial Capitalism," pp. 199–207. © 2004 by Jagdish Bhagwati. A Council on Foreign Relations Book. By permission of Oxford University Press, USA.

explanations is a desire to continue to maintain ideological positions in favor of a policy of free capital flows or to escape responsibility for playing a central role in pushing for what one might aptly call gung-ho international financial capitalism. Let me consider first the wrong explanations and then the right ones.

The Wrong Explanations

A benign but wrongheaded explanation was that the Asian crisis was a result of these countries' long-standing economic miracle running out of steam. That miracle, it may be recalled, was a result of long-sustained and phenomenally high rates of productive investment at levels that had no precedent in history. But if rapid accumulation of capital through rates of high investment was the source of growth, economists would fear that the growth would slow down because of diminishing returns—that is, as capital accumulated relative to labor, further investment would produce progressively less output. A man with a spade could plow an acre a day, but an extra spade, with the man not given a comrade, would add little to the work done. Economists know that this gloomy scenario can be foiled if there is technical progress that adds to output what diminishing returns subtract from it: instead of an extra spade, imagine that a motor is added to the man's spade. But my Columbia student Allwyn Young had estimated that the Asian countries had no technical change to speak of.

The layperson is bound to wonder how this could possibly be true. After all, these countries had registered huge advances in technology by importing foreign equipment embodying massive advances in technology. Just contrast the images of the hamlets and rickshaws in South Korea at the time of the Korean War, for instance, with the skyscrapers in Seoul, built no doubt with the latest cranes, that filled our screens when Korea advanced to the quarterfinals of the World Cup, to national delirium. Or look at the flood in Western markets of Hyundai cars and Samsung TVs, which cannot have been manufactured except with sophisticated technology.

The way economists calculate productivity change, however, is to attribute to investment the effects of technical change embodied in newer equipment, as in the example of the motorized spade earlier. They virtually assume that new and more productive equipment must be treated as if investment had increased: that a spade twice as productive is to be treated as if it were two spades. But the consequence is that it is somewhat startling to those who are not economists to say that the region had "no technical change"! So the pessimistic conclusions about diminishing returns are somewhat exaggerated when such equipment-embodied technical change is quite dramatic, as it has been and continues to be in Asia.

But even if the Asian economic miracle had been based on investment rather than technical progress, it is hardly plausible that the miracle would have vanished precipitously. As capital accumulated relative to labor, the future return to capital would decline only slowly, except in the most singular circumstances. But what happened in reality was that the economies *crashed*. Instead of slowly winding down, they went rapidly, within a matter of months, into negative growth rates. If you were to draw a chart of the actual growth rates of per capita incomes in the affected Asian countries, with the growth rates on the vertical axis and the years on the horizontal axis, that chart would go not into a gentle flattening out and then a steady fall, but dramatically into what everyone should remember from their geometry classes as the second quadrant, which plots negative growth rates.

The parallel with the Soviet Union was eerie. There, economists had seen per capita income growth rates decline over almost two decades, and the favored explanation was diminishing returns to capital accumulation. But with the arrival of President Gorbachev and his adoption of *perestroika* (economic restructuring) and *glasnost* (political reform), the economy went crashing into negative growth rates.

The sharp, discontinuous reversal of fortune was mind-boggling in both cases. In the case of East Asia, the economists who had predicted a decline were happy to claim foresight. But to claim credit for having foreseen a crash when all one had asserted was that a decline would soon set in was not exactly persuasive. The question still remained: why did a financial crisis, and then an economic one, break out when these countries had been doing so well until then?

Yet another argument, albeit a lame one, was that these countries were afflicted by crony capitalism, which led to malfeasance that produced the financial crisis under financial liberalization. As many experts on East Asia remarked, however, crony capitalism had produced the economic miracle earlier; why was it now a cancer that killed the patient? Besides, it is indeed true that many of these leaders had cronies, but which politicians do not? Are President Suharto's entourage "cronies," whereas people at Bechtel and Halliburton are Vice President Dick Cheney's "friends"? Are Barbra Streisand and Steven Spielberg President Clinton's "friends," while President Mahathir's celebrity friends are his "cronies"? What is the difference? If it is about patronage in exchange for contributions, is it not true that Hollywood has managed to get extraordinary rewards from its lobbying in opening foreign markets for its movies . . . ?

I wrote at the time in Singapore an op-ed essay titled "A Friend in the United States, but a Crony in Asia," which drew attention to the self-serving rhetoric that was coming out of Washington as the ideologues who had pushed for international financial liberalization without adequate safeguards were rushing for cover. This type of talk also fueled the notion that corruption was to be found there, not here. James Wolfensohn, president of the World Bank, took to attacking corruption around the same time, an activity that I warmly welcome, and I noticed that his staff's attention was selectively focused away from the rich countries. So I suggested that if he opened his window in Washington, D.C., and looked out, Wolfensohn would see plenty of the corruption that he and his staff were looking for in the poor countries instead. But I fully understand that it is hard to look in the face the ones whose money you must accept in order to stay in business; morality is more easily thrown at those who borrow than at those who lend.

But if these explanations of the crisis were implausible, then one had a puzzle on one's hands. After all, these economies had excellent fundamentals. Between 1991 and 1996, budgets generally showed surpluses, the investment and growth rates were as impressive as they had been since the 1960s, the inflation rate was in single digits, and current account (i.e., trade) deficits were extremely small as a percentage of national income. In November 1994, when the Mexican peso crisis erupted, requiring extensive rescue efforts by the United States, the fundamentals were unsound, and the turmoil that came was not entirely surprising. East Asia was exemplary; Latin America rarely has been.

Problems with Free Capital Flows

The reason why capital inflows are tricky is simply because when confidence is shaken, the fact that the situation is inherently one of imperfect information implies that the actions of a few can initiate herd action by others.

Economists have amusingly instructive models of herd behavior under imperfect information now. If you do not know which of three restaurants in a mall is good, you could pick one at random and hope for the best. But then you see that two are empty and the third has a table taken by a well-dressed couple. You will think that they know something you don't, and therefore you will go in. The next fellow deciding on which restaurant to pick will now see two tables taken, so he will go in too, occupying a third. And pretty soon, you will have herd behavior benefiting that restaurant generously, even if it is, objectively speaking, not the best one.

This is probably the best explanation of what happened in Asia despite the splendid fundamentals. The huge borrowing of short-term capital was perhaps manageable, objectively speaking, but its sheer size had within it the seeds of panic behavior. Since there was no transparency on how much had been borrowed, the panic spread fast, feeding on itself.

The other problem with the Asian economies was that their institutional practices had not been suitably modified for transition to a regime of free capital flows. In South Korea, for instance, the debt-equity ratios in the industrial enterprises, including the big conglomerates known as *chaebols,* were traditionally twice as high as in the developed countries, where corporations relied for financing far more on equity. If the financing was with debt in wons, a panic-fed crisis could be met by conventional intervention by the central bank extending necessary cash as a lender of last resort. But if the debt was borrowed from abroad and denominated in foreign currency, this meant that there would be a balance-of-payments crisis: dollars to pay the recalled loans cannot be printed in Seoul. This should have been anticipated, and regulations to monitor and prevent massive accumulation of short-term foreign debt to dangerous levels should have been put in place before South Korea was encouraged by the IMF [International Monetary Fund], and required by the OECD [Organization of Economic Cooperation and Development] as a price of membership, to turn to the free-capital-mobility regime.

At the same time, a lack of banking and financing regulation compounded the problem. Many commercial banks borrowed short-term from abroad, given the new ability to do so as capital flows were freed from control, and lent the borrowed funds long-term to domestic private investors, often in real estate, without adequate safeguards. "In the five . . . economies, short-term borrowing amounted to almost a quarter of bank loans to the private sector in 1996."[1] So when the panic set in and capital began to flow out rather than in, the banks were forced to recall their loans. The central banks also cut the money supply as their foreign exchange reserves shrank due to the capital outflow. Both factors led to closing businesses and, in turn, to collapsing banks.

By contrast, India and China, which had been chalking up high growth rates through the decade prior to the Asian crisis while rejecting the calls for the elimination of capital controls, escaped the crisis altogether. One must therefore ask why the crisis-afflicted countries undertook this shift, which would soon prove expensive, to fulsome integration into the world's financial markets.

The Wall Street-Treasury Complex

The rush to abandon controls on international capital flows—economists call this a policy of capital account convertibility—was hardly a consequence of finance ministers and other policy makers in the developing countries suddenly acknowledging the folly of their ways. It reflected instead external pressures.

These came from both the IMF and the U.S. Treasury (where the leadership was doubtless provided by Treasury secretary Robert Rubin, the most influential financial figure in the Clinton administration). The economists in leadership positions in these institutions were among the most accomplished today. They could not be accused of unfamiliarity with the need for caution and prudence when it came to leaning on countries to free capital flows.

In fact, in 1989, Lawrence Summers (who was deputy to Rubin and succeeded him as Treasury secretary) and his lawyer wife, Victoria, had written a classic article about "excessive speculation," quoting with approbation statements such as:

> The freeing of financial markets to pursue their casino instincts heightens the odds or crises. . . . Because unlike a casino, the financial markets are inextricably linked with the world outside, the real economy pays the price.

and the celebrated words in 1936 of John Maynard Keynes:

> As the organization of investment markets improves, the risk of the predominance of speculation does increase. In one of the greatest investment markets in the world, namely New York, the influence of speculation is enormous. Speculators may do no harm as bubbles on a steady of enterprise. But the position is serious when enterprise becomes the bubble on a whirlpool of speculation. When the capital development of a country becomes the by-product of the activities of a casino, the job is likely to be ill-done. The measure of success attained by Wall Street, regarded as an institution of which the proper social purpose is to direct new investment into the most profitable channels in terms of future yield cannot be claimed as one of the outstanding triumphs of laissez-faire capitalism, which is not surprising if I am right in thinking that the best brains of Wall Street have been in fact directed towards a different object.

If Summers had been eloquent about free capital mobility's downside, Stanley Fischer, who was the main theoretician at the IMF as its first deputy managing director, was surely familiar with the scholarly work on financial and currency crises. So why did they go along optimistically with the notion that the time had come to hasten the elimination of barriers to capital mobility worldwide?

I suspect that this had much to do with the general shift to markets and away from controls that had occurred in the 1970s and 1980s as disillusionment grew with knee-jerk interventions worldwide. They were likely caught in the usual swing of the pendulum—one extreme follows the other. So, I am sure, was Secretary Rubin. But the explanation of his complacency is possibly more complex. His working life had been on Wall Street, with Goldman Sachs. He clearly believed that America's financial markets had brought unusual venture-capital-financed prosperity to the United States. It was natural for him to see that countries practicing capital account inconvertibility, and regulating and inhibiting the inflows of capital, were denying themselves these benefits. It was inevitable that, as with most of us, his outlook was shaped by his experience.

Then again, one must reckon with the energetic lobbying of Wall Street firms to pry open financial markets worldwide. These firms argued that their profits and social good were in sync. If they had any doubts, these were carefully concealed!

The euphoria was widespread. In the exasperated words of the Nobel laureate James Tobin, a great figure in macroeconomics:

> U.S. leadership . . . gives the mobility of capital priority over all other considerations.

And Paul Volcker, the legendary chairman of the Federal Reserve whom Alan Greenspan succeeded, remarked in consternation:

> The visual image of a vast sea of liquid capital strikes me as apt—the big and inevitable storms through which a great liner like the U.S.S. United States of America can safely sail will surely capsize even the sturdiest South Pacific canoe.

It was impossible to puncture the balloon because few with dissenting opinions could penetrate what I have called the Wall Street-Treasury complex. This is the loose but still fairly coherent group of Wall Street firms in New York and the political elite in Washington, the latter embracing not just the Treasury but also the State Department, the IMF, the World Bank, and so on. There is constant to-and-fro between these two groups. For instance, Rubin moved from Wall Street to the Treasury and back; Wolfensohn at the World Bank moved there from his investment firm in New York; Stanley Fischer has moved in the reverse direction from the IMF to Citigroup; Ernest Stern, the senior vice president and acting president of the World Bank, moved to Morgan Stanley; and one could go on.

I think of the Wall Street-Treasury complex not as a conspiracy but very much in the spirit of C. Wright Mills's "power elite." They wear similar suits, not just similar ties; they interact on boards and in clubs; they wind up sharing the same sentiments, reinforced by one another's wisdom. So on capital mobility, like lemmings, they took other lemmings, and us, merrily down a dangerous path.

The phrase "Wall Street-Treasury complex" has proven popular not just among radical critics of NGOs [nongovernmental organizations]. Robert Wade, an influential writer on financial crises who teaches at the London School of Economics, has adopted it, calling it the "Wall Street-Treasury-IMF complex." But "Treasury" in my phrasing stood for Washington; adding just the IMF therefore unwittingly narrows, not widens, the meaning. Barry Eichengreen, a noted economic historian and occasional consultant to the IMF, has instead called it diplomatically the "Wall Street complex," but this is to leave out half of the culpable parties!

In a lighter vein, remember that Dwight Eisenhower, who surprisingly launched the radical phrase "military-industrial complex," was the president of Columbia University. C. Wright Mills, the author of *The Power Elite,* taught sociology at Columbia. It was at Columbia also that I wrote about the Wall Street-Treasury complex. Consequently many talk now of the "Columbia trio." I suppose this is the next best thing to being 'N Sync!

The Question of Malaysian Capital Controls

But the Asian crisis called into question not just the wisdom of a rapid freeing of capital flows in countries that still had capital controls. It also raised the somewhat separate question of whether a country that *already* had this freedom would be wise to temporarily abandon it and to adopt capital controls in response to panic-fueled capital flows.

As it happens, Malaysia did just that, imposing selective exchange controls in September 1998. Though the IMF disapproved, Prime Minister Mahathir stuck to his guns, therefore losing IMF support but gaining freedom from its conditionality. Most observers agree that IMF conditionality was in error, requiring deflation when an expansionary response was called for. So the other crisis-afflicted Asian economies went into a deep dive and recovered later, but Malaysia managed to get to the correct, expansionary policies earlier and avoided the gratuitous deepening of the downturn.

Economists have debated whether Malaysian controls played a significant role in allowing Dr. Mahathir to expand when others were contracting under the wrong IMF medicine. That is certainly what theory would say. Just as an import tariff enables you to segment domestic from foreign markets and to raise the domestic price above the foreign price, capital controls segment the domestic capital market from the world market and this can enable you to lower interest rates (to inflate the economy) without fearing further outflows of capital because interest rates are higher abroad. The theory is not far removed from reality, in my view.

Where Do We Stand?

By now, the IMF has abandoned its excessive pre-crisis enthusiasm for free capital mobility. It has learned the role of prudence in opening domestic financial markets to global integration, and the need to strengthen banking structures and practices prior to the opening. It has informally accepted the possible wisdom of measures such as a tax on incoming capital flows (an innovation of Chile) if they get too large. Finally, it has painfully learned the need for diversity of responses and conditionalities should crises erupt despite the prudence and safeguards. In short, while a watchful eye over the Wall Street-Treasury complex remains a necessity, the days of gung-ho international financial capitalism are probably past.

I can do no better than to cite *The Economist,* the most influential opinion magazine today on economics and finance:

> If any cause commands the answering support of *The Economist,* it is that of liberal trade. For as long as it has existed, this newspaper has championed freedom of commerce across borders. Liberal trade, we have always argued, advances prosperity, encourages peace among nations and is an indispensable part of individual liberty. It seems natural to suppose that what goes for trade in goods must go for trade in capital, in which case capital controls would offend us as violently as, say, an import quota on bananas. The issues have much in common, but they are not the same. Untidy as it may be, economic liberals should acknowledge that capital controls—of a certain restricted sort, and in certain cases—have a role.

* * *

LESSONS FROM THE CURRENT CRISIS

The current crisis—or perhaps two crises, one financial or Wall Street, the other macroeconomic or Main Street, both are intertwined—has caused not only panic, but also much anguished thought about its implications for capitalism

Source: Reprinted from Jagdish Bhagwati. "Lessons from the Current Financial Crisis," *KULTURAUSTAUSCH,* December 2008. Reprinted by permission of KULTURAUSTAUSCH and the author.

and globalization. Clear thinking is necessary to prevent both of these principles being undermined in the populist reaction that seems to have emerged.

Market Fundamentalism

The financier George Soros and the economist Joseph Stiglitz, in particular,
have gone around saying that the crisis has put an end to "market fundamentalism," and that it represents for capitalism and globalization what the collapse of
the Berlin Wall did for communism. Both arguments must be rejected.

The post-war shift to more reliance on markets, greater integration of
national economies into the world economy (which we call *globalization*), and
shift away from knee-jerk expansion of public-sector enterprises into activities
beyond utilities that are "natural monopolies" was a shift from "anti-market
fundamentalism" towards a more pragmatic center. It was not, as these critics
claim, a shift from pragmatism to "market fundamentalism."

Besides, the analogy with the collapse of the Berlin Wall is laughable. The
Wall's collapse signified the epitaph of a failed communism, which had landed
its supporters in authoritarianism and economic wilderness. The current crisis
follows instead decades of post-war prosperity, ushered in by the shift to the
pragmatic center and away from anti-market fundamentalism. It also follows
a steady shift of more of the world's nations to democracy, with economic and
political liberalization often reinforcing each other.

Globalization and Financial Innovation

Again, we must avoid the fallacy of aggregation. Globalization, in the shape of
freer trade and multinational investments, has been generally a force for good and
economic prosperity. But it has also advanced, rather than harmed, social agendas
such as gender equality and reduction of child labor, as demonstrated in my 2004
book, *In Defense of Globalization*. But, as every sophisticated economist knows,
the financial sector offers asymmetries vis-à-vis international trade and, while it
provides credit, which is the lifeblood of capitalist (or indeed any) systems, it can
also lead to huge downsides and requires monitoring and informed regulation.

In relation to freeing capital flows and capital account convertibility that led
to the East Asian financial crisis in the 1980s, I illustrate this asymmetry by
using a couple of analogies.

Regarding trade, if I exchanged some of my toothbrushes for some of your
toothpaste, and we both remembered to brush our teeth, we would both have
white teeth and the probability of our teeth being knocked out in the process
would be pretty slim.

However, the analogy for free capital flows is different. It is like fire, which enables me to turn veal into delicious "wiener schnitzel," but it can also burn down my house. The downside is huge, as we discovered at the time of the East Asian crisis.

This insight applies to financial innovation, which underlies recent crises, including the one we are in right now, perfectly. The long-term capital management crisis was precipitated by the financial innovation of derivatives which few understood. The innovation, and its downside when things got rough, had gone beyond comprehension by most, including the regulators. Currently, we have had similarly dangerous financial innovations like the credit default swaps and securitized mortgages. I am afraid few people realized the downside potential of these instruments. Yes, there were some warning voices. But they did not belong to what I have called the Wall Street-Treasury Complex: players who go back and forth, like Treasury Secretary Robert Rubin, between the Treasury and Wall Street (in his case, he went from Goldman Sachs to the Treasury and back to Citigroup). This Complex shared the euphoria about the financial innovations. So, they took us right into what turned into the bonfire.

The point we need to learn is that nonfinancial and financial innovations have important differences. Nonfinancial innovations (such as the innovation of the personal computer) raise the issue of what Schumpeter called "creative destruction" (i.e. smoothing into obsolescence the typewriter). With financial innovations, the problem is that there is a potential downside which can turn it into a "destructive creation." Therefore, we need a high-level "Standing Committee of Experts" whose job would be to look hard at the potential downside of whatever is the latest innovation being created by Wall Street.

Again, an analogy helps. The United States, under the Cheney-Rumsfeld leadership, went to war against Iraq based on the assumption that the war would last six weeks. They did not have a scenario where it would last six years, which it has! They had not worked out the downside scenarios, and the cost of that omission, as with the current financial crisis, has turned out to be enormous. We may not be able to figure out the downside with prescience; after all, Keynes once said, with characteristically brilliant exaggeration: "The inevitable never happens. It is always the unexpected." The task of the "Standing Committee of Experts" which I have proposed would be to reduce the unexpected whenever possible.

Financial Regulation

We therefore need to fix the financial sector and the problems that affect it. In this vein, let me also say that the U.S. Congress was remiss in encouraging home ownership through its quasi-governmental agencies Freddie Mac and Fannie Mae, in effect regardless of adequate collateral, with many mortgages being given to people who could not possibly have qualified under normal commercial criteria. These agencies also "bribed" congressmen from both political parties with political contributions into effectively providing lax oversight. And again the big investment banks, such as Goldman Sachs, pressured the Securities and Exchange Commission into exempting them from the prudential reserve requirements, leading to gross over-leveraging. In turn, politicians like Senator Schumer of New York supported such irresponsible actions by arguing that, if New York imposed prudential requirements on the investment banks, the business would go to London, suggesting that the new financial architecture must seek some basic coordination of regulations so we do not get a dangerous "race to the bottom."

Free Trade, Not Protectionism

The current crisis has also made the critics of free trade more confident. But trade did not cause the crisis, and protectionism will not cure it. The East Asians were smart enough to know that premature capital account convertibility (i.e. freeing of capital flows, which is the "financial sector") caused the crash from their remarkable growth for nearly three decades, which was attributable to outward orientation in trade. So, after the crisis, they refused to throw the trade baby out with the financial bath water. Surely, we are not going to be less smart than they were. So, the G-20 has been right to urge that protectionism must be kept at bay.

On the other hand, the U.S. has failed to provide the lead in holding the line on protectionism, with the Congress working with the Buy America provisions in its Stimulus Bill. President Sarkozy, in keeping with the French skepticism over free trade, has even gone so far as to suggest that French firms should return to France from Eastern Europe. Apart from that, many leaders face demands to fire legal and illegal workers first, and to hire them last. So, the protectionism and anti-foreigner discrimination is showing incipient signs of breaking out, in trade, in foreign investment, in immigration, and labor markets. Only determined leadership will hold the line; and only time will tell whether it will be forthcoming in the way it should.

Morality in the Financial Sector

One final word is necessary. Many populists have concluded that the current crisis shows that markets are incompatible with morality. This is, of course, an old debate, ever since Adam Smith's time. Let me make just two observations.

First, markets affect our morality less than morality affects how we behave when we work in these markets. Our morality comes from our family, school, church, and even from literature, such as the great Russian novels which explore the ethical dilemmas of its characters. In turn, this affects how we conduct ourselves in the marketplace. Thus, we observe different types of capitalism: the Scandinavian version reflects egalitarianism, for example. In the same industry, again, we find some practicing corporate social responsibility, whereas others do not. It is therefore nothing short of vulgar quasi-Marxism to claim that where and how we work affects our morals.

Second, the corruption that we have seen in the financial sector should to be put down not to greed (which suggests compulsive pursuit of self-interest to the exclusion of other virtues and vices) but often to the mere fact that the financial sector offers such enormous returns to skullduggery that, given the same propensity to cheat, the actual cheating is far greater than it would be without such returns. The greater the temptation, the greater the likelihood that you will succumb to it. So, you observe that, in agriculture, the display of "greed" is less than in the manufacturing sector, and it is the worst in the financial sector.

NOTE

1. Padma Desai, *Financial Crisis, Contagion, and Containment: From Asia to Argentina* (Princeton University Press, 2003), p. 94.

NO: Philip I. Levy, *Columbia University School of International and Public Affairs*

INTRODUCTION

In the wake of the recent global financial crisis, there were ringing calls to action for greater international coordination of financial rules and practices. At gatherings such as the G-20 group of leading nations, there were solemn vows taken that the countries would work together, shore up dilapidated financial regulatory schemes, and create a new coordinated structure that would prevent—or, at least, mitigate—future financial crises.

The logic behind such calls seemed fairly straightforward. The September 2008 failure of Lehman Brothers, a highly leveraged financial institution, seemed to be the precipitating spark that set off a global conflagration. The vast bulk of the world that was not privy to the inner workings of global finance was horrified to find that institutions such as Lehman, Bear Stearns, Fannie Mae, and AIG were entangled in an opaque and alarming web of mortgages, collateralized debt obligations, and credit default swaps. As they fell, one by one, they threatened to pull the global financial system down with them. Banks stopped lending to each other and businesses found themselves without credit.

How could this have happened? Weren't there restrictions on the quality of assets these institutions could hold? Regulatory failure: AAA-rated financial instruments proved virtually worthless. Weren't banks required to hold capital in reserve against such contingencies? Regulatory failure: the reserves proved inadequate. Weren't mortgages backed by homes as collateral? Regulatory failure: standards and collateral had dropped, a situation exacerbated by falling home prices.

If regulatory failures were undeniable, then so, too, were the international aspects of the crisis. The tottering financial institutions were global players. Chinese savings had helped fund a U.S. mortgage boom that ultimately ended up threatening the European banking system. When the crisis became acute, it climaxed in agonized conversations between U.S. and European officials about who, if anyone, had the legal or political authority to stop Lehman from falling.[1]

Yet the experience of international financial cooperation has not matched the ambitious promises issued in mid-crisis summit statements. Countries have certainly undertaken financial reforms and they have certainly continued to meet and talk, but the reforms are neither undertaken in unison nor are they substantively equivalent. If such tight coordination were really a prerequisite for future financial stability, this would bode ill for global financial prospects. Fortunately, such tight coordination is not a prerequisite for preventing future crises. It may not even be constructive.

To make this case, Section 2 considers more carefully what we mean by international financial coordination and how we can determine whether or not it is required. Section 3 addresses the motivating experience of the recent global financial crisis and discusses some of the arguments that have been put forward about how economic shocks were transmitted and the relative importance of financial regulation. Section 4 asks whether any country had the ability to insulate itself from the financial shocks of the recent crisis (preview answer: yes—Canada). Section 5 considers the obstacles to international coordination in financial regulation and whether this is cause for regret or a blessing in disguise. Section 6 concludes.

WHAT DOES IT MEAN TO "REQUIRE" COORDINATION?

To take the question seriously—whether preventing future financial crises will require international cooperation—it may help to parse it. We can first restate the question as is it possible to escape a crisis in the absence of international cooperation? If so, that cooperation was not required. If not, it was.

But this begs the question of what it means to escape a financial crisis. We live in a world with many layers of linkages between countries. Nations will exchange goods and services through trade and will engage in cross-border investments from bank loans to setting up businesses. Each of these linkages can serve as a transmission mechanism in a time of crisis. If the United States economy slows down, for whatever reason, it is very likely to have an impact on Europe and Canada as major trading partners. Businesses and consumers in a slowing economy demand less of everything, including imports. With or without international coordination and rulemaking, a macroeconomic shock to a country like the United States will be felt by all of its trading partners. It has long been a goal of macroeconomists to perfect their policy tools to such an extent as to be able to tamp down all such unpleasant swings through the business cycle. After the recent crisis, that goal seems as elusive as ever.

Usually, though, when one talks about escaping the transmission of a financial crisis, the discussion revolves around a particular transmission mechanism: the interlinkage of financial institutions. Banks and other financial institutions play a particularly important role in the functioning of an economy. As the suppliers of credit, they can direct resources from one sector to another. They provide the basic sustenance that businesses need to survive.

They also inevitably take risks. The fundamental banking act of borrowing for a short period of time (taking in a deposit) and lending for a longer period of time (issuing a mortgage, for example) is risky. The potential harm to an economy from bank failure (or even widespread suspicion of bank failures) prompts countries to both backstop their financial institutions and to regulate their behavior.

Here we come to the basic transmission mechanism that concerns advocates of closer coordination. Imagine a scenario in which "Safety Bank" in Europe is well-regulated, takes no unnecessary risks, and follows best financial practices. Suppose, though, that Safety Bank lends money to "Wild Cowboy Bank" in the United States.

One might well ask whether lending money to Wild Cowboy Bank is in keeping with our depiction of Safety Bank as prudent and careful. Let us set that aside and assume for the moment that Safety Bank makes the erroneous assumption that Wild Cowboy Bank is subject to the same regulation that it faces. Thus, Safety Bank is excessively trusting and becomes excessively dependent on the financial well-being of Wild Cowboy Bank. That bank, living up to its name and poorly supervised, behaves recklessly and manages to fail.

This is the mode of transmission of principal concern. Safety Bank is put at risk because of lax financial regulation abroad, potentially importing a U.S. financial crisis into Europe. If only there had been coordination, one might think, this hypothetical European crisis could have been averted. But that sort of claim relies on some particular assumptions about what coordination would entail—assumptions that are revealing about the limits of coordination.

One possibility is that coordination could mean identical financial regulation between the United States and Europe: equivalent laws, regulations, and powers. But would even this high level of mimicry suffice? Discussing the poor regulatory decisions that led to the recent financial crisis, Levine (2010) argues that "On the whole, these policy decisions reflect neither a lack of information nor an absence of regulatory power." Rather, for a variety of reasons, he argues that regulators did a poor job of wielding the powers they had.[2] That poses a dramatically more difficult coordination problem. It suggests that not only would coordination require similar rules and powers across countries, it would require similar behavior by regulators.

Furthermore, as optimists, we might presume that coordination means that the wayward or reckless country would alter its rules to conform to those of the prudent country. It is not obvious why that should happen. It is equally possible that the reckless country persuades its wary counterpart to loosen its regulations, a point raised by Rodrik (2009). He writes that the prospect of converging on the wrong set of regulations

> is not just a hypothetical possibility. The Basel process, viewed until recently as the apogee of international financial co-operation, has been compromised by the inadequacies of the bank-capital agreements it has produced. Basel 1 ended up encouraging risky short-term borrowing, whereas Basel 2's reliance on credit ratings and banks' own models to generate risk weights for capital requirements is clearly inappropriate in light of recent experience.[3]

We could, of course, adopt a much looser definition of *coordination*. We could take it to mean that central bank authorities and regulators would compare notes at regular intervals, informing each other of relevant actions and concerns. If we set the bar for coordination that low, it is far more likely that we will see instances of "coordination." Such minimal coordination will also very likely have some beneficial effect. But a simple exchange of views would not prevent the financial crisis transmission mechanism discussed earlier. Therefore, we will interpret the term *coordination* to mean a sufficient harmonization of policies and practices that permissible financial behavior is essentially the same across countries.

The next section considers whether the lack of such coordination was a principal cause of the recent global financial crisis.

DID A LACK OF COORDINATION CAUSE THE GLOBAL FINANCIAL CRISIS?

Resolving the question of what caused the financial crisis of 2007–2008 is well beyond the scope of this paper. For our purposes, the relevant point is that there are sharply differing views. We have already hit on one potential split: was the problem that regulators had insufficient powers or that they failed to make good use of the powers they had? The former argument helped motivate the Dodd-Frank financial legislation in the United States in 2010. We have already seen Levine argue that regulators often did have the power they needed; they just neglected to use it properly.

There are other arguments about the fundamental causes of the crisis, however. Taylor (2008) attributes a major role to excessively low interest rates that spurred the U.S. housing bubble.[4] Taylor shared the view that the problem lay far more with misapplication of existing powers than inadequate authority. He wrote critically of the Dodd-Frank legislation in 2010:

> The biggest misdiagnosis is the presumption that the government did not have enough power to avoid the crisis. But the Federal Reserve had the power to avoid the monetary excesses that accelerated the housing boom that went bust in 2007. The New York Fed had the power to stop Citigroup's questionable lending and trading decisions. . . . The Securities and Exchange Commission (SEC) could have insisted on reasonable liquidity rules to prevent investment banks from relying so much on short-term borrowing through repurchase agreements to fund long-term investments. And the Treasury working with the Fed had the power to intervene with troubled financial firms.[5]

Other prominent authors emphasize a balance of forces driving the crisis. Obstfeld and Rogoff (2009) give substantial weight to macroeconomic imbalances in the world economy. In their conclusion, they also describe a need for more coordination:

> [D]evelopment of a globally more effective framework for financial regulation is an urgent priority. It is well understood that a rational and politically robust regulatory framework will have to be based on more extensive international cooperation than currently exists.

They follow this call for coordination with the pessimistic assessment that "international agreement on further concrete common (policy) measures is far away."[6]

Thus, while inadequate financial regulation is certainly cited as a contributing factor in some accounts, others either substitute or complement this with explanations such as problematic macroeconomic policies and poor judgment on the part of regulators and policymakers.

While this may put the linkage between international financial coordination and crises in perspective, it does not provide a dispositive answer to whether such coordination is necessary to prevent crises. To argue decisively in the negative, we would need an instance in which a country went its own way with financial regulation and managed to insulate itself from the recent crisis. The next section discusses just such an example.

WERE COUNTRIES CAPABLE OF INSULATING THEMSELVES?

If it were possible for a country to avoid having a financial crisis in the midst of all the recent turmoil, this would provide strong evidence that international coordination might be helpful but is certainly not necessary to prevent financial crises. Canada provides just such an example.

Bordo, Redish, and Rockoff (2011) write, "In Canada, there were no bank failures or government bank bailouts and the recession has been less severe than either that of the early 1980s or early 1990s."[7]

This is not to say that Canada was untouched by the global downturn. As discussed above, Canada, as a major trading partner of the United States, will inevitably be affected by any major economic shocks to its southern neighbor. Yet the question at hand is whether financial crises can be avoided; Canada seemed to do just that.

Canada's accomplishment was certainly not the result of advanced international coordination in financial practice. If anything, Canada benefited from having taken its own distinctive approach. Contrasting the Canadian approach with that of the United States, Bordo, Redish, and Rockoff (2011) write:

> The Canadian concentrated banking system that had evolved by the end of the twentieth century had absorbed the key sources of systemic risk—the mortgage market and investment banking—and was tightly regulated by one overarching regulator. In contrast, the relatively weak and fragmented U.S. banking system that had evolved since the early nineteenth century led to the rise of securities markets, investment banks and money market mutual funds combined with multiple competing regulatory authorities.[8]

Earlier, we noted that one of the obstacles to financial harmonization and coordination was that not only rules but their implementation would need to be copied for there to be true international parity in financial practice. We can now add two additional obstacles to this list: differences in political structures and differences in financial structures across countries.

Bordo, Redish, and Rockoff stress the deep historical roots of differences in U.S. and Canadian banking practices. They recount attempts to set up national banking in the United States dating back to the early years of the country. When Alexander Hamilton proposed the First Bank of the United States in the late 18th century,

> there was strong opposition. Partly that opposition was based on constitutional issues: The Constitution had merely said that the federal

government could coin money and regulate its value; it said nothing about setting up banks. The heat behind the constitutional debate reflected the fundamental political question of how power would be divided between the federal government and the states.[9]

Canada, of course, had a different political tradition. So, too, does the modern European Union, though Europe's tradition has left bank regulation at the national level. In fact, this European federalism is a significant obstacle to a more concerted European response to the banking component of its ongoing financial crisis: European policymakers report that it would be politically unacceptable for a Brussels-based banking authority to declare a major French bank (for example) in default and to take it over. In this sense, European bank regulators are more encumbered than their U.S. counterparts.

The point is that for comprehensive international financial coordination to take place, one could not simply have all the attendees at a G-20 summit sign up to a new model text. The attendees' nations would differ in their political structures, as the United States differs from Canada and Europe. Regulatory frameworks can only operate within those political structures.

The second, related point is that countries differ in their financial structures. In Euro Area in 2010, bank assets accounted for more than 50 percent of total financial assets.[10] For Canada, the comparable figure is roughly 35 percent; for the United States, it is just over 20 percent. As Bordo, Redish, and Rockoff note, the United States has developed alternative means of finance, formally known as "non-bank credit intermediation" and informally known as the "shadow banking system." This can include hedge funds, money market funds, or real estate investment trusts. The implication, again, is that it becomes very difficult to adopt a single set of measures across countries to regulate financial practices, since particular measures may work better in a bank-dominated financial scene than in one in which nonbank actors predominate.

These points that arise from analyses of why Canada was different—the importance of political and financial structures—speak more to the difficulty of international financial coordination than to its necessity. But Canada's ability to maintain the health of its financial institutions, while its nearest neighbor and much of the world experienced a financial crisis, is direct evidence of the ability to avoid crises in independent fashion.

To reinforce the point, we can return to the fanciful example of Section 2 with Safety Bank naively and unwisely investing in Wild Cowboy Bank. In that discussion, we deferred the question of why a well-regulated financial institution would do such a thing. The Canadian example demonstrates that well-regulated banks *need not*. Canadians were certainly geographically well-positioned to stock up on the sort of toxic financial instruments coming out of the United

States, as a significant number of European financial institutions did. Yet they largely refrained. Through their nonconformist approach to *caveat emptor,* the Canadian financial system largely managed to insulate itself. This suggests that the key ingredient in avoiding financial crises is not global coordination but rather the quality of national financial regulation and practice.

The frequent counterargument is that in an unregulated global financial marketplace, there will be a race to the bottom and the wildest, riskiest practices will prevail. But this is really the risk-return tradeoff that is fundamental to finance. A skeptical purchaser of financial instruments who sees one offering twice the yield of another will stop to ask whether the additional yield is compensating for additional risk. A naïve purchaser will, in general, get fleeced. There can and should be a space in which ill-informed naïve depositors can function safely, as with domestic deposit insurance for banks and securities and exchange regulation for investors. But the idea that this safety net should be extended around the globe and is necessary to protect large sophisticated financial market participants is problematic.

The next section describes some of the troubled efforts that have taken place in the wake of the financial crisis to extend such a safety net through coordination of regulation.

WEAK PROSPECTS FOR COORDINATION

As noted at the outset of this piece, the global financial crisis of 2007–2008 led to very public efforts to enhance international financial coordination. The G-20 was elevated as a forum to address such issues, in large part because it brought significant new economic actors to the table, such as the People's Republic of China. In the years since, there have been numerous summits, each concluded with some sort of declaration, often containing deadlines and highlighting financial issues that should be addressed. Over the same time period, countries have undertaken financial reform, often addressing those issues mentioned in the summit declarations. Does this mean that we have successful international financial cooperation?

The meager record of achievement can suffice for some enthusiasts of the process, but the hurdle is awfully low. If countries each do what they think is in their individual interest and then issue a joint summit declaration congratulating themselves, then "coordination" will be trivially easy to achieve. A more reasonable standard of achievement might be that countries jointly decide to cooperate in a given set of regulatory areas. Then, for full marks, we would require evidence that the countries had adapted their plans to conform to the joint requirements.

Far more common has been the experience of countries doing whatever they liked, then defining cooperation as urging others to follow their example. Consider, for example, recent testimony by Lael Brainard, U.S. Undersecretary of the Treasury for International Affairs:

> The United States moved fast and first to repair and reform our financial system. . . . By contrast, Europe opted to move more slowly on stress test disclosures and measures to build capital and improve funding. As a result, many euro area banks were less resilient in the face of shocks last year, putting pressure on funding and credit and raising financial stress in a negative spiral. . .
>
> Moving first and ensuring that others enact reforms consistent with our own are the best ways to reduce opportunities for regulatory arbitrage and a race to the bottom, to prevent firms from exploiting gaps in regulation, to provide a fair and level playing field for U.S. firms, and to protect our economy from risks emanating beyond our shores.[11]

While this may have been sound strategy—there are arguments about the efficacy of U.S. reforms, as noted above—it hardly conforms to any more demanding notion of coordination.

In a survey of financial reform efforts after the crisis, Verón (2012) writes:

> during the first G-20 summit in Washington (November 2008) . . . 39 out of 47 items in the final declaration were about financial regulation in the sense used in this paper. The specific impact of the G-20 in this field is not easy to assess precisely. Some initiatives were given G-20 endorsement but would probably have gone ahead anyway. In other cases, the G-20 set deadlines that the authority of the heads of state and governments effectively made binding.[12]

Verón places greatest emphasis on the Basel II Capital Accord as a real achievement in international coordination, the process that Rodrik dismissed above as substantively inappropriate. Verón goes on to note that the Basel III accords have been contentious, raising concerns about implementation in Europe and the United States. While bank capital regulation is important, it is given particular attention in this case because it is one of the very few instances put forward of successful coordination meeting the standard set out above. As demand for coordination surged, the act itself seemed to become more difficult and rare.

This mounting difficulty has led to calls for rethinking academic analyses of cooperation. In a review essay, Helleiner and Pagliari (2011) suggest:

> Theoretical innovation and new empirical research are required to address important limitations revealed by the crisis in existing understandings of interstate power relations, the influence of domestic politics, and the significance of transnational actors within international regulatory politics. Recent developments in all three policy arenas also suggest that researchers need to be prepared to shift from explaining

the strengthening of official international standards to analyzing their
weakening in the post crisis world.[13]

Among the arguments discussed by Helleiner and Pagliari is the idea that
financial regulation has become increasingly the subject of domestic political
debate and that there is a decreased willingness to leave decisions in the hands
of international technocrats (as was done with the Basel talks).

In the United States Senate, the Dodd-Frank financial legislation of 2010
passed with 60 votes, the minimum necessary to cut off debate. The legislation
was then and remains controversial. This is significant, because it dramatically
limits the flexibility the administration has in international negotiations.
Consider Figure 1 (this page), a conventional set of Venn Diagrams in which
each circle can be taken to represent the range of financial regulatory policies
that one group finds acceptable. The left panel depicts a situation in which
there is some degree of consensus about acceptable financial regulation.

The right panel depicts a more contentious policy landscape in which there may
be barely a single point in policy space that can draw the requisite degree of support.

If we think of these two panels as showing the domestic political landscape, the
shaded area on the left represents the flexibility that a national government would
have as it heads to international conclaves to search for mutually acceptable,
coordinated policies. If the contentious depiction applies, the government will
have little or no room to maneuver. One would expect approaches such as that
described by the U.S. Treasury: set policy first, then seek to get others to agree.

Figure 1

Financial Regulatory Policies

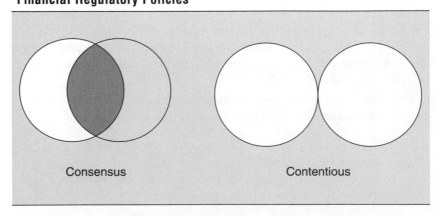

It is tempting to think that the heightened contentiousness of financial regulatory policy stems from political partisanship or dysfunctional politics. While that may play some role, there is also honest disagreement about the efficacy and desirability of regulatory reform measures. The Dodd-Frank legislation in the United States has been attacked by critics from Simon Johnson, who argues that it does not eliminate "too big to fail," to Peter Wallison, who concurs and goes on to argue that identifying institutions that are too big to fail will have deleterious effects on the financial system by encouraging their growth.[14] These are honest disagreements over policy, in which dissenters see "reforms" as moves in the wrong direction.

Nor is this degree of disagreement confined to the United States. Europe has struggled with finding acceptable reforms that both address ongoing crises and respect national sovereignties and regulatory jurisdictions. One person's financially prudent government backstop is another's reckless invitation to moral hazard.

CONCLUSION

International financial coordination is not necessary to prevent future financial crises. In the most recent severe crisis, Canada avoided a financial crisis of its own by following a set of prudent and successful regulatory policies. Had others imitated Canada's approach *ex ante,* they too might have avoided the pain of failing financial institutions. On the other hand, had Canada imitated the policies of its neighbors, it might have succumbed to the same fate they suffered.

There are a number of reasons why international financial coordination is very difficult. First, the impact of a regulatory regime depends on its implementation, not just the statutory language, and implementation practices are even harder than statutory language to replicate. Second, countries have different political structures and jurisdictions, implying that measures that are legally feasible in one country may well not work in another. Third, differing financial structures across countries mean that a given regulatory regime is likely to have different economic effects across different economies. Finally, there is honest and significant disagreement over what regulation would be appropriate. This disagreement has helped politicize the issue and limit the room national governments have to compromise with their international counterparts.

The record of international financial coordination in the wake of the global financial crisis is a meager one, unless one is content to accept summit declarations as a sufficient measure of progress. This has left countries in the position of keeping open lines of communication with each other but searching individually for the set of regulations that best fit their politics, financial structure, and understanding of how the economy works. That may, in fact, be the optimal approach. Since we cannot coordinate very well, it should serve as a relief that it is not truly necessary.

NOTES

1. James Quinn, "Hank Paulson blames FSA for Lehman failure," *The Telegraph,* January 30, 2010.
2. Ross Levine, "An Autopsy of the US Financial System: Accident, Suicide, or Negligent Homicide," *Journal of Financial Economic Policy* 2, no. 3 (2010): 196–213.
3. Dani Rodrik, "A Plan B for Global Finance," *The Economist,* March 12, 2009.
4. John B. Taylor, "The Financial Crisis and the Policy Responses: An Empirical Analysis of What Went Wrong," *Bank of Canada, Festschrift in Honour of David Dodge,* November 2008.
5. John B. Taylor, "The Dodd-Frank Financial Fiasco," *Wall Street Journal,* July 1, 2010.
6. Maurice Obstfeld and Kenneth Rogoff, "Global Imbalances and the Financial Crisis: Products of Common Causes" (December 2009, CEPR Discussion Paper, No. DP7606) p. 39.
7. Michael D. Bordo, Angela Redish, and Hugh Rockoff, "Why Didn't Canada Have a Banking Crisis in 2008 (or in 1930, or 1907, or . . .)?" (NBER Working Paper 17312, August 2011).
8. p. 30.
9. p. 5.
10. FSB, *Shadow Banking: Strengthening Oversight and Regulation: Recommendations of the Financial Stability Board,* October 27, 2011. In particular, see Exhibit 1–5, p. 29.
11. "Written testimony of Under Secretary Lael Brainard before the Senate Committee on Banking, Housing, and Urban Affairs on 'International Harmonization of Wall Street Reform: Orderly Liquidation, Derivatives, and the Volcker Rule,'" March 22, 2012. http://www.treasury.gov/press-center/press-releases/Pages/tg1460.aspx
12. Verón, Nicolas, "Financial Reform after the Crisis: An Early Assessment" (Peterson Institute for International Economics Working Paper 12–2, January 2012).
13. Eric Helleiner and Stefano Pagliari, "The End of an Era in International Financial Regulation? A Postcrisis Research Agenda," *International Organization 65* (Winter 2011): 169–200.
14. Simon Johnson, "Too Big to Fail Not Fixed, Despite Dodd-Frank," *Bloomberg,* October 9, 2011. Peter J. Wallison, "Dodd-Frank's Threat to Financial Stability," *Wall Street Journal,* March 25, 2011.

terrorism and security

Is International Terrorism a Significant Challenge to National Security?

YES: Charles Duelfer, *Omnis, Inc.*

NO: John Mueller, *Ohio State University*

Terrorism is the use of violence for political ends. Rather than seeking to directly control territory (for which they lack resources), terrorists seek to instill terror in the citizens of the target, hoping to destabilize the government or to undermine the society's willingness to conduct a sustained war. Terrorism stands in stark contrast to more traditional wars of territorial occupation, such as World War II.

Since the attacks of September 11, 2001, terrorism has attracted much more attention in the United States and elsewhere than it drew in the past. In response, the United States has focused part of its security strategy on al-Qaeda and the war on terror. This focus may make it seem that terrorism is a new or renewed security threat, but terrorism is not new. There is a long history of terrorist attacks across borders going back millennia, and many other terrorist organizations besides al-Qaeda operate today. The United Kingdom long faced terrorism from the Irish Republican Army, as Turkey has from separatist Kurds; Israel is a target of both Hamas and Hezbollah; and many attacks in Iraq occur between Sunnis and Shi'ites. In the 1970s and 1980s, the radical Red Army Faction operated in Western Europe, seeking to challenge the ability of elected governments to protect their citizenry and thus to undermine the democratic state and capitalism in Western Europe. Indeed, as Figure 1 (p. 132) makes clear, terrorist attacks are reasonably common.

However, what is distinctive about recent terrorism directed at the United States is that it occurs on multiple fronts: attacks on U.S. citizens, assets, and allies have occurred in Beirut (1991), Kenya (1998), Aden (2000), and the United States (2001)—and this list does not include the failed 1993 World

Figure 1

Number of Terrorist Incidents throughout the Globe, 1968–2008

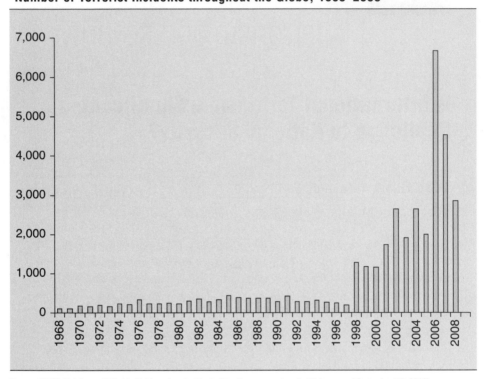

Source: RAND Database of Worldwide Terrorism Incidents, http://smapp.rand.org/rwtid (accessed December 15, 2011).

Trade Center bombing. In addition, although the data reveal that there are far more terrorist incidents than those targeting only the United States, some terrorist activities on foreign soil are addressed at the United States through its allies, such as attacks in Spain (2004) and the United Kingdom (2005).

Many terrorist attacks are reported annually. Casualties from terrorism soared after the mid-1990s, although the majority of them resulted from sectarian violence within Iraq. The 9/11 bombings in the United States, while tragic, were only a small proportion of total terrorist attacks and casualties. Table 1 (p. 133) presents the distribution of terrorist attacks from 1968 to 2008.

The policy challenge today is to understand the reasons for such attacks, to assess and respond proportionately to the terrorist threat to national security relative to other possible threats, and to appreciate the array of potential responses to punish terrorists and to deter future attacks.

Terrorists typically have a relatively small resource base. They lack the ability for sustained traditional assaults as in conventional warfare. They do not

Table 1

The Most Frequent Geographical Targets of Terrorist Attacks, 1968–2008

	Incidents	Injuries	Fatalities
Iraq	10,763	53,590	28,971
West Bank/Gaza	2,038	1,620	560
Afghanistan	2,025	4,789	4,200
Thailand	2,009	3,371	1,442
Colombia	1,913	2,748	1,615
Israel	1,687	7,355	1,360
Spain	1,425	1,567	297
Turkey	1,279	2,541	605
Pakistan	1,277	8,669	2,692
World Total	40,129	146,365	64,236

Source: RAND Database of Worldwide Terrorism Incidents, http://smapp.rand.org/rwtid (accessed December 15, 2011).

have a lot of highly trained warriors—although the U.S. response to the ten-year Soviet occupation of Afghanistan led to the training of numerous potential terrorists for future engagements and to the circulation of missiles and explosives of use for terrorism. Thus the terrorists must rely on highly visible, possibly symbolic attacks that will undermine the will of the target population. Consequently, they typically focus on random bombings or other attacks aimed at civilians.

The responses available to possible targets are limited. Nonstate terrorists cannot be deterred in the same way that states can—for instance, by threats of military and economic retaliation against specific states—which limits the options available to countries for trying to deter terrorism. Close monitoring of movements of people and goods seems necessary, but the vast numbers of those entities moving through the world economy with globalization make such controls logistically daunting and would seriously slow the delivery of goods that are deemed necessary for national economies. Good military surveillance and policing is, of course, critical, requiring multiple sources and informants on the ground both in the United States and abroad. Thus, modern terrorism may be a security threat that is not easily addressed through traditional modes of military security policy, which relies on overwhelming material force.

Consequently, some argue that fighting terrorism requires proactive efforts. Yet such efforts in the United States have already entailed significant challenges to civil rights. If they are to be regarded as legitimate elsewhere in the international community, proactive efforts have to accurately target real threats without collateral civilian casualties—a very demanding standard when ambiguous intelligence is often involved. Finally, some authors say that the threats from terrorism may be overdrawn and are not worth the significant constraints on democratic societies that proactive efforts would require. The recent debates in the United States concerning the USA PATRIOT Act, and the debate in the international community about the legality of Guantanamo detentions, are clear examples of how some responses to fighting terrorism can infringe on civil liberties and human rights.

Recently, the defense community has begun to worry about threats from **cyberterrorism**. Rather than targeting civilians, terrorists may resort to hacking computer sites in order to destroy the virtual infrastructure of their targets. Such cyberterrorism requires an entirely new mode of response—one for which traditional military responses may be inappropriate, because they involve careful information collection and policing and coordination with foreign police forces (such as **International Criminal Police Organization [INTERPOL]**) to arrest possible terrorists based on good documentary evidence.

The authors of the two articles that follow address questions such as the degree to which fighting terrorism warrants overriding other foreign policy considerations, whether terrorism is a significant threat to national security, and what are the most effective means of combating terrorism. Although they agree that policies that exacerbate the fear of terrorism only fuel potential terrorists, the authors differ in their assessment of terrorism's place on the international agenda and how terrorism can be combated most effectively. Charles Duelfer argues that the consequences of terrorism warrant the saliency of the war on terrorism. John Mueller argues that the threats of terrorism are greatly exaggerated and that high-profile efforts to publicize or address them have the effect of creating the very threat that we fear.

Discussion Questions

1. What are the differences between state (or conventional) threats and nonstate threats? Do they require different policy approaches? What are they?
2. What are the root causes of terrorism? What policies would address these causes?
3. Has globalization changed the goals and means of terrorism? How?
4. What points does John Mueller make to refute the idea that terrorism is a major national security threat? What does he mean when he says that America aids terrorists? Do you agree with his assessment?
5. Why do the authors disagree about the risks and consequences of terrorist attacks on the U.S. or the West?

YES: Charles Duelfer, *Omnis, Inc.*

I t is certain that among the current and coming threats to American national security will remain something termed *international terrorism*. However, that threat and the global context are changing. This threat will manifest itself in different ways, coming from different sources and directions in the years ahead. Moreover, our reaction to terrorism will also evolve, particularly in recognition of other, more potent sources of risk to our nation and its way of life.

Over the next decade, many factors will cause international terrorism to drop from primacy on the global threat model. However, bureaucratic and other sources of inertia in Washington will cause a substantial lag between the change in the threat and the recognition and reaction to that change.

The Global War on Terror, like the War on Drugs and the War on Poverty announced by past presidents, will not suddenly terminate. It will gradually recede into the normal pulse of government and societal life. This is not to say that hypersensitivity to terrorist attacks—especially via nonstate actors potentially in possession of any weapons of mass destruction (WMDs)—will not remain at the top of the threat board. However, the magnitude and sources of international terrorist threats have changed, and our responses with respect to national security strategies, plans, intelligence, and defense programs need to be recalibrated. More prosaically put, the lumbering mass of bureaucracy, think tanks, defense contractors, academics, cable news pundits, and bloggers will slowly drift on to other threats as they become more lucrative financially, in prestige, and in publicity.

DYNAMICS OF THE POST-9/11 DECADE

There are several fundamental dynamics coming out of the last decade that can be highlighted to support this projection.

First, the global balance of ideologies has evolved. Most conspicuously, Arab Spring was a tipping point reached during 2011 whereby autocratic regimes in Arab countries that have not been responsive to their citizens became destabilized by popular uprisings. Populations were electrified by the discovery of their own powers—largely through social media. Notably, these uprisings had virtually nothing to do with American policies. America was largely irrelevant. These popular revolutions did, however take the energy, purpose, and quite possibly much of the recruitment base from Islamic extremist groups that seek through violence to expunge "American" influence and power in the region. This trend has certainly reduced the threat from international terrorism. And

Washington had very little to do with it. In fact, one could argue that some American policies and actions, like the war in Iraq, may have delayed the emergence of these popular uprisings.

The blossoming of communications outside any government control has had as much or more to do with the eruption of the Arab Spring than any policy (or war) hatched in Washington. Likewise, the globalization of commerce and, indeed, capitalism has permeated all but the most hermitic regimes on earth. This has also awakened the latent energy among populations previously viewed as more docile. Such global trends tend to diminish the perception that the United States is the primary enemy to the aspirations of many millions in the Middle East. Now, the salience of the United States compared to other global actors such as Russia, and even China, is becoming smaller from an ideological standpoint.

Still, the popular revolutions are by no means necessarily good from the perspective of United States security and values. Egyptian parliamentary elections results announced in January 2012 showed that Islamist parties took 77 percent of the vote. Secular candidates did surprisingly bad—about 18 percent of the vote.[1] Women did worse still and will occupy about only a handful of seats. Consequences may be long term, since this new parliament will have a major role in drafting the new Egyptian Constitution. Where the Egyptian or other revolutions eventually land is still uncertain. Revolutions and elected governments can spin off in various unpredictable directions. Hamas was freely elected to govern in Gaza in 2006. Elections in Iraq have been part of a painful and uncertain process that may still turn out very badly.

Moreover, building an economy that can support growing populations is no mean task. It is easy to see how Egypt, for example, could spiral out of control if the economy cannot provide employment and education for its 80 plus million citizens. Before the revolution, when Egypt still attracted tourists, the average per capita income was about $2 a day. Since then the economy has plunged. Investment has dropped dramatically.

So while the Arab Spring phenomena may tend to reduce the ideological antipathy toward the United States, there may be other longer-term consequences with respect to enlarging the territory where terrorists might operate freely—potentially dwarfing Afghanistan or Somalia. All would fuel instability in the region with unpredictable reactions among Arab Gulf states and the Islamic Republic of Iran.

Another massive change in 2011 was the withdrawal of United States military forces from Iraq. This eliminated one of the most salient grievances for those who argued that the United States was seeking to take over, dominate, or otherwise subject the local population to its will.

The exit of American forces removed a very large physical target for those seeking to attack America. A long discussion of the merits and success of the invasion of Iraq is beyond the scope of this essay. However, since the Bush administration took the step of removing Saddam by force, stating among its reasons that Saddam supported "terrorism,"[2] it is important to mention here that whatever terrorism Saddam supported (and it wasn't al-Qaeda), there was much less of it when he was around then after he was removed and the United States began an occupation and the several-year deployment of a hundred thousand troops.

An important effect of these changes is that those who would organize violence against the United States are losing their organizing principle (to say nothing of their organizers, in the case of al-Qaeda—more on that below). Particularly with respect to al-Qaeda (recently fracturing into more decentralized elements, but which remains the central terrorist threat to the United States, according to the Director of National Intelligence— though now often termed the "global jihadist movement"[3]), their ideological raison d'être was to establish a caliphate run according to the principles they elicited from their brand of Islam.

The United States represented a major impediment to their vision. American influence was seen as exporting its apostate lifestyle and corrupting power to the region. As Fawaz A. Gerges[4] describes in detail, for al-Qaeda and Osama bin Laden, the United States was "the enemy from afar" and should be attacked in its homeland. With the changes during the decade between 2001 and 2011, this image of the United States that was central to al-Qaeda under bin Laden has changed. The killing of bin Laden also removes one of the major advocates of this narrative. Al-Qaeda leaders still endeavor to promote "a U.S.-specific narrative that motivates individuals to violence,"[5] especially via the Internet, but the prospect of spectacular attacks on the homeland is apparently diminished.

The al-Qaeda affiliates that are now active concentrate upon local governments and opportunities to strike local Western targets[6] (although they have not forgotten the "enemy from afar").[7] Al-Qaeda in the Arabian Peninsula is perhaps most dangerous as evidenced by the attempt of Umar Farouk Abdulmutallab to blow up an airliner in Detroit on December 25, 2009, and the attempt to send explosive ink cartridges to the United States via UPS in October 2010. However, like al-Qaeda cells elsewhere, there seems to be greater activity aimed against the local governments and not primarily mounting operations to target the American homeland. This may especially be the case since the American al-Qaeda leader Anwar Al-Awlaki was killed in Yemen on September 30, 2011.

The concentrated efforts of the United States intelligence community and military to capture or kill[8] leaders and operators in core al-Qaeda in Pakistan have become very effective. The obvious high point was the killing of Osama bin Laden in May 2011 after a decade-long search. This capability to identify, locate, and kill al-Qaeda leaders has become remarkably good . . . but took time and resources to develop. Director of National Intelligence (DNI) James Clapper stated that "We judge that al-Qaeda's losses are so substantial and its operating environment so restricted that a new group of leaders, even if they could be found, would have difficulty integrating into the organization and compensating for the losses."[9] Al-Qaeda has evolved in response by dispersing and attempting to motivate recruits to act on their own without being brought back to al-Qaeda camps. This response has had only marginal effect to date, and al-Qaeda leaders continue to have brief life expectancies, which impedes organizational control.

There are some metrics of terrorism used by the State Department that also indicate a shifting threat. The most blunt is the designated list of State Sponsors of Terrorism. The trend here during the past decade has been good—to the point where the list has become almost meaningless, since most terrorism is no longer state-sponsored (the major exceptional cases are Iran and, to a lesser extent, Syria and Sudan). The State Department list has contracted from seven countries in 2001 to four in 2011 (Cuba, Iran, Syria, and Sudan). Cuba remains on the list for political reasons.

Perhaps more relevant is the State Department list of Foreign Terrorist Organizations. This has grown during the last decade from 28 in 1999 to 49 in 2011. The trend this suggests is quite general, and caution must be exercised about drawing any conclusions for two reasons. One, the listed organizations often have only local objectives and do not target the United States per se. Second, it is far easier to get on the list than off. Legislative changes made post-9/11 (to the Immigration and Nationality Act, section 219, for example) have made it far more difficult to get removed from the list. Also, the number of members and activity levels of these groups vary widely. Still, there are many nonstate groups that pursue their objectives through terror.

In congressionally mandated annual reports, the State Department publishes statistics (aggregated by the National Counterterrorism Center [NCTC]) about the global number of attacks and casualties. In 2010, they marked 11,604 terrorist attacks in 72 countries, totaling 13,186 deaths.[10] Taken on a global scale, these data do not suggest much of a threat compared to other military threats. Moreover, in the statistics that NCTC has published, during the period 2006–2010, the trends have all been downward (e.g., the number of attacks in 2006 was 14,371, with 20,487 deaths).

In spite of the above trends, as of 2012, the United States intelligence community still puts terrorism at the top of its list of global threats in the annual

"Worldwide Threat Assessment."[11] Director of National Intelligence James Clapper said that al-Qaeda "aspires to spectacular attacks" and continues to pursue "a range of attack methodologies and recruit operatives familiar with the West." However, the intelligence community now views al-Qaeda regional affiliates, like those in the Arabian Peninsula, Somalia, and the Maghreb, as an emerging threat. Reports of United States attacks on al-Qaeda members in both Yemen (as the demise of al-Awalki demonstrates) and Somalia indicate an extension of the threat and the United States response.

We will continue to suffer the handicap of not being able to clearly define what a "war on terrorism" means. The critical legal structure that has evolved for facilitating the handling of enemies—foreign and domestic—will continue to be at odds with some national principles . . . especially as regards domestic freedoms. The growing prominence of concern about "homegrown" terrorists and self-radicalizing individuals illustrate the morphing of international terrorism into something else. Domestic agencies have ramped up their domestic collection capabilities in response to this theme. The notion of "Homegrown Violent Extremists (HVE)" was given sudden prominence in the worldwide threat briefing for 2012.[12] This threat focus will drive domestic surveillance in ways that may eventually be questioned with respect to privacy rights.

So far, there have been relatively small incidents of domestic terror in spite of the encouragement from al-Qaeda propagandists. In effect, the risk to national safety has not been much different than the acts of crazed individuals. Ted Kaczynski, the "Unabomber," might fall into the category of "terrorist" if he were active today.

The war on terrorism will not end nor will anyone declare it over. At best, it will just fade away as budgets are reduced and attention distracted to other issues—perhaps global economic conflicts or more traditional inter-state conflicts. It is worth noting that during the decade of the Global War on Terror, the Department of Defense (DoD) budget has totaled over $6.6 trillion (fiscal year 2001–2011 inclusive in constant fiscal year 2012 dollars).[13] This is over $20,000 for every man, woman, and child.

Obviously, that is not all directly aimed at countering terrorism, but certainly, the vast growth of defense funding post-9/11 was justified to counter the terrorist threat. This buildup of spending inevitably creates strong groups interested in sustaining their funding. This is a simple bureaucratic law of nature. The more funding in support of a mission, the more difficult it is to change due to the broad number of stakeholders in the dominant threat assumptions.

Thus, the massive bureaucratic and industrial interests that have developed during the past decade will tend to sustain the image of a global terrorist threat irrespective of the physical threat. Defense contractors do not have a financial interest in saying there is less of a terrorist threat—unless they can replace it with some other threat that will justify their business. (In fact, think tank analysts may also be similarly motivated.) Money, careers, contracts, publicity, and so on do not accrue to those who say the problem is not all it used to be. Nevertheless, the reality of a diminution in the effectiveness of al-Qaeda and the concomitant reduction in the incentives to attack the United States for such nonstate actors will eventually reduce the focus on the threat we term "terrorism."

ANALYZING THE TRENDS

So how does a policy or intelligence analyst sort through these (and perhaps other) dynamics? One approach for a structured analysis is to borrow the methodologies of risk analysis applied in commercial and financial worlds. There are many specific analytic approaches depending upon the frame of reference.[14] A risk analysis for a nuclear power plant might include assessments of natural hazards such as earthquakes or floods as well as political or terrorist threats. Likewise, an oil company would evaluate natural hazards, political uncertainties, and terrorism threats before investing in an oil development field in Africa. Private companies make these calculations routinely in a disciplined way, because they must determine what risks exist and whether to spend resources to mitigate the risks (or their potential consequences) or to simply live with them.

This analytic process can help in assessing national security priorities. If nothing else, it can provide order to the discussions.

There are common factors in all risk analyses. The methods of evaluating them vary depending upon the client system or enumeration of the assets of interest. Obviously, trying to conduct a structured analysis of all threats to the assets of the United States and then make decisions to mitigate some and accept others would be impossible—although, in essence, that is what the combined decisions of the Administration and Congress amount to. Still, considering the factors of risk analysis can help put various phenomena in a rationale perspective.

The most basic statement of risk is the likelihood of an undesirable event occurring and the consequences of the event occurring, or

$$\text{Risk} = \text{Likelihood} \times \text{Consequence}$$

The factors included in most security (vice natural hazards) risk assessments to determine likelihood are *threat* (which is often defined as intent combined with capability) and *vulnerability* (which is often defined as the product of profile or visibility and exposure).

The expression of these factors may be seen as:

$$\text{Risk} = [(\text{Intent} \times \text{Capability}) \times (\text{Profile} \times \text{Exposure})] \times \text{Consequence}$$

It is important to appreciate that some risk assessments attempt to achieve a quantitative outcome, which is to say, the output is an expected cost to the client system of some dollar value over a given period of time. This can then be compared with an evaluation of the costs of mitigating or buying down that risk. However, it is also frequently the case that structured risk analysis is conducted to simply lay out an order of quantitative judgments about greater or lesser threats and attendant risks and thereby order them in relative terms. Risk models can become quite complicated very quickly, and quantitative risk analyses rapidly become very sensitive to input assumptions and factors such as dependencies among the assets that are difficult to anticipate, let alone quantify. For the simple illustrative purposes here, it is worth only considering how factors relate in relative ways.

In a systematic risk assessment, an analyst would create a registry of assets of concern and apply the risk equation to each asset—making evaluations of threat, vulnerability, and consequence for each asset in the enterprise being studied. For illustrative purposes here, just consider the asset to be the United States.

Taking the changes to the dynamics noted above and thinking of them in the terms of the risk equation might give some notion of whether we should worry more or less about international terrorism. Moreover, if the notion of a risk matrix were considered, it might be useful to rack up a series of identified risks to the United States and make a judgment about whether international terrorism is rising or falling relative to other risks.

Threat (Capability x Intent). During the last decade, the nature of the components of threat—capability and intent—have trended lower.

Capability. With respect to capability, those organizations that have expressed the intent to attack the United States have been seriously degraded. Their operating bases are more limited; their leaders, particularly those of al-Qaeda, have been killed or arrested with great regularity—not just Osama bin Laden but many of the critical operational directors have been killed. Funding and weapons and training opportunities have been reduced, according to the reports of American officials.[15]

Intent. The expressions of direction from al-Qaeda leaders have been largely inspirational and have tended to encourage sympathetic members of their

Internet audiences to act independently. The rhetoric of the leadership has adapted to the shifting political situation in the Middle East largely saying that the enemy has not changed. On balance, the intent as expressed by the leaders of al-Qaeda remains threatening to the United States homeland.[16]

Vulnerability (Profile x Exposure). U.S. vulnerability to terrorism is a function for both profile and exposure.

Profile. The profile, or desirability of attacking the United States, when evaluated in context of the expressed objectives of the most prominent Islamic extremist organizations, would seem to have receded. The current administration has been less supportive of the regimes and policies in the Middle East that al-Qaeda has opposed. Certainly, they still vigorously denounce the United States, but the prominence of the United States in the region as a partner to autocratic regimes has clearly declined following the withdrawal from Iraq and the change of regimes in Egypt, Libya, and Tunisia. The United States has not been standing against the apparent will of the broader populations, and this must attenuate the desire of attacking the United States.

Vulnerability. American vulnerability to foreign terrorist attacks has clearly been reduced as well. The absence of troops in Iraq is one obvious change. There are fewer American targets located in proximity to poorly controlled territories with lots of munitions and explosives readily available.

During the past decade, the United States, at enormous expense, has sought to protect its commercial airline operations and prominent domestic facilities and cities. New York City has devoted more effort to preventing terrorism than any other United States city, but it is not unique in focusing on domestic protective measures.

However, the vulnerability of the United States to severe disruption and costly damage from relatively small-scale attacks remains, even after the creation of the Department of Homeland Security and all the attendant national and local measures undertaken. The political imperative to do something (usually measured by the expenditure of resources) outweighs concerns over the effectiveness of the expenditures. It is now much more difficult for a group to orchestrate the hijacking of multiple commercial airliners and use them as bombs. However, the number of ways small groups with minimal resources could attack the United States in conspicuous and highly costly manners remains. It takes little imagination to think of ways New York could again be disrupted. To many experts, it is a surprise that the techniques prevalent overseas have not appeared in New York. It's not that hard. Why are there no attacks on such major transit points as Grand Central Station? Why has there not been even a very rudimentary chemical attack, using something as simple as chlorine? It is not for lack of vulnerability.

The few attempted attacks have been remarkable for their ineptness. This absence of action provokes a consideration of the threat.

TERRORISM AND SECURITY POLICY

On balance, the country (at substantial cost in dollars and efficiency) has mitigated some vulnerabilities. But for committed terrorist groups or individuals, it would not be difficult to conduct a variety of significant and damaging attacks on the United States.

Policies are just words until decisions are made to allocate resources to support them. Budget decisions, which may seem the purview of accountants and financial experts, are in fact a superior indicator of national direction and intent. Budgets will reflect and, indeed, force decisions on recalibrating threat priorities. The $6 trillion-plus spent during the last decade on defense represents an expression of our national will and priorities. Obviously, this was a massive allocation of national resources that could have been spent on other things. Our competitive position in the world is affected by putting resources into things that do not produce income. Such expenditures may be necessary for national survival, but they come at a tremendous direct and even greater indirect cost. A trillion dollars spent on overseas deployments does not advance the United States economy.

By comparison, China did not spend a trillion dollars on military operations. The United States will pay a price in its economic competitive position for these expenditures. The United States has typically been willing to shoulder a much greater defense burden than any other country. Throughout the Cold War, there was a constant rub with our **North Atlantic Treaty Organization (NATO)** allies over whether they were carrying their fair share of the defense burden. And, in the Global War on Terror, no country comes anywhere near the United States in terms of allocating national treasure against that threat. If such decisions reflect their judgments of threat, it is clear they see the threat in far different terms.

To illustrate the magnitude of our commitment to this threat, consider the defense budgets at other times in our recent history compared with the DoD budget of $700.1 billion in 2011.[17]

In 1968, at the height of the Vietnam War and the midst of the Cold War, the defense budget was $539.7 billion. For context, consider that in 1968, there

Table 1

Department of Defense Budget in 1968, 1981, and 2011

	1968	1981	2011
DoD Budget	539.7	444.1	700.1
% of GDP	8.9	5.1	4.8

Note: Budget figures are in billions of constant 2012 dollars.

were over 500,000 American troops in Vietnam and 16,592 killed in action that year.[18] In FY 1981, in the midst of the Reagan defense buildup that some credit with winning the Cold War, the DoD budget was $444.1 billion. Some like to compare the level of defense effort not in absolute terms but in relative terms to the overall size of the United States economy as measured by the gross domestic product (GDP). In that comparison, the 1968 DoD budget represented 8.9 percent of the GDP, dropping to 5.1 percent in 1981 and standing at 4.8 percent in 2011. During the face-off with the former Soviet Union, the risk of wartime casualties was not in the thousands but in the millions. If our defense policies and forces structure were wrong, entire cities could have been incinerated. In this light, it is reasonable to ponder whether our efforts to mitigate the vulnerabilities from international terrorism are proportionate to the potential consequences.

Consequences. The consequences component of analyzing risk from international terrorism must take into account many tangible and intangible factors. Most poignant and perhaps most important was the psychological effect upon American citizens whose sense of security was shattered on 9/11. Other countries such as the United Kingdom have a history of domestic terrorism from the Irish Republican Army's attacks—including a nearly fatal 1984 bomb attack on Prime Minister Thatcher. While the United States had experienced the bombing of the federal building in Oklahoma City in April 1995 by Timothy McVeigh as well as the 1993 bombing of the World Trade Center, the magnitude of the 9/11 attacks seemed to rip the sense of individual safety in a way that was slow to recover. Placing a value on that is impossible.

Likewise, there are political consequences that are impossible to quantify. However, one manifestation of political reaction is the change of laws permitting more intrusive actions by the government to pursue terrorists within and outside the U.S. The trade-off between individual privacy and security actions by government agencies adjusted sharply after 9/11. This may be viewed as a substantial cost by many.

It is also noteworthy that these effects are reactions on the part of the U.S., not direct actions by those committing the terrorism. We could elect to do nothing in response to such acts and simply accept the damage as a cost of existing in the world today.

Economic consequences have been examined in several studies over the last decade. Generally, the conclusions are that the United States economy was quite resilient to the 9/11 attacks. For example, a Congressional Research Service study published a year after the attacks concluded, "The loss of lives and property on 9/11 was not large enough to have had a measurable effect on the productive capacity of the United States even though it had a very significant localized effect on New York City and, to a lesser degree, on the greater Washington, D.C. area." The study observes that it was impossible to distinguish direct effects of 9/11 from changes in broader economic indicators like aggregate demand. Whatever effects there were got lost in broader dynamics and other market effects.[19]

A few bits of data illustrate this. The Dow Jones Industrial Average (DJIA) dropped 1369.7 points between September 10, 2001, and September 21, 2001, to 8,236—a drop of 14.3 percent. However, it had recovered all of that and more by the end of the year, closing at 10,021 on December 30, 2001. For context, it is notable that the DJIA dropped far more in 2008–2009, when it sank from 13,000 in January 2008 to just over 6,600 in early March 2009. The United States equities markets have been subject to far more massive turmoil from the mortgage-backed securities debacle and massive risk miscalculations by investment banks and hedge funds during 2008–2009 than anything having to do with terrorism.

A look at resources shows that prices are largely driven by other factors. Oil prices spiked very briefly after 9/11 but ultimately *fell* in price from $24.44 to $23.73 a barrel. Gasoline at the pump was about $1.40 a gallon in the United States and did not fluctuate substantially. Prices a decade later hovered around $100 a barrel.

Gold jumped significantly from $215.50 to $287 an ounce but backed off to about $275 at the end of the year. However, the larger upward trend in gold prices since 2001 (it was selling for $1,530 per ounce at the close of 2011) has also been a consequence of larger macroeconomic dynamics such as the shrunken value of the dollar.

It is worth observing that during the past decade, the relative position of China (as another potential threat to the security and well-being of the United States) in the world economy has grown rapidly. China passed Japan as the second largest economy in 2001, according to the CIA World Factbook. There are various estimates of when (but not if) China's economy will surpass the

United States economy. Based on World Bank data, estimates are that the Chinese economy will surpass the economy of the United States sometime in the period 2016–2021.[20] These estimates vary, based upon how the comparisons of GDP are made, but China's real GDP growth rate for the period 2001–2010 was 10.48 percent, compared with a rate of only 1.58 percent for the U.S.[21] The CIA World Factbook puts recent China GDP at 9.6 percent, 9.2 percent, and 10.3 percent for the years 2008–2010 respectively.[22]

Further, China held 7 percent of United States debt in 2001—a total of about $65 billion—and by 2010, it had grown to 27 percent—a total of about $1.2 *trillion*. A few observations can be made on this point. One, foreign investment in the United States has not been diminished by the threat of terrorism. Second, the importance of China relative to our economic well-being greatly exceeds that of international terrorism. Not all threats to United States national security are kinetic. Third, the massive incapacitating national debt at the end of the decade would have been massively less if the American GDP had been a more "normal" 4 percent.

SUMMARY

In conclusion, the international terrorist threat will continue and will require efforts and resources in response. However, it seems to have attracted attention and resources beyond what may be needed for a balanced response. If policy makers, like business owners, seek risk-parity among the variety of risks during the coming decade, then a reordering of the prominence of international terrorism is essential.

The relative threat posed by international terrorism to the United States will shrink in absolute terms because of the changed dynamics related to the United States in the world and as a relative risk compared to other threats. The decade following 9/11 was one in which the United States far overinvested in the global terrorist threat. The opportunity cost has been substantial. We need to course correct now. Intelligence and some military programs are extraordinarily good and effective against the terror threat. We should sustain them.

However, in thinking about other present and emerging threats in a structured way, such as the risk analysis process illustrated here, it is clear that international terrorism should not remain the top priority threat as currently listed by the DNI in his list of worldwide threats. There are other risks that can have greater consequences on the well-being of the United States. We need to concentrate more attention on nonterrorist threats. They will have far more material effect on United States security and its way of life.

NOTES

1. Results are drawn from posting at http://www.aljazeera.com/indepth/interactive/2012/01/201212392416169247.html (accessed January 24, 2012).

2. President Bush did not draw fine (or even rough) distinctions between terrorist groups. Support to Palestinian suicide bombers was equivalent to al-Qaeda. For Saddam, however, these were two completely different things, and Saddam in postwar debriefings made clear his antipathy to Islamic fundamentalists. In fact, his initial reaction to 9/11 was to think that Washington would now recognize the need to deal with Iraq, since in his view, America and Iraq shared a common threat in that regard—an impression nurtured by his experience of United States sympathy and support during the Iran–Iraq war from 1980–1988. For President Bush's views, see George W. Bush, *Decision Points* (New York: Crown Publishers, 2010) p. 228. For discussion of Saddam's reaction, see Charles A. Duelfer and Stephen Benedict Dyson, "Chronic Misperception and International Conflict: The U.S.–Iraq Experience," *International Security* 36, no. 1 (Summer 2011): 82.

3. See James R. Clapper, Statement for the Record on the Worldwide Threat Assessment of the US Intelligence Community for the Senate Select committee on Intelligence by the Director of National Intelligence, January 31, 2012, p. 1.

4. Fawaz A. Gerges. *The Far Enemy: Why Jihad went Global* (New York: Cambridge University Press, 2009).

5. See James R. Clapper, Statement for the Record on the Worldwide Threat Assessment of the U.S. Intelligence Community for the House Permanent Select Committee on Intelligence by the Director of National Intelligence, February 10, 2011, p. 3.

6. James R. Clapper, Statement for the Record on the Worldwide Threat Assessment of the US Intelligence Community for the Senate Select Committee on Intelligence by the Director of National Intelligence, January 31, 2012, p. 3.

7. Marc Sageman, *Understanding Terror Networks* (Philadelphia: University of Pennsylvania Press, 2004). See also, his later book, *Leaderless Jihad: Terror Networks in the Twenty-First Century* (Philadelphia: University of Pennsylvania Press, 2008).

8. Often, al-Qaeda targets in Pakistan have been killed by the United States (rather than captured), since it has become legally and politically difficult to deal with detainees. Osama bin Laden was only the most prominent example of this.

9. Op. Cit., Clapper statement of January 31, 2012, p. 2.

10. See the "Country Reports on Terrorism 2010," of the United States Department of State, especially the annex "National Counterterrorism Center: Annex of Statistical Information" at http://www.state.gov/j/ct/ris/crt/2010/170266.htm Retrieved January 25, 2012.

11. Op. Cit., Clapper statement of January 31, 2012, p. 1.

12. Ibid., p. 4

13. From the National Defense Budget Estimates for FY 2012, Office of the Undersecretary of Defense (Comptroller), March 2011 ("The Green Book"), pp. 133–134. The figures used are for Budget Authority in constant 2012 dollars.

14. There are various treatments of risk analysis for various applications. Those most relevant here are for security of business enterprises (vice financial instruments). The International Standards Organization (ISO) has published ISO 31000:2009. This is very useful to understand best practices. A detailed examination of risk modeling to large enterprises can be found in Christina Ray, *Extreme Risk Management: Revolutionary Approaches to Evaluating and Measuring Risk* (Columbus: McGraw-Hill, 2010). Also, a general treatment is covered in James F. Broder, *Risk Analysis and the Security Survey*, 3rd ed. (Oxford: Elsevier Butterworth-Heinemann, 2006).

15. For example, the Assistant to the President for Homeland Security and Counterterrorism, John O. Brennan, stated in a speech on September 16, 2011, that core al-Qaeda was "severely crippled" though "it retained the intent and capability to attack the United States and our allies." Text is at: http://www.whitehouse.gov/the-press-office/2011/09/16/remarks-john-o-brennan-strengthening-our-security-adhering-our-values-an (accessed January 24, 2012).

16. Testimony by Director of National Intelligence James R. Clapper, February 10, 2011, before the House Permanent Select Committee on Intelligence, p. 3 of statement for the record.

17. All Defense budget figures are from the National Defense Budget Estimate for FY 2012, Office of the Undersecretary of Defense (Comptroller), March 2011, the so-called "Green Book." The figures are in constant FY 2012 dollars unless otherwise noted. The figures for DoD budget authority totals are from pages 136–140.

18. Killed in Action figure is from the Combat Area Casualties Current File at the National Archives (www.archives.gov/research/military/vietnam-war/casualty-statistics.html). The number of United States troops deployed in Vietnam for 1968 is from the DoD Historical Office series on Secretaries of Defense, Clark Clifford March 1, 1968–January 20, 1969 (http://osdhistory.defense.gov/SODs/clifford.html). It is relevant that personnel costs were lower because of the draft during the Vietnam War.

19. Gail Makinen, Coordinator, Government and Finance Division, "The Economic Effects of 9/11: A Retrospective Assessment," September 27, 2002. See also a later study: Professor Olivia A. Jackson, "The Impact of the 9/11 Terrorist Attacks on the United States Economy," *The Journal of 9/11 Studies* 19 (January 2008). http://www.journalof911studies.com/volume/2008Olivia.Jackson911and US-Economy.pdf

20. John Ross, "The Central Date for China's GDP to Overtake the US at Market Exchange Rates is 2019—a Study of Growth Assumptions and Analyses," *Key Trends in the World Economy*, February 15, 2011. http://ablog.typepad.com/key_trends_in_the_world_e/2011/02/index.html

21. These rates are drawn from the United States Department of Agriculture Economic Research Service historical data files; see http://www.ers.usda.gov/data/macro economics/

22. The CIA World Factbook, www.cia.gov/library/publications/the-world-factbook/geo/ch.html (accessed January 22, 2012).

NO: John Mueller, *Ohio State University*

I n a 2008 interview, Homeland Security czar Michael Chertoff thundered that the "struggle" against terrorism is a "significant existential" one—carefully differentiating it, apparently, from all those insignificant existential struggles we have waged in the past.[1] International terrorism hardly seems to justify such extreme proclamations. It scarcely represents an existential challenge—or even, perhaps, a significant one—to just about any country's national security. The main challenges stem less from terrorism than from the tendency to self-destructively overreact to it.

EVALUATING THE CHALLENGE

Ten years after 9/11, the most costly and determined manhunt in history finally culminated in Pakistan when a high-tech hit squad killed Osama bin Laden, one of the chief authors of 9/11 and one of history's most storied and cartooned demons. Taken away with bin Laden's bullet-shattered body, which was soon to be ceremoniously dumped at sea, were written documents and masses of information stored on five computers, 10 hard drives, and 100 or more thumb drives, DVDs, and CD-ROMs. This, it was promised, was a "treasure trove" of information about al-Qaeda—"the mother lode," said one official eagerly—and it might contain plans for pending attacks. Poring through the material with great dispatch, however, a task force soon discovered that the members of the group were primarily occupied in dodging drone missile attacks, complaining about the lack of funds, and watching a lot of pornography.

The Wizard of Oz conclusion of the 10-year quest for bin Laden suggests that Glenn Carle, a 23-year veteran of the Central Intelligence Agency where he was deputy national intelligence officer for transnational threats, got it right in 2008, when he warned: "We must not take fright at the specter our leaders have exaggerated. In fact, we must see jihadists for the small, lethal, disjointed and miserable opponents that they are." Al-Qaeda "has only a handful of individuals capable of planning, organizing and leading a terrorist organization," and although they have threatened attacks, "its capabilities are far inferior to its desires."[2]

Indeed, it is not all that clear that al-Qaeda central, now holed up in Pakistan, has done much of anything since 9/11 except issue videos filled with unfulfilled, self-infatuated, and essentially delusional threats. The tiny group of perhaps 100 or so does appear to have served as something of an inspiration to some

Muslim extremists, may have done some training, has contributed a bit to the Taliban's far larger insurgency in Afghanistan, and may have participated in a few terrorist acts in Pakistan.

Overall, with 9/11 and subsequent activity, bin Laden and his gang seem mainly to have succeeded in uniting the world, including its huge Muslim portion, against their violent global jihad. No matter how much they might disagree on other issues (most notably on America's war on Iraq), there is a compelling incentive for states—including Arab and Muslim ones—to cooperate to deal with any international terrorist problem emanating from groups and individuals connected to, or sympathetic with, al-Qaeda. Although these multilateral efforts, particularly by such Muslim states as Sudan, Syria, Libya, Pakistan, and even Iran, may not have received sufficient publicity, these countries have had a vital interest, because they felt directly threatened by the militant network, and their diligent and aggressive efforts have led to important breakthroughs against al-Qaeda.[3]

This post-9/11 willingness of governments around the world to take on terrorists has been much reinforced and amplified as they reacted to subsequent, if sporadic, terrorist activity within their own countries. Thus a terrorist bombing in Bali in 2002 galvanized the Indonesian government into action and into extensive arrests and convictions. When terrorists attacked Saudis in Saudi Arabia in 2003, that country seems, very much for self-interested reasons, to have become considerably more serious about dealing with internal terrorism, including a clampdown on radical clerics and preachers. Some inept terrorist bombings in Casablanca in 2003 inspired a similar determined crackdown by Moroccan authorities. The main result of al-Qaeda-linked suicide terrorism in Jordan in 2005 was to outrage Jordanians and other Arabs against the perpetrators. Massive protests were held, and in polls, those expressing a lot of confidence in Osama bin Laden to "do the right thing" plunged from 25 percent to less than 1 percent. In polls conducted in 35 predominantly Muslim countries, more than 90 percent condemned bin Laden's terrorism on religious grounds.

In addition, the mindless brutalities of al-Qaeda types in Iraq—staging beheadings at Mosques, bombing playgrounds, taking over hospitals, executing ordinary citizens, performing forced marriages—eventually turned the Iraqis against them, including many of those who had previously been fighting the American occupation either on their own or in connection with the group. In fact, they seem to have managed to alienate the *entire* population: data from polls in Iraq in 2007 indicate that 97 percent of those surveyed opposed efforts to recruit foreigners to fight in Iraq, 98 percent opposed the militants' efforts to gain control of territory, and 100 percent considered attacks against Iraqi civilians "unacceptable." In Iraq, as in other places, "al-Qaeda is its own worst enemy," notes Robert Grenier, a former top CIA counterterrorism official. "Where they have succeeded initially, they very quickly discredit themselves."[4]

Other terrorist groups around the world affiliated or aligned or connected to al-Qaeda may be able to do intermittent mischief, but nothing that is very sustained or focused. One way to evaluate the challenge is to focus on the actual amount of violence perpetrated around the world by Muslim extremists since 9/11, outside of war zones. This is, of course, the kind of terrorism that really concerns people in the developed world. Included in the count would be terrorism of the much-publicized and fear-inducing sort that occurred in Bali in 2002; in Saudi Arabia, Morocco, and Turkey in 2003; in the Philippines, Madrid, and Egypt in 2004; and in London and Jordan in 2005. Three think-tank publications have independently provided lists of such incidents. Although these tallies make for grim reading, the total number of people killed comes to some 200 or 400 per year.[5] That, of course, is 200 or 400 per year too many, but it hardly suggests that the perpetrators present a major threat, much less an existential one. For comparison: over the same period, more people have drowned in bathtubs in the United States alone.

At present rates (but including 9/11 in the consideration), an American's chance of becoming a victim of terrorism stands at about one in 3.5 million per year. And, judging from the pronouncements of public leaders, this low likelihood will, if anything, become even smaller in the future: although they continue to worry about small-scale attacks, they say they are now less concerned about large-scale ones like 9/11.

Any threat appears, then, principally to derive from what Marc Sageman calls "leaderless jihadists": self-selected people, often isolated from each other, who fantasize about performing dire deeds.[6] Despite post-9/11 estimates that there were thousands of al-Qaeda operatives and supporters at loose in the United States, the FBI now acknowledges that it had been unable to uncover a single true al-Qaeda sleeper cell anywhere in the country, despite years of intense and very well-funded sleuthing.

Moreover, many of the people who have been picked up on terrorism charges within the country do not seem likely, despite quite a bit of official hype when they were arrested, to have presented much of a threat at all. There is, for example, the diabolical would-be bomber of shopping malls in Rockford, Illinois, who exchanged two used stereo speakers (he couldn't afford the opening price of $100) for a bogus handgun and four equally bogus hand grenades supplied by an FBI informant. Had the weapons been real, he might actually have managed to do some harm, but he clearly posed no threat that was existential (significant or otherwise) to the United States, to Illinois, to Rockford, or, indeed, to the shopping mall.[7]

THE PROSPECT OF A TERRORIST NUCLEAR BOMB

For dire scenarios—or fantasies—to become even remotely plausible, terrorists would have to become *vastly* more capable of inflicting damage. In fact, they would pretty much need to acquire an atomic arsenal and the capacity to deploy and detonate it. Nuclear weapons can inflict massive destruction, of course, and an atomic bomb in the hands of a terrorist or rogue state could kill tens of thousands of people or even, in exceptional circumstances, more.

Warnings about the possibility that small groups like terrorists or mafias could fabricate nuclear weapons have been repeatedly uttered at least since 1946, when A-bomb maker J. Robert Oppenheimer agreed that "three or four men" could smuggle atomic bomb units into New York and "blow up the whole city." With the stimulus of 9/11, dire warnings about nuclear terrorism have escalated, even though the terrorists used weapons no more sophisticated than box-cutters on that terrible day. And by 2008, Defense Secretary Robert Gates was assuring a Congressional committee that what keeps every senior government leader awake at night is "the thought of a terrorist ending up with a weapon of mass destruction, especially nuclear."

These cries of alarm have obviously so far proven to be much off the mark, and it is essential to note that making a nuclear weapon is an extraordinarily difficult task.[8] As the Gilmore Commission, a special advisory panel to the President and Congress, stressed in 1999, building a nuclear device capable of producing mass destruction presents "Herculean challenges." The process requires obtaining enough fissile material, designing a weapon "that will bring that mass together in a tiny fraction of a second, before the heat from early fission blows the material apart," and figuring out some way to deliver the thing. And it emphasizes that these merely constitute "the *minimum* requirements." If each is not fully met, the result is not simply a less powerful weapon, but one that can't produce any significant nuclear yield at all or can't be delivered. And, after assessing this issue in detail, physicists Christoph Wirz and Emmanuel Egger conclude that fabricating a nuclear weapon "could hardly be accomplished by a subnational group" because of "the difficulty of acquiring the necessary expertise, the technical requirements (which in several fields verge on the unfeasible), [and] the lack of available materials and the lack of experience in working with these [weapons]."[9]

The task would also require the fabrication of a vast conspiracy, at once leakproof and foolproof, that would necessarily include the subversion of a considerable array of criminals, corrupt officials, and opportunists, each of whom has every incentive to push the price for cooperation as high as possible. And even at that, there would be a considerable risk that those so purchased would, at an exquisitely opportune moment of their choosing, decide to take the money and run—perhaps to the authorities representing desperate governments with essentially bottomless bankrolls and an overwhelming incentive to expend resources to arrest the atomic plot and to capture or kill the scheming perpetrators.

It is also worth noting that although nuclear weapons have been around now for well over half a century, no state has ever given another state—even a close ally, much less a terrorist group—a nuclear weapon (or a chemical, biological, or radiological one either, for that matter) that the recipient could use independently. Donors understand that there is always the danger that the weapon or its elements would be traced to their source using nuclear forensics or that the bomb would be used in a manner the donor would not approve—or even, potentially, on the donor itself.

Nor is it likely that a working nuclear device could be stolen. "A theft," note Wirz and Egger, "would involve many risks and great efforts in terms of personnel, finances, and organization" while safety and security systems on the weapons "ensure that the successful use of a stolen weapon would be very unlikely." Of particular concern in this are Russia's supposedly missing suitcase bombs. However, a careful assessment by the Center for Nonproliferation Studies has concluded that it is unlikely that any of these devices have indeed been lost and that, regardless, their effectiveness would be very low or even nonexistent because they require continual maintenance.

Moreover, no terrorist group, including al-Qaeda, has shown anything resembling the technical expertise necessary to fabricate a bomb. Few of the sleepless, it seems, found much solace in the fact that an al-Qaeda computer seized in Afghanistan in 2001 indicated that the group's budget for research on weapons of mass destruction (almost all of it focused on primitive chemical weapons work) was some $2,000 to $4,000. In the wake of the killing of Osama bin Laden, officials now had many more al-Qaeda computers, and it appears that nothing in their content suggests that the miserable little group had the time or inclination, let alone the money, to set up and staff a uranium-seizing operation as well as a fancy, super-high-tech facility to fabricate a bomb.

In testimony before the Senate Select Committee on Intelligence on January 11, 2007, FBI Director Robert Mueller, who had been highly alarmist about the terrorist potential in previous testimony, stressed that his chief concern within the United States was now homegrown groups and that, while remaining concerned that things could change in the future, "few if any terrorist groups" were likely to possess the required expertise to produce nuclear weapons—or, for that matter, biological or chemical ones.

Given the destructive capacity of nuclear weapons, it is sensible to expend some policy effort to increase the difficulties for any would-be nuclear terrorists, particularly by seeking to control the world's supply of weapons-grade uranium or plutonium material. But the difficulties for the terrorists persist, and their likelihood of acquiring the weapon remains very low—even assuming they try hard.

THE CHALLENGE FROM WITHIN

What we mostly get from what might be called "the terrorism industry"—politicians, bureaucrats, journalists, and risk entrepreneurs who benefit in one way or another from exacerbating anxieties about terrorism—is fearmongering and doomsaying, and much of it borders on hysteria.[10]

Actually, the subtexts (or sometimes the texts) of the warnings issued by members of the terrorism industry often suggest that, insofar as international terrorism presents a significant challenge to national security, this arises not so much from what the terrorists would do to us but what we would do to ourselves in response.

For example, Michael Ignatieff warns that "inexorably, terrorism, like war itself, is moving beyond the conventional to the apocalyptic," and he helpfully explains how the process will play itself out. Although Americans did graciously allow their leaders one fatal mistake in September 2001, they simply "will not forgive another one." If there are several large-scale attacks, he confidently predicts, the trust that binds the people to its leadership and to each other will crumble, and the "cowed populace" will demand that tyranny be imposed upon it and quite possibly break itself into a collection of rampaging lynch mobs devoted to killing "former neighbors" and "onetime friends."[11] It seems, then, that it is not only the most-feared terrorists who are suicidal.

We seem to need a reality check here. All societies are "vulnerable" to tiny bands of suicidal fanatics in the sense that it is impossible to prevent every terrorist act. But the United States is hardly "vulnerable" in the sense that it can be toppled by dramatic acts of terrorist destruction. In all probability, the country can readily, if grimly, absorb even extensive damage—as it "absorbs" some 40,000 deaths each year from automobile accidents—without instantly becoming a fascist state. Israel, of course, has absorbed a great deal of sustained terrorism on its soil and still manages to have a functioning democracy. As President Barack Obama candidly observed in a 2010 interview, "We can absorb a terrorist attack. We'll do everything we can to prevent it, but even a 9/11, even the biggest attack ever . . . we absorbed it and we are stronger." Any death is tragic, but it is not at all obvious that even another 9/11 would have necessarily triggered societal suicide. Actually, of course, the lesson of 9/11 is that disasters tend to pull people together, not splinter them into warring bands.

However, although the alarmists may exaggerate—a proclivity that is by nature (and definition) central to their basic makeup—the subtext of their message should perhaps be taken seriously: ultimately, the enemy, in fact, appears to be us. Terrorism is rather rare and, appropriately considered, not generally a terribly destructive phenomenon.

As military analyst William Arkin points out forcefully, although terrorists cannot destroy America, "every time we pretend we are fighting for our survival, we not only confer greater power and importance to terrorists than they deserve but we also at the same time act as their main recruiting agent by suggesting that they have the slightest potential for success."[12]

There is also a strong tendency to overspend to deal with the problem, however illusory it often seems. Thus, even ignoring overseas costs such as the wars in Afghanistan and Iraq, the United States has increased domestic homeland security expenditures since 9/11 by a total of $1 trillion. Using convention cost-benefit approaches, this outlay would be justified only if it can be determined that it succeeded in deterring, thwarting, or protecting against four attacks (similar to the one attempted on Times Square in 2009) *per day*.[13]

A key element in a policy toward terrorism, therefore, should be to control, to deal with, or at least to productively worry about the fear and overreaction that terrorism so routinely inspires. Policy approaches that exacerbate fears of terrorism not only very often do more harm than anything the terrorists have accomplished but play into their hands.

NOTES

1. Shane Harris and Stuart Taylor Jr., "Homeland Security Chief Looks Back, and Forward," *Government Executive.com*, March 17, 2008.
2. Glenn L. Carle, "Overstating Our Fears," *Washington Post*, July 13, 2008.
3. Fawaz Gerges, *The Far Enemy: Why Jihad Went Global* (New York: Cambridge University Press, 2005).
4. Joby Warrick, "U.S. Cites Big Gains against Al-Qaeda," *Washington Post*, May 30, 2008.
5. John Mueller and Mark G. Stewart, *Terror, Security, and Money: Balancing the Risks, Costs, and Benefits of Homeland Security* (New York: Oxford University Press, 2011), ch. 2.
6. Marc Sageman, *Leaderless Jihad* (Philadelphia: University of Pennsylvania Press, 2008).
7. See John Mueller, ed., *Terrorism Since 9/11: The American Cases* (Columbus: Mershon Center, Ohio State University, 2011).

8. For a fuller discussion, see John Mueller, *Atomic Obsession: Nuclear Alarmism from Hiroshima to al-Qaeda* (New York: Oxford University Press, 2010), chs. 12–15.

9. Gilmore Commission, *Terrorism Involving Weapons of Mass Destruction*, December 15, 1999. Christoph Wirz and Emmanuel Egger, "Use of Nuclear and Radiological Weapons by Terrorists?" *International Review of the Red Cross*, September 2005.

10. See John Mueller, *Overblown: How Politicians and the Terrorism Industry Inflate National Security Threats, and Why We Believe Them* (New York: Free Press, 2006); Ian S. Lustick, *Trapped in the War on Terror* (Philadelphia: University of Pennsylvania Press, 2006).

11. Michael Ignatieff, *The Lesser Evil: Political Ethics in an Age of Terror* (Princeton: Princeton University Press, 2004).

12. William M. Arkin, "Goodbye War on Terrorism, Hello Long War," *washingtonpost.com*, January 26, 2006.

13. Mueller and Stewart, op. cit.

nuclear weapons

Should the United States or the International Community Aggressively Pursue Nuclear Nonproliferation Policies?

YES: Scott D. Sagan and Reid Pauly, *Stanford University*

NO: Todd S. Sechser, *University of Virginia*

Nuclear nonproliferation is a recent world problem. Only since the 1950s have governments been able to destroy vast numbers of citizens of another country with a relatively small number of warheads and at such a distance. The increasing proliferation of nuclear weapons in succeeding decades is cause for increasing concern about national security.

Nuclear nonproliferation policies attempt to ensure that nuclear threats and exchanges—or worse, nuclear war—do not occur. Historically, only two nuclear weapons have been used: the United States dropped atomic bombs on Hiroshima and Nagasaki, Japan, on August 6th and 9th, 1945. Since then, the destructive power, numbers, and delivery systems of these weapons have grown extensively, making it far easier in principle to cause massive damage from great distances. Nuclear warheads can now be delivered not only by bombs carried on long-distance aircraft but also by intercontinental land-based missiles and those launched from submarines as well as by smaller tactical battlefield missiles and even bulky suitcase bombs.

A significant set of multilateral treaties has been introduced to try to contain nuclear proliferation. The **International Atomic Energy Agency (IAEA)** seeks to prevent the spread of nuclear states beyond the original five (the United States, the Soviet Union, the United Kingdom, France, and China) that had nuclear weapons at the time of its creation in 1970. The agency administers a large-scale bargain: in return for agreeing not to develop nuclear weapons, countries are given access to civilian nuclear power (for commercial energy generation). The IAEA also closely tracks the circulation of fissile materials. Its inspectors can visit power plants, and the Nuclear Suppliers Group keeps close tabs on who purchases fissile materials. In addition, countries that are seen to be violating IAEA rules face stiff economic sanctions.

The original nuclear states were the United States (1945), the USSR/Russia (1949), the United Kingdom (1952), France (1960), and China (1964). Subsequently, India (1974), Israel (1979), Pakistan (1998), and North Korea (2006) have developed nuclear arsenals of at least several warheads.

Table 1 (this page) shows the numbers of nuclear warheads existing in the 1990s and 2009 and projections of the estimated numbers in 2012.

But not all countries aspire to possession of a nuclear arsenal. Indeed, there are few good reasons for actually having one—it is extremely expensive to develop nuclear weapons, and the political costs of becoming a nuclear power are economically onerous, as the IAEA sanctions can be severe. Countries pursue nuclear weapons, nonetheless, as a possible deterrent against nuclear-armed adversaries (India, Pakistan, Iran), as status symbols (Libya, Pakistan), or as potential bargaining chips in international diplomacy (North Korea). There are also instances, however, of countries deciding that nuclear proliferation made no sense and abandoning their programs. Brazil, Argentina, and Chile established a nuclear-free zone in the Southern Cone of South America in the

Table 1

Number of Warheads by Country, 1990s–2012

Country	Early 1990s	2009	2012
United States	9,680	3,575	1,700–2,200
Russia	10,996	3,113	1,700–2,200
United Kingdom	260	~160	<160
France	538	300	<300
China	100–200	>125	Replacing with more capable warheads
India	N.d.	~50	Building more
Pakistan	N.d.	~60	Likely to build more
Israel	100–200	~80	100–200
Iran	None	Presumed to be 2–10 years away from nuclear capability	
North Korea	Possibly 1–2	<10	0
South Africa	6	0	0

Sources: *The Economist*, March 29, 2008, 80; *New York Times*, March 25, 1993, A1, A12. and The Carnegie Endowment for International Peace, World Nuclear Arsenals 2009, http://www.carnegieendowment.org/2009/02/03/world-nuclear-arsenals-2009/fr5.
Note: N.d. = No data.

1980s. South Africa dismantled its few nuclear warheads in 1991. Libya finally halted its program in 2003, in the face of Western sanctions.

A multitude of approaches have been devised in the attempt to promote nonproliferation. The centerpiece is the IAEA, which verifies which states have nuclear capabilities and which do not and administers sanctions for violators. During the Cold War, the United States and the Soviet Union signed a number of bilateral treaties that were intended to build mutual confidence so that a nuclear exchange could not occur accidentally (see the 1964 movie *Doctor Strangelove* for a satiric demonstration of this possibility) and to reciprocally reduce their arsenals.

Alternative approaches have stressed the role of **deterrence** in preventing the use of nuclear weapons. Kenneth Waltz, a major international relations scholar, famously argued that if everyone has a weapon, then no one will initiate out of fear of retribution.[1] Scott Sagan argues here that the most likely source of nuclear crisis is not bungled deterrence but mishandled communications in case of a crisis. For Sagan, the focus of nonproliferation efforts should be on management and communication rather than on counting the number of warheads.

Recently, the spread of nonstate criminal groups, such as al-Qaeda, has inspired a new fear of nonstate actors gaining access to nuclear weapons, either by building them or by stealing or by buying them from a nuclear state. Few of the policies that have been developed to influence behavior by states would likely be effective for such nonstate actors, who are beyond the influence of many states and are not accountable to citizens and thus would not suffer from sanctions.

The authors of the essays that follow discuss the principal reasons for nuclear proliferation as well as alternative means for achieving nonproliferation. Todd Sechser argues that the case against deterrence may not stand up to close empirical scrutiny and that deterrence may well limit states' willingness to pursue nuclear weapons. Scott Sagan and Reid Pauly elaborate on Sagan's opinion that the most serious threat of nuclear Armageddon may arise from mistakes and the mindless pursuit of organizational routines.

Discussion Questions

1. Why do countries decide to pursue nuclear weapons despite their considerable costs? Why do some countries decide against it?
2. Is it hypocritical for the United States to pursue nuclear nonproliferation policies when it currently possesses nuclear weapons? Why or why not?

3. What four requirements for stable nuclear deterrence do Scott Sagan and Reid Pauly lay out? What points do they make in rejecting the likelihood that these requirements will be met? Do you agree with their position?

4. What questions does Todd Sechser raise in making his argument on nuclear proliferation and U.S. foreign policy? What policies does he recommend to address these questions? Do you agree with him?

5. Both authors recognize the dangers of a nuclear North Korea or a nuclear Iran. They also describe the dangers of a terrorist group acquiring nuclear weapons. Which situation presents the bigger threat? What policies should be put in place to prevent these parties from acquiring nuclear weapons? Are the same policies appropriate for both kinds of adversaries?

NOTE

1. Kenneth Waltz, "The Spread of Nuclear Weapons: More May Be Better," *Adelphi Papers* no. 171 (London: International Institute for Strategic Studies, 1981).

YES: Scott D. Sagan and Reid C. Pauly, *Stanford University*

Yes, both the United States and the international community should aggressively pursue nuclear nonproliferation policies. This affirmative answer follows from two key considerations that must be made when evaluating the question. First, what are the consequences of further nuclear weapons proliferation? Second, are nuclear nonproliferation policies pursued by the United States and the international community likely to be effective in curbing the spread of nuclear weapons?

To answer the first question, this chapter will explicate the cases of three countries whose pursuit of nuclear weapons technology were or are great cause for concern and demonstrate the obvious dangers of nuclear proliferation in the 21st century: Iraq, North Korea, and Iran. With regard to the second question, given the nature of the threat and the dramatically high consequences of failure in controlling nuclear weapons and material, the U.S. has pursued nonproliferation policies for decades but has not always been successful. The key is that nuclear nonproliferation policies can be led by the United States but must be pursued in conjunction with the rest of the international community in order to be effective. Furthermore, this section will explain how combating proliferation fatalism in Washington, DC and elsewhere is necessary to secure a safer global nuclear future.

Both Republican and Democratic administrations have recognized the risks of allowing the unchecked spread of nuclear technology. President George W. Bush in his 2002 State of the Union address focused on Iraq, Iran, and North Korea, saying, "By seeking weapons of mass destruction, these regimes pose a grave and growing danger."[1] Assessing the nuclear threat in 2009, President Barack Obama remarked, "Today, the Cold War has disappeared but thousands of those weapons have not. In a strange turn of history, the threat of global nuclear war has gone down, but the risk of a nuclear attack has gone up."[2] Both administrations recognized that terrorist organizations seek to buy, build, or steal nuclear weapons or material and that new governments with nuclear weapons pose serious dangers.

Thankfully, there is much to be done about these consequential threats. The United States should pursue nonproliferation as a high priority goal and can succeed in its efforts.

WHY WORRY?[3]

A prominent group of scholars (known as *proliferation optimists*) argues that the spread of nuclear weapons promotes peace and stability by raising the costs of war to an unacceptable level. Following the logic of rational deterrence theory, optimists contend that statesmen know that a nuclear exchange would be catastrophic for their states and will thus be deterred from starting any military conflict that could escalate to nuclear war. These scholars point to the Cold War as evidence for their claims: despite deep political animosity, numerous crises, and a massive arms race, they argue, the superpowers avoided nuclear war. They then wonder: why should we expect the experience of future nuclear powers to be any different?

It is common today to look back nostalgically on those years as "the long peace." But this oversimplifies the challenges of the Cold War. Nuclear weapons did seem to have a sobering influence on the **great powers**, but that effect was neither automatic nor foolproof. Both the Soviet and the Chinese governments originally hoped that having the bomb would allow them to engage in more aggressive policies with impunity. Moscow repeatedly threatened West Berlin in the late 1950s and early 1960s, for example, confident that its growing arsenal would dissuade the United States from coming to West Germany's defense. Soviet Premier Nikita Khrushchev also believed that if the Soviet Union could place nuclear weapons in Cuba, the United States, faced with the fait accompli, would be deterred by the Soviet arsenal from attacking Fidel Castro's regime. This dangerous learning by "trial and error" was far from a stable or desirable international system.

Proliferation optimists place too much faith in deterrence based on mistaken nostalgia and a faulty analogy. Although deterrence did work with the Soviet Union and China, there were many close calls; maintaining nuclear peace during the Cold War was far more difficult and uncertain than U.S. officials and the American public seem to remember today. Nuclear weapons have been a mixed blessing, a dangerous deterrent. The Cold War witnessed many close calls; new nuclear states will be even more prone to deterrence failures.

Nuclear weapons are not controlled by the abstract entities we call states but rather by normal, imperfect individuals and normal, self-interested organizations within the state. To understand the effects of nuclear proliferation, therefore, one should pry open the black box of decision making inside states to look at who issues commands and who actually controls the nuclear weapons that are being built. Organization theory provides a useful lens to focus attention on how governments in different states are differently organized (and sometimes disorganized) and therefore how and why they might contemplate the use of nuclear weapons in different manners.

Historical evidence supports the pessimistic view of organization theorists. Organizational proclivities sparked numerous near-catastrophes during the Cold War, despite the strong mechanisms of civilian control that both super powers developed. The danger of such incidents is likely to be even greater in future nuclear-armed states, because many current and emerging proliferators have either military-run or undemocratic civilian-led governments that lack the checks and balances necessary to produce prudent decision making. Moreover, the small size and primitive technology of new nuclear states increases the security and safety risks associated with their arsenals. Finally, the spread of nuclear weapons into regions that have unstable governments and Islamic radical terrorist organizations creates especially frightening prospects.

Over the past decade, the U.S. government and much of the international community have greatly feared the dangerous consequences should Iraq, North Korea, or Iran acquire nuclear weapons. Such fears have been and remain utterly warranted. Each of these dangerous proliferators will be analyzed in turn.

Iraq

Soon after the March 2003 U.S. invasion of Iraq, American arms inspectors were startled to discover that the government of Saddam Hussein had in fact destroyed all Iraqi nuclear weapons facilities in the years following the 1991 Gulf War and had not restarted a covert program. The great secret that Saddam was hiding from international inspectors was not the existence of a covert nuclear, chemical, or biological weapons program; the great secret was that the Iraqis and international inspectors had in fact already dismantled all the nuclear, chemical, and biological weapons of mass destruction (WMD) development facilities that Saddam had earlier constructed prior to the 1991 war. Saddam Hussein did not want Iran and his own people to know that he had effectively disarmed under the ceasefire agreement and subsequent UN inspection system. He clearly was looking forward to restarting these programs in the future if UN sanctions were lifted against his regime; but that future fortunately never arrived.

We now know a great deal about Saddam's motivations to pursue nuclear weapons and the story is alarming. Saddam Hussein secretly taped many of his meetings with the cabinet and military officers, and his statements reveal that he was not primarily motivated by defensive security concerns vis-à-vis Iran or Israel. Instead, Saddam envisioned nuclear weapons as a strategic shield behind which Iraq would be able to engage in conventional aggression against Israel. Before the invasion of Kuwait in 1990, for example, Saddam predicted that Iraq would get nuclear weapons within five years and rhetorically asked his colleagues that "if the Arabs were to have a nuclear bomb, wouldn't they take the territories that were occupied after 1967?"[4] This was a long-standing theme for Saddam Hussein. For example, in the late 1970s, Saddam told other high-level Iraqi leaders that nuclear weapons would allow Iraq to engage in a war of attrition against Israel to reclaim the West Bank and Golan Heights. Iraqi nuclear weapons would counter Israeli nuclear weapons and thereby permit Iraq to launch a conventional war against the Zionist state without fear that Israel would, in desperation, retaliate with its nuclear arsenal. The transcript of Saddam's secret speech is chilling:

> We want, when the Israeli enemy attacks our civilian establishments, to have weapons to attack the Israeli civilian establishment. We are willing to sit and refrain from using it [a nuclear weapon], except when the enemy attacks civilian establishments in Iraq or Syria, so that we can guarantee the long war that is destructive to our enemy, and take at our leisure each meter of land and drown the enemy with rivers of blood. We have no vision of war that is any less than this. . . . We should consider losses in the thousands, so that we plan to be prepared to lose in those 12 months 50,000 martyrs and keep going.[5]

Proliferation optimists believe that nuclear weapons only serve a deterrent function for all states, but for Saddam Hussein, a nuclear deterrent was sought so that he could more safely engage in conventional aggression.

An additional frightening insight is apparent when one looks inside the Iraqi government's decision-making process: the tyrant created such a climate of fear that his subordinates wove an intricate web of lies and delusions to please him. Saddam Hussein tolerated no disagreements, spurned professional military advice, and trusted his own mystical intuition more than objective intelligence reports. Anyone who questioned Saddam's assumptions or decisions, or those of his brutal sons, was likely to be severely punished, and that climate of fear produced constant exaggerations about Iraqi military capabilities and self-serving reports of interactions with foreign governments. He made virtually all of his major strategic decisions on his own and actively discouraged advisors from delivering intelligence or counsel that contradicted his wisdom and what he called his "politician's alertness." According to one taped conversation after the 1990 invasion of Kuwait, for example, Saddam told his colleagues

> I forbade the intelligence outfits from deducing from press and political analysis anything about America. . . . I said I don't want either intelligence organization to give me analysis—that is my specialty. . . . We agree to continue on that basis . . . which is what I used with the Iranians, some of it out of deduction, some of it through invention and connecting the dots, all without having hard evidence.[6]

Saddam compartmentalized strategic decision making and refused to let military commanders coordinate operational plans before conflicts, lest they challenge his authority or even prepare coup attempts. This produced remarkably poor military planning and operations. Before the 1980 invasion of Iran, Iraqi commanders received only days or weeks of warning to prepare and, according to Saddam's later testimony, neither the defense minister nor the army chief of staff were informed of the 1990 invasion of Kuwait prior to the attack.[7] Saddam's strategic decisions were made in a haze of delusions: in 1991, he insisted that the chemical weapons that Iraq had just developed were 200 times more powerful than those he used against the Kurds and Iranians and could "make fire eat up half of Israel"; he insisted after the 1991 Gulf War that Iraqi military forces had actually won the battle against the U.S.-led coalition forces, due to their superior "fighting spirit"; and he insisted prior to the U.S. invasion in 2003 that Washington would not send forces all the way to Baghdad and would once again settle for a limited victory without imposing regime change.[8]

These observations about Saddam Hussein's pathological decision-making style are a warning sign that nuclear weapons would not have contributed to stable deterrence in the region had Iraq acquired them through the covert nuclear program, which was uncovered after the 1991 Gulf War. Saddam without nuclear weapons attacked Iran in 1980. Saddam without nuclear weapons invaded Kuwait in 1990. Saddam without nuclear weapons launched missile strikes against Israel in 1991. It strains credibility to believe that Saddam with nuclear weapons would have behaved more cautiously.

North Korea

The George W. Bush Administration cannot be blamed for the Democratic People's Republic of Korea (DPRK) government's initiation of a nuclear weapons program. That program began many years ago and was, after a tense crisis during the Clinton Administration, significantly curtailed by the Agreed Framework, under which the North Koreans dismantled their plutonium-producing graphite reactor and permitted International Atomic Energy Agency (IAEA) inspectors to verify that the reactor's fuel rods were kept in spent fuel pond storage at the Yongbyon facility. The Bush Administration can, however, be at least partially blamed for the abandonment of the Agreed Framework. For when Bush Administration officials confronted the DPRK in 2002 with evidence that Pakistan had helped Pyongyang develop a secret uranium enrichment program, North Korean officials abruptly withdrew from the **Nuclear Nonproliferation Treaty (NPT)** and reinvigorated their nuclear weapons program, separating plutonium from the fuel rods and then conducting nuclear weapons tests in 2006 and 2009.

Today, North Korea is estimated to have extracted enough plutonium from its now dismantled graphite reactor to build approximately eight nuclear weapons. We know that much because we know the amount of plutonium that was in the spent fuel coming out of the one North Korean reactor. What the U.S. government does not know is how much progress North Korea has made toward constructing small nuclear warheads that could be placed on the long-range missiles that it clearly has in abundance. Pyongyang officials have continued to insist that they need to increase the strength of their national deterrent given the perceived threats from the United States and South Korea. In 2010, they surprised both U.S. intelligence agencies and western scholars by taking Stanford professor and former Los Alamos National Laboratory Director Siegfried Hecker on a tour of what had until then been a secret uranium enrichment facility.[9] Once completed, this facility—jam-packed with centrifuges based on Pakistani designs—will give the North Koreans the ability to expand its nuclear arsenal significantly. Indeed, North Korea is a severe nuclear danger for three related reasons.

First, we should not be optimistic that the DPRK, which has been quite aggressive when weak, will suddenly become more cautious when strong. Within months of the March 2010 North Korean sinking of the *Cheonon*, which killed forty-six South Korean seamen, the leadership in Pyongyang apparently ordered North Korean artillery units to shell the South Korean island of Yeonpyeong, an attack that killed two marines and two civilians and wounded nineteen others. It is true that these incidents occurred in disputed waters and that the North Koreans did not escalate the operations afterwards, even though in the Yeonpyeong incident, the South Koreans retaliated by shelling the artillery units on the North Korean mainland. Given this track record, there is no reason for optimism in this regard about the effect of nuclear weapons on North Korean behavior and even less reason to predict increased caution once North Korea acquires a larger and more effective nuclear arsenal.

And this is the second reason to be worried—the DPRK seems determined to do exactly that: expand its nuclear arsenal, create smaller warheads that can fit on its existing missiles, and develop and deploy longer-range missiles capable of hitting the United States as well as South Korea and Japan. This is the main explanation for North Korea's development of its new uranium enrichment facilities: after the dismantlement of their gas-graphite nuclear reactor, the DPRK lacked the ability to produce more plutonium, and the alternative Highly Enriched Uranium (HEU) route to making the bomb became far more attractive. Moreover, U.S. intelligence agencies discovered in 2003 that A.Q. Khan had sold the bomb blueprints of an HEU implosion device (based on a tested Chinese design) to Libya, and there is no reason not to assume that

Khan included such blueprint designs in the package of materials and technology that he sold to North Korea. If that is the case, the North Koreans may actually prefer to use HEU for their emerging arsenal, because using a proven design would make miniaturization of new warheads for long-range missiles significantly easier.[10] Finally, in October 2010 in a parade in Pyongyang, the North Koreans displayed a new road-mobile Intermediate Range Ballistic Missile (IRBM), reportedly based on a Russian submarine-launched missile, with an estimated range of 3,000 to 5,000 kilometers.[11]

These observations about how military technology imports are leading to North Korea's enhanced nuclear capabilities leads us directly to the third and most important reason to be alarmed by a nuclear DPRK. North Korea is such a basket case economically that its government has been led to sell virtually anything to other nations that have cash available. Pyongyang started with production and smuggling of counterfeit currency, fake pharmaceuticals, and illicit drugs but has moved quickly into the even more lucrative missile and nuclear technology smuggling business. Smuggling is a tough business, however, and the need for covert and decentralized operations is leading to a shift away from the traditional North Korean reliance on centrally managed operations. Sheena Chestnut, in the most thorough study of the North Korean smuggling networks, notes a disturbing trend: "An examination of patterns in illicit activity, however, reveals that although North Korean criminal smuggling has been centrally inspired and sanctioned, it is not always centrally controlled; the state has shifted over time from using solely state agents and assets to contracting out transportation and distribution of smuggled goods to criminal partners over whom it has less control."[12] North Korea has been observed shipping missiles to Pakistan and Iran and is known to have sold nuclear materials or technology to Syria and Libya. Other deals with other countries are suspected. We hope that Kim Jong-Il and Kim Jong-Un, his son and chosen successor, maintain tight control over North Korean nuclear exports in the future, but that is only a hope and not a confident expectation.

Instead of welcoming North Korean nuclear developments as a force for stability, the U.S. should continue to use sanctions, negotiations, and deterrence to try to contain the DPRK nuclear threat and attempt to reverse it.

Iran

This leads to the most recent and the most serious case of a state trying to acquire nuclear weapons: Iran.[13] Proliferation optimists believe that the Iranians will behave cautiously if they acquire nuclear weapons, the way that Cold War adversaries did. But Iran does not have the internal characteristics that communist China and the communist Soviet Union had: an ideology eschewing risks, centralized collective decision making, and tight civilian control of the military. Instead of using a Cold War analogy, we should look back at more recent cases of nuclear proliferation or attempted nuclear proliferation—Pakistan and Iraq—in order to predict the effects of a nuclear Iran. First, we should worry that Iranian leaders with nuclear weapons will see them as a shield behind which they can more safely engage in aggression against neighbors and the United States. Iran already is a major arms supplier to Hezbollah, the Lebanese-based Shi'a militia, and supports its attacks against civilian and military targets inside Israel. Iranian officials already provided support for the 1996 Hezbollah bombing of the U.S. barracks at the Khobar Towers in Saudi Arabia. Iran already covertly armed and supported Iraqi Shi'a militia who were fighting U.S. troops combating the insurgency inside Iraq after 2003. Iranian leaders have already called for revolutions against many Arab governments in the region. Iran is already suspected by U.S. officials of having provided special artillery shells to Muammar Qaddhafi's regime in Libya, which were then filled with mustard gas.[14]

If Iran acquires nuclear weapons, will it behave more or less aggressively in the Middle East? On the one hand, we know that the United States and Israel would be more reluctant to attack Iran if it had nuclear weapons—and indeed, it is likely that Tehran's concerns about forced regime change is its central motivation for wanting to acquire nuclear weapons. On the other hand, however, even if that is true, it is also likely that various Iranians—especially those in the Islamic Revolutionary Guard Corps (IRGC)—may feel that it would be safer for them to act aggressively, to attack American troops in the region, to support terrorist attacks against Israel, and to attempt to destabilize Arab regimes in the neighborhood.

The second crucial question is who would control nuclear weapons in Iran: the mullahs, the elected politicians, the professional military, or the IRGC? The evidence suggests that the IRGC will be the guardians of the Iranian arsenal, for it is the Iranian Revolutionary Guard Corps—not the professional Iranian military—that has been covertly purchasing nuclear technology, guarding the nuclear facilities, conducting research on weapon delivery systems, and managing the nuclear weapons activities. And it is the IRGC leadership that has been responsible for running Iran's relationship with terrorist organizations in the Middle East. That is a deadly mixture—nuclear command and control responsibilities and terrorist ties in the same organization.

There is no reason to assume that, even if they wanted to, central political authorities in Tehran could completely control the details of nuclear operations by the Islamic Revolutionary Guard Corps. The IRGC recruits young "true believers" to join its ranks, subjects them to ideological indoctrination and—as the IAEA discovered when it inspected Iran's centrifuge facilities in 2003—gives IRGC units responsibility for securing production sites for nuclear materials. The IRGC also has ties with the most radical clerics in Iran, including some who have argued (in contrast to the views of many traditional Shi'ite clerics) that nuclear weapons acquisition and use is justified under Islamic law.[15]

Concerns about whether the IRGC can be controlled by the Tehran government is not just a theoretical proposition, for there have been numerous cases in the past decade of senior IRGC commanders acting aggressively on their own authority, without the apparent sanction of the central authorities. In January 2002, for example, the Israeli Navy intercepted a ship that was delivering weapons from Iran to the Palestinian territories, an act that many Western officials believed was a rogue IRCG operation, launched without the knowledge or approval of the Iranian President Mohammad Khatami.[16] In September 2007, in a similar incident, IRGC-controlled naval vessels captured a group of British sailors, holding them hostage for two weeks and claiming that they were in Iranian waters. British and American officials believed at the time that this capture was "probably not directed from the upper reaches of government."[17] Finally, there are suspicions in the U.S. that the 2011 Iranian plot to assassinate the Saudi Ambassador in Washington was a rogue operation: "It's a rogue plan or they're using very different tactics. We just don't know," a senior U.S. official told a reporter.[18]

For nuclear weapons to provide even a semblance of stability, the government must maintain tight command and control. These incidents are disturbing warnings that Iranian nuclear weapons operations would be dangerous in this regard. The central government in Tehran might not be in command; the IRGC might be out of control.

Nuclear Terrorism

Today, the threat posed by nuclear materials and nuclear weapons is no longer one of just state proliferation but of nuclear terrorism. The risk of terrorists unleashing catastrophic damage on a nuclear scale is too frightening to ignore. It is important to recognize as well that nuclear terrorism anywhere is a threat to everyone, everywhere. As Kofi Annan, former Secretary-General of the UN, stated in 2005, "Were such an attack to occur, it would not only cause widespread death and destruction, but would stagger the world economy and thrust tens of millions of people into dire poverty. . . . Any nuclear terrorist attack would have a second death toll throughout the developing world."

Regardless of what happens to the al-Qaeda organization after the killing of Osama bin Laden, the danger of nuclear terrorism is one that existed long before Bin Laden formed al-Qaeda and will exist long after the threat of al-Qaeda is significantly weakened. In 1977, the Red Army Faction in West Germany attacked a U.S. military base, hoping to steal the tactical nuclear weapons there. The Aum Shinrikyo apocalyptic cult in Japan sought recruits in the Russian military in the 1990s to get access to loose nukes and only settled on using sarin gas chemicals in the Tokyo subway when their nuclear efforts failed. Today's threat is even more alarming. It is well-known that Osama bin Laden proclaimed that Islamic jihadists have a duty to acquire and to use nuclear weapons against the West. And al-Qaeda is known to have recruited senior Pakistani nuclear scientists in the past and may now have "sleeper agents" in Pakistani laboratories to help in that effort.

Terrorists are not likely to be deterred by threats of retaliation. Stopping them from purchasing a nuclear weapon, stealing one, or getting the materials to make their own is a much better strategy. If aspiring nuclear-weapons states—such as Iran and Syria (and some suspect Myanmar)[19]—get nuclear weapons in the future, the danger that terrorists will get their hands on one will clearly increase. And if the United States and other nuclear-weapons nations are seen to be hypocritical by not following our NPT commitments and maintaining that we (but only we) are responsible enough to have them, it will reduce the likelihood of ensuring the broad international cooperation that is needed to reduce these proliferation risks.

EFFECTIVE NONPROLIFERATION POLICIES

Proliferation optimists are like individuals whistling past the graveyard. The United States and regional powers may have to live with nuclear weapons in North Korea or with nuclear ambiguity in Iran or other nations in the future, but we should certainly not welcome it. The United States should ensure that nonproliferation policies are pursued multilaterally to ensure their effectiveness and mitigate the threat of nuclear weapons use.

In the past, the United States has effectively pursued nonproliferation policies that have shown real results in the international system. Some of the cases involve regime changes, as in the case of South Africa, where the apartheid state fell and the new government got rid of their clandestine nuclear weapons program. Other cases have involved effective pressures being applied by the United States. For example, in the case of Taiwan, the U.S. threat to end its special relationship with the government was enough to convince Taipei to change course. Similarly, in the case of South Korea, threatening to bring U.S. troops home from the peninsula was enough to dissuade South Korea from further pursuit of nuclear weapons. U.S. pledges of extended deterrence have also played an important role in convincing U.S. allies to forgo the expenses of building an independent nuclear weapons capability.

Sometimes military operations have been necessary to stop determined nuclear proliferators. For example, the Israeli bombing of the Osirak reactor in Iraq in 1981 set back the program for a number of years, and we now know that coalition forces ended the Iraqi nuclear program after the 1991 Gulf War.

The case of Iran is particularly apropos. Given how far Iran has gone already with its nuclear program, some are tempted to advocate preventive air strikes, or even a preventive war, against Iran. But such a military option is unlikely to be completely successful, as former Secretary of Defense Robert Gates has said in Washington and former Mossad intelligence chief Meir Dagan has warned in Israel.[20] Continued pressure, through UN Security Council sanctions when possible and U.S. and allied nations' sanctions when necessary, is more attractive. Continued sabotage efforts, such as the Stuxnet computer virus attacks, are more promising. Greater support for government opposition forces inside Iran to promote an Iranian Spring should be considered. More vigorous trade embargoes, including embargoes on Iranian imports of refined petroleum, should be explored. The U.S. and the world community are not yet at the crucial crisis point when it faces only the horrible options of going to war with Iran or living with a nuclear-armed Iran. Our policy objective should be to push that horrendous day of reckoning as far as possible over the distant horizon to create time for these other options to be effective.

The best way to stop proliferation, however, is to do so before it starts. The U.S. and the international community should therefore be particularly careful to sell nuclear technology only to states that have agreed to strict inspection systems under the Additional Protocol and that have agreed to forgo sovereign uranium enrichment and reprocessing programs.[21]

PROLIFERATION FATALISM

The reasoning of scholars and officials struggling to deal with Iran's nuclear ambitions too often displays both creeping fatalism about the United States' ability to keep Iran from getting the bomb and excessive optimism about the United States' ability to contain Iran if it does become a nuclear power. Such proliferation fatalists argue that over the long term, it may be impossible to stop Iran—or other states for that matter—from getting the bomb. Given the spread of nuclear technology and know-how and the right of parties to the NPT to enrich uranium and separate plutonium, the argument goes, any foreign government determined to acquire nuclear weapons will eventually do so. Moreover, the 1981 Israeli attack on the Osirak nuclear reactor in Iraq may have delayed Iraq's progress, but similar air strikes today are unlikely to disable Iran's capacities completely, since its uranium enrichment facilities at Natanz are buried underground and many specialists suspect that there are covert facilities hidden elsewhere as well.

Such proliferation fatalism overlooks the impressive track record of nonproliferation policies since the signing of the NPT in 1968, during which time at least nineteen states that considered the nuclear option chose instead to forgo it and four additional states—Belarus, Kazakhstan, Ukraine, and South Africa—surrendered or destroyed the nuclear weapons in their possession.[22] Many other countries that have the technical capability to develop nuclear weapons have, at least for now, decided not to pursue that option.

Given the case of Iran and its development of significant amounts of Low Enriched Uranium (LEU), it is understandable that many analysts are turning their attention to how best to deter a nuclear Iran. A Bush administration official in the executive branch anonymously told *The New York Times* in March 2006, "The reality is that most of us think the Iranians are probably going to get a weapon, or the technology to make one, sooner or later."[23] According to *The New York Times* again, Obama administration officials have also discussed whether a nuclear-armed Iran is inevitable and, if so, how the U.S. should best provide deterrence and containment against Tehran.[24] But that analysis should be considered long-term contingency planning against an undesirable outcome, not an excuse for accepting that Iran's nuclear ambitions are acceptable or inevitable. Indeed, proliferation fatalism and deterrence optimism interact in a particularly diabolical manner: the more we think it inevitable that Iran is going to acquire nuclear weapons, the more we are tempted—through wishful thinking—to say, "Well, maybe it won't matter." And, the more we bolster our belief that it won't matter, the less willing we are to take the necessary diplomatic and strategic steps that could potentially stop Iran from getting nuclear weapons.

GLOBAL ZERO

Finally, we should acknowledge that any effective nuclear nonproliferation policies must go hand-in-hand with good-faith efforts toward nuclear disarmament. The question of how to manage a slow disarmament movement with the maintenance of credible deterrence is a great challenge for the next generation of leaders, but the disarmament vision itself is one that requires aggressive leadership on the part of the United States. On April 5th, 2009, President Barack Obama laid out the Prague Agenda in Hradčany Square at the heart of historic Prague, Czech Republic with four main objectives: (1) reduce the total number and role that nuclear weapons play in the defense postures of nuclear-armed nations; (2) strengthen the international nonproliferation regime by holding rogue states accountable; (3) secure loose and vulnerable nuclear materials around the world while strengthening international cooperation on nuclear security; and (4) support the safe and secure growth of nuclear power in ways that reduce the spread of dangerous technologies.

The disarmament vision—codified in the Nuclear Nonproliferation Treaty—remains key to ensuring the safety and security of the United States and bolstering our nonproliferation efforts. Indeed, by proclaiming that America seeks a world without nuclear weapons, Obama is simply reaffirming that we will follow our treaty commitments: states that joined the 1970 NPT agreed "to pursue negotiations in good faith on effective measures relating to cessation of the nuclear arms race at an early date and to nuclear disarmament." And since Article 6 of America's Constitution says that a treaty commitment is "the supreme Law of the Land," at a basic level, Obama is simply saying that he will follow U.S. law.

The abolition aspiration is not, however, based on such legal niceties. Instead, it is inspired by two important insights about the global nuclear future. First, the most dangerous nuclear threats to the United States today and on the horizon are from terrorists and potential new nuclear powers, not from our traditional Cold War adversaries in Russia and China. Second, the spread of nuclear weapons to new states, and indirectly to terrorist organizations, will be made less likely if the United States and other nuclear-armed nations are seen to be working in good faith toward disarmament.

Officials in the George W. Bush administration believed that there was no link between U.S. arsenal size or military posture and nonproliferation decisions made by nonnuclear-weapons states. The Obama administration's April 2010 Nuclear Posture Review maintains that the connection is strong, even if it is often indirect and hard to measure: "By demonstrating that we take seriously our NPT obligation to pursue nuclear disarmament, we strengthen our ability to mobilize broad international support for the measures needed to reinforce the nonproliferation regime and secure nuclear materials worldwide."[25]

There are now many signs that the Obama administration is correct in its assessment that progress in disarmament enables progress in nonproliferation. The April 2010 Nuclear Security Summit brought forty-six countries to Washington, where they reached agreement on a number of concrete steps to better protect nuclear materials from terrorists. And in stark contrast to the Bush-era 2005 NPT Review Conference, which ended in failure, the May 2010 review took place in a cooperative atmosphere and produced a final document that called on all states to sign onto improved safeguards for their reactors and encouraged governments not in compliance with their treaty commitments to change their ways. The successful efforts to get additional rounds of sanctions against Iran in the UN Security Council can be credited, in part, to the new spirit of cooperation, including the progress on arms-control agreements between the United States and China and the United States and Russia.[26]

Despite major successes like the Nuclear Posture Review, the Nuclear Security Summit, and the New START (Strategic Arms Reduction Treaty) Treaty, much work remains to be done on the Prague Agenda. Ratification of the Comprehensive Test Ban Treaty (CTBT) is necessary to stem the production of new nuclear weapons and limit dangerous and destabilizing posturing between nuclear states. The negotiation of a Fissile Material Cutoff Treaty must move forward (with or without the Conference on Disarmament) to stop the flow of the dangerous ingredients for nuclear warheads. The United States and Russia must reach an agreement to cooperate on ballistic missile defense in order to build confidence for further reductions of nuclear weapons, both strategic and nonstrategic. None of this will be easy.

Moreover, a nuclear-weapons-free world will not be a world free of conflicts of national interest nor will it be a utopia in which governments never feel tempted to cheat on their international obligations. A world without nuclear weapons will not be a world without war. Indeed, the maintenance of global zero will require that conventionally armed major powers be prepared to enforce nuclear disarmament and nonproliferation commitments in a fair and vigorous manner. Potential proliferators may have to be "forced to be free."

In medieval times, European mapmakers placed the words *hic sunt dracones* (here be dragons) at the edge of the known world. Disarmament critics today are like those medieval mapmakers, fearing that we are entering unknown territory fraught with hidden nuclear monsters. But these dragons are fantasies. The genuine strategic challenges we face in creating a secure nuclear-free world—adequate verification, enforcement of violations, and mutual-defense deployments—are challenges that can be met over time. And the world we are heading toward if we fail to find safe paths to mutual and verifiable disarmament—a world crowded with nuclear-weapons states and terrorist temptations—is even more fraught with danger.

CONCLUSIONS

As long as nuclear weapons exist, we will have to maintain some form of nuclear deterrence. But long-term nuclear deterrence is a risky way of ensuring global security. Nuclear weapons may have been a dangerous necessity to keep the Cold War cold, but scholars and policymakers who are nostalgic for the brutal simplicity of that era's nuclear deterrence do not understand how much the world has changed. The United States and the international community should aggressively pursue nuclear nonproliferation policies to confront the security challenges of the 21st century.

NOTES

1. George W. Bush, "State of the Union Address." Washington, DC, January 29, 2002.
2. Barack Obama, Speech in Prague, Czech Republic, April 5, 2009.
3. This section is based on a chapter on Iraq, North Korea, and Iran appearing in the third edition of Scott D. Sagan and Kenneth N. Waltz, *The Spread of Nuclear Weapons: An Enduring Debate* (New York: W.W. Norton, 2012).
4. Hal Brands and David Palkki, "Saddam, Israel, and the Bomb: Nuclear Alarmism Justified?" *International Security* 36, no. 1(Summer 2011): p. 156.
5. David D. Palkki, Mark E. Stout, and Kevin M. Woods, *The Saddam Tapes*. New York, NY: Cambridge University Press, 2011, pp. 223–4.
6. Kevin M. Woods et. al., *The Iraqi Perspectives Report* (Annapolis: Naval Institute Press, 2006), p. 12.
7. Hal Brands and David Palkki, "Saddam, Israel, and the Bomb: Nuclear Alarmism Justified?" *International Security* 36, no. 1 (Summer 2011): 152–3.
8. See *The Saddam Tapes*, pp. 211, 238, 240; and *The Iraqi Perspectives Report*, p. 31.
9. Siegfried S. Hecker, "A Return Trip to North Korea's Yongbyon Nuclear Complex," CISAC, November 20, 2010. http://cisac.stanford.edu/publications/ north_koreas_yongbyon_nuclear_complex_a_report_by_siegfried_s_hecker/ (accessed November 22, 2011); and Robert Carlin and Siegfried Hecker, "2011: North Korea's Countdown to Kim Il-Sung's Centenary," *Bulletin of the Atomic Scientists*, 2012.
10. Robert Carlin and Siegfried Hecker, "2011: North Korea's Countdown to Kim Il-Sung's Centenary," *Bulletin of the Atomic Scientists*, 2012.
11. See Joshua Pollack, "North Korea Debuts an IRBM," *Arms Control Wonk*, October 10, 2010. http://pollack.armscontrolwonk.com/archive/3351/north-korea-debuts-an-irbm (accessed November 22, 2011).
12. Sheena Chestnut, "Illicit Activity and Proliferation: North Korean Smuggling Networks," *International Security* 32, no. 1 (Summer 2007): p. 81.
13. This section builds upon Scott D. Sagan, "How to Keep the Bomb from Iran," *Foreign Affairs* (September/October 2006), pp. 45–59.
14. R. Jeffrey Smith et al., "Iran may have sent Libya shells for chemical weapons," *The Washington Post*, November 20, 2011. http://www.washingtonpost.com/world/ national-security/iran-may-have-sent-libya-shells-for-chemical-weapons/2011/11/18/ gIQA7RPifN_print.html (accessed November 23, 2011).
15. Safa Haeri and Shahram Rafizadeh, "Iranian Cleric Okays Use of Nuclear Weapons," *Iran Press Service*, February 20, 2006. http://www.iran-press-service .com/ips/articles-2006/february-2006/iran_nuke_20206.shtml (accessed

November 17, 2011). For analysis of this and other statements, see Shmuel Bar, "Can Cold War Deterrence Apply to a Nuclear Iran?" *Strategic Perspectives*, November 7, 2011. http://www.jcpa.org/text/cold_war_deterrence_nuclear_iran.pdf (accessed November 17, 2011).

16. Annie Samuel and Daniel Tavana, "Going Rogue in Iran?" *CNN.com*, October 14, 2011. http://belfercenter.ksg.harvard.edu/publication/21402/going_rogue_in_iran.html?breadcrumb=%2Fexperts%2F2320%2Fdaniel_tavana (accessed November 17, 2011).

17. David E. Sanger, "No Diplomatic Change After Britons' Release," *The New York Times*, April 6, 2007. http://www.nytimes.com/2007/04/06/washington/06policy.html (accessed November 17, 2011).

18. Charlie Savage and Scott Shane, "Iranians Accused of a Plot to Kill Saudis' U.S. Envoy," *The New York Times*, October 11, 2011. http://www.nytimes.com/2011/10/12/us/us-accuses-iranians-of-plotting-to-kill-saudi-envoy.html?pagewanted=all (accessed November 17, 2011).

19. "Myanmar Sought Nuke Aid from North Korea, Lugar Asserts," *Global Security Newswire*, November 28, 2011. http://gsn.nti.org/gsn/nw_20111128_8201.php (accessed December 11, 2011).

20. David Blair, "Robert Gates: Bombing Iran Would Not Stop Nuclear Threat," *The Telegraph*, May 1, 2009. http://www.telegraph.co.uk/news/worldnews/middleeast/iran/5257343/Robert-Gates-bombing-Iran-would-not-stop-nuclear-threat.html (accessed November 23, 2011); and Boaz Fyler, "Dagan: Iran Strike—Only as Last Resort," *YnetNews*, June 1, 2011. http://www.ynetnews.com/articles/0,7340,L-4077239,00.html (accessed November 23, 2011).

21. For more on reforming international institutions to combat proliferation before it starts, see Scott D. Sagan, "Shared Responsibilities for Nuclear Disarmament," *Daedalus Special Issue: On the Global Nuclear Future Vol. 1* (Fall 2009), pp. 157–168.

22. Scott D. Sagan, "The Causes of Nuclear Weapons Proliferation," The Annual Review of Political Science (March 2011), pp. 225–244.

23. David E. Sanger, "Suppose We Just Let Iran Have the Bomb?" *The New York Times*, March 19, 2006. http://www.nytimes.com/2006/03/19/weekinreview/19sanger.ART0.html?pagewanted=all (accessed November 22, 2011).

24. David E. Sanger, "Debate Grows on Nuclear Containment of Iran" *The New York Times*, March 13, 2010. http://www.nytimes.com/2010/03/14/weekinreview/14sanger.html (accessed November 22, 2011).

25. *U.S. Nuclear Posture Review Report*, Department of Defense, April 2011. www.defense.gov/npr/ (accessed November 20, 2011).

26. "Arms, Disarmament and Influence: the International Impact of the 2010 U.S. Nuclear Posture Review," *The Nonproliferation Review Special Section* (March 2011), coedited by Scott D. Sagan and Jane Vaynman (Routledge, Taylor & Francis Group).

NO: Todd S. Sechser, *University of Virginia*

S hould the United States try to prevent the spread of nuclear weapons to states that do not already have them? At first glance, this appears to be a fairly uncontroversial proposition. After all, nuclear weapons are the most horrific and destructive weapons ever invented—how could the world possibly be better off with more fingers on the nuclear trigger? Indeed, for decades, official U.S. national security policy has embraced the doctrine of universal nonproliferation codified by the 1968 Nuclear Nonproliferation Treaty (NPT), aiming to prevent friends and enemies alike from acquiring nuclear weapons.

The idea that the United States should aggressively pursue nuclear nonproliferation rests in part on a widespread belief that the spread of nuclear weapons would destabilize international relations. But this pessimistic view confronts one incontrovertible fact: nuclear weapons proliferated to thirteen states[1] during the six decades since the dawn of the nuclear age, yet the world has not witnessed a single preventive or preemptive nuclear war, accidental nuclear attack, or instance of nuclear terrorism. Motivated by this striking observation, scholars known as "proliferation optimists" have suggested that nuclear proliferation may, in fact, exert a stabilizing force on international politics. They argue that nuclear states new and old will be highly motivated to avoid taking actions that might risk nuclear conflict.

The core of the optimists' position is that the cost of a nuclear war would be so grave that even the world's most risk-prone leaders will find themselves reluctant to risk fighting one. As Kenneth N. Waltz, perhaps the most prominent proliferation optimist, has argued, nuclear states quickly recognize that engaging in aggressive or risky behavior that could prompt nuclear retaliation is "obvious folly" (Sagan and Waltz 2003, 154). Because a nuclear conflict could place a state's very survival at risk, national leaders have powerful incentives to manage their arsenals with care and caution. Moreover, according to this view, even a few nuclear weapons constitute such a powerful deterrent to aggression that they obviate the need for high levels of spending on conventional arms. According to the optimists, then, the spread of nuclear weapons is likely to deter large-scale wars, restrain conventional-arms races, and produce greater international stability.

Here I contend that the historical record supports this optimistic position. I divide my argument into three parts. First, I present empirical data suggesting that nuclear proliferation is unlikely to destabilize international politics and may in fact be stabilizing. Second, I evaluate the body of evidence cited by more pessimistic scholars and conclude that it is insufficient to bear out their skepticism. Finally, I consider the implications of my argument for U.S. foreign policy. In the end, I conclude that further nuclear proliferation would probably bolster—not undermine—international stability. If the lessons of the nuclear age are to be believed, a world with more nuclear states is likely to be, on balance, a more stable, peaceful, and secure world than one without.

PROLIFERATION AND THE HISTORICAL RECORD

Will additional nuclear proliferation stabilize world politics, or will it worsen the problem of interstate conflict? We cannot answer this question with certainty, of course, since we cannot collect data about the future. We can, however, learn from events that have already happened. Imagine that, at the advent of the nuclear age in 1945, today's proliferation optimists and pessimists had put forth their competing predictions about the likely consequences of the spread of nuclear weapons. Whose predictions would be borne out? In this section, I argue that historical data confirm the predictions of proliferation optimism while offering little corroboration for rival perspectives.

Scholars who take the view that proliferation bolsters global stability argue that the spread of nuclear weapons produces three observable effects.[2] First, by deterring aggression, nuclear weapons reduce the *frequency* with which wars occur. Second, nuclear weapons induce caution among leaders in crises and during wartime, thereby mitigating the *intensity* of wars. Third, nuclear weapons defuse arms races and obviate the need for high levels of *conventional-arms spending*. I consider each claim below with respect to five proliferators: China, Israel, India, South Africa, and Pakistan. These five states provide a useful laboratory for examining the behavior of proliferators, because they more closely resemble the types of states most likely to proliferate today. The United States, the Soviet Union, Great Britain, and France were all major industrialized powers when they acquired nuclear weapons, but these five proliferators were weaker, poorer, and less internally stable—much as today's proliferators are likely to be.

The Frequency of Armed Conflict

The optimist camp's first and most important claim is that the presence of nuclear weapons suppresses international conflicts. Nuclear weapons, in this view, differ from conventional military tools in two central ways. First, nuclear weapons carry enormous destructive power. Whereas the targets of conventional weapons necessarily tend to be small in size (for instance, an airfield, communications center, or ammunition depot), the most powerful nuclear weapons can place entire cities at risk. The use of even a few nuclear weapons could destroy hundreds of thousands (if not millions) of human lives in a short span of time. Second, defenders have little control over the level of destruction they endure during a nuclear conflict. Without a reliable means to destroy incoming ballistic missiles or to shield cities from nuclear attack—neither of which exists today—nuclear combatants must rely on an enemy's restraint to limit the amount of damage they suffer. These two characteristics—colossal destructive capacity and the lack of an effective defense—combine to induce caution among leaders facing the prospect of nuclear retaliation. Leaders will behave less aggressively and will more eagerly seek peaceful solutions to crises, the logic goes, since they do not want to endure even a small risk that a conventional war might become nuclear.

These propositions can be evaluated empirically by comparing the rates at which proliferators have participated in interstate conflicts both before and after their acquisition of nuclear weapons. If the optimists are correct, nuclear states should experience fewer conflicts after they acquire nuclear weapons. One way to measure the turbulence of a state's foreign affairs is to calculate its participation in *militarized interstate disputes*, defined here as conflicts involving at least one military fatality. Figure 1 (p. 180) considers five proliferators and charts how much their involvement in military conflicts changed after they became nuclear states. In this chart, each conflict is counted once for every year it persisted, to account for the fact that more severe disputes often last many years. Israel, for instance, participated in an average of 1.33 conflicts per year as a nonnuclear state but entered into only 0.40 conflicts per year after becoming a nuclear state in 1972, so its bar in Figure 1 drops below zero to illustrate that Israel has been involved in fewer interstate conflicts since acquiring nuclear weapons.

Optimists predict that states will participate in fewer conflicts after going nuclear, since they expect nuclear weapons to deter aggression and dissuade opposing leaders from escalating crises. And indeed, three of the five states examined here participated in significantly fewer interstate conflicts, on average, once they became nuclear states. For example, Israel fought four interstate wars against its neighbors before acquiring nuclear weapons but just two afterward. India and Pakistan have gone to war against one another four times since achieving independence, but only one of those wars occurred after the two rivals acquired nuclear weapons. Indeed, India and Pakistan saw the average incidence of militarized disputes between them decline by a factor of two-thirds (from 0.51 disputes per year to 0.17) once both states had acquired nuclear weapons. Both South Africa and China experienced minor increases in their conflict participation rate after achieving nuclear status, but the magnitude of these changes (+0.03 and + 0.04 conflicts per

Figure 1

Changes in Average Interstate Dispute Rates after Acquiring Nuclear Weapons

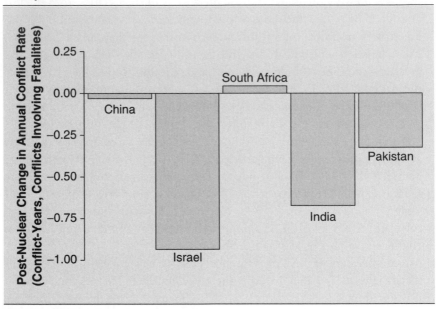

Source: Militarized Interstate Dispute dataset, http://vow2.la.psu.edu.

Table 1

Wars between India and Pakistan

War	Year	Fatalities
Kashmir I	1948–1949	7,500
Kashmir II	1965	6,000
Bangladesh/East Pakistan	1971	11,223
Kargil	1999	1,200

Note: Military fatalities only. Battle deaths data available from the Peace Research Institute, Oslo.

year, respectively) are trivial compared to the reductions in conflict experienced by the other three proliferators.

These data tell us that proliferation optimists are right to expect an overall decline in the frequency of interstate wars as more states acquire nuclear weapons. Admittedly, this analysis cannot demonstrate that these declines were caused entirely by nuclear weapons, but the strength of the correlation cannot be ignored. At a minimum, the data cast considerable doubt on the argument that nuclear weapons undermine conventional military stability.

The Intensity of Military Conflict

What about conflicts which, despite the shadow of nuclear weapons, nevertheless occur? Proliferation optimists argue that even if nuclear-armed states fight one another, their wars will be less severe: leaders will prevent such conflicts from escalating to avoid the risk that nuclear weapons might be used. As Waltz writes, "Everyone knows that if force gets out of hand all the parties to a conflict face catastrophe. With conventional weapons, the crystal ball is clouded. With nuclear weapons, it is perfectly clear" (Sagan and Waltz 2003, 114).

This reasoning was borne out by the 1999 Kargil War between India and Pakistan—the only war ever to occur between two nuclear states. The episode is instructive because the war entailed far fewer casualities than any of the prior wars between India and Pakistan (see Table 1, p. 180), owing in part to the restraint of the Indian military in expelling Pakistani insurgents from the Kargil region. The Indian military could have reduced its own losses and ended the war more quickly by attacking critical communication and supply lines in Pakistani controlled Kashmir, yet because crossing into Pakistani territory might have widened the war and risked provoking a Pakistani nuclear response, Indian leaders instead opted for caution.

It is not hard to find other military crises in which the risk of nuclear escalation induced restraint. In March 1969, Chinese forces ambushed Russian troops along the Ussuri River in northwest China, prompting a Soviet counterattack. But one important reason we do not read about the catastrophic Sino–Soviet War of 1969 is that a Soviet threat to launch preventive strikes against Chinese nuclear targets induced Chinese leaders to enter into negotiations over a volatile border dispute. Despite having initiated the challenge, China backed down rather than risk letting events get out of hand. The Soviet Union, of course, had itself recently backed down from a crisis it precipitated, when Nikita Khrushchev agreed in 1962 to remove Soviet missile bases from Cuba rather than risk a potentially nuclear conflict with the United States.

These examples make clear that nuclear weapons cannot prevent all conflicts: indeed, the Cuban Missile Crisis, the Ussuri River crisis, and the Kargil War all came about because one nuclear power was bold enough to challenge another. But in a world without nuclear weapons, these clashes might have escalated to large-scale conventional wars. Instead, in each case the shadow of nuclear weapons helped to cool tempers and contain the crisis: retaliation remained limited, escalatory options were rejected, and eventually, the challenger backed down.

Conventional-Arms Spending

A final question asks whether possession of nuclear weapons encourages states to restrain their spending on conventional arms and avoid arms races. Optimists argue that even a few nuclear weapons will provide adequate deterrence and security for new proliferators. As a result, those states will not need to remain as carefully attuned to the balance of forces as they would in a purely conventional world. Moreover, since nuclear weapons negate the offensive advantages of conventional forces, nonnuclear-arms racing among rivals will become both unnecessary and unlikely.

Does the evidence bear out this prediction? The charts in Figure 2 (p. 183) provide a tentative answer by tracking the proportion of gross domestic product (GDP) that China, Israel, South Africa, India, and Pakistan each devoted to military spending from 1960 to 2007. If the optimistic view is correct, then these states should exhibit general declines in military expenditures following the acquisition of nuclear weapons. Indeed, this prediction is largely vindicated: all five of these states spent a smaller share of their GDP on defense in 2007 than in the year they first acquired nuclear weapons. To be sure, military spending did not immediately decline in all cases. But the acquisition of nuclear weapons appears to be associated with significant long-run declines in conventional military spending. Indeed, none of these states has exhibited any inclination to participate in the sort of tit-for-tat nuclear arms competition that characterized U.S.–Soviet relations during the Cold War. Even China, the only major power in this group, has remained content for decades with the security provided by its small strategic nuclear force (Lewis 2007).

DO NEAR MISSES COUNT?

The evidence in the above section tells against the view that the spread of nuclear weapons engenders instability. Yet proliferation pessimists nonetheless point to a very large body of empirical support for their arguments. Through years of painstaking archival research, scholars such as Bruce G. Blair (1994), Peter D. Feaver (1997), and especially Scott D. Sagan (1993) have amassed an extraordinary collection of data about "near-catastrophes"—incidents that almost resulted in nuclear accidents or outright nuclear war—that occurred in

Figure 2

Military Spending as a Share of Gross Domestic Product, 1960–2007

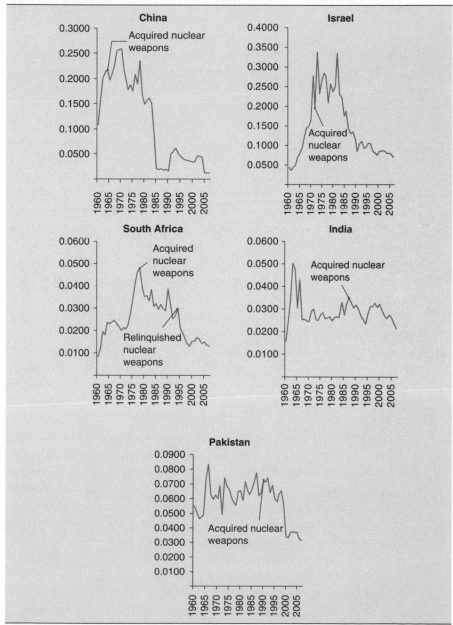

Sources: Nuclear acquisition data are from Sonali Singh and Christopher R. Way, 2004. "The Correlates of Nuclear Proliferation: A Quantitative Test." *Journal of Conflict Resolution* 48(6): 859–885. Military spending data are from the Correlates of War Project (http://www.correlatesofwar.org).

the United States, China, India, Pakistan, and elsewhere during the Cold War and afterward. In the "yes" section, for instance, Sagan and Reid Pauly tell of military officers who sought to provoke war with aspiring nuclear rivals, organizational missteps that inadvertently left nuclear forces vulnerable to attack, and blunders that nearly led to accidental nuclear detonations or launches.[3]

While doubtless worrisome, nuclear near misses are insufficient to corroborate with proliferation pessimism, because they provide no information about the risk of *actual* accidents. Consider the following analogy. Imagine that an insurance company official is assigned to evaluate the accident risk for cars that use a particular brand of tires. After interviewing customers who have used these tires for many years, she writes a report concluding that clients using the tires in the future will suffer a high risk of accidents. She bases her conclusion on reports that customers' cars sometimes skidded while taking tight turns or when stopping rapidly, although none of the customers in her study ever experienced an actual crash.

Would the researcher's conclusion be a reasonable inference from her data? It would not. The reason is that in the researcher's sample, experiencing skidding—that is, a "near-accident"—was not in fact associated with a higher likelihood of an actual accident. Cars that skidded had exactly the same likelihood of being involved in a crash—zero—as those that did not skid. Without having studied any actual crashes, the researcher can draw no inferences about the relationship between skidding and accidents. It may seem like common sense to assume that skidding cars have a greater likelihood of crashing, but intuition is no substitute for empirical data. Indeed, just the opposite might be true: perhaps skidding provides such a jolt to drivers that they become more cautious and attuned to road conditions as a result of the skid, thereby making a subsequent crash less likely.

So it is with the study of nuclear proliferation. Since none of the close calls in the data collected by proliferation pessimists led to an actual nuclear detonation, it is inappropriate to infer that close calls raise the likelihood of nuclear accidents.[4] The only conclusion supported by such data is that states possessing nuclear weapons have a greater likelihood of near misses than nonnuclear states. But near misses, while dramatic and unnerving, are ultimately of little consequence if they never escalate to outright catastrophes.

A common response to this criticism holds that even a tiny risk of nuclear catastrophe is sufficient to justify a policy of universal nonproliferation. This is a staggering burden of proof, and it is flawed for two reasons. One reason is that scholars have not actually demonstrated that the risk of nuclear accidents or inadvertent nuclear war in a proliferated world is greater than zero.

Of course, the absence of nuclear catastrophe in the past does not assure its absence in the future. But theories ultimately aim to predict real-world outcomes, and despite unearthing a valuable trove of nuclear near misses, the theory of proliferation pessimism has not succeeded in accomplishing this task. To be sure, existing research has shown that the theory's predicted *causal mechanisms*—that is, organizational biases and mishaps—have appeared in organizations that handle nuclear weapons, but these mechanisms, thankfully, have never produced the theory's predicted *outcomes*. Safeguards and cooler heads have always prevailed—albeit sometimes at the last minute.

Second, the appropriate question is not whether the spread of nuclear weapons would result in *any* nuclear disasters, but whether a world with proliferation would *on balance* be more peaceful and more stable than a world without it. In other words, we must ask: will the gains outweigh the costs? Even if one of the terrible events feared by proliferation pessimists does occur at some point in the future (as indeed it may), this outcome will not necessarily imply that the costs of proliferation outweigh the benefits. If the spread of nuclear weapons also would prevent numerous conventional wars, then it may be entirely reasonable to conclude that the net overall benefit justifies a more relaxed nonproliferation policy. In deciding whether nuclear proliferation would be stabilizing or destabilizing for international politics, it is not enough to merely point out that risks exist—one must weigh those risks against potential rewards.

Another objection to my critique holds that the nuclear age has not yet provided enough data to test theories of proliferation. In other words, it is simply too early to evaluate the theories' predictions (see Sagan 1993, 12). This argument is unpersuasive. The nuclear age is now more than sixty-five years old, and more than a dozen nations have possessed nuclear weapons at one time or another. If we imagine that every operational nuclear warhead in existence provides, say, one "disaster opportunity" per year, then since 1945 there have been nearly *two million* opportunities for an accidental explosion, preemptive nuclear strike, nuclear terrorist attack, or preventive war against an emerging proliferator. At the very least, the fact that none of these scenarios has yet occurred should suggest that the risk is low enough to warrant a plausible cost-benefit case against universal nonproliferation.

Of course, the absence of a nuclear catastrophe to date does not "prove" that proliferation pessimism is wrong. But it is important that we recognize the sharp limits to the inferential leverage that near misses provide. Each year that passes without a preemptive nuclear attack, preventive war against an aspiring nuclear power, nuclear accident, or act of nuclear terrorism must cast additional doubt on the theory. Ultimately, proliferation pessimism remains burdened by the contrast between the ubiquity of organizational pathologies and the absence of the disastrous nuclear outcomes it expects them to cause. This gap should make us skeptical of its claims.

PROLIFERATION AND U.S. FOREIGN POLICY

What are the implications of the preceding argument for U.S. foreign policy? There are two separate policy questions to consider: first, whether the United States should try to prevent its adversaries from acquiring nuclear weapons; and second, whether it should continue to adhere to a doctrine of universal nonproliferation.

The answer to the first question is unequivocally affirmative. The arguments in this section do not imply that the United States should stop trying to prevent its adversaries from acquiring nuclear weapons. Even if nuclear weapons are stabilizing overall, they could nevertheless permit hostile states to counter the power and influence of the United States, potentially threatening U.S. interests. A nuclear Iran, for example, might seek to deter, resist, or blackmail the United States. Stopping proliferation to U.S. adversaries will therefore remain an essential pillar of U.S. foreign policy, even if the proliferation optimists are correct. On this, the optimists and pessimists can probably agree.

But a second—and distinct—question is whether the United States should maintain its commitment to preventing proliferation not only to its adversaries but to *all* states. The answer is significant, because it carries implications for how the United States should treat new members of the nuclear club—in particular, whether the United States should assist new nuclear states in making their arsenals safe, secure, and reliable. Scholars in the pessimist tradition have noted that new nuclear nations may lack the resources and knowledge necessary to equip their nuclear arsenals with safety devices, survivability measures, and adequate command-and-control arrangements. Timely assistance from the United States could help to secure and protect nascent nuclear arsenals, thereby mitigating these problems.[5] But one barrier to a policy of direct technical assistance to new or aspiring proliferators has been a concern that it would violate the NPT's requirement that states not "assist, encourage, or induce any nonnuclear-weapon State to manufacture or otherwise acquire nuclear weapons." Providing technical assistance, the logic goes, could undermine the international nonproliferation regime.

For this reason, proliferation pessimists have been hesitant to advocate a policy of nuclear safety assistance, reasoning that it would further encourage the spread of nuclear weapons. In contrast, proliferation optimism suggests that we should consider replacing the doctrine of universal nonproliferation with a more nuanced approach that is designed to safely *manage* proliferation when it occurs.[6] If the spread of nuclear weapons would not necessarily be destabilizing, after all, then preventing proliferation to all states (rather than only to U.S. adversaries) is unnecessary; instead, U.S. foreign policy should focus on containing its risks.[7]

CONCLUSION

The historical data presented here suggest that nuclear weapons have had a sobering effect on international politics. They have bolstered stability by quelling conventional-arms races and by making wars less intense and less frequent. Although it is impossible to know what a world without nuclear weapons would have looked like in the decades following World War II, it is reasonable to conclude from these data that the existence of nuclear weapons has restrained some international conflicts and prevented others from igniting altogether. In contrast, despite a sizable number of "close calls" experienced by the United States and other nations, the absence of preventive, preemptive, and accidental nuclear attacks casts doubt on gloomy predictions about the consequences of proliferation.

The spread of nuclear weapons undoubtedly entails extraordinary risks. Nuclear weapons are the most horrific weapons humanity has ever known, and one of the foremost priorities of the United States should be to prevent them from ever being detonated by accident or in anger. But an accurate assessment of the risks of further proliferation requires that we acknowledge that nuclear weapons carry both costs and benefits to international stability. Weighing these costs and benefits, in turn, demands a sound empirical basis for evaluating the effects of nuclear weapons. If we are to make informed predictions about the nuclear future, we must first acknowledge the lessons of the past.

NOTES

1. States currently possessing nuclear weapons include the United States, Russia, Great Britain, France, China, Israel, India, Pakistan, and possibly North Korea. South Africa, Kazakhstan, Belarus, and Ukraine acquired and then relinquished them.
2. See Waltz's chapters in Sagan and Waltz 2003 for an in-depth discussion of these claims.

3. See Sagan and Pauly's section in this volume.

4. It should be noted that in his book, *The Limits of Safety* (1993, pp. 11–13), Sagan quite explicitly acknowledges the difficulty of evaluating the risk of an event that has never happened.

5. Indeed, shortly after the September 11, 2001, terrorist attacks, the United States reportedly offered technical nuclear assistance to Pakistan in an effort to prevent its nuclear weapons from falling into terrorist hands (Sanger and Broad 2007).

6. Elsewhere I have argued for precisely such a policy (Sechser 1998).

7. Universal nonproliferation may still be preferable, of course, if one believes that permitting some states to have nuclear weapons would undermine efforts to prevent U.S. adversaries from acquiring them.

military intervention and human rights

Is Foreign Military Intervention Justified by Widespread Human Rights Abuses?

YES: Jack Donnelly, *University of Denver*

NO: Doug Bandow, *The Cato Institute*

The issue of legitimizing military intervention has bedeviled the United Nations since its founding. Clear justification is required for the UN Security Council to authorize military intervention in a sovereign country. When the UN does attempt to provide legitimacy to an intervention in a member government's territory, however, it suffers both from the political difficulty of achieving consensus within the constraints of **veto powers** wielded by the **P5** (the five permanent members of the Security Council: the United States, Russia, France, China, and the United Kingdom) and from the lack of a standing army. Instead, it has to rely on contributions of troops and finances from member states. Over the past sixty years and more, Security Council principles for military intervention have been selectively applied, and the justification for intervention has evolved to fit the current political climate.

During the Cold War, interventions were undertaken primarily to resolve civil wars or to impose cease-fires under the overall rubric of peacekeeping. Most interventions in those years came at the request of states, and many either were vetoed or never came to a vote, because the United States and the Soviet Union both regarded them in light of support for their proxies in the Third World. Secretaries-general of the United Nations initiated interventions in Korea (1950–1953) and the Congo (1960–1964). Since the end of the Cold War, emphasis has shifted to two possible justifications for intervention: to offer humanitarian protection or to manage **failed states**.

Along with the war in the Balkans (1991–1995), the Rwandan **genocide** of 1994—and the UN's limited and delayed response to it—catalyzed the development of new norms for **humanitarian intervention**. The UN's 1992 *Agenda for Peace* tried to expand the definition of intervention and the conditions under which it was warranted to include failed states. The 2005 World Summit, enabled by United Nations Security Council (UNSC) Resolution 1674 of April 28, 2006, asserted the responsibility to protect populations from genocide, war crimes, ethnic cleansing, and **crimes against humanity**. There are strong legal norms in the **UN Charter** and in human rights treaties banning genocide and holding political leaders individually responsible for genocide. But the rules adopted so far have been aimed at enforcement after the fact, putting such criminals before tribunals or the **International Criminal Court**. As experience with humanitarian interventions grew over the 1990s, the UN learned that effective and lasting humanitarian protection required not just interventions to separate the parties and punish the guilty but also to transform the underlying conditions that caused distress (peacemaking). These policy lessons led to more complex peacekeeping missions as well as to greater reluctance on the part of many Security Council members to commit resources to interventions that were now understood to require lengthy and complex operations.

Recently, attention has shifted to failed states—cases of domestic collapse, wherein no one with authority can invite assistance or intervention. Failed states create political problems within the country, which collapses into a state of anarchy and civil **warlordism**, as well as problems for neighboring states, which have to face the prospects of receiving large numbers of refugees or repelling rebel forces that may seek to establish safe enclaves outside the failed state from which to launch their campaigns. In such instances, there is no legal authority able to ask for intervention, so the UN Security Council or the secretary-general must impose it. The first failed state to attract the UN's attention was Somalia (1991–1995, following the U.S. involvement there from 1988 to 1991). In 2011, *Foreign Policy* magazine estimated that there were seventy-two failed or close to failing states—largely countries located in Africa but also including Colombia, Haiti, the Dominican Republic, Iraq, Afghanistan, Bangladesh, and North Korea.[1]

Dealing with failed states involves a daunting array of responsibilities: recreating a working economy; combating poverty; disarming militias; providing food, education, and shelter; and hosting elections. In addition, intervention in such cases creates an ethical conundrum for the international community: how can they protect the rights of individuals in a failed state without violating the legal integrity of national sovereignty? Some scholars have argued that foreign intervention to deal with failed states or to punish genocidal leaders is a new stage of imperialism while others suggest that failed states carry no legal or moral authority and that individual rights trump sovereignty.

Still other observers have worried that humanitarian intervention can lead to a slippery slope of justifiable interventions. If it is acceptable to intervene to protect human rights and save lives, is it also permissible to invade a state to prevent or mitigate famine? How about to provide humanitarian assistance after a natural disaster when the state's government lacks the resources to do so? Intricate considerations such as these have made *ex ante* actions before intervention difficult to legitimize without a clear framework for intervention.

The following essays address this complex question, addressing international norms, international law, and questions of morality and ethics in their responses. Jack Donnelly offers a highly nuanced argument that, when the interventions are reserved for the purpose of addressing abuses banned by UN treaties, humanitarian intervention is consistent with broad international norms on human rights. He also points out the pragmatic justification for intervention: that political order is preferable to conditions of anarchy and civil war, such as those that now persist in Somalia and the Congo. Conversely, Doug Bandow questions the consistency with which the argument for intervention is made and cautions that it seldom achieves the intended purposes.

Discussion Questions

1. Most would agree that human rights violations do cause moral concern. Given that general consensus, why do you think nations do not intervene to stop such violations more often? Are there situations that would justify nonintervention? What are they?
2. The United Nations recognizes state sovereignty but also authorizes state interventions in some cases of humanitarian violations. Are these positions contradictory? Why or why not?
3. Are principles of nonintervention universal? What are some of the country-specific considerations that might shape the decision to intervene or not?
4. Jack Donnelly says that good things done for the wrong reasons may not be as justified as good things done for the right reasons. What does he mean? How does he explain this judgment? Do you agree?
5. What are the four standards that Donnelly says must be considered in regard to humanitarian intervention? Which does he think is most important? Do you agree?
6. Does Doug Bandow argue that humanitarian intervention is allowed by international law? What evidence does he give to prove his point?

NOTE

1. Failed States Interactive Grid, *The Fund for Peace.* http://www.fundfor peace.org/global/?q=fsi-grid2011

YES: Jack Donnelly, *University of Denver*

1. JUSTIFICATION

Justification is a complex and multifaceted exercise. At least four standards of evaluation are relevant to humanitarian military intervention: morality or justice (I will use these terms interchangeably), law, order, and politics.

There is little disagreement that at least some massive violent human rights violations, such as the genocide in Rwanda in 1994, provide a moral cause for military intervention. That is not, however, the only relevant standard of justification.

International society has a body of law that governs the behavior of states and other international actors. Particularly relevant is the principle of territorial state sovereignty: each state has exclusive jurisdiction over its territory and the activities that take place there. Massive human rights violations, which characteristically involve a state mistreating its own citizens on its own territory, seem on their face to be protected exercises of sovereignty.

States, however, in order to better realize their interests, regularly create legal obligations for themselves. For example, a military alliance may restrict a state's right to choose when, where, and for what purposes it will fight. Alliances, however, are an exercise of, not an infringement of, sovereignty.

In the case of human rights, there is an extensive body of law, rooted in the 1948 **Universal Declaration of Human Rights** and given binding legal form in two International Human Rights Covenants (adopted in 1966) and a number of single-issue treaties (most notably on racial discrimination, women's rights, torture, and rights of the child). States, by becoming parties to these treaties, accept obligations to protect and implement a wide range of internationally recognized human rights. Today, on average, 88 percent of the world's states are parties to these six treaties.[1]

This establishes a legal right of the international community and its members to be concerned with the human rights practices of states. State sovereignty, however, remains a powerful bar to action—especially military action—to implement and enforce those rights. The human rights practices of states are monitored through periodic reports to committees of experts and in various activities of the United Nations Human Rights Council. But these multilateral monitoring bodies have only the most limited powers to receive and pass judgment on complaints of violations from individual citizens. Furthermore, such judgments are not legally binding. (Nongovernmental organizations and foreign states also engage in extensive monitoring. They too, however, lack rights to implement or enforce internationally recognized human rights.)

We thus have a system of *national implementation of international human rights norms.*[2] States have retained for themselves sovereign authority to implement and enforce internationally recognized human rights on their own territories. When they violate their international human rights obligations, there is no agency or actor authorized to punish them or compel them to comply with their obligations. In the next section, I will argue that a genocide exception was created in the 1990s. The legal bar to the use of foreign military force to implement internationally recognized human rights, however, remains high. And considerations of order and politics suggest keeping it high.

International relations is a domain of anarchy in the literal sense of absence of hierarchical rule or a ruler. (The United Nations, for example, is not a world government but an organization whose members are sovereign states.) States thus regularly face potentially hostile neighbors as well as distant great powers, some of which have the interest and capability to intervene. Exclusive territorial jurisdiction helps to keep states out of each others' way in the absence of international government.

Order, we must remember, is a value, no less than (although different from) the values of morality and legality. The absence of higher ruling authority makes order an especially pressing concern in international relations. This creates a characteristic tension between the values of order and justice, with international law usually leaning more toward order.

In the case of armed humanitarian intervention, pursuing the just moral cause of intervening often would undermine the ordering (and legal) principles of sovereignty and nonintervention. In addition, both increased international disorder and disrespect for international law are likely to have serious antihumanitarian consequences. Thus states—which ordinarily are more interested in order than justice—tend to put law and order over morality in their decision making.

Morality, law, and order, as I have considered them here, operate at the level of the international system; they are practices of the society of states or the international community. States, however, also face national evaluation according to standards that I will call *political.* (We have no need here to consider the national dimensions of law, order, and morality.)

The leaders of states, by the nature of their office, are charged primarily with pursuing the *national* interest. States, however, may define their national interests to include alleviating international suffering. Many states, especially in the past quarter century, have indeed done that. But when faced with a conflict between these broader humanitarian interests and more particularistic interests, national leaders typically choose—and are usually expected by their citizens to choose—the narrower national interest.

States, in other words, frequently have not merely good but compelling foreign policy reasons not to intervene against gross and persistent systematic human rights violations. They may even have good reasons to intervene in ways that harm human rights. As a result, a surfeit of politically motivated *anti*humanitarian intervention has been at least as serious a moral problem as the shortage of genuinely humanitarian interventions. A strong principle of nonintervention thus may help to protect not only states but foreign citizens from self-interested intervention by the powerful.

Considering these conflicting standards, it is easy to see how the international community has come down generally on the side of nonintervention. Although neither uncontroversial nor unproblematic, a strong principle of nonintervention is almost universally endorsed by states for reasons of both national interest and international order. And many (if not most) individuals and nonstate groups agree that this is the least unappealing compromise. A strong principle of nonintervention is an unfortunate sacrifice of humanitarian ideals that helps to preserve international law and order and to protect states and people against armed states pursuing selfish national interests in the absence of international government.

2. THE GENOCIDE EXCEPTION

So far, we have not considered international rules on the use of force. The two central rules, laid out in the United Nations Charter, are that (1) only states (and the United Nations Security Council) may use force internationally and (2) such force may be used only in self-defense. This poses substantial additional constraints on armed humanitarian intervention.

The monopoly of states on the legitimate use of force is relatively uncontroversial. Allowing private groups such as multinational corporations or individuals to use force would be a recipe for not just disorder but disaster.

Restricting the use of force to self-defense is intrinsically attractive: it is the one case in which there is little controversy over its legitimacy. It also strongly supports the principle of nonintervention, both as a legal norm and as a principle of order, and is a notable normative constraint on self-interested political action.

Nonetheless, since the end of the Cold War, we have seen substantial movement toward legal recognition of a limited humanitarian exception. The moral basis for this exception is clear. The idea that force can be used only in *self*-defense is (morally) deeply problematic. In the right circumstances, most people would agree that, considering only morality or justice, some things in addition to self-defense—for example, dramatically reducing crushing poverty, eliminating severe and systematic gender discrimination, or stopping genocide—are worth fighting for. There has thus always been considerable moral disquiet with the international legal requirement that interested and capable actors stand idly by while foreigners suffer at the hands of their own government.

This requirement, however, began to change with the end of the Cold War. The cessation of bipolar superpower rivalry both removed external protection from many severely rights-abusive regimes and reduced (although did not eliminate) the likelihood of partisan abuse of a principle of humanitarian intervention. It also came at a time in which increasingly assertive international human rights policies were becoming norm among liberal democratic states. And the 1990s presented the international community with several prominent instances of genocidal conflicts, especially in Europe and Africa, where international action seemed increasingly problematic.

No explicit decision was taken to change the rules. Nonetheless, in the course of the 1990s, a limited legal exception allowing armed humanitarian intervention against genocide emerged. In Somalia and Bosnia, UN-authorized international military action produced significant (if limited) humanitarian benefits. In Rwanda, the failure of international action led to the (probably preventable) deaths of more than three-quarters of a million people. This quickly came to be understood as not merely a tragic but an avoidable failure. Thus when ethnic cleansing in Kosovo and genocidal violence in East Timor occurred in 1999, they were met with armed humanitarian action.

The Kosovo intervention was certainly problematic, as we will see in the next section. There was little international disagreement, however, that the Security Council acted within its legitimate authority in sending (primarily Australian) armed forces to stop the violence in East Timor and to manage its transition to independence. These instances of practice, which were widely seen as not merely legitimate but desirable, were central to establishing an international legal exception to the principle of nonintervention and the restriction of the legitimate use of force to self-defense.

This exception, however, applies only to genocide—which is defined in Article 2 of the 1948 Genocide Convention as actions "committed with intent to destroy, in whole or in part, a national, ethnical, racial or religious group, as such"—and comparable mass killing. There is no evidence of widespread support for military action against other kinds of human rights violations. Even massive repression does *not* (legally) justify international military action.

(Consider, for example, Robert Mugabe's Zimbabwe, North Korea, or, until recently, Myanmar.) Only the unusual death of a large number of people in a small place over a short time is widely accepted as legally justifying armed humanitarian action.

A limited genocide exception causes few problems of order. It may even increase order, as genocide typically leads to a disorderly flow of refugees across state borders and the risk of the spread of violence. A limited genocide exception also is relatively immune to partisan abuse. And it has few undesirable spillover effects on the basic principles of sovereignty and nonintervention.

Morally, of course, prioritizing genocide over other forms of suffering is problematic. (Compare, by analogy, the fact that malnutrition is a far more serious threat to the lives of many more people than famine, yet the international community today responds relatively effectively to famine but does a rather poor job in combating malnutrition.) But there is even a moral argument for a narrow genocide exception.

Self-determination can be seen as providing the moral basis for the rights of sovereignty and the correlative duties of nonintervention. It is impossible to imagine, however, that any free people would freely consent to a government that practices genocide. Genocide thus strips away the underlying moral basis of nonintervention.

Some other practices—slavery and imperialism come immediately to mind—may fall into this category. Most injustices, however, do not involve such an uncontroversial denial of the principle of self-determination. Therefore, there is a moral case—a controversial case to be sure, but a (not im)plausible one—to be made for something similar to the narrow genocide exception.

A narrow genocide exception to the principles of nonintervention and the restriction of the use of force to self-defense thus has come to seem like a reasonable way to balance the competing standards of justification. And powerful concerns about disorder and partisan abuse suggest that any additional exceptions should also be narrowly drawn.

3. AUTHORITY, INTENTIONS, CONSEQUENCES, AND MEANS

So far, we have considered only whether genocide is an appropriate occasion for armed international action. Having a just cause, however, is not enough to act justifiably, all things considered. A fully justified military action must also be undertaken by those with the authority to use force (domestically, the police may do different things than ordinary citizens), be done for the right reasons, and employ means that are appropriate in both quantity and kind.[3]

There is little controversy today that humanitarian military action by the Security Council is properly authorized. There is heated disagreement, however, about genuinely humanitarian action in the absence of Security Council authorization. Assessing such interventions requires drawing further distinctions concerning justification.

Most legal experts today agree that armed humanitarian action that is not authorized by the United Nations is illegal on its face. Nonetheless, there is also a widespread belief, which I endorse, that an unauthorized intervention may be excusable—(not un)justified, all things considered—if it is based on a just cause and carried out justly. Consider an analogy of a poor person stealing only what is necessary to feed his or her family.

Many saw the North Atlantic Treaty Organization (NATO) intervention in Kosovo in these terms. For example, the Independent International Commission on Kosovo described it as "illegal but legitimate."[4] Many responded similarly two decades earlier, when Tanzania invaded Uganda to depose Idi Amin (and then quickly withdrew). The underlying intuition is that good intentions, in certain stringently defined circumstances, are a valid excuse for *prima facie* impermissible actions.

The two-step nature of this evaluation process, however, must be emphasized. Armed humanitarian intervention not authorized by the Security Council is illegal. Thus, on its face and by this standard of evaluation, it is unjustified. The intervener, however, ought to be given the opportunity to rebut this presumption through appeals to other relevant standards. The burden of proof lies with those who commit a *prima facie* illegal act. Nonetheless, illegal behavior, even in domestic courts, may be excusable.

We also need to recognize the possibility of an international equivalent to "jury nullification," in which the interests of justice lead to setting aside an otherwise unquestioned legal rule. For example, many critics of international inaction against the genocide in Rwanda argued that when hundreds of thousands of lives could be saved by the judicious application of modest international legal force, "the law be damned." And when faced with what they saw as imminent genocide in Kosovo just five years later, the leaders of the United States and Britain, the principal proponents of NATO intervention, seem to have acted—at least in part—out of this understanding.

Humanitarian interests and motivations were clearly predominant in the decisions to intervene in Kosovo and East Timor. In East Timor, the international community backed a small, poor, and strategically insignificant former Portuguese colony against large, oil-rich, and strategically significant Indonesia. Often, however, humanitarian interventions involve more mixed motives. But even where self-interested motives prevail, considerations of consequences can establish a certain kind of justifiability.

I label such interventions (merely) tolerable. Consider, for example, India's intervention in East Pakistan in 1971 that helped to create Bangladesh. Although it stopped genocidal violence against Bengalis, which had forced some ten million to flee, India seemed much more concerned with weakening Pakistan, its principal enemy. Similarly, Vietnam's invasion of Cambodia in 1979, ending the **Khmer Rouge's** four-year reign of terror, seems to have been largely a geopolitical move with a very thin, and not very consistently pursued, humanitarian veneer.

Good things done for the wrong reason may not be as justified as good things done for the right reasons. Improper motives alone, however, do not make an action simply or completely unjustified, particularly when tens or hundreds of thousands of lives are saved. Intentions, consequences, authority, and just cause all need to be factored into a final judgment of justifiability.

Finally, fully justified action must be carried out with proper means. More particularly, the means used must be proportional to the ends pursued. Prohibited means must not be used. And the special immunities of civilians (noncombatants) must be respected.

A justified intervention must not cause more suffering than it alleviates. There must be a reasonable prospect that, with the actual means used, more suffering is likely to be eliminated than caused. Interveners are responsible for the predictable consequences of their actions, both negative and positive.

Proportionality focuses on the consequences of the means used. The prohibition of the use of certain means reflect a categorical substantive ("deontological") judgment. Poison gas, for example, cannot legitimately be used. Period. Soldiers who surrender must be treated according to the laws of war.

Noncombatant immunity is also a substantive principle of justice in war (although it also has an important consequential dimension). Military action must minimize damage to or suffering imposed on civilians. In fact, soldiers, because they are soldiers, are required to take some additional risks in order to minimize certain unintended but predictable injury to civilians.

For example, during the Kosovo campaign, bombing was carried out at an altitude above the reach of Serbian antiaircraft weapons, in order to minimize NATO casualties (out of fear of losing public support). This led in at least one instance to a civilian train being destroyed on a targeted bridge. Had the plane in question been flying lower, the pilot probably would have identified, and avoided destroying, the train. This is a striking example of a conflict between legal and moral standards requiring the protection of noncombatants and political standards that needed to be met in order to effectively initiate and maintain the intervention.

4. JUSTIFYING ARMED HUMANITARIAN INTERVENTION

The more one considers *justification*, the more complicated it becomes. Morality, law, order and politics, authority and means, and intentions and consequences are all centrally relevant. Few actual interventions, however, are unproblematic under all of these standards. And there simply is no agreement about which standard is "most important." Neither the law nor the national interest nor any other single consideration is "the" essential element of justifiability.

It would be unreasonable, however, to say that only interventions that fully meet all relevant standards of justification are justified. We live in a world of multiple competing values and standards that can only be resolved through acts of judgment, not appeal to lists of rules.

I have argued for giving considerable weight to considerations of order and law. Disorder may, all things considered, be worse than injustice. (Perhaps the only thing worse for human rights than an evil state is a failed state.) And justice that undermines order rarely is good for justice in the long run (unless that order is very deeply and systematically unjust).

In some severe cases, however, law and even order appropriately give way to the demands of justice. A limited humanitarian intervention exception for genocide allows us to respond to a severe injustice that undermines the moral rationale for sovereignty. It also is unlikely to increase—and may actually decrease—disorder. It therefore is not surprising that such an exception has become fairly well established in contemporary international law.

The special priority accorded to order arises from the absence of international government. The special priority accorded to law arises in part from its consensual nature. With few exceptions, international law binds only those who have directly consented to it directly (through a treaty) or indirectly (through the process of customary norm formation). Consensus hardly guarantees justice, especially when it is a "lowest common denominator" consensus. It is, however, an important protection against certain kinds of injustice rooted in partisan interests.

Law also merits special weight, because it is a domain where considerations of order, justice, power, and interest can be authoritatively adjudicated. Law frequently diverges from justice but rarely as much as partisan political self-interest. And when law and order are not equally distant from justice, law is more frequently the closer of the two.

Nonetheless, as I have suggested above, sometimes the right course of action, all things considered, is "law be damned"—especially when a major injustice can be prevented at little cost to order. And it must be emphasized that partial justification—excusable or tolerable intervention—is justification (of a sort).

Partially justified actions are precisely that: partially justified, not unjustified. And often, the most appropriate evaluation of armed humanitarian intervention, as with many other kinds of international acts, is that, all things considered, it is (not un)justified.

5. THE RESPONSIBILITY TO PROTECT

My argument for a limited right to intervene militarily against genocide and comparable humanitarian crises is a *long* way from a responsibility to protect. This idea has become a common theme in discussions of armed humanitarianism since the 2001 report by that name, issued by the International Commission on Intervention and State Sovereignty.[5] I want to conclude by arguing that a responsibility to protect can be justified only as an aspirational moral principle.

A responsibility to protect is just that: a responsibility, an obligation, a duty. There is no evidence, however, that states in fact acknowledge such a duty as a matter of either domestic or international law. Likewise, the practice of the UN Security Council shows no support for an obligation to protect the victims of genocide, as the continued suffering in Darfur tragically illustrates. A true responsibility to protect would also raise serious order problems, especially if the victims reside in states that are not failed or failing.

Further difficulties are posed by the idea of protection. Protect against what? A narrow answer raises serious problems of morally inappropriate selectivity. A broad answer poses serious conflicts with other no less important values. What is required for protection? Stopping the killing? Establishing a rights-protective regime? Both answers seem both right and wrong. There are also serious issues of cost.

A *right* to military intervention carries with it no obligation. Right-holders usually are free to choose not to exercise their rights. If one chooses to act, the right provides justification. A right to intervene, however, imposes no duty to intervene.

Nonetheless, advocacy of a *moral* responsibility to protect, understood as one set of claims that need to be balanced against competing moral, legal, order, and political claims, does push the Security Council and states (appropriately, in my view) toward exercising their right to humanitarian intervention more frequently than they might otherwise. Such a moral responsibility also can be seen as implicit in the basic framework of international human rights law.

As we noted above, states have created a system of national implementation of international human rights. Citizens are presumed to receive protection of their rights from "their own" government. This foundational legal fiction, however, becomes hopelessly implausible in the case of genocide. When this occurs, one can understand the international community as having a residual moral responsibility to protect.

Consider the analogy with refugee law. Those with a well-founded fear of persecution have a right to asylum. More precisely, they have a right not to be returned to "their own" country. In other words, when the assumption of state provision of human rights becomes perversely implausible, refugees have a claim—in this case, a legal claim—against other states and the international community.

Why not, then, recognize a legal right of victims of genocide to international protection? The principal reason is much higher costs. Few refugees with a well-founded fear of persecution are able to get to any particular asylum country. When they do, accommodating them usually imposes largely financial costs that are generally modest. In particular, receiving states are not required to risk the lives of their own citizens or bear the other costs of war. Furthermore, asylum in no way infringes sovereignty and any impact on order tends to be positive rather than negative.

Genocide thus provides a true dilemma. Given not simply the imperfections of the world of practice but also the competing values of justice, law, order, and politics, intervening on behalf of victims of genocide is almost always likely to be in some ways problematic. But so is *not* intervening.

Why, then, don't we pose the question as "Is *failure* to intervene militarily against widespread human rights abuses justified?" Because, for better or worse, sovereignty, nonintervention, and the restriction of force to self-defense have been accepted in international law and political practice as a baseline and starting point for discussion. The burden of proof lies with those who would infringe sovereignty, practice military intervention, or use force for reasons other than self-defense. As we have seen, though, this burden sometimes can be met, even in some cases of unauthorized intervention by individual states or groups of states.

6. DARFUR

Darfur, the western region of Sudan, was the most prominent case of international action against genocide in the first decade of the twenty-first century. Beginning in 2003, the central government, based in the largely Arab and Muslim north, carried out sustained and brutal military operations against the primarily non-Arab and non-Muslim residents of Darfur, who saw the Sudanese government as a largely external and oppressive force. Relying on local militias (*janjaweed*) backed by Sudanese air and logistical support, Sudan forced over 100,000 refugees to flee Darfur by the time the conflict began to receive significant international attention, early in 2004.

The Sudanese government pursued a strategy of what in Bosnia and Kosovo was called *ethnic cleansing.* A conscious effort seems to have been made both to limit the killing, which was aimed primarily at causing targeted populations to flee, and to engage diplomatically with critics in order to forestall an effective, full-scale multilateral intervention. But even this "restrained" violence forced more than two and a half million people—forty percent of the prewar population—to flee and killed perhaps a third of a million people (three-quarters of those deaths being from disease among refugees).

The international response was in many ways rapid and robust. In April 2004, Chad brokered a ceasefire, which African Union (AU) peacekeepers began monitoring in August 2004. The following month, the Security Council condemned the government for its actions in Darfur. In 2005, the AU peacekeeping force was expanded to almost 7,000 troops. In August 2006, the Security Council authorized a force of over 17,000 peacekeepers. Numerous efforts at cease-fires and final resolution were undertaken by both bilateral and multilateral actors inside and outside of the region, including (prominently) the United States. A major nongovernmental organization response mobilized substantial pressure both on Sudan and especially on Western governments. Charges were even brought in the International Criminal Court against leaders of the violence, including the sitting president of Sudan, Omar al-Bashir. And a new, more promising peace agreement was signed by all the major parties in Doha, Qatar in July 2011.

Compared to Kosovo and East Timor, though, these responses were somewhat mild and noticeably less successful. Genocidal violence continued for more than half a decade. And as I write this in early 2012, it is by no means certain that the conflict is finally over.

Part of the explanation lies in the distraction of the United States in wars in Afghanistan and Iraq—and the unwillingness or inability of any other state to play a leading role in a more robust response. China and Russia were unwilling to allow armed action by the Security Council; and support for Sudan within the Arab League undermined regional efforts. But even had there been the political will, more forceful action would have been extremely difficult. Darfur is a huge area (more than 190,000 square miles; roughly the size of Spain) with primitive infrastructure. The substantial majority of the population lived in widely scattered villages in a flat, semiarid terrain. A large and difficult ground operation thus would have been required to provide protection. (A small, lightly armed force, such as would have made such a huge difference in Rwanda, could not provide protection against mobile militias backed by air support.)

Furthermore, the government in Khartoum was an astute and effective opponent. It appears to have carefully studied previous interventions. And it had a clear appreciation of the strengths of its position. Khartoum thus calibrated its actions, both internally and externally, to allow it to continue the ethnic cleansing of Darfur. It had the oil resources to support such policies both internally and externally. It brooked no opposition to its rule, which even in the north of the country was highly repressive (although much less violent). It did not care much what the rest of the world thought of its actions. It needed nothing from outside (other than to sell its oil—which proved no problem). And it pursued its policies with considerable skill.

In other words, Sudan shows that a relatively effective and committed government can largely flout the international community, so long as it is willing to inflict sufficient suffering on "its" people. North Korea, Burma, and Zimbabwe present different variants of this pattern—which has no connection at all with genocides in "failed" states such as Somalia and Congo. Politically possible actions simply were inadequate to stop the killing.

But even in Darfur, the international response had a limited positive impact. The number of people directly killed numbered "only" several tens of thousands. Horrible as that figure is, it almost certainly would have been much higher had the international community not been watching carefully. And if the Doha agreement proves durable and effective, the conflict will have ended with the government failing to achieve many of its objectives—in significant measure because the international community, even though unable to stop the violence, would not allow it to succeed.

Darfur has been, at best, a tragically limited success for international humanitarian action. National and international politics made armed humanitarian intervention impossible. But the transformed normative and legal environment made inaction equally impossible. And, for all its limitations, international action in Darfur has saved the lives of tens of thousands, and probably hundreds of thousands, of innocent civilians.

7. CONCLUSION

A limited right to humanitarian intervention against genocide is a good thing. So is a more frequent and forceful exercise of that right, especially by the Security Council. We must be careful, however, not to confuse the exception with the rule. Not all widespread human rights abuses justify armed humanitarian intervention. And while lamenting the injustices that are tolerated out of considerations of law, order, and politics, we must remember that these values too are important and deserving of respect.[6]

NOTES

1. These and other treaties can be found at http://www2.ohchr.org/english/law/; up-to-date data on ratification can be found at treaties.un.org/Pages/Treaties.aspx?id=4
2. For introductory overviews of the international human rights machinery, see (Forsythe 2012, ch. 3) and (Donnelly 2013, ch. 5). Different procedures exist regionally, but only in Europe are they significantly stronger. See (Forsythe 2012, ch. 5) and (Donnelly 2013, ch. 6).
3. These criteria—of just cause, right intention, authorization, and just means—are rooted in the Christian tradition of just way thinking. Thomas Aquinas provides a succinct classic expression in *Article 1 of the Second Part of the Second Part [sic] of the Summa Theologica*, available online at http://www.ccel.org/a/aquinas/summa/SS/SS040.html#SSQ40OUTP1. For a contemporary secular updating of this body of thought, with extensive historical applications to hard cases, see (Walzer 1977), chapter 6, which explicitly addresses issues of humanitarian intervention.
4. http://sitemaker.umich.edu/drwcasebook/files/the_kosovo_report_and_update.pdf
5. http://www.iciss.ca/pdf/Commission-Report.pdf
6. Two good book-length introductions to humanitarian intervention, which provide good starting points for those interested in reading further, are (Hehir 2010) and (Weiss 2012).

NO: Doug Bandow, *The Cato Institute*

Nations go to war for a variety of reasons. Many conflicts reflect simple greed and avarice or national ego. Sometimes vital necessity is claimed—most obviously, self-defense. Today's wars, at least those initiated by America, are increasingly justified as humanitarian. Although very different in their details, Bosnia, Kosovo, Iraq, and Libya all were sold by U.S. political leaders as saving lives and promoting human rights and democracy.

Yet hard experience demonstrates that war is a dubious humanitarian tool. There are few causes more appealing than helping the helpless, but loosing the dogs of war is more likely to do harm than good, setting off a cascade of always expensive and often deadly unintended consequences. Comparing moral evils can be difficult, but the U.S. government bears responsibility for harms that result from its actions, as in Iraq.

U.S. foreign policy always has had a moral component. Even as they were killing Native Americans, Mexicans, and Filipinos in aggressive campaigns, the early Americans claimed to occupy the moral high ground. The U.S. justified war as achieving manifest destiny, vindicating the rights of wronged American citizens, Christianizing savages, overthrowing tyrants, and spreading liberty. Still, most of Washington's early wars arguably advanced one U.S. national interest or another, even if they were of the American nation state rather than of the American people. And Washington's military reach remained limited. The U.S. did not attempt to reorder countries and societies throughout Africa, Asia, Europe, and the Middle East.

That changed under Woodrow Wilson, who became the great proponent of war to spread democracy and even end war. He long was a liberal icon, criticized by conservatives for his disregard of U.S. interests and international realities. His counterproductive decision to enter World War I and egregious bungling at the Versailles peace conference created popular disillusionment in the U.S.; the new international order that he helped create led directly to World War II, worse slaughter, and the triumph of totalitarian communism.

In the latter conflict, there were heavy moral overtones from the crusade against Nazism and Japanese militarism. Nevertheless, that fight, along with the Korean War and Vietnam War in the following decades, was seen as essentially defensive. Only with the collapse of the Soviet Union did Washington feel free to undertake wars of choice for less than important, let alone vital, reasons.

The GOP initially was skeptical of humanitarian war making, such as when President Bill Clinton initiated the bombing of Yugoslavia, a small state that had threatened neither the U.S. nor any of its allies. The regime of Slobodan Milosevic may have been thuggish, but it was not dangerous to anyone but those who were in—or were attempting to secede from—Yugoslavia. The Clinton administration appeared to support military action although it advanced no significant U.S. security interest. Michael Mandelbaum of the School of Advanced International Studies (SAIS) talked of "foreign policy as social work,"[1] which reflected a stream of liberal thought that advocated war as a means to achieve progressive ends—in this case, ending Belgrade's brutal anti-insurgency campaign and ultimately creating a new ethnic-Albanian state. Congressional Democrats who once inveighed against Republican presidential war making endorsed Democratic presidential war making.

Although some Republicans, such as Sen. John McCain (R-Ariz.)—perhaps the Senate's leading militarist—supported the administration, then-House Majority Leader Tom Delay (R-TX) famously called Kosovo "Bill Clinton's war."[2] The Republican-dominated Congress refused to declare war or otherwise back the administration's efforts.

In 2003, however, President Bush, with congressional Republicans acting as a Greek chorus, dressed himself in full warrior garb. If you didn't believe that Saddam Hussein was more dangerous than Hitler and armed with nuclear weapons, unmanned aerial vehicles capable of hitting America, and massive stocks of biological weapons, no problem: it was America's duty to take out Hussein because he was a killer. Indeed, once it became evident that Iraq had possessed no weapons of mass destruction and had posed no threat to America, humanitarianism became the chief ex post facto justification for the conflict as the occupation descended into debacle.

The humanitarian sincerity of the president and his Republican supporters was hard to credit. After all, there were many ugly regimes around the world. Republicans hadn't seemed terribly concerned about mass slaughter in Rwanda, bloody civil war in Liberia, bitter Kurdish resistance in Turkey, years of conflict in Sudan, horrific civil war and international war killing millions in the Congo, large-scale murder and imprisonment in North Korea, decades of brutal repression in Burma, or a host of other conflicts. In these cases, the GOP's passion for liberating the helpless and dying was largely absent.

In fact, at the time Washington embarked upon the Iraq war, America's ally, Saudi Arabia, was probably killing as many people as was Iraq. But the ruling Saudis were routinely feted in Washington, including at President Bush's Texas ranch.

Even the commitment to safeguarding Iraqis was well-concealed before 9/11. Had the administration been focused on saving Iraqi lives, the president should have asked the Pentagon to begin drafting war plans after he took the oath of office on January 20, 2001. After all, lives were at stake: if the president believed the U.S. had to go to war to save Iraqis, why did he wait more than two years to liberate them?

The only logical conclusion is that administration officials weren't particularly interested in suffering Iraqis and that humanitarianism was primarily a politically popular gloss for a war that the president was determined to undertake for other reasons. Finding an alternative justification was particularly important when it became evident that Hussein had no weapons of mass destruction (WMDs).

Still, rank hypocrisy does not necessarily make the argument illegitimate. Hussein was a tyrant; Human Rights Watch figured between 250,000 and 290,000 people died under his regime.[3] He also started two wars—though, frankly, few Americans shed many tears for his first victim, Islamist Iran; and the Reagan administration, represented by special envoy (and future George W. Bush administration Defense Secretary) Donald Rumsfeld, avidly aided Hussein in that conflict.

Yet humanitarian intervention traditionally has been envisioned as stopping ongoing genocide or at least mass slaughter. In March 2003, Hussein was oppressing his people but not killing huge numbers of them. One can argue that the West should have previously stopped him from cracking down on the

Kurds, crushing the Shiite insurgency, and embarking upon other murderous expeditions. But those campaigns were long over and the resulting mass graves were long overgrown. However attractive the prospect of bringing him to justice, doing so would have been a dubious ground for going to war.

Although Barack Obama criticized the Iraq war, he appeared to sympathize with the idea of coercive humanitarianism when he proposed an extensive democracy-promotion program and advocated concerted action in humanitarian crises, such as Darfur, Sudan. As president, he unleashed bombers and drones on Libya and entertained arguments for intervening in Syria. His secretary of state, Hillary Clinton, who carried out the forgoing policies, was a strong proponent of attacking Yugoslavia as First Lady. Before being nominated as United Nations Ambassador, Susan Rice advocated action to end the "human devastation" in Darfur.

In short, humanitarian intervention seems to have become a bipartisan mistake.

Killing and destroying for charitable ends might seem attractive in theory, but going to war is deadly, expensive, and risky—usually far more so than expected at the start, as in Iraq's case. Good intentions are not enough when it comes to war. The presumption always should be against military action.

As a matter of principle, American resources should not be spent and American lives should not be risked unless doing so advances a fundamental interest of the American polity, including those serving in the military. War inherently conflicts with constitutional governance and individual rights.

Indeed, it is hard to imagine how a free society could long survive at home if the government pursued an unabashedly imperialist policy abroad, even in the name of liberal objectives. Sacrificed are human life and dignity, individual liberty, economic prosperity, limited government, constitutional stability, and republican government. As social commentator Randolph Bourne pointed out and Robert Higgs documented so well in *Crisis and Leviathan*, war is the health of the state. War is the most important excuse used by politicians to conscript the young, restrict civil liberties, punish free speech, limit public disclosure, expand government secrecy, raise taxes, expand government spending, regulate economic activity, limit democratic debate, and curtail the Constitution.

Going to war for reasons unrelated to America's interests also conflicts with the U.S. government's responsibility to the American people. The lives of Americans are of no greater moral value than those of other people. However, Washington is directly responsible to its own citizens: they fund its operations, man its military, are accountable for its actions, and expect its protection. However, war puts them at risk. Despite the promises of politicians, war inevitably costs lives and money. These days, the dangers of intervening often come home. For instance, officious and violent foreign intervention is the most important cause of terrorism, which typically reflects an attempt by a weaker power to achieve political ends, usually in response to military or political dictates. (This is an explanation, not justification, of what remains a horrid tactic.)

The U.S. government's responsibility to guard the interests of Americans includes the lives of America's fighting men and women. They are not pawns to be sacrificed in a global chess game, and their lives should not be forfeit when policymakers, especially those happily insulated from the rigors and risks of combat, imagine a glorious crusade involving objectives largely irrelevant to the interests of the Americans whose protection is the fundamental objective of government.

It might be extreme to contend that one American life is too many to sacrifice, no matter how many other lives would be saved. Surely, however, the risk of even one death requires that decisions involving war be made seriously, not frivolously, and that the costs and risks to Americans be weighed very heavily. It is not right, morally or practically, to turn 18-year-old U.S. military personnel into guardians of distant outposts in a new global empire, even if such an enterprise is advanced in glowing moral terms.

Expecting others to make such sacrifices is particularly dubious, given how rarely humanitarian intervention works as planned. The justification for humanitarian intervention is fundamentally utilitarian. More people will live than die as a result. Given the uncertainties of war, however, the result of no conflict is ever certain. This is why few people believe America should have attacked Nazi Germany before World War II or either the Soviet Union or the People's Republic of China during the Cold War. There were many lives to be saved, many more than were at stake in Iraq or most any other secondary conflict in this or the last century. But the potentially catastrophic consequences of another global conflict were too great to risk.

Humanitarian intervention is most commonly advocated for regimes with little or no serious military capability. Targets are usually despotic but decrepit Third World dictatorships, weak governments wracked by internal conflict, or failed states with a disorganized or absent state—such as Haiti, Libya, or Somalia. Even former Warsaw Pact member Yugoslavia could offer only minimal resistance in 1999 against the world's greatest military alliance.

Still, the utilitarian calculus remains uncomfortable even then. Some people who otherwise would live—American soldiers, coalition forces, enemy combatants, foreign civilians—will die. Are their deaths okay because some others will live?

At the same time, many supposed benefits of war prove evanescent at best. Wars of choice have been common in U.S. and world history. In most cases, even the winners suffered greatly, with any gains far overshadowed by losses and the causes of new conflicts sown amid the wreckage left by old ones.

This should come as no surprise: no matter how rosy the scenario painted by war advocates, social engineering internationally is far more difficult than social engineering domestically. It is hard enough to manipulate people within a single society; it is far more difficult to reach across international, cultural, historic, ethnic, religious, and social lines to transform people.

Even against weak powers, the U.S. can rarely simply intervene and leave. Nation building becomes an inevitable ancillary duty of humanitarian war making. Kosovo has been one tragic example: the ethnic Albanian majority engaged in two episodes of ethnic cleansing under *allied* occupation and has created what is widely viewed as the "black hole" of Europe, a fount of crime and even terrorism.

But, for a moment, assume that humanitarian intervention is justified so long as more are saved than killed (or substantially more, anyway). That is the traditional calculus for humanitarian intervention: strong states have an obligation to intervene to prevent genocide (at least) and other forms of mass murder (perhaps). The "Responsibility to Protect" doctrine, recently promoted by the United Nations, lowered the standard but nevertheless promoted limited rather than unlimited intervention. Indeed, such a doctrine could hardly apply to every badly managed state in which hundreds or thousands of people were murdered by, with the acquiescence of, or due to the incompetence of, the governing authorities. Otherwise, there are scores of nations that at one point or another might thereby qualify, even some significant powers—consider Russia in Chechnya or Turkey in Kurdistan.

More recently, however, almost any serious criterion appears to have disappeared. The humanitarian underpinnings of allied intervention in Libya were nonexistent. There was no mass murder, let alone genocide. Instead, Libyans were dying in the hundreds in the sort of combat common to a low-grade, low-tech civil war. Moammar Qaddafi had engaged in no orgy of slaughter in any of the cities that he retook, and his much-criticized florid rhetoric was directed against armed fighters, not civilians, in Benghazi. The allies appeared to use humanitarianism as a convenient gloss to push a cheap campaign for regime change, which ended up costing tens of thousands Libyan lives because it dragged on for months.

Intervention in Kosovo looked equally cynical. A couple of thousand people died in a typically brutal guerrilla campaign before allied intervention. A U.S. diplomat even called the Kosovo Liberation Army "terrorist"[4] (although the State Department explicitly avoided such a depiction) before Washington decided that Slobodan Milosevic was the latest reincarnation of Hitler. Allied intervention—including military forces from Turkey, which killed thousands while suppressing Kurdish insurgents—triggered the mass expulsion of ethnic Albanians and killed a few hundred or thousand Serb civilians, followed by ethnic cleansing of Serbs.

Far worse were the consequences of Iraq. Never mind the supposed good intentions and manifold might-have-beens. The Iraq conflict damaged fundamental American security interests—Washington's most basic duty to the American people—by creating new grievances, encouraging more terrorism, weakening U.S. military forces, undermining America's reputation, discouraging allied cooperation, and wasting financial resources. Ironically, the country most empowered by the Iraq invasion was Iran, a repressive state thought to be interested in developing nuclear weapons.

The war's humanitarian impact also was negative. Tens or hundreds of thousands of Iraqis died who would have lived had the U.S. not invaded. What moral calculus could justify that bloody human trade-off?

Indeed, the more one looks at Iraq, the more one doubts the moral justification of aggressive war. For an argument that is largely utilitarian, the place to start is American casualties. The 4,700 deaths and more than 30,000 wounded are a sobering reminder of the cost of war. (Thankfully, medical and technological advances lowered mortality rates in Iraq, though many survivors have lost limbs or suffered grievous head injuries.) The U.S. government had a direct obligation to these soldiers, a duty not changed by the fact that they volunteered for military service. Their lives should have been risked for the defense of their own community, not to crusade on behalf of others.

But the number of dead Iraqis raises even more profound doubts as to the humanitarian justification of the conflict and others allegedly waged on behalf of the oppressed. No one knows for sure how many Iraqis died—and continue to die—but the toll is extraordinary. Unfortunately, in early 2012, after America's withdrawal, the trend lines were moving in the wrong direction, with violence rising.

President George W. Bush once acknowledged 30,000 Iraqi dead, a significant admission for someone who steadfastly avoided mentioning the slightest hint of bad news in his war of choice. Early in the occupation, the Pentagon suggested civilian death tolls of 50,000 and 60,000. During the worst of the violence, the Iraqi Health Ministry figured 150,000 dead civilians. The *Washington Times*, which consistently editorialized in favor of the war, cited the estimate of 128,000 dead between the war's start and July 2005 from the Iraqi group, Iraqiyun. Extrapolated to later in the decade, noted the *Times*: "the figure would be in the high 100,000s or low 200,000s."[5]

The website *Iraq Body Count* (IBC) attempts to track reported deaths. It estimates between 106,000 and 116,000, with possibly another 14,000 derived from an analysis of the WikiLeaks disclosures. But since many deaths likely go unreported, IBC has acknowledged that doubling the public number may offer a more accurate figure for total casualties. A study out of the Johns Hopkins Bloomberg School of Health using survey techniques figured the number of additional deaths at 654,000; a survey by the Opinion Research Business put the likely toll at about one million.[6] (The methodologies for the latter two have been sharply criticized.)

Whatever the exact toll, most of the additional deaths resulted from the U.S. invasion. American forces obviously did not kill most of those people directly. However, the U.S.-led coalition broke Iraqi society, loosing the forces of death. Washington ripped away the thin veneer of order that gave Iraqis a sense of security, if not liberty, in Hussein's Iraq. The result was an orgy of murderous kidnappings, revenge killings, incidental wounding from military actions and errant bombings, and other deaths. Iraqis no longer risked death from resisting the regime but faced a much greater possibility of death from merely going about their normal lives. Family, community, civic, and political life became difficult, if not impossible.

Not only notable politicians risked death. Journalists, barbers, religious minorities, and even garbage collectors were regularly killed. (The latter were targeted by insurgents seeking to prevent the discovery of explosives hidden in the trash.) Businesspeople and bureaucrats alike were kidnapped and held for ransom; Shi'a and Sunni were killed because they were Shi'a and Sunni. Nor was it enough to murder: many bodies were found with evidence of torture.

The destruction of the economic and social infrastructure that remained after a decade of sanctions caused more hardship. The lack of stable services can kill. The Johns Hopkins study observed: "Aside from violence, insufficient water supplies, nonfunctional sewerage, and restricted electricity supply also create health hazards. A deteriorating health service with insecure access and the flight of health professionals adds further risks."[7]

Many Iraqis fled the bloody chaos. Upwards of four million, including much of Iraq's historic Christian population, gave up their homes. Many of the latter went to Syria, where they now fear the potential of upheaval in another once-reasonably-stable secular dictatorship.

When they fight, the U.S. and Europeans do attempt to minimize civilian casualties. Still, civilian deaths are inevitable, and Washington cannot escape responsibility for them. The problem continues in Afghanistan. Cars filled with civilians speeding towards military checkpoints are riddled with bullets. While commanding U.S. forces in Afghanistan, General Stanley McChrystal admitted,

"We've shot an amazing number of people and *killed* a number and, to my knowledge, none has proven to have been a real threat to the force."[8] Aerial bombing raids sometimes still fail to distinguish between insurgent and civilian—or Pakistanis across the ill-defined border.

The problem also was evident even in Libya, where allied military action was much more limited. Yet the United Nations has complained that the North Atlantic Treaty Organization (NATO) refused to investigate air attacks that killed civilians.

Moreover, if Washington intervenes, it is ultimately responsible for the actions of the local governments that it supports and especially those that it creates. Iraq again offers a sobering lesson. The problem is not that Prime Minister Nuri al-Maliki's administration is imperfect. The problem is that Maliki may be turning into an authoritarian, sort of a housebroken Saddam Hussein. Maliki's respect for parliamentary process appears modest at best. He attempted to arrest the country's Sunni vice president based on testimony that may have been procured by torture. He used the highly sectarian security forces for political gain. His government arrested critical journalists and violently suppressed public protests. Although overall violence is well below its peak during the U.S. occupation, it remains higher than before the war. And smoldering resentment among the minority Sunnis could trigger a new round of sectarian violence.

That the U.S. wanted none of this matters not. It was entirely predictable and, indeed, was predicted by many analysts. But for the invasion, none of the violence would have occurred. But for the blundering afterwards, the violence would not have been as great. The administration's war of choice pushed Iraq off a cliff into an abyss.

Most of Washington's other supposedly humanitarian interventions have had dubious results. U.S. bombing in Bosnia helped end the conflict but forced three warring groups, all of which had committed atrocities, to remain together in an artificial state that remains widely hated. In Kosovo, Washington empowered the ethnic Albanians who murdered and ethnically cleansed Serbs, Roma, and Jews and created a quasi-gangster state. In Libya, armed factions wreaked revenge on those associated with or were thought to support the Qaddafi regime and violently struggled for power afterwards. The victorious rebels included both Islamists and former fighters with al-Qaeda (Iraq).

David Rieff, once a strong supporter of humanitarian intervention, was sobered by the results in Rwanda as well as Kosovo. While in both cases the victors were not as bad as those they replaced, the results were far more mixed than enthusiasts for war typically admit with war crimes, murder, repression, and other human rights abuses. Such results are particularly disappointing when they result from military intervention that is otherwise unjustified. As noted earlier, Iraq was even worse.

Perhaps the most fundamental question posed by allegedly humanitarian intervention is who decides? After spending years making sunny predictions, President Bush acknowledged: "I know that a lot of innocent people have died and it troubles me and grieves me."[9] But he ignored his role in bringing about the deaths. When confronted with the Johns Hopkins study, President Bush dismissed its findings and added: "I applaud the Iraqis for their courage in the face of violence. I am, you know, amazed that this is a society which so wants to be free that they're willing to . . . you know, that there's a level of violence that they tolerate."[10]

Yet no Iraqi—except, perhaps, Ahmed Chalabi and other exiles hoping to take power while riding on American tanks after the latter disposed of Hussein—had any role in shaping American policy. With some asperity, analyst Ximena Ortiz observed in the *National Interest*:[11]

> The President, in referring to a war he launched, is marveling at the Iraqi society's willingness to tolerate the violence he has in effect brought to their country—*willingness* and *tolerate* of course being the operative words. Perhaps he should next wonder why they don't ask for cake. The breadth of his misunderstanding and naivety is simply astounding.

In some swerve of logic, Bush has decided for the Iraqis that they see the death of, say, their child or children, husband, wife, the descent of their entire country into chaos and hell—all worth it for the sake of what Bush deems to be freedom. It should go without saying that the president's conclusion begs a question: what choice do the Iraqis have? Does the president really believe that, given such a choice, the Iraqis would choose ruinous war in exchange for his own vision of freedom?

In retrospect, one wonders how many Iraqis who were killed or maimed, or who lost loved ones or friends, would view their liberation as "worth it." Some extraordinary people might consider freedom to be a prize for which no sacrifice is too high, but they are likely to be few indeed—especially since liberty may eventually have come anyway, just not so quickly.

Some larger number of Iraqis might have been prospectively willing to take the risk, at least, if they thought the odds of success to be reasonable. Alas, the last nine years have demonstrated that despite the fantasizing that passed for planning in the Bush administration, the odds of creating a liberal, democratic state in Iraq always were long.

More importantly, though, no one ever asked the Iraqis what they desired. A handful of officials in Washington had a vision and bloodily imposed it on 26 million people half a world away. The goodness of Washington's intentions doesn't matter. The war with Iraq was not humanitarian.

Americans should always treat war as a last resort rather than a first choice. War still might sometimes become an ugly necessity. But it cannot be justified on humanitarian grounds.

No one can, or should, feel comfortable standing by in the face of oppression and murder in other lands. But humanitarian intervention inevitably fails the tests of both morality and practicality. Some wars may result in some good, but military action is not an appropriate tool to try to promote good. In practice, humanitarian intervention just isn't humanitarian.

NOTES

1. Michael Mandelbaum, "Foreign Policy as Social Work" *Foreign Affairs* January/February 1996.
2. Doug Bandow, "The Painful Death of Humanitarian Intervention," *Antiwar.com* November 4, 2006. Available at http://original.antiwar.com/doug-bandow/2006/11/03/the-painful-death-of-humanitarian-intervention/
3. Shaun Waterman, "Disputed Iraqi Bodycount," *Spacewar.com*, October 23, 2006. Available at http://www.spacewar.com/reports/Disputed_Iraqi_Bodycount_999.html
4. http://rpc.senate.gov/releases/1999/fr033199.htm
5. http://www.washingtonpost.com/wp-dyn/content/article/2006/10/10/AR2006101001442.html; For general surveys of Iraqi casualties, see Les Roberts, Riyadh Lafta, Richard Garfield, Jamal Khudhairi, and Gilbert Burnham, "Mortality before and after the 2003 Invasion of Iraq: Cluster Sample Survey," *The Lancet* 364, no. 9448 (November 20, 200): 1857–1864. See also Gilbert Burnham, Riyadh Lafta, Shannon Doocy, and Les Roberts "Mortality after the 2003 Invasion of Iraq: A Cross-Sectional Cluster Sample Survey," *The Lancet* 268, no. 9545 (October 11, 2006): 1421–1428.
6. http://www.jhsph.edu/news/news-releases/2009/iraq_review.html
7. http://www.jhsph.edu/news/news-releases/2009/iraq_review.html
8. Stanley McChrystal, "We've Shot 'an Amazing Number' of Innocent Afghans" *Huffington Post*, June 2, 2010. Available at http://www.huffingtonpost.com/2010/04/02/mcchrystal-weve-shot-an-a_n_523749.html
9. http://www.youtube.com/watch?v=GF6hYsMsC1o
10. Ibid.
11. Ximena Ortiz, "Obama's Speech," *The National Interest*, June 4, 2009.

maritime security

Does Controlling Piracy and Other Criminal Activities Require Systematic State Interventions?

YES: Scott McKenzie, *World Affairs Council of New Orleans*

NO: Karl T. Muth, *London School of Economics and Political Science*

History has witnessed all manner of piracy, from medieval Vikings to the Barbary pirates off North Africa to the infamous Blackbeard in the Caribbean. Today, piracy at sea is a growing business involving far more actors than historical images or the pirates commonly pictured in open air boats off the Somalian coast, now one of the most dangerous shipping lanes in the world. A long chain of financiers, enablers (e.g., government officials), land- and marine-based support, detention facilities, and ransom negotiators undergird a business that relies on financial rewards that far exceed wages that pirates could expect to receive through legal employment. Far from ragtag groups that prey on unsuspecting tourists on pleasure boats, modern piracy is a highly organized business threatening high-valued targets like oil tankers and container ships. Increased trade has enhanced opportunities for piracy, and the threat is global, reaching from South China and the Indian Ocean through West Africa, the Caribbean, and South America. Geopolicity estimates that in 2010, the cost to the international community from piracy was $4.9–8.3 billion, an amount expected to more than double over the next four years.[1]

Overall, piracy is an expanding problem, with one year's reduction in East African attacks offset by increases elsewhere (and likely increases in 2011 in East Africa as well). As Figure 1 (p. 216) shows, piracy incidents have increased considerably in nearly all regions of the world, and an

Yearly Piracy Incidents since 1984

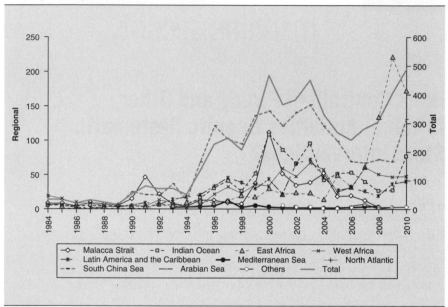

Source: International Maritime Organization, *Reports on Acts of Piracy and Armed Robbery Against Ships, Annual Report 2010.* April, 2011.

overall dip in the last decade (mid-2000's) was replaced by strong increases beginning in 2007.

Besides evasive maneuvers that individual ships may take—speed being among the most effective—avoiding capture increasingly involves improved training and awareness and hiring onboard security, though that is expensive. These measures have met with some success, such as the reduced number of successful piracy attacks in Somali waters from 2009 to 2010. However, individual shipping lines/owners recognize that coordinated efforts are essential to avoiding and repelling attacks, which entail sharing information about the location and nature of attacks and coordinating responses. Warships from the European Union, United States, China, and elsewhere patrol the Gulf of Aden, yet pirates simply move to other, less-patrolled regions. Some pirates seek cargo while others rely on kidnapping for ransom money. And while attacks off the Somali coast are explained by "supply side" factors such as political instability, attacks in West Africa, where governments such as Ghana are relatively prosperous and stable, are explained more by demand for the region's oil. Piracy is elusive, flexible, and well organized.

Modern pirates often use small boats supplied by "motherships" nearby at sea to attack large targets with small crews, often armed with automatic weapons and rocket-propelled grenades (RPGs). While most piracy results in ransoms paid and hostages released, in some cases, hostages are beaten and shot. The typical pattern is that the ship is seized, followed by weeks of negotiations between pirate negotiators and consultants and insurance companies. For a relatively small "investment" of tens of thousands of dollars, pirates can command $2–10 million or more for a vessel, particularly large oil tankers. The cash is air-dropped in large plastic containers in the ocean where it is counted—it can take all day—and then divided amongst the maritime pirates and the ground crew, with the bulk of it to bosses, investors, and sometimes government officials. Modern piracy is a business.

The challenges in meeting this problem are significant. First, the economic incentives for piracy are substantial, so apprehending pirates will likely encourage others with limited employment opportunities seeking relative riches. In one example, an estimated investment of $50,000 netted pirates $13.5 million after holding the oil tanker *Irene SL* for 58 days, a return of over 26 thousand percent.[2] While many hijackings fail, success rates over the past five years range from 17 to 45 percent.[3] Second, the vast majority of piracy raids occur in international waters, where national laws are replaced with the concept of "universal jurisdiction," allowing states to punish piracy as an "enemy of mankind." Nongovernmental interventions, such as information coordination and dissemination through the Piracy Reporting Center in Malaysia, assist by reporting pirate attacks and alerting local law enforcement officials combatting piracy. The United Nations facilitated the development of the Contact Group on Piracy off the Coast of Somalia in early 2009 to coordinate organizational and state responses to piracy in the region. Despite significant numbers of arrests and prison terms, pirate attacks continue to increase.

An important issue is whether systematic state interventions are necessary to effectively address the problem. Scott McKenzie, of the World Affairs Council of New Orleans, argues that ad hoc state intervention has been ineffective and that combatting piracy requires increased state coordination efforts. In contrast, Karl Muth, of the London School of Economics and Political Science, argues that allowing aggrieved parties to contract with nonstate actors—in essence, privatized law enforcement—to address the problem is a far better solution.

Discussion Questions

1. Do you think piracy is a rational response to economic deprivation, or is there another explanation?
2. What explains the increase in piracy incidents over the past 15 years?
3. Do states need international law to address the problem of piracy?
4. Should states intervene preemptively, e.g., by attacking pirate staging areas, or does that violate national sovereignty?
5. How should states handle the problem of piracy when pirates are often based in "failed states"?
6. Can pirates be "rationally" deterred?

NOTES

1. "The Economics of Piracy," *Geopolicity,* May 2011. www.geopolicity.com/upload/content/pub_1305229189_regular.pdf
2. Robert Young, "Sea Dog Millionaires: Somali Pirates' Rich Returns," *Bloomberg Businessweek,* May 12, 2011. http://www.businessweek.com/magazine/content/11_21/b4229064090727.htm?link_position=link3
3. Ibid.

YES: Scott Mckenzie, *World Affairs Council of New Orleans*

The Roman statesman, orator, and lawyer, Cicero, said that pirates were *hostis humani generis,* or "enemies of the human race."[1] Since the time when all roads led to the Eternal City, the international community has made impressive progress in cooperation and worldwide communication. But, even with technology that would have awed the legislators in the Forum, the world has not erased the scourge of pirates and international crime. It seems that as rapidly as technology has grown, criminals have kept pace and found new ways to exploit weaknesses. Today, in an increasingly interconnected world, a person is more likely to be robbed by a "Nigerian prince" on the Internet than a masked street thug. Just as lumbering cargo ships have been over-powered by nimble Somali fishermen with AK-47s, states have been slow to coordinate a unified strategy and engage in systemic intervention against international criminals.

Piracy and other international crime proliferate in areas functionally out-side of state control. Piracy has long been considered an *international* crime under customary international law. Today this crime is most common around Somalia, a failed state in the warm coastal waters in the Gulf of Aden. Other crimes that stem from a lack of state control are *transnational* crimes, because they cross national borders. Modern hackers navigate the uncharted and vast virtual world of the Internet, which by design does not have strong barriers along national borders. These areas and means of access are not easily suscep-tible to regulation by any one actor, and looking at the type and scope of crimes committed alongside the pitfalls of the current regulatory system shows that there is a strong need for international action to be taken.

Many would call for a reliance on single state actors to solve these issues of crimes. Every criminal does live in a state, and the crimes can be policed by states. However, a patchwork approach to state intervention produces procedural gaps that result in civil and human rights violations. Furthermore, it does little to attack the leaders of these crimes or to deal with the root issues of these activities.

There are two different types of state intervention required to solve the prob-lem of piracy and international crime. First, there must be increased coordina-tion to deal with modern criminals in a consistent way that bridges national borders as easily as they do. This can be through conferences and meetings that lead to closer state-to-state cooperation. Second, coordinated state intervention is needed to create international laws and protocols that deal with criminals in a consistent way that upholds generally accepted expectations of civil and human rights. The crimes that the accused violated should be roughly consistent, the trial must be fair, and the sentence must be just. The enforcement of international law could also help tackle some of the underlying causes that give rise to this illegal activity. Addressing only the superficial criminal activity will likely prove ineffective if the conditions persist.

SOMALI PIRATES—FAILED STATES

Pirates in the Gulf of Aden are a salient example of the connection between weak central governments and rampant international crime. Piracy was a problem that many people associated with the high seas, galleon ships, and men with names like Red Beard. However, since at least 2005, this classic form of economic terrorism has been making a comeback in the warm waters off the coast of Somalia.

Civil strife in Somalia is now decades long and has destroyed the economy and the ability of the government to extend the rule of law throughout its territory. Since the independence of various areas and their unification in 1960, it has had few years of peace. Starting in 1969, it was led by a series of military governments. The country was under this undemocratic leadership until Major General Mohamed Siad Barre was overthrown by armed revolutionaries in December of 1990. The country has not yet recovered from this civil war and has generally been without a consistent government.

In 1992, Somalia experienced a tremendous famine that killed as many as 300,000 people and required extensive United States and United Nations intervention to control. While initially successful at slowing the rate of starvation, the UN mission was never able to create a stable government and was ended in 1995. The next fifteen years saw constant fighting between rival warlords. The formation of the Transitional Federal Government (TFG) in 2004 created a faint glimmer of hope, but its strength has been weak. In reality, it controls little area outside of the capital city, Mogadishu.

Opposing the TFG is a powerful faction known as Al-Shabaab, which was formed out of the Islamic Court Union. Al-Shabaab fighters have pushed as far as Mogadishu, and it has proven that it has an iron grip on the southern part of the country, where they have implemented their strict interpretation of *sharia* law. The economy in the area under Al-Shabaab control has been pushed so far that in 2011, it fell into another famine that rivals the one experienced in 1992.[2] This fighting has filled the country with a Pandora's box of firearms that are cheap and available.

The TFG is even unable to control itself. It has failed to close ranks and promote domestic stability. The parliament is so divided that a violent fistfight broke out on the floor of the parliament between rival political factions because of acrimony over the election of a new speaker.[3] As the government is slowly falling apart, its ability to uphold the rule of law has diminished. This centralized federal power became so weak that two northern areas, Somaliland and Puntland, broke away and became semiautonomous.

Given the combination of desperate economic need, easy access to guns, and little police power to limit them, it is not surprising that some people would turn making their living though banditry. U.S. Assistant Secretary of State for African Affairs Johnnie Carson described the situation:

> The African community has borne the brunt of the piracy, and the international response, particularly on the legal side, has been very, very minimal. . . . Piracy continues to persist for two reasons. One is the lack of a government and an economy on shore, and the other one is an absence, the continuation of impunity and the absence of punishment for people who are caught engaged in piracy.[4]

Mr. Carson's explanation points to two areas that can clearly be dealt with through an increase in international state intervention.

Unlike the pirates in children's books, this new generation usually stays close to land. These Somali pirates generally do not sail around the world to plunder new ships, though new reports indicate that they have continued to evolve their methods using more sophisticated techniques that increase their range. They leave the coast in larger "motherships," then zoom in for an attack with speedboats, brandishing machine guns and rocket launchers against usually poorly armed merchant ships. After commandeering the boats, they are brought to the coast, where the vessel, along with its cargo and crew, are held for ransoms that average $2 million.[5]

This pirate problem is regionally isolated, but it has global impacts. The shipping lanes that run though the Gulf of Aden are used to move cargo to points around the earth, and the ships and crews captured have included citizens from a wide number of countries. Similarly, shipping companies have paid more for increased security and ransoms and have passed this final cost along to consumers, who have seen higher prices on goods that have passed through this commercial zone. The chances of being stopped by pirates rose so high that Gulf of Aden was labeled a "war risk" by some insurance companies. This label resulted in higher prices to insure the cargo.[6] This can have more than just monetary impacts. The World Food Program (WFP), for example, brings 90 percent of the food it delivers for humanitarian relief through this area. Now each ship must have an armed military escort. This, in turn, has increased costs to the WFP and has decreased the amount of food aid it has been able to deliver.

The quest for money has always been a motivating factor of pirates. But the Somali situation requires a more detailed consideration of the root causes. Pirates captured after attacking an Iranian ship simply said, "In Somalia, we have no jobs. . . . That's the reason to go to sea. Our country has a civil war, and I don't have skills [to find work]."[7] In interviews with many of the pirates themselves, they claim that they can no longer continue making their living as fishermen. Pirates say that ships have been dumping toxic waste into Somali waters, harming the ecosystem. There are also accusations that fishing trawlers from other countries have been entering the exclusive economic zone around Somalia and illegally harvesting fish in those waters. They charge that ships from other countries have been taking advantage of the almost nonexistent enforcement of marine law. The TFG can scarcely devote resources to raise a Coast Guard, and some pirates have taken up this mantle. In the words of one, "We are simply patrolling our seas. Think of us like a coast guard."[8]

ANONYMOUS AND THE INTERNET—NEW AND UNREGULATED TERRITORY

The Internet presents a different lens to look at the issue of how transnational crime has become prevalent in areas outside of state control. It has taken less than a human lifetime for the power of the Internet to make instantaneous global communication a reality. Unlike a physical territory that is conventionally susceptible to the rule of law and regulation, the Internet is more ethereal. As the reach of the Internet has expanded rapidly from its origins in the 1960's to become a transformative force in modern society, regulation has always been a few steps behind the curve.

The Internet was designed as an open system, with no center point holding it together. This was originally intended to create a redundant system that would be impossible to shut down, even in the event of a nuclear attack. While all the elements of the Internet such as servers, cables, and computers exist in the physical world, its functions such as reading e-mail, surfing the web, or watching movies are transnational and incorporeal. This means that it is as simple for a hacker working from China to break into a computer in San Francisco as it is in Shanghai. The difficulties for prosecution are clear and require new ways of thinking about the governance of this important resource. As the CEO of Unilever, Paul Polman said, "This is an example of technology developing faster than the frameworks and sometimes the regulations around that."[9]

The Internet's unique decentralized spirit is clearly reflected though its governance or lack thereof. The only governance at the international level concerns the system of Internet names and technical requirements. These two bodies are the Internet Corporation for Assigned Names and Numbers (ICANN) and the Internet Engineering Task Force (IETF). ICANN is a registered nonprofit group in the state of California.[10] The IETF is a nonprofit group and is operated in a remarkably open governance system by allowing "any interested person . . . [to] participate in the work, know what is being decided, and make his or her voice heard on the issue."[11] Clearly, these are organizational systems that do not desire to exert a tremendous amount of control.

Paralleling every great milestone for the Internet has been a shadow history of hackers, thieves, and criminals, whose technical creativity rivals that of any computer professional. Hackers have always been loosely allied with each other in a loose-knit community. They have extensive discussions online over e-mail and on message boards, but they also have trade magazines and even hold well-attended conferences. It is important not to confuse the fact that organization has flourished with a social sanction for hacker activities. Many have been subject to criminal prosecution for the damage they have created to physical computer systems and for theft and fraud that is every bit as real as if they had robbed a bank. For example, the United States Department of Justice reached a plea agreement with Kevin Mitnick, its most wanted hacker in 1999, and accused him of "millions of dollars in damages resulted from lost licensing fees, marketing delays, lost research and development, and repairs made to compromised computer systems."[12]

At various times, these criminals have coordinated their work. Starting in 2008, one of the biggest groups, Anonymous, made headlines for their orchestrated attacks and civil disobedience against targets ranging from multinational companies (such as Sony) to governments that it found repressive and hostile (such as Syria). Anonymous is not similar to a formal alliance that would be organized by a hierarchy. The actions of Anonymous are carried out by volunteer participants who use the Anonymous moniker but who have little or no connection to each other. This mirrors the decentralized and volunteer-based organization of the Internet itself. One unnamed member described the composition of the group as "'the first internet-based superconsciousness.' Anonymous is a group in the sense that a flock of birds is a group. How do you know they're a group? Because they're travelling in the same direction. At any given moment, more birds could join, leave, or peel off in another direction entirely."[13]

In 2011, Anonymous launched several attacks that resulted in police responses from governments around the world. After Internet commerce companies restricting the accounts of their *cause de celebrate* Julian Assange, Anonymous launched significant attacks on the computer networks, primarily PayPal, Visa, and MasterCard. These attacks were not designed to steal funds from the sites but to disable their websites and restrict their ability to conduct business. Other attacks, as in Spain, came against government targets as a result of proposed legislation that would limit the ability of citizens to maintain their anonymity on the Internet.

Similar to Somali pirates, there were economic harms to private companies. These were then passed along to consumers around the world both in real terms and in restricted access to these services.

Unlike in Somali, there is no entity that could be resurrected to provide regulation. In this respect, the Internet is *sui genius*. However, this does not mean that it is incapable of oversight or that rules and regulations cannot be mutually agreed on by all nations that would form a system of governance that could prevent these types of attacks in the future. This could also be helpful in preventing at least some of the issues that lead up to these attacks by setting standards for privacy and the extent of government intervention.

FAILURE OF INTERNATIONAL CONTROL RESULTS IN VIOLATIONS OF CIVIL AND HUMAN RIGHTS

Pirates, Anonymous, and other crime groups that exist outside of regulation by the state fall into two categories. Piracy is an international crime, because it is so serious that it rose to a level that all nations could equally condemn throughout history. Crimes such as hacking are transnational, because they cross national borders. There are two roadblocks to combating international and transnational crime. First, there are jurisdictional concerns about where the criminal will be prosecuted. It could be in a number of different states: the one they are physically in, the state of the person they attacked, or perhaps a country that is only an outside third party. Or, as will be discussed later, they might also be prosecuted under international law. Related to the venue where prosecution takes place are concerns about the criminal proceedings themselves and punishment that will be meted out if they are found guilty. While the individual criminal laws are the purview of each state, the application of laws of one state to nationals of another can easily lead to miscarriages of justice that most reasonable countries want to avoid. In the example of piracy, the accused are subject to a hodgepodge of jurisdictions, and the country that does try them more often reflects state or international politics or random luck than the locations of the crimes or the victims. The present system does not provide a uniform system of proceedings—arrest, detention, and trial in the United States are far different than those conducted in Kenya or Seychelles. The second problem in combating international and transnational crime comes from finding and dealing with the criminal and any related criminal organizations. The Anonymous hackers have been equally difficult to trace and bring to trial. Many who have been arrested were guilty for a small portion of the overall attack, doing little more than allowing their computer to be used by others. Meanwhile, those who are organizing and planning the attacks often go free. Some states do not adequately respond to the problem.

The jurisdictional problems are clearly shown in Somalia. To fight the pirates, a number of countries have stepped forward and began patrolling the waters in the Gulf of Aden. The military answer to the growing pirate problem has come together slowly and disjointedly. As more foreign nationals were captured and held for ransom, countries began to respond by moving armed naval ships into the area. They relied on United Nations Security Council Resolution 1838, which calls on nations with naval and air power in the region to suppress the pirates. A coalition including the United States, South Korea, Canada, Denmark, France, Germany, Pakistan, and the United Kingdom have formed the Combined Task Force 150. Another force operating to combat piracy is the European Union Naval Forces in Somalia (EU NAVFOR). Similar to the Combined Task Force, this is comprised of members from EU countries. Finally, China, India, and Russia all have their own independent antipiracy operations in the Gulf of Aden.

This military answer has only created a partial solution. It has captured many pirates and potentially deterred other pirate attacks but has failed to adequately answer what to do with these modern pirates. In today's world, walking the plank has gone out of fashion. Ensuring a fair trial for these often young, uneducated, and impoverished men has proven to be a difficult task.

The trial of the Maersk Alabama demonstrates the jurisdictional issues confronting the prosecution of pirates. This attack received a great deal of attention in the Western press and was even turned into a movie. The attack against the Maersk Alabama was launched on April 8, 2009, and in a dramatic rescue, Navy SEALs shot and killed three pirates holding Captain Richard Phillips. They also captured a fourth pirate, Abdul Wali Muse. Because he attacked Americans and was captured by Americans, he was taken to New York City and was indicted on numerous counts. This led to the first piracy trials in the United States in 100 years. Court observers were surprised and intrigued by how the case would play out, because in the United States, the crime of piracy is vaguely "defined by the law of nations."[14] However, on May 18th, 2010, Mr. Muse pled guilty and was sentenced later that year. The outcome of this trial can be compared to the case of *the United States v. Mohamed Ali Said*, a different American case involving a captured Somali pirate. This court decided that attempted piracy was not the same as actual piracy. The judge interpreted the law of nations to only include the actual act of robbery at sea. Since the defendant had only attempted, but not completed, the robbery, he was not guilty of a charge.

Trial and imprisonment in the United States was not the only option. Mr. Muse or Mr. Said could have been tried in Kenya, where the courts have also been adjudicating cases of suspected pirates. In 2009, Kenya signed Memorandums of Understanding (MOUs) with the United States, the United Kingdom, the European Union, Denmark, Canada, and China. These MOUs stipulated that pirates captured by these foreign powers would be taken to Kenya and tried in domestic Kenyan courts under Kenyan law. In exchange for its service as a tribunal, Kenya was promised technical, judicial, and financial support. However, within a year, Kenya backed out of the agreement, citing a number of issues including security concerns, a judicial backlog, and other countries not living up to their end of the agreement.[15]

Many countries such as Denmark have laws that stipulate that they can only prosecute pirate attacks when there have been attacks on their own nationals or national interests. After a Danish warship stopped one pirate attack, they had to release the pirates due to a lack of jurisdiction. In another case, they had to hand them over to authorities in the Netherlands, a country that did have jurisdiction. Despite pirate attacks being an age-old problem, the evolutions in law and self-protection mean that for some countries, there are new debates about the limits of engagement. In the United Kingdom, a member of parliament, Richard Ottaway, framed the question slightly differently, asking, "If a private armed guard on board a U.K.-flagged vessel sees an armed skiff approaching at high speed, can the guard open fire? The government must provide clearer direction on what is permissible and what is not."[16]

Additionally, Mr. Muse or Mr. Said could have been tried in a number of other countries. Drawing on the "enemies of the human race" idea, some countries such as the Seychelles have laws that confer universal jurisdiction on the crime of piracy and allow them to prosecute suspects, regardless of the territory where they were found or the nationality of the ship they attacked. In a time before GPS and satellite imagery, it was prohibitively difficult to require a Spanish warship to deal with a pirate attack if an Italian ship was at the scene. Allowing for universal jurisdiction was an early form of international cooperation and helped countries that relied on oceangoing ships to carry on the trading that made up a large part of their economy needed to ensure the world's oceans were pirate free.

A problem with universal jurisdiction is that not all countries currently accept it. General principles of territorial sovereignty say that each state should respect the territory of others. For example, the 2009 Djibouti Code of Conduct on Countering Piracy states that "any seizure made in the territorial sea of a Participant . . . should be subject to the jurisdiction of that Participant." The results of one country encroaching on another can range from a diplomatic flap to an act of war.

The punishment phase of a trial also differs from country to country. Under Kenyan law, the maximum sentence a pirate could receive is life in jail. Capital punishment is not an option that the judge or prosecutor could have. In all cases, the accused are given legal representation. This is easily contrasted with the case of a pirate in the autonomous area in northern Somalia, Puntland, who was sentenced to death for his role in the murder of Sayid Jacfar, a Pakistani skipper of the cargo ship MV QSM Dubai.[17]

A concerning issue is that a lack of international coordination can lead to dangerous lapses of rights on the high seas. In a 2010 example, Russia took up the role of Cicero when it captured 10 suspected pirates. Russia claimed there were not sufficient legal grounds to take the suspects back to Russia for a trial. They were left adrift in a small rubber boat in the middle of the Indian Ocean without navigational equipment and likely perished at sea. Rumors in Somalia claimed that this was a cover story and the pirates were executed. Either way, it is unlikely they survived.

In dealing with the second issue, there are dramatic problems with state-to-state coordination to find the perpetrators of crimes committed on the Internet. As a result of the Anonymous hacking events, there were numerous arrests in countries around the world. These included the Netherlands, the United States, the United Kingdom, Australia, Spain, and Turkey. In each of these cases, the arresting country relied on its own laws to arrest its own citizens, though the victims of the crime might be elsewhere.

In fact, there has been little internationally coordinated action against cyber-crime. Recently, however, there has been a growing push for countries to work together to fight back. North Atlantic Treaty Organization (NATO) declared that "[t]he time it takes to cross the Atlantic [via the Internet] has shrunk to 30 milliseconds, compared with 30 minutes for ICBMs [intercontinental ballistic missiles] and several months going by boat. . . . Meanwhile, a whole new family of actors are emerging on the international stage, such as virtual 'hactivist' groups. These could potentially lead to a new class of international conflicts between these groups and nation states, or even to conflicts between exclusively virtual entities."[18] This might be hyperbole, but it hints at an underlying stress from many experts who feel not enough is being done to combat this problem.

Somali pirates who operate in international waters and hackers whose work crosses national boundaries show that there is a variety of individual state-run command and control techniques, which creates concerns about lapses at the margins. There is serious concern about civil and human rights. There are many examples that show that when there is a lack of systemic state intervention, abuse is rampant.

INTERNATIONAL SOLUTIONS

The current methodology for dealing with piracy and other international crimes can be summarized as a focus on the responsibility of states, with ad hoc enforcement programs for states unable to shoulder the burden. Clearly, this has not been effective.

Following in the direction already set, there are clear solutions for systemic state intervention. First, to deal with international crime, states need to seriously consider treaties and frameworks that would address and deal with the problems that caused the crime and with the criminals themselves. Second, for transnational crime, there needs to be increased state cooperation and coordination to make sure that the true criminals are prosecuted and there is not a differential enforcement of justice from country to country.

Laws have had centuries to adapt to the issues raised by piracy. But, as was discussed, these have not solved many issues that have been raised, such as violations of civil and human rights caused by inadequate or nonexistent trials. Additionally, the rise in piracy shows that current methods have not proven effective.

More recently, other responses to piracy involving some international policy options have been created. These point the way forward not only for this specific problem but for other types of international crime. The United Nations Convention on the Law of the Seas (UNCLOS) is an example of systemic state intervention, which would be effective in combating this crime.

Constructing this convention was not easy or simple. It took states and stakeholders 10 years of discussion to draft and did not come into effect until 1994. Today, despite being in force, the full legal weight of this treaty has not yet been felt, because some provisions have not yet been used.

UNCLOS provides a general outline for dealing with pirates. For example, it has provisions that deal with boarding suspected pirate ships. Additionally it contains a provision for the creation of an International Tribunal for the Law of the Sea (ITLS) in Hamburg, Germany. Currently the ITLS has only handled cases dealing with mineral rights on the sea bed. But Luis Jesus, the president of the ITLS, has indicated that this body could handle the cases of pirate attacks.

An international tribunal would have the benefit of encouraging greater monetary participation by member states while maintaining consistent due process standards and an attention to human rights. In addition, it could cut down the number of pirates set free or wrongly punished because of a lack of or inconsistent application of national laws.

The process of building states and regulating international law is difficult. However, it is a process that is difficult for a state to do by itself. If Somalia had not experienced decades of civil war, it would likely not be a staging ground for these attacks. Similarly, if it was able to protect its territorial waters and prevent ships from other nations from fishing its waters and polluting them by dumping waste, it might also have not been given an impious for these actions. In these situations, other nations need to step in and help Somalia through this difficult period until it can govern its territory.

In the wild west of the Internet, states have been reluctant to work together for this common purpose. One example of closer state coordination came in 2011 at the London Conference on Cyberspace, which was organized by British Foreign Secretary William Hague to bring together stakeholders from around the world to discuss an international approach to combating cyber-crime. This highly select cadre of 700 officials and business leaders focused on issues such as digital espionage, cybercrime, and electronic surveillance. However, the London Agenda was designed to only "shape the debate" about the future of the Internet. It was not designed to set rules for the future of security online but to provide a groundwork for future action. Reflecting that all states need the Internet, Mr. Hague, the United Kingdom's Foreign Secretary, said that all countries had to remember "not [to] treat cyberspace as if it belongs to you."[19]

CONCLUSION

Somalia is not much closer to a stable government today than it was 20 years ago, and the Internet will only take on a greater importance in the future. The crimes of the future may come from other lawless regions or from other unregulated markets. Every problem has a solution, and to solve piracy, hack-ing, and other international crime, systemic state intervention is needed. As these examples indicate, when state intervention is not coordinated, it results in violations of the civil and human rights of the accused and does not effectively deal with root causes and actors. To solve international crimes, the global com-munity must work together to implement international laws that can be used to evenly and fairly prosecute criminals. When the problems are more transna-tional, states must work closer together to coordinate their responses to these criminals. There are risks to increased state intervention to be sure, but it is also the only effective way to solve these problems.

NOTES

1. Keith Johnson, "Who's a Pirate? U.S. Court Sees Duel over Definition," *Wall Street Journal* (2010). http://online.wsj.com/article/SB20001424052748703988304575413 470900570834.html (accessed January 6, 2012).

2. Jeffrey Gettleman, "Somalis Waste Away as Insurgents Block Escape from Famine," *The New York Times*, August 1, 2011. http://www.nytimes.com/2011/08/02/world/ africa/02somalia.html?_r=1 (accessed January 6, 2012).

3. "Somali MPs Brawl over Election of New Speaker," *BBC*, January 5, 2012. http:// www.bbc.co.uk/news/world-africa-16430025 (accessed January 6, 2012).

4. Charles Corey, "Africa: Maritime Piracy Off Somali Coast a Global Problem," *AllAfrica.com* (2010). http://allafrica.com/stories/201010150169.html (accessed January 6, 2012).

5. Robyn Hunter, "Somali Pirates Living the High Life," *BBC*, October 28, 2008. http:// news.bbc.co.uk/2/hi/africa/7650415.stm (accessed January 6, 2012).

6. Githua Kihara, "Reduced Risk of Pirate Attacks to Cut Freight Costs," *Business Daily* (2012), http://www.businessdailyafrica.com/Corporate+News/Reduced+risk +of+pirate+attacks+to+cut+freight+costs+/-/539550/1299106/-/bp9ikrz/-/index. html (accessed January 6, 2012).

7. C. J. Chivers, "For Iranians Held by Pirates, U.S. to the Rescue," *The New York Times*, January 6, 2012. http://www.nytimes.com/2012/01/07/world/middleeast/for-iranians-held-by-pirates-us-to-the-rescue.html (accessed January 7, 2012). Complicating the Somali narrative is a rise in 2011 of piracy in other countries. In many of these places, the draw seems to be entirely monetary rather than as a result of dramatic onshore instability. Joshua Keating, "The Stories You Missed in 2011," *Foreign Policy* (2011). http://www.foreignpolicy.com/articles/2011/11/28/the_stories_you_missed_ in_2011?page=0,6 (accessed January 6, 2012).

8. Jeffrey Gettleman, "Somali Pirates Tell Their Side: They Want Only Money," *The New York Times*, October 1, 2008. http://www.nytimes.com/2008/10/01/world/ africa/01pirates.html (accessed January 8, 2012).

9. Peter Apps, "IMP Cyber Attack Boosts Calls for Global Action," *Reuters* (2011). http://www.reuters.com/article/2011/06/13/us-imf-cyberattack-idUSTRE75A207 20110613 (accessed January 8, 2012).

10. Ibid.

11. Mission Statement, *Internet Engineering Task Force*. http://www.ietf.org/about/mission .html (accessed January 8, 2012).

12. United States Department of Justice, "Kevin Mitnick Sentenced to Nearly Four Years in Prison; Computer Hacker Ordered to Pay Restitution to Victim Companies Whose Systems Were Compromised" (2010). http://www.justice.gov/criminal/ cybercrime/mitnick.htm (accessed January 6, 2012).

13. Chris Landers, "Serious Business: Anonymous Takes on Scientology: (And Doesn't Afraid of Anything)," *Baltimore City Paper* (2008). http://www2.citypaper.com/ columns/story.asp?id=15543 (accessed January 6, 2012).

14. United States Code: Title 18,1651. Piracy under law of nations | LII / Legal Information Institute. http://www.law.cornell.edu/uscode/18/usc_sec_18_00001651----000-.html (accessed January 6, 2012).
15. Jeff Davis, "Kenya: Country Cancels Piracy Trial Deals," *AllAfrica.com* (2010). http://allafrica.com/stories/201010010009.html (accessed January 6, 2012).
16. "'Clarify Piracy Defence Laws,' say MPs," *BBC,* January 5, 2012. http://www.bbc .co.uk/news/uk-politics-16410671 (accessed January 6, 2012).
17. "Pirate Ringleader Faces Execution in Somalia," *BBC,* September 28, 2010. http:// www.bbc.co.uk/news/world-africa-11426560 (accessed January 6, 2012).
18. Lord Jopling, "074 CDS 11 E – Information and National Security." *NATO Parliamentary Assembly.* http://www.nato-pa.int/default.asp?SHORTCUT=2443
19. "Nigeria: Conference Highlights Usage of Text Messaging in Country," *AllAfrica.com* (2011). http://allafrica.com/stories/201111031207.html (accessed January 8, 2012).

NO: Karl T. Muth, *London School of Economics and Political Science*

A ttempts at a state-driven resolution to the piracy issue will only energize, fund, and legitimize Somalia's aspiring amphibious kleptocrats. Allowing harmed parties to contract directly with those with the resources and ability to eliminate pirates—whether through specific arrangements, general bounties, or other means—is a cost-effective, desirable, elegant, and feasible resolution to the piracy issue.

Law enforcement has long been subject to privatization, and not only in the West. From Africa's diamond mines[1] to Western cities' parking meters[2] to a global trend toward prison privatization, governments already delegate to private enterprises the running of traditionally state-controlled law enforcement functions. Key industrial assets, including the harbor in Hong Kong[3] and petroleum infrastructure in the United Arab Emirates (UAE),[4] are administered, controlled, and patrolled by private enterprises and their privately hired security forces.

The contemporary problem of piracy in the western Indian Ocean, and particularly near the Gulf of Aden, is less a failure of the Somali government and more a failure of the international community.

There are two reasons that private actors engaging in bilateral transactions are best positioned to provide security in many areas.

First, the incentives of state actors are not well aligned with those suffering from many of the world's big problems. Shipping companies have interests they are willing to spend billions to protect, whereas many countries' governments do not have enough of an interest in shipping to patrol distant shores. Film studios and software companies are willing to combat software piracy and protect their property through extraordinary means, while governments are unlikely to break down doors and detain hundreds or thousands of people for copyright violations. Governments have proven inefficient and impotent in the war against illegal drug manufacture and distribution, but large pharmaceutical companies have compelling commercial reasons to destroy their illicit competitors. By allowing these corporations to defend their commercial and property interests, governments can better protect their citizens (which include resident corporations), shift costs to private actors, and conserve state resources.

Second, the actions of security forces controlled by private actors are narrowly tailored to their commercial purpose. An international conglomerate hiring mercenaries is unlikely to find itself mired in peacekeeping, preoccupied with state building, or expending time and resources on aid projects. Instead, it is in the commercial interest of the corporation hiring a mercenary force to channel that force's energy into securing valuable assets, be they container ships, harbors, or oil fields.

In order to understand why now is the time to largely remove the state from the commercial security equation, one must first review and understand the history of mercenary intervention.

A BRIEF HISTORY OF PRIVATE SECURITY

During the late seventeenth (and throughout the eighteenth) century, England, France, the Netherlands, Spain, the United States, and other governments issued letters of marque and reprisal (*lettres de course*) to privateers (*corsairs*). Many of the privateers were tasked with defensively protecting merchant fleets or offensively exacting retribution where the identity and position of pirates was known. In high-profile cases, dead-or-alive bounties demanded the body of a pirate (*corps précieux*), providing rewards in the form of cash, gold, or land in return.

Later nineteenth century bounty systems—famously used in the American "wild west"—proved dramatically more efficient than the hiring of privateers but still faced some of the same limitations as letters of marque. As with letters of marque, nineteenth-century bounties required state sanction: the rewards were provided by the state, only fugitives from courts of law could be hunted (rather than highwaymen and pirates not yet tried), and the posters were affixed to notice boards at government buildings, including town halls and post offices.

In the wake of the World Wars, many private soldiers found work in the employ of the Western allies and the Soviet states, sometimes enjoying the patronage of both within a single career—or, in places from Afghanistan to Congo, within a single decade. Others worked for corporations hoping to exploit the resources of exotic locales populated by natives too ambitious, incompetent, savvy, or untrustworthy to be trusted on garrison duty. Still more worked on security details in nameless convoys of black vehicles holding new millionaires from Kowloon to Kabul, Mexico City to Monrovia.

In this young millennium, mercenaries of various flavors are parts of a growing industry worth hundreds of billions of dollars.[5] This industry looks more conventional than that of eighteenth-century privateers, with established firms, trade associations, and lobbying groups. Both the private security providers and those who employ them are sophisticated businesspeople, able to negotiate and reduce to writing complex arrangements. Hence, the state is an unnecessary intermediary between the buyer (those wanting pirate-removal services) and the seller (those able to provide pirate removal).

In the past, state actors took the lead on pirate hunting and other flavors of pest control on the high seas. This role was not one states were eager to fill or one states guarded particularly jealously. Simply put, pirates were a problem and, before the rise of the privateer, only states had the men and materiel to destroy pirates in open water.

Today, state actors are reluctant to fill the role of maritime policeman, while private actors have more resources at their disposal than ever before. While the Somali piracy crisis is fluid and ongoing, as of this writing, at least ten ships of substantial size are in pirate custody, along with nearly 250 hostages.[6] These ships are the property of corporations, and these hostages are their employees. While no one nation may have an incentive to intervene and recapture either ships or personnel, these corporations have incentives to reclaim both swiftly and safely. When achieved by force, the action should be respected by states as a mechanism of replevin rather than considered an event of extrajudicial violence.

THE FAILURE OF STATE COOPERATION

If one envisions the social network of nation-level diplomacy, one quickly realizes states work in concert at three levels. The simplest is the bilateral understanding or reciprocity arrangement, which involves only two actors and may settle a regional dispute, make concrete a porous border, or formalize a trade relationship. The second is the treaty or accord, which may be bilateral or multilateral and may be commercial, military, or otherwise in its orientation. The highest level of state collaboration is that of a widely supported or adopted resolution before the United Nations.

In 2008, the international community used this highest level of collaboration in the form of Resolution 1838, which was adopted by all parties under Chapter VII of the UN Charter. In Resolution 1838, the Security Council asked member states with naval military assets to repress pirates off the Somali coast. Viewed as a companion resolution to Resolutions 1814 and 1816 from earlier that year, member states were allowed to use "all necessary means" to "actively fight piracy" in the area, including in Somali territorial waters.[7]

Though "gravely concerned by the recent proliferation of acts of piracy and armed robbery at sea against vessels off the coast of Somalia,"[8] state actors failed to kill or capture any substantial number of pirates in the months following Resolution 1838. During 2008, over one hundred attacks resulted in over forty successful hijackings of vessels near Somalia.[9]

Figure 1

Prevalence of Somali Pirate Activity, 2008

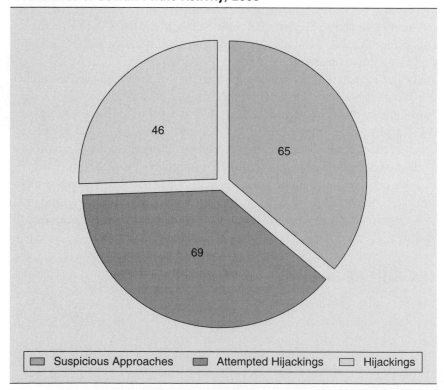

Source: "Pirates Hijack Two Tankers Within 24 Hours Off Somali Shore," *FOX News*, March 26, 2009. http://www.foxnews.com/story/0,2933,510766,00.html (accessed November 30, 2011).

Due to continuing failures to coordinate and launch naval attacks against pirates, a naval surface task force was created, Combined Task Force 151,[10] similar to the earlier Combined Task Force 150.[11] Combined Task Force 151 captured sixteen Somalis on or about February 11, 2009. Despite successful international cooperation in capturing the sixteen February pirates, only two months later, the Dutch navy captured twenty pirates off the coast of Somalia and later released them because they believed they lacked legal jurisdiction to detain them.[12]

Alongside the efforts of the Combined Task Forces, roughly a quarter billion dollars was given to Somalia's government to combat piracy.[13] Whether this funding was squandered, stolen, or spent on Somalia's impotent military remains unclear, but no pirates were captured or killed as a direct result of this funding.

Despite interventions involving billions of dollars' worth of cash, equipment, and personnel, pirate revenue grew after Resolution 1838 from about sixty million dollars around the time of the resolution's passage to four times that in 2010.[14] In the third quarter of 2008, while UN member states meandered toward agreement as to the wording of Resolution 1838, pirates successfully carried out 26 hijackings off the coast of Somalia.[15]

Member states' governments have lost little from their failed intervention, however. Their politicians are not elected by the terrorized people of Somalia. Their constituents are preoccupied with other issues and are not concerned with the stability of the shipping and logistics industries or with a civil conflict in a faraway land.

Meanwhile, corporations and their investors have suffered. While costs stemming from piracy are difficult to estimate, a figure around ten billion dollars is likely in the right order of magnitude.[16] Several studies have examined the economic cost of maritime piracy, many coming to the conclusion that a number between $7 and $12 billion[17] is plausible once one considers increased costs in ransoms, insurance premiums, and goods transported by sea as well as the distortions of shipping routes and the future impact on regional economies. These costs are borne primarily by consumers, corporations, and shareholders and only secondarily by national treasuries. Whether the harm is more or less than $10 billion is an accounting question not relevant to the broader philosophical debate; the harmed parties must be allowed to directly intervene and capture or kill pirates in order to protect the security of their assets. The access to Somali waters and ability to use "all necessary means" to "actively fight piracy" given to—but used ineffectively by—governments under UN Resolutions 1814, 1816, and 1838 should be transferred, licensed, or auctioned to private security companies whose clients demand and deserve the protection government actors have failed to provide.

THE FIRST CONTENTION

Believers in a strong, altruistic state will take issue with the first contention, that the incentives of state actors are not well aligned with those suffering from many of the world's big problems—or, at minimum, that private corporations' interests are better aligned with citizens' needs than the interests of the state.

"What of the Congo Free State?" opponents of privatization frequently ask. The Belgian colonial experience in Africa is often held up in academic debate (particularly by historians and anthropologists) as Charles Marlow's pillar of salt that should warn others of treading too close to privatization of what have historically been state functions. The profit motive of King Leopold in extracting valuable rubber from the vines of dense Congolese jungles is often cited as a case of greed paving the way for other sins.

However, a review of the atrocities in the Congo Free State shows this experiment was a failure of management rather than a failure of privatization—and mismanagement is a problem that afflicts state enterprises to the same (or greater) extent as their private cousins.

The most notorious mismanagement in Congo involves the obsession among officers surrounding the collecting of amputated hands and the rape, terrorism, and killings in Congolese villages. Though the seizure of severed hands may have originally been driven by economic concerns (the enforcement of rubber quotas and the conservation of ammunition, which was heavy and difficult to transport from factories in Europe), the methods used by the *Force Publique* quickly exceeded the bounds of any purely economic justification.[18] In short, the abuse of the Congolese people became more akin to the hunter who does not bother to collect his game; any economic reason for the Belgians' behavior in Congo was eclipsed by the failure of officers to manage their platoons and the implementation of brutality as sport and, eventually, as the organizational culture of the (unprofitable) rubber enterprise.

Many of the atrocities that the international community would today consider war crimes or genocide reported by George Washington Williams and, later, by E.D. Morel were at best peripherally related to the economic productivity of Congo.[19] These activities of brutality, murder, and slavery were more similar to the activities of a totalitarian state actor than the role of an international industrial conglomerate. Without state sponsorship, no private corporation can engage in violence on this scale, to this degree, or for this duration, as it is an unprofitable activity.

Indeed, the efforts to suppress the people of Congo treated them as a homogenous *capite censi* rather than a group of market participants or consumers. Had the Belgian rubber business been wholly untethered from the Belgian state, it would have been forced to focus on its business mission and would not have had capital, time, or men to devote to its violent frolics. Instead, the rubber enterprise was allowed to rely upon an unrealistically low cost of capital and the use of Belgian government infrastructure, inviting waste.

One microeconomic falsehood still widely believed (and oft-cited in debates concerning Belgian Congo) is that slavery is a system with a marginal labor cost of zero (but marginal productivity of labor greater than zero). If this were true, slavery would offer a very competitive economic model. However, it is not true: the costs of disciplining, feeding, housing, replacing, and transporting slaves in Congo almost certainly exceeded the cost of paying a tiny wage to each worker that approximated this marginal product of labor.

Perhaps most telling is the conclusion to the Congo Free State story. The falling price of rubber, rising security costs, and diminishing productivity of the workforce (due to environmental destruction, resource scarcity, unrest, and other factors) ended Leopold's experiment in rubber extraction in Congo. The Congo Free State's rubber business did not end because it was immoral or unpopular; it ended chiefly because it was unprofitable. It is worthwhile to note that—despite an international quorum[20] of celebrities, organizations, philan-thropists, and politicians much larger than the group active in opposing Somali piracy—market forces, rather than policymaker ingenuity, forced an end to the Belgian terror in Congo.

THE SECOND CONTENTION

Advocates of state intervention would oppose the second contention's premise, that a private company's involvement will be limited in scope and minimally disruptive to the target market.

"How does one explain the East India Company?" the opposition might inquire.

The East India Company grew from its original charter of 1600[21] to become the primary conduit for English (and, more broadly, Imperial and Anglophone) trading with India and the Orient. Over time, it assumed authority over mili-tary functions on behalf of the Crown. Like its contemporary, the Dutch East India Company,[22] it had assumed powers historically vested in state actors, such as the ability to conduct war, control colonial outposts, and mint nego-tiable instruments with cash value.

There is no doubt that the East India Company's range of operations included enterprises of questionable commercial value and even wholly unprofitable ventures, such as control over garrison forces in coastal India. Most problematic was the East India Company's size—it may have been, to utilize an anachronistic term—the first corporation "too big to fail" as its interests became inexorably intertwined with those of Imperial Britain[23] during the eighteenth century.

The cycle of reciprocity between the Company and the state eventually evolved into an intractable symbiosis indispensable for the survival of both. The British government and the company also aligned their activities, their policy positions, and, eventually, their *weltanschauung*. Due to comingling of funds between Crown treasuries and the Company, the choices made by the British government and by the East India Company were subject to similar capital constraints. This led to an economic *folie à deux* shared by the Company and the Crown but increasingly different from reality—particularly when one compares Company activities to the changing commercial and competitive landscape.

While the East India Company defended its ships from pirates (sometimes with its own resources and sometimes by calling upon the Royal Navy), it did so both actively (in battle) and passively (through the steady militarization of its fleet). By the close of the eighteenth century, the vessels of the Company resembled the surface inventory of a merchant navy rather than the transport assets of a shipping firm. By comparison, today's shipping lanes are populated with vulnerable vessels manned by skeleton crews.

The *Taunton Castle*, a merchantman in service with the Company beginning in or about 1800, was 182 feet in length[24] and about 1,450 metric tons (about 1,600 short tons), with a complement of 140 hands to man the ship and 26 for her cannon.[25] Meanwhile, the *Maersk Alabama*, taken by pirates off the coast of Somalia in 2009, carried 17,000 metric tons of cargo and a civilian crew of 20.[26] Because today's large commercial ships are shorthanded and more similar to the often-unarmed Spanish *Galeones de Manila-Acapulco*[27] than East India Company merchantmen, it is unreasonable to expect these ships to act in self-defense.

Because shipping firms today are generally only loosely allied to a given country and because ships often fly flags of convenience, today's crews cannot depend upon protection from any particular country's navy. In many ways, shipping companies today suffer from the opposite of the East India Company's problem. The East India Company eventually suffered from its irreversible entanglement with unprofitable British colonial ventures. Today, there is often no state interested in becoming entangled with the international shipping industry or interested in protecting a shipping company's employees and property. Hence, shipping firms must be allowed to privately contract with mercenaries who can guarantee the security of their cargo, their men, and their ships.

FROM TRIAGE TO TREATMENT

No doubt there have been small victories—recaptured ships and freed sailors—in the war against modern piracy, but states are managing symptoms rather than curing the disease. Negotiating with pirates who already have the upper hand and attempting to free ships already anchored along the Somali coast does not help protect investors, ships, or sailors. Paying ransoms for captured ships only strengthens the pirates; this transaction is the modern pirate's *raison d'être.*

If the cost of piracy near Somalia is on the order of ten billion dollars, then even paying $500,000 dead-or-alive bounties on 15,000 pirates (or $50,000 bounties on 150,000 pirates, depending upon one's estimation of how many pirates or potential pirates there may be and where one would prefer to place the zero) would be economically preferable to suffering the economic costs of piracy. The social and network effects of eliminating thousands of pirates would likely have an effect on the availability of new pirate recruits. Open bounties would be preferable to hiring a specific mercenary for a specific task, as anyone can claim the reward for a bounty. Competition among bounty hunters—including pirates who learn it is more profitable to hunt other pirates than to hunt merchant ships—would be helpful in destroying any trust between pirate leaders and their coconspirators.

There are two cases of the English using open bounty systems in the early eighteenth century for pirate hunting, each worthy of brief discussion.

- England offered a series of handsome general pirate bounties to cleanse the West Indies of pirates. Some of these pirates were offered by His Majesty's Treasury while others were matched or contributed by merchants in London. Soon after bounties were announced, many pirates were captured, thrown into brigs of Royal Navy Men O' War,[28] hanged from cross members of carracks, or killed in battle. While Edward Teach, better known as Blackbeard, escaped the bounty hunters,[29] many of his contemporaries were not so fortunate. Often, pirates would turn on one another to claim bounties.

- An open bounty system was used by the English East India Company in the winter of 1695, which offered £1,000 for the capture of pirate Henry Every, who had stolen the Ganj-i-Sawai from the company's fleet, which was carrying half a million pieces in gold and silver, most of which have never been recovered but are believed by some to have been melted into bullion measures. Despite an extraordinary bounty, Every retired and evaded capture for the balance of his life. Even contemporary accounts[30] question whether the great price on his head may have driven Every into early retirement in pirate havens in the Bahamas and elsewhere. England never again issued a bounty of similar value (in adjusted pounds sterling) for a single criminal.

In the 1980's, the United States instituted an open bounty system for information regarding the activities, enterprises, and whereabouts of persons of interest in terrorism cases. While the highest-profile recent bounty was the (unclaimed) $25 million reward for Osama Bin Laden, the U.S. offers bounties for information on a regular basis. The "Rewards for Justice" program, established under the 1984 Act to Combat Terrorism, has paid over $100 million to informants and turncoat agents. The United States does not itemize or disclose specifically how many people have been captured, detained, or killed as a result of the bounties offered through its "Rewards for Justice" program.

Some may be uncomfortable with an open bounty system for capturing or killing pirates and may prefer a system that holds a contractor directly accountable for a given pirate-removal operation. If a specific contractor must be chosen, the most efficient system would involve contractor mercenaries participating in a reverse auction to set the price of pirate contracts. Assuming mercenary

An informant is handed a briefcase full of cash by a U.S. government representative in exchange for information under the United States Department of State's "Rewards for Justice" program.

companies operating in the region have a good sense of the marginal cost per pirate, the auction value should approach the marginal cost of eliminating one pirate. Many large companies already use reverse auctions of this type to locate suppliers, source materials, or choose between similar service providers; there is no reason "pirate removal" could not be sourced alongside other services.

The insurance industry could accelerate this process, rewarding companies posting bounties with lower premiums, recognizing the positive effects of these contracts on the larger commercial fleet. Insurers already make these adjustments to reward drivers who purchase vehicles with better safety ratings or health insurance customers who refrain from smoking cigarettes. As insurance is a substantial (and rising) cost for shipping firms, insurers are well positioned to incentivize desirable behaviors. A shipper may consider that offering an extra $5,000 per pirate in bounty money is reasonable, if he saves more than this amount on his next insurance invoice.

CONCLUSION

The question presented for debate asks, "Does controlling piracy and other criminal activities require systematic state interventions?" However, not all state interventions are systematic and not all systematic interventions are state led; thus, a fine scalpel of distinction is needed to separate "systematic" from "state." The argument *supra* should not be mistaken for anarchic advocacy—it is the opposite. No doubt piracy and other epidemic criminal acts must be tackled in an orderly method, but the method need not involve the state. Countless historical examples, including the Congo Free State and the East India Company, illustrate that even a well-intentioned state (and more quickly a greedy or careless state) will eventually meddle in, distract from, or become a parasite upon the business of a sizable enterprise. More recent examples from American sugar price controls to Icelandic banking deregulation follow this pattern of tampering and interdependence—one might say capitalism with state-symbiotic characteristics.[31] But for unfortunate state intervention, the Belgian enterprise would have been destroyed by competition[32] and been punished with insolvency rather than unpopularity. By 1903, investors were already skeptical of ABIR's wild appreciation.[33] Without omnipresent and intrusive government involvement in its affairs, the East India Company would have been guided by corporate strategy rather than national policy.

Currently, ships and their owners must beg state actors for appropriate intervention. Even when these appeals are successful, they receive sporadic assistance and little satisfaction. If those with an interest in shipping could allocate a fraction of their losses from piracy toward hiring able assistance in eliminating pirates, the piracy problem would be quickly resolved. Those harmed by piracy, an ongoing threat to life and property, should be allowed to directly purchase violence against pirates in bilateral arrangements to which states contribute only contractual enforcement.

NOTES

1. African mines have been guarded by private security firms for over a century.
2. The City of Chicago recently sold its parking meters—and the revenue associated with their future operation—to overseas investors.
3. Victoria Harbour and its Kwai Chung facility are primarily administered by a network of shipping and logistics corporations and were largely privatized during the British colonial period.
4. Petroleum exploitation infrastructure in the UAE is typically controlled and managed by a mixture of private corporations, individual investors, and public-private partnerships.
5. Scholars cited $120 billion US dollars (USD) as the value of the mercenary industry nearly ten years ago, prior to the growth of the business during the wars in Afghanistan and Iraq, recent conflicts in Africa, and the drug wars in South America. See, e.g., Peter Singer, "War, Profits, and the Vacuum of Law: Privatized Military Firms and International Law," *Columbia Journal of Transnational Law* 42, no. 2 (2004).
6. These vessels, as of November 21, 2011, included *MV Iceberg 1* (Panama), *MV Olip G* (Malta), *MV Albedo* (Malaysia), *MV Orna* (Panama), *MV Savina Caylyn* (Italy), *MV Rosalina d'Amato* (Italy), *MV Gemini* (Singapore), *MV Fairchem Bogey* (Marshall Is.), *MV Liquid Velvet* (Marshall Is.), and *FV Ardie* (Seychelles). See EU NAVFOR Somalia report dated November 21, 2011, available at http://www .eunavfor.eu/wp-content/uploads/2011/08/Pirated-Vessel-21.11.2011.pdf (last accessed November 27, 2011 and on file with the author).
7. As of this writing, countries including France, India, and the United States have entered Somali territorial waters for pirate-hunting purposes with permission from Somalia. During intervention operations, the *INS Mysore*, an Indian destroyer, captured 23 pirates near the Somali coast. "Indian Navy 'Captures 23 Pirates,'" *BBC News*, December 13, 2008.
8. *Report from 5987th Meeting of UN Security Council*, available at http://www.un.org/ News/Press/docs/2008/sc9467.doc.htm (last accessed November 28, 2011 and on file with the author).
9. "Pirates Hijack Two Tankers Within 24 Hours Off Somali Shore," *FOX News*, March 26, 2009. http://www.foxnews.com/story/0,2933,510766,00.html (accessed November 30, 2011).
10. Combined Task Force 151 operates in a theater covering over a million square miles and American ships within the Task Force operate under an Executive Order to capture pirates. As of this writing, the most recent Order in this lineage is Executive Order 13536 authorized by President Barack Obama on April 15, 2010.

11. Combined Task Force 150 was assembled from German, Italian, Japanese, New Zealand, Spanish, and American naval assets to execute tasks associated with Operation Enduring Freedom. The Combined Task Force ships were primarily smaller frigates and destroyers, with the exception of the large Vietnam-era Spruance-class American destroyer *USS Cushing* (DD-985), which served its final tour with the task force and was replaced with the more advanced *USS Bunker Hill* (CG-52).

12. The United States opposed the release of the pirates by the Dutch navy, with Secretary Clinton asserting that the release might send "the wrong signal" about international cooperation regarding the pirate problem. See Elise Lambott, "Clinton Says Releasing Pirates Sends 'Wrong Signal'," *CNN*, April 20, 2009. http://articles.cnn.com/2009-04-20/politics/clinton.pirates_1_somali-coast-maersk-alabama-pirates?_s=PM:POLITICS (accessed November 30, 2011).

13. Though the precise value is in dispute and may never be known, the donation to Somalia to improve its security with regard to the pirate situation was on the order of a quarter billion dollars, see "Donors Pledge over $250 Million for Somalia," *USA Today*, April 23, 2009. http://www.usatoday.com/news/washington/2009-04-23-somalia-donors_N.htm (accessed November 30, 2011).

14. Pirate revenues in 2009 were estimated at $58 million (see http://www.spiegel.de/panorama/justiz/0,1518,741573,00.html); pirate revenues in the following year grew to an estimated $238 million (see http://www.eyefortransport.com/content/maritime-piracy-costs-global-community-12-billion-year).

15. See http://online.wsj.com/article/SB122754608281053435.html (*The Wall Street Journal* quoting statistics offered by the Piracy Reporting Centre of the International Maritime Bureau).

16. See "Maritime Piracy Costs Global Community up to $12 Billion a Year," *Eye for Transport*, January 20, 2011. http://www.eyefortransport.com/content/maritime-piracy-costs-global-community-12-billion-year

17. See, e.g., Anna Bowden et al., 2010. *The Economic Cost of Maritime Piracy*, Working Paper at p.25. http://oceansbeyondpiracy.org/sites/default/files/documents_old/The_Economic_Cost_of_Piracy_Full_Report.pdf and on file with the author.

18. "The collection of hands became an end in itself. *Force Publique* soldiers brought them to the [officers] in place of rubber; they even went out to harvest them instead of rubber[.]" Peter Forbath, *The River Congo* (Harper & Row 1977).

19. The tenuous relationship between brutality in Congo and economic productivity, particularly in later years, is explored in a narrative context in Adam Hochschild's excellent book, *King Leopold's Ghost* (Pan Macmillan 1998), which draws upon the work of Williams and other contemporary sources.

20. Those high-profile celebrities urging an end to Belgian rubber operations in Congo included millionaire William Cadbury, novelist Joseph Conrad, statesman Booker T. Washington, and writer Mark Twain.

21. Charter Endorsed by Elizabeth I, "Ordered, Queen's Majestie [*sic*]" (St. James's Palace, December 31, 1600).

22. *Dutch*: Vereenigde Oost-Indische Compagnie.

23. The author uses Britain in the context of the period following the Acts of Union (1707) and England to refer to the Crown, its government, and its possessions prior to the Acts of Union.

24. Jean Sutton, *Lords of the East; The East India Company and Its Ships* (London: Conway Maritime Press, 1981), p.166.

25. RJH Griffiths, *Indiaman* (2010; on file with the author).

26. The *Alabama* had no weaponry for ship-to-ship combat.

27. The *Galeones de Manila-Acapulco* customarily displaced around 2,000 short tons (about 1,800 metric tons) and were lightly armed or unarmed (but escorted by heavily-armed war galleons with 250 or more bronze cannons and artillery power of more than 500 tons).

28. The rules of engagement of the Royal Navy allowed engaging, capturing, and killing pirates at will. When bounties were on offer, it was accepted practice for Naval vessels to pursue pirates.

29. Teach may have been waiting for a "pyrate [*sic*] amnesty," which were occasionally offered by the Crown during the early eighteenth century. See, e.g., the Rogers pardons in the Bahamas (known outside the Caribbean as "the Queen Anne indies pyrate [*sic*] pardons"), which are discussed at length in the literature. Teach received a pardon for his previous piracy from Charles Eden, Governor of the Colony of North Carolina. Despite an end to Teach's piracy having been a condition upon which pardon was offered, Blackbeard soon returned to taking ships for both plunder and ransom.

30. Charles Johnson, *A General History of the Robberies and Murders of the Most Notorious Pyrates* [*sic*] (London: Clopeham Imprint, 1724).

31. A construction I use with conscious reference to 黄亚生 (Huang Yasheng)'s work.

32. This competition would likely have come from the better-organized British, who enjoyed more efficiency in agricultural operations at scale and may have enjoyed a lower cost of capital, though this is disputed among scholars in economic history.

33. ABIR (formerly BAIR) (Abir Congo Company) traded at 500 gold francs on its first day of trading, floating 1,000 shares. These publicly-traded shares appreciated 3,000 percent (appreciation calculated in non-inflation-adjusted gold francs) in the following ten years. Despite peak profits of approximately 3 million gold francs in 1903, no reasonable growth estimate—particularly given the nature of this business and its tendency to quickly exhaust its key resources—would support the share prices in 1902–1903. Pieces of ABIR (BAIR) history and performance statistics within this footnote taken from Robert Harms, "The World Abir Made: The Margina-Lopori Basin, 1885–1903," *Journal of African Economic History* 12 (1983):125–139.

9

international conflict

Is War Likely Between the Great Powers?

YES: John F. Copper, *Rhodes College*

NO: Joshua S. Goldstein, *School of International Service, American University*

History is full of wars between great powers. Great-power wars are likely to be more severe than those between other parties or between great powers and lesser powers. Such conflicts are often destabilizing and have widespread effects, because great powers are allied and their conflicts often have global consequences. Great powers have been engaged in the most number of conflicts and sustained the greatest number of deaths and casualties. Because the strongest nations are able to devote the most resources to defense, wars with each other tend to be more brutal.

Global wars are not new. While one often thinks of World War I (1916–1919) and World War II (1939–1945) as typifying major global conflicts between great powers, there is a long history of such conflicts. The Thirty Years' War (1618–1648) was a period of widespread bloodshed across Europe. The Seven Years' War (1756–1763) involved the French against England on a global canvas; the U.S. revolution and battle for independence became a colonial minor sideshow as the French supported American revolutionaries seeking to overstretch the British. The Napoleonic Wars (1803–1815) pitted the major European powers against one another.

Writers agree that the states listed in Table 1 (p. 246) have been the significant great powers in the international system.

Yet, why does great-power conflict persist? While the conduct of war is subject to emotion and uncertainty, the decision to go to war is often carefully calculated. As Prussian general and military analyst Karl von Clausewitz (1780–1831) wrote, "War is the continuation of politics (or policy) by other means."[1] States choose whether the risky application of scarce resources against an enemy is likely to yield discernible benefits. The choice is often distilled down to

Figure 1

Number of Wars by Starting Year, 1820–2003

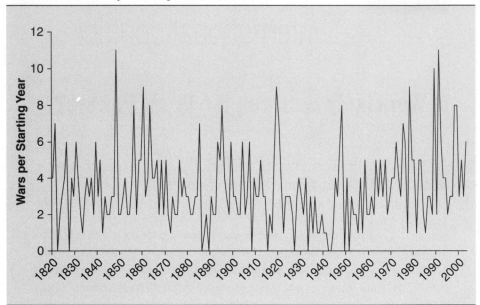

Table 1

Great Powers in History

Power	Period
Netherlands	1609–1713
Hapsburg Dynasty	1495–1519; 1519–1556; 1556–1918
Spain	1495–1519; 1556–1808
Sweden	1617–1721
France	1495–present
Ottoman Empire	1495–1699
Prussia/Germany/West Germany	1740–present
England	1495–present
USA	1898–present
Russia/USSR	1721–present
Italy	1861–1943
Japan	1905–1945
China	1949–present

Source: Jack Levy, *War in the Modern Great Power System* (Lexington: University of Kentucky Press, 1983), Table 2.1.

Figure 2

Battle-Related Deaths by War Starting Year, 1820–2003

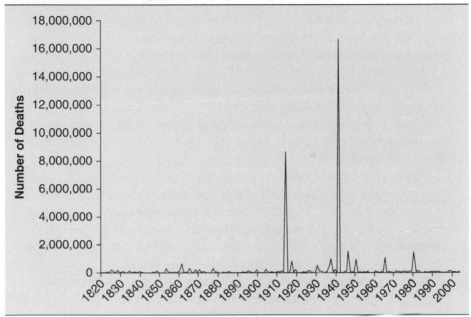

Sources: Data compiled from Correlates of War databases. http://www.correlatesofwar.org/ (accessed February 25, 2012).

a simple cost-benefit calculation: does the net benefit outweigh the cost? Still, historically, states have been most likely to miscalculate during periods of great power transitions (when they are entering the scene or declining). At such moments, great powers are likely to miscalculate and exaggerate their capabilities and likelihood of winning a war, thus precipitating a major conflict.

Various factors influence these decisions. Authors still disagree about the relative importance of these factors, though. Classical realists, including such recent articulate proponents as Kenneth Waltz, John Mearscheimer, and Steve Walt, argue that a state's prime consideration is ensuring the integrity of its borders and that secondary factors associated with socialization and economics are unlikely to make a difference. Liberals, on the other hand, are more likely to believe that a state's choices will be shaped by factors other than military capabilities. Liberal diplomats with great foresight, such as Hillary Rodham Clinton, seek to promote these factors (many related to globalization) out of a hope that they will contribute to peace by deterring the decision to initiate war. Whereas realists are worried about connections between states—economically or because of population flows—because such connections are likely to make each country feel more vulnerable and less in control of its borders, liberals see such mutual sensitivities and vulnerabilities as potentially transformative, reducing great powers' willingness to fight one another.

Alliances help defend a country. And yet alliances can be seen as aggressive to an insecure country and generate compensatory alliance building and arms races that make all parties feel less secure and more prone to initiating violence.

The prevalence of nuclear weapons (Chapter 6 in this book) may serve as a strong deterrent to war between the super powers and may have contributed to keeping the Cold War from turning hot.

Economic interdependence between powers elevates the costs of war by increasing the material benefits that will be lost to a country through fighting its commercial partners.

Democratic Peace may also be a pacifying factor. Academics have noted that democracies tend not to fight wars with other democracies for a variety of reasons that may have to do with better mutual understanding, a sense of common identity, and the fact that democracies enjoy greater economic connections with one another. The proliferation of democracies since the end of the Cold War is thus potentially a pacifying force worldwide.

Thus, debates about the future of great power rivalries and the potential for conflict are highly consequential. Current concerns focus most heavily on relations between the U.S. and China, as the U.S. is a stable or declining great power and China is expected to greatly increase its global stature over the next 20 years. And yet analysts disagree widely about the likelihood of conflict between these great powers. John Copper argues that historical trends suggest the strong possibility of armed conflict between the U.S. and China within the next 20 years. Joshua Goldstein argues that the world has significantly changed, in large part due to concerted responses to globalization, deliberate efforts to promote international interdependence, and the role of an impartial United Nations peacekeeping role; thus the prospects for a great-power war are also diminished.

Discussion Questions

1. Do you believe the trend away from great-power wars is likely to continue?
2. What can the international community do to deter great-power conflicts?
3. To what extent is Copper's argument a realist argument?
4. To what extent is Goldstein's argument a liberal argument?

NOTE

1. Karl von Clausewitz, *On War* (New York: Penguin, 1982).

YES: John F. Copper, *Rhodes College*

DEFINING THE GREAT POWERS AND WAR

Before proceeding to make the argument that war is probable between or among the contemporary great powers and which ones, it is appropriate to define *great power* and suggest how many there are. It is also necessary to note some different perspectives concerning what war is and is not.

A great power is a nation that can exert global influence and is able to cause other nations to concur with its views and/or do what it asks or demands. Great powers are considered to possess military, economic, diplomatic, and cultural power.[1] Sometimes great power has a formal definition; sometimes it does not. The Congress of Vienna defined a great power; so did the United Nations (by granting permanent membership on the Security Council). More commonly today, however, a great power is simply a nation that is perceived as that.

Currently, the number of great powers in the world is very much in dispute. Those who define a great power as a superpower and view the global system as unipolar in structure argue that there is only one great power—the United States. Those who define the global system as bipolar (which it was to most observers between 1945 or 1947 and 1991) and see it as having since been recreated (with China having replaced the Soviet Union) contend there are two great powers or superpowers. Those that advocate or believe a **multipolar global structure** prevails say there are more than two powers, though they do not agree on the number.[2]

Some multipolarists contend there are three great powers, now blocs instead of nations, if the system is defined in terms of economic power: the European Union, the United States (or North American Free Trade Agreement [NAFTA]), and the Pacific Rim (or Asia more broadly, if India is included) led previously by Japan and now by China.[3] Most, however, define power more in military terms or by combining all of the qualities (though in different proportions) of a power mentioned above rather than simple economic power. They frequently cite the U.S. and China plus the European Union, Russia, and Japan as the great powers. Others add India, the Association of Southeast Asia (ASEAN), and sometimes Brazil. If possession of nuclear weapons is seen as an essential qualification, they include Pakistan and Israel.[4]

War is defined as a situation that exists when two or more nations declare that hostilities exist between or among them, though it is more often thought of as an organized, armed conflict that results in considerable damage and disruption plus injuries and deaths where it occurs.[5] Some scholars define war to include smaller conflicts that result in as few as one thousand deaths.[6] Wars are commonly thought of as being between or among nations, although many of the worst wars have been civil wars.[7]

If one agrees with the multipolarist view; namely that one accepts their thesis that there are a considerable number (possibly ten) of great powers, adheres to a fairly long timeline (twenty years in the future is often seen as the maximum time frame for assessment of international politics, but some say it should be longer), and defines war as not meaning a huge number of dead, then war between two great powers or among more than two great powers seems extremely likely—perhaps close to a certainty.

It need also be noted that the current definition of (serious) war does not require the use of nuclear weapons, since many regard them as obsolete. They have not been used in the current era (and perhaps cannot be), and there are other weapons just as destructive as a nuclear weapon.[8] In counterpoint, a radiation device (certainly a kind of nuclear weapon) used by a terrorist would not necessarily constitute a "serious war" with global consequences.

Or, if war can be defined as a serious struggle against terrorism (the term "war on terrorism" being common) by one or more great power, then a serious war is already in progress. The same may be said of other kinds of war (of which there are many).

However, many scholars do not accept war as so defined since it would make the inevitability of war an argument that cannot be refuted. Hence, war in the sense of comporting with the generally understood meaning of the question whether there will be a war between two great powers needs to be a conflict that is large in its dimensions and dangerous to the global community.

In any case, in recent years, predicting a serious war means, to most scholars, calculating the probability of a serious conflict between the United States and China.[9] Most other possibilities of a serious war (as just defined) occurring in the near term at least are not viewed as very likely. For example, it is difficult to conceive of a serious conflict, certainly what we would call a dangerous war, between the European Union and Japan, Brazil, or ASEAN. A war between the U.S. and Japan, Brazil, or ASEAN would be so lopsided it would not likely occur and would not be very meaningful if it did.

Even a nuclear exchange between India and Pakistan, which seems a fairly high probability, given that the two countries have gone to war more than once in recent years, would not be ultimately dangerous to the planet if the U.S. and China (or Russia, for the time being) were not to take opposite sides and join in fighting the war. The same can be said of an Israeli attack on Iran or another Middle East country to preclude it going nuclear (which many say is highly probable).[10]

Therefore the continuation of this discussion will be on the prospects for a U.S.–China war. There are three realms where currently the causes for war are palpable: the state level, the global-system level, and the human level.[11]

A U.S.–CHINA WAR: THE STATE LEVEL OF ANALYSIS

Most specialists that study warfare say that confrontation between competitive nation states is the leading cause of war. In anticipating a serious conflict, they examine *flashpoints* or places where a war (involving using weapons of mass destruction) is likely. Importantly, the places or countries where the U.S. and China have different and opposing interests and where war will likely occur involving the two are the same as the most dangerous flashpoints. The top three are Taiwan, the Korean Peninsula, and the South China Sea.[12]

Taiwan, or the Taiwan Strait, is generally regarded as the most serious flashpoint in the world. China regards Taiwan as part of China or Chinese territory that has not yet been recovered. According to Chinese leaders, "American imperialists" prevented it from being incorporated by China at the end of the Chinese Civil War between the Communists and the Nationalists that followed WWII. In 1950, U.S. President Truman sent the U.S. Seventh Fleet to the Taiwan Strait to block a Chinese invasion of the island. Two crises followed in 1954–1955 and 1958, when China attacked the Offshore Islands near the coast of China held by the Chiang Kai-shek government in Taiwan, ostensibly as a prelude to invading Taiwan. The U.S. threatened China with an attack using nuclear weapons. This was something China did not forget.[13] It may be viewed as the beginning of China and the U.S. becoming true enemies.

In 1954, the U.S. concluded a defense treaty with Chiang Kai-shek, formalizing America's protectorate relationship with Taiwan. This was terminated in 1979 but for all intents and purposes was replaced by a law passed by Congress called the Taiwan Relations Act (TRA). The TRA arguably broadened America's commitment to the island.[14] In 2005, China's parliament passed a law called the Anti-Secession Law that declared China would use "non-peaceful means" to recover Taiwan if peaceful means did not succeed over a certain period of time.[15] In short, China and the United States have established formal policies, based on binding legal commitments, which compel their policymakers to take a hard stance on the "Taiwan issue," thereby making it likely that the two countries will come to loggerheads on the Taiwan matter.

To China, recovering Taiwan is not only a matter of preserving its territorial integrity (one of the most common causes of war), but it has grown in salience as a strategic goal in China since the country has become infused with virulent Chinese nationalism.[16] Taiwan is now said to be a Chinese "core interest"—something China is willing to go to war over. It is also a major objective of China's military, which has been considerably more assertive and more involved in politics in recent years.[17]

In addition, control over Taiwan relates to China's "Malacca Strait" problem—its oil lifeline to the Middle East that passes through a narrow strait in Southeast Asia. As well, it connects intimately to China's military strategy of expanding its navy (including, importantly, its submarine fleet), which might use Taiwan as an important base.[18]

To the United States, Taiwan is a working democracy—more importantly, one that the U.S. created and nourished. Therefore, to Americans, Taiwan deserves to decide its own future. Since most citizens in Taiwan prefer not to be part of China or want to keep the status quo, which is *de facto* independence of China, the U.S. position is diametrically opposed to China's. In 1996, the U.S. and China nearly went to war when China conducted threatening missile tests off Taiwan's coast during the run-up to a major national election. A Chinese leader at this time warned that China might nuke Los Angeles.[19]

Another consideration is that America's "loss of Taiwan" would undermine its credibility in East Asia such that its military alliances and its other strategic ties with countries in the region would be damaged beyond repair. American strategists also see Taiwan under Chinese rule as affording the latter a base from which its submarines can quickly enter deep waters in the Pacific Ocean and proceed from there to locations proximate to the U.S. West Coast undetected, putting the U.S. under threat of attack by short-range missiles.[20] Something similar to this happened during the Kennedy administration, which created a crisis and nearly a war between the U.S. and the Soviet Union—arguably the closest the two came to nuclear exchange during the Cold War.

Still another American perspective on Taiwan's importance is that it is part of a chain of islands off the coast of China that pits the littoral nations of East Asia against the continental power; if that chain is broken, it would result in an important advantage to China and a serious disadvantage to America's allies, especially Japan and the Philippines. Still another view is that of the historian and the geopolitician: Taiwan represents the last of China's territorial concerns. When the U.S. finally resolved its territorial matters after the last of the Indian Wars in the late 1800s, it became an ambitious and aggressive global power— which China may well mimic after it incorporates Taiwan.[21]

In the case of Korea, China and the United States went to war (called a *police action* under the guise of a United Nations' operation, though few saw it as that) in 1950. China supported North Korea, and thus when U.S. forces neared the Chinese border, it reacted by sending troops to wage war. United States forces suffered more than thirty thousand deaths and more than one hundred thousand wounded. The war left bitterness in the U.S. toward China. The war had another shocking effect: In the minds of Americans, the United States had never before failed to win a war. (This was not true, but it was widely believed.)[22] Now, for the first time the U.S. did not win. America was profoundly embarrassed and its global image was sullied. To China, the Korean War was an American war of aggression. China suffered many more casualties than the U.S.—over one million; Mao's son was among those killed.[23]

Moreover, the Korean War did not end. There was no peace treaty, only an armistice. North and South Korea are still at war. China and North Korea have a defense treaty, making China bound to protect North Korea. The United States has a defense pact with South Korea. This means a conflict between the two Koreas, which are implacable enemies, will draw Washington and Beijing into war.

North Korean leaders, with Chinese connivance (in American eyes), have since killed American soldiers in the demilitarized zone, shot down U.S. planes, seized American naval vessels, and committed acts of terrorism. China has aided North Korea in building nuclear weapons and missiles to deliver them. The North Korean regime is run by the army, starves its citizens, disregards human rights, refuses to accept the notion that communism should be extinct, flaunts its obligations under international agreements, and reneges on its promises to denuclearize. Its leaders, in the American view, are partially or wholly insane.[24] It is fair to say that North Korea is the most unpredictable country in the world and a provocateur.

Without China's economic aid, North Korea would have to come to terms with the U.S. and join the community of peace-loving nations or implode. Notwithstanding China's close ties and support, the U.S. has contemplated military action against North Korea on a number of occasions and likely will in the future, given that the "North Korean problem" has not been resolved or dampened in its severity.[25]

Finally, there is widespread hope for the unification of the two Koreas (rightfully so) if done primarily on South Korea's terms—which is likely, given that it is bigger and more prosperous. This would possibly put some thirty thousand U.S. troops on China's border. Or, if U.S. troops were withdrawn, China would be impelled to fill the vacuum, and Korea would then become a threat to Japan (with whom the U.S. has a defense treaty and with whom relations with China have deteriorated in recent years).[26]

The South China Sea constitutes a vortex of conflicting U.S. and Chinese core principles that could easily lead to conflict. China claims the South China Sea is its territory, and in 1992, its legislature passed a law to that effect. Its claim is serious.[27] Furthermore, the U.S. declares that the South China Sea is international waters. The United States Navy must use the area freely, lest American naval power be reduced to insignificance in the Far East and Washington dramatically lose its influence in the region and beyond. Hence the aims of the two powers clearly conflict.[28]

As in the case of Taiwan, China's territorial integrity is at issue. More than that, there are oil and other resources undersea that China desperately needs to feed its continued industrialization and economic growth. In addition, China's "oil lifeline" to the Middle East passes through the South China Sea.[29]

China is trying to get the nations of Southeast Asia to acquiesce to its claim. It has spent billions in aid, built regional infrastructure projects that connect China and the region, and has concluded a trade agreement (in January 2010) that has created the world's largest common market, one that poignantly excludes the United States. Washington has recently declared it is returning to the region in force and is in the process of bolstering its military and other ties with nations in the region.[30] U.S.–China competition in the South China Sea and in adjacent countries has recently escalated.[31]

The U.S. and China have already faced off against each other in the South China Sea. One of the two most important instances happened in April 2001, when a U.S. reconnaissance plane collided with a Chinese fighter. The former was damaged and had to land on China's Hainan Island; the latter crashed and the pilot was killed. This, the EP-3 Incident, resulted in a serious deterioration of relations between the U.S. and China, with both making threatening statements toward the other. A similar crisis occurred in 2009, when the U.S. ship *the Impeccable* came close to a new Chinese submarine base on Hainan Island and was challenged and harassed by Chinese vessels. In both cases, China challenged the U.S. right to spy on China in what the U.S. considered above or in international waters but what China says is China's exclusive economic zone.[32]

Some observers see the winner in the South China Sea dispute between the U.S. and China as determining who will win dominance in the region—the most dynamic area of the world and one that will determine the direction of world politics in the future. Dominance there is worth fighting for.

The India–Pakistan standoff and a possible Israeli attack on Iran's nuclear facilities are regarded as less serious or are considered secondary flashpoints, because the U.S. and China are not clearly on opposite sides nor do they have very serious conflicting national interests. Conditions could, of course, change. A war between China and Russia would be a serious matter that the U.S. could not ignore, though the two are friends or allies at the moment.

A U.S.–CHINA WAR: THE GLOBAL LEVEL OF ANALYSIS

To assess further the chances of a war between the U.S. and China, one needs to consider the context of the relations between the two countries. In other words, the international system, it will be argued, makes a U.S.–China war more likely.

The belief that a U.S.–China conflict is likely is based on how a majority of scholars in the field look at the current structure of the international system. Most describe it as dominated by one superpower (the United States) and one fast-rising power (China). Both from observing history and the various kinds of academic analyses (including computer modeling, gaming, etc.) of this kind of system, it is seen to be a very unstable one and one that will likely result in conflict.[33]

Not only is the international system defined as one superpower and one rising (and challenging) power but changes favoring the rising power and disfavoring the superpower are prominent; in fact, they are overwhelming. China is very fast on the rise; American is fast, relatively at least, on the decline.[34]

The salience of this can hardly be overstated. Scholars of international relations tell us their studies prove that war does not follow from a situation of countries building arms and increasing their military power or doing the opposite (cutting their armaments). Rather, war happens when there is unevenness or lack of balance between or among the competing powers' military strength.[35] This is also true of economic power and power generally.

Assessing the two major elements of power—economic power and military power—it is obvious there is a "great transition" in progress in U.S.–China relations—a dangerous transition. The question is can the two powers handle this shift peacefully? The evidence so far suggests it is unlikely.

China has been growing economically at a miracle rate of speed since 1978, when it made the transition from extreme, egalitarian communism under Mao to capitalism, sometimes described as "wild west capitalism," under Deng Xiaoping. The increases in China's gross domestic product have been in the double-digit range for more than forty years. During that period, China's worst year economically (1989—the year of the Tiananmen Square Incident) has been better than America's best. China's growth in most years during this period was between three and five times that of America's growth.[36]

As a consequence, it is a matter of predicting when—not if—China will pass the United States to become the world's foremost economic power. If China is defined to include Hong Kong (which is a part of China but considered separate when citing economic data), Taiwan, Singapore, and the Overseas Chinese (all Chinese or Chinese entities) and using purchasing power parity (PPP), "China" passed the U.S. five or so years into the new millennium. When using the PPP measurement for the People's Republic of China (not including the Chinese entities just mentioned), it passed the U.S. in 2010. Using simply absolute (U.S. dollars) figures the People's Republic will pass the U.S. in a decade or so, giving China economic dominance in the world.[37]

China catching up with and passing the U.S. so far has not been a pretty sight. And it portends to get worse. America accuses China of exploiting its cheap labor, saving too much, investing too much, raping the environment, stealing intellectual property, and undervaluing its currency. China feels that America is jealous and wants to prevent its rise and that China is singled out for demonization. This situation is a classic (and dangerous) example of a rising economic power seeking a higher status (if not hegemony) in the global system and the status quo power resisting.[38]

America has a choice (but not really) between implementing very serious reform—such as abolishing the minimum wage, ending unemployment benefits, getting rid of labor unions, cutting taxes, reigning in regulations and lawyers, drastically trimming its military and using it only in desperate situations or when it is profitable, shedding its vast entitlement system, making its penal system self-financing, and much more—and losing the economic war to China. America won't do these things; they are too radical and would make the U.S. like China. Americans would prefer to vilify China and/or fight.

The magnitude of China's growing economic power and America's precipitous (relative) economic decline can hardly be overestimated. U.S. debt of over $15 trillion and future entitlement obligations of several times that juxtaposed beside China's trillions in foreign exchange, savings, and investments abroad (including U.S. debt to China) translates into the fast rise of China and the precipitous decline of the United States.[39]

The U.S., while further ahead in military power, is losing the power contest to China in this realm even faster. U.S. defense spending has recently been cut by billions of dollars. Given the magnitude of the U.S. debt, the military budget will undoubtedly be cut much more in the future. China, meanwhile, has been upping its defense budget by double-digits every year. It can afford it. Its spending on its navy and air force, which compete directly with the U.S., has increased by much larger figures.[40]

The U.S. currently has no new manned aircraft under development (for the first time in its aviation history). It has no new surface ship or attack submarine in the design stage. Over the last two years, it has cancelled thirty defense programs.[41] Meanwhile, China has developed new weapons or weapons systems at short intervals. It has put into use its space weapons by shooting down a satellite and recently put on display its stealth capabilities—both to the consternation and/or embarrassment of the United States.[42]

Some U.S. military leaders have talked of reconfiguring America's defense strategy to take into consideration China's rise; but this is now little more than stage-planning thinking.

Meanwhile, the U.S. has spent vast quantities of its military force, funds for structure, and personnel in Middle East wars. And yet, Washington has painfully ignored East Asia, the only region of the world where there is a real challenge to the U.S.[43]

Recently, American leaders seem to have come to the realization that the U.S. cannot match the growth of Chinese military power in Asia. Its recourse has been to seek allies and try to manage a balance of power system in Asia by aligning with Japan, ASEAN, and India against China.[44]

Power balancing is what adherents to the realist school of thought, the most popular view of global politics espoused by both scholars and diplomats in the West, do. Balancing means confronting and challenging. Thus many American realists believe war with China is likely or inevitable.[45] Chinese leaders tend to be realists too, but their realism is based on quite different premises.[46] They see U.S. balancing efforts as a means to contain China and prevent its rise.[47] This is a deadly combination.

Diplomacy might help ameliorate the situation, but only if there is considerable understanding and equity in the relationship. The gaps between the U.S. and China in diplomatic and cultural power are closing fast. China has vast sums of money to use to give foreign aid; America can afford much less than it has been giving. Chinese language and culture are growing in popularity throughout the world. Chinese, which is spoken by roughly threefold the number of native English speakers in the world, is being taught in more and more countries, in many cases, replacing English. China is overall making rapid progress in the pursuing the diplomatic/culture war; some say it is winning.[48]

One might summarize the changing power relationship between the U.S. and China as profound and shocking. America is a country that believes that its political system, culture, and much more are superior and should be universal. It is a country that has a "superbowl mentality": winners are those in first place; losers finish in second place. Chinese are a people that are humble on the outside and arrogant on the inside, and the latter becomes dominant when China does well. China, like the United States, sees its culture as universal.[49] This means the two will ultimately engage in a showdown.

A U.S. WAR WITH CHINA: THE HUMAN LEVEL OF ANALYSIS

At the human level, the lack of understanding as well as the level of misunderstanding between the two peoples abounds. This stems, in large measure, from the fact that China sees itself as singular or unique, and its citizens espouse this view of themselves and their culture.[50] Americans use the word *exceptional* to depict themselves and the U.S.[51] Feelings of superiority that are the product of these self-perceptions are ingrained into the souls of the people of each country.

In fact, the record of relations between the U.S. and China reveals a plethora of grievous misinterpretations based on their different histories and cultures. The results are slights and insults of each other, both deliberate and unintentional and public and private. The term *barbarian* describes how Chinese see Americans; the terms *Chinaman* and *heathen* depict how Americans see Chinese.

Pointing out some of the more egregious examples of ill will growing out of this misunderstanding will help elucidate the nature of the relationship; but it also suggests that there are past grievances that make war now likely.

When evoking the name "Franklin Delano Roosevelt," Americans think of an icon, an American wartime hero. Chinese see the name "Delano." Warren Delano was an American businessman who sold opium in China in the 1800s, causing unspeakable suffering to the Chinese people in the 1800s; in fact, he took over much of the British trade when the latter were banned from it. FDR's fortune was inherited from Delano, his grandfather, hence his middle name.[52]

To Americans, World War I was a war fought in Europe, which America joined to save the world's democracies from tyranny. Most Americans do not know China was a participant in the war. The Chinese view is quite different: China was on America's side and should have enjoyed the fruits of victory, the most important being the return of Shandong Province (the home of Confucius and considered by most Chinese as a sacred place). It was a German leasehold. President Woodrow Wilson negotiated the peace at Versailles and advanced his famous Fourteen Points to change the world. But when Japan suggested adding another point, banning racism, Wilson (one of America's most racist presidents) gave Japan Shandong for retracting its proposal.[53]

World War II, in American history texts, was a war whose cause was to defeat German/Italian and Japanese fascism alike. But to the Chinese it was not alike; rather, it was an example of America's strategy to win the war in Europe first—because liberating white people took precedence.[54] To make matters worse, at the close of the war, FDR committed a second betrayal of China by giving Chinese territory and special privileges in China (at Yalta) to the Soviet Union.[55]

Chinese know and often recall the Chinese Exclusion Act of 1882 as blatant American racial discrimination against Chinese. Most Americans, if they know about the law at all, view it as something the state of California did and as something that presently has little or no relevance, since there is currently no prejudice against Chinese in the United States. Chinese perceive racial discrimination in the U.S. against them as having changed very little over time. They cite the fact that illegal Chinese in the U.S. are apprehended and quickly deported. Not so are the ten million or so white-race people from countries south of the United States. Chinese are seldom seen on American television, and when they appear in Hollywood's movies, they are often depicted in an unfavorable light—quite in contrast to other minorities in the United States.

Chinese feel the vilest form of racism against Chinese is the quota systems used against them when they apply for admission to America's best universities.[56] Americans see this as fair and proper affirmative action.

Americans sees China as a site of vast human rights abuses: persecution of large numbers of people for their political beliefs or expression of them, lack of legal protections, forced abortions, executions, and so on. China sees America as a land where there is rampant racial discrimination, the incarceration of the largest number of people by percent of the population anywhere, a high frequency of women injured or killed by men, and horrendous rates of abuse of children and the elderly (the latter being segregated in the society and/or fear to take a walk on the streets of any large city).[57] This difference in perspective is an especially sensitive matter to the U.S., as America is losing the "human rights crusade" against China. More and more nations and more people are espousing China's position on human rights.[58] Yet the U.S. persists in invoking the human rights agenda with China. China can only think that Americans fear China's recent successes and espouse evil intentions toward China.

Americans view China as being undemocratic. They are vexed by the reality that its economic development has not produced a "freer" political system. In counterpoint, China's economic success (along with most of Asia) has fostered the view (prevalent in the Third World) that a democratic system is not the best way to develop. Rather, China is now the model.[59] Chinese note that there has been profound political change in China in recent years—freedom to do business, to travel, and much more; local elections; a new legal system; more transparency; and decentralization of political power—that America has not noted or does not respect.[60]

A salient point in this regard is the fact that Americans think that if China were to democratize, as they advocate, relations would improve and war between the two countries would be less likely. There are two problems with this view. One, America's policy of democratizing China is not working well, if at all. China is not putting democratic reforms into practice. Returning students are not taking American democratic values with them.[61] Two, the empirical research reveals that new democracies, which arguably China is or is becoming, are *more* likely to start a war than other countries, including autocratic ones.[62]

The Tiananmen Square Incident ("Massacre" to Americans) was a watershed event in U.S.–China relations. To Americans, it marked a turnaround in China democratizing and a return to an authoritarian politics. China perceived the "event" as the product of foreign efforts to subvert China and prevent its rise and was turned into a Western "anti-Chinese epoch" by a hostile Western media. The event caused a permanent deterioration in U.S.–China relations.[63]

The huge majority of Chinese believe the U.S. bombing of the Chinese embassy in Belgrade in 1999 was a calculated act. The smart bomb that did the deed killed Chinese and no one else. America expressed little remorse and said it was an accident. Chinese often ask: how could such a highly technological nation as the U.S. have made such a mistake? Their answer: it didn't; America did it deliberately.[64]

Currently, many Americans think that America's image has improved in the eyes of other countries, including China, with the end of the George W. Bush administration and the demise of the neocons. On the other hand, the Chinese government has not been so affected. It insulted President Obama when he visited in 2009.[65] The Internet in China has been full of Obama insults, many of them racist. China's aggressive foreign policy has accelerated coinciding with Obama taking office.

Popular opinion in the two countries, as measured by opinion surveys, has become more negative toward each other. This, of course, reflects trade relationships and other frictions and the fact that the two countries are competing for global influence. But it also mirrors ill will at the grassroots level.[66] This, in fact, explains why U.S. politicians running for office demonize China—it helps win votes. Likewise, Chinese officials who criticize America find they have a more friendly audience.

Many U.S. scholars expect (and hope) that the tension that might otherwise lead to conflict between the U.S. and China will be ameliorated by the increased use of soft (people's) power by each, thereby reducing the likelihood of employing hard power (the military). The reality is that the U.S. cannot afford to increase its spending on soft power, while China has found the results from soft power lacking, thus creating advocates of relying more on hard power from both countries.[67]

All of this relates to China's search for status in the world, which, at least in the eyes of Chinese, America seeks to deny. *Image* (or *face* to China), which has long been related to the outbreak of war, is certainly a possible cause of war between China and the United States. China is the most status-conscious nation in the world. The U.S. woefully misunderstands this and frequently, in arrogance, dismisses it.[68]

CONCLUSIONS

The likelihood of war between the U.S. and China is large. A host of indicators point in that direction. There are also other reasons, in addition to those cited, to think that a small conflict can and will expand.

China's strategy (about which much has been written) to fight the United States involves using "asymmetric warfare." This style of war involves disrupting computers and communications facilities, wrecking financial markets, employing terrorism, using chemical and biological weapons, engaging in counterfeiting, and much more. In other words, striking at the enemy's weak points using unconventional weapons is China's strategy for victory. Adopting such a strategy means that neither side can accurately calculate the power of the other nor can they anticipate the winner in a conflict. This makes a U.S.–China war more dangerous and more difficult to control.[69]

It can also be said that the U.S. and China are already at war. Most people in both countries, as well as many academics, perceive there is already an economic war in progress.[70] There is a resource war.[71] There is also a cyber war.[72] There is a spy war.[73] There is a contest for the domination of space, which many other countries have opted out of or will soon, due to the high cost and the fact their weapons research funds (which are connected to space research) have declined. (Which country will colonize Mars?)[74] All of these constitute what may be called *modern warfare*. Moreover, they are likely to escalate and encourage other forms of warfare.

Meanwhile, the means for the U.S. and China to avoid war are fraught with obstacles. One way out of this dangerous downward spiral between the two countries heading for a hot war is for them to cooperate (collude), as China (along with some American scholars) often said the U.S. and the Soviet Union did during the bipolar years.[75] Some observers suggest that both countries currently need war (or at least an enemy) to control their economies and deal with unemployment, their restless populations, and more. If this happens, there will be a new bipolarity and a new Cold War. But a new cold war is war as it has generally been defined. Moreover, given the vast cultural and other divides, the collusion needed to make the system stable will likely be much more difficult to sustain than it was for the U.S. and the Soviet Union.

If, on the other hand, the global system evolves into a multipolar one, which will happen if China does not continue to rise as it has been or deliberately curtails its ambitions, China's role in that system will be uncertain. It could be a supporter of the system, a spoiler, or a shirker. The latter two would contribute to instability and make war more probable.[76] In any event, a multipolar system requires balancing to work and, as indicated, there are serious difficulties for China and the U.S. doing this.

Finally, there is the possibility that China will become the world's dominant power. Some suggest that U.S. debt, slow economic growth, and a waning desire to play a dominant role in the world will end the era of American supremacy, just as the role of the United Kingdom declined after World War II—the Suez crisis in 1954 marking the turning point.[77] The rise of China (along with the rest of Asia) means the American global system will be supplanted by a Chinese world order—one that is very different from that of the U.S. (not based on equality, universalism, and other Western principles) and is generally unacceptable to the United States. America will oppose this system and will fight rather than submit.[78]

NOTES

1. A host of scholars have written about the elements of power and have listed them. See, for example, Hans J. Morgenthau, *Power and International Relations: The Struggle for Power and Peace* (New York: Alfred A. Knopf, 1967). John Copper applies the concept to China during the Mao period. See John F. Copper, *China's Global Role: An Analysis of Peking's National Power Capabilities in the Context of an Evolving International System* (Stanford: Hoover Institution Press, 1980). For a more recent assessment, see David M. Lampton, *The Three Faces of Chinese Power: Might, Money, and Minds* (Berkeley: University of California Press, 2010). For a more general discussion of great powers, see John J. Mearsheimer, *The Tragedy of Great Power Politics* (New York: W.W. Norton, 2001).

2. The structure of the international system, of course, does not determine absolutely who the great powers are or the number of them, but it is a strong indicator. See G. John Ikenberry, Michael Mastanduno, and William C. Wohlforth, "Introduction: Unipolarity, State Behavior, and Systemic Consequences," in *International Relations Theory and the Consequences of Unipolarity* (London: Cambridge University Press, 2011).

3. Lester C. Thurow, *Head to Head: The Economic Battle among Japan, Europe, and America* (New York: Morrow, 1992).

4. Normally a *nuclear nation* is defined as one that has tested a nuclear weapon. Israel has not done a test in the conventional sense of that word, although it has done many computer-simulated tests and is considered to have a sizeable number of operational nuclear weapons.

5. See Jack C. Plano and Roy Olton, *The International Relations Dictionary* (Santa Barbara: ABC-CLIO, 1982), p. 198. The authors note there are many different kinds of war, including guerrilla war, civil war, accidental war, limited war, etc.

6. See Melvin Small and J. David Singer, "Patterns in International Warfare, 1816–1965," *Annals of the American Academy of Political and Social Science* (September 1970): 45–55.

7. World War II resulted in the largest number of deaths of any war. However, two civil wars in China are close, and the death counts in both were much larger in terms of the percentage of people living on the planet at the time that were killed. It is sometimes thought that China is a peaceful country (as it often claims) and has not been involved in wars very much. This is definitely not true. For example, see Stephen Mosher, *Hegemon: China's Plan to Dominate Asia and the World* (San Francisco: Encounter Books, 2003).

8. In 1946, President Truman spoke of an "insect age" or an "atmosphere-less planet" after he dropped atomic bombs on Japan. Joseph Stalin said something similar. In the Korean War, the Vietnam War, and other wars that followed, nuclear weapons

were not used. See Niall Ferguson, *The War of the World: Twentieth-Century Conflict and the Descent of the West* (New York: Penguin, 2006), p. 597.

9. This has been the subject of several recent books, including Aaron L. Friedberg, *A Contest for Supremacy: China, America, and the Struggle for Mastery in Asia* (New York: W.W. Norton, 2011); Martin Jacques, *When China Rules the World: The End of the Western World and the Birth of a New Global Order* (New York: Penguin, 2009); Henry Kissinger, *On China* (New York: Penguin, 2011); and Michael D. Swaine, *America's Challenge: Engaging a Rising China in the Twenty-First Century* (Washington, DC: Carnegie Endowment for Peace, 2011).

10. China, of course, is aligned with Pakistan against India, but the two have no defense treaty. China has not entered directly in past conflicts. The U.S. has close ties with Pakistan as well as India and would probably be in a position to try to dampen or stop any conflict between them. Finally, China and the U.S. have not expressed serious disagreements regarding India–Pakistan relations. China is aligned with Iran but would not likely get directly involved if Israel were to strike its nuclear facilities.

11. Kenneth N. Waltz, *Man the State and War: A Theoretical Analysis* (New York: Columbia University Press, 2001).

12. Since 2008, with a new president in Taiwan and problems in Korea, some say that Korea is the number one flashpoint.

13. Thomas E. Stolper, *China, Taiwan, and the Offshore Islands* (Armonk: M.E. Sharpe, 1985), pp. 89–90; and A. Doak Barnett, *Communist China and Asia: A Challenge to American Policy* (New York: Vintage, 1960), p. 116. China immediately embarked on a nuclear weapons program at this time to ensure this would not happen again.

14. See John F. Copper, *China Diplomacy: The Washington–Taipei–Beijing Triangle* (Boulder: Westview Press, 1992). I argue that because the TRA promises to keep U.S. troops in Asia (which the treaty did not) and expresses concern over human rights (through democratization) that the U.S. is very committed to Taiwan.

15. See Richard C. Bush and Michael E. O'Hanlon, *A War like No Other: The Truth about China's Challenge to America* (Hoboken: John Wiley and Sons, 2007), p. 109. According to the authors, the law represented a willingness on China's part to use force. The U.S. Congress voiced opposition to the law, seeing it as a threat and conflicting with the Taiwan Relations Act. It was also viewed as an indication of the rising influence of the military in China.

16. For details concerning the rise of Chinese nationalism, see Peter Hays Gries, *China's New Nationalism: Pride, Politics, and Diplomacy* (Berkeley: University of California Press, 2004); and Yongnian Zheng, *Discovering Chinese Nationalism in China: Modernization, Identity, and International Relations* (Cambridge: Cambridge University Press, 1999). A number of books published in China recently, such as *The China That Can Say No*; *China is Unhappy*; *China Dream*; and *China's Path under the Shadow of Globalization*, underscore this trend.

17. See Michael D Swaine, "China's Assertive Behavior—Part One: On 'Core Interests,'" *China Leadership Monitor*, February 22, 2011 (online at chinaleadershipmonitor.org).

18. Toshi Yoshihara and James R. Holmes, *Red Star over the Pacific: China's Rise and the Challenge to U.S. Maritime Strategy* (Annapolis: Naval Institute Press, 2010), pp. 19–20.

19. See John F. Copper, *Playing with Fire: The Looming War with China over Taiwan* (Westport: Praeger, 2005), chapter 1; and John W. Garver, *Face Off: China, the United States, and Taiwan's Democratization* (Seattle: University of Washington Press, 1997).

20. Yoshihara and Holmes, *Red Star over the Pacific,* pp. 6–7.

21. John F. Copper, "Why We Need Taiwan," *The National Interest online,* August 29, 2011 (http://nationalinterest.org/commentary/why-we-need-taiwan-5815).

22. See Gordon Tullock, *Open Secrets of American Foreign Policy* (Singapore: World Scientific, 2007), p. 67.

23. Michael Schaller, *The United States and China in the Twentieth Century* (Oxford: Oxford University Press, 1990), p. 143.

24. The U.S. Department of State and the Central Intelligence Agency have documented North Korea's state sponsorship of terrorism, its infiltration and sabotage in South Korea, its trafficking in persons and drugs, and much more. See "Background notes" (online at http://www.state.gov/r/pa/ei/bgn/2792.htm) and CIA World Factbook (online at https://www.cia.gov/library/publications/the-world-factbook/index.html). The U.S. government has condemned North Korea's nuclear tests, as has the United Nations.

25. Peter Navarro, *The Coming China Wars: Where They Will Be Fought, How They Will Be Fought* (Upper Saddle River: Financial Times Press, 2007), p. 214.

26. Ibid.

27. See Andrew J. Nathan and Robert S. Ross, *The Great Wall and the Empty Fortress: China's Search for Security* (New York: W.W. Norton, 1997), pp. 114–15.

28. Yoshihara and Holmes, *Red Star over the Pacific,* pp. 87–97. The authors even suggest war scenarios related to this conflict.

29. See Robert D. Kaplan, "The South China Sea Is the Future of Conflict," *Foreign Policy,* September/October 2011, pp. 76–86; and Robert D. Kaplan, *Monsoon: The Indian Ocean and the Future of American Power* (New York: Random House, 2010), p. 8.

30. See for example, Hillary Clinton, "America's PacificCentury," *Foreign Policy,* November 2011, pp. 56–63.

31. See Richard Weitz, "Nervous Neighbors: China Finds a Sphere of Influence," *World Affairs,* March/April 2011, pp. 6–14.

32. Robert G. Sutter, *Chinese Foreign Relations: Power and Policy since the Cold War* (Lanham: Rowman and Littlefield, 2010), p. 66.

33. This view is based on the various works on power transition theory in the field. For a recent update, see Margit Bussmann and John R. Oneal, "Do Hegemons Distribute Private Goods? A Test of Power-Transition Theory," *Journal of Conflict Resolution,* February 2007, p. 89.

34. See sources cited in footnote #1.

35. A number of writers have made this point. See, for example, Robert Gilpin, *War and Change in World Politics* (New York: Cambridge University Press, 1981); A. F. K. Organski, *World Politics* (New York: Alfred A. Knopf, 1958); and A. F. K Organski and Jack Kugler, *The War Ledger* (Chicago: University of Chicago Press, 1980).

36. See William H. Overholt, *The Rise of China: How Economic Reform is Creating a New Superpower* (New York: W.W. Norton, 1993) for an analysis of how China's economic boom began.

37. See "How to Get a Date," *Economist*, December 31, 2011. According to this article, China has already passed the U.S. in half of twenty-one criteria and will overtake America in virtually all of them within a decade.

38. See Samuel P. Huntington, *The Clash of Civilizations and the Remaking of the World Order* (New York: Simon and Schuster, 1996), p. 229. It should also be noted that the rules of global trade do not prohibit most of China's trade policies; they are domestic issues off-limits to America's efforts to create a level playing field.

39. For the salience of this, see Arvind Subramanian, *Eclipse: Living in the Shadow of China's Economic Dominance* (Washington, DC: Peterson Institute, 2011), chapter 1. The author argues that America's economic dominance in the world is about to end as a result of China's rise.

40. Richard D. Fisher, Jr., *China's Military Modernization: Building for Regional and Global Reach* (Stanford: Stanford University Press, 2010), pp. 16–17.

41. See "Ten Questions on the Future of U.S. Defense Spending Priorities for Secretary of Defense Nominee Leon Panetta," *Articles and Commentary* (American Enterprise Institute), June 7, 2011; and Mackenzie Eaglen and Bryan McGrath, "A Day Without Sea Power," *The Weekly Standard*, June 6, 2011, p. 22.

42. Friedberg, *A Contest for Supremacy*, p. 222.

43. It is the opinion of many pundits that the U.S. is not equipped to fight two kinds of war at the same time. See Kurt M. Campbell and Michel E. O'Hanlon, *Hard Power: The New Politics of National Security* (New York: Basic Books, 2006), p. 186. Also see Joshua Kurlantzick, "How Obama Lost His Asian Friends," *Newsweek*, July 16, 2010 (online at newsweek.com).

44. Henry Kissinger suggested this should be U.S. policy some time ago. See Henry Kissinger, *Does the United States Need a Foreign Policy? Toward a Diplomacy for the 21st Century* (New York: Simon and Schuster, 2001), p. 110–18.

45. Almost all realists accept this view to some degree. See Mearsheimer, *The Tragedy of Great Power Politics*. Elsewhere, Mearsheimer has stated: "To put it bluntly, China cannot rise peacefully." See John Mearsheimer, "The Gathering Storm: China's Challenge to US Power in Asia," Michael Hintze Lecture, University of Sydney, August 5, 2010 (online at usyd.edu.au/ews/84.html?news-storyid=5351).

46. See Wang Shuzhong, "The Post-War International System," in Harish Kapur, *As China Sees the World* (New York: St. Martin's Press, 1987), p. 22. China's realism is based on its version of dialectic and historical materialism.

47. Richard Bernstein and Ross H. Monro, *The Coming Conflict with China* (New York: Alfred A. Knopf, 1997), p. 9.

48. Joshua Kurlantzick, *Charm Offensive: How China's Soft Power Is Transforming the World* (New Haven: Yale University Press, 2007), p. 226. The author notes that in a short period of time, China has proven it can "woo the world," has become the "preeminent power in parts of Asia, and can develop China-centered spheres of influence in other parts of the globe."

49. See Mark Mancall, *China at the Center: 300 Years of Foreign Policy* (New York: Free Press, 1984), chapters 1 and 2.

50. Kissinger, *On China*, chapter 1.

51. This is a term used frequently by American politicians in boasting of the U.S. See, for example, Newt Gingrich, *A Nation like No Other: Why American Exceptionalism Matters* (Washington, DC: Regnery, 2011).

52. Bill Bryson, *At Home: A Short History of Private Life* (New York: Random House, 2010).

53. Jonathan D. Spence, *The Search for Modern China* (New York: Norton and Company, 1999), pp. 288–89.

54. See I-cheng Loh, "China and the United States—Friends or Adversaries in the New Millennium?" in *Through Asian Eyes: U.S. Policy in the Asian Century*, ed. Sol W. Sanders (Lanham: University Press of America, 2001), 44.

55. See Frank Costigliola, *Roosevelt's Lost Alliances: How His Personal Politics Helped Start the Cold War* (Princeton: Princeton University Press, 2012), pp. 232–50; and Freda Utley, *The China Story* (Chicago: Regnery, 1990), p. 5. The author notes that millions of Chinese died during WWII to deny Japan "rights on their soil" only to have the area be given to the Soviet Union. Chinese also mention the fact that FDR was a big supporter of Chiang Kai-shek.

56. See Iris Chang, *The Chinese in America: A Narrative History* (New York: Viking, 2003), pp. 329–33; and Melanie Jeralds, "Asians May Face Tougher Admissions Policies, Study Finds," *The Daily Princetonian*, October 12, 2009 (online at http://www.dailyprincetonian.com/2009/10/12/24103/). According to this report, blacks need (on average) an SAT score of 1150, whites need 1460, and Asians need 1600.

57. The U.S. Department of State publishes its "country reports" on human rights annually delineating human rights abuses in China. Amnesty International and Freedom House also report on human rights in China. All are, as a rule, critical of China. For a rebuttal, see Yu Quanhu, "China Leads the U.S. in Human Rights," *Beijing Review*, October 3–9, 1994. The Chinese view on this subject is almost unknown to Americans.

58. See Richard Gowan and Flanziska Brantner, "A Global Force for Human Rights? An Audit of European Power at the UN," European Council on Foreign Relations, September 2007, pp. 1–2 and pp. 24–25; and Stephan Halper, The Beijing Consensus (New York: Basis Books, 2010), p. 116. Support for China's position on human rights has increased from less than fifty percent at the beginning of this century to seventy-four percent in 2008. Recently, forty-one countries that were seen as U.S. supporters on human rights shifted to support China.

59. Halper, *The Beijing Consensus*, pp. ix–x.

60. See Friedberg, *A Contest for Supremacy*, pp. 49–52.

61. Copper, *Looming War with China over Taiwan*, pp. 226–27.

62. Edward D. Mansfield and Jack Snyder, *Electing to Fight: Why Emerging Democracies Go to War* (Cambridge: MIT Press, 2005).

63. Copper, *The Looming War with China over Taiwan*, chapter 2.

64. See Kissinger, *On China*, p. 477.

65. It was reported in China that President Obama lavishly praised his hosts when he visited China and did not criticize China for human rights abuses, as had other U.S. presidents, because he needed Chinese money. Some described the president as a supplicant. The Internet has been full of insults, including racist comments. See "Leaders: The Pacific (and Pussyfooting) President;" and "Barack Obama in Asia," *Economist*, November 21, 2009, p. 16.

66. See Leonard A. Kusnitz, *Public Opinion and Foreign Policy: America's China Policy, 1949–1979* (Westport: Greenwood Press, 1984) for background. Also see "Rising Concern over China's Increasing Power: Global Poll," *BBC*, March 29, 2011 (online at worldpublicopinion.org).

67. For the latter argument, see Joseph S. Nye, Jr., *The Future of Soft Power* (New York: Public Affairs, 2011), pp. 88–90.

68. Joseph A. Camilleri, *Chinese Foreign Policy: The Maoist Era and Its Aftermath* (Seattle: University of Washington Press, 1980), p. 8. See also Yong Deng, *China's Struggle for Status* (Cambridge: Cambridge University Press, 2008), p. 2 and p. 7. Deng notes the difficulty for Chinese leaders in balancing China's rise and its great power status.

69. See Fisher, *China's Military Modernization*, pp. 218–25.

70. See James Rickards, *Currency Wars: The Making of the Next Global Crisis* (New York: Penguin, 2011). The author cites two previous currency devaluations that created crises. The first was by Germany after World War I and led to the Great Depression and World War II. The second was President Nixon's devaluation of the dollar, which led to an economic crisis involving recession, inflation, and high unemployment. The current U.S. "quantitative easing" has created serious antagonisms between the U.S. and China.

71. Michael T. Klare, *Resource Wars: The New Landscape of Global Conflict* (New York: Henry Holt and Company, 2001), pp. 16–17, 135–36.

72. See "Foreign Spies Stealing U.S. Economic Secrets in Cyberspace, Report to Congress on Foreign Economic Data Collection and Industrial Espionage, 2009–2010," Office of the National Counterintelligence Executive, October 2011.

73. Ibid. This report connects digital hacking and spying. The Cox Report also goes into detail about this issue. See "U.S. National Security and Military/Commercial Concerns with the People's Republic of China," Select Committee of the House of Representatives, May 25, 1999.

74. See Baohui Zhang, "The Security Dilemma in the U.S.–China Military Space Relationship," *Asian Survey*, March/April 2011, pp. 311–32.

75. See Friedberg, *A Contest for Supremacy*, p. 254, for a discussion of the possibility of a U.S.–China bipolar system emerging from their present conflict.

76. Randall L. Schweller and Xiaoyu Pu, "After Unipolarity: China's Visions of International Order in an Era of U.S. Decline," *International Security*, Summer 2011, p. 42.

77. See Subramanian, *Eclipse*, chapter 1.

78. See Jacques, *When China Rules the World*, pp. 413 and chapter 12. This view is also expressed in Fareed Zakaria, *The Post-American World: Release 2.0* (New York: W.W. Norton, 2011), and earlier in Paul Kennedy, *The Rise and Fall of the Great Powers* (New York: Vintage, 1987).

NO: Joshua S. Goldstein, *School of International Service, American University*

G*reat powers* are the handful—usually about half a dozen—of countries with the greatest power in the international system. Their alliances, conflicts, and cooperation largely define world order and affect the lives of people worldwide. In recent decades, there have been, by my definition (Goldstein and Pevehouse 2012, 54–55), five military great powers (the United States, Russia, China, France, and Britain—i.e., the permanent UN Security Council [UNSC] members) and two economic great powers with limited military roles (Germany and Japan).

Great-power wars can be among the most lethal and destructive of all wars, if only because the great powers possess so much military might. Today's seven great powers account for 75 percent of the world's military expenditures, 30 percent of the soldiers, a quarter of the tanks, half the warships, and 98 percent of the nuclear weapons worldwide (Goldstein and Pevehouse 2012, 195).

For centuries, the great-power system, rooted in Europe but later extended to the world, kept an overall stability that prevented any single power from conquering all and establishing a universal empire. However, this stability came at the cost of recurrent wars, some of which defy comprehension in their scale of violence.

Historically, the great powers fought almost constantly. Political scientist Jack Levy's data for 1495–1975 show European great powers at war with each other in 60 percent of the years. Over these five centuries, a new war between great powers began, on average, every seven or eight years (Levy 1983, 97–98). In this long-term historical perspective, great-power war was *always* likely.

But this constant drumbeat of great-power war across the centuries only highlights the extraordinary change that has occurred in the past sixty years. During those six decades, great powers have been at war zero percent of the time. The last time great powers directly met on the battlefield was in 1953, when Chinese and American forces clashed in the Korean War. The question is whether this remarkable sixty years of great-power peace will endure.

Critics could argue that the recent lull in great-power war resembles previous historical periods of temporary peace, followed in the end (and inevitably) by a new outbreak of war. For instance, the period of the Concert of Europe in the early 19th century, after the Napoleonic Wars, saw high levels of cooperation among the great powers, somewhat like today's world. But after some decades, new rivalries and escalations led to the Franco-Prussian War and, after a few more decades, the World Wars. The current sixty-year peace among the great powers seems long to the great majority of people alive today who have never lived through a great-power war, but in historical time, it might be just an interlude.

Shortly before World War I, British journalist and activist Norman Angell published *The Great Illusion,* to public acclaim (Angell 1910, vii). He argued that economic interdependence, with wealth deriving not from territory but from credit and commerce, had made war and conquest self-defeating and pointless. At that time, relative great-power peace had prevailed for almost four decades, since 1871. A massive-scale great-power war had not occurred in nearly a century. It was easy to think, in 1910, that war had withered away. Instead, the World Wars followed, even though they created the economic devastation in Europe that Angell had foreseen.

Given these historical realities, we clearly must be cautious in concluding that peace is at hand, based on a quiet sixty years. If we ask the question, "Is great-power war possible?" the answer is clearly "yes." All the great powers, and indeed all the world's major countries, remain armed to the teeth, with vast arsenals of firepower at the ready—thousands of tanks, artillery, airplanes, ships, rockets, nuclear weapons, bayonets, and almost every other known means of destruction. Also, the great powers do have some conflicts about ideas such as human rights and about more material interests such as oil and gas. So nobody can say with certainty that a great-power war will not take place in the future. As long as states remain armed and have not categorically and enforceably renounced violence, war remains in the repertoire. As Hobbes (1651, 88–89) wrote, "the nature of War, consisteth not in actuall fighting; but in the known disposition thereto, during all the time there is no assurance to the contrary."

But the possibility of great-power war is not the question here. It is whether such war is *likely* in the future. All evidence indicates it is extremely unlikely. The causes that underlie the past sixty years of great-power peace are durable and will likely strengthen in the future.

EXPLAINING THE GREAT-POWER PEACE

The reasons for this peace are several, and probably all contribute something to the positive trend of recent decades.

Strengthening Norms against Violence

For starters, norms and attitudes about war have changed dramatically since the time of Norman Angell. During the 19th century, an active peace movement in Europe and North America pressed the idea that war was a bad thing and that alternatives such as arbitration could replace it. But this movement represented a minority opinion in a world in which war was considered normal, even desirable—a way not only to secure national interests but also to uplift society, to prove manhood, and to keep nations hard-edged and strong. After World War I, that attitude never really recovered, outside of fascist countries. Populations increasingly viewed war as an evil—perhaps a necessary evil at times, but something to be avoided.

The changing attitudes about war and peace have been accompanied by long-term shifts in attitudes toward all kinds of violence, from torture and slavery to capital punishment and colonialism (Crawford 2002; Pinker 2011). War, like cannibalism and human sacrifice (but lagging centuries behind them), was once utterly normal worldwide but is no longer considered "cool." Over the past century or two, humanitarianism has also developed as part of this process of evolving norms, expanding the circle of human beings whom we care about (Smillie and Minear 2004). The explosion of information technologies in recent years has brought reports of war zones to billions of people around the world who, in past times, would never have known or cared about distant conflicts.

The long-term trend away from violence contrasts with the extremely high rates of war and violence in early prestate human societies. Many theories claim that our "true" peacefulness has been obscured by capitalism, the state, or some such interfering reason (Engels 1884). This is clearly not the case. The human species has been fighting since the get-go, and our "true" nature includes the potential for lethal violence (as well as capacities to avoid or overcome this potential). In moving away from war in recent decades, we are not falling back on our true selves but rather redefining ourselves and developing new rules over time.

Nuclear Weapons

A second factor that contributes to great-power peace is the invention of nuclear weapons after World War II, which changed the great-power calculus dramatically. Once the great powers all had nuclear weapons (or, in the case of Japan and Germany, came under the "nuclear umbrella" of a superpower that did), an all-out great-power war became synonymous with national suicide. On the few occasions when the United States and Soviet

Union came close to war, as during the 1962 Cuban Missile Crisis, their leaders appear to have realized the folly of taking risks that carry such catastrophic potentials.

Since the U.S. destruction of Hiroshima and Nagasaki in 1945, no two nuclear-armed states have fought even a single battle against each other anywhere in the world. This is not coincidental. Policy planners have thought about methods for fighting limited, conventional wars among nuclear powers that do not escalate to nuclear weaponry, but absolutely nobody has wanted to test those theoretical methods with hundreds of millions of lives on the line. (During the Cold War, the U.S. policy deliberately created conditions for any conventional war with the Soviet Union to escalate to nuclear war, such as by integrating tactical nuclear weapons among front-line forces in Europe. This policy was intended to prevent conventional conflict from breaking out, and ultimately, it worked, though at the risk of catastrophe had it failed even once.)

Since the height of the Cold War arms race, the great powers have made good progress in reducing the hair-trigger standoff of tens of thousands of nuclear weapons (the vast majority of them held by the United States and Russia). Since 1980, the number of nuclear weapons worldwide has dropped by three-quarters, and the recent New START treaty (Strategic Arms Reduction Treaty) that entered into force in 2011 will reduce these levels further. If additional efforts could push the number of warheads below 1,000 on each side, the risk of accidental or conspiratorial use of nuclear weapons would be reduced and a more stable deterrence among the world's nuclear powers might be realized.

Another indicator of the strengthening of norms against nuclear weapons is that the great powers carried out dozens of nuclear test explosions each year during the Cold War era, but in the 21st century, they have carried out zero (the only two tests being those of North Korea). The fact that great powers have stopped testing nuclear weapons and are sharply reducing their numbers indicates that a "nuclear taboo" continues to strengthen as the decades pass. Rather than the powers' becoming more relaxed and perhaps reckless about nuclear weapons as Hiroshima fades into historical memory, the opposite is happening.

Prosperity and Interdependence

A third factor stabilizing great-power relations and contributing to an overall decline of armed conflict worldwide is the changing nature of wealth creation as technology evolves. Historically, wealth came from land, so conquest was profitable. Today, wealth comes from trade, and war only hurts. National leaders' power now rests on delivering prosperity, be it China's leaders trying to sustain a high growth rate or an American president trying to bring down the unemployment rate. The globalization of manufacturing, for all its disruption to traditional patterns and cultures, has brought great economic benefit overall and would suffer tremendously if a great-power war occurred.

In recent years, four great powers—the United States, Britain, France, and Russia—have carried out military actions in their backyards or former colonies and in the decade-long wars in Iraq and Afghanistan. These actions, especially the isolated and nonstrategic ones, such as French and British deployments in West Africa, carry a low risk of triggering great-power war. However, even the limited war in Iraq turned out to be extremely expensive, with close to a trillion dollars in direct costs and additional trillions of lost economic activity as oil prices spiked on regional insecurity (Stiglitz and Bilmes 2008). This lesson further deters any great-power war, which would be vastly more expensive still.

The United Nations

A fourth factor in the great-power peace is the role of the United Nations (UN) in managing world order and, as the UN Charter puts it, trying "to save succeeding generations from the scourge of war." The UN's 100,000 deployed peacekeepers have measurably improved the success of peace agreements in civil wars (Fortna 2008), reducing the "kindling" that could lead to a great-power conflict. The peacekeepers represent the world's second largest deployed army, after the American one. Of course, peacekeepers have little direct relevance in great-power conflicts, since the powers can veto authorization of a peacekeeping force and since peacekeepers are never a match for great-power military forces.

More than peacekeeping, the nature of the UN itself has helped stabilize great-power peace. The permanent five have veto power and thus security and status in the system. The UN Charter did not create the Security Council to represent the people of the world but rather to represent *military power*. Partly because of President Franklin D. Roosevelt's insistence on giving China a seat (Ruggie 1996, 28–29), partly by luck, and partly because these things change slowly, today's **Permanent Five (P5)** members still represent the world's military power very well indeed.

The UN has strengthened international norms against interstate aggression and the alteration of borders by force. Indeed, in all the UN's years, not a single member state has gone out of business as a result of being conquered and annexed by another state—what Saddam Hussein tried to do to Kuwait in 1990. Furthermore, almost no borders have changed as a result of the use of force since a few years after the UN's founding in 1945. The Korean War caused a million battle deaths, but the border ended up where it started. The Iran-Iraq War killed 650,000 with the same result. Iraq's annexation of Kuwait in 1990 backfired. Israel seized land in 1967, but since then, most has been returned and the rest remains contested. The effort to create a Greater Serbia in parts of Croatia and Bosnia in the 1990s failed, and the architects of that effort ended up before a war-crimes tribunal in The Hague.

The UN's success contrasts markedly with the failures of the **League of Nations**, which the United States did not join and which did not stop aggression in the 1930s or prevent World War II. Today, the United States participates actively in the UN and serves as its host country and largest single contributor. Public opinion polls of Americans show that about 80 percent support strengthening the UN.

GREAT-POWER WAR SCENARIOS

If we think concretely about how a great-power war would occur, it is hard to imagine any of the various scenarios actually happening. Great-power war is possible, but in truth, it is extremely unlikely in the foreseeable future.

The top of the list of potential war scenarios is that a rising China will inevitably come to blows with the United States as the former hegemonic power declines. The analogy is to the rise of Germany and the challenge it posed to Britain. Political scientist and leading realist John Mearsheimer (2010, 382) wrote recently that "to put it bluntly: China cannot rise peacefully." But realism generally assumes the rationality of national leaders in pursuing the national interest and does not assume that war generally serves those interests. (Indeed, Mearsheimer and other realists published a *New York Times* advertisement in 2002 against war in Iraq because it would not be in the national interest, a prescient argument.) A peaceful rise by China is not contrary to any principle of realism.

China, quite contrary to 19th-century Germany, follows a declared "peaceful rise" strategy and has not fought a single military battle in 25 years (something no other permanent UNSC member can say). Also, Germany felt denied its due status in the international system, as it came late to the colonial game and had few overseas possessions. But China has its due status as a permanent veto-wielding member of the UNSC, thanks to the foresight of Franklin D. Roosevelt in the creation of the UN (at a time of great Chinese weakness).

China's leaders derive their legitimacy from delivering economic prosperity based on international trade. A future war against the United States or another great power would wreck the pursuit of trade-based wealth. That would be irrational on the part of China's leadership, which has so far proven both peaceful and generally rather cautious in world affairs. Given that a great-power war in the nuclear age would be absolutely catastrophic for the participants, one would have to assume a level of craziness or stupidity from China's leaders, which completely departs from their behavior in recent decades. They may be exasperating as negotiating partners or brutal as human-rights abusers, but they are not crazy.

The most likely China scenario for a future great-power war would involve an accidental or unintended escalation of a U.S.-Chinese conflict over Taiwan. The American position is deliberately ambiguous about whether the United States would come to Taiwan's defense in the event China attacked to reintegrate the island by force. On the one hand, the United States has for decades officially recognized that Taiwan is part of "one China" and does not recognize Taiwan as an independent country. On the other hand, the United States sells arms to Taiwan and implies that it might use military means to prevent forceful reintegration.

Fortunately, China-Taiwan trade and communication have been increasing rapidly, and the chances of a declaration of independence, or some other reason for a Chinese attack, are decreasing. A Taiwan crisis that precipitated a U.S.-China war belongs in the category of possible but unlikely events.

What about Russia? Here we can see a clearer case for a future scenario in which legitimacy based on economics or ideology crumbles and a Russian government whips up nationalism to stay in power. But who would be the enemy? China once fought border skirmishes with the Soviet Union (in the 1960s) but is today Russia's best friend in the great-power system. This was evident in early 2011, when China voted with Russia in the UN against a Syria resolution supported by most of the world. China and Russia have major, expanding trade ties that can only grow as the vast natural resources of Siberia flow to the vast labor force of a growing China. As for Russia and Europe, they enjoy strong economic ties and have few really serious conflicts, certainly nothing worth fighting a war about in the foreseeable future. Where decades ago, a militarized standoff marked the length of the Iron Curtain, now Russia and Europe squabble about natural gas prices.

Japan has not fought a battle in sixty years. Japan does have a territorial dispute with Russia, which occupied the Kuril Islands at the end of World War II and claims them as Russian. They are part of a string of islands protecting the

Sea of Okhotsk where Russian submarines hide, so they have strategic value to Russia. However, with Japan "pacified" and Russia—the stronger and more aggressive power—in possession of the islands, it is extremely unlikely that this dispute could lead to war. Japan also has disputes with China about tiny islands that carry economic zones containing oil, fish, and other resources. These disputes are purely economic and so seem more likely to end in negotiated settlements that divide the pie rather than an expensive war that would shrink the available pie.

Then there is Europe, which for centuries generated many of the world's most destructive wars. In recent decades, Europe has built an extremely stable peace as it transformed itself over decades into the European Union (EU). In 2007, the border between Germany and Poland, the scene of centuries of violent contention and the starting line for World War II in 1939, withered away with not a checkpoint left behind as Poland joined the borderless zone within the EU known as the Schengen Area. Any historian or political scientist familiar with Europe knows that what has happened there over the decades since the World Wars ended in 1945 (and since the Cold War ended in 1989) is something completely new and enormously important in the history of the world.

Some writers predicted that the end of the Cold War would lead to a period of greater instability and violence. Mearsheimer (1990, 6) famously predicted in 1990 that "the next decades in a Europe without the superpowers would . . . probably be substantially more prone to violence than the past 45 years." He argued that we would soon miss the stability of the Cold War. Robert Kaplan foresaw a "coming anarchy" as ethnic and religious wars proliferated and globalization heightened inequality (Kaplan 1994). Clearly, Europe and the world have moved in the opposite direction in the past twenty years.

As for the United States, it will continue to fight armed conflicts around the world, but on a small scale. In 2011, Robert Gates, the former secretary of defense, said, "any future defense secretary who advises the president to again send a big American land army into Asia or into the Middle East or Africa should have his head examined" (Shanker 2011). War between America and Europe or Japan is unthinkable and between America and China or Russia unlikely.

The United States takes the possibility of armed conflict with Russia or China extremely seriously and avoids it carefully. For example, early in George W. Bush's presidency, a Chinese fighter jet bumped into a U.S. surveillance plane off the Chinese coast and the plane had to make an emergency landing on Chinese territory, where China initially held the crew and plane captive. The U.S. response was quite patient, and eventually, the crew was returned (as was the plane after a thorough going-over by Chinese intelligence). Similarly, when

Russia and Georgia got into an armed conflict in 2008, the United States did not risk fighting Russia on behalf of its friend Georgia, despite previous declarations of support for Georgia's people.

PROXY WARS

Perhaps the most likely route to a great-power war is the involvement of two or more great powers on opposite sides of a smaller war. In the past six decades, great powers have been drawn into local conflicts on numerous occasions. This involvement may start with political support and the provision of money and weapons to one side but, in various cases, has resulted in the direct participation of a great-power military force in the fighting. This occurs, not infrequently, in conflicts where different great powers back different sides in a conflict. For example, the Soviets fought in Afghanistan against rebels backed by the United States, as American troops had fought in Vietnam against forces backed by the Soviet Union.

So far, these cases have not resulted in both sides simultaneously participating in direct combat on the two sides, which could bring the two great-power militaries into face-to-face combat. (Indeed, since 2004, no two regular uniformed militaries of any state, not just of great powers, have fought directly, except for the Soviet and Georgian armies for five days in 2008.) But we know this kind of escalation is possible, because it happened in the Korean War (1950–1953), which started as a fight between the North Korean and South Korean forces but developed into direct combat between China and the United States. At that time, China was a new great power—not yet even a great power by some accounts—and did not have nuclear weapons. And it was the last time direct fighting of this kind occurred.

The situation with regard to proxy wars has improved substantially since the Cold War decades, when the opposing superpowers used to pour in arms and money to sustain and escalate conflicts in such places as Angola, Nicaragua, and the Arab-Israeli conflict (and, of course, Vietnam and Afghanistan). The cessation of the tendency to fuel opposing sides in local wars has made the past twenty years far more peaceful than the preceding decades. The trend is toward smaller wars, with fewer casualties worldwide (Goldstein 2011).

CONCLUSION

A cautionary note is in order. Although great-power war is indeed very unlikely, we should remain vigilant and not discount the possibility altogether. Psychological studies have shown that people tend to wrongly estimate the risks associated with very improbable but high-impact events (Kahneman and Tversky 1979, 286). A nuclear war, accidental nuclear attack, or, indeed, any great-power war belongs to that category of potentially catastrophic outcomes that have a nonzero probability of occurrence. Stanford engineer Martin Hellman (2011) makes a convincing case for taking very seriously the nonzero probability of an accident or miscalculation that could trigger a nuclear attack and for taking steps now to reduce that risk.

While avoiding complacency about these risks—and continuing to work hard to reduce them—we should not overestimate them either. Sound policies, including defense budgets, must not be driven by irrational fears or a sense that hugely devastating wars are inevitable. Great-power war should be treated neither as inevitable nor as something definitively retired and permanently stored in a museum. Rather, we should see it as a real but diminishing risk that needs attention in order to sustain recent trends.

climate change and the environment

Can International Regimes Be Effective Means to Restrain Carbon Emissions?

YES: Brent Ranalli, *The Cadmus Group*

NO: Samuel Thernstrom, *Clean Air Task Force*

It may come as a surprise that it has been only twenty-five years since the prospect of climate change—now widely acknowledged both as a global problem and as one that is caused largely by the recent, and increasing, impact of human activity—was first popularized in the U.S. media and brought to the broader public's attention. James Hansen, a NASA scientist testifying before Congress during the very hot summer of 1988—and in a deliberately overheated hearing room—presented data showing the relationship between greenhouse gases and increasing global temperatures as well as projections indicating that further increases could lead to substantial global warming, with significant ecological impacts.

While scientific data supporting these claims were at least eighty years old, media coverage of climate change began to increase significantly only after this startling exposure. Since then, a steadily building scientific consensus maintains that humans—through greenhouse-gas emissions as well as deforestation and other land-use changes—have caused increasing global temperatures and that unabated fossil-fuel consumption will have profound environmental impacts across the globe in the future. The most recent manifestation is the Fourth **Intergovernmental Panel on Climate Change (IPCC)** report that termed anthropogenic climate change "unequivocal." Indeed, the issue of climate change has so increased in prominence worldwide that, in November 2007, UN Secretary-General Ban Ki-moon called it "the defining challenge of our age."[1]

The belated recognition of climate change heralded both a new and important environmental problem and one that is qualitatively different from others: the fact that humans could alter the entire earth's climate was far different from pollutant-specific contaminants that had constituted most environmental perils to date. But, although recognition of a problem may be a necessary condition for arousing concern, it is far from sufficient as a spur to action. Part of the problem of generating a more appropriate response to this looming disaster stems from the paradox known as the "**tragedy of the commons**": when costs are spread widely and benefits concentrated locally, the incentive for individuals (or nations) is to continue to overproduce/pollute. In terms of global warming, each rational actor (individual or nation) seeks to encourage all other nations to restrict their total greenhouse-gas emissions—to the benefit of all—while it continues to enjoy the economic advantages (and only a fraction of the costs) of its own unabated emissions. Thus, in the absence of a concerted effort of some kind, individual incentives lead to ruinous collective behavior.

A further difficulty inhibiting effective management of climate change stems from the current and future distribution of carbon emissions. As Figure 1 (p. 280) indicates, total carbon emissions are highest in OECD nations, while Figure 2 (p. 281) shows that although the United States continues to be the leading producer of carbon dioxide (CO_2), China is quickly catching up, and many nations in the developing world are expanding their output considerably. This two-sided dynamic presents twin problems. First, the high-producers have economies that heavily depend on fossil-fuel consumption, so change will be costly. Second, developing nations resent pressures placed on them to restrict carbon emissions by the wealthy West, in full recognition that those older economies were built and enriched by burning petroleum, coal, and other fossil fuels.

Yet another driving force behind global warming is the worldwide growth not only in economic output but in population as well—almost all of it emerging in the developing world. Thus, the twin impacts of rising populations and quickly growing economies produce strong incentives to continue to produce greenhouse gases. These are powerful incentives to overcome, and international institutions lack the enforcement capabilities to compel behavioral changes. While the Organization of Economic Cooperation and Development (OECD) nations' share of world CO_2 emissions fell in the decades since 1990, emissions shares in East and South Asia are rising quickly. Many OECD countries have begun to reduce their CO_2 emissions per unit of economic growth, yet the challenge remains to fully decouple economic growth from emissions and to encourage developing countries to adopt cleaner, new green technologies.

Figure 1

Total Carbon Dioxide Emissions by Region, 1990–2008

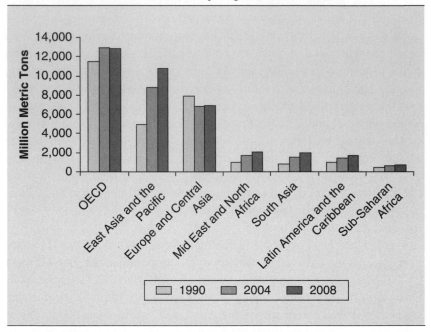

Source: The World Bank, "CO2 emissions (kt)" database, http://data.worldbank.org/indicator/EN.ATM.CO2E.KT/countries/ES-1W?display=graph. Rankings determined by the Carbon Dioxide Information Analysis Center.

To make things worse, much of the current population growth is occurring among the middle classes of India and China, many of whom aspire to consumer lifestyles akin to those in the United States.

International institutions have enjoyed some success in addressing environmental problems by adopting initiatives such as the **Montreal Protocol** to limit ozone-producing gases. But the stakes in climate change are considerably higher and the number of producers far greater than can be addressed by such narrow-focused efforts, while the variety of sources—both natural and man-made—greatly complicates efforts to address the fundamental causes of global climate change. There are many possible technical paths to improving matters—from carbon sequestration to nuclear power to alternative vehicle fuels—yet the challenges are not simply technical; they involve requiring a sufficient number of nations to reduce carbon emissions to a significant degree in a verifiable manner.

Figure 2

Top 20 Carbon Dioxide Emitters, 1990–2008 (total fossil-fuel emissions)

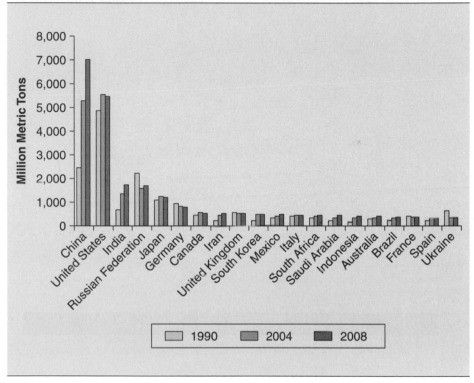

Source: The World Bank, "CO2 emissions (kt)" database, http://data.worldbank.org/indicator/EN.ATM.CO2E.KT/countries/ES-1W?display=graph. Rankings determined by the Carbon Dioxide Information Analysis Center.
Note: Russian Federation and Ukraine represent 1992 data.

The two articles that follow provide differing perspectives on the likelihood of achieving meaningful results through international institutions. Brent Ranalli reviews the diplomatic history of multilateral negotiations over a climate change treaty and argues that a well-designed treaty can provide economic incentives for technological change as well as a recognition of different North–South priorities, while providing for stronger enforcement and social learning over time. Samuel Thernstrom also emphasizes national differences that must be considered in implementing climate-change policy; because some nations stand to lose (or even gain) from climate change and because compliance with any international agreement is voluntary, climate-change policy must respect national differences if it is to be effective.

Figure 3

Energy Intensity (Selected Countries), 1980–2004

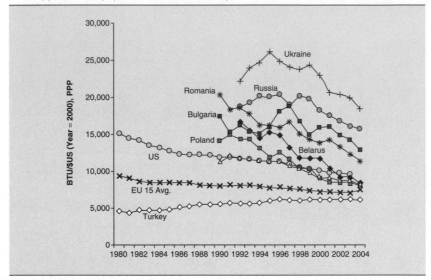

Source: U.S. Energy Information Administration (EIA).
Note: BTU stands for British Thermal Unit. PPP stands for Purchasing Power Parity.

Discussion Questions

1. Is climate change a problem that is best addressed on a global, national, or subnational level? Why?
2. What policies can governments implement to address climate change? How will these policies impact different stakeholders? What are the obstacles to implementing these policies?
3. Who is responsible for climate change? Who bears the responsibility to stop it? What role should industrial nations have? What about developing nations?
4. What does Brent Ranalli propose as a new and complementary approach to ensuring the effectiveness of international regimes for curbing greenhouse-gas emissions? What are the characteristics of his proposal? Do you agree with his approach?
5. What reasons does Samuel Thernstrom cite to explain why past international efforts to curb carbon emissions, particularly the **Kyoto Protocol,** have failed? What does he propose for the future?

NOTE

1. "Climate Change Poses 'Defining Challenge' of Our Time," *UN News Centre*, October 7, 2008. Available at http://www.un.org/apps/news/story .asp?NewsID=28458

YES: Brent Ranalli, *The Cadmus Group*

TODAY'S SORRY SITUATION

The Kyoto Protocol of 1997 is generally considered, if not an outright failure, at least a grave disappointment. The largest emitter of greenhouse gases in the world at the time of adoption, the United States, failed to ratify it. China, which now surpasses the United States in emissions, has no meaningful obligations under the Protocol; nor does India, with over a billion people, or any other developing country.

It gets worse. Emission-reduction targets that were established under Kyoto were, it was widely agreed from the beginning, wholly inadequate to meet the threat of climate change—they were just a "good start." And even so, many nations are on track to fail to meet their 2012 targets, some by a wide margin. Anticipating failure, Canada has formally withdrawn from the Protocol. Canada, Russia, and Japan have all indicated their intention to "opt out" of the second commitment period, which is scheduled to last from 2013 to 2020, leaving only a straggling remainder of European and other countries planning to make any sort of formal commitment to mitigation action in the next decade.

Upon close inspection, even many nations that are on track to meet their Kyoto targets do not impress. Consider that targets for most countries are set in relation to 1990 baseline emissions. Russia and the Eastern European nations easily meet their own targets, since they suffered industrial collapse when the communist regimes fell in the early 1990s. And since the bar is set so low for these nations, they have emission credits to spare (*hot-air credits*) that can be sold abroad, enabling other nations to meet their own targets without making any substantive changes at home. England gets credit for a transition from coal to cleaner-burning natural gas that took place in the 1990s, before Kyoto was signed. Germany gets credit for having swallowed post-Communist East Germany and its hot-air credits; and worse: as Germany has decarbonized, factories disassembled in the Ruhr Valley have been reassembled in China (resulting in *leakage*—a shifting of pollution from countries with targets to countries without targets), where poor environmental management and lax government controls have resulted in a net *increase* in emissions—increases of up to 300 percent for some industrial processes.[1]

At the climate summit in Durban, South Africa, in late 2011, negotiators agreed to let Kyoto expire in 2020 and failed to reach a firm agreement on what would replace it. They pledged to give themselves until 2015 to work that out. In the meantime, countries are invited, if they feel like it, to participate in a lame-duck second commitment period of Kyoto under the old rules. The climate diplomacy community put a brave face on this announcement, but there is palpable despair among climate activists of seeing any bold and meaningful action. Those skeptical of the diplomatic effort are able to gloat that "the proverbial can has been dented so hard and kicked so far down the road that it's no longer fit for the recycling bin."[2]

At this nadir in the climate negotiation process, it is tempting to wonder—is it wasted effort? Perhaps the international community, with its diverse agendas and interests and sheer weight of bureaucracy, is simply incapable of action that is bold enough and comprehensive enough to address the problem. Perhaps nations should give up efforts at climate change mitigation and focus on adaptation instead, saving themselves and their neighbors as best they can. Perhaps we should look on the bright side—if crops fail in some parts of the world, think how much wheat Canada and Russia will be able to plant in what is now tundra. Or perhaps we should hold on to some ray of hope that the prognosis may change—after all, the science is never complete or 100 percent certain.

In this essay, I will argue that in spite of the disappointing performance of climate diplomacy to date, there is every reason for cautious optimism that the international community can and will take meaningful action toward mitigating climate change.

PRELIMINARIES

To start out, we should reiterate *why* mitigation is important and why international collaboration is essential to mitigation. Here, we address ourselves to some of the points raised a few paragraphs ago, in reverse order:

- *Should we take the science seriously?* Although the scientific enterprise is indeed never complete and climate modeling is subject to uncertainty, it would be foolish not to take prudent action based on the evidence available. Today, the best available evidence indicates that the climate is changing, that anthropogenic greenhouse-gas emissions play a role, and that the pattern of anthropogenic emissions in the coming decades could mean the difference between mild climate change and catastrophic climate change.

- *Won't there be benefits?* Although some localized benefits are anticipated from climate change (especially in the milder scenarios), they are balanced by costs; and in the more extreme scenarios, the costs are overwhelming.[3] To take the example mentioned above: mild-to-moderate warming of northern latitudes would indeed create expanded opportunities for agriculture, but it would also melt the permafrost, making many current settlements uninhabitable and causing huge economic damages in the form of corrosion of oil infrastructure. The cost in Alaska has been estimated at approximately $35 million annually, or 1.4 percent of the state budget; costs in Canada and Russia may be comparable or greater.[4] In addition, climate change poses costs that are rarely monetized (e.g., species and ecosystem loss).

- *Why not just adapt?* Adaptation is an essential element of any strategic thinking about climate change. Adaptation has already begun—for example, in Papua New Guinea, rising sea levels have led to the evacuation and resettlement of some island communities. Many countries have begun to prepare national adaptation plans, and structures are in place for cooperative international action, including technology transfer and financial aid to poorer nations. This is one of the underappreciated success stories of the international climate diplomacy process. But adaptation can only be one piece of the puzzle. The difference between mild climate change, under which orderly adaptation is possible, and catastrophic change, under which it is not, lies in mitigation.

Given that mitigation is necessary, does it have to be internationally coordinated? In the abstract world of economics and game theory, greenhouse-gas emissions are a classic example of a *negative externality* (a cost imposed on others) that leads rational actors to make choices that leave everybody worse off. The economic benefit of emitting greenhouse gases accrues to emitter, and costs are distributed all around the globe. So no one has a rational incentive to curb emissions—and if everyone emits, everyone suffers. Only a public or community solution—"mutual coercion, mutually agreed upon," in the phrase of Garrett Hardin[5]—can bring about an optimal solution.

One might balk at the pessimism implied in that analysis. People are not bloodless "rational actors," bent solely on the pursuit of narrow self-interest, narrowly defined. Real human beings have an altruistic streak and are susceptible to moral arguments. They can be moved to action by righteousness, indignation, and reciprocity.[6] Is it not possible that in the absence of an international regime, nations might set aside economic self-interest sufficiently to pitch in to do their part to mitigate climate change? There are examples we might point to: in the United States, for example, numerous states, cities, and regional associations have pledged to reduce emissions in spite of U.S. non-participation in Kyoto.

I am very sympathetic to the argument that *homo economicus* is a thin abstraction and that real people are capable of surprising degrees of solidarity and altruism. But as an argument against making the effort to achieve an international climate regime, this line of reasoning fails on at least two counts. First, prominent among the complex motivations of the state and local authorities who have taken voluntary action was a desire to fulfill their share of the U.S.'s neglected Kyoto obligations. That is, the voluntary action *presupposed* an international understanding of shared obligations. Second, the scenario in which nations are willing to pitch in to solve a common problem voluntarily, described above, is exactly the optimal condition for establishing an international regime[7] to turn those intentions into commitments. Conversely, if a coordinated regime fails, there is virtually no hope that voluntary action alone will succeed.

If we accept that coordinated international action is necessary for successful mitigation, we come to the thorny part of the problem: how has climate diplomacy failed so badly in recent years, and what prospect is there of improvement?

SOLID FOUNDATIONS

Before diagnosing the weaknesses of the current climate regime, it is worth assessing and acknowledging its strengths. What is being done right? I highlight four pieces of diplomatic accomplishment that lay a solid foundation for future success.

1. A strong, versatile framework: convention and protocol

The nations of the world did not attempt to solve the problem of global warming overnight. They started, in 1992, by agreeing on a convention (the **United Nations Framework Convention on Climate Change [UNFCCC]**) that established a consensus on the need for international action and laid down some basic principles to guide that action. The UNFCCC stipulates (Article 7, paragraph 4) that there will be regular (annual) conferences of the parties (COP) to work out further arrangements.[8] UNFCCC does not get into the nuts and bolts of how to solve the problem of climate change, but it authorizes the parties to negotiate such detailed agreements in the form of protocols. There can be as many protocols as necessary.

Having a strong undergirding framework, in the form of the UNFCCC, provides for continuity of climate negotiations, even as specific protocols come and go. Thus, while Kyoto has limped along, spurned and abandoned by important nations, the underlying convention has nevertheless been remarkably strong and resilient, and there is no question of abandoning climate negotiations altogether. Thanks to the convention/protocol framework, nations that are not parties to the Kyoto Protocol, notably the United States, have still had a role to play and have remained active in climate diplomacy.

2. Differentiated responsibility

Among the core principles enshrined in the UNFCCC is an acknowledgment that different nations have different levels of capacity for action. The Convention (preamble and Article 3) calls on all nations to cooperate and participate "in accordance with their *common but differentiated responsibilities and respective capabilities*" (emphasis added). This is a concession to realism, one that steers negotiations away from making technically and politically impossible demands on poor nations and failed states. It is also a concession to the moral argument that the wealthier nations bear the greatest responsibility for historical anthropogenic emissions.

In the Kyoto Protocol, this principle was put into operation by dividing nations into two groups: one group (roughly, the wealthier/developed nations) was expected to set targets for emissions reductions, while the other (roughly, the poorer/developing nations) was not. The somewhat crude division of nations into two groups and the exemption of developing nations (even the most rapidly developing nations) from any responsibility for setting and meeting targets has come in for criticism, as we will see below. But most observers would agree that the underlying principle of differentiated responsibility is sound. In one form or another, it will undoubtedly inform any future protocol.

3. Meaningful commitments

The Kyoto Protocol established a precedent of setting concrete national targets and timetables for reducing emissions of greenhouse gases. Not all nations set goals under Kyoto, and many of the current goals will not be met, but the principle of goal setting is important, for at least two reasons. First, setting measurable targets and timetables for emissions reductions (or other concrete mitigation actions such as afforestation/reforestation, carbon sequestration, etc.) enables nations to focus their efforts. All the sincere intentions and optimistic energy generated by the establishment of UNFCCC, for example, under which nations agreed that mitigation was important and necessary, led to very little concrete action. It was this lack of action that convinced many that a formal protocol was necessary.

Second, setting concrete goals and targets makes it possible to connect concrete actions with science-based targets (e.g., peak concentrations of atmospheric carbon dioxide that are estimated to be low enough to ward off catastrophic risk). Goals set under Kyoto were not science based, but under a future protocol, they may be.

Goals should be ambitious but realistic. Arguably, the Kyoto goals were not realistic, given the current state of technology. Economic modeling suggests that the efficient path would be to set goals of progressively increasing stringency over the course of decades, taking advantage of progressively more climate-friendly technologies as they come online.[9]

Talk of goals raises the question of enforcement. Is it necessary to establish sanctions and penalties for nations that fail to meet their goals? Experience to date suggests that too much emphasis should not, indeed cannot, be placed on sanctions and penalties. Fear of sanctions will drive nations to set unambitious goals or to drop out rather than risk failure, as Canada has done.[10] What matters ultimately are environmental outcomes. Failure to meet an ambitious target by a few percentage points may be better than hitting a "safe" target.

Since climate change mitigation is an effort that will span decades, goals should also ideally be set in the long term. Kyoto has been criticized as "too little, too fast," setting goals on a horizon of only years and leaving future targets in doubt. It is argued that industries that make capital investments with a lifespan of decades need to be given the right incentives to plan for a low-carbon economy.[11] That some industries appear to be doing this even in the absence of explicitly negotiated long-term targets[12] can be credited in at least some part to the stability of the underlying UNFCCC (see the discussion of convention and protocol above). Protocols may come and go, but international action on climate appears inevitable.

4. Flexible implementation

Another important precedent set in the Kyoto Protocol is that of subsidiarity—that is, letting nations decide for themselves how to meet the goals they set, rather than micromanaging. As is discussed in more detail below, there are many policy tools nations can use to reduce emissions, from comprehensive approaches like a **cap-and-trade system** or a carbon tax to more piecemeal regulatory options, institutional arrangements, and incentive programs.

As Kyoto has been amended over time, it has evolved in directions that provide even greater flexibility for meeting targets: for instance, nations get credit for investing in mitigation actions made in one another's territory (*Joint Implementation* [JI]) and for investment in emissions-limiting projects in the developing world (the *Clean Development Mechanism* [CDM]). And, as noted above, nations are allowed to buy and sell emissions credits (*International Emissions Trading* [IET]). They are granted credit for afforestation and reforestation and penalized for deforestation (under provisions for Land Use, Land-Use Change, and Forestry [LULUCF]). These moves toward flexibility should be applauded, even as policymakers remain vigilant to close loopholes and prevent gaming.

ECHOES OF THE MONTREAL PROTOCOL

These foundations for success in the international climate treaty architecture are not unprecedented. They echo the highly successful diplomatic effort to tackle the ozone problem in the late 1980s. The ozone negotiators first established a general convention (the Vienna Convention of 1985), and then they hammered out a detailed plan of action in a protocol (the Montreal Protocol of 1987). The Montreal Protocol made special provisions for developing countries, giving them extra time to convert their infrastructure and promising financial assistance. It set concrete targets and timetables for phasing out the ozone-depleting chemicals and left it largely up to each nation to decide how best to manage its own phase-out.[13]

The resemblance between the two efforts is hardly accidental. The ozone negotiations and the documents they produced are considered a model of international environmental diplomacy, and they were fresh in the minds of early climate negotiators. Scholars—foremost among them Richard Benedick, who at the time of Montreal was the chief U.S. ozone negotiator and had a panoramic insider's view—have published books and articles assessing the factors that led to success in Vienna and Montreal and suggesting how these might apply in the climate context.[14]

In addition to serving as a model of best practices in environmental diplomacy, the ozone negotiations set some precedents that may guide our thinking about what is desirable and achievable in the climate context. For example, the Vienna Convention and Montreal Protocol were negotiated as precautionary measures at a time when ozone science was evolving rapidly, far less settled than climate science is today.[15] And perfectionists who wish for simplicity or elegance or perfect equity and efficiency in a climate treaty will find in Montreal a salutary example of a treaty that *works*—not because it represents a Platonic ideal of elegance or efficiency (it surely does not) but because in the heat of negotiation, a compromise was forged, warts and all, that was both environmentally effective and minimally satisfactory to all parties.

In the remainder of this essay, we will have occasion to make additional comparisons with the ozone and greenhouse gas diplomacy efforts.

STUMBLING BLOCKS IN CLIMATE NEGOTIATIONS

We now turn to an analysis of the real weaknesses and problems of the current international climate regime and examine prospects for ameliorating them. These weaknesses and problems can be placed in three main classes: those concerned with the *effectiveness* of the tools used by and available under the regime, those concerned with *procedure* under the regime, and those concerned with *participation* of nations in the regime. These three sets of problems are intertwined; we will treat them in the order in which they are listed above.

Effectiveness

Much of the debate and academic literature that has grown up around the Kyoto Protocol in the last decade or so has been preoccupied with the mechanisms that should be used to reduce emissions and whether they will be adequate to the task. To an extent, this debate has informed the shape of the treaty (e.g., the incorporation of flexible mechanisms, described above). But for the most part (in accordance with the principle of subsidiarity, described above), Kyoto does not prescribe particular policies.

There are many policy tools available. The two approaches that are most frequently discussed are *tradable permits* (sometimes called *cap-and-trade* or *carbon markets*) and a *carbon tax*. In addition to being economically efficient (encouraging lowest-cost emissions reductions to be made first), these two policy tools have the special feature that they can be calibrated to achieve specific emission-reduction targets. Below, we discuss the feasibility and relative merits of carbon trading and carbon taxes, followed by the importance of considering a wide spectrum of other policy options as well. We close with discussion of implementation.

Permits and taxes

The idea behind a market for tradable permits and a carbon tax is that it sends a consistent price signal to the regulated community, inducing individual firms to make cost-effective investments in emissions-reducing technologies or practices rather than buying extra permits or paying extra taxes. In each case, it is a relatively simple matter to relax or (more likely) tighten restrictions over time: the number of available permits could be enlarged or reduced, and the tax rate could be adjusted downward or upward. Each policy option has known advantages and disadvantages:

- *Ease of implementation.* A permit regime is far more challenging to implement than a tax. Taxation is an everyday function of government, while a market for permits requires technology, administrative capacity, and auditing capacity that may be challenging to assemble. Furthermore, there are technical considerations in setting up a carbon market that are particularly thorny. For instance, decisions must be made about the initial assignment of permits. Those decisions can have huge implications both in terms of fairness and in terms of efficiency (consider the assignment of hot-air credits to Russia and Eastern European nations, effectively subsidizing those ailing national economies without providing a spur to carbon-efficiency). Furthermore, permit market administrators must gauge the right quantity of permits to allow in circulation: too many and the market goes slack (as the price of a permit falls, so does the incentive to reduce emissions), too few and the market freezes up (permits are expensive and hard to obtain, and the cost of compliance with program requirements becomes ruinous for participants).[16]

- *Revenue generation.* Both regimes would carry administrative costs; the costs of the tradable permit regime would be considerably higher. Even more significantly, a carbon tax would *generate public revenue* that could then be spent on related priorities.

- *Acceptance.* A final factor is political acceptability. A tax, whatever relative advantages it may offer vis-à-vis tradable permits, is likely to be a harder sell with the public in most democratic nations.

Implementation at the international level (among nations). Kyoto's IET program is an example of **emissions trading** among nations. Problems with this regime, as noted above, include leakage and questionable initial allocations.

There have been calls for an international carbon tax, possibly as part of a future protocol. In actuality, this would not be a single international tax (no such authority or collection mechanism exists) but a system of harmonized national carbon taxes. Such a regime would eliminate problems of leakage and initial allocation and would generate income that could be earmarked for climate mitigation and/or climate adaptation. However, as a practical matter, the idea of a harmonized carbon tax is a political nonstarter. As Richard N. Cooper, an advocate of harmonized carbon taxes, has himself observed, taxation is a sovereign prerogative; national legislatures are unlikely to let an international agreement dictate tax policy.[17]

Implementation at the national or subnational level (among firms). As noted above, it is a principle of climate diplomacy that each sovereign nation may choose how to achieve its targets. So the result of international target setting has been, and is likely to continue to be, a patchwork of national policies that include tradable permits and carbon taxes.

Several proposals for carbon taxes have foundered on political opposition (e.g., in New Zealand, Japan, Canada, and the U.S.). Those that have been implemented (e.g., in Costa Rica, India, and several European nations as well as subnational Canadian and U.S. jurisdictions) are generally considered successes.

The most ambitious carbon emission permit trading scheme to date is the European Emissions Trading Scheme (ETS), which takes advantage of the efficiencies gained by merging multiple national markets into a single market. ETS was established around the same time that Kyoto went into effect, covering industries that represented around 40 percent of carbon dioxide emissions from the 15 participating nations. While ETS has had its setbacks (including a too-slack market during the first trading period of 2005–2007), it is continually improving and is generally considered a success story. Today, it encompasses 30 nations and has been expanded to include the aviation sector, and there are plans to broaden it further.

To sum up: Both permit trading and carbon taxes, the key policy options for achieving emission-reduction targets, can be made to work. Markets for trading emissions credits have been established both among nations (under Kyoto) and among firms, including cross-border trading among firms under ETS. Carbon taxes, which offer some distinct benefits, have been implemented successfully at the national and subnational level. In future years, we can expect that these key tools will be used with increased effectiveness.

Beyond permits and taxes: other policy instruments

Carbon markets and carbon taxes can and should be supplemented by a wide range of other policy instruments. Options available include subsidies and assorted tax incentives, traditional command-and-control regulation of targeted industries, and changes to procurement rules as well as "soft," nonregulatory approaches like public/private partnerships, technical assistance, and grants to civil society. Moving to a low- or zero-carbon economy will involve changes in the way agriculture is practiced, changes in transportation infrastructure, and changes in the way buildings and communities are designed. Much activity is already underway, but we have barely scratched the surface of what is possible. Business, civil society, and almost every department of government will need to be engaged; local and regional governments have important roles as well.

Public investment in research and development is particularly important. Economic analysis and practical experience suggest that price signals from carbon markets and carbon taxes will be insufficient to generate technological innovation from the private sector on the necessary scale.[18] "Given the stakes," Benedick argues, "energy research arguably merits a degree of public sector commitment comparable to that devoted not long ago to aerospace and telecommunications."[19] Presumably, it will also stimulate comparable levels of private-sector activity and wealth creation.

Implementation

Often, in discussions of climate policy, too little attention is paid to the ability of governments and international regimes to effectively carry out the policies they enact.[20] Especially in poorer countries, civil servants may lack adequate training and tools. In every country, both firms and government agencies will be subject to temptation to find and exploit loopholes in the climate regime and otherwise game the system.

Some of this can be helped: capacity development efforts, including training and technology transfer, can be undertaken. Further, policy recommendations can and should take into account the possibility of gaming; robust monitoring and verification should be standard. It is also important to recognize local customs and norms, especially in developing countries, and adapt policy recommendations to fit those customs and norms.[21]

Procedural Issues

Earlier, we discussed the strengths of the UNFCCC process. The process has some well-known weaknesses as well.

Consensus and obstruction

One weakness is the employment of standard UN consensus rules, which in essence gives any nation the power to veto cooperative action on the part of other nations. Political scientist Peter M. Haas blames this partly on the "reflexive application of UN procedural norms" by diplomats accustomed to them. But he also credits the "strategic efforts" of some nations "to prevent binding commitments." It appears that "the weak institutionalization on this issue is deliberate."[22]

Other ways are possible or might have been possible. The ozone negotiations provide a telling contrast. One important difference is that there were fewer active participants in the early stages—this will be discussed below. Another was that discussions took place under the auspices of the United Nations Environmental Programme (UNEP). UNEP did not merely provide meeting space; it actively shepherded the discussions along. Benedick refers to the "catalytic and mediating functions" of the institution and indicates that UNEP Executive Director Mustafa Tolba, in particular, played a very important personal role behind the scenes in brokering the eventual consensus.[23]

Before the UNFCCC was established, UNEP was seen as having a possible role in the climate negotiations. Haas reports that the U.S. and other nations deliberately sidelined UNEP, knowing that it would favor aggressive targets.[24]

Could the current lethargic forum or rules of procedure be abandoned or revised? Haas wrote optimistically in 2008 that "moving outside the UN is still

an option" and that UN procedures could still be "replaced with other procedural and substantive norms, such as coordinating UN negotiations with
discussions elsewhere, or going beyond consensus voting rules."[25] This is perhaps too optimistic. There is no real prospect of abandoning the current basic
framework for discussion today any more than there was in 2008. But Haas's
suggestion of coordinating the UN negotiations with additional discussions
has merit. It is possible for the plenary discussions to be supplemented by additional official and unofficial discussions.

"Thicker" discussions

There is every reason to expect that what we might call "thicker" discussions—
multitrack discussions on a range of topics, working in smaller groups within
and outside the UNFCCC framework and engaging stakeholders who are currently not represented in the negotiations—would yield improved results. To
be sure, the current climate diplomacy process involves committee work. But a
much more ambitious vision is possible. Benedick writes:

> An architecture of parallel regimes, involving varying combinations of
> national and local governments, industry, and civil society on different
> themes, could reinvigorate the climate negotiations.... By focusing on
> specific sectors and policy measures in smaller, less formal settings with
> varying combinations of actors and by not operating under UN consensus
> rules, the possibilities for achieving forward motion would be increased.
> The process and results could be termed protocols or forums or agree-
> ments, but their essential character would more closely resemble a prag-
> matic working group than a formal diplomatic negotiation.... Providing
> reports on these activities to the wider audience of the annual Conference
> of Parties to the Framework Convention could stimulate other countries
> to join one or another regime of interest and could gradually transform
> the Convention into a forum for dissemination of new ideas and practical
> results, rather than instrument for illusory consensus, rhetoric, and delay.[26]

The participation of civil society and business leaders in global discussions
on climate mitigation would open up new realms of possibility. "Is it not
conceivable," Benedick writes, "that the 15 or 20 automakers of the world,
together with the ministers of industry of their respective nations, could
convene in a medium-sized conference hall and hammer out a schedule for
introducing low-carbon and then no-carbon vehicles? The topics could range
from new fuels and engines to strong but lightweight structural materials. No
auto manufacturer could complain of being at a disadvantage, for they would
all operate under the same constraints."[27] He recalls that this is essentially what

happened among chemical manufacturers at the time of the ozone negotiations: they pooled their knowledge and experience to help hammer out a realistic but ambitious timetable for the elimination of CFCs and the development of alternative technologies.

As newsworthy as the participation of auto manufacturers in climate negotiations would be, participation by "ministers of industry" would be equally revolutionary. As surprising as it may seem, given the scope of the climate problem and the range of activities that mitigation would require (see the discussion of "other policy instruments," above), government agencies responsible for industry, commerce, energy, agriculture, transportation, and urban planning have been almost entirely absent from the UNFCCC climate negotiations. This fact goes a long way toward explaining lackluster performance under Kyoto. The environmental agencies represented at UNFCCC just don't have much clout at home. There have been calls to break the impasse by further empowering environmental ministries.[28] A more credible solution, though, would be to "get the right actors to the table."[29]

This vision of thicker negotiations, both within and outside of the UNFCCC process, is compelling. But would it be politically feasible?

There is doubt in some quarters. Climate consultants Nigel Purvis and Andrew Stevenson argue on the one hand that key nations like the U.S. and China prefer a forum that promotes obstruction (and presumably would be reluctant to give it up) and on the other hand that switching to a different forum would make little difference anyway, since the underlying problem is the attitude of the participants.[30] The bloc of large developing countries known as BASIC (Brazil, South Africa, India, and China) have affirmed that "the only legitimate forum for negotiation of climate change is the UNFCCC" and that breakout groups must not be allowed unless they meet stringent criteria.[31]

Such rhetoric appears to be overblown, however, and pessimism about the possibility of thicker discussions appears to be mostly unfounded. Both China and the U.S. were founding members of the Asia–Pacific Partnership on Climate and Clean Development, established in 2005 to promote cooperative climate-friendly research and development (R&D) and technology transfer among major nations of the Pacific Rim and South Asia. And even as the BASIC nations claim UNFCCC is the only legitimate forum for climate discussions, they happily collaborate with each other on "the creation of an on-going [BASIC] forum, including work on adaptation and mitigation action plans,"[32] and they participate in climate policy discussions with other key players in extracurricular settings like the 2009–2010 Major Economies Forum.[33]

Several analysts argue that the most effective way to engage developing nations, or at least the key players among the developing nations (see the discussion of "minilateral diplomacy" below), is to work directly with each of them on tailored packages of aid and investment and technology transfer.[34] This is particularly important, as the greatest opportunities for low-cost mitigation are in the developing world,[35] and CDM projects have barely scratched the surface of those opportunities.[36]

It appears that in the high-stakes game of targets and timetables, there is no escaping the cumbersome UN rules. But in the multitude of cooperative actions that are needed to meet those targets and timetables, a thousand flowers may yet bloom outside the UN process. It should be remembered that the failure of Kyoto was not primarily a failure to set goals but a failure to meet them. The emergence of thicker discussions and the prospect of engaging an even wider range of actors provides reason for optimism that future goals, as ambitious as those under the first commitment period of Kyoto, may yet be met with effective action.

Participation

Finally, we turn to the question of participation: in particular, participation in a protocol that establishes targets and timetables. Kyoto was greatly handicapped by the failure of the United States to ratify it. It was weakened as well (in terms of anticipated environmental outcomes, leakage, and morale) by the lack of any requirement for developing nations to establish targets and timetables.

"Minilateral" diplomacy

Does participation need to be universal? Ultimately, universal participation is an ideal worth striving for, but as a practical matter, what is most important—again, in terms of expected outcomes, avoidance of leakage, and morale—is participation by the largest emitters. In fact, given the dysfunctions of the plenary UN process discussed above, the most effective route might be for the large emitters to work out a scheme among themselves first and then invite other nations to join. This is essentially what happened in the ozone negotiations.[37] Legal expert Thomas Heller has coined the term *minilateral* to describe this kind of diplomacy.[38]

Which nations, then, are the critical actors for climate mitigation? Heller suggests a group consisting of the U.S., the EU, China, Russia, Japan, and India, which together were responsible for 65 percent of global greenhouse-gas emissions in 2008. Haas suggests that the Organization of Economic Cooperation and Development (OECD) nations plus India and China would be a good core group. Benedick calculates that "25 nations, about half of them in the 'developing' category, are responsible for about 85 percent of the world's greenhouse-gas emissions. None of the other 160-plus countries accounts for even 1 percent."[39]

If any minilateral climate diplomacy is to take place today, it will have to be outside the official UNFCCC process. This was attempted before Copenhagen in 2009, with the establishment of the Major Economies Forum (MEF). Seventeen "major economies" participated, including the BASIC countries and Indonesia. This did not result in a breakthrough at Copenhagen, but it could be tried again. The BASIC countries, as leaders and spokespersons for the bloc of developing nations known as **Group of 77 (G77)**, officially say that no negotiations should take place outside the UNFCCC process where the full G77 is represented, but (as noted above) they participate eagerly in bilateral and regional talks, so further minilateral discussions are not out of the question.

In any case, whether a deal is worked out in the plenary discussions or in minilateral discussions, participation by major emitters is essential to success. Below, we discuss the prospects of future participation by the United States and China, arguably the two "keystone" nations. The U.S. and China are not only the world's largest emitters of greenhouse gases, they have also been perceived as among the most obstructionist in negotiations to date. In addition, it has been argued, China and U.S. are thought to be among the major nations with least to lose from climate change, so they may have less of an incentive than others to work for a viable international regime.[40] If these two nations were to agree to set targets and timetables, there is every reason to be optimistic that others would follow.

United States

There is plenty of goodwill toward action on climate change in the U.S. What is missing is leadership at the national level. Conventional wisdom is that Democratic administrations are more likely to provide this than Republican. Certainly there is a climate-leadership vacuum among possible Republican presidential candidates at the time of this writing, in early 2012; these individuals hold positions ranging from opposition to Kyoto to avowal that global warming is a hoax. On the other hand, the Democratic administration of President Obama has not provided the strong leadership that many climate activists had anticipated.

The truth is that the obstacles to U.S. participation are not only or primarily partisan. At the outset, opposition to joining Kyoto was bipartisan; a resolution to that effect in the Senate passed unanimously, 95–0. What, then, are the obstacles to U.S. participation?

In the simplest terms, the U.S. has been unwilling to participate on terms that would be economically disadvantageous. At the time of the Kyoto meeting, this meant two things, primarily: first, the U.S. wanted market mechanisms that would enable it to meet its target by investing in inexpensive emissions reductions abroad (e.g., in Russia's hot air and in developing countries) rather than imposing onerous costs on businesses at home. Second, and more importantly, the U.S. wanted what it considered a level playing field. The Senate explicitly opposed binding the nation to targets and timetables if developing countries were not similarly bound.

Could U.S. reservations be overcome? Since the initial negotiations in Kyoto, flexible mechanisms have been incorporated into the treaty. As for a level playing field, this is still a sticking point. But at Durban, an agreement in principle was reached that the successor protocol to Kyoto will include mitigation commitments from developing countries.[41] There was also a sense at Durban that participation by the largest and wealthiest of the developing nations (or even participation by China in particular)—rather than universal participation— would be sufficient to ensure U.S. participation.

If those primary objections are overcome, there are plenty of reasons why U.S. participation in a climate treaty could come to be seen as advantageous and even enjoy bipartisan support. The U.S. would be in a position to take up its accustomed leadership role in the international community and to profit from its accustomed leadership in technological innovation. Liberals may continue to view climate mitigation as a moral issue, and conservatives may increasingly come to view it (as the Department of Defense already does[42]) as a security issue. With the principle of subsidiarity intact, obligations under a climate treaty would be far less intrusive than, say, obligations as a member of the World Trade Organization.

China

Policymaking is far less transparent in authoritarian China than in the world's democracies. Nevertheless, some reliable inferences can be made about what principles currently guide Chinese climate policy and what could change that policy in the future.

Two primary concerns appear to have shaped China's climate policy in recent years. The first is an intense preoccupation with increasing economic growth and employment in order to absorb the surplus population that is continually migrating to the urban centers. In a sense, this economic priority is ultimately a security priority: if the government fails to provide adequate employment in a society with no social safety net to speak of, it could find a revolution on its hands. The result of this principle is that China has steadfastly refused to accept any climate mitigation obligation that could impede domestic economic growth.

The second apparent principle behind China's climate policy is a desire to assume a more significant international leadership role. Whereas most nations send environmental ministers to climate negotiations, China's climate negotiations are conducted by its foreign ministry.[43] China exercises *de facto* leadership among the G77 and has positioned itself as a spokesperson for that bloc in the larger negotiations.

Given this starting point, there is reason to be optimistic that over time, China will come around to the view that taking on meaningful mitigation targets is in its interest. (Indeed, the experience at Durban indicates that this shift is underway.)

In the first place, having enjoyed tremendous economic growth in recent years and having surpassed the United States as the leading emitter of greenhouse gases, China can hardly retain its credibility among the G77 nations (which include small island nations and others most vulnerable to climate change) unless it supplements tough words against the wealthier nations with mitigation commitments of its own.[44]

In the second place, the Chinese leadership is getting a clearer picture of the potential downsides of climate change. As noted above, projections from around 2000 suggested that China—like the United States—did not stand to lose as much from climate change as most other major countries;[45] prospects of improved agricultural production may even have led some in China to perceive net benefits from climate change.[46] But more recent reports, including reports produced internally by Chinese scientists, are not so sanguine. These suggest significant risks of drought and desertification in the interior North, river flooding in the South, and sea level rise. The fact that domestic scientists are sounding the warning bells is significant: it is increasingly less possible for Chinese authorities to dismiss climate change as a mere foreign distraction.[47]

Drought and flooding are bad enough in themselves, but they also could be potentially destabilizing forces. In the calculus of economic growth and national security, Chinese leaders may decide that the risks associated with global inaction may outweigh the costs of action.[48]

Veteran China-watcher Martin Sieff reminds us that the nation is extremely volatile.[49] Throughout its modern history, China has been subject to swift and dramatic changes in foreign and domestic policy, often to the surprise and bewilderment of outsiders. If the Chinese leadership were to make climate mitigation a top priority, the result would undoubtedly be dramatic. The world's largest national bureaucracy would be mobilized to reduce emissions at home, and the tone of international negotiations would be altogether changed.

DIPLOMATIC WINDOWS OF OPPORTUNITY

The above analysis suggests that meaningful, coordinated international action on climate mitigation is possible and offers some specific reasons to expect that the chances of meaningful action will improve. But it provides no assurance.

Here, a final lesson from the ozone negotiations is apropos.

Diplomacy, like politics, is the art of the possible. In hindsight, the Montreal Protocol appears to have a masterstroke of diplomacy. And in many ways, it was: key players at UNEP and in national diplomatic missions aimed high, worked hard, and made good strategic and tactical decisions. But they also were incredibly lucky. The U.S. business community was uncharacteristically supportive. Cutting-edge scientific advances arrived just in time to deliver answers to critical technical questions. An attempt by the antiregulatory faction within the Reagan administration to withdraw U.S. support for the emerging consensus at the Vienna negotiations narrowly failed. Within the bitterly divided European Community, rotating leadership passed to sympathetic nations just months before the Montreal negotiations began. Between Vienna and Montreal, initial reports of the giant seasonal ozone hole over Antarctica began to hit the newsstands, creating a groundswell of public interest and support.[50]

In other words, there are windows of diplomatic opportunity. In the ozone negotiations, those windows opened up in quick, serendipitous succession, enabling an international agreement that many had believed was impossible on its face[51] to be negotiated and put into effect with astonishing speed.

Climate is a more complex and challenging issue than ozone in many respects. Carefully weighed arguments about the efficacy of policy instruments and the attitudes of key nations, such as I have tried to offer above, may suggest possibilities and probabilities of action on climate mitigation, but ultimately, what action is taken will depend on the alignment of multiple windows of opportunity. In almost 20 years of climate diplomacy under the UNFCCC, many important steps forward have been taken, but a breakthrough to strong, coordinated action that will be environmentally effective has remained elusive. The last few years of negotiation have been largely devoid of progress. This may continue for many more years—or, if internal developments in key nations like China and the U.S. alter the terms of debate, it could change overnight.

The plenary discussions under UNFCCC, though procedurally flawed, will remain—for better or worse—the one and only forum for making commitments to targets and timetables. But while progress on national commitments in the UNFCCC forum is stalled, there are many other opportunities for climate diplomacy on other fronts, in other fora—including the nuts and bolts of effective actions that national and local governments, regional coalitions, specific industries, and civil society can undertake. Thicker discussions and coordinated actions outside UNFCCC are already underway and prospects for expanding them are good.[52] It is likely that the sum of these actions taken on the periphery—the development of needed technologies, the demonstration of dramatic emissions reductions by pioneering cities and countries, and the increasing sensitivity of major global corporations to climate in their operations and their public image—will open up new windows of opportunity at the center, creating conditions under which nations find it advantageous to participate and find it possible to make and keep ambitious commitments.

NOTES

1. Jonathan B. Wiener, "Climate Change Policy and Policy Change in China," *UCLA Law Review* 55 (2008): 1809.
2. Steven F. Hayward, "The Slow, Agonizing Death of Europeanism," *American Enterprise Institute,* December 20, 2011 (http://www.aei.org/article/the-slow-agonizing-death-of-europeanism/).
3. Intergovernmental Panel on Climate Change (IPCC), *Climate Change 2007: Impacts, Adaptation and Vulnerability.* Working Group II Summary for Policymakers, p. 17.
4. Anna Korppoo, Jacqueline Karas, and Michael Grubb, eds., *Russia and the Kyoto Protocol: Opportunities and Challenges* (London: Chatham House, 2006), 22–23.
5. Garrett Hardin, "The Tragedy of the Commons," *Science* 162 (1968): 1243–1248.
6. Jedediah Purdy, "Climate Change and the Limits of the Possible," *Duke Environmental Law & Policy Forum* 18 (2008): 289–305.
7. See Thomas Heller, "Climate Change: Designing an Effective Response," in *Global Warming: Looking Beyond Kyoto,* ed. Ernesto Zedillo (Washington, DC: Brookings Institution Press, 2008), 130.
8. Each year's UNFCCC meeting is held in a different city. Since the Kyoto Protocol went into effect, members of that treaty have held their annual meetings at the same time and location. So the December 2011 meeting in Durban, South Africa, for example, was simultaneously the 18th conference of the parties to the UNFCCC (COP8) and the 8th meeting of the parties to the Kyoto Protocol (MOP8).
9. Sheila M. Olmstead and Robert N. Stavins, "A Meaningful Second Commitment Period for the Kyoto Protocol," *Economists' Voice* (May 2007): 2.
10. The sanctions under Kyoto are both relatively mild and somewhat self-defeating—nations that fail to meet targets in the first commitment period are required to take on more onerous targets, under stricter conditions, in the second commitment period. Under such rules, what penalized nation would choose to participate in the second commitment period?
11. See, e.g., Olmstead and Stavins 2007, op. cit., pp. 2–3.

12. See William A. Pizer, "Practical Global Climate Policy," in *Architectures for Agreement,* ed. Joseph E. Aldy and Robert N. Stavins (Cambridge: Cambridge University Press, 2007), 297. Another indicator of expectations in the private sector: in a 2011 survey of Global 500 companies, over two-thirds report that climate issues inform their "overall business strategy" (https://www.cdproject.net/en-US/Results/Pages/CDP-Global-500-Report-2011.aspx).

13. There are significant differences too, of course. One is the absence of flexible mechanisms for international trading of production and consumption allowances under Montreal. Flexible mechanisms produce economic efficiency, ensuring that the lowest-cost reductions are made first. With the relatively short time frame for the complete phase-out of chlorofluorocarbons (CFCs) under Montreal (as amended), it mattered relatively little whether low-cost or higher-cost reductions were made first. There were some (e.g., in Europe and Japan) who wanted to adopt this strict and simple approach under Kyoto as well, and indeed, this is how Kyoto was initially written. But since the aim of Kyoto is to reduce rather than eliminate emissions, the gains in efficiency produced by flexible mechanisms are enormous, theoretically reducing the overall cost of compliance by as much as 50 percent, according to Olmstead and Stavins (2007, op. cit., p. 4).

14. Richard Benedick, *Ozone Diplomacy* (Cambridge: Harvard University Press, 1991); Richard Benedick, "The Diplomacy of Climate Change: Lessons from the Montreal Ozone Protocol," *Energy Policy,* March 1991; Richard Benedick, "Avoiding Gridlock on Climate Change," *Issues In Science and Technology,* Winter 2007; Scott Barrett, "Montreal versus Kyoto: International Cooperation and the Global Environment," in *Global Public Goods: International Cooperation in the 21st Century,* ed. Inge Kaul, Isabelle Grunberg, and Marc Stern (Oxford: Oxford University Press, 1999); Cass Sunstein, "Of Montreal and Kyoto: A Tale of Two Protocols," *Harvard Environmental Law Review* 31 (2007); and Daniel Esty, "Beyond Kyoto: Learning from the Montreal Protocol," in Aldy and Stavins 2007, op. cit.

15. Benedick 2007, op. cit., p. 38

16. It is possible to protect against this last hazard by allowing firms to purchase credits directly from the government when the price hits a predetermined ceiling. Since this sort of "safety valve" raises public revenue like a tax, a carbon market with a safety valve is sometimes considered a hybrid "trade-and-tax" scheme. Over time, as stronger price signals are desired and businesses have had time to adapt, the ceiling price can be raised or eliminated entirely.

17. Richard N. Cooper, *Alternatives to Kyoto: The Case for a Carbon Tax* (2006) p. 20.

18. Pizer in Aldy and Stavins 2007, op. cit., p. 292.

19. Benedick 2007, op. cit., p. 38.

20. For a useful antidote, see Heller in Zedillo 2008, op. cit., pp. 130.

21. Ruth Greenspan Bell, "What to Do about Climate Change," *Foreign Affairs* 85, no. 3 (May–June 2006).

22. Peter M. Haas, "Climate Change Governance after Bali," *Global Environmental Politics* 8, no. 3 (August 2008): 4–5.

23. Benedick, *Ozone Diplomacy*, 1991, p. 95.
24. Haas 2008, op. cit., p. 5.
25. Haas 2008, op. cit., pp. 4–6.
26. Benedick 2007, op. cit., pp. 38–40.
27. Benedick 2007, op. cit., pp. 39.
28. E.g., Bell 2006, op. cit.
29. Heller in Zedillo 2008, op. cit., 140. Bringing finance ministers to the table could bring extraordinary results. "Changes in macroeconomic practices, financial liberalization, security arrangements, international trade reform, or other indirect influences on important climate input markets could have a far greater impact on climate-relevant choices than more direct and obvious policy measures" (Heller in Zedillo 2008, op. cit., p. 141). Government procurement policy is another area where a lot of good could be done. A simple conference of government bureaucrats to share ideas and best practices could revolutionize procurement practices in participating nations, with immediate effects. Again, Benedick is able to point to precedents in ozone history, where "the U.S. Department of Defense played an unexpectedly critical role in accelerating the phase-out of CFC 113 by revising its procurement standard" (Benedick 2007, op. cit., p. 40).
30. Nigel Purvis and Andrew Stevenson, "Rethinking Climate Diplomacy," Brussels Forum Paper Series (March 2010), pp. 11–13.
31. "BASIC Group Wants Global Deal on Climate Change by 2011," *The Hindu,* April 26, 2010.
32. "BASIC Group . . . ," *The Hindu, op. cit.*
33. For additional examples, see Sjur Kasa, Anne T. Gullberg, and Gørild Heggelund, "The Group of 77 in the International Climate Negotiations: Recent Developments and Future Directions," *International Environmental Agreements* 8 (2008): 120–122.
34. Heller in Zedillo 2008, op. cit., pp. 130; Purvis and Stevenson 2010, op. cit., p. 29.
35. Olmstead and Stavins 2007, op. cit., p. 1.
36. Pizer in Aldy and Stavins 2007, op. cit., pp. 305–06.
37. Benedick 2007, op. cit., p. 38. Montreal, he writes, was "negotiated by only about 30 nations in nine months. . . . I doubt whether the ozone treaty could have been achieved under the currently fashionable global format."
38. Heller in Zedillo 2008, op. cit.
39. Heller in Zedillo 2008, op. cit., p. 131; Haas 2008, op. cit., pp. 4–5; and Benedick 2007, op. cit., p. 37. Earlier, Benedick (1991, "The Diplomacy of Climate Change," op. cit., p. 96) proposed that "the countries of North America, USSR, EU, and Japan" could get things started and then be joined by China, Brazil, India, and Indonesia.
40. Sunstein 2007, op. cit., p. 48.
41. There has been discussion of how this should be managed; some analysts have proposed that targets be conditional and graded, phased in as countries achieve certain development thresholds, such as per-capita income thresholds (e.g., Robert Stavins, "An International Policy Architecture for the Post-Kyoto Era," in Zedillo 2008, op. cit., p. 147).
42. E.g., U.S. Department of Defense, *Quadrennial Defense Review Report* (February 2010).

43. Kasa, 2008, op. cit., p. 120.
44. China has taken some significant steps in domestic policy but remains leery of committing to targets. See Purvis and Stevenson 2010, op. cit., p. 11.
45. As described by Sunstein 2007, op. cit., p. 48.
46. Wiener 2008, op. cit., pp. 1810, 1816.
47. See Myanna Lahsen, "Trust Through Participation? Problems of Knowledge in Climate Decision Making," in *The Social Construction of Climate Change*, ed. Mary E. Pettenger (Surrey: Ashgate, 2007).
48. Other factors that may enter into the calculus include the public health co-benefits of action (e.g., in urban air quality) and the possible problem of climate refugees (Wiener 2008, op. cit., p. 1822) plus the effect of climate change on Chinese investments around the globe, including in vulnerable African nations.
49. Martin Sieff, *Shifting Superpowers* (Washington, DC: Cato Institute, 2010).
50. Benedick 1991, *Ozone Diplomacy*, op. cit., pp. 19–20, 30, 36, 46, 77–79.
51. Benedick 1991, *Ozone Diplomacy*, op. cit., p. 94.
52. See, e.g., Haas 2008, op. cit.; Radoslav S. Dimitrov, "Inside UN Climate Change Negotiations: The Copenhagen Conference," *Review of Policy Research* 27, no. 6 (November 2010), pp. 795–821; Radoslav S. Dimitrov, "Inside Copenhagen: The State of Climate Governance," *Global Environmental Politics* 10, no. 1 (March 2010).

NO: Samuel Thernstrom, *Clean Air Task Force*

THE QUIXOTIC QUEST FOR UNIFORM NATIONAL EMISSIONS STANDARDS

We stand at a critical point in the development of policies to protect the global climate. In 2008–2009, significant new national and international climate policies were widely expected. They did not materialize: despite holding the White House and both Houses of Congress, Democrats failed to enact legislation, and the much-anticipated international climate conference in Copenhagen in 2009 ended without agreement on a binding successor to the Kyoto Protocol, which expires in 2012. The wave of momentum toward ambitious domestic and international action on climate seems to have crested, at least for the moment. After legislation died in the Senate in spring 2010, Democrats virtually abandoned the issue, and the president appears reluctant to even mention the issue. The longstanding climate policy agenda has collapsed; the critical question is where to go from here.

Note: An earlier version of this essay appeared in the first edition of this book, while the author was at the American Enterprise Institute. This essay represents the opinion of the author alone, and does not necessarily reflect the institutional perspectives of either the American Enterprise Institute or the Clean Air Task Force.

While momentum toward and support for new climate policies has slowed dramatically, the need for action has not diminished in the slightest. Global emissions continue to rise at unprecedented rates, with no sign of diminishing in the forseeable future. Policymakers have struggled to find ways to curtail greenhouse-gas emissions for twenty years, with little to show for their efforts. The Kyoto Protocol has had a negligible effect on global emissions—its targets were unpalatable for America, undemanding for energy-inefficient Russia, and impractical for the countries that were missing their targets, while also being far too modest to have a meaningful effect on warming—and the failure to reach consensus on new targets and timetables for emissions reductions at the international climate conferences in 2009 and 2011 is still further evidence of the political infeasability of that approach. And yet, the dream does not die. Many environmental advocates, and the European nations that are Kyoto's strongest supporters, continue to seek a further extension of that style of treaty in the coming years.

Coming out of the Copenhagen and Durban climate summits in 2009 and 2011, the course of international climate policy does remain legitimately unsettled. While the main thrust of the Copenhagen and Durban Accords was to move past the Kyoto model in key respects, Kyoto's advocates can still point to the fact that the option to adopt future emissions targets and timetables does remain on the table in international negotiations. The art of international diplomacy is such that the Copenhagen and Durban Accords represented substantial departures from (and therefore, implicit rejections of) the Kyoto approach—but nothing even approaching a definitive statement on this question emerged from either conference.

So despite more than two decades of debate, the core questions of climate policy remain unresolved: how much, and how quickly, should each nation cut its emissions if we are to prevent significant warming? Is there a fair and feasible way of allocating emissions reduction obligations among all nations— and enforcing those terms? Can differing national interests be harmonized in a single global system?

Casual observers of the issue might well assume that the basic direction of American and international policy is very clear, given how single-minded the public debate has been. Attention is almost exclusively focused on consideration of various cap-and-trade proposals modeled on the Kyoto approach.[1] The key elements of this concept are (1) the establishment of targets and timetables for emissions reductions and (2) the concept of *common but differentiated responsibilities,* (in diplomatic terms) which establishes the expectation that industrialized nations would accept emissions targets but that developing nations would not.

Central to the international debate over the structure of any climate treaty are questions of fairness and efficacy. How far to extend the reach of a treaty, and on what terms, remain highly contentious questions. While some would be satisfied with a treaty that included all major global economies, others argue for a more radical goal: universal—and, ideally, equal—participation in emissions reductions. Climate change is a global problem, the reasoning goes, so each country should contribute equally to solving it. Any country that avoids emissions reduction obligations could potentially become a haven for energy-intensive industries seeking to circumvent emissions limits. Countries could benefit economically by eschewing emissions limits while enjoying the benefits of the sacrifice of others—the classic "free rider" problem. An equal standard for all countries would, therefore, be the fairest and most effective approach.

In fact, universal participation in any emissions reduction effort is critical to its success. As William Nordhaus, one of the leading economists studying climate change, has written,

> Our modeling results point to the importance of near-universal participation programs to reduce greenhouse gases. Because of the structure of the costs of abatement, with marginal costs being very low for the initial reductions but rising sharply for higher reductions, there are substantial excess costs if the preponderance of sectors and countries are not fully included. We preliminarily estimate that a participation rate of 50 percent, as compared with 100 percent, will impose an abatement-cost penalty of 250 percent. Even with the participation of the top 15 countries and regions, consisting of three-quarters of world emissions, we estimate that the cost penalty is about 70 percent.[2]

While this argument has a theoretical logic and a certain emotional appeal, it would be a poor basis for negotiating a meaningful climate treaty that all nations might actually accept and implement. There is no way to compel

Table 1

Projected Damages from 2.5°C Warming, as a Percentage of GDP

India	4.93
Africa	3.91
Organization of Economic Cooperation and Development (OECD) Europe	2.83
High-Income OPEC	1.95
Eastern Europe	0.71
Japan	0.50
United States	**0.45**
China	**0.22**
Russia	**−0.65**

Source: Cass R. Sunstein, "The Complex Climate Change Incentives of China and the United States" (working paper 07-14, Washington, DC: AEI-Brookings Joint Center for Regulatory Studies, August 2007) p.11, Table 3.

participation—or adherence to—such a treaty; each nation must choose to join voluntarily.[3] Countries have widely differing national interests, abilities, and preferences when it comes to the broad range of issues related to climate policy. While climate change is, indeed, a global concern, it does not have equal implications for all countries. This has profound implications for the prospects of any future global agreement. There is a wealth of data to illustrate this point, but to pick just one key metric, consider the differences in the amount of economic damage the countries and regions listed in Table 1 (p. 306) expect to suffer, as indicated by expected impact on gross domestic product (GDP).

As Table 1 shows, some countries stand to lose much more from climate change than others; China and Russia might even benefit from warming.[4] Just looking at those numbers, it is not hard to conclude that China and Russia are unlikely to accept significant emissions limitations at any time in the foreseeable future or to bear the cost of mitigation. The United States may be a somewhat different story, due to its political system and current preferences—but only somewhat. It seems implausible that the three countries that stand to lose the least from climate change will be as eager to bear the cost of mitigation as other countries with different national interests. These differences in national interests will inevitably limit the potential for a harmonized international climate treaty. As Harvard Law School professor Cass Sunstein observed,

> An agreement that is in the interest of the world as a whole is unlikely to be in the interest of China and the United States, the world's leading contributors. It is increasingly clear that the costs and benefits of emissions reductions are highly variable across nations. On prominent projections, neither China nor the United States is anticipated to be among the principal victims of climate change. The circumstances for an international agreement are distinctly unpromising if the leading emitters do not perceive themselves as likely to gain a great deal from emissions reductions.[5]

Furthermore, there is no way to compel participation—or adherence to—such an agreement; each nation must choose to join voluntarily. Kyoto was essentially toothless in that it had no meaningful enforcement mechanism for countries that missed their targets; it seems unlikely that future treaties will provide for much stronger enforcement. (Indeed, Canada withdrew from the Kyoto Protocol in late 2011 rather than face multibillion-dollar fines for missing its emissions targets—highlighting the perverse and ineffective structure of the treaty.)

In the face of these fundamental political obstacles, the challenge for policymakers is to be realistic about crafting policies that will attract some form of participation by the broadest range of nations, recognizing that each will necessarily prefer to respond differently to climate change. Emissions limits are naturally the primary focus of a sound climate policy—but not the only one.

Some nations might want to focus nearly exclusively on one approach—adaptation to the effects of rising temperatures, for instance—while others may choose to combine different elements of these strategies. As it would be difficult (if not impossible) to measure accurately the comparative value of different approaches, each nation would necessarily make different judgments about what policies would be the most cost-effective and appropriate for its circumstances.

Proponents of the one-size-fits-all approach to emissions reductions have no solution to the participation problem beyond hoping that it will improve in time. Some imagine that a major developing nation such as China might be induced to join an international emissions regime within the next twenty-five years. The possibility cannot be dismissed, but there is little reason to expect it.

Kyoto's exemption of the entire developing world from any emissions obligations is the most conspicuous example of how fundamentally flawed the protocol's structure is. But Kyoto's problems hardly stop there: Even among the countries that did choose to ratify it, many are missing their (quite modest) emissions reduction targets. We can only conclude that nations' willingness to accept targets may well exceed their abilities to meet them—which bodes ill for the effectiveness of future agreements.

Even if the United States had rejoined the Kyoto regime and all countries set stricter targets for the next commitment period and—truly wishful thinking—actually met them, the growth in emissions from the developing world, if left unchecked, would mean that total global emissions will continue to rise for decades to come. China has at last overtaken the United States as the world's leading emitter of greenhouse gases, a symbolic turning point that policymakers cannot ignore, and is on pace to increase its emissions by 13 percent a year in this decade, far more than had been expected.[6] Given the persistence of greenhouse gases in the atmosphere (carbon dioxide can last for a century or more), the continued rise in emissions that is expected in the coming decades will commit the planet to a century or more of warming. Americans are concerned about "the China problem"—how to make a treaty work without China's participation; in Europe, they talk of "the American problem." The American problem may well resolve itself (at least in some form) over time; the China problem may prove the more persistent.

THE FUTILITY OF EQUITY ARGUMENTS

Faced with the participation problem, many advocates turn to exhortations, often framed in terms of moral obligations rooted in a sense of fairness. These arguments are primarily directed at the United States, the most conspicuous holdout from the Kyoto regime. But their lasting strength and effectiveness will depend more upon their applicability to the China problem—and there they seem weakest.

Even though China has taken over as the world's leading emitter of greenhouse gases, the United States (we are often reminded) long held that position and remains by far the leading emitter on a per-capita basis. It is easy—and politically popular in the international community—to argue that America has a unique obligation to lead the effort in reducing emissions. Former United Nations Secretary-General Kofi Annan, for instance, has called for "climate justice"—that is, requiring reductions from the countries most responsible for past emissions rather than those whose emissions are growing fastest now. "We must recognize," says Annan, "that the polluter must pay, and not the poor and vulnerable."[7]

Certainly this was the logic, if not effect, of the Kyoto Protocol. And over time, it seems likely that Americans will indeed undertake more aggressive measures to reduce their emissions; the U.S. **Environmental Protection Agency** is expected to issue greenhouse-gas regulations on new electric power plants before the end of 2012. But if *climate justice* means repeating Kyoto's errors in emissions allocations, particularly its exemption of the developing world, then we can be certain that global emissions will continue to rise. And if climate change is truly a moral issue, the obligation to act against it must fall on all shoulders, regardless of economic circumstances, since inclusion is the key to effectiveness.

Some believe that American leadership would inspire China, India, and other major developing countries to accept emissions limits as well. If we give any credence to the historical record and the current position of those governments, however, we would have to conclude that, if anything, unilateral acceptance of emissions limits by America would only reinforce China and India's incentives to reject limits of their own. The more inclusive and stringent the Kyoto regime becomes, the stronger the incentive for energy-intensive industries to relocate to developing nations that have no emissions limits. Further financial incentives to refuse emissions caps are provided by Kyoto's Clean Development Mechanism (CDM), which generates emissions reduction credits by funding projects in the developing world.[8] Unfortunately, the CDM actually creates perverse incentives for developing countries: The less initiative a country takes to cut its own emissions voluntarily, the more it can earn from the CDM.

Advocates argue that, in time, rising standards of living in the developing world and growing evidence of the effects of climate change will persuade at least the major developing economies to accept emissions caps. One can never know what the future will bring, but it seems unlikely that such a transformation will occur quickly. But it does raise again the question: even if all nations agree that action of some sort is desirable, what principles can guide us to a fair and practical international agreement?

Equity, while naturally appealing to a simplistic sense of fairness, seems particularly ill-suited to the multifaceted challenges of global climate policy. There are both practical and conceptual problems with using equity—or any of the common alternatives, such as Annan's fairness argument—as a guide to allocating international obligations for climate policy.

The simplest application of the equity argument, for instance, is the idea that all nations should cut their emissions of greenhouse gases by equal amounts. Poorer and more populous countries, however, argue that emissions should be equalized on a per-capita basis. Surely an Indian is entitled to emit as many greenhouse gases as an American? The industrialized world is largely responsible for the manmade greenhouse gases currently in the atmosphere; shouldn't it be responsible for solving the problem?

There is certainly a logic in their perspective—but as a practical matter, if we accept that claim, we accept a future of virtually unlimited global emissions. Until we invent technologies that can remove greenhouse gases from the atmosphere, there is no way to undo historical emissions; we can only seek to prevent future emissions, the majority of which will come from developing countries such as India. There is no end to the fairness arguments, but as a practical matter, they are irrelevant. It will be impossible to stabilize global atmospheric concentrations of greenhouse gases without significant emissions limits in the developing world.

One recent study projects that, absent an agreement to limit its emissions, China's greenhouse-gas emissions in 2030 will be equal to the entire world's current emissions.[9] This staggering fact underscores the fundamental reality: without a means of controlling emissions from China, India, and other major developing economies, efforts to halt warming through emissions reductions are doomed to failure. The Kyoto Protocol's exemption of China and other developing countries from any emissions reduction obligations may well prove to be the single most damaging precedent in climate policy; the prospects for reversing it in future negotiations seem poor.

On the other side of the fairness argument, some have argued that it would be both unfair and simply unrealistic not to recognize differences in the size of national economies when calculating environmental obligations. Yes, America has been the leading global emitter—but it is also the largest economy in the world. In fact, not surprisingly, its share of the global economy corresponds precisely with its share of global emissions. Separating those trend lines is the goal of climate policies, but progress has been slow.

In February 2002, President Bush proposed reducing the greenhouse-gas "intensity" of the American economy—that is, the amount of emissions per unit of GDP.[10] This metric has a logical appeal as well—it recognizes the fundamental fact that economic activity inevitably generates greenhouse-gas emissions and that consequently, emissions targets should reflect differences in the size and nature of each nation's economy. But, as with the per-capita approach, this metric can also be used to justify continued emissions rather than curtailing them. Developing nations may object that this concept constitutes *carbon colonialism*, reinforcing existing differences in global economic status through an economically controlling emissions regime.

In sum, accepting existing differences in economic growth and associated emissions levels would disadvantage less-developed countries, discouraging them from accepting emissions limits; allocating emissions obligations on an equal per-capita basis would sanction decades of additional growth in developing-world—and, hence, global—emissions.

The obstacles to a "fair" allocation of emissions burdens don't end there, however. Some countries (Japan, for example) have highly energy-efficient economies, with far fewer opportunities for cost-effective emissions reductions. Should Japan be punished for its progress by asking it to cut its emissions as much as a country with an aging, highly inefficient industrial infrastructure?

There are nearly endless variations on this theme. America has enjoyed stronger economic and population growth than other countries. Shouldn't we expect American emissions to grow? France happens to have the benefit of a strong nuclear power sector; Britain shifted away from coal in favor of natural gas for reasons unrelated to climate change. Should those countries be given credit for those facts—or should they be expected to expend an equivalent effort at reducing emissions in other areas of their economies?

On the other side of the coin, Russia, of course, only ratified the Kyoto Protocol because it was bribed with generous credits based on its Soviet-era emissions levels. Russia's participation in Kyoto, in other words, was purchased at the price of granting it the right to emissions far in excess of its current level. The leading proposals to entice China into a new global agreement tend to replicate that example, although they obviously sacrifice effectiveness for the sake of achieving nominal participation. But without such favorable terms, countries like China and Russia are unlikely to accept any emissions limits—and, from their perspective, why should they? Clearly, fairness is in the eyes of the beholder when it comes to these issues.

The ultimate futility of the equity argument becomes even clearer when one considers the impossibility of accurately measuring the merit of each nation's investments in climate protection. Even if nations were simply to agree that each should make an equivalent effort at combating warming, a meaningful measure of a nation's effort would have to be far more complex than merely totaling annual emissions levels. It is a grave mistake to treat climate change as a single problem with a single solution; in fact, it is a much more complex and multifaceted group of issues requiring a much more complex policy response.

DIFFERING INTERESTS, ABILITIES, AND APPROACHES TO CLIMATE POLICY

Agreeing on what level of comparable effort might be a fair distribution of burdens among nations—and finding a way to measure that effort—is hard enough, but the task becomes impossible if there is also no way to measure progress objectively in the short term. Different nations would be wise to choose a variety of different climate policies, depending on their interests and abilities, with some emphasizing adaptation to warming more than mitigation and some vice versa. Some countries would favor aggressive action to reduce emissions, while others might prefer investing in research efforts that might have an equal or greater effect in the long run. Each nation would have countless different decisions to make in crafting its policies. Determining what mix of actions is "fair" would involve an endless array of subjective, uncertain calculations—and what country would accept the judgment of others in that assessment?

Some countries have greater opportunities than others to reduce their emissions at relatively modest cost. Others may have different visions for achieving the same goals. How should we value differing national investments in emissions reductions, scientific and technological research and development, and adaptation measures to protect public health? For many countries, particularly in the developing world, it would make most sense to invest significant resources in programs to protect their citizens from the effects of climate change. Foremost on that agenda would be economic growth, which would raise living standards and protect citizens from the effects of climate change—while necessarily contributing to ever-rising global emissions.

Even within the industrialized world, different countries would rationally prefer different approaches to climate change, depending on their interests and abilities, which might be equally valid. If a wealthy, innovative country, for instance, were to invest heavily in an intensive research-and-development program for climate-related technologies that would make massive emissions reductions cost-effective in the long run—while eschewing ambitious emissions reductions in the short term—the long-term benefits of that approach could be far greater than another country's comparably costly effort to cut emissions as quickly as possible.[11] But there is no way to predict reliably which of these efforts would be more effective.

Since the key question is not necessarily how *quickly* we reduce global emissions but rather how *much* they can be reduced over the course of the rest of this century, nations might reasonably choose different emissions pathways that could ultimately have equivalent effect—or could not, if unexpected obstacles arise along one of the chosen routes. Measuring progress in a century-long effort in annual increments can easily give a distorted picture—but that is how political institutions tend to see these questions.

Ultimately, each country will have to make its own judgments. Purists may call for universal participation in an emissions control regime, but there is no way around the fact that each country has different interests, abilities, and agendas; and when it comes to designing an architecture and agenda for a global climate policy, it is not clear that uniformity or equality should be primary concerns. In a global economy, where innovation in energy and climate-friendly technologies is driven largely by private companies operating in multinational markets and drawing upon the intellectual and economic capital of multiple nations, efforts to precisely allocate national credit for specific contributions to such complex, intermingled efforts seem painfully reductionist.

THE QUEST FOR A COMPREHENSIVE INTERNATIONAL CLIMATE POLICY

The global population is expected to grow by 2.5 billion by mid-century.[12] Energy use is expected to increase by 57 percent by 2030. Within countries outside the OECD, that figure is 95 percent.[13] Despite two decades of effort to constrain them, global emissions continue to rise inexorably, and fundamental differences in the ability and motivation of countries to reduce emissions continue to undermine the level of consensus needed for effective global action.

Given those facts, it is far from clear that it is even possible to craft a truly effective international climate treaty, so vast is the scale of economic, social, and technological transformation that would be necessary and so fundamental the political and economic obstacles to success. If there is any hope of making such a treaty broadly attractive to a wide range of countries, it cannot be rigidly committed to universal and equal targets. Widely varying national circumstances should determine the nature of each nation's climate policies. It would be madness, for instance, for Bangladesh to focus its resources on emissions reductions; its environmental conditions dictate that adaptation to warming is the only rational priority for its government. Even if it was possible to force the world into a uniform emissions reduction scheme, therefore, it is far from clear that it would be desirable.

The Kyoto Protocol was intended to be the first step in constructing a single, harmonized emissions limitation regime. Although it was understood that its initial scope would be limited, advocates imagined it could be slowly expanded and refined until it became complete. But with this goal remaining elusive, perhaps a better approach would be to stop trying so hard. A growing number of scholars recognize that a single, harmonized approach to climate policy might not be preferable, even if it were feasible. William Pizer of Resources for the Future has noted three lessons we can take from our experience with Kyoto and other national efforts at emissions reductions:

> First, a binding international agreement is neither necessary nor sufficient for domestic actions. . . . Second, whatever action a country takes, the form of that action is likely to be dictated by domestic features and forces. . . . Third, even without formal mechanisms to equalize marginal costs across countries—e.g., international trading or a single, agreed-upon tax rate—various forces seem to keep those costs in line.[14]

Pizer suggests we set aside the quest for a single, all-encompassing structure for an international emissions limitation regime and focus instead on encouraging countries to take action in whatever form seems most appropriate and most effective, given their national circumstances. "We need to recognize," he explains,

> that domestic circumstances and opportunities [for action on climate] differ; that, at least right now, at the beginning of a perhaps century-long global effort to address climate change, binding emission limits, prices, or standards are unlikely to be helpful; and that formal mechanisms to equalize marginal costs (at this initial phase) are less important for efficiency than suggested in the literature. Instead, we should encourage countries to make some commitment to mandatory action, and focus our energy on a clear commitment to evaluate what actually happens.[15]

Gwyn Prins and Steve Rayner, two British scholars of climate policy, have made similar recommendations in a landmark paper entitled "The Wrong Trousers: Rethinking Climate Policy." They offer seven key principles by which a new approach to climate policy might be guided, the first of which is to use a "silver buckshot" approach—by which they mean, adopt "a wide variety of climate policies—silver buckshot—and nonclimate policies with climate effects. Each would have the potential to tackle some part of the overall problem, although it would not be clear which would be the most successful."[16]

Prins and Rayner suggest abandoning the pursuit of a universal treaty in favor of a focus on just the major emitters, with more emphasis on state and regional initiatives, more research and development, and greater investment in adaptation. Freed from an international treaty, nations could learn from their experiences and adjust their policies accordingly. "Sometimes the best line of approach," they conclude, "is not head-on, if one seeks long-lasting impact."

In an ideal world, a single, unified emissions regime might be the most effective and efficient approach to the climate problem—but given the fundamental political and economic factors at work in our less-than-ideal world today, a less-coordinated and more creative approach may be our only hope of success. There is little prospect for successfully cutting global emissions dramatically in the near term, so long-term success must depend upon our ability to learn from our successes and failures and to respond to changing conditions over the course of the century. Flexibility and innovation, not equity and arbitrary standards, should be our watchwords in designing national and international climate policies.

Samuel Thernstrom was a resident fellow at the American Enterprise Institute when this essay was originally written. He is currently senior climate policy advisor to the Clean Air Task Force, a nonprofit organization that works to protect the atmosphere through research, advocacy, collaboration, and innovation. This essay reflects his personal opinions, not necessarily those of either his current or former employers.

NOTES

1. A "cap-and-trade" system is an innovative way of reducing pollution while providing companies the freedom to find the most cost-effective means of improving their environmental performance and the incentives to exceed conventional emissions standards if there are cost-effective opportunities to do so. The idea was first adopted in the 1990 **Clean Air Act** amendments, and while it was highly controversial at the time, it has proven to be quite successful in that context, leading many people to assume—perhaps falsely—that it is the ideal mechanism for reducing greenhouse-gas emissions. The basic idea is simple: Set an overall emissions limit for a given pollutant and industry—say, the total amount of sulfur dioxide emissions that electric power plants on the East Coast can emit—and a target for how much that pollutant should be reduced in order to meet environmental standards. Distribute "emissions credits"—the right to emit a given amount of pollution—to each power plant and, with each year, reduce the number of credits available to plants until the

desired target is met. Plants that have affordable opportunities to reduce their emissions will do so, freeing up credits that can be sold to other power plants that cannot economically reduce their own emissions. The end result is that overall pollution targets are met while giving companies the flexibility to find the most cost-effective opportunities to cut their emissions. The Clean Air Act's **emissions trading** system has been effective at reducing the pollutants that cause smog; the analogous system established under the Kyoto Protocol by European nations has not, for complicated reasons having to do with the scale of the system, the technological and economic limitations on companies' abilities to substantially reduce their greenhouse-gas emissions, and the difficulty in allocating credits and verifying the value of projects certified to earn emission reduction credits. Emissions trading systems seem best suited to drive deployment of moderately innovative technologies in a narrow range of applications and less suited to drive more radical, long-term innovation of technologies in a wider range of applications and fields.

2. William Nordhaus, *A Question of Balance* (New Haven & London: Yale University Press, 2008) p.19.

3. Some people have advocated the use of trade sanctions as a means of compelling participation—by either the United States or China, for example—in an emissions control regime. Such an approach would, of course, tread on dangerous ground. It is far from clear that such an effort would be legal under the terms of the World Trade Organization (WTO); even if the WTO did sanction carbon tariffs, the result could well be a green trade war that could do significant damage to free trade without producing the desired effect.

4. Richard B. Stewart and Jonathan Weiner, *Reconstructing Climate Policy: Beyond Kyoto* (Washington, DC: AEI Press, 2003) 15.

5. Ibid., p. 2

6. Roger Pielke Jr., Tom Wigley, and Christopher Green, "Dangerous Assumptions," *Nature* 452 (April 3, 2008): 531–532.

7. The Associated Press, "Former UN Chief Calls for Climate Justice," *International Herald Tribune*, June 24, 2008. http://www.iht.com/bin/printfriendly.php?id=13961173

8. The value of the CDM program itself has also been questioned, as there is evidence that many of the credits it issued were essentially fraudulent; see, for instance, Michael W. Wara and David G. Victor, *A Realistic Policy on International Carbon Offsets* (working paper #74, Program on Energy and Sustainable Development, Stanford University) http://pesd.stanford.edu

9. Ning Zeng, Yihui Ding, Jiahua Pan, Huijun Wang, and Jay Gregg, "Climate Change—the Chinese Challenge", *Science* 319, no. 5864 (February 8, 2008): 730–731.

10. President George W. Bush, "Clear Skies and Climate Change Initiatives," February 14, 2002, available at http://www.whitehouse.gov/news/releases/2002/02/20020214-5.html; supporting materials available at http://www.whitehouse.gov/news/releases/2002/02/clearskies.html

11. Bjorn Lomborg's 2007 book, *Cool It: The Skeptical Environmentalist's Guide to Global Warming*, provides a detailed and approachable exposition of this argument.

12. Andrew C. Revkin, "Budgets Falling in Race to Fight Global Warming," *New York Times*, October 30, 2006.

13. Energy Information Administration, *International Energy Outlook 2008*, available at http://www.eia.doe.gov/oiaf/ieo/highlights.html

14. Joseph E. Aldy and Robert N. Stavins, eds., *Architectures for Agreement: Addressing Global Climate Change in the Post-Kyoto World* (Cambridge: Cambridge University Press, 2007), 302–03.

15. Ibid., 304.

16. Gwyn Prins and Steve Rayner, *The Wrong Trousers: Rethinking Climate Policy* (James Martin Institute for Science and Civilization, University of Oxford, and the MacKinder Centre for the Study of Long-Wave Events, London School of Economics), 26. See also Gwyn Prins and Steve Rayner, "Time To Ditch Kyoto," *Nature* 449 (October 25, 2007): 973–75, available at http://www.nature.com/nature/journal/v449/n7165/full/449973a.html

11

the future of energy

Should Governments Encourage the Development of Alternative Energy Sources to Help Reduce Dependence on Fossil Fuels?

YES: Christopher Flavin, *Worldwatch Institute*

NO: Michael Lynch, *Strategic Energy & Economic Research, Inc.*

The twin problems of high (and potentially rising) energy prices and climate change present an enormous challenge: how can countries find and use sustainable sources of economically efficient energy without releasing environmentally destructive greenhouse gases? And the challenge is exacerbated by other conditions that should ideally attend these changes: absence of significant risks, ease of transition from petroleum-based transportation to alternatives, ensuring that adjustment costs are not unequally distributed, and so on. Meeting future energy needs will be a formidable task; Figure 1 (p. 319) shows how significantly total world energy demands have increased and are expected to continue to increase over time. Taken together, energy consumption and climate change are technical as well as political challenges that confront the so-called developed and developing nations alike.

Expected growth in energy demand stems from rising world populations—mostly in the developing world—and from increasing wealth, which is strongly correlated with greater energy use. Figure 2 (p. 320) shows past energy use for several large nations, and it reflects particularly high energy growth in China. Even more alarming for those who seek to limit fossil-fuel use is the projected future consumption of coal, oil, and gas, which constitute the vast majority of energy resources tapped for current and future needs. Therefore, reducing dependence on fossil fuels will necessitate reversing long-standing trends, which will likely require significant economic and political dislocations.

Figure 1

Total World Primary Energy Demand, 1971–2030

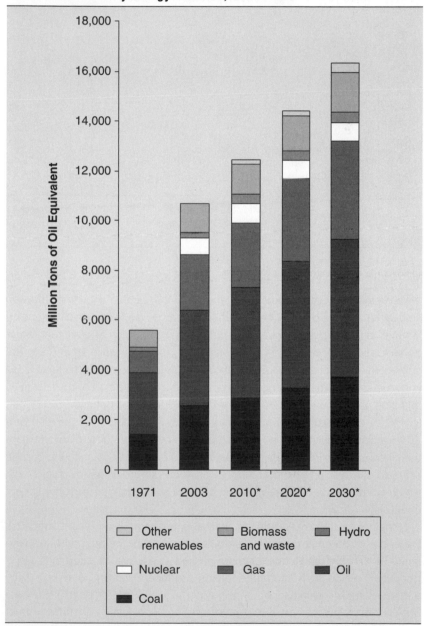

Source: International Energy Agency, World Energy Outlook 2005, Paris, 2005, 82.
*Predicted Values.

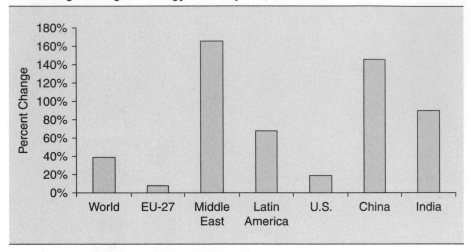

Figure 2

Percentage Change in Energy Consumption, 1990–2008

Source: International Energy Agency, Key Energy Statistics, 2010.
Note: EU-27 is the 27 member states in the European Union.

While the problems of increasing energy use are clear, choosing between solutions presents challenges. Increasing energy use is not inherently problematic, but continued burning of fossil fuels contributes to climate change as well as to the realization that fossil-fuel reserves, while abundant, are subject to eventual exhaustion. Means to address these problems tend to fall into one of two broad categories. The first is market driven and essentially relies on rising energy prices to force technological and behavioral changes in energy production and consumption. Of course, such changes also produce economic dislocations and disparities as the poor suffer disproportionately from sudden increases in prices. Relying on energy costs to encourage shifts to alternative fuels also introduces a certain irony, as low fuel costs, which are politically attractive to most citizens, inhibit longer-term investment in alternative fuels.

Nonetheless, the market-driven model is a powerful argument, because increases in prices are quickly distributed throughout the economy, creating immediate incentives to drill for more oil and to explore for alternatives and because the incentives to change rely on producers wanting to make money and consumers looking to purchase energy at the lowest possible prices. Supporters claim that there is no fear of running out of fossil fuels (or any other type of fuel), since scarce supplies will drive prices so high as to restrict consumption and spur innovation in recovery techniques for fuels that are commercially attractive only at high prices. Therefore, by allowing higher prices to stimulate attempts to produce economically viable alternative energy sources, the market approach is said to stimulate innovation most effectively. Other related approaches recognize that greenhouse-gas (GHG) intensities vary with different fuels and that policies can discriminate (for example, through taxes) based on the GHG intensity of various fuels.

One problem with the market model is that, in many instances, energy prices fail to reflect the full social costs of energy production and consumption. In the absence of significant taxes or other policies to discourage certain types of energy use, the burning of fossil fuels is typically underpriced. In other words, when individuals or institutions purchase energy, they are rarely, if ever, paying the full social cost of its consumption. For example, driving your gasoline-powered car costs you money for upkeep and gasoline, but you do not pay (and therefore do not fully account for) the social costs of pollutants. Under these circumstances, reliance on markets to produce innovation actually leads to overconsumption of energy, because it is priced too low in relation to its full social costs. Furthermore, allowing market prices to regulate consumption produces economic and political dislocations as the poor—whether measured as individuals or as nations—tend to bear the brunt of the reduced consumption.

Some observers have called instead for significant governmental intervention into energy markets, to spur the sort of innovation that they believe the markets alone will never produce. Pointing both to successes of some government-led innovations (such as the Internet) and to the myopia of markets (as well as their heavy discounting of social costs and benefits), supporters of a stronger industrial policy suggest government involvement as a superior means of delivering important social priorities such as abundant and clean energy sources. Others ridicule this kind of industrial policy as forcing governments to pick winners, which, they argue, is a politically disputatious enterprise, based on developments that are difficult to foresee and increase the potential for political manipulation.

The two articles that follow outline different approaches to improving our production and use of energy. Christopher Flavin argues that markets are crucial to energy development, but he favors public-private partnerships as the most effective way to address the severe energy needs facing the global economy. Michael Lynch argues that many renewable energy sources are poor substitutes for oil in addressing future energy needs. Promoting technologies that are not economically viable wastes scarce resources, which, in his view, are better expended on improved battery technology and other innovations that will assist a broad range of energy sources.

Discussion Questions

1. What are the consequences of a dependence on fossil fuels? Consider the potential effects on the environment, the economy, public health, and national security.
2. Who should lead the initiative for reducing dependence on fossil fuels? The government? The market? The private sector? The consumer? Why?
3. To help reduce U.S. dependence on foreign sources of fossil fuels, some advocate increased offshore drilling and drilling in the Arctic National Wildlife Refuge (ANWR). Are there benefits to this strategy? Drawbacks? As a policymaker, what stakeholders would you have to consider or consult when making your decision?
4. What does Christopher Flavin say are the three elements of an effective climate strategy? In what ways does he think the government can help to implement this strategy? Do you agree with his approach?
5. What four general arguments does Michael Lynch describe as often being made by those who promote alternative energies? What evidence does he give for rejecting each of these arguments? Do you agree with his assessment?

YES: Christopher Flavin, *Worldwatch Institute*

The world is entering uncharted territory.

Fossil fuels made the modern economy and all of its material accomplishments possible. But soaring energy prices, concern about climate change, and an expected decline in production of crude oil in the next few decades makes the building of a low-carbon economy the central challenge of our age. Meeting that challenge will require that governments encourage the development of alternative energy sources and the restructuring of the global energy industry through technological, economic, and policy innovations that are as unprecedented as the climate change they must address.

Driven by the perfect storm of soaring energy prices and concern about climate change, companies around the world are now investing tens of billions of dollars in a wide array of clean-energy technologies with the potential to reduce dependence on fossil fuels. Solar energy, wind power, green buildings, and electric cars are among the pivotal technologies now entering the global marketplace on a grand scale. A combination of private-sector innovation and proactive government policies are making this new energy revolution possible: from the Federal Republic of Germany to the State of Texas and the People's Republic of China, government policies are being implemented that allow new energy technologies to overcome the head start that a century of public support has provided for fossil fuels.

The sheer magnitude of the transformation ahead requires bold action. Across the political spectrum, respected voices are calling for the United States to undertake a national commitment to reducing dependence on oil and coal—replacing it with indigenous energy sources such as solar and wind power and biofuels. Real change hinges on government policies that will stimulate production, increase efficiency, and reward investment in renewable energy.

AVOIDING CATASTROPHE

Only recently have scientists understood that changes in the concentration of carbon dioxide, methane, and other less common gases could trigger an ecological catastrophe of staggering proportions. Past climate changes have been caused by tiny alterations in Earth's orbit and orientation to the sun—providing, for example, just enough added energy to warm the planet over thousands of years, increasing the concentration of carbon dioxide in the atmosphere, and in turn triggering even larger changes in the temperature. Today's massive release of CO_2 and other greenhouse gases is leading to far greater changes to the atmosphere in a period of decades.[1]

Scientists now project that within the decades immediately ahead, the capacity of land and ocean to absorb carbon emissions will decline, while vast changes in the Arctic may further accelerate warming. Melting tundra will release millions of tons of methane, a greenhouse gas that is more powerful than CO_2. And as the Arctic ice pack recedes each summer—nearly half is already gone—it will be like removing a large air conditioner from the Northern Hemisphere. This effect will further warm the climate and could mean the end of the million-year-old Greenland ice sheet—which by itself contains enough water to raise worldwide sea levels by more than seven meters.[2]

When the world will reach such a tipping point remains uncertain. But it is already clear that ecological change of this magnitude would lead to unprecedented disruptions to the world's economies. A groundbreaking 2006 study led by former World Bank chief economist Nicholas Stern concluded that climate change could cut global economic output by between 5 and 20 percent. In his 2007 book, *The Age of Turbulence*, Alan Greenspan, the leading free-market economist of the day, included climate change as one of five forces that could derail the U.S. economy in the twenty-first century.

In 2006 the combustion of fossil fuels released 8 billion tons of carbon to the atmosphere—nearly a million tons every hour—of which coal and oil contributed roughly 40 percent each, while natural gas accounted for the rest. Global fossil-fuel carbon emissions have increased fivefold since 1950; they are up 30 percent just since 1990. Today, fossil fuels provide four-fifths of the energy that powers the global economy.[3]

Burning fossil fuels on this scale is a vast and risky experiment with Earth's biosphere. Scientists are still not sure when our environment will cross an invisible but catastrophic threshold of no return, but growing evidence suggests that it may be close. James Hansen, director of the NASA Goddard Institute of Space Studies, is among a growing group of climate scientists who believe that the world should make every effort to avoid pushing the atmospheric concentration of CO_2 beyond 450 parts per million and the effective concentration (including methane and trace gases) beyond 500 parts per million. This restraint would limit the increase in the average global temperature to 2.4–2.8 degrees Celsius above preindustrial levels. The increase so far is just under 0.8 degrees Celsius.[4]

At the July 2008 G8 summit in Japan, the world's leading industrial nations called for a 50 percent cut in global emissions of greenhouse gases by 2050. This is an ambitious goal—achieving it will require reversing the upward trend in emissions that has been underway for a century and a half. The G8 statement marked a growing political consensus that the fossil-fuel economy will have to be substantially restructured in the decades ahead.

Providing energy services for the much larger global economy of 2050 while reducing emissions to 4 billion tons of carbon will require an energy system that is very different from today's. If the world as a whole is to cut emissions in half by 2050, today's industrial countries will need to cut theirs by more than 80 percent. Getting there depends on three elements in a climate strategy: capturing and storing the carbon contained in fossil fuels, reducing energy consumption through new technologies and lifestyles, and shifting to carbon-free energy technologies. This strategy will not be successful if left strictly to the market; a combination of government initiative and market demand are required.

Phasing out oil, the most important fossil fuel today, may turn out to be the easiest part of the problem. Production of conventional crude oil is expected to peak and begin declining within the next decade or two. By 2050, output could be a third or more below the current level. Reliance on natural gas, which has not been as heavily exploited as oil, and which releases half as much carbon per unit of energy as coal, is meanwhile likely to grow.

But the slowdown in the rate of discovery of oil and gas is pushing world energy markets toward dirtier, more carbon-intensive fossil fuels. The greatest problems for the world's climate are coal, which is both more abundant and more carbon intensive than oil, and "unconventional" energy sources such as tar sands and oil shale, which, given current oil prices, have become economically accessible.

The central role of coal in the world's climate dilemma has led policymakers and industrialists to focus on **carbon capture and storage (CCS)**. Although this process is likely to be feasible only for large, centralized uses of fossil fuels, many energy planners are counting on it. They hope to build a new generation of power plants equipped with devices that capture carbon either before or after the combustion of fossil fuels and then pipe the CO_2 into underground geological reservoirs or into the deep ocean, where it could, in principle, remain for millions of years.

Expert opinion on the eventual commercial viability of carbon capture and storage is severely divided, but one thing is certain: it won't happen soon. In light of the lead times required for technology development and demonstration, it will be the 2020s at the earliest before significant numbers of carbon-neutral coal plants come online. That means that during the critical next decade, when emissions growth must turn downward in industrial countries—and begin to level off in developing countries—CCS will not be able to help. In the meantime, a growing number of climate experts are calling for a moratorium on building new coal-fired power plants unless or until CCS becomes available.

THE CONVENIENT TRUTH

Many energy industry executives argue that reducing carbon emissions as rapidly as scientists now urge would risk an economic collapse. According to conventional wisdom, the available alternatives are just too small, unreliable, or expensive to do the job. In 2001, for example, Vice President Dick Cheney described saving energy as a moral virtue but not important enough to play a major role in the national energy policy proposals he was developing at the time. The World Energy Council, which represents the large energy companies that dominate today's energy economy, declared in 2007 that renewable energy has "enormous practical challenges. It is unlikely to deliver a significant decarbonisation of electricity quickly enough to meet the climate challenge."[5]

However, a thorough review of studies that assess the potential contribution of new energy options, as well as the rapid pace of technological and policy innovation now under way, points to the opposite conclusion. Improved energy productivity and renewable energy are both available in abundance—and new policies and technologies are rapidly making them more economically competitive with fossil fuels. In combination, these energy options represent the most robust alternative to the current energy system, capable of providing the diverse array of energy services that a modern economy requires.

The first step in establishing the viability of a climate-safe energy strategy is assessing the available resources and the potential role they might play. Surveys show that the resource base is indeed ample; the main factors limiting the pace of change are the economic challenge of accelerating investment in new energy options and the political challenge of overcoming the institutional barriers to change.

ENERGY PRODUCTIVITY AND SUPPLY

Energy productivity measures an economy's ability to extract useful services from the energy that is harnessed. From the earliest stages of the Industrial Revolution, energy productivity has steadily advanced. In the United States, the economy has grown by 160 percent since 1973, while energy use has increased by 31 percent, allowing the nation's energy productivity to double during the period; Germany and Japan, starting with higher productivity levels, have achieved comparable increases. But even today, despite these advances, well over half the energy harnessed throughout the world is converted to waste heat rather than being used to meet energy needs.[6]

This vast inefficiency suggests enormous potential to improve energy productivity in the decades ahead. Light bulbs, electric motors, air conditioners, automobiles, power plants, computers, aircraft, and buildings are among the hundreds of systems and technologies that can be made far more efficient, in many cases just by using already available technologies more widely—such as compact fluorescent light bulbs and hybrid electric vehicles. Further gains can be made by altering the design of cities—increasing the role of public transport, walking, and cycling, while reducing dependence on automobiles.

The greatest potential turns out to lie in the most basic element of the energy economy—buildings—which could be equipped with better insulation, more efficient lighting, and better appliances, at costs that would be more than paid for by lower energy bills. With technologies available today, such as ground-source heat pumps that reduce the energy needed for heating and cooling by 70 percent, it is possible to construct zero-net-energy buildings, which do not require fossil fuels at all. All countries have this untapped potential to increase energy productivity, but the largest opportunities are found in the developing nations, where current energy productivity tends to be lower. Enhancing that productivity will not only reduce consumption of fossil fuels but will make it easier and more affordable to rapidly increase the use of carbon-free energy sources.[7]

On the supply side, renewable energy relies on two primary energy sources—sunlight and the heat stored below ground—that are available in vast abundance. The sunlight alone that strikes Earth's land surface in two hours is equivalent to total human energy use in a year. While much of that sunlight becomes heat, solar energy is also responsible for the power embodied in wind, hydro, wave, and biomass sources, each with the potential to be harnessed for human use. Only a small portion of that enormous daily, renewable flux of energy will ever be needed by humanity.[8]

Several studies have assessed the scale of the major renewable resources and estimated what their practical contribution to the energy economy might one day be. One study by the National Renewable Energy Laboratory in the United States, for example, concluded that solar thermal power plants built in seven states in the U.S. Southwest could provide nearly seven times the nation's existing electric capacity from all sources. And mounting solar electric generators on just half of the suitable rooftop area could provide 25 percent of U.S. electricity. In the case of wind power, the Pacific Northwest Laboratory found that the land-based wind resources of Kansas, North Dakota, and Texas could meet all the nation's electricity needs, even with large areas excluded for environmental reasons.

These reports demonstrate that resource availability will not be a limiting factor as the world seeks to replace fossil fuels. With improved technologies, greater efficiency, and lower costs, renewable energy could one day replace virtually all the carbon-based fuels that are so vital to today's economy.

MAKING ENERGY MARKETS WORK THROUGH GOVERNMENT

Although consumers should in theory be interested in making investments in energy efficiency whenever it is economical, they face many obstacles, including a lack of capital to invest in conservation and a lack of information about which investments make sense. Perceiving the lack of demand, potential manufacturers and installers of energy-efficient equipment have little incentive to scale up production or build businesses that would facilitate efficiency improvements. This lack of impetus is where government becomes important in this issue.

One of the easiest ways to overcome these kinds of market barriers is government mandates. Since the 1970s, many governments have required that home appliances, motor vehicles, and buildings meet minimum efficiency standards in order to be sold, and these standards have been gradually ratcheted up over time. Additional tightening is now in order, and many governments are moving quickly in that direction. Average auto efficiency standards, for example, will soon move to 47 miles per gallon in Japan and 49 miles per gallon in Europe, and in 2007 Congress raised the U.S. standard, which had remained at 27.5 miles per gallon for over two decades. Another approach to requiring efficiency can be seen in the law recently passed in Australia to phase out the use of most incandescent light bulbs, which can be replaced by compact fluorescent bulbs that are four times as efficient.

Government mandates are also being used to compel the construction of more energy-efficient buildings and to require the introduction of renewable energy into electricity grids as well as the markets for liquid fuels. Several national governments and twenty-four U.S. states now have binding "renewable portfolio standards" requiring that specified amounts of renewable electricity be added to their grids. In Spain, a recent update of building codes requires all new buildings to incorporate solar water heaters. As of April 2008, the state government of Baden-Wurttemberg, Germany, began requiring that 20 percent of new buildings' heating requirements be met with renewable energy. Brazil, the United States, and the European Union are among the jurisdictions mandating that a minimum proportion of biofuels be blended with gasoline and diesel fuel, spurring growth in their use.

Mandates such as these are a useful backstop to ensure that minimal rates of change occur and to remove the very worst technologies from the market. However, it is also essential that markets reward innovation and investment that strive for the best possible performance. To achieve this goal, some regulation is needed. One important step in this direction is to decouple electric utilities' profits from the amount of power they sell by introducing a regulatory formula that instead rewards utilities for providing the best service at the least cost. California regulators have already made this change; as a result of this and other policies, Californians use less than half as much electricity per person as other Americans do.

Governments outside the United States have successfully promoted investment in renewable energy. Beginning in the early 1980s, Denmark decided to reduce its dependence on oil-fired generation by encouraging its agricultural industry to enter the power business by selling wind- and biomass-based electricity to the utilities at prices set by government. This government intervention stopped the utilities from thwarting potential competitors, and over two decades it reduced Denmark's dependence on fossil fuels and made it a leading generator of renewable power.[9]

Germany and Spain adopted similar market access laws in the 1990s, and they too moved quickly into the leading ranks of renewable energy development. Over time, the prices governments set have been adjusted downward as the cost of renewable technologies has fallen. As a result of this law, Germany now holds the inside track in solar photovoltaics and wind-generating capacity—despite the fact that it has modest resources of sun and wind.[10]

THE FINAL TIPPING POINT

There are good reasons to think that the world may be on the verge of a major transformation of energy markets. The powerful interaction of advancing technology, private investment, and policy reform have led to a pace of change unseen since pioneers such as Thomas Edison and Henry Ford created the last great energy revolution a century ago. But is it enough? Will the coming years bring the accelerated change and level of capital that are needed to reverse the tide of climate change?

The answer to that question will likely be found not in the messy world of economics but in the even messier world of politics. But time is growing short: in the United States alone, 121 new coal-fired power plants have been proposed; if built, they could produce 30 billion tons of carbon dioxide over their sixty-year lives. And China is building that many plants every year.[11] However, in 2007 there were growing signs that the years of political paralysis on climate change may be coming to an end, spurred by the warnings of scientists and the concerns of citizens. One sign of the changing times is that many of the planned coal plants are under attack by local and national environmentalists, and some have already been scrapped. Germany recently announced that its centuries-old hard coal industry will be closed by 2018. Several other potentially game-changing political developments are worth noting:

- Twenty-seven major U.S. companies—from Alcoa and Dow Chemical to Duke Energy, General Motors, and Xerox—announced support for national regulation of CO_2 emissions. Meanwhile, seventeen U.S. states moved toward adopting regulations on CO_2 emissions, thereby increasing pressure on Congress, which was considering national legislation.

- The European Union committed to reducing its CO_2 emissions to 20 percent below 1990 levels by 2020, and member states are ramping up their energy-efficiency and renewable-energy programs in order to achieve these goals.

- China announced its first national climate policy, pledging to step up its energy-efficiency and renewable-energy programs and acknowledging that earlier policies were not sufficient.

- Brazil recognized the threat that climate change poses to the country's economically crucial agriculture and forestry industries and signaled a new commitment to strengthening international climate agreements.[12]

CONCLUSION

As negotiations begin on the international climate agreement that will supplant the Kyoto Protocol after 2012, the world's political will to tackle climate change will be put to an early test. The politics of climate change are advancing more rapidly than could have been imagined a few years ago. But the world has not yet reached the political tipping point that would ensure the kind of economic transformation that is required. And the divide between industrial and developing countries over how to share the burden of action must still be resolved.

As people around the world come to understand that a low-carbon economy could one day be more effective than today's energy mix at meeting human needs, support for the needed transformation is bound to grow. Urgency and vision are the twin pillars on which humanity's hope now hangs.

NOTES

1. E. Jansen et al., "Palaeoclimate," in Intergovernmental Panel on Climate Change (IPCC), *Climate Change 2007: The Physical Science Basis* (New York: Cambridge University Press, 2007), p. 449.
2. IPCC, *Climate Change*, pp. 342, 350, 537, 543; M. Serreze et al., "Perspectives on the Arctic's Shrinking SeaIce Cover," *Science*, March 16, 2007, 1533–1536.
3. "Summary for Policymakers," in IPCC, *Climate Change*; International Energy Agency, *Key World Energy Statistics* (Paris: 2007), 6; recent carbon emissions cited

by Worldwatch, based on G. Marland et al., "Global, Regional, and National Fossil Fuel CO2 Emissions," in Carbon Dioxide Information Analysis Center (CDIAC), *Trends: A Compendium of Data on Global Change* (Oak Ridge, Tenn.: Oak Ridge National Laboratory, U.S. Department of Energy, 2007); BP, *Statistical Review of World Energy* (London: 2007).

4. J. Hansen et al., "Dangerous Humanmade Interference with Climate: A GISS Model E Study," *Atmospheric Chemistry and Physics* 7, no. 9 (2007): 2287–2312; 0.8 degrees Celsius is the midpoint of estimates of warming, as reported in IPCC, op. cit. note 1, p. 5.

5. Remarks by U.S. Vice President Cheney at the annual meeting of the Associated Press, Toronto, Canada, April 2001; World Energy Council, *Energy and Climate Change Executive Summary*, London, May 2007, 5.

6. U.S. Department of Energy, *Monthly Energy Review*, Washington, D.C., September 2007, 16; energy productivity based on data from International Monetary Fund (IMF), *World Economic Outlook* (Washington, D.C., April 2007); International Energy Agency, *Energy Technology Perspectives—Scenarios and Strategies to 2050* (Paris: 2006), pp. 48–57; U.S. Department of Energy, *International Energy Annual 2004*, Washington, D.C., 2006, Table E.1; BP, *Statistical Review of World Energy* (London: 2007); estimate of useful energy from G. Kaiper, *U.S. Energy Flow Trends—2002* (Livermore, Calif.: Lawrence Livermore National Laboratory, 2004).

7. B. Griffith et al., *Assessment of the Technical Potential for Achieving Zero-Energy Commercial Buildings* (Golden, Colo.: National Renewable Energy Laboratory, 2006); Bressand et al., *Curbing Global Energy Demand Growth: The Energy Productivity Opportunity* (McKinsey Global Institute, May 2007), 13.

8. S. Mufson, "U.S. Nuclear Power Revival Grows," *Washington Post*, September 2007.

9. J. Sawin, "The Role of Government in the Development and Diffusion of Renewable Energy Technologies: Wind Power in the United States, California, Denmark and Germany, 1970–2000" (PhD diss., The Fletcher School of Law and Diplomacy, Tufts University, Somerville, Mass., September 2001).

10. M. Ragwitz and C. Huber, *FeedIn Systems in Germany and Spain and a Comparison* (Karlsruhe, Germany: Fraunhofer Institut fr Systemtechnik und Innovationsforschung, 2005); ranking based on Travis Bradford, Prometheus Institute, emails to Janet Sawin, April 5–8, 2007.

11. E. Shuster, *Tracking New Coal-Fired Power Plants* (Washington, D.C.: National Energy Technology Laboratory, U.S. Department of Energy, October 2007).

12. "Germany to Close Its Coal Mines," *Spiegel Online*, January 30, 2007; United States Climate Action Partnership, "U.S. Climate Action Partnership Announces Its Fourth Membership Expansion," press release, Washington, D.C., September 2007; European Council, "The Spring European Council: Integrated Climate Protection and Energy Policy, Progress on the Lisbon Strategy," press release, Brussels, March 12, 2007; National Development and Reform Commission, *China's National Climate Change Programme* (Beijing, June 2007); Pew Center

on Global Climate Change, "Climate Change Initiatives and Programs in the States," press release, Arlington, Va., September 11, 2006; "Statement of H. E. Luiz Incio Lula da Silva, President of the Federative Republic of Brazil, at the general debate of the 62nd Session of the United Nations General," press release (New York: Ministry of External Relations, September 25, 2007).

NO: Michael Lynch, *Strategic Energy & Economic Research, Inc.*

> We shall answer their demands for a gold standard by saying to them,
> you shall not press down upon the brow of labor this crown of thorns.
> You shall not crucify mankind upon a cross of gold.
>
> William Jennings Bryan, July 9, 1896

In recent years, a combination of high energy prices and concerns about global warming has led to calls for an array of new energy sources from across the political spectrum. Ralph Nader, John McCain, and both T. Boone Pickens, the Texas oilman, and Al Gore, the environmentalist, have announced plans involving a heavy emphasis on renewable energies such as solar and wind power. Even the Bush administration called for an end to our "addiction" to foreign oil.

It is a real oddity of the current craze for renewable energies that petroleum was originally considered a "green" fuel that reduced coal-based pollution in the United Kingdom. In fact, oil got its start by replacing biofuels—primarily whale oil used in lamps. Presumably, no one would now suggest replacing electric lighting with whale oil, but other examples, not as absurd, abound. In a more modern example, Haitians suffering from deforestation undoubtedly envy their neighbors in the Dominican Republic, who have access to propane for cooking.

While renewable energy sources have an important role to play in energy supply, the reality is that they are all too often given a free pass, analytically. Many proposals that would not stand the laugh test if made by large private companies are embraced by a variety of activists and politicians without serious thought as to their costs or benefits. I reject the notion that encouraging alternative energy sources is always positive. Instead, I want to emphasize here the need for economic efficiency when it comes to energy.

FINITE RESOURCES: MALTHUS REDUX

The renewable nature of wind, solar, and biomass power sources is often cited as a prime factor in making them desirable. But simply being renewable is a poor argument. Whale oil, after all, was a renewable resource, and, in fact, there are a lot more cases of scarcity among renewable resources than among nonrenewable ones, whether the resource in question be tuna or polar bears.

The best example of the irrelevance of the finite nature of nonrenewable resources is probably copper: the Bronze Age began about 5,000 years ago, and during the Trojan War, if Homer is to be believed, men would fight and die to retrieve valuable bronze armor. Today, most Americans would not stoop to pick up a copper penny.

In recent times, many have seized on the so-called peak oil theories—which maintain that oil production has already peaked and is currently in decline—to justify the desperate need to switch away from finite fossil fuels. But those arguments are based on simplistic analysis that is demonstrably false (Lynch 2003). The petroleum resource base is approximately 8 to 10 trillion barrels of conventional oil (that found in liquid oil fields), of which 1 trillion has been used in 150 years. Another 2.5 trillion barrels of the remaining resource are recoverable (from tar sands and shale oil) with current technology. The amount of the resource that is recoverable will easily increase, perhaps adding another 3 trillion barrels, even without considering the 10 or 15 trillion barrels of shale oil that is technically but (apparently) not economically recoverable.

The 2008 collapse of the financial industry was one more reminder that the finite resource most constraining the global economy is the lack of sufficient money to do everything we need to do, let alone everything we would like to do. The world faces enormous social, economic, and environmental problems—far beyond what can be resolved with existing government finances. Thus, it behooves us not to waste money on inefficient energy policies.

BENEFITS: GREEN PIE IN THE SKY?

The general arguments put forth by the great majority of proponents of alternative energies are these:

- Most alternative energies are environmentally beneficial because they are approximately carbon-neutral and therefore lessen global warming.

- High energy prices are here to stay; therefore renewable energy will be economically more attractive in the future than in the past.

- Because they are largely produced domestically, alternative energies improve the energy security of the United States.

- Renewable energy improves American economic competitiveness and provides jobs.

Though renewable energy and other new fuels certainly have a role to play, these strong assertions deserve critical scrutiny.

Pollution Reduction

While there is no doubt that many new energy sources reduce pollution, the issues are, first, whether the pollutants they reduce are the most needful of reduction, and, second, whether the benefits are the best that can be achieved for the expenditure involved. Not all pollution does the same level of environmental harm, and different fuels and technologies obviously deliver different amounts of benefits. Simply stating that any approach that reduces any pollution should be pursued is wildly inefficient; comparisons of the relative costs and benefits will allow for much more efficient use of our scarce financial resources.

Bjorn Lomborg's "Copenhagen Consensus" is one laudable attempt to develop such broad social priorities. Given our finite budget, and the advances in our understanding of environmental—and social—challenges since the first Earth Day in 1969, this type of consideration should be applied to our energy policymaking.

Unfortunately, those developing new energy sources are unlikely to recommend diverting resources to health care, clean water supplies, and so forth—nor are proponents of these causes likely to defer to the renewable energy imperative. Such narrow-focused advocacy is simply human nature. But it doesn't mean that the proposals of new-energy promoters should be blindly accepted.

High Prices: Déjà Vu All Over Again

The energy crisis has not yet overwhelmed us, but it will if we do not act quickly. . . . The most important thing about these proposals is that the alternative may be a national catastrophe. Further delay can affect our strength and our power as a nation.

President Jimmy Carter

We have been here before. On April 18, 1977, President Jimmy Carter made his famous speech declaring the energy crisis to be the moral equivalent of war and proposing various measures in response, including setting up the Synthetic Fuels Corporation to promote alternative energies (primarily shale oil and coal gasification), while subsidies for solar and wind energy were implemented. Carter also encouraged conservation and more coal use. Solar thermal panels sprouted across the nation, even on the White House roof. Oil companies developed (or bought) solar power divisions. Windmills were erected in many places, and research into a variety of exotic energy sources was funded. The electric car was described as just around the corner, and Chrysler, for one, abandoned its large car line.

Most of these responses proved unwise, to put it mildly. All the computer models, all the economists and consultants, government organizations, and oil companies, turned out to be wrong about ever-rising prices and scarce resources. The belief that markets were myopic in not raising prices high enough to make crucially needed synthetic fuels viable turned out to be hubris on the part of the many experts.

The Synthetic Fuel Corporation was a bust; solar thermal panels and windmills had numerous technical problems; and Americans returned to their love of large vehicles, rewarding Ford and GM for their "prescience" (and punishing Chrysler). Meanwhile, electric cars are still "just around the corner." Some high-priced alternatives were later attacked by consumer advocates, who objected to the above-market prices being paid for them.

Has anything changed? Just go back to Christopher Flavin's 1979 "The Future of the Automobile in an Oil Short World"—its arguments are nearly identical to those still being heard today. Everyone at that time, including the oil industry, was sold on the notion of ever-rising prices and projects such as extraction of shale oil were thought not only wise but essential.

Jobs

> A century ago, the story goes, a construction foreman was approached by a union representative who demanded that he not use a steam shovel, but instead, a hundred men with shovels. He responded, "Why not a thousand men with teaspoons?"

Following the 2008 presidential election and in the face of our current economic problems (the perfect recipe for policy disaster), the job-creating properties of renewable energies such as wind and solar power are being heavily touted. But if these energy technologies are not self-supporting economically without significant subsidies, their job-creating properties should not be sufficient cause to pour billions of dollars of new subsidies into them.

In fact, since the days of the Great Depression and the Public Works Administration, it has been common practice among conservatives to decry "ditch-digging"—hiring the unemployed for meaningless tasks, just to give them a paycheck—as a prime example of government waste. Yet the suggestion that money should be provided for renewable energy is only sinning to a lesser degree. Why not dig a massive ditch and pour water down it to generate hydroelectric power? (And it could be dug with teaspoons to generate even more jobs.) Because it would be wasteful. How is buying jobs with federal subsidies for inefficient and economically unsustainable energy sources any better than ditch-digging jobs? The losses may be smaller, but they are not inconsequential.

Energy Security

The talk of energy independence by the 2008 candidates represents the triumph of rhetoric over reality. The likelihood that the United States could reduce its oil imports by 12 million barrels per day—which is what energy independence would look like—without doing major economic damage is fanciful, as is the expectation that renewable energy would be the primary reason for such a reduction. President Nixon's 1973 Project Independence report sensibly noted that becoming energy independent not only would be prohibitively expensive but would not eliminate our need to protect global energy supplies, given our interdependent economy and many alliance commitments. Only countries such as Albania under Communism and North Korea have developed autarky to that degree, and their examples are hardly to be emulated.

More poignantly, recalling that President George W. Bush, a Texas oilman and friend of the Saudi royal family, embraced Ariel Sharon as a great friend, it is all but impossible to see where our energy dependence has constrained our foreign policy significantly. Fears about resource wars are similarly overblown: international markets are so well-developed that "access" merely requires payment. The belief in scarcity of mineral resources, including energy, is based on simplistic analysis. In fact, fears about resource scarcity are not new, and they have been proven wrong repeatedly.

COMING DOWN TO EARTH

In the 1960s, it was considered unacceptable to criticize labor, but that
changed by the 1980s. Could the same thing happen to environmentalism?

Denny Ellerman, MIT [Massachusetts Institute of Technology]

Zealotry is the negative side of public policy, as racism is the negative side
of nationalism. Given the obvious benefits of pollution reduction, it cannot be
surprising that many environmentalists take on the role of crusaders. However,
this role inflation has caused them not only to adopt a moralistic tone, but also
to yield to the temptation to overstate their case.

Probably the most extreme case is pundit/activist Jeremy Rifkin's advocacy
of the hydrogen economy—he argues that since we built the Internet, we can
build a hydrogen economy (Rifkin 2003). The comparison is meaningless,
implying that building a hydrogen economy, which would require vast investments of money and manpower, would be trivial.

Rationalizing the shortcomings of new energy sources has a long history.
The extremely poor performance of electric cars has long been overlooked
by their proponents. Yet it is hard to think of other products that are considered desirable despite similar limitations: a television that worked only
sixteen hours a day? Or could operate for only three hours before shutting
down for eight?

An article in *The Economist* ("Electrifying," December 18, 1997) described
the situation clearly:

> Only two years ago, electric vehicles (EVs) seemed the answer to worries
> about the noise, pollution and environmental destruction that the internal-
> combustion engine leaves in its wake. California had plans to require
> the car industry to build and sell tens of thousands of EVs a year in the
> Golden State. Then, regulators reluctantly accepted that drivers would
> revolt if they were forced to drive cars powered by expensive batteries that
> had a range of less than 100 miles and took up to eight hours to recharge.
>
> Now, EVs are back in fashion. The biggest change in their prospects has
> come from the sudden emergence of affordable fuel-cell technology ... the
> new consortium hopes to produce an initial 10,000–50,000 cars a year
> powered by fuel cells, starting commercially in 2004.

Amazingly, a technology as incredibly complex and expensive as hydrogen-fuel-
cell cars was seen as on the verge of being ready for the marketplace in 1997,
although hydrogen production was not yet economical, a distribution system

for hydrogen fuel was not in place, fuel-cell technology was still prohibitively expensive, and storage systems remained bulky and inefficient.

A typical response to the charge that these shortcomings make the electric car impractical for now is that technologies that are not currently attractive should be mandated or subsidized to allow them to achieve economies of scale and thus lower costs. However, this argument appears to be overselling. Nearly all consumer products achieve acceptance without mandates, and the fact that some technologies are said to need mandates implies that the industry does not believe that the economies of scale will lower costs enough to make them attractive; otherwise, they would undertake to do so themselves.

ECONOMICS: NOT THE ONLY THING, BUT AT LEAST SOMETHING

While conservatives are inclined to focus entirely on the relative costs of various energy sources, proponents of alternative energies take a different tack. They usually assert that (a) economics isn't very important; (b) the technologies are roughly economically viable already (or can be made so through government policy); or (c) intangible benefits outweigh the poor economics.

Engineers tend to adopt the first approach, especially academics. Renowned conservation proponent Amory Lovins often argues for technologies that are technically viable but far too expensive, which is why his predictions of huge efficiency increases in recent years have proved invalid.

But the debate should not be over straight cost and benefits, but over relative costs and benefits. The United States has many opportunities to reduce energy consumption, carbon emissions, and/or oil imports, and its budget is finite. Therefore, careful judgments will be required to produce the most efficient expenditure of funds, assuming that it is necessary to provide taxpayer or consumer dollars to accomplish these goals.

As Table 1 (p. 339) shows, the cost of wind power is nearly competitive with that of other sources, while photovoltaics are still far too expensive to be competitive outside of niche uses, such as generating energy for farms or towns that are distant from power lines. The government subsidies for both new sources are huge despite the fact that wind power doesn't require them and photovoltaics are simply not ready to make a significant contribution to our energy needs.

Yet many, such as Representative Bernie Sanders of Vermont, argue that renewable energy is the answer to the problem of high energy costs, which is

| Table 1 |

Costs and Subsidies for Electricity Generation (Cents per Kilowatt-Hour)

	Generation cost	Federal subsidies
Pulverized Coal	4.3	0.044
Geothermal	4.4	0.092
Natural Gas Combined-Cycle	4.7	0.025
Wind	4.8	2.337
Open-Loop Biomass	5.1	
Nuclear	6	0.159
Solar-Thermal	12.6	
Photovoltaic	21	2.434
U.S. wholesale electricity price in 2006	5.9	

Source: Howard Greuenspecht, Statement Before the Subcommittee on Select Revenue Measures, Committee on Ways and Means, U.S. House of Representatives, May 24, 2005.
Note: Nuclear costs are for a plant entering service in 2013; all others are for 2010.

rather like Marie Antoinette suggesting that peasants who don't have bread should eat cake.

OTHER SHORTCOMINGS

It is rare to hear the admission that renewable energy sources have shortcomings, except from contrarians. Unfortunately, there are a variety of problems with renewable energy sources that are usually ignored, including the large land requirements, competition with food inputs, intermittency, and pollutants.

One example is ethanol. While ethanol may offer a net environmental benefit, it does impose a variety of negative consequences, including high energy needs for fertilizer, processing, and transportation, although these consequences are often exaggerated. The recent rise in global food prices has been partly driven by biofuel production, although that effect should be mitigated over the long term. Another example is gasoline with ethanol, which is associated with a variety of pollutants—not only higher levels of acetaldehyde and formaldehyde compared to regular gasoline, but also higher volatile organic compounds (VOCs) compared to gasoline with the additive MTBE [methyl tertiary butyl ether].

Furthermore, photovoltaic cells can contain hazardous materials that can be released by accident, while solar concentration plants typically use oil or molten salts, and nearly all wind power installations require substances such as lubricants and hydraulic fluids.

CONCLUSION

Promoting technologies that are not yet ready for the marketplace will only waste money and damage their reputation with consumers. Our finite budget resources should be redirected, leaving sharply lower subsidies for wind power (which doesn't need them) and photovoltaics (which are not broadly viable). The money saved should be spent on research to reduce the costs of photovoltaics and to improve battery technologies, which would make a variety of energy sources and uses more attractive. But, especially, it must be recognized that it is a given energy technology's economic viability that results in widespread adoption by consumers, accomplishing far more than government mandates. Otherwise, consumers and taxpayers will simply be crucified on a cross of biomass.

hiv/aids

Should the Wealthy Nations Promote Anti-HIV/AIDS Efforts in Poor Nations?

YES: Mead Over, *Center for Global Development*

NO: Mark Heywood, *AIDS Law Project*

The worldwide devastation from AIDS is staggering—the World Health Organization estimates that more than 25 million people have died of AIDS since the early 1980s. Currently, roughly 33.5 million men, women, and children are infected with HIV (see Figure 1, p. 342); about 1.8 million individuals die annually of the disease (see Figure 2, p. 343) and even more contract it every year (see Figure 3, p. 344). There has been a steady increase in those living with HIV worldwide, rising from approximately 8 million in 1990 to more than four times that number in less than twenty years.

HIV/AIDS is thus a global killer whose effects are so overwhelming as to have had substantial impacts on the overall demographic profiles of some nations. For example, Swaziland—where the prevalence rate is 26 percent—has the largest percentage of its population living with HIV, followed by Botswana, where nearly one-fourth are infected. The average life expectancy in Swaziland has dropped from fifty-seven to forty-nine years (2011); in Botswana, life expectancy fell from sixty-five to fifty-three years in a single decade. Yet the devastation is not spread equally around the world, as is indicated in Figure 4 (p. 345). More than two-thirds of those living with HIV reside in sub-Saharan Africa, where adult prevalence rates are 5 percent of the entire adult population. (This figure compares with prevalence rates of 0.6 percent in the United States, 0.4 percent in Europe, 0.1 percent in East Asia, and 0.8 percent worldwide.)

The impacts on nations such as Botswana and Swaziland extend far beyond the individuals infected; they also contribute to social disturbances and threats to government effectiveness. Family members forsake work to tend to the sick; children are orphaned—Swaziland alone has tens of thousands of orphaned

Figure 1

Estimated Numbers of Adults and Children Living with HIV Globally in 2009

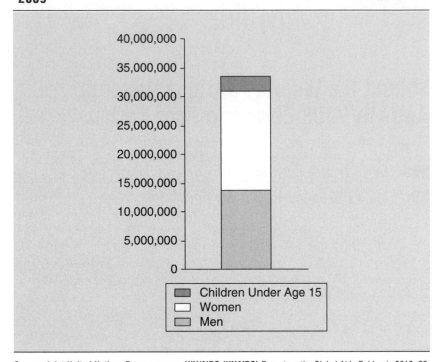

Source: **Joint United Nations Programme on HIV/AIDS (UNAIDS)** Report on the Global Aids Epidemic 2010, 23.

children, many left to fend for themselves—and governments struggle to cope with providing health care and other social services. Hospitals are overrun with patients suffering from HIV-related diseases, and, as a consequence, hospital workers, including midwives, are particularly susceptible to infection.

In the United States in 2009, 49 percent of diagnosed AIDS cases were found among African Americans (a group that makes up just 14 percent of the population), 16 percent among Hispanics (who comprise 16 percent of the population), and 28 percent among white, non-Hispanic residents (who comprise two-thirds of the population). And higher concentrations of the disease are found in large states (California, Texas, Florida, New York), while more rural states have lower rates. A recent **Center for Disease Control and Prevention (CDC)** study suggests that AIDS cases are substantially underreported in the United States.

To date, most of the immediate effects of AIDS have occurred nationally, because few people with AIDS travel abroad. Consequently, efforts have

Figure 2

Estimated Numbers of Adult and Child Deaths Due to AIDS Globally in 2009

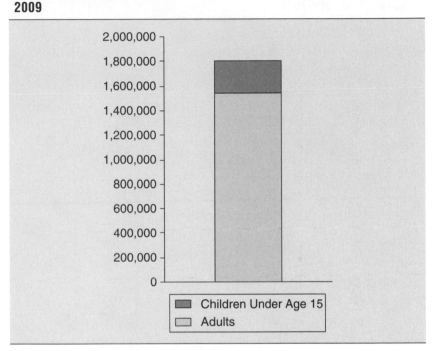

Source: UNAIDS Report on the Global Aids Epidemic 2010, 19.

focused on treating patients and on containing the spread of the disease within countries rather than across borders. A major problem—particularly in Africa—is the lack of administrative and financial resources by the national governments. Foreign aid—from governments, international organizations, and private foundations—has been solicited as a way to fill the void.

Multiple strategies have been proposed and adopted for coping with the disease and preventing its expansion. These approaches include condom distribution (which sometimes faces obstacles of local practice and custom), widespread HIV testing, government-sponsored efforts that target highly mobile populations, attempts to modify behavior, and providing antiretroviral drugs. The impact of these strategies has been mixed, and their reach has been limited by the high costs of drug treatment.

Yet, for all the recognition of its horrible impact around the world (and particularly in sub-Saharan Africa), AIDS is not the only deadly disease threatening

Figure 3

Estimated Numbers of Adults and Children Newly Infected with HIV Globally, 2001 and 2009

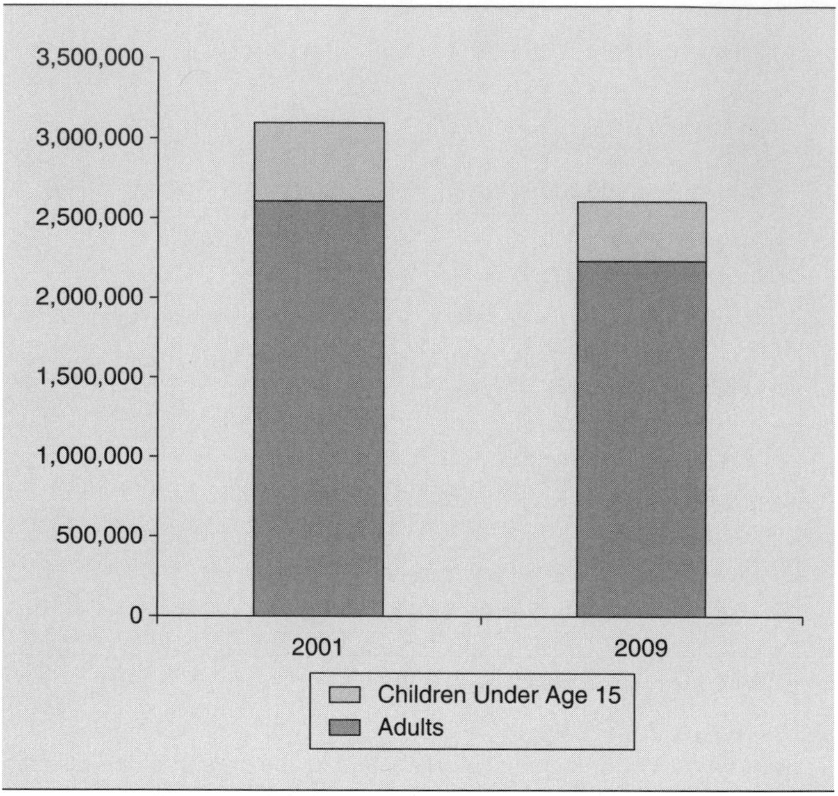

Source: UNAIDS Report on the Global Aids Epidemic 2010, 21, 64.

populations globally. Another is tobacco use, which the World Health Organization characterizes as the most preventable cause of death worldwide. The basic provision of clean water would save millions of lives per year in developing nations, and even modest immunization efforts would make significant public health inroads. Therefore, the articles that follow do not suggest that HIV/AIDS is unimportant, but their authors take different sides on the relative importance of narrowly focusing public health efforts on this one disease rather than adopting a more diversified approach. Mead Over argues that treatment has taken precedent over preventing new infections and that coordinated donor incentives to avert new infections would be a prudent use of limited funds for combatting AIDS. Mark Heywood argues that Western attempts to address the problem have been sorely inadequate and may eventually do more harm than good.

Figure 4

Estimated Numbers of Adults and Children Living with HIV, 2001 and 2009

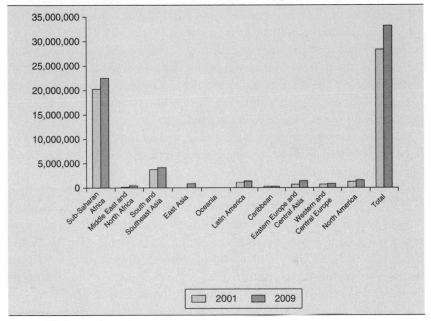

Source: UNAIDS Report on the Global Aids Epidemic 2010, 20–21.

Discussion Questions

1. Should funding for anti-HIV/AIDS efforts be directed toward prevention or toward treatment? What are the risks of inadequately funding one or the other?

2. The world is faced with many public health issues and diseases—from HIV/AIDS to tuberculosis to malnutrition to unsanitary drinking water—and finite resources to address them. As a policymaker, how would you decide where to allocate resources? What criteria should be used?

3. Are wealthy nations responsible for alleviating suffering due to poor health in developing nations? Are there moral arguments for or against? What about economic arguments? What role does politics play?

4. What is the distinction, made in both essays, between global health and international health? Do the authors think a global health approach or an international health approach is the best way to fight the spread of HIV/AIDS?

5. Mark Heywood makes a direct link between health and the economy and health and politics. How does he see the economy and politics influencing public health?

YES: Mead Over, *Center for Global Development*

There was much to celebrate on World AIDS Day last week. Over the last decade, an unprecedented surge in donor support for HIV/AIDS treatment has lengthened and improved the lives of millions of people living with the disease. The number of people receiving anti-retroviral treatment worldwide stands at more than six million in 2011, a 16-fold increase since 2003. Accordingly, those affected with HIV/AIDS are living, on average, longer lives than at any point since the dawn of the pandemic.

But celebration is premature. Success in treatment is great, but the underlying strategy of focusing resources on treatment is flawed. The rate of new infections now outpaces the rate of AIDS-related deaths, so the number of people living with AIDS—and therefore the number of people needing treatment—is growing faster than the funding needed to provide care. In 2010, some 1.8 million people died from AIDS-related illnesses, but about 2.7 million were newly infected, increasing the total number of people living with the disease by approximately 900,000. In other words, although there is no question that focusing on treatment prolongs lives, it's just not a financially feasible strategy to manage the spread of the disease—much less to eradicate it altogether.

It is unfortunate that so many have focused on treatment alone, because there is a way to end the global scourge of HIV/AIDS: by conditioning the rate of expansion of treatment programs on the reduction of new infections. This much-needed shift would lead to what I call an *AIDS transition*—the day on which the rate of new infections falls below the rate of AIDS-related deaths so that the number of people living with HIV/AIDS decreases year-on-year. Getting to the transition would require vast changes in policy and practice for donors, recipient governments, and health practitioners. But if these changes were made effectively, after about a decade of keeping new infections ever lower than deaths, we would see AIDS taking its place among treatable chronic diseases such as diabetes, cancer, and heart disease.

The number of people infected with HIV grew from a few million in 1981 to about 34 million by the end of last year. The number of annual new infections peaked at 3.2 million in 1997 and has recently declined at a rate of about two percent each year. Meanwhile, annual deaths due to AIDS have slowed considerably—from 2.1 million in the mid-2000s to 1.8 million in 2010. This is thanks to more widespread care: some six million individuals in low- and

Source: Reprinted by permission of *Foreign Affairs*, December 8, 2011. Copyright 2011 by the Council on Foreign Relations, Inc. www.ForeignAffairs.com.

middle-income countries received treatment last year. Over the last decade, financing from the President's Emergency Plan for AIDS Relief (PEPFAR), with contributions from other bilateral donors and from the Global Fund to Fight AIDS, Tuberculosis, and Malaria, catapulted the donor-financed AIDS treatment budget from a few million dollars in 2000 to more than four billion dollars in 2010. Eight countries, including two in sub-Saharan Africa, have achieved universal access to treatment. All this has created a narrative of success, so much so that last month U.S. Secretary of State Hillary Clinton declared, "The goal of an AIDS-free generation is ambitious, but it is possible."

It is, indeed. But not if treatment continues to take precedence over prevention. In recent years, HIV/AIDS advocacy has focused heavily on achieving universal access to treatment. Donor-funded programs followed suit, increasing the number of people receiving treatment in poor countries by more than 20-fold between 2001 and 2010. But in 2008, AIDS financing plateaued. Given the current global financial climate, that trend looks like it is here to stay. As new infections continue to increase around the world, the current scope of treatment will be difficult to maintain, let alone scale up. The prospect of expanding treatment beyond the six million who now receive it to most of the remaining 34 million is financially, not to mention logistically, impossible. As HIV-infected people live longer and require more costly second- and third-line treatments, the total cost of treatment will skyrocket, often in countries that lack good public health services to begin with.

Of course, treatment is not entirely distinct from prevention. Evidence shows that anti-retroviral medication can prevent new infections by reducing either the infectivity of people with the virus or the susceptibility of uninfected people. But treatment works to reduce infectivity only if the patient adheres closely to the prescribed regimen, has enough food, and begins treatment within weeks of infection.

A way to think about an AIDS transition is to consider the demographic transition that took place in high-income countries after the Industrial Revolution. As health improved and life expectancy increased, countries seemed headed for unsustainable population explosions. It was not until birth rates dropped, due to a number of factors including higher educational attainment, women's entry into the labor force, and other social transformations such as access to family planning, that population growth dropped to sustainable levels.

A similar dynamic is at work with HIV/AIDS cases: the number of people living with the disease will continue to grow until the rate of new infections is finally brought down. And that would demand a revolution in policy at both the national and individual levels.

Specific policies will vary in response to local demands, but some principles apply across the board. Proposals for HIV/AIDS treatment programs should project not only the number of lives a program will extend but also the number of infections it will avert. Likewise, proposals for prevention programs should demonstrate that they are cost-effectively reducing the number of new infections, thereby freeing financial resources for treatment. Additionally, the transition should become an international milestone: donors should make a multiyear commitment to fund AIDS treatment only within the framework of a plan to push new infections below AIDS mortality by a specific projected date. Independently verified national monitoring will be required to provide planners the information they need to update their projections—and to suggest how the AIDS transition could be reached more quickly.

Well-designed incentives are essential as well. At the donor level, incentives can be offered to countries that show they have accelerated the date of their AIDS transition—and thus reduced the expected future costs of AIDS treatment—by offering a portion of future savings to finance expanded access to AIDS treatment now. Such an arrangement would align the incentives of the donor and the recipient government, because both would gain financially from improved prevention. Donors and countries can also agree on a cash-on-delivery aid program that would reward the country with, say, $100 for every averted HIV infection, with the understanding that the country could use the reward to address urgent public needs in any sector.

Incentives can also work at lower levels of program implementation, both on the demand side (in the form of vouchers for HIV testing or for transportation to AIDS treatment centers) and on the supply side (in the form of pay-for-performance contracts with HIV/AIDS treatment or prevention providers). A review of early evidence suggests that such incentives can be remarkably powerful at eliciting more socially responsible behavior. Rwanda, for example, has instituted incentive payments to doctors and nurses for HIV tests as well as other health services. USAID is including conditional cash transfers among the interventions to be tested in one of its trials of combination prevention. The World Bank has developed a new lending instrument called "results-based financing," which it would be willing to deploy for HIV/AIDS if recipient governments request it.

Washington and capitals in Western Europe are strapped for cash. Foreign assistance is on the chopping block. In turn, donor commitments to provide HIV/AIDS treatment to the 34 million in need is becoming more and more unrealistic. It would be a tragedy if donors responded to the infeasibility of these demands by turning their backs on the pandemic and consigning to early death the millions infected now and in coming years. An AIDS transition offers a reasonable, achievable, fiscally prudent, and necessary stepping stone toward a future where a world without AIDS will become a reasonable goal—instead of the fantasy it seems to be today.

NO: Mark Heywood, *AIDS Law Project*

Wealthy nations do have a legal and moral responsibility to promote anti-AIDS efforts in poor countries. However, arguments touting these moral and legal responsibilities often have fatal flaws: they overlook the role of AIDS activists in bringing about a truly global response to the problem and the role they must continue to play, and they pay insufficient attention to the politics of health in developing countries and therefore to the reasons for the evolution of what is frequently called a "vertical" response—one that channels resources directly to the problem, in this case HIV, rather than through the expansion and strengthening of existing health systems. Finally, they oversimplify the reasons why HIV treatment programs have been able to deliver more tangible benefits than HIV prevention.

My argument, therefore, focuses on what "promoting anti-AIDS efforts" actually entails, as well as how, Schneider and Garrett[1] see the "excitement, energy, and dollars" mobilized in the wealthy world to address HIV/AIDS as "possibly the single greatest achievement to date in the Age of Globalization." But the reality is that the wealthy world's response to HIV has been *ad hoc*, prescriptive, paternalistic, and, at times, contradictory. If this approach continues, it may ultimately do more harm than good.

IS THERE A NEW COMMITMENT TO GLOBAL HEALTH?

Something is happening around the issue of health care, but is it froth or something more fundamental? Since the late 1980s, the HIV/AIDS epidemic has forced Third World health back onto global political agendas. The death of millions of poor people, mostly in Africa, is seen as a morally repugnant blight that, in the words of a former UN Special Envoy for AIDS in Africa, Stephen Lewis, "shames and diminishes us all."[2]

Initially in the United States, and later within the UN, AIDS activists have pressured politicians to open up new resources and commitments for tackling neglected diseases, including malaria and tuberculosis, around which there had been decades of fatalistic resignation and inertia. Significantly, the demands of AIDS activism evolved from advocacy for equal rights and nondiscrimination for people in the United States with HIV in the 1980s and 1990s to calling for action on social and economic rights for people in the Third World. At the beginning of the new century, activist campaigns were mainly about the right of access to affordable medicines. But, increasingly, they demand investment in health systems and health workers. It was a direct result of these campaigns that anti-retroviral (ARV) drug prices were made affordable to developing countries, and that bodies such as the Global Fund on AIDS, TB [tuberculosis] and Malaria (GFATM) were established.

Activist pressure also re-ignited debates about health governance. The 2002 appointment, by the UN Commission on Human Rights, of a Special Rapporteur on the right of everyone to the highest attainable standard of physical and mental health, and the establishment in 2005 of the Commission on the Social Determinants of Health (CSDH) were positive signals. So, too, are signs that a number of developing-country governments have begun to accept and assert their duty to protect and fulfill the human right to health, particularly when it comes to the clash between intellectual property law and the affordability of essential medicines.

Those wanting to claim that there is a commitment to global health will also point to a number of bi- and multi-lateral governmental initiatives around the issue of health. For example, in March 2007, the governments of Brazil, France, Indonesia, Norway, Senegal, South Africa, and Thailand issued a statement describing health as "one of the most important, yet still broadly neglected, long-term foreign policy issues of our time," and promising henceforth "to make impact on health a point of departure and a defining lens that each of our countries will use to examine key elements of foreign policy and development strategies."[3]

Another feature of the past decade has been the emergence of a range of governance institutions and vertical health programs that aim to staunch aspects of the health hemorrhage. Mechanisms such as the GFATM and the U.S. President's Emergency Program for AIDS Relief (PEPFAR)[4] have stepped into the breach created by state and multilateral failures around issues of health. On July 30, 2008, President Bush signed a congressional authorization of $48 billion for PEPFAR. Side-by-side with these mechanisms are the global health programs of late-in-the-day philanthropists such as Bill and Melinda Gates and Bill Clinton.

These initiatives have a positive impact on millions of lives, but they entail risks. By tacitly accepting developing-state failure in relation to health, they fragment and further weaken national health systems. In some cases, they even compound the crisis by sucking scarce health workers out of public health systems—an effect that was contemplated in a recent article analyzing

PEPFAR: "The effect on the wider health care system of funding a disease-specific programme is harder to quantify."[5] This mixed result is why global and national health programs must be judged not by surface impressions or wishful thinking but by critical analysis.

These developments beg some questions. Why, despite the centrality of health to the Millennium Development Goals (MDGs), and the flurry of new health initiatives, is health aid declining?[6] Why are African governments not meeting their own pledges to increase spending on health as a percentage of total expenditures?[7] Why are First World governments not fixing their own health systems, given that the doctor/nurse shortage in poor countries is directly linked to their diversion to rich countries that are not training enough of their own health care workers?

These questions force us to face a sober reality: much as we may be inclined to misty-eyed approval of the contributions wealthy nations and wealthy individuals make to the fight against HIV/AIDS, we must ask (a) whether those contributions are sustainable for the millions of people whose lives now depend on them, and (b) whether they will bring about any change in the ability of governments to promote and protect health at a national level—or in citizens' power to demand the right to health and health care services. The answer to the first question is uncertain, particularly in the context of a global financial crisis. The answer to the second is "maybe—maybe not."

Morally and legally, wealthy nations do have a duty in relation to HIV/AIDS. But realpolitik and the future of public health require that we do more to ascertain the political and economic factors that are determining of health. In this way we may begin to shape a global response to health care issues, including better guidance to maximize the potential outcomes from the giving habits of wealthy nations.

FROM STATE TO NONSTATE

Health care has made itself global because disease has gone global, as evidenced by HIV. But this situation in itself is not new. Throughout history, economic expansion has spread disease; indeed, the notion of public health arose from the need of the state to prevent and treat this phenomenon. Protecting armies, navies, settler populations, and the aristocracy from being wiped out by "foreign" diseases about which there was no knowledge—or for which people had no immunity—was a necessity both for the "progress" of colonialism and for the expansion of national economies. Over time, this necessity led to vaccination campaigns, investment in water and sewerage systems, public health legislation, and the creation of rudimentary public health services. Growing state involvement with health led to declines in mortality.

But if such engagement was once the case, it is so no longer. Something has changed. Today, there is a deficit of coordination, investment, and planning in health care. Ironically, however (as we see later), the explanation for this health care deficit may still rest in the relationship between national governments and economic expansion. Many governments now neglect key functions of the state, such as health care and education—as is illustrated by the changing pattern of research and development of new medicines. At the start of the twentieth century, governments of industrialized countries—particularly those in Europe—invested heavily in research, which contributed significantly to such medical breakthroughs as the treatment of TB. However, since the early 1990s, there has been a dramatic decline in medical innovation that has been attributed, at least in part, to declining investments by European governments in pharmaceutical research, development, and application.[8]

Except in times of crisis or threat, the dominant politics of health care today seems to be one in which responsibility for the protection, maintenance, and improvement of public health is being separated from the state. In the so-called First World, this privatization movement is driven by a complacent assumption that infectious disease has largely been conquered.

GLOBAL DISEASE THREATS: SELF-INTEREST FIRST

Following upon the advent of neoliberal economic policies in the 1980s, wealthy countries underwent a transition away from proactive, state-driven strategies in public health, adopting instead a largely passive and technical approach that aims to manage the maintenance of health systems and infrastructure, while avoiding periodic disease outbreaks. The consensus is that, as long as major public health threats are held at bay or contained in developing countries, the *actual* health of their citizens—who are getting less healthy, but no longer primarily as a result of communicable disease—is of less concern to the state.

Thus, within developed countries, but to significantly varying degrees, the state supports health systems that maintain a high standard of health care "at home," such as the National Health System (NHS) in England or Medicaid in the United States. Compared with health systems in the Third World, these systems offer an undreamt-of standard of care. However, they, too, have been subject to attacks by government that have reduced the quality of care and, in countries such as the United States, have left millions of people uninsured and grossly disadvantaged in access to decent health services.

But even the praiseworthy parts of these state-run health systems overlook how infectious and communicable diseases take advantage of the explosion of inter- and intra-national travel to move pathogens swiftly, from causing localized to generating globalized epidemics. Most wealthy governments seem to believe that their duty to provide health care and their budgetary responsibilities and health policies end abruptly at national boundaries. What happens on the other side of these porous borders is not the responsibility of health departments but of "development aid."

The health services of wealthy nations are not linked to an integrated global strategy that recognizes the transnational nature of both good and bad health. Although the world has acknowledged the impact of health on development—and vice versa—there is still no globally agreed *political* strategy on states' duty to tackle health care issues or the interventions and standards that will be required to achieve the MDGs. Thus, although funding for health programs, including the prevention and treatment of HIV/AIDS, represents a growing portion of development aid, such efforts continue to be implemented through vertical programs that often ignore or work around the larger political paralysis on health care.

Consequently, foreign assistance for health is rarely driven by precisely identified and quantified local needs, but is instead determined by what wealthy nations consider those needs to be. New imbalances and inequalities arise because donor funds end up being transferred only to those organizations in recipient countries that have the capacity to design and (usually) implement these programs. This situation leads to further distortions and imbalances between urban and rural areas or between developing countries. A symptom of the want of coordination in the financing of health care is the lack of funding for TB, which derives from the fact that HIV may have initially squeezed out this less prominent disease in the "competition" for donor funds.[9] Given that TB is now the primary cause of death in people with HIV in developing countries, this distortion is particularly grotesque.

The wheel has come full circle. A century ago, the state actively intervened to improve public health. Today, in both the industrialized and the developing worlds, it is the lack of action that influences patterns of disease. This is the politics that needs to be addressed both in relation to funding from wealthy nations and to the legitimate expectations of developing country governments by their citizens.

DEVELOPING COUNTRIES: HEALTH AT THE MARGINS

Schneider and Garrett call for "investment in strong health systems" and for a stepping-up of "targeted evidence-based" prevention interventions to replace the "religious and moral ideologies . . . that are ever-present on the design of anti-AIDS programming."[10] They are right to make these demands. But they overlook the lassitude of the governments of developing countries toward health and HIV, as well as the realities of what has happened to our health care systems over the past few decades.

In this context, it is unfortunate but relevant that the largely laissez-faire approach to health care adopted by industrialized-country governments has been mimicked by the governments of most developing countries. The rot started under the old policies of the International Monetary Fund and the World Bank, which in the 1980s and 1990s required cuts in social investment and in public goods, including health care. But today, the neglect of health takes place not under the whip of international financial institutions but as a voluntary policy of government. Many developing countries replicate the First World approach to health care policy by attempting to maintain expensive but still underfunded tertiary-care systems in urban centers (which are wrongly considered to be the template of a health care system), while throwing in an ingredient of what some describe as "selective primary health care" in rural and peri-urban districts.[11] In the spaces that public health should occupy, there have arisen large and profitable private health care sectors that cater to the health needs of the wealthy and the employed.

It is an unpalatable fact that public health is rarely regarded as a political priority by developing-country governments. Planning to improve health is not integrated into development or economic planning, or vice versa. For example, in South Africa, the media statements that are released after government cabinet meetings reveal no record of discussions of health broadly. Although there are discussions about HIV/AIDS, generally they have taken place only in response to activists' criticism of the country's response to that particular problem. Despite a burgeoning AIDS epidemic, former South African President Mbeki's annual State of the Nation speech to Parliament, given in February each year, often barely touched on health. Indeed, in 2004 and 2005, the issue of health occupied only a fraction of the time given to matters of economy, international affairs, and poverty.

This low prioritization of public health issues is borne out by the way in which, in many countries, poor performance and corruption are tolerated from health ministers and their departments. As a rule, developing-country governments approach health reactively rather than proactively. Their passive attitude is evidenced by the almost complete dependence of many African governments on wealthy nations for health investment; the absence of serious and consistently driven public health strategies; the acceptance of very high rates of maternal mortality; the neglect of primary health care; and the failure to control infectious diseases. The failure therefore is not limited to the "foreign aid architecture" around health funding that is referred to by Schneider and

Garrett,[12] but is also found in the domestic architecture. The two constitute a vicious and mutually reinforcing circle.

HEALTH AND UNDERDEVELOPMENT: GLOBALIZATION AND ITS CONSEQUENCE FOR PUBLIC HEALTH

Developing-country governments cannot feign ignorance about the linkages between politics, health, and development. A succession of commissions—notably, the [World Health Organization] WHO's Commission on Macro Economics and Health (CMEH 2002) and its Commission on Social Determinants of Health (CSDH 2008), as well as the United Kingdom-sponsored Commission on Africa (2005)—has drawn attention to the linkages. For example, the report of the CMEH offers the following warning:

> As with the economic well-being of individual households, good popula-
> tion health is a critical input into poverty reduction, economic growth,
> and long-term economic development at the scale of whole societies.
> This point is widely acknowledged by analysts and policy makers, but
> is greatly underestimated in its qualitative and quantitative significance,
> and in the investment allocations of many developing country and donor
> governments.[14]

Why then, in the face of this repeatedly restated evidence, is health care failing so signally in so many countries? Why are U.S. donor dollars—which by March 2008 claimed to be keeping alive 1.7 million people with HIV—not altering the underlying determinants of health? Is there an explanation other than the wiles of politicians? Why has a period in history that has seen the advance of democracy been accompanied by declines in health? Why have the citizens of the new democracies not forced health issues into greater focus?

Modern health care, or the want of it, is rooted in economy and politics, as is population vulnerability to disease. Since the late 1980s, there have been rapid and important changes in economy and society. Improvements in technology and communications have been the primary drivers of a new phase of economic globalization and integration. What Karl Marx called "the means of production" (factories and technology) have become more and more capital-intensive—and less and less dependent on labor. Linked to this evolution—and enabled by it—were profound political developments, notably the end of the so-called cold war and the collapse of "communism," which opened new markets for economic expansion, especially in Asia. New technologies have been introduced to new and old markets, creating new consumption "needs." These new commodities depend less on the labor of human beings to produce them—making them cheaper. Yet they can be enormously profitable, by virtue of new economies of scale unleashed by the global economy.

How does this economic revolution relate to health? It has diminished the relative importance of human labor (and thus humans) to the production of wealth: more profit can now be made by fewer and fewer workers. In many emerging markets—including India, China, and South Africa—this devaluation of the human factor has left an enormous surplus population, who have little prospect of ever getting gainful employment. These people have no role in the formal economy. In South Africa, for example, despite a decade of rapid economic growth, unemployment remains at 40 percent. High and permanent unemployment will be a feature of the twenty-first-century economy. Thus, inadvertently perhaps, it is the health of the few—those who produce wealth—that matters in the modern economy, rather than the health of the population as a whole.

Because the health of poor people has been delinked from productivity and profit, developing-country governments behave as if they no longer have an economic interest in using the state's resources and power to improve public health. Investments in AIDS prevention and treatment have rarely been voluntary decisions of government—generally, they have been decisions taken under the pressure of local and international activists. Countries such as Botswana and Uganda, where political leadership has been more far-sighted, are the exception, not the rule. And even in these countries, AIDS programs and public health continue to exhibit enormous deficiencies and inequalities.

The past two decades have taught governments and capitalists that it is possible to sustain economic growth while generally ignoring general population health—a lesson in neglect that is also applicable in education and other areas of social welfare. This sorry spectacle seems to confirm the arguments of those political economists who claim that capitalism "generates economic growth, prosperity, [and] employment as side-effects. It also causes much misery and destruction in its tendency towards incessant change."[14]

Thus, the same economic logic that discourages private investment in the research and development of new medicines for the poor because their sale will yield no profitable return works to deny public investment in population health—which is also thought to have no direct benefit to the state or the economy. Health may be a social necessity, but it is not necessarily an economic one.

IS INVESTING IN HEALTH AN ECONOMIC NECESSITY?

Failure to recognize the reality of governmental neglect may be the fatal flaw in the recommendations of commissions such as the CMEH and the CSDH, which may be astute and accurate but do not take sufficient account of, or speak honestly about, how national politics and economics influence health. In its executive summary, for example, the CMEH relays this finding:

> We estimate that approximately 330 million DALYs [disability adjusted life years] would be saved for each of the 8 million deaths averted. Assuming, conservatively, that each DALY saved gives an economic benefit of 1 year's per capita income of a projected $563 in 2015, the direct economic benefit of saving 330 million DALYs would be $186 billion per year, and plausibly several times that.[15]

This perceived benefit would seem to provide a huge incentive for governments to invest in health care. The problem is that it does not, because most of those ill or at risk of illness are outside the modern economy. Influenced by economists such as Amartya Sen, the CMEH's recommendations assume that governments attach an economic value to sick people who could be healthy, and that most of the people who are healthy but poor will be able to find a place in the modern economy. Neither assumption may prove true. If economic growth can be achieved by relatively small segments of the population utilizing increasingly capital-intensive technologies for ever-larger markets, then these assumptions are mistaken.

Crudely put, illnesses such as those caused by the HIV/AIDS epidemic, while causing widespread suffering and social dislocation, do nothing to further economically disable those segments of the population that are already socially disabled by the fact that there is no place in the modern economy for them.

The lack of a purely economic motive for investment in health care is further compounded by the fact that in many developing countries the financial cost to the state of treating illness is avoided because the collapse of health services means that most people die at home—burdening their families, but not necessarily requiring public expenditure. In South Africa, for example, as illustrated by Table 1 (p. 358), there has been a dramatic rise in mortality, most of it caused by HIV/AIDS and TB.[16] But despite this trend, as seen in Table 2 (p. 358), there was an overall decline in hospital admissions between 2001 and 2007.

This discrepancy suggests several things: that hospitals are saturated; that people are being admitted for longer periods (because they are sicker); and that many people are bypassing the lower rungs of the health system in order to access tertiary care. However, the net effect is that a large portion of the growing burden of disease is displaced onto the families of poor people—reports show that nearly 50 percent of deaths occur at home. This pattern probably exists in many other developing countries with high HIV prevalence.

Table 1

Mortality Trends in South Africa, 1997–2005

Year	Deaths	Deaths as % of total population	Deaths as % of uninsured population
1997	316,507	0.8%	0.9%
1998	365,053	0.9%	1.0%
1999	380,982	0.9%	1.1%
2000	414,531	1.0%	1.2%
2001	453,404	1.0%	1.2%
2002	499,925	1.1%	1.3%
2003	553,718	1.2%	1.4%
2004	572,350	1.2%	1.4%
2005	591,213	1.3%	1.5%

Source: *Statistics South Africa.*

Table 2

Hospital Admissions in South Africa, 2000–2007

	2000/01	2001/02	2002/03	2003/04	2004/05	2005/06	2006/07
District	1,624,425	1,593,010	1,524,585	1,513,924	1,529,946	1,600,115	1,439,544
Regional	1,388,042	1,545,566	1,487,031	1,518,548	1,463,930	1,507,511	1,327,711
Central and tertiary	568,585	603,677	612,556	599,796	610,344	572,943	698,518
Total	3,581,052	3,742,253	3,624,172	3,632,268	3,604,220	3,680,569	3,465,773

Note: Reclassification in Eastern Cape for 2006/07 accounts for changes between regional and central.

HEALTH IS A HUMAN RIGHT AND A LEGAL ENTITLEMENT

I have drawn a rather pessimistic and tragic picture in response to Garrett and Schneider's[17] affirmation that wealthy nations should promote anti-AIDS efforts in developing countries. I have done so because, while there must be no doubt that wealthy nations have a moral and legal duty to promote such efforts, more is required than just throwing money or medicines at the problem. It is incumbent on wealthy nations to take steps and adopt policies that aim to resuscitate global health.

The vertical response to HIV and treatment for AIDS, which is criticized by Garrett and Schneider[18] as the "pursuit of quick fixes and easily measurable treatment outcomes," was necessary initially because AIDS presented the global system with a disease emergency that was unprecedented in modern times. HIV arrived at a time when the health systems of poor countries were dilapidated and without capacity to generate their own effective response. An externally driven, vertical response was necessary to save lives.

But developing countries are now in a catch-22 situation. Donor funding remains necessary to save millions of lives, but it fuels a vicious circle: because of the collapse of "horizontal" health systems, there is often no alternative other than the vertical funding streams. But funding health in this way further weakens the local base of health systems.

Reviving the world's failing health systems will require that health care reform and investment be demanded and driven by a recognition of legal duties that arise from the international human rights framework. Such an understanding should form the foundation of the efforts of wealthy nations to address the problem of HIV/AIDS.

In this respect, it is worth drawing attention to a proposal made by health law scholar Larry Gostin, who has argued for a Framework Convention on Global Health, which would set global norms and standards of health, as well as seeking to calculate the investment that is necessary for both health systems and priority-disease programs.[19] It is necessary to recognize in practice (and not just in prayers) the interconnectedness of developing- and developed-country health—a lesson that the AIDS epidemic has made glaringly apparent.

NOTES

1. Kammerle Schneider and Laurie Garret, "Yes," in *Controversies in Globalization*, eds. Peter M. Haas, John A. Hird, and Beth McBratney (Washington, DC: CQ Press, 2009), 253–264.

2. S. Lewis, *Race against Time* (Toronto: Anansi, 2005).

3. The Oslo Ministerial Declaration, "Global Health: A Pressing Foreign Policy Issue of Our Time," www.thelancet.com, April 2, 2007.

4. See www.theglobalfund.org and www.pepfar.gov.

5. W. El Sadr and D. Hoos, "The President's Emergency Plan for AIDS Relief—Is the Emergency Over?" *New England Journal of Medicine* 359, no. 6 (August 7, 2008).

6. A recent report has pointed out that, within the European Union, funding for health dropped from 7 percent of Overseas Development Assistance in 1996 to 5 percent in 2005 and that "only one third of these commitments were actually disbursed." Action for Global Health, "An Unhealthy Prognosis: The EC's Development Funding for Health," May 2007.

7. See African Union, "Abuja Declaration on HIV/AIDS, Tuberculosis and Other Infectious Diseases, April 2001," which pledged to set a target of "at least 15% of our annual budgets to the improvement of the health sector."

8. R. Laing, *Priority Medicines for Europe and the World*, World Health Organization, November 2004.

9. S. Kaufmann and S. Parida, "Changing Funding Patterns in Tuberculosis," *Nature Medicine* 13 (2007).

10. Kammerle Schneider and Laurie Garret, "Yes," in *Controversies in Globalization,* eds. Peter M. Haas, John A. Hird, and Beth McBratney (Washington, DC: CQ Press, 2009), 253–264.

11. D. Werner and D. Sanders, *Questioning the Solution: The Politics of Primary Health Care and Child Survival* (Palo Alto, Calif.: HealthWrights, 1997). The concept of primary health care, which originally rested in human rights, has been starved of imagination and funds. In South Africa, the concept has been perverted and now refers to "health centres" or "clinics" that are "close to the community" but under-funded, ill-equipped, understaffed, and rarely involved in community health pro-motion. Not surprisingly, a 2007 report by the South African Human Rights Commission (SAHRC) found that "many patients are by-passing clinics and going straight to hospitals. This seems to indicate that despite clinics being geographi-cally accessible, they are unable to meet patient needs."

12. Kammerle Schneider and Laurie Garret, "Yes," in *Controversies in Globalization,* eds. Peter M. Haas, John A. Hird, and Beth McBratney (Washington, DC: CQ Press, 2009), 253–264.

13. WHO, "Report of the Commission on Macroeconomics and Health, Macroeconomics and Health: Investing in Health for Economic Development, 2001," 21–22.

14. M. Desai, *Marx's Revenge: The Resurgence of Capitalism and the Death of Statist Socialism* (London and New York: Verso, 2002), 313.

15. Ibid., Executive Summary, 12–13.

16. Statistics South Africa, "Mortality and Causes of Death in South Africa, 2005: Findings from Death Notification," July 2007.

17. Kammerle Schneider and Laurie Garret, "Yes," in *Controversies in Globalization,* eds. Peter M. Haas, John A. Hird, and Beth McBratney (Washington, DC: CQ Press, 2009), 253–264.

18. Ibid.

19. L. Gostin, "Meeting the Survival Needs of the World's Least Healthy People: A Proposed Model for Global Health Governance," *JAMA,* July 11, 2007, Vol. 289, 2, 225–228.

gender

Should the United States Aggressively Promote Women's Rights in Developing Nations?

YES: Isobel Coleman, *Council on Foreign Relations*

NO: Marcia E. Greenberg, *Independent Gender Mainstreaming Consultant*

Women have suffered from numerous forms of discrimination through the ages. While some inroads have been made in recent years in terms of political entranchisement and entry into the workforce, widespread disparities persist between women's and men's wages and between the social status accorded to women and men in most societies. As of 2011, only 19.5 percent of legislators in the world's parliaments were women. Also, in most countries, girls receive less education than boys (see Figure 1, p. 362) and are viewed as subservient in many ways.

From the 1970s on, international attention has become focused on women's rights and the need to achieve women's equality. Activist nongovernmental organizations (NGOs) at UN conferences on population (1974, 1984, 1994) and women (1975, 1980, 1985, 1995) generated global publicity and national campaigns. While there have been no further International Conferences on Population and Development since 1994, there was a 15-year review in 2009, and the next planned conference is in 2014. Globalization has contributed to the rapid and universal spread of these ideas as well as facilitating the creation of formal networks of activists to promote the ideas and coordinate their activities.

The 1994 Cairo Conference on Population and Development marked a serious change in attitudes about women's rights. The resulting **Cairo Declaration** maintained that women's equality was a necessary condition for economic

Figure 1

Populations with at Least Secondary Education, 2011

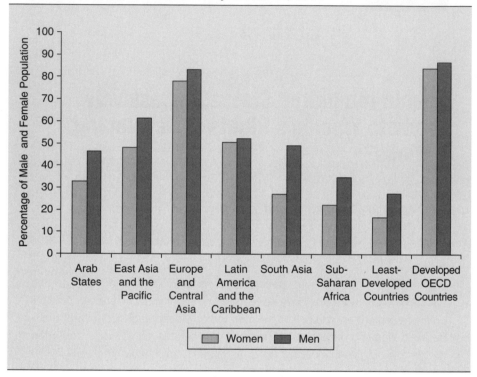

Source: United Nations Development Programme (UNDP), Human Development Report 2011 (New York: Palgrave Macmillan, 2011), 142.

development as well as for reducing population growth rates. In order to limit population growth rates, particularly in developing countries, women had to be empowered to play an equal role in family-planning choices. In addition, the new policy consensus held that women's equality was necessary for economic development; that in order to combat poverty, women's wages had to be equal to men's; and that women needed to play a more influential role in the economy.

Women's equality became enshrined as an international aspiration in the Millennium Development Goals of 2000—one of which calls for reducing gender inequality and empowering women for development. The main target is to eliminate gender disparity in primary and secondary education by 2005 and at all levels of education by 2015. Current studies indicate significant movement toward achieving these goals in most areas other than Africa, Oceania, and southern Asia (UN Millennium Development Goals [MDG] Report, 2011). However, considerable gains must still be made, as the 2005 goals have yet to be fully met and gender equality in tertiary education is even further behind in the lagging regions.

Women's equality thus serves a dual purpose. In the West, where individual rights are dominant, it is seen as a principled goal in and of itself. But more universally, it is now regarded as instrumentally desirable in order to promote economic development and limit population growth rates. Despite a consensus on the necessity of promoting gender equality, policy debates have ensued on how to achieve these goals, and many observers have lamented the limited financial resources that have been committed to the struggle.

Actively including women in shaping family-planning decisions—by providing relevant information and contraception—has been strongly opposed by the Republican right in the United States; social conservatives believe that foreign aid should not be spent on any activities that disseminate information about abortion. Therefore, even those pursuing women's literacy projects encounter questions about funding priorities, even though it is now conventional wisdom among development economists that more literate women enjoy greater influence over family-planning decisions, because they are able to earn more money and thus enjoy greater social status as well as being able to read family-planning materials. Moreover, while empowering women in developing societies is now regarded as a desirable policy instrument and objective, in practice, it is extremely difficult to reverse traditional social habits based on male supremacy.

Women's equality spans a wide array of issues, and it is difficult to separate them. For instance, does promoting women's rights require improved literacy, increased focus on women's health issues, greater political empowerment, higher wages, and more job opportunities? Do all of these goals have to be pursued in combination, or can they be disentangled?

Analysts ask about the appropriate political channels through which to promote women's equality. National governments control much of the money for such activities, yet the involvement of powerful foreign governments such as that of the United States is often met with resentment abroad. International organizations (such as the **United Nations Population Fund [UNFPA]**) and national foundations and networks of NGOs (such as **Planned Parenthood**) can provide lower-profile channels to provide resources directly to target groups in developing countries.

The matter of women's rights is a complex issue. The articles that follow take differing positions on whether the United States should aggressively pursue its various aspects in developing countries in light of the normative justification for such efforts and the possible indirect and unanticipated political consequences of such policies.

1. Is it possible to promote women's rights in some countries yet still respect cultural and religious beliefs and practices?
2. Why are women's rights important? Are there reasons beyond a moral right to equality? Is there a reason to focus on women's rights rather than human rights more generally?
3. Is promoting women's rights a development objective or a foreign policy objective?
4. Besides supporting education for girls and women, what other ways of promoting women's rights does Isobel Coleman propose? What strategy does she suggest for accomplishing these goals? Do you agree?
5. Marcia Greenberg makes a distinction between *rights-based* and *rights-focused* initiatives. What are the differences? What reasons does she give to explain why rights-focused initiatives often fail? What does she propose as alternatives to women's rights initiatives?

YES: Isobel Coleman, *Council on Foreign Relations*

Should the United States move aggressively to promote women's rights and education in developing nations? On the surface, it seems almost odd to be asking this question. Women's rights are not distinct from human rights, and since 1948, when the United States led the international community in adopting the Universal Declaration of Human Rights, the promotion of human rights has been a core U.S. foreign policy value. This is not to say that the United States has consistently backed human rights. On countless occasions, Washington has prioritized other foreign policy objectives over the promotion of human rights—a "sell-out," cynics might say, or, from a realist perspective, the inevitable result of hard strategic choices. When it comes to women's issues, cultural and religious constraints add additional complexities. But this is no reason to shy away from the imperative of women's rights. In our increasingly global world, the empowerment of women is critical to addressing the most serious issues of our time: the rise of global extremism, the persistence of crushing poverty, the spread of deadly infectious diseases, and environmental degradation.[1] So the question on women's empowerment is not "whether," but "how."

If we define women's empowerment as increasing women's access to quality education, opportunities to generate income, political voice, and health, there are ample opportunities for the United States to promote the role of women in global society in ways that support its other foreign policy objectives. The word *aggressively* in the question posed is somewhat vexing. Promoting women's rights in traditional societies must be done with sensitivity and caution, given the highly controversial nature of women's issues. The United States cannot simply impose its own understanding of women's rights on developing countries. Instead, it should support existing local women's groups and work through multilateral organizations to foster change from within. Even in the most conservative societies, there are leaders working to improve the status and opportunities of women in their communities. The benefits of promoting women's rights, and especially of investing in women's education, are so clear that it behooves U.S. policymakers to support these efforts.

SUPPORT FOR GIRLS' EDUCATION: A FOREIGN POLICY "NO-BRAINER"

In the early 1990s, Lawrence Summers, then the chief economist of the World Bank, made the economic case that investing in girls' education was the "highest return investment available in the developing world."[2] Numerous studies before and since corroborate that assertion. The World Bank, for example, has shown through its research that women's education improves the health and survival of both the mother and child.[3] According to its *Engendering Development* report, "there is a strong negative association between mother's average schooling and child mortality."[4] The report goes on to explain that a woman's schooling specifically increases the likelihood that she will immunize her children and give them proper medical care. Educated mothers are certainly more likely than uneducated mothers—and even more likely than educated fathers—to ensure that all their children, both boys and girls, attend school.

As numerous studies also show, female education leads to a decrease in fertility rates. A woman who is educated is likely to marry later (and therefore have fewer childbearing years), to have the confidence to make her own reproductive decisions, and to take better care of the children she already has. Since high fertility often exacerbates the problems associated with poverty and strains already limited government resources, educating women and realizing lower fertility rates is an important step in ending the vicious cycle of poverty in the poorest countries of the world.

Female education is also critical for economic productivity and growth. Development economist Stephan Klasen's work shows that when girls do not attend school, a society loses the productive capacity of some of its most able and competent members. Klasen concludes that gender equality in education, specifically at higher levels, improves the overall quality of education in a society and eventually leads to significant economic growth.[5] Although some economists continue to challenge the link between girls' education and economic growth, several other studies support Klasen's research.[6] David Kucera, a labor economist at the International Labour Organization, has found that gender equality in education also positively impacts foreign direct investment (FDI) in developing countries.[7] Many of the light manufacturing and service-sector jobs created in developing countries through FDI tend to employ women. These jobs are often an extended family's ticket to the middle class.

Agnes Quisumbing, a researcher at the International Food Policy Research Institute, has published several studies on the connection between female literacy and agricultural productivity, an important driver of economic growth, given agriculture's central role in many developing countries. Quisumbing's research demonstrates that raising the educational level of female farmers—more so than that of male farmers—increases the probability that new technologies and methods will be adopted.[8]

Ultimately, educated women are more productive members of society who can better improve the health of their families, lower fertility rates, contribute to economic growth, improve agricultural productivity, and attract foreign direct investment. Even in the most conservative societies, if women are able to contribute to the economy and health of the community, their status undoubtedly improves. The more active they become in the public sphere, the more they are able to impact policies and issues facing women across the country. Education gives women the skills and confidence they need to become active agents of change in their own local communities.

Many developed countries and international organizations are finally recognizing the benefits of investing in education in the developing world, particularly for girls and women. Universal primary education is one of the UN's Millennium Development Goals, to be achieved by the year 2015. Representatives from 164 countries gathered in 2000 for the World Education Forum in Dakar, Senegal, where they announced a platform of action for expanding quality education worldwide. Education promotion is central to the World Bank's long-term development strategies. The various UN agencies are at the forefront of this struggle, promoting literacy and quality education. Supporting this effort, the Bush administration pledged $525 million over five years specifically to educate the poorest children of the world.

Still, the problem is large: 781 million adults in the world are illiterate, and more than two-thirds of them are women. While many countries have made great strides in closing their persistent gender gaps, there are still millions of fewer girls in school today than boys.[9] Even worse, of those girls who are lucky enough to attend school, one out of five does not complete her primary education. The majority of the children not in schools are from just three regions of the world: sub-Saharan Africa, South Asia, and the Middle East. Girls' education is particularly neglected in these regions.

The United States should increase funding for both boys' and girls' education, particularly in the three regions most in need. Policymakers seem to be waking up to the strategic benefits of supporting universal education: in May 2007 several congressmen introduced an "Education for All" bill that would increase U.S. funding for primary education in the developing world to $10 billion over the next five years.[10] This unprecedented move would undoubtedly lead global efforts to provide universal primary education. Interestingly, the arguments put forward by the bill's supporters included an explicit appeal to U.S. national security interests. As Democratic congresswoman Nita Lowey, one of the four legislators to push for the bill, put the case, "Unstable societies are a breeding ground for terrorists. In countries plagued by violence and strife, diseases like HIV/AIDS and malaria, and poverty, education is an equalizing force. Today more than ever, education is a national security issue. It is the key to turning back the spiraling tide against fanaticism."

Despite such national security arguments, the bill has not been passed, and might never be approved at such an ambitious level of funding. That the bill was introduced at all, however, reflects a growing recognition on the part of policymakers that educating the world's poorest inhabitants, including its girls, makes sense economically, politically, and strategically. The proposed bill would support activities to train teachers, build schools, develop effective curricula, increase access to school lunch and health programs, and increase parent and community involvement in schools—all critical components of a sound plan to achieve universal education.[11]

The good news is that when the international community finally is beginning to rally behind universal education, we have a much better understanding today of what works with respect to building sustainable education programs. There is also an emerging consensus that the unique physical and cultural obstacles facing girls must be explicitly addressed in any attempt to promote girls' education. For example, studies show that, both for security and economic reasons, girls are less likely to attend school if they must walk more than a few kilometers from home. Girls also need flexible schedules to boost their enrollment. The reality is that across developing countries, girls do much of the household work, including carrying water and firewood, caring for younger siblings, and tending farm animals. School schedules that allow them to finish their chores cater to this reality. Providing latrines with privacy is also important. Whereas boys can easily use the surrounding fields, girls are reluctant to do so, for reasons of hygiene, modesty, and personal safety. As girls reach adolescence and begin menstruating, private latrines become essential; without toilets, girls simply will not attend school during menses, which causes them to fall behind and increases female drop-out rates.

In some societies, cultural constraints require girls to attend school separately from boys, or at least at different times of day. Active community and, specifically, parent involvement in choosing teachers, determining schedules, and setting curriculum also improves female enrollment. So, too, does the availability of female teachers.[12] Most communities encourage girls to attend school when their safety and privacy concerns are met.

Promoting universal education, and specifically girls' education, is a win-win proposition for U.S. foreign policy. Strengthening education improves the economic trajectory of poor countries and provides a better opportunity for the next generation to pull themselves out of economic instability. Educated girls become educated mothers, who are more likely to lift their families out of poverty. They also become active female citizens and members of civil society, strengthening the foundations of democracy.

BEYOND EDUCATION: HEALTH AND JOBS

The United Nations Development Program provides an annual **"Gender Empowerment Measure"** (GEM) ranking for countries, which reflects women's economic and political participation and decision making and their power over economic resources.[13] Each year, sub-Saharan African countries have the lowest rankings, followed closely by South Asian and Middle Eastern countries. Violence against women is high in these regions, educational gender gaps are largest, economic participation is low, and political participation is only recently occurring with any critical mass. Maternal mortality in many of these countries is also shockingly high. A recent global report by the World Health Organization (WHO), United Nations Children's Fund (UNICEF), and the United Nations Population Fund (UNFPA) shows that a woman in sub-Saharan Africa has a 1-in-16 risk of dying from maternal causes, compared with a 1-in-2,800 chance for a woman in a developed country and a 1-in-28,000 risk for Scandinavian women.[14] Getting pregnant in many of these countries is the most dangerous risk a woman can take, since childbirth is the No. 1 killer of women of child-bearing age.

Clearly, these three regions are not alone in their gender discrimination. Serious abuses are committed against women all over the world. Sex-trafficking, rape, and domestic violence affect hundreds of millions of women regardless of their country or culture.[15] However, specific forms of violence against women—including female genital mutilation (FGM), acid burning, and honor killings—are more prevalent in these regions, where they are often justified on religious and cultural grounds. In numerous countries, the official laws reflect the fact that women's lives are valued less than men's lives, since they impose weak punishments for men killing women. Also, parents perpetuate the cycle of denigrating female life. So strong is the desire for sons over daughters that the spread of inexpensive sonogram technology has led to millions of sex-selective abortions. Nobel Prize–winner Amartya Sen has drawn the world's attention to "100 million missing women," mainly in India and China, where strong cultural preferences for male children have led to the abuse and neglect of female children. Girls in these countries may be denied medical care, proper nutrition, and education. And while there are laws in most countries outlawing such violence and discrimination against women, enforcement is still a problem. Most governments have signed the Convention to Eliminate Discrimination against Women (CEDAW), the most comprehensive international treaty to promote women's rights, yet they continue to allow gross violations of CEDAW's basic precepts.

For U.S. policymakers, addressing many of these sensitive topics is certainly more complicated than supporting girls' education, especially when the promotion of women's rights treads on cultural or religious landmines. In many societies today, issues related to women's rights are particularly fraught for a number of reasons: colonial legacies, the rise of religious fundamentalism, and suspicion of anything Western, including ideas of Western feminism. Western criticisms of specific cultural practices such as FGM are denounced as neocultural imperialism.

And any initiative related to women's health gets immediately caught up not only in conflict with local customs, but also in vitriolic domestic U.S. politics about women's sexual and reproductive rights. How can the United States most effectively promote women's rights in this highly charged context?

U.S. policymakers would be well-advised to adopt the foreign policy equivalent of the Hippocratic Oath: Do no harm. When American officials publicly condemn practices and traditions that are seen, often incorrectly, as being religiously rooted, their words can create a backlash effect. It did not help women in Egypt, for example, when Laura Bush publicly called for an end to the practice of FGM. Her condemnation was manipulated by local proponents of the practice to prove that indigenous forces working to end FGM are under foreign sway and that their efforts are therefore illegitimate. The 2005 Egypt Demographic and Health Survey shows that 96 percent of Egyptian women between 15 and 49 years of age have been circumcised—indicating little or no decline from a decade earlier, when ending FGM first became a cause for numerous international women's groups.[16] On such controversial issues, working discreetly with local NGOs usually leads to more productive outcomes. Indeed, more recently, the U.S. government has been quietly backing Egyptian NGOs dedicated to ending FGM. In the long term, this strategy will have much more of an impact than strident denunciations by foreign dignitaries.

Given the much-maligned position of the United States in the world today, working through multilateral institutions on such sensitive topics as violence against women, legal discrimination, and women's health promotion is often the best strategy. This approach requires providing more financial support for UN agencies, regional organizations, and international NGOs that can distribute money to local community groups. In order to achieve results, the promotion of women's rights should not be tied too closely to the politics of the U.S. government. By working with groups such as UNFPA and the United Nations Development Fund for Women (UNIFEM), U.S. policymakers can often have a greater impact than by supporting these efforts directly through U.S. embassies or USAID [U.S. Agency for International Development] programs, which are often perceived with mistrust and cynicism by the local population.

However, the fact that the United States is one of only a handful of countries—along with pariah states such as Iran, Sudan, and Somalia—that have not ratified CEDAW, the most important international treaty for women, undercuts its role in multilateral institutions and hurts its international image. Since the treaty was drafted in 1979, opposition in the United States has been small but vociferous. Critics of the treaty argue that the United States already protects the rights of women sufficiently, and that ratifying the treaty would only undermine American sovereignty. President Carter signed CEDAW in 1980, but his unpopularity with the American public left him without the political weight needed to push the treaty through Congress. Since then, CEDAW has been brought before the Senate on several occasions but blocked each time by a conservative minority.

As in the case of other international treaties, conservative critics contend that CEDAW represents a liberal conspiracy to impose "world government." They also falsely argue that based on its implementation in other countries, the treaty would force governments to decriminalize prostitution, give money in support of abortion, and even do away with Mother's Day on the grounds that it reinforces stereotypes of women. Such unfounded allegations about CEDAW continue to circulate today. In 2002 the U.S. State Department notified the Senate Foreign Relations Committee that CEDAW is "generally desirable and should be ratified," but the Bush administration publicly refused to push for its ratification.

U.S. credibility in promoting women's rights was further undermined by the Bush administration's refusal to fund UNFPA, the agency dedicated to reproductive health and family planning, and other similar organizations focused on sexual and reproductive health. Beginning in 2002, officials in the administration withheld UNFPA funds that had been appropriated by Congress, basing their action on spurious claims that UNFPA supports coercive abortion in China. The U.S. State Department itself investigated these allegations and issued a report stating that "based on what we heard, saw and read, we find no evidence that UNFPA has knowingly supported or participated in the management of coercive abortion or involuntary sterilization in the PRC (People's Republic of China). Indeed, UNFPA has registered its strong opposition to such practices."[17] Nevertheless, kowtowing to domestic anti-abortion groups and conservative Republicans in Congress, the Bush administration continued to deny funding to UNFPA.

By linking sexual and reproductive health to their anti-abortion credo, such conservatives in the Bush administration and in Congress ignored a critical issue that needs more U.S. support: maternal health. More than 500,000 women worldwide die every year from problems related to pregnancy and childbirth—equating to the death of one woman every minute, every day. WHO estimates that in addition to these tragic deaths, nearly 10 million women are seriously injured or contract a debilitating infection during childbirth. Millions of children are orphaned as a result, and a high percentage of them die within two years of their mother's death.

Improving maternal health worldwide should be a bipartisan priority for moral, political, economic, and social reasons. Furthermore, this is an issue on which developed countries can provide meaningful assistance, since the majority of deaths and injuries caused by childbirth are preventable. In particular, the United States can help to train health professionals, provide money to build better and more accessible prenatal and natal centers for women, and distribute information on reproductive health. By addressing this critical problem, the United States could help to improve the status of women worldwide.

Another less controversial but very important way for the United States to promote women's rights would be to provide more economic opportunities for women in developing countries. International polls show that women themselves prioritize jobs and their ability to earn income above less tangible notions of women's rights. Making explicit efforts to create jobs for women would be smart public diplomacy for the United States. Moreover, the long-term impact of putting income in the hands of women is highly positive. Studies have shown that, like education, earning income greatly improves a woman's status within her community and family. Female access to money also has a positive effect on the well-being of society. According to the World Bank's *Engendering Development* report, "additional income in the hands of women enlarges the share of the household budget devoted to education, health, and nutrition-related expenditures."[18] Marginal income in the hands of a mother improves child survival twenty times more than in the hands of a father. Improving women's economic status can be a non-threatening way for the United States to further women's rights around the world.

One way to accomplish this goal would be to increase support for micro-finance organizations, which extend credit primarily to women. Although microfinance has grown considerably in the past decade, there are still more than a billion people in the world with no access to credit. Supporting the growth of the microfinance industry by providing access to capital, subsidizing new technologies, and promoting a sound regulatory environment are all important activities for U.S. policymakers to undertake. Also, the United States should increase funding to those microfinance institutions that are committed to serving the poorest of the poor.

The U.S. private sector also has an important role to play in women's empowerment. Some of the most effective drivers of change are U.S.-based multinational companies, which quietly but firmly bring their workplace practices to local markets. In Saudi Arabia, for example, global companies such as Kimberly-Clark and McKinsey & Company hire, train, and promote female professionals, creating opportunities for women and leading by example. Microsoft recently started a training program in Egypt, which has trained over 100 women to become computer technicians.[19]

In 2002 Cisco Systems launched an innovative project designed to get more women into the IT sector in Jordan, a country where less than 15 percent of women were economically active. In conjunction with UNIFEM, Cisco established ten Networking Academies across the country to train women in computer technologies and connect graduates with the job market. The program's explicit goal is to give women an edge in Jordan's job market, where cultural barriers to women's advancement remain high. The U.S. government can encourage such efforts through public-private partnerships that support scholarships for women to receive higher education, targeted vocational training, and leadership programs for women. Ultimately, women's success in the workplace will be an important catalyst for long-term change.

CONCLUSION

Women's empowerment in the developing world is not only a moral imperative, but also a pressing economic, social, and political issue, and one that the United States should stand behind firmly. Undoubtedly, some components of such an agenda are controversial, and they may create backlash in regions of the world where the United States is already battling unprecedented levels of anti-Americanism. But there are ample opportunities to promote the status of women in ways that contribute positively to the U.S. image abroad: by supporting girls' education, maternal health, economic opportunities for women, and even political and civic training for women in countries that are already encouraging women's political participation.

Empowering women is clearly associated with alleviating poverty, with undermining the conditions that foster human-trafficking, with stemming the spread of AIDS, and even with cleaner, less corrupt government. And there is some evidence that women's empowerment is negatively correlated with authoritarian government and tempers extremism.[20] Given that the payoff from enhancing women's rights is so compelling, women's empowerment should be a consistent priority of U.S. foreign policy.

NOTES

1. Isobel Coleman, "The Pay-Off from Women's Rights," *Foreign Affairs* 83, no. 3 (May–June 2004).
2. L. H. Summers, "Investing in All the People: Educating Women in Developing Countries," EDI Seminar paper no. 45, World Bank, Washington, D.C., 1994, 1.
3. Elizabeth King and Andrew Mason, *Engendering Development* (Oxford: World Bank/Oxford University Press, 2001), 79.
4. Ibid.
5. Stephan Klausen, "Does Gender Inequality Reduce Growth and Development?" World Bank, 1999, 23, http://siteresources.worldbank.org/INTGENDER/Resources/wp7.pdf.

6. It should be noted, though, that the link between girls' education and economic growth has been challenged by some economists.

7. David Kucera, "The Effects of Core Workers Rights on Labour Costs and Foreign Direct Investment: Evaluating the 'Conventional Wisdom,'" International Institute for Labour Studies, 2001.

8. Agnes Quisumbing, "Gender Differences in Agricultural Productivity: A Study of Empirical Evidence," International Food Policy Research Institute, 52, http://www .ifpri.org/divs/fcnd/dp/papers/dp05.pdf.

9. UNICEF estimates that of the roughly 93 million children in the world who are not in school, the majority are girls. "Basic Education and Gender Equality: The Big Picture," http://www.unicef.org/girlseducation/index_bigpicture.html.

10. DATA Press Releases, "Bono Joins Lowey, Clinton, Smith and Bachus in Unveiling Education for All Act," May 1, 2007, http://www.data.org/news/press_20070501.html.

11. Ibid.

12. Gene Sperling and Barbara Herz, "What Works for Girls' Education," Council on Foreign Relations, 2004, 9–13, http://www.cfr.org/content/publications/attachments/ Girls_Education_full.pdf.

13. UNDP, "Gender Empowerment Measure," 2003, http://hdr.undp.org/statistics/ data/indic/indic_229_1_1.html.

14. Global Health Council, "Women's Health," www.globalhealth.org.

15. In the U.S. alone, an estimated 5.3 million women are abused each year; http:// www.aidv-usa.com/Statistics.htm.

16. UNICEF, "Egypt FGM/C Country Profile," November 2005, http://www.childinfo. org/areas/fgmc/profiles/Egypt/Egypt%20FGC%20profile%20English.pdf.

17 "Report of the China UN Population Fund (UNFPA) Independent Assessment Team," U.S. State Department, http://www.state.gov/g/prm/rls/rpt/2002/12122.htm.

18. King and Mason, *Engendering Development*, 81.

19. Sarah El Sirgany, "Microsoft Opens Technology Center to Train Youth, Women," *Daily News of Egypt*, June 14, 2006, http://www.dailystaregypt.com/article .aspx?ArticleID=1882.

20. Steven Fish, "Islam and Authoritarianism," *World Politics* 55 (October 2002): 4–37.

NO: Marcia E. Greenberg, *Independent Gender Mainstreaming Consultant*

INTRODUCTION

Presumably most readers of this essay believe in respecting and protecting the rights of women and girls. Similarly, most probably agree that the United States, with its power and resources, should exercise global leadership in support of human rights in general and for women and girls in particular. In fact, in recent years, many of us have admired how Hillary Rodham Clinton has used her position as U.S. Secretary of State to focus attention on the needs, contributions, and rights of women and girls.[1]

Yet while we may share the firm conviction that the U.S. government should take action to prevent violations of women's rights undertaken by actors and institutions that include governments, communities, combatants, and even families, stopping pervasive discrimination or changing entrenched attitudes is not so simple. In both the public and private sectors, principles of Results-Based and Evidence-Based Management (RBM & EBM) now challenge us to determine whether "business as usual" is indeed as effective as we have liked to believe (i.e., whether accepted approaches have in fact been achieving the objectives expected). In fact, aggressively promoting women's rights in developing countries has not.

That is not to deny the major achievements of the last 30 years. The global movement that included four world conferences on women from 1975–1995 and culminated with the Beijing Platform for Action was critical for raising worldwide awareness, building global partnerships, and engaging women's rights advocates in all nations.[2] Subsequent milestones have included the 1997 Resolution by the UN's Economic and Social Council [ECOSOC] that defined and called for gender mainstreaming, particularly the last line: "The ultimate goal is to achieve gender equality" (ECOSOC 1997/2);[3] the ever-increased visibility and decrial of violence against women[4] and inclusion in the founding statute of the International Criminal Court (the Rome Statute) that rape is a crime against humanity;[5] and United Nations Security Council (UNSC) Resolution 1325 (2000) on Women, Peace, and Security,[6] calling for women's leadership in defining and securing peace. Each has established globally agreed norms that reinforce women's rights and supports the passage of gender quality legislation by nations around the world.[7]

Moreover, whereas campaigns for human rights and programs for economic development used to be entirely separate realms (until the 1990s, the World Bank interpreted its legal mandate to preclude any attention to or meddling in issue of human rights), today economists and World Bank leaders recognize that violations of women's rights not only hurt women but also undermine the economic well-being of families and nations. In its 2012 World Development Report,[8] the World Bank has assessed linkages between development and women's rights and how development has closed some gender gaps—including "dramatic improvements" in female life expectancy at birth, "unprecedented reduction in fertility in developing countries,"[9] the entrance of over half a billion women into the world's labor force over the last thirty years, and major strides in gender parity in primary education.[10] In its sixth annual Global Gender Gap Report in 2011, the World Economic Forum noted progress (though also "conclud[ing] that women remain well behind men in two crucial areas: economic equality and political power").[11]

At the same time, however, there have been some limitations, disappointments, or frustrations. The World Bank characterizes areas of frustration as being "sticky domains" attributed to three reasons: a single institutional or policy fix that is difficult to implement or easily blocked, disparities caused by "multiple and reinforcing constraints that combine to block progress," and gender differences that persist from being "rooted in deeply entrenched gender roles and social norms." These domains may be found in places and cultures where accepted rights approaches have not been effective, where the approach has generated backlash, and where ostensible women's rights successes may not be sustainable. United States Agency for International Development (USAID) points out five areas where "much more remains to be done," including the following: (1) sixty-four percent of the 774 million adults worldwide who lack basic literacy skills are women, "a share virtually unchanged since the early 1990s"; (2) seventy-two percent of the world's 33 million refugees are women and children; (3) approximately 800,000 people are trafficked across national borders annually while millions are trafficked within their own national borders; (4) most studies estimate that 20 to 50 percent of women experience partner violence at some point in their lives; and (5) one in 61 women in developing countries die during pregnancy and childbirth (and 1 in 17 in least developed countries).[12]

Further, the last decade has been characterized by a proliferation of religious fundamentalist attacks on women's rights. The most visible challenge to women's rights in the early 21st century, the proverbial "elephant in the room," is the pervasive and powerful role of fundamentalist religious sects within nearly every religion. Women in Iraq have seen their rights and freedoms decrease ("Saddam Hussein's Baath Party espoused a secular Arab nationalism that advocated women's full participation in society. But years of war changed that."),[13] women and men in Turkey face uncertainty about the future of women's rights ("Secular opposition lawmakers voted against the change [lifting a ban on head scarves]. . . . Crowds of secular Turks backed them on the streets of the capital, Ankara, chanting that secularism—and women's right to resist being forced to wear head scarves by an increasingly conservative society— was under threat."),[14] women and men in India persist in aborting the girl-child,[15] and in Israel, ultraorthodox Jews are threatening women's rights not only within their own communities but among less religious or secular Israeli communities.[16] Within the United States as well, the laws restricting women's control of their reproductive health increasingly constrain women's ability to control their health and destiny.[17]

Hence while this essay absolutely supports the proposition that the United States should formulate policies and undertake proactive measures to support women and girls around the world, it takes issue with three aspects: "aggressive," "promoting rights," and "in developing countries." The argument for "no," that the U.S. should not aggressively promote women's rights in developing countries, focuses on three considerations: (1) whether we understand the root causes or enablers of rights violations in developing countries, (2) whether the traditional focus on rights as legal mechanisms is effective, and (3) the need to identify more effective ways for the U.S. to use its power and resources on the world stage.

A PRELIMINARY CLARIFICATION REGARDING THE OBJECTIVE: "RIGHTS" OR THE WELL-BEING OF WOMEN AND GIRLS?

As a first step in considering whether the U.S. should promote women's rights, it is important to take a step back to consider the very objective of "promoting women's rights." Is the goal to promote rights as legally defined and enforced, or is it the broader objective of rights themselves, namely the resulting quality of life, self-esteem, capabilities, and opportunities? While a wealthy or worldly woman might call for improved respect for her rights, a woman living in the Plan Alto of Angola, in a rural village of Sri Lanka, or in Port-au-Prince in Haiti will more likely call for food, security, electricity, or access to healthcare or safety on the streets. In fact, deciding the rights-related goals for women in developing countries requires that we shed our own expectations in order to hear what those women want. For example, an American specialist who began working with Afghan women well before September 2011 noted that whereas Americans focused on freeing Afghan women from the miseries of wearing a *burka*, Afghan women prioritized healthcare, education, and economic opportunities over the *burka*—while also noting that it often protects them from indignities and violence by men in the streets.

Hence while the foundations for this essay are *"rights-based,"* it takes issue with approaches that are *"rights-focused."* This essay is *rights-based* in a normative sense, in that the concern for women stems from a conviction that women should enjoy a complete range of rights as human beings, including any particular to their sex. It emanates both from respect for positive law and from a natural law perspective on rights: that these rights are inherently and fundamentally the "right thing to do," anchored in morality.

In contrast, a *rights-focused* approach looks particularly to positive law. It recognizes and relies on international laws that include the Universal Declaration of Human Rights; the Covenant on Civil and Political Rights; the Covenant on Social, Cultural, and Economic Rights; and the Convention to Eliminate Discrimination against Women (CEDAW).[18] It seeks to ensure on the national level that Constitutions, laws and regulations are consistent with international norms and requirements. Primary targets or partners are legislators, judges and magistrates, lawyers, and women's rights advocates. For the most part, legal mechanisms become both the final objective and programmatic focus.

In reframing the objective, therefore, what does a goal of "women's rights" really mean? Short term, it may mean improving the well-being of girls and women, as articulated in the Beijing Platform for Action. Some may suggest that the real objective is "empowerment" or girls' education, both raised within the "yes" essay responding to this question. Another way of recasting the objective is in terms of human capabilities, as suggested by Martha Nussbaum in *Women and Human Development: The Capabilities Approach.*[19] Nussbaum's "core idea is that of the human being as a dignified free being who shapes his or her own life in cooperation and reciprocity with others, rather than being passively shaped or pushed around by the world in the manner of a 'flock' or 'herd' animal. A life that is really human is one that is shaped throughout by these human powers of practical reason and sociability."[20] Another approach is the focus on *agency*, defined as the ability to make choices to achieve desired outcomes, put forward by the World Bank's World Development Report as one of three basic domains of gender equality along with assets and economic opportunities.

Long term, it may call for more than legal rights to achieve cultures of gender equality and respect—such that men and women relate to one another with mutual respect and collaborate for the greater well-being of families, enterprises, communities, and nations. Whatever the specifics of the goal, achievements should be sustainable. To be so, they should be "owned" not only by girls and women but also by boys and men.

Thus the objective is not simply to promote rights *per se* but rather to translate those rights into the well-being of girls, adolescent girls, women, and older women.

ADDRESS THE CONTEXTS AND CAUSES THAT ENABLE OR GENERATE VIOLATIONS OF WOMEN'S RIGHTS

Despite marked improvements in respect for women's rights in some nations or regions, many women still face intransigence, setbacks, and purposeful discrimination and attacks. In what are arguably the worst cases, women and girls are targeted for physical and psychological violence ranging from rape to honor-killings, bride-burning, forced prostitution, and acid attacks. In others, they are forbidden to go out or travel without male accompaniment, to sign contracts on their own behalf, or to hold political office. In many cases, they lack access to economic resources such as capital or land or to decision-making authority.

Yet violations of women's and girls' rights do not happen in a contextual vacuum. In fact, conditions are worst for women and girls in countries characterized by three factors: extreme poverty, armed conflict, and nondemocratic governments[21]—as reflected in Table 1 (this page), reflecting rankings in the UN Development Report's 2011 Gender Inequality Index.[22] Within the very worst (ranking from lowest-ranked Yemen to 123rd-ranked Haiti), governments are ineffective, corrupt, and oppressive; basic living conditions are terrible; and people are terrorized and victimized by rampant violence, much of which is sex- or gender-based violence (SGBV).[23]

As will be discussed below, this suggests that focusing narrowly on the legal aspects of rights may fail to address the circumstances that undermine the well-being of girls and women. Broader approaches, focused on socioeconomic situations, peace, and good governance, may be more effective ways to "promote women's rights."

Table 1

Countries with Lowest Gender Inequality Index (GII) Rankings

Country	GII Rank
Yemen	146
Chad	145
Niger	144
Mali	143
DPR of Congo	142
Afghanistan	141
Papua New Guinea	140
Liberia	139
Central African Rep	138
Sierra Leone	137
Cote d'Ivoire	136
Saudi Arabia	135
Cameroon	134
Benin	133
Congo	132
Zambia	131
Kenya	130
India	129
Sudan	128

RETHINK RELIANCE ON LEGAL SYSTEMS AND COURTS

*Avoid basing decisions on untested but strongly
held beliefs, what you have done in the past, or on
uncritical "benchmarking" of what winners do.*

EBM Principle #5

For years, women's rights programs have focused on the traditional locuses for rights creation and enforcement: legislatures and courts. In many countries where women's rights are denied and violated, the legal system may have laws that violate women's rights or authorize systems that violate rights, such as prohibiting a woman from traveling unless she has obtained her husband's permission or is accompanied by a male relative or precluding women from owning real property, serving as guardians, or running for public office. The system may have institutions that are incapable of applying and enforcing the law—both of a lack of resources (whether courts exist in rural areas or whether rural or poor or illiterate populations have any possibility of gaining access to courts) and because the personnel in the institutions (judges, magistrates, police officers, etc.) are not committed to following or applying the law on women's behalf (such as judges who "exercise their discretion" to ignore legal remedies and instead send home a woman who seeks protection from domestic violence, because they deem it a "family matter" that should be resolved there).[24] Consequently, most efforts focus on drafting laws that recognize women's rights, removing laws that abrogate women's rights, removing gender bias from judicial systems responsible for interpreting laws, and building more effective mechanisms for enforcement.[25]

Yet those programs are often not effective. When such legalistic efforts fail, the typical explanation is that "unfortunately" enforcement is weak or magistrates and judges need sensitization. Yet if one recognizes the weaknesses of the legal system from the start, why invest in legalistic, rights-focused strategies? It is like insisting on building on a major earthquake fault but asserting that the building was beautifully designed. In fact, the legal systems themselves are often unable to support an effective rights-focused approach. Women's rights projects are ineffective because, as is the case for other rule-of-law programs, they are grounded in assumptions of a liberal legal paradigm and legal culture that are weak or nonexistent in many key contexts.

One must recognize from the outset that rights-focused approaches presume legal systems consistent with a liberal legal paradigm, expecting a legal system of laws, institutions, and culture that are similar to or building toward those of the United States or Western Europe. The paradigm presumes six components, as flagged by David Trubek and Marc Galanter back in 1973,[26]

- that there are *intermediate groups* between a society of individuals and the State

- that the *State exercises control* over individuals through law—but according to rules by which State itself is constrained

- that the *rules are intended* to achieve social purposes and principles

- that when applied, the rules are *enforced equally for all citizens* and for the purposes for which they were designed

- that *courts are central* to functioning of the legal system

- that social actors *tend to conform to those State-generated rules* (both leaders and people)

All too often, however, that paradigm fails: In many contexts where women's rights are not respected, the State does *not* exercise control over individuals by law; instead, it may be a particular religious institution or customary law at a local level.[27] In many instances, the legal system serves those who live in capital cities and who have education and wealth—but means little to girls and women in rural areas. In many countries, courts do not serve as primary institutions of dispute resolution and/or may focus more on commercial issues than on "family" or social issues. (And many of those failing relate back to the underlying correlates or causes of gender inequality as discussed above: extreme poverty, armed conflict, and undemocratic governance.) Once those components are in doubt, it puts into question whether a "rights-focused approach" has the requisite institutional foundations to be meaningful.[28] All too often, the U.S. (and others) invest expertise and resources in improving legal institutions that have little or no impact on most women's lives.

Yet beyond institutions, there are often issues of legal culture.[29] Even if the laws and institutions exist, people may not turn to state-sponsored courts to support them or recognize rights. Instead, they may find other ways to resolve issues, relying on religious institutions or traditional community or family leaders. This may vary from whether women who are subjected to home-based violence or who are raped would turn to courts and whether women whose employers discriminated against them in terms of wages or benefits or even sexual harassment will sue them to whether attitudes regarding women's participation in political life are molded by civil society organizations or religious organizations. Often, state-supported courts simply do not play a role in their lives.

If those countries or communities where violations of women's rights are greatest (i.e., where women's circumstances of exclusion and disempowerment are most severe) are also those where the liberal legal model does not exist, then investing in promoting women's rights is often an ineffective way to achieve the objective of improving women's lives. The concepts of rights and legal systems presume that the state plays a major role in peoples' lives. In many developing countries, however, the State can be irrelevant, dysfunctional, or pose more threat than protection.

For most women striving for greater opportunities, education, respect, and dignity, the State's legal system does not offer either short-term or effective support. Rights and laws should be regarded as tools that are effective in some contexts and not in others: As those who own a hammer may wish to see everything as a nail, rights advocates ought not to regard all rights violations as legal challenges.[30]

SHIFT FOCUS FROM RIGHTS TO DEVELOPMENT, BUT ALSO FROM WOMEN TO GENDER EQUALITY THAT INCLUDES MEN AND BOYS AS WELL

If rights violations are not simply legal challenges, they involve a wide range of social, economic, and governance challenges. No matter what is done in courts or no matter how much one promotes girls' education or women's health, countries without effective justice systems, without schools and teachers for all children, and lacking basic healthcare are failing all of their citizens. And those inflicted with vicious armed conflict are destroying lives and livelihoods for all. The steps to protect and ensure the rights of women and girls must include steps to alleviate extreme poverty, build effective governance, and establish peace.

In fact, this was the message captured by the Beijing Platform for Action (the BPfA), endorsed in 1995 by "17,000 participants, including 6,000 delegates from 189 countries, over 4000 representatives of accredited non-governmental organizations . . . [and] more than 30,000 people" at the NGO Forum.[31] While the platform addresses "human rights of women," that is but one of twelve planks that range from women and poverty, education, health, and violence to women and armed conflict and women and the environment. Advocates for women recognized that advancing the rights of women and female children requires a holistic approach that addresses the contexts that are harmful to women while also recognizing the particular needs of women and girls and their potential contributions.

The recommended mechanism for implementing the BPfA and thereby advancing women's rights was *gender mainstreaming*. The "mainstream" includes various contextual factors that determine the well-being and opportunities for women and girls, make their particular needs visible, call for incorporating their perspectives and participation, and focus on the "ultimate goal" of achieving gender equality.[32] Achieving the strategic objectives requires actions by all sectors and actors of society, including governments, UN agencies or donors, and civil society. In many ways, gender mainstreaming is what was applied to the Millennium Development Goals (MDGs), where MDG #3 is to Promote Gender Equality and Empower Women, but all goals are to benefit women and benefit from their contributions and from respectful gender relations.[33]

Moreover, however, gender mainstreaming also brings boys and men back into the picture. Collecting sex-disaggregated data and undertaking gender analyses of social and economic problems results in better understanding of the respective roles and responsibilities of girls and boys, women and men. This enables context-particular assessments of disparities: whether girls and women suffer as a result of gender bias or whether they suffer along with boys and men— allowing as well for cases where boys or men may be suffering more, such as the fact that "girls outnumber boys in secondary schools in 45 developing countries."[34] Further, recognizing that there are still many ways in which culture or tradition perpetuate disparities for girls and women, engaging men is a way to enlist men as allies rather than enemies—by demonstrating the win-win of social and economic units that engage the skills and perspectives of men and women. Finally, gender mainstreaming and gender analysis have increased attention to relations between women and men, thereby suggesting ways in which improving relations between women and men may improve the well-being of both.

Rather than allowing the promotion of women's rights to suggest that it is "women versus others" or encouraging movements engaging only women for women, gender equality initiatives may engage men and women together within programs that benefit them all. These may foster collaboration and communication by women and men together, whether as family farms in Macedonia, as coleaders for super-cyclone drills in India, as protectors of natural resources, or as parents taking joint responsibility for the nutrition and well-being of their children. Rather than focusing on laws and State power, gender mainstreaming may focus attention on how women and men exercise power in relation to one another. Such approaches are oriented more toward people, relations, and what is critical in their daily lives than are rights- and law-focused approaches. While the objective may still be women's rights, the approach is inclusive; rather than suggesting a zero-sum game in which women win only as men lose, the ultimate goal suggests a win-win for all.

Finally, all too often, promoting women's rights fails to achieve long-lasting, deeply rooted, and widely accepted change. With rights-based approaches, laws can be overturned, courts can be moribund or corrupt, and enforcement can be reluctant, lax, or even obstructionist.[35] In contrast, efforts to build cultures of gender equality suggest more focused attention toward long-term impacts and sustainability.

THE U.S. ON THE WORLD STAGE

Look for the risks and drawbacks in what people
recommend —even the best medicine has side effects.

EBM Principle #4

Beyond determining which sorts of interventions may be most effective, the U.S must also consider the effectiveness of proactive, visible intervention (even when not fully "aggressive"). In seeking to do good, the U.S. must be cognizant of how it is regarded. In many respects, the U.S. has the opportunity to use its power, resources, and prestige to achieve laudable goals. Often, other nations and their people wish to have some of the lifestyle advantages enjoyed in the U.S. Many do respect and emulate some hallowed principles—from Constitutional protections of minorities to an economic environment that supports entrepreneurship and innovation. There was admiration and amazement around the globe when a man born to an American mother and African father, without either royal pedigree or millions in the bank, was able to become President of the United States.

However, while there have been some improvements in recent years, in the years following 9/11, the United States lost some of its credibility as a leader for human rights and rule of law. The lack of due process accorded prisoners held at Guantanamo; the U.S. treatment of prisoners at Abu Ghraib in disregard of the **Geneva Conventions**; the practice of *extraordinary rendition*; and the U.S. refusal to ratify such international treaties as the Convention to Eliminate Discrimination against Women (CEDAW), the Convention on the Rights of the Child, and the Rome Statute have undermined the power and legitimacy of U.S. calls to respect women's rights.[36]

At the same time, the rest of the world is often ambivalent about U.S. power. On the positive side, the world eagerly adopts some aspects of American culture, including McDonald's hamburgers, Levi's jeans, music, and technology. On the other hand, however, the U.S. way of doing things is often characterized as "foreign," "Western," or offensive—and thus flatly rejected as inappropriate. While it may not seem logical, opponents of women's rights are quick to use the "foreign" label to generate hostility.[37] Whereas they may be glad to accept other changes to their culture, they readily say that outsiders should not meddle with their culture regarding women's roles. Although there may be contradictions and purposeful manipulation by opponents of women's rights, if the U.S. wants to improve women's lives, it must recognize and address this political context.

What this means for U.S. policy, and in particular for promoting women's rights, is that aggressive, targeted actions may backfire. "Naming and shaming" by calling out leaders who are nationally and locally already recognized as violators of women's rights may not help local efforts—or worse, it may be counterproductive. Similarly, openly supporting leaders of gender equality or of women's organizations may put into question their independence and credibility. In fact, the promotion of women's needs and rights has spread throughout the world. As was demonstrated by participation at the International Conference on Population and Development (ICPD) in 1994, the Beijing Conference in 1995, and subsequent meetings to review implementation of their recommendations, women's organizations and women's rights advocates around the world are working to promote gender equality. They need to be able to promote change without being weakened by opponents' claims that they are doing the bidding of the U.S. or introducing culturally inappropriate change. Often, the more the United States is associated with rights and with pushing to change the treatment of women, the more strongly there is pushback. Recalling a key adage for humanitarian work, "Do no harm," it is important to recognize that forceful intervention by the U.S. may backfire, hurting national or local leaders and organizations striving to improve women's lives.

That does not mean, however, that the U.S. should take no action. Instead, it means that actions should be taken in two different ways: First, the U.S. should stand for women's rights worldwide by purposefully and consistently stating its commitment to women's rights and its concerns for the well-being of women and girls. This is what Secretary of State Hillary Clinton has done— in no uncertain terms and around the world. Yet U.S. expectations should be the same for *all* countries. By not targeting some with naming and shaming, the U.S. would also avoid making distinctions between Iran and Saudi Arabia (foe and friend) when both are responsible for appalling and widespread violations of women's rights.[38]

Second, regarding the need for targeted criticism of rights violators or support for gender equality, the U.S. should put its weight and resources behind multilateral mechanisms like the United Nations or the Organization for Security and Co-operation in Europe (OSCE). The U.S. should support the new UN Women,[39] which combines the four smaller agencies of the Division for the Advancement of Women (DAW), Office of the Special Adviser on Gender Issues Advancement of Women (OSAGI), **United Nations Development Fund for Women (UNIFEM),** and International Research and Training Institute for the Advancement of Women (INSTRAW)[40] as well as United Nations Population Fund (UNFPA), United Nations Children's Fund (UNICEF), the Organization of Economic Cooperation and Development (OECD), and the World Bank as they institutionalize gender mainstreaming and undertake gender equality initiatives.[41] While many advocates for women's rights and gender equality have questioned U.S. leadership for women's rights in international aid in the past, increased United States support would enable the U.S. to take its place among those who have provided consistent support to women's rights in the international arena (predominantly the Nordic countries, the Netherlands, Canada, and the U.K.), while working through international organizations would distinguish the message from the messenger and preclude rejection of pro-women messages simply because they come from the U.S.

SUPPORT WOMEN'S RIGHTS AND WELL-BEING THROUGH U.S. MANAGEABLE INTERESTS AND TAKING RESPONSIBILITY FOR IMPACTS

Beyond considering how the U.S. might influence other governments, actors, and initiatives, the U.S. has opportunities to support women's rights by looking inward rather than outward, assessing the impacts of U.S. policies and practices rather than those of other countries. The U.S. has many opportunities to promote gender equality (even for women outside the U.S.) by demonstrating how Americans value and respect women at home. The U.S. may model women's leadership, respect for women's contributions, and the benefits of gender equality in myriad situations, such as women serving as ambassadors or members of the President's cabinet, Fortune 500 companies touting the value of mixed leadership teams, U.S. states gaining from women governors working side-by-side with both male and female advisors, and U.S. women athletes performing in the Olympics. Similarly, American women scientists at international conventions and specialists in international agencies demonstrate the value of girls' and women's education.

Further, however, the U.S. has impacts on women around the world as a result of gender-neutral policies that may nevertheless have impacts on women. For example, trade policies that encourage free trade zones but omit any labor standards may result in women working in conditions and earning wages that violate their rights.[42] A gag rule affects women and men when it causes the withholding of support from organizations that help men and women to understand and manage their reproductive health and decisions. Immigration policies may keep husbands and wives or mothers and children separate. Agricultural policies make it difficult for family farms in Africa, many of which may be managed by husbands and wives and extended families working together to compete, and drive the men to earn wages in urban areas, leaving women behind to fend for themselves and their children alone. As was demonstrated by boycotts against South Africa to protest apartheid, the private sector may influence policies affecting women. There are many ways in which the U.S. may promote women's rights and gender equality by assessing our own policies, rather than focusing on laws and policies abroad.

CONCLUDING THOUGHTS

For those aiming to improve the status, well-being, and opportunities for women and girls around the world, there are some basic principles to follow:

- Be clear about the objective: is it legal rights or overall well-being?

- Before prescribing solutions, consider the causes of rights violations or the inability of women and girls to enjoy their rights.

- Approaches should be tailored rather than one-size-fits-all. Any initiatives should begin with gender analysis to achieve an understanding of women's and men's roles, responsibilities, and relations within a given society.

- Work should begin by connecting with thoughtful partners in each country or region and by engaging in a partnership of equals to explore options and debate strategies.

- Approaches that involve rights must anticipate that rights require legal systems to support them. If such systems are weak or nonexistent, then improving the situations of girls and women in the short term requires action in other arenas.

- U.S. efforts to lead with regard to women's rights should take into account how they will be perceived and whether they may inadvertently cause harm.

- Quick results, such as passing new laws, may look good in the short term but prove worthless if not sustainable. Sustainability requires time, ownership, and tailoring to local context, much like appropriate technologies.

- Achieving gender equality and respectful relations requires the involvement of men as well as women (and adolescent boys as well as adolescent girls).

- U.S. policymakers should assess their own laws and programs for whether they may undermine women's rights—or whether modifications might support the rights and opportunities of women in developing countries.

So should the U.S. be committed to assisting women whose rights are being violated? Yes, absolutely. But should the U.S. help women by "aggressively promoting women's rights in developing countries"? No. The objective is broader than promoting the legal manifestations of rights. The U.S. goal should use the normative foundations of women's rights to compel actions to improve women's lives, should be strategic, and should aim for sustainable gender equality that will benefit future generations of boys and girls.

NOTES

1. See the State Department's Office for Global Women's Issues at http://www.state .gov/s/gwi/index.htm for two 2011 speeches: "Asia Pacific Economic Cooperation Women and the Economy Summit" in San Francisco on Sept. 16th and "Women, Peace, and Security" at Georgetown University in Washington, DC on Dec. 19.

2. For a history of the women's conferences, see Peggy Antrobus, *The Global Women's Movement: Origins, Issues and Strategies* (London: Zed Books, 2004).

3. For more and details, see http://www.un.org/womenwatch/daw/csw/critical.htm

4. See, e.g., Susanne Gusten, "Turkish Charity Tells Battered Women How to Save their Lives—with a Gun," *NY Times*, January 18, 2012; Roni Caryn Rabin, "Nearly 1 in 5 Women in U.S. Survey Say They Have Been Sexually Assaulted," *NY Times*, December 13, 2011.

5. Section (g) of the definition of Crimes against Humanity specifies: "Rape, sexual slavery, enforced prostitution, forced pregnancy, enforced sterilization, or any other form of sexual violence of comparable gravity."

6. For 1325 and further information, see http://www.unifem.org/gender_issues/ women_war_peace/

7. "In all, 136 countries now have explicit guarantees for the equality of all citizens and nondiscrimination between men and women in their constitutions." *WDR Overview*, p.2

8. World Development Report 2012: Gender Equality and Development ("WDR") http://wdronline.worldbank.org//worldbank/a/c.html/world_development_ report_2012/abstract/WB.978-0-8213-8825-9.abstract

9. WDR, page xxi.

10. WDR, page 8.

11. See Luisita Lopez Torregrosa, "Progress for Women, but a Long Way to Go," *NY Times*, November 1, 2010.

12. http://blog.usaid.gov/category/cross-cutting-programs/

13. See, e.g., Nancy Trejos, "Women Lose Ground in the New Iraq," *The Washington Post*, December 16, 2006.

14. See, e.g., Ilene Prusher, "Turks Tangled in Politics of Scarves," *The Christian Science Monitor*, October 28, 2002; Sabrina Tavernise, "Turkey's Parliament Lifts Scarf Ban," *New York Times*, February 10, 2008.

15. See, e.g., Scott Baldauf, "Indians Crack Down on Gender Abortions," *Christian Science Monitor*, March 31, 2006, http://www.csmonitor.com/2006/0331/p07s02-wosc.html; Sen, AK, "Missing women," *BMJ* 304 (1992): 586–7; and Sen, AK, Editorial, *BMJ* 2003, 327 (December 6, 2003): 1297–1298.

16. Beyond attention commonly paid to Islam, there are fundamentalist threats to women's rights in other religions. See, e.g., Ethan Bronner and Isabel Kershner, "Israelis Facing a Seismic Rift Over Role of Women," *NY Times*, January 14, 2012, http://www.nytimes.com/2012/01/15/world/middleeast/israel-faces-crisis-over-role-of-ultra-orthodox-in-society.html (quoting Moshe Halbertal, a professor of Jewish philosophy at Hebrew University: "This is an immense ideological and moral challenge that touches at the core of life, and just as it is affecting the Islamic world, it is the main issue that the rabbis are losing sleep over."); Susan Berns, "Women's Rights are in Jeopardy Maintains Israel's Top Feminist," *The Jewish News Weekly*, April 4, 1997, http://www.jewishsf.com/ ("It is the religious courts, however, that cause real concern for Shalvi and the IWN. 'We have made no progress whatsoever,' Shalvi said, citing as particularly troublesome the areas of divorce and 'who is a Jew,' which in turn affects marriage, health and other family matters that are under the jurisdiction of the religious courts."). See also, Susan M. Shaw, "Gracious Submission: Southern Baptist Fundamentalists and Women," *NWSA Journal* 20, no.1 (September 2008): 51–77. http://muse.jhu.edu/login?uri=/journals/nwsa_journal/v020/20.1.shaw.html ("In 1979, fundamentalists began a movement to take control of the sixteen million-member Southern Baptist Convention. At the heart of their social agenda was the appropriate place of women in church, home, and society.")

17. See *New York Times* editorial of January 8, 2012: "Republicans versus Reproductive Rights." http://www.nytimes.com/2012/01/09/opinion/republicans-versus-reproductive-rights.html?emc=eta1

18. http://www.un.org/womenwatch/daw/cedaw/

19. Martha Nussbaum, *Women and Human Development: The Capabilities Approach* (Cambridge: Cambridge University Press, 2000).

20. She proposes the importance of ten "central human functional capabilities": (1) Life—being able to live to the end of a human life of normal length, (2) Bodily health—including nourishment, reproductive health, and shelter, (3) Bodily integrity—including the ability to move freely from place to place and to be free from violence, (4) Senses, Imagination, and Thought—in ways informed and cultivated by adequate education, (5) Emotions—including not having one's emotional development blighted by overwhelming fear and anxiety or by traumatic events or abuse or neglect, (6) Practical Reason, (7) Affiliation, (8) Other species—being able to live with concern for and in relation to animals, plants, and the world of nature, (9) Play—being able to laugh and enjoy recreation, and (10) Control over one's environment. Nussbaum, p. 72.

21. This is not at all to deny that in developed countries and richer countries, there are also setbacks (such as how the revolution in Egypt has increasingly targeted women and threatens them with substantial restrictions on their rights and how

ultraorthodox communities in Israel are flexing their muscles to restrict the rights of all Israeli women).

22. The Gender Inequality Index (GII) reflects women's disadvantage in three dimensions—reproductive health, empowerment, and the labor market—for as many countries as data of reasonable quality allow. The health dimension is measured by two indicators: maternal mortality ratio and the adolescent fertility rate. The empowerment dimension is also measured by two indicators: the share of parliamentary seats held by each sex and by secondary and higher education attainment levels. The labor dimension is measured by women's participation in the work force. The Gender Inequality Index is designed to reveal the extent to which national achievements in these aspects of human development are eroded by gender inequality and to provide empirical foundations for policy analysis and advocacy efforts.

23. Note that there are some countries for which data is not available, including Angola, Egypt, Ethiopia, Eritrea, Guinea, and Nigeria and Somalia.

24. Akua Kuenyehia, "Legal Literacy and the Law Enforcement Agencies in Ghana," *Legal Literacy: A Tool for Women's Empowerment*, edited by Margaret Schuler and Sakuntala Kadirgamar-Rajasingham, *UNIFEM* (1992): 301–312

25. For a range of programs addressing women's rights, see, e.g., American Bar Association, Rule of Law Initiative Gender Issues Program (http://www.abanet.org/rol/programs/gender-issues.html); Global Rights (http://www.hrlawgroup.org/); Human Rights Watch (http://www.hrw.org/women/); Open Society Institute's International Women's Program (http://www.soros.org/initiatives/women).

26. D. Trubek and M. Galanter, "Scholars in Self-Estrangement: Some Reflections on the Crisis in Law and Development Studies in the United States," *Wisconsin Law Review* 1974 (1975): 1062–1102. Note that in "Lessons Not Learned: Problems with Western Aid for Law Reform in Post-Communist Countries," Wade Channell argues that the rule of law "industry" continues to rely on those assumptions and follow the problematic paradigm. See Carnegie Papers #57, The Rule of Law Series, Democracy and Rule of Law Project, Carnegie Endowment for International Peace (May 2005).

27. And in some cases, the context is a "failed state," where there is little if any presence or power of a State and the situation is fundamentally lawless from a State-law perspective.

28. This brings to mind an analogy from Barbara Kingsolver's *Poisonwood Bible*: The missionary father, who is also a minister, seeks to plant seeds in his garden in Africa that had thrived in the U.S.—but the soil conditions were such that the seeds fail. So, too, "planting" rights in a legal system that lacks the fundamental conditions means that the rights, culture, and practices and protections are at risk of failing.

29. Lawrence Friedman and Stewart Macaulay, "Legal Culture and Social Development," (Law and Culture), *Law and the Behavioral Sciences* (1970): 1000–1017.

30. Where legal systems do offer meaningful recourse, however, there are two issues: First, do they reach demographic groups like rural populations or women for whom they are not meaningful? If not, they do not protect women's rights without determined attention to access. See Stephen Golub, "Beyond Rule of Law Orthodoxy: The Legal Empowerment Alternative," *Rule of Law Series*, Democracy and Rule of Law Project, Carnegie Endowment for International Peace, no. 41, October 2003. Second, in a world of limited resources, would resources focused on legal systems be more effective for women and girls if invested in different sorts of programs?

31. Introduction by Boutros Boutros-Bhali, UN Secretary General to the *Platform for Action and the Beijing Declaration*, Department of Public Information, New York: United Nations (1996), p. 1.

32. Agreed Conclusions 1997/2, 18 July 1997.

33. See http://www.unmillenniumproject.org

34. See WDR, p. 8–9.

35. And in some cases, the context is a "failed state," where there is little if any presence or power of a State and the situation is fundamentally lawless from a State-law perspective.

36. See also Adam Liptak, "U.S. Court, a Longtime Beacon, Is Now Guiding Fewer Nations," *New York Times*, September 18, 2008.

37. Leaders may also use U.S. involvement as a way of discrediting local wishes and initiatives, as has been the case in Iran, recently in Egypt regarding election preparations, or in Syria. See, e.g., Steven Lee Myers and David D. Kirkpatrick, "Egypt Vows to End Crackdown on Nonprofits," *NY Times*, December 30, 2011. One further example is how Putin blamed Hillary Rodham Clinton for demonstrations in Russia against fraudulent elections and Putin himself.

38. Admittedly there are direct tensions between the visibility necessary to ensure domestic constituencies that the U.S. government is taking action on behalf of women around the world and behind-the-scenes support preferred by local advocates.

39. In July 2010, the United Nations General Assembly created UN Women, the United Nations Entity for Gender Equality and the Empowerment of Women. "UN Women, among other issues, works for the elimination of discrimination against women and girls; empowerment of women; and achievement of equality between women and men as partners and beneficiaries of development, human rights, humanitarian action and peace and security." http://www.unwomen.org/

40. Division for the Advancement of Women (DAW), International Research and Training Institute for the Advancement of Women (INSTRAW), Office of the Special Adviser on Gender Issues and Advancement of Women (OSAGI), and United Nations Development Fund for Women (UNIFEM).

41. Attention is also being paid to gender by such newcomers at *The Economist* and the World Economic Forum. The World Economic Forum released a Global Gender Gap Index (GGI) in November 2011. It differs from the Human Development Report's GII in two ways: (1) Using different dimensions and indicators and (2) measuring gender gaps without taking into consideration a

country's level of development. The *Economist* Intelligence Unit has developed a Women's Economic Opportunity Index (WEOI) that focuses on laws and regulations about women's participation in the labor market and social institutions that affect women's economic participation. It used five dimensions—labor policies and practice, women's economic opportunity, access to finance, education and training, women's legal and social status, and general business environment. "Like the OECD's Social Institutions and Gender Index (SIGI), the WEOI complements the GII by helping us understand the underlying causes of gender inequalities in economic participation." http://hdr.undp.org/en/statistics/gii/ (FAQs)

42. For more information, see "African Women and Trade: Helping End Poverty in Africa" from the organization *Women Thrive Worldwide,* http://www.womensedge.org/index.php?option=com_content&task=view&id=391&Itemid=152

immigration

Should Countries Liberalize Immigration Policies?

YES: James F. Hollifield, *Southern Methodist University*

NO: Philip Martin, *University of California, Davis*

The vast majority of people live in the country in which they were born, with immigrants comprising 3.2 percent of total population, or 216 million in 2010. Yet international migration has expanded considerably in recent decades, from 81.5 million in 1970 to 175 million in 2000. Just over 48 percent of immigrants are women, and 7.6 percent of immigrants (or 16.3 million) are refugees. Among physicians, 4.2 percent are immigrants—over 336,000 worldwide—with more than 20,000 emigrating from India, 12,200 from the United Kingdom, and more than 8,000 each from the Philippines and Germany. Over 97 percent of physicians trained in Grenada and Dominica emigrate and over half in St. Lucia and Cape Verde.[1]

Many in the United States focus on immigration to the U.S., the world's largest recipient, and think of immigrants as mostly from Latin America. In fact, the majority of those who immigrate to the United States today do come from Latin America—it is expected that more than 38 million U.S. residents (12.5 percent of the population) are foreign born, including more than 11.5 million from Mexico, the largest source. (At the turn of the twentieth century, most immigrants were from northern and western Europe, with shifts early in the century to larger numbers from southern, eastern, and central Europe.) However, the Americas actually account for a relatively small portion of international migration today, as is evident in Figure 1 (p. 394).

The largest immigrant host nations include the United States, Russian Federation (much of which is to/from former Soviet republics), Germany, Saudi Arabia, and Canada (see Figure 2, p. 395). In some nations, such as Qatar, Monaco, and the United Arab Emirates, more than 70 percent of the population

Figure 1

Percentage Distribution of International Migrants by Region, 1970 and 2000

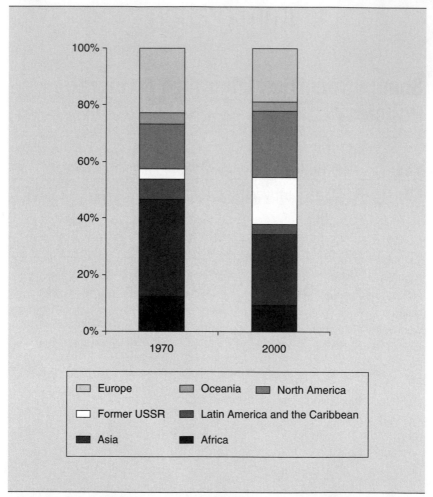

Source: UN Secretariat, *World Migration 2005: International Migration Data and Statistics* (New York: Department of Economic and Social Affairs, Population Division, 2005), 396.
Notes: (1) "Asia" excludes Armenia, Azerbaijan, Georgia, Kazakhstan, Kyrgyzstan, Tajikistan, Turkmenistan, and Uzbekistan. (2) "Europe" excludes Belarus, Estonia, Latvia, Lithuania, the Republic of Moldova, the Russian Federation, and Ukraine.

in 2010 is made up of immigrant populations that represent a critical source of labor. Other nations with more than half of their populations comprised of immigrants include Kuwait, Andorra, the Cayman Islands, the Northern

Figure 2

Top Ten Immigration Countries, 2010

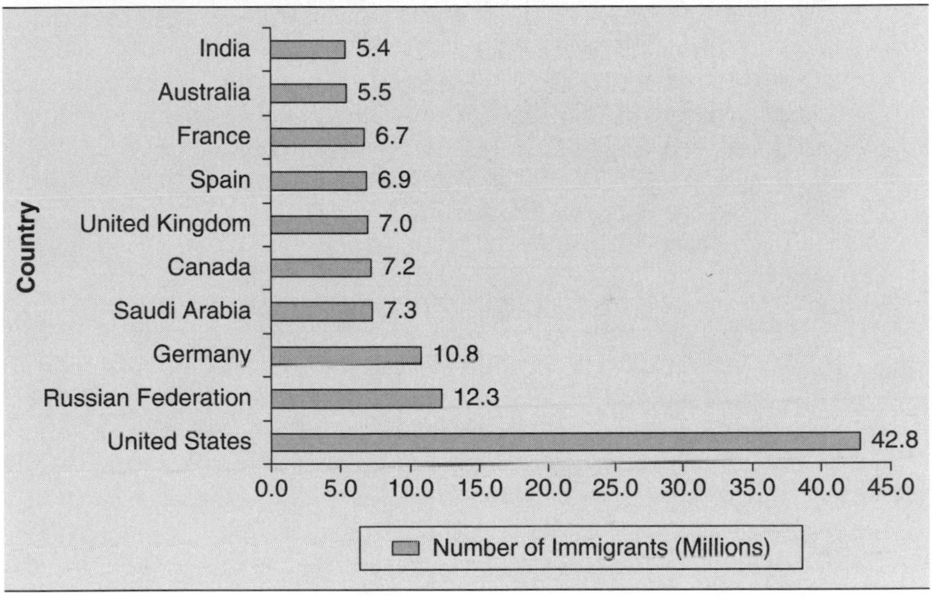

Source: World Bank, *Migration and Remittances Factbook*, 2011.

Mariana Islands, the U.S. Virgin islands, Macao, and the Isle of Man. The top emigrant nations are Mexico, India, and the Russian Federation in 2010, as measured by number of people (see Figure 3, p. 396); though as a percentage of the population, the largest emigrant regions include the West Bank and Gaza, Samoa, and Grenada, all at approximately two-thirds of their population. The largest migration corridors, excluding the former Soviet Union, include Mexico–US, Bangladesh–India, and Turkey–Germany; Figure 4 (p. 396) shows the top ten worldwide, five of them including the U.S.

Immigration and free trade are not often discussed simultaneously, but some of the same arguments can be marshaled to support and oppose each position, although the political fault lines are not typically consistent. The proposition that free trade brings prosperity can hold for immigration as well. While libertarians tend to support free movement of both capital and labor, political conservatives and liberals often disagree on issues of free trade (for which there is greater support among political conservatives) and free immigration (more support among political liberals). Nonetheless, many views of immigration policy stem from a pragmatic rather than a doctrinaire perspective, hinging, finally, on the perceived benefits and costs.

Figure 3

Top Ten Emigration Countries, 2010

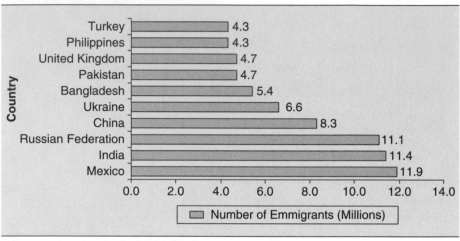

Source: World Bank, *Migration and Remittances Factbook*, 2011.

Figure 4

Top Ten Migration Corridors, Excluding the Former Soviet Union, 2010

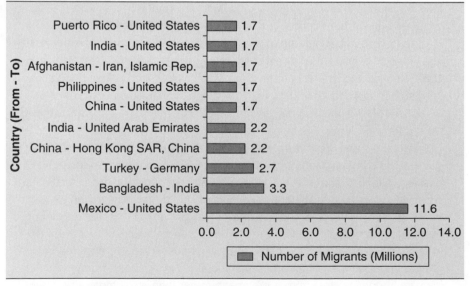

Source: World Bank, *Migration and Remittances Factbook*, 2011.
Note: SAR stands for special administrative region.

The perceived benefits of immigration are considerable. Even setting aside the important cultural enrichment (food, language, historical perspectives, and so on) offered by a diverse population, immigrants provide substantial economic and demographic advantages to host nations. Immigrants tend to be younger than native populations—a substantial boon to the aging populations of the wealthy West—and they often work in fields that are unacceptable to many natives, such as domestic assistance, construction, agriculture, and food services. Some of this work (such as janitorial service) is immovable, while some (including low-skilled manufacturing or assembly jobs) might easily be exportable to other nations were it not for immigrants willing to fill these positions. Therefore, liberal immigration policies can inhibit outsourcing by retaining jobs within the host country.

Also, because immigrants are younger, they improve the demographic profile of host nations—an important consideration in terms of public health care and pensions. Indeed, to a considerable extent, the United States is far better positioned than much of Europe and Japan—whose populations are considerably older—largely due to the influx of immigrants. The replacement ratio (the number of workers per retiree) is a key factor in the political and economic support for public pensions, and those nations with aging populations face considerable hurdles in maintaining generous support systems for retirees. Finally, many migrants send payments, or remittances, back home to the benefit of families left behind. Four nations—India, China, Mexico, and the Philippines—each received more than $20 billion in 2010 in remittances (see Figure 5, p. 398), while the top four remittance-sending countries were the United States ($48 billion), Saudi Arabia ($26 billion), Switzerland ($19.6 billion), and the Russian Federation ($18.6 billion) in 2009; see Figure 6 (p. 398) for additional details. For a number of developing countries, these remittances account for a significant proportion of their country's foreign exchange earnings; Tajikistan, Tonga, and Lesotho each receives more than 25 percent of its gross domestic product (GDP) from remittances, and the Philippines and Bangladesh receive 12 percent each. Total estimated inward remittance flows in 2010 were $325 billion in all developing nations and $440 billion worldwide.

On the other hand, immigration presents some serious challenges. In addition to the personal difficulties of mutual adjustment to new cultures, immigration is perceived as presenting economic, public health, and security challenges as well as forcing the host nation to confront and potentially adjust its national identity. Tensions arise when immigrants are perceived to take jobs from natives, often because of their willingness to work at lower pay, for longer hours, or in inferior conditions. However, most studies indicate that immigration,

Figure 5

Top Ten Remittance-Receiving Countries, 2010

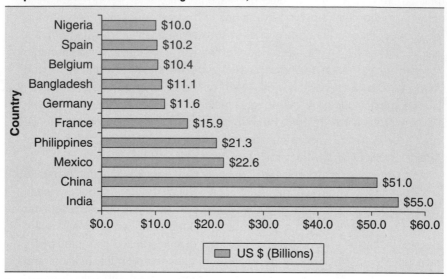

Source: World Bank, *Migration and Remittances Factbook*, 2011.

Figure 6

Top Ten Remittance-Sending Countries, 2009

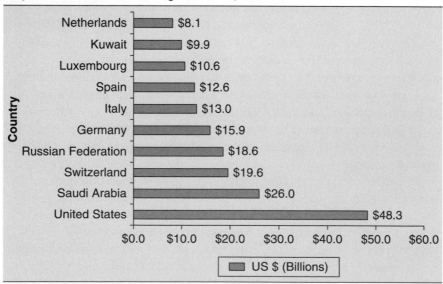

Source: World Bank, *Migration and Remittances Factbook*, 2011.

while it can sometimes cause economic dislocations, has a slightly positive or, at worst, a neutral impact on a host country's overall economic conditions.

The potential for exploitation—whether among Bangladeshi domestic servants in Saudi Arabia or among Mexican migrant farmers in the United States—is even more pronounced when migrants enter nations illegally. Furthermore, security considerations post-9/11 affect perceptions of immigration's impacts and drive policies that make residency and citizenship difficult for some subpopulations. Finally, there are impacts on the migrants' nations of origin, including concerns about a "**brain drain**" when highly educated emigrants leave developing nations for wealthy alternative destinations.

Immigration is inherently a political issue, as the movement of people becomes "immigration" only when it transcends a political boundary—that is, a national border. While Canada has the highest per capita net immigration in the world, the United States is the destination for the largest number of immigrants. One of the central immigration policy issues is how many immigrants a nation such as the United States should permit each year (recognizing the interrelationship between legal and illegal immigration). Another issue involves nations' policies for permitting entry and allowing foreigners to gain residency and citizenship. Countries such as Canada and Australia have used point systems based on potential economic contributions to their nations to assess potential immigrants, while the United States has made national origin and family ties the paramount considerations.

The impacts of immigrants (on both home and host countries) are considerable and complex, and therefore, their political impacts are complicated. Liberalization of immigration policy produces costs and benefits—for host nations and for the migrants themselves—that defy easy political categorization. The articles that follow take alternating positions on the desirability of liberalizing immigration policies worldwide. James Hollifield argues that the manner in which immigration is managed by powerful liberal states will determine whether society benefits from or is harmed by increased migration, and he urges broader international frameworks for managing migration. Philip Martin argues that immigration has very small economic impacts, and that most immigrants earn higher wages abroad but cannot climb the economic ladder. Thus, he suggests that the costs of change may exceed the perceived benefits of expanding immigration for host states.

Discussion Questions

1. What motivates people to emigrate from their home countries? What impact has globalization had on their motivations? Is there a link between free trade and immigration?

2. Many immigrants strive to retain their cultural traditions and beliefs rather than integrating fully into their new country's culture. Does this tendency bring benefits or costs to the new country? What other benefits or costs do immigrants bring to a society?

3. Many countries would like to curb illegal immigration. What are the challenges to doing so? What policies should be adopted to meet this goal?

4. What is the *liberal paradox*, as defined by James Hollifield? Is this something that states still struggle with or have they escaped from this dilemma? What policies or strategies have countries adopted to deal with the liberal paradox?

5. Philip Martin predicts that economically motivated migration is likely to increase in the future. What evidence does he cite to support his prediction? What impact does he say that immigrants have on the economy?

NOTE

1. World Bank, *Migration and Remittances Factbook,* 2011.

YES: James F. Hollifield, *Southern Methodist University*

INTRODUCTION

Today tens of millions of people cross borders on a daily basis. International mobility is part of a broader trend of globalization, which includes trade in goods and services, investments and capital flows, greater ease of travel, and a veritable explosion of information. While trade and capital flows are seen as the twin pillars of globalization, migration often is overlooked, especially among scholars of international relations (Hollifield 2008). Yet migration is a defining feature of the global era in which we live. Although it is linked in many ways to trade and investment, it is profoundly different. Some clever person once observed that "people are not shirts," which is another way of saying that labor is not a pure commodity. Unlike goods and capital, individuals can become actors on the international stage, whether through peaceful transnational communities or violent terrorist/criminal networks. Migration and mobility can be a threat to the security of states, as we have been reminded daily since the terrorist attacks of September 11, 2001; but migrants also are an asset. Immigrants bring human capital and new ideas and cultures to their host societies, and they come with a basic package of (human) rights that enables them eventually to become members of society, if not citizens, of their adoptive countries. Conversely, they may return to their countries of origin, where they can have a dramatic effect on economic and political development (Hollifield et al. 2007). And lest we forget, not all migration is voluntary—in any given year, millions of people move to escape political violence, hunger, and deprivation, becoming refugees, asylum seekers, or **internally displaced persons**. At the beginning of 2011, UN estimates put the global refugee population at 10.5 million—down considerably from the turbulent decade of the 1990s and trending slightly downward. The total population of concern to the UN High Commission for Refugees stands at almost 35 million, up slightly due to increases in the number of internally displaced persons. Because it is so complex and multifaceted, migration poses an enormous regulatory challenge for states and the international community.

How can we explain the rise in international migration and mobility when governments in every region of the globe are under pressure to limit the influx and reverse the flows? It might be tempting to argue that international migration is simply a function of the inexorable process of globalization. Demand for labor—both skilled and unskilled—is high in the principal receiving countries of North America, Europe, and Australia, and the supply of workers in Asia, Latin America, and Africa willing to fill this demand is unlimited. Demand-pull and supply-push forces seem to account rather well for the surge in international migration. Yet we know that individuals are risk averse and migration is fraught with risks—the transaction costs alone should be enough to deter most people from moving, and indeed, this is the case. Two hundred and fourteen million people live outside their country of birth, and this represents just over three percent of the world's population. Yet despite efforts to restrict migration, people are moving in increasing numbers, and in many receiving countries, there is a sense of crisis and loss of control. Sociologists and anthropologists have helped us to understand how individuals reduce the risks associated with migration (Massey et al. 2002). Individuals are more likely to migrate if they have friends or relatives in the destination country willing to help ease the process of transition. Social networks lower the transaction costs associated with emigration, making it less risky and connecting supply and demand, like two poles of a battery.

Is this the end of the story? If so, there would appear to be no room for the state in managing migration. Policy, some say (Sassen 1996), may be irrelevant, playing at best only a marginal role in the migration process, and the institutions of sovereignty and citizenship are increasingly outdated (Soysal 1994). According to this logic, we are entering a post-national era, and migration is redefining the international state system. I shall argue, however, that it is a mistake to eliminate the state from our analysis. *The necessary conditions for migration to occur may be social and economic, but the sufficient conditions are political and legal.* States must be willing to open their borders to the movement of people, and as people move, they can acquire rights. Immigration has profound political implications, and states are critical in shaping migration outcomes. I want to develop this argument in three steps: (1) we need to look at the causes and consequences of international migration, with an eye to understanding (2) how states have tried to manage migration and (3) the emergence of what I have termed the *migration state.* First, let us put the contemporary migration crisis into historical perspective.

THE GLOBAL MIGRATION "CRISIS"

Migration, like globalization, is *not* a new phenomenon. Throughout history, the movement of populations has been the norm. Only with the advent of the nation state in sixteenth- and seventeenth-century Europe did the notion of legally tying populations to territorial units (states) and to specific forms of government become commonplace. In the twentieth century, passport and visa systems developed and borders were increasingly closed to nonnationals (Torpey 1998). Almost every dimension of human existence—social-psychological, demographic, economic, and political—was reshaped to conform to the dictates of the nation state. The migration "crises" of the late twentieth century pale by comparison with the upheavals associated with the industrial revolution, the two world wars, and decolonization, which resulted in genocide, irredentism, the displacement of massive numbers of people, and the radical redrawing of national boundaries, not only in Europe but around the globe. This process was repeated with the end of the Cold War and the breakup of the Soviet Empire.

Myron Weiner (1995) argued that the increase in international migration in the postwar period posed a threat to international stability and security, especially in those areas of the globe where nation states are most fragile—the Balkans, Transcaucasia, the Middle East, the great lakes region of Africa, and Southern Africa. Weiner extended his argument to the western democracies, pointing out that the rise in xenophobic and nationalist politics in Western Europe showed that even the most advanced and tolerant democracies risk being destabilized politically by an influx of unwanted immigrants. Weiner postulated that there are limits on how many foreigners a society can absorb. Samuel Huntington of the "clash of civilizations" fame has argued that failure to control American borders is the single biggest threat to the national security of the United States (Huntington 1996; 2004). Weiner and Huntington echo the sentiments of Arthur Schlesinger, Jr. (1992) and others (Brimelow 1995), who fear that immigration and multiculturalism will lead to the "disuniting of America." In this line of reasoning, nation states are threatened by globalization from above and multiculturalism from below.

At the heart of the migration crisis are concerns about sovereignty, citizenship, national security, and identity. The ability or inability of a state to control its borders and hence its population is the *sine qua non* of sovereignty. With some notable exceptions—such as the international refugee regime created by the 1950 Geneva Convention in the aftermath of World War II—the right of a state to control entry and exit of persons to and from its territory is an undisputed principle of international law. But this political and legal principle immediately raises several questions: why are some states willing to accept rather high levels of immigration when it would seem not to be in their interest to do so (Hollifield 1992; Cornelius et al. 2004)? Does this influx pose a threat to the institutions of sovereignty and citizenship (Joppke 1998) and should we view migration primarily as an issue of sovereignty and national security (Rudolph 2006)?

MIGRATION AND GLOBALIZATION

In international relations theory, states are defined primarily by their security or military function. The **Westphalian state** is above all else a *garrison state*. Realists and neorealists (Waltz 1979) view the state as a unitary rational actor, with the overriding responsibility to maximize power, protect its territory and people, and pursue its national interest. Since the beginning of the industrial revolution in Europe, however, the state has taken on an increasingly important economic function. Ensuring material wealth and power has required states to risk greater economic openness and to pursue policies of free trade, giving rise to what Richard Rosecrance (1986) has called the *trading state*. As a result, states have been partially liberated from their dependence on territory and the military as sources of power. International relations theory has moved away from the narrow realist view of the state, recognizing that in an increasingly interdependent world, power is more diffuse (Keohane and Nye 1977). In this neoliberal view, states are linked together by international trade and finance, forcing them to alter their grand strategies and seek new ways to cooperate. I (Hollifield 2000) argue that migration and trade are inextricably linked—two sides of the same coin. Hence, the rise of the trading state necessarily entails the rise of the *migration state*, where considerations of power and interest are driven as much by migration (the movement of people, human capital, and manpower) as they are by commerce and finance.

For centuries, states have been in the business of organizing mass migrations for the purposes of colonization, economic development, and to gain a competitive edge in a globalizing economy. Recent attempts by states like Canada and Australia to recruit highly skilled foreign workers are but the latest chapter in the long history of globalization and migration. Looking at the eighteenth and nineteenth centuries—a period of relatively free migration—many states with open frontiers, like the United States and Russia, were happy to receive immigrants; whereas overpopulated societies, with a growing rural exodus and burgeoning cities, were happy to be rid of masses of unskilled and often illiterate peasants and workers.

By the early twentieth century, however, some of the traditional sending countries in Europe were well into the industrial revolution and entering a demographic transition, with falling birth rates and more stable populations. The great transatlantic migrations were drawing to a close (Nugent 1992), nationalism was on the rise, and it was increasingly important (in terms of military security) for states to be able to identify their citizens and to construct new demographic regimes (Koslowski 2000). The need to regulate national populations, for purposes of taxation and conscription, led to passport and visa systems and the concomitant development of immigration and naturalization policies (Torpey 1998). Every individual was expected to have one and only one nationality; and nationality, as a legal institution, would provide the individual with a measure of protection in a hostile and anarchic world of nation states. Countries of emigration, like Germany, tended to opt for nationality laws based upon *jus sanguinis* (blood, kinship, or ethnicity), whereas countries of immigration, like the United States and France, developed a more expansive political citizenship based upon *jus soli* (soil or birthplace). The German nationality law of 1913 had a strong ethnic component, and it was designed specifically to accommodate return migration; whereas birthright citizenship in the United States, as codified in the Fourteenth Amendment to the Constitution, was more inclusive (Brubaker 1989, 1992; Schuck 1998). It is important to remember that the Fourteenth Amendment was adopted in the aftermath of the Civil War, and its primary purpose was to grant immediate and automatic citizenship to former slaves (Kettner 1978). Moreover, American immigration policy in the late nineteenth and early twentieth centuries evolved along racial lines, culminating in the Chinese Exclusion Act of 1882 and the National Origins Quota system, enacted in 1924 (Smith 1997; King 2000).

Until 1914, international migration was driven primarily by the dynamics of colonization and the push and pull of economic and demographic forces (Hatton and Williamson 1998), even though receiving countries like the United States were struggling to put in place regulatory schemes to manage immigration (Tichenor 2002). Illegal or unauthorized immigration was not recognized as a major policy issue, and there were virtually no provisions for political migration (i.e., refugees and asylum seekers). To a large extent, efforts to regulate immigration would be rendered moot by the outbreak in 1914 of war in Europe, which stopped economic migration in its tracks. However, the Great War fostered the rise of intense and virulent forms of nationalism—often with a strong ethnic dimension.

War in Europe sparked irredentism and the redrawing of national boundaries, which in turn fostered new kinds of migration. Millions of displaced persons and refugees would cross national boundaries in the twentieth century to "escape from violence." (Zolberg, Suhrke, and Aguayo 1989). World War I marked a critical turning point in the history of migration and international relations. States would never return to the relatively open migration regimes of the eighteenth and nineteenth centuries, when markets (supply-push and demand-pull) were the driving force of international migration. Instead, the twentieth-century world would be increasingly closed, and travel would require elaborate documentation. World War I also marked the beginning of the end of imperialism, with struggles for independence and decolonization in Asia and Africa—movements that would eventually result in the displacement of millions more people.

In the interwar years, the Westphalian system of nation states hardened and became further institutionalized in the core countries of the Euro-Atlantic region, and it continued to spread around the globe with the creation of new states (or the reemergence of old ones) in Asia, Africa, and the Middle East. Old and new states guarded their sovereignty jealously, and peoples in every region gained a stronger sense of citizenship and national identity. Because of these developments, international migration took on more of a political character, with diaspora and exile politics coming to the fore. Henceforth, crossing borders had the potential of being a political as well as an economic act, and states reasserted their authority with a vengeance. The rise of antistate revolutionary movements, such as anarchism and communism, provoked harsh crackdowns on immigration and the rollback of civil rights and liberties in the name of national security and identity (Smith 1997; King 2000).

The events of the 1930s and 1940s in Europe radically changed legal norms governing international migration. The Holocaust and World War II led to the creation of the United Nations and a new body of refugee and human rights law. Although states retained sovereign control over their territory and the principle of noninterference in the internal affairs of others still holds, the postwar international order created new legal spaces (i.e., rights) for individuals and groups. The 1951 Geneva Convention Relating to the Status of Refugees established the principle of asylum, whereby an individual with a "well-founded fear of persecution," once admitted to the territory of a safe state, cannot be arbitrarily expelled or sent back to the state of his or her nationality. Under international law, the individual is entitled to a legal hearing; but it is important to remember that no state is compelled to admit an asylum seeker. If, however, the state is a signatory of the Convention, it cannot legally send an individual back to his or her country of origin if he or she is threatened with persecution and violence. This is the principle of *non-refoulement.*

The United Nations Charter as well as the Universal Declaration of Human Rights, which was adopted by the UN General Assembly in December 1948, reinforced the principle of the rights of individuals "across borders" (Jacobson 1996). Likewise, as a direct response to the Holocaust and other crimes against humanity, the international community in 1948 adopted and signed the Convention on the Prevention and Punishment of the Crime of Genocide. Alongside these developments in international law and politics, we can see a growing "rights-based liberalism" in the politics and jurisprudence of the most powerful liberal states in Europe and North America. These liberal developments in international and municipal law feed off of one another, creating new rights (legal spaces) for migrants at the international and domestic level (Hollifield et al. 2008).

Why are these legal developments so important? Unlike trade and financial flows, which can be promoted and regulated through international institutions like the World Trade Organization (WTO) and the International Monetary Fund (IMF), the movement of individuals across borders requires a qualitatively different set of regulatory regimes—ones based squarely on the notion of rights. It is almost a truism to point out that individuals, unlike goods, services, or capital, have a will of their own and can become subjects of the law and members of the societies in which they reside (Hollifield 1992; Weiner 1995). They also can become citizens of the polity (Koslowski 2000). The question is how far are states willing to go in establishing an international regime for the orderly (legal) movement of people, and to what extent would such a regime rely upon municipal as opposed to international law (Hollifield 2000)?

MANAGING MIGRATION IN A NEW ERA OF GLOBALIZATION

The last half of the twentieth century has marked an important new chapter in the history of globalization. With advances in travel and communications technology, migration has accelerated, reaching levels not seen since the end of the nineteenth century. With more than half the world's migrant population in the less-developed countries (LDCs), especially those rich in natural resources like oil, gold, or diamonds, the biggest challenge confronts states like South Africa or the United States, which share land borders with overpopulated and underdeveloped states. Supply-push forces remain strong while the ease of communication and travel have reinforced migrant networks, making it easier than ever before for potential migrants to gather the information that they need in order to make a decision about whether or not to move.

To some extent, supply-push forces are constant or rising and have been for many decades. Demand-pull forces are variable, however, both in the Organization of Economic Cooperation and Development (OECD) world and in the wealthier LDCs, many of which suffer from a shortage of skilled and unskilled labor. The oil sheikdoms of the Persian Gulf are perhaps the best examples, but increasingly, we have seen labor shortages in the newly industrialized countries (NICs) of East and Southeast Asia as well. Singapore, Malaysia, and Taiwan, for example, have become major importers of cheap labor from other LDCs in Southeast Asia, particularly the Philippines and Thailand.

With very few exceptions, however, these LDCs have not evolved elaborate laws or policies for managing migration. Wealthier LDCs have put in place contract or guest worker schemes, negotiated with the sending countries and with no provisions for settlement or family reunification. These types of pure manpower policies leave migrants with few if any rights, making them vulnerable to abuse and arbitrary expulsion. The only protections they have are those afforded by the negotiating power of their home countries, which may choose to protest the treatment of their nationals. But, more often than not, the sending countries are unwilling to provoke a conflict over individual cases of abuse for fear of losing access to remittances, which are one of the largest sources of foreign exchange for many LDCs (Hollifield, Orrenius, and Osang 2007). Hence, economics and demography (forces of supply-push and demand-pull) continue to govern much of international migration in the developing world. Summary deportations and mass expulsions are viable options for controlling immigration in these nonliberal states.

In the advanced industrial democracies, immigration has been trending upward for most of the post-World War II period to the point that well over forty percent of the world's migrant population resides in Europe and America, where roughly ten percent of the population is foreign born (Castles and Miller 1998). Postwar migration to the core industrial states of Europe and North America has gone through several distinct phases, which make these population movements quite different from the transatlantic migrations of the nineteenth century or economic migrations in the Third World today. The first wave of migration in the aftermath of World War II was intensely political, especially in Europe, where large populations were displaced as a result of the redrawing of national boundaries, irredentism, and ethnic cleansing. Much of the remaining Jewish population in Central Europe fled to the United States or Israel, whereas large ethnic German populations in East Central Europe flooded into the newly created Federal Republic of Germany. The partition of Germany, the Cold War, and the division of Europe contributed to the exodus of ethnic populations, seeking refuge in the democratic west. Until the construction of the Berlin Wall in 1961, twelve million German refugees arrived in West Germany.

Once this initial wave of refugee migration had exhausted itself and Europe began to settle into an uneasy peace that split the continent between the superpowers—thus cutting (West) Germany and other industrial states in Western Europe off from their traditional supplies of surplus labor in East Central Europe—new economic forms of migration began to emerge. The massive effort to reconstruct the war-ravaged economies of Western Europe in the 1950s quickly exhausted indigenous supplies of labor, especially in Germany and France. Like the United States, which launched a guest worker (*bracero*) program (1942–1964) during World War II to recruit Mexican agricultural workers (Calavita 1992), the industrial states of Northwest Europe concluded bilateral agreements with labor-rich countries in Southern Europe and Turkey, which allowed them to recruit millions of guest workers during the 1950s and 1960s (Hollifield 1992).

The guest worker phase ended in the United States with the winding down of the *bracero* program in the 1950s, whereas in Europe, it continued until the first signs of economic slowdown in 1966. However, the big shift in migration policy in Western Europe came in 1973–1974, following the first major oil shock and recession, which rapidly spread around the globe. European governments abruptly suspended all foreign worker recruitment and took steps to encourage "guests" to return home. Policies were put in place to discourage or, wherever possible, prevent settlement and family reunification. The prevailing sentiment was that guest worker migrations were primarily economic in nature and that these workers constituted a kind of economic shock absorber (*Konjunkturpuffer*). They were brought into the labor market during periods of high growth and low unemployment, and they should be sent home during periods of recession. In these circumstances of recession and rising unemployment, it seemed logical that guest workers should behave, like all commodities, according to the laws of supply and demand.

The difficulty of using guest workers for managing labor markets in Western Europe is a perfect illustration of what I call the *liberal paradox* (Hollifield 1992). States need labor for economic growth, hence the need for openness; but they need to maintain a degree of closure to protect the social contract and the institutions of sovereignty and citizenship. Importing labor to sustain high levels of noninflationary growth during the 1950s and 1960s was a logical move for states and employers. This move was in keeping with the growing trend towards internationalization of markets for capital, goods, services, and labor; and it was encouraged by international economic organizations, particularly the OECD. But, as the Swiss novelist, Max Frisch, pointed out at the time, the European governments had "asked for workers, but human beings came." Unlike goods or capital, migrants (qua human beings) can and do acquire rights, particularly under the aegis of the laws and constitutions of liberal states, which afford migrants a measure of due process and equal protection.

The settlement of large foreign populations transformed the politics of Western Europe, giving rise to new social movements and political parties demanding a halt to immigration (Givens 2005). Public opinion was by and large hostile to immigration, and governments were at a loss how to manage ethnic diversity (Lahav 2004; Messina 2007). Problems of integration began to dominate the public discourse, amid perceptions that Muslim immigrants in particular posed a threat to civil society and to the secular (republican) state. The fear was (and is) that dispossessed and disillusioned youth of the second generation would turn to radical Islam rather than following the conventional, secular, and republican path to assimilation (Klausen 2005). European societies looked increasingly like the United States, where older, linear conceptions of assimilation had given way to multiculturalism and an increasingly uneven or segmented incorporation, whereby large segments of the second generation, particularly among the unskilled and uneducated, experienced significant downward mobility (Hollifield 1997; Portes and Rumbaut 1996; Alba and Nee 2003; Messina 2007).

In spite of xenophobic pressures that were building in the last two decades of the twentieth century, European democracies maintained a relatively strong commitment to the international refugee and human rights regime; and in the 1980s and 1990s, asylum seeking became the principal avenue for entry into Western Europe, in the absence of full-fledged legal immigration policies and in the face of growing fears that large numbers of asylum seekers would undermine the refugee regime and destabilize European welfare states (Freeman 1986; Ireland 2004). In this atmosphere of crisis, control policies shifted in the 1990s to stepped up external (border) control—Operations Gatekeeper and Hold the Line on the U.S.–Mexican border and the Schengen system in Western Europe to allow states to turn away asylum seekers if they had transited a "safe third country"—internal regulation of labor markets (through employer sanctions and the like), and integrating large, established foreign populations (Brochmann and Hammar 1999; Cornelius et al. 2004).

Controlling borders in Europe required a renewed emphasis on international cooperation, especially among the member states of the European Community (EC). The EC (soon to become the European Union [EU]) was committed to building a border-free Europe, relaxing and eventually eliminating all internal borders in order to complete the internal market. This process of integration was given new impetus by the Single European Act of 1986—which called for the elimination of all barriers to the movement of capital, goods, services, and people within the territory of the EC by January 1992—and by the **Maastricht Treaty** on Economic and Monetary Union (EMU), which, ratified in 1993, established a new kind of European citizenship (Geddes 2003). Given the desire of member states to stop further immigration, creating a border-free Europe meant reinforcing external borders, building a "ring fence" around the common territory, and moving towards common asylum and visa policies.

A series of conventions dealing with migration and security issues were drafted to help construct a new European migration regime, including the Schengen Agreement of 1985, whereby EU governments committed themselves to eliminating border checks, in exchange for common visa requirements to control the movement of third-country nationals (TCNs). In the same vein, the Dublin Convention of 1990 required asylum seekers to apply for asylum in the first "safe country" where they arrive. Schengen and Dublin helped to establish buffer states in the formerly communist countries of Central Europe. EU member states could return asylum seekers to these now-safe third countries, without violating the principle of non-refoulement. The Dublin and Schengen Conventions also were designed to eliminate "asylum shopping" by requiring signatory states to accept the asylum decision of other member states. Thus an asylum seeker is permitted to apply for asylum in only one state, assuming he or she did not transit a safe third country before arriving on the common territory.

Project 1992, together with the Maastricht process, launched the most ambitious program of regional integration and economic liberalization in European history. But just as this process was taking off in 1989–1990, the strategic situation in Europe was turned upside down with the end of the Cold War and the collapse of the USSR and its communist satellites in East Central Europe. This change in the international system, which had begun in the 1980s during the period of glasnost under Mikhail Gorbachev, made it easier for individuals wishing to emigrate from the east to leave and seek asylum in the west. The result was a dramatic increase in the number of asylum seekers in Western Europe, not just from Eastern Europe, but from all over the world.

International migration had entered a new phase in the 1980s and 1990s, with refugee migration and asylum seeking reaching levels not seen since the period just after World War II. The situation in Europe was further complicated by a resurgence of ethnic nationalism, by war in the Balkans, and by a dramatic increase in the number of refugees from almost every region of the globe. By the mid-1990s, there were over 16 million refugees in the world, with two-thirds of them in Africa and the Middle East. The UN system for managing refugee migration, which had been created during the Cold War primarily to accommodate those fleeing persecution under communist rule, suddenly came under enormous pressure (Teitelbaum 1980; Gibney 2004). The **United Nations High Commission for Refugees (UNHCR)** was transformed virtually overnight into one of the most important international institutions. The UNHCR was thrust into the role of managing the new migration crisis, as the Western democracies struggled to contain a wave of asylum seeking. The claims of the vast majority of those seeking asylum in Western Europe and the United States would be rejected, leading Western governments (and their publics) to the conclusion that most asylum seekers are in fact economic refugees. By the same token, many human rights advocates feared that genuine refugees would be submerged in a tide of false asylum seeking.

Whatever conclusion one draws from the high rate of rejection of asylum claims, the fact is that refugee migration surged in the last two decades of the twentieth century, creating a new set of dilemmas for liberal states (Gibney 2004). A large percentage of those whose asylum claims were refused would remain in the host countries either legally—pending appeal of their cases—or illegally, simply going underground. With most of the European democracies attempting to slow or stop all forms of *legal* immigration, the number of *illegal* immigrants—many of whom are individuals who entered the country legally and overstayed their visas—has increased steadily. Closing off avenues for legal immigration in Western Europe led to a surge in illegal migration. But with the perception among Western publics that immigration is raging out of control, and with the rise of right wing and xenophobic political parties and movements, especially in Western Europe, governments are extremely reluctant to create new programs for legal immigration or to expand existing quotas.

Instead, the thrust of policy change in Western Europe and the United States has been in the direction of further restriction. To give a few examples, Germany in 1993 amended its constitution in order to eliminate the blanket right of asylum that was enshrined in Article 16 of the old Basic Law. France in 1995–1996 enacted a series of laws (the Pasqua and Debré Laws) that were designed to roll back the rights of foreign residents and make it more difficult for immigrants to naturalize (Hollifield 1997; Brochmann and Hammar 1999). Also in 1996, the Republican Congress enacted the Illegal Immigration Reform and Immigrant Responsibility Act, which curtailed social or welfare rights for all immigrants (legal as well as illegal) and severely limited the due process rights of illegal immigrants and asylum seekers.

At the same time that the U.S. Congress was acting to limit immigrant rights, it took steps to expand legal immigration, especially for certain categories of highly skilled immigrants. The H-1B program, which gave American businesses the right to recruit foreigners with skills that were in short supply among native workers, was expanded in the 1990s. In France in 1997 and in Germany in 1999, laws were passed to liberalize naturalization and citizenship policy (Hollifield 1997). Most European governments accepted the reality of immigration. Moreover, with stagnant or declining populations and a shortage of highly skilled workers, European governments have enacted new recruitment programs, seeking to emulate some aspects of American and Canadian immigration policy and make their economies more competitive in a rapidly globalizing world.

How can we make sense of these seemingly contradictory trends? Have states found ways of escaping from the liberal paradox, or are they still caught between economic forces that propel them toward greater openness (to maximize material wealth and economic security) and political forces that seek a higher degree of closure (to protect the *demos*, maintain the integrity of the community, and preserve the social contract)? This is a daunting task—for states to find the appropriate equilibrium between openness and closure—and these states also face the very real threat of terrorism. The attacks of September 11, 2001, on the United States served as a reminder that the first responsibility of the state is to provide for the security of its territory and population.

THE EMERGING "MIGRATION STATE"

International migration is likely to increase in coming decades, unless there is some cataclysmic international event such as war or economic depression. Even the 9/11 terrorist attacks on the United States and the ensuing "war on terrorism" has not led to a radical closing of borders. Global economic inequalities mean that supply-push forces remain strong, while at the same time demand-pull forces are intensifying. The growing demand for highly skilled workers and the demographic decline in the industrial democracies create economic opportunities for migrants in the industrial democracies. Transnational networks have become more dense and efficient, linking the sending and receiving societies. These networks help to lower the costs and the risks of migration, making it easier for people to move across borders and over long distances. Moreover, when legal migration is not an option, migrants have increasingly turned to professional smugglers, and a global industry of migrant smuggling— often with the involvement of organized crime—has sprung up. Hardly a week passes without some news of a tragic loss of life associated with migrant smuggling (Kyle and Koslowski 2001).

Regulating international migration requires liberal states to be attentive to the (human or civil) rights of the individual. If rights are ignored or trampled upon, the *liberal* state risks undermining its own legitimacy and *raison d'être*. As international migration and transnationalism increase, pressures build upon liberal states to find new and creative ways to cooperate, to manage flows. The definition of the national interest and *raison d'Etat* have to take this reality into account as rights become a central feature of domestic and foreign policy. New international migration regimes will be necessary if states are to risk more openness, and rights-based (international) politics will be the order of the day.

Some politicians and policymakers, as well as international organizations, continue to hope for market-based/economic solutions to the problem of regulating international migration. Trade and foreign direct investment—bringing capital and jobs to people, either through private investment or official development assistance—it is hoped, will substitute for migration, alleviating both supply-push and demand-pull factors. Even though trade can lead to factor-price equalization in the long term, as we have seen in the case of the European Union (Straubhaar 1988), in the short- and medium term, exposing LDCs to market forces often results in increased (rather than decreased) migration, as is evident with the North American Free Trade Agreement (NAFTA) and the U.S.–Mexican relationship (Martin 1993; Massey et al. 2002; Hollifield and Osang 2005). Likewise, trade in services can stimulate more "high end" migration, because these types of products often cannot be produced or sold without the movement of the individuals who make and market them (Bhagwati 1998; Ghosh 1997).

In short, the global integration of markets for goods, services, and capital entails higher levels of international migration; therefore, if states want to promote freer trade and investment, they must be prepared to manage higher levels of migration. Many states (like Canada, Australia, and Germany) are willing, if not eager, to sponsor high-end migration, because the numbers are manageable, and there is likely to be less political resistance to the importation of highly skilled individuals. However, mass migration of unskilled and less educated workers is likely to meet with greater political resistance, even in situations and in sectors such as construction or health care, where there is high demand for this type of labor. In these instances, the tendency is for governments to go back to the old guest worker models, in hopes of bringing in just enough temporary workers to fill gaps in the labor market but with strict contracts between foreign workers and their employers that limit the length of stay and prohibit settlement or family reunification. The alternative is illegal immigration and a growing black market for labor—a Hobson's choice.

The nineteenth and twentieth centuries saw the rise of what Richard Rosecrance (1986) has labeled the *trading state*. The latter half of the twentieth century has given rise to the *migration state*. In fact, from a strategic, economic, and demographic standpoint, trade and migration go hand in hand; because the wealth, power, and stability of the state is now more than ever dependent on its willingness to risk both trade and migration (Hollifield 2004). In launching a new "blue card" program to attract highly skilled foreign workers, the European Union is clearly seeking to emulate the United States and Canada, on the premise that global competitiveness, power, and economic security are closely related to a willingness to accept immigrants.

Now more than ever, *international security and stability are dependent on the capacity of states to manage migration*. It is extremely difficult, if not impossible, for states to manage migration either unilaterally or bilaterally. Some type of multilateral/regional regime is required, similar to what the EU has constructed for nationals of the member states. The EU model, as it has evolved from Rome to Maastricht to Amsterdam and beyond, points the way to future migration regimes, because it is not based purely on *homo economicus* but incorporates rights for individual migrants and even a rudimentary citizenship, which continues to evolve. The problem, of course, in this type of regional migration regime is how to deal with third country nationals.

In the end, the EU, by creating a regional migration regime and a kind of supranational authority to deal with migration and refugee issues, allows the member states to finesse, if not escape, the liberal paradox (Geddes 2003). Playing the good cop/bad cop routine and using symbolic politics and policies to maintain the illusion of border control help governments fend off the forces of closure, at least in the short run (Rudolph 2006). In the end, however, it is the nature of the liberal state itself and the degree to which openness is institutionalized and (constitutionally) protected from the "majority of the moment" that will determine whether states will continue to risk trade and migration (Hollifield 2008; Hollifield et al. 2007).

Regional integration reinforces the trading state and acts as a midwife for the migration state and blurs the lines of territoriality, lessening problems of integration and national identity. The fact that there is an increasing disjuncture between people and place—which in the past might have provoked a crisis of national identity and undermined the legitimacy of the nation state—is less of a problem when the state is tied to a regional regime like the EU. This does not mean, of course, that there will be no resistance to freer trade and migration. Protests against globalization and nativist or xenophobic reactions against immigration have been on the rise throughout the OECD world. Nonetheless, regional integration—especially when it has a long history and is deeply institutionalized as it is in Europe—makes it easier for states to risk trade and migration and for governments to construct the kinds of political coalitions that will be necessary to support and institutionalize greater openness.

Mexican leaders, like former Presidents Raul Salinas de Gortari and Vicente Fox, looked to Europe as a model for how to solve problems of regional integration, especially the very delicate political issue of illegal Mexican immigration to the United States. Their argument is that freer migration and a more open (normalized) border are logical extensions of the North American Free Trade Agreement (NAFTA). But the U.S. has been reluctant to move so fast with economic and political integration, especially after the attack of September 11, 2001, preferring instead to create new guest worker

programs or to continue with the current system, which tolerates high levels of unauthorized migration from Mexico (Massey et al. 2002). Clearly,
however, North America is the region that is closest to taking steps towards
an EU-style regional migration regime, and the U.S. is facing the prospect
of another amnesty comparable to the one carried out as part of the 1986
Immigration Reform and Control Act. In the long run, it is difficult for liberal states, like the U.S., to sustain a large, illegal population. For this reason,
amnesties, legalizations, or regularizations have become a common feature of
the migration state.

Even though there are large numbers of economic migrants in Asia, this
region remains divided into relatively closed and often authoritarian societies, with little prospect of granting rights to migrants and guest workers. The
more liberal and democratic states, like Japan, Taiwan, and South Korea, are the
exceptions; but they have only just begun to grapple with the problem of immigration, on a relatively small scale (Cornelius et al. 2004). In much of Africa
and the Middle East, which have high numbers of migrants and refugees, there
is a great deal of instability, and states are fluid with little institutional or legal
capacity for dealing with international migration.

In conclusion, we can see that migration is both a cause and a consequence
of globalization. International migration, like trade, is a fundamental feature
of the postwar liberal order. But as states and societies become more open,
migration has increased. Will this increase in migration be a virtuous or a
vicious cycle? Will it be destabilizing, leading the international system into
greater anarchy, disorder, and war; or will it lead to greater openness, wealth,
and human development? Much will depend on how migration is managed
by the more powerful liberal states, because they will set the trend for the
rest of the globe. To avoid a domestic political backlash against immigration, the rights of migrants must be respected and states must cooperate
in building an international migration regime. I have argued that the first,
halting steps towards such a regime have been taken in Europe, and that
North America is likely to follow. As liberal states come together to manage
this extraordinarily complex phenomenon, it may be possible to construct
a truly international migration regime. But I am not sanguine about this
opportunity in the short term because the asymmetry of interests, particularly between the developed and the developing world, is too great to permit
states to overcome problems of coordination and cooperation. Even as states
become more dependent on trade and migration, they are likely to remain
trapped in a liberal paradox, needing to be economically open and politically closed, for decades to come.

NO: Philip Martin, *University of California, Davis*

MIGRATION AND LABOR

International migrants, people who move from one country to another for a year or more, are the exception, not the rule. The United Nations estimated 214 million international migrants in 2010, meaning that 3 percent of the world's people left their country of birth or citizenship for a year or more— a very inclusive definition that embraces naturalized citizens (such as Henry Kissinger), legal immigrants, and long-term visitors (such as foreign students and unauthorized migrants).[1] About 20 percent of the world's migrants—almost 40 million—are in the United States.

Most people never leave the country in which they were born. However, international migration for employment is increasing. Most migrant workers move from poorer developing countries to richer industrial countries, and more want to move.[2] Almost 20 percent, or 600 million, of the world's workers are in the industrial countries, leaving 2.5 billion workers and almost all labor force growth in developing countries. The sheer force of numbers suggests that most new workers in developing countries will have to find jobs there. Between 2007 and 2020, industrial-country labor forces are expected to remain at about 600 million, while developing-country labor forces expand by 500 million— making the *growth* in developing-country work forces almost equal to the current industrial-country labor force.

Not all migrant workers settle in the country in which they work. For example, a million Filipinos a year leave for overseas jobs, but there are fewer than 3 million Filipino contract workers abroad, meaning that many return after two or three years abroad.

Table 1

International Migrants in 2010 (millions)

Origin	Destination	
	Industrial	Developing
Industrial	55	13
Developing	73	74
Total	128	87

Source: UN Population Division. 2010. *International Migration Report.*

Here I will explore current global migration patterns and issues, explaining why economically motivated migration is likely to increase, examining the effects of migration on labor-sending and labor-receiving countries, and concluding that countries can adjust to the presence or absence of additional migrants. The most important policy challenge is to avoid allowing migration policy to shift from a national interest to a special interest, as occurred when the United States restricted imports of sugar from Caribbean islands in the 1950s and then allowed Florida sugarcane growers to import cane-cutters from Jamaica.[3] Finally, I will consider how these conclusions relate to the debate on liberalizing immigration policies. Advocates of liberalization argue that immigration speeds economic growth. More immigrants do produce a larger economy, but the net economic benefits of immigration in migrant-receiving countries are very small.

DIFFERENCES MOTIVATE MIGRATION

Migration is the movement of people from one place to another. Migration is as old as humankind wandering in search of food, but international migration is a relatively recent development, since it was only in the early twentieth century that the system of nation states, passports, and visas developed to regulate the flow of people over national borders.[4]

The No. 1 form of migration control is inertia—most people do not want to move away from family and friends. The second form involves governments, who have significant capacity to regulate migration, and they do so with passports, visas, and border controls. One item considered by many governments when deciding whether to recognize a new entity that declares itself a nation state is whether it is able to regulate who crosses and remains within its borders.

Nonetheless, international migration is likely to increase in the twenty-first century for reasons that range from persisting demographic and economic inequalities to revolutions in communications and transportation that increase mobility. There are also more borders to cross. There were 193 generally recognized nation states in 2000, four times more than the 43 that existed in 1900.[5] Each nation state distinguishes citizens and foreigners, has border controls to inspect those seeking entry, and determines what foreigners can do while inside the country, whether they are tourists, students, guest workers, or immigrants.

Most countries discourage immigration, meaning that they do not anticipate the arrival of foreigners who want to settle and become naturalized citizens. Some also discourage emigration, as when Communist nations tried to prevent their citizens from fleeing to the West during the Cold War—as symbolized by the Berlin Wall between 1961 and 1989—and the continuing effort of North Korea to keep its citizens from leaving.

Five countries plan for a significant annual inflow of immigrants: the United States (which accepts about 1.2 million immigrants a year), Canada (250,000), Australia (125,000), New Zealand (50,000), and Israel (25,000). The number of newcomers arriving in industrial countries exceeds this planned total of 1.5 million a year, suggesting that many newcomers are temporary visitors or unauthorized foreigners.

There are two extreme perspectives on the rising number of migrants in industrial countries. At one extreme, the *Wall Street Journal* advocates a five-word amendment to the U.S. Constitution: "There shall be open borders."[6] Organizations ranging from the Catholic Church to the World Bank have called for more migration, arguing that people should not be confined to their countries of birth by man-made national borders and that more migration would speed economic growth and development in both sending and receiving countries.

At the other extreme, virtually every industrial country has organizations such as the Federation for American Immigration Reform (FAIR) and Numbers USA that call for sharp reductions in immigration on the economic and social grounds that unskilled newcomers especially disadvantage low-skilled native workers, that increasing numbers of people have negative environmental effects, and that those from different cultures threaten established norms. Many European countries have political parties that call for reducing immigration, such as the National Front in France, which proposed removing up to 3 million non-Europeans from France during the 1995 presidential campaign, mainly in order to reduce the number of Muslim residents.[7]

Amid regular reports of migrants dying in deserts and drowning at sea, some pundits see governments as powerless to manage international migration, for migrants seem determined to go over and under the walls that try to keep them out. The late President Boumedienne of Algeria appealed for more foreign aid on behalf of the Group of 77 developing countries, warning that if industrial countries did not respond, "no quantity of atomic bombs could stem the tide of billions . . . who will someday leave the poor southern part of the world to erupt into the relatively accessible spaces of the rich northern hemisphere looking for survival."[8]

Most people do not want to migrate to another country: international migrants make up 3 percent of the world's residents, not 30 percent. Furthermore, economic growth can turn emigration source nations into destinations for migrants within decades, as it has done in Ireland, Italy, and Korea. The challenge is to speed up such migration transitions and to manage migration so as to reduce the differences that encourage people to cross borders over time. Planned immigration can produce socioeconomic dividends, but unplanned mass migration can be manipulated by special interests seeking cheap labor or more people from particular countries.

WHY PEOPLE MIGRATE

International migration is usually a carefully considered individual or family decision. The major reasons to migrate to another country can be grouped into two categories—economic and noneconomic—while the factors that encourage a migrant to actually move fall into three categories: demand-pull, supply-push, and networks. An economic migrant may be encouraged to move by employer recruitment of guest workers (a demand-pull factor), while migrants crossing borders for noneconomic reasons may be moving to escape unemployment or persecution (supply-push factors).

For example, a worker in rural Mexico may decide to migrate to the United States because a friend or relative tells him of a job, highlighting the availability of higher-wage jobs as a demand-pull factor encouraging a person to cross a national border. The worker may not have a regular job at home or may face debts from a family member's medical emergency, examples of supply-push factors that encourage emigration. Networks encompass everything from the moneylenders who provide the funds needed to pay a smuggler to cross the border to employers or friends and relatives at the destination who help migrants find jobs and places to live.

Demand-pull, supply-push, and network factors rarely have equal weight in an individual's decision to migrate, and their respective weights can change over time. Generally, demand-pull and supply-push factors are strongest at the beginning of a migration flow, while network factors become more important as migration streams mature.

The first migrant workers of a given migration stream are often recruited. For example, the U.S. government sent recruiters to rural Mexico in the 1940s to encourage Mexicans to move to the United States to fill jobs on U.S. farms. Many of these migrants then returned home with savings, encouraging more Mexicans to seek U.S. jobs and fueling unauthorized migration. Network factors ranging from settled friends and relatives to the expectation that young men, in particular in rural areas, should "go north for opportunity" sustained migration between rural Mexico and rural America after the Mexico–U.S. *bracero* program ended in 1964. A similar process played out in Western Europe, where governments stopped recruiting Turks and other southern European guest workers in 1973–1974, but others from those countries continued to arrive under family unification laws or came to France or Germany and asked not to be sent home to face persecution.

One of the most important noneconomic motivations for crossing national borders is family unification—the desire of a father settled abroad to have his wife and children join him. In such cases, the anchor immigrant is a demand-pull factor for family migration, and the immediate family may be followed by parents and brothers and sisters, creating a *chain migration.*

Globalization has made people everywhere more aware of conditions and opportunities abroad. Tourism has become a major industry as people cross national borders to experience new cultures, different weather, or the wonders of nature. Many young people find a period of foreign study or work experience enriching, and this initial exposure encourages them to migrate. In some cases, former colonies have become independent nations, but traditional migration patterns persist, as between India and Pakistan and the United Kingdom or between the Philippines and the United States.

Immigration policies aim to facilitate wanted migration, such as tourism, and deter unwanted migration, including those who arrive on tourist visas and do not depart as scheduled. However, it is often hard for inspectors at ports of entry to distinguish between legitimate and illegitimate migrants. Who is a legitimate tourist and who is a potential unauthorized worker? Most countries require visas from foreigners wishing to enter and maintain consulates abroad to screen potential visitors to determine if they truly intend to return home. At many U.S. consulates around the world, most applicants for tourist visas are rejected.

DIFFERENCES AND LINKAGES

Globalization has increased linkages between countries, as evidenced by sharply rising flows of goods and capital over national borders and by the growth of international and regional bodies to set rules for such movements. However, although controlling the entry and sojourn of travelers is a core attribute of national sovereignty, flows of people are not governed by a comprehensive global migration regime. Most nation states do not welcome newcomers as immigrants, but almost all of the industrial or high-income countries have guest-worker programs that allow local employers to recruit and employ temporary foreign workers. Many also have significant numbers of unauthorized or irregular migrant workers.

Most of the world's people—and most of its population growth—are to be found in developing countries. The world's population, which reached seven billion in October 2011, is growing by 1.2 percent (84 million a year), and 97 percent of that growth occurs in developing countries.[9] In the past, significant demographic differences between areas prompted large-scale migration. For example, as Table 2 (p. 422) shows, Europe had 21 percent of the world's almost one billion residents in 1800, and the Americas had 4 percent. When there were five Europeans for every American, millions of Europeans emigrated to North and South America in search of economic opportunity as well as religious and political freedom.

Will history repeat itself? Africa and Europe have roughly equal populations today, but by 2050, Africa is projected to have three times more residents than Europe (see Table 2, p. 422). If Africa remains poorer than Europe, the two

Table 2

World Population by Continent, 1800–2050

	1800	1999	2050
World (in millions)	978	5,978	8,909
Percentage shares:			
Africa	11	13	20
Asia	65	61	59
Europe	21	12	7
Latin America and Caribbean	3	9	9
North America	1	5	4
Oceania	0	1	1

Source: United Nations, "The World at Six Billion," 1999, Table 2, http://www.un.org/esa/population/publications/sixbillion/sixbillion.htm.

Note: Figures for 2050 are approximate.

continents' diverging demographic trajectories may propel young people to move from overcrowded cities such as Cairo and Lagos to Berlin and Rome, where there may be empty apartments.

The economic differences that encourage international migration have two dimensions, one fostered by inequality *between* countries and the other by inequality *within* countries. The world's almost 200 nation states had per capita incomes, according to the World Bank, that ranged in 2010 from less than $500 per person per year in sub-Saharan countries such as Burundi to more than $85,000 in Norway—a difference that provides a significant incentive for young people especially to migrate in search of higher wages and more opportunities.[10]

The thirty high-income countries had 1.1 billion residents in 2010, over a seventh of the world's population, while their gross national income was $43 trillion, which was 80 percent of the global total of $62 trillion.[11] The resulting average per capita income of $39,000 in high-income countries was nearly 12 times the average $3,300 in low- and middle-income countries (see Table 3, p. 423). Furthermore, despite rapid economic growth recently in China and some other developing countries, the gap between per capita incomes in high- and low-income countries has been increasing.

A second dimension to economic inequality between nation states adds to international migration pressures. The world's labor force of 3.1 billion in 2005 included 600 million workers in the high-income countries and 2.5 billion in the lower-income countries. Almost all growth in this area between 2005 and 2015 is projected to occur in lower-income countries, whose labor force is projected to increase by about 425 million, while the labor force in high-income countries is projected to remain stable at just over 600 million.

Table 3

Global Migrants and Per Capita Income Gaps, 1975–2010

	Migrants (millions)	World Population (billions)	Migrants as % of World Population	Annual Migrant Increase (millions)	Countries Grouped by Per Capita GDP ($)			Ratio High-Low	Ratio High-Mid
					Low	Middle	High		
1975[a]	85	4.1	2.1%	1	150	750	6,200	41	8
1985	105	4.8	2.2%	2	270	1,290	11,810	44	9
1990[b]	154	5.3	2.9%	10	350	2,220	19,590	56	9
1995	164	5.7	2.9%	2	430	2,390	24,930	58	10
2000	175	6.1	2.9%	2	420	1,970	27,510	66	14
2005[c]	191	6.4	3.0%	3	580	2,640	35,131	61	13
2010[c]	214	6.9	3.1%	5	510	3,765	38,660	76	10

Sources: UN Population Division and World Bank Development Indicators. www.un.org/esa/population/publications/publications.htm; http://go.worldbank.org/LOTTGBE9I0.
[a] 1975 income data are from 1976.
[b] The 1990 migrant stock was raised from 120 million to 154 million because of the breakup of the USSR.
[c] 2005 and 2010 data are gross national income.

Figure 1

Economically Active Populations (EAPs), 1980–2020

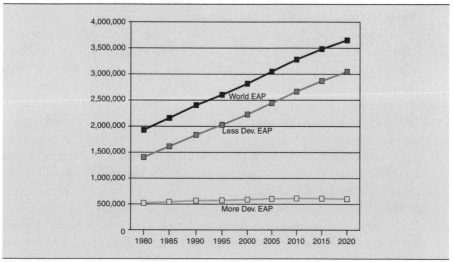

Source: ILO Laborsta, http://laborsta.ilo.org/.

In the lower-income countries, 40 percent of workers are employed in agriculture, a sector that is often taxed despite the fact that farmers and farm workers usually have lower-than-average incomes.[12] Because these taxes help to keep farm incomes lower than nonfarm incomes, there is often rural-urban migration—a major reason why the urban share of the world's population surpassed 50 percent for the first time in 2008.[13]

The United States and European countries had "Great Migrations" off the land in the 1950s and 1960s, providing workers for expanding factories and fueling population growth in cities. Similar Great Migrations are underway today from China to Mexico, and this rural-urban migration has three implications for international migration. First, ex-farmers and farm workers everywhere are most likely to accept "3-D" (dirty, dangerous, difficult) jobs, both inside their countries and abroad.[14] Second, rural-urban migrants often make physical as well as cultural transitions, and many find the transition as easy abroad as at home, as when Mexicans from rural areas find adapting to Los Angeles as easy as navigating Mexico City. Third, rural-urban migrants get one step closer to the country's exits by moving to cities, where it is usually easiest to obtain visas and documents for legal migration or to make arrangements for illegal migration.

Differences encourage migration, but it takes networks or links between areas to encourage people to move. Migration networks are a broad concept that has been shaped and strengthened by three revolutions of the past half century: in communications, transportation, and rights.

The communications revolution helps potential migrants to learn about opportunities abroad. The best information comes from migrants who are already established abroad, since they can provide family and friends with information in an understandable context. Cheaper communications enable migrants to quickly transmit job information as well as advice on how to cross national borders to friends and relatives at home. For example, information about vacant California farm jobs may be received in rural Mexico, thousands of miles away, before it spreads to nearby cities that have unemployment rates of over 20 percent.[15] Meanwhile, films and television programs depicting life in high-income countries may encourage young people especially to assume that the grass is greener abroad or that migration will lead to economic betterment.[16]

The transportation revolution accounts for the declining cost of travel. British migrants unable to pay one-way passage to North American colonies in the eighteenth century often indentured themselves, signing contracts that obliged them to work for three to six years for whoever met the ship and paid the captain. Transportation costs today are far lower—typically less than $2,500 to travel anywhere in the world legally and $1,000 to $20,000 for unauthorized migration. Most studies also reflect faster payback times for migrants today, so that even migrants who have paid high smuggling fees can usually repay them within two or three years.

The communications and transportation revolutions help migrants to learn about opportunities and to cross national borders, while the rights revolution affects their ability to stay abroad. After World War II, most industrial countries strengthened the constitutional and political rights of residents to prevent a recurrence of fascism, and most did not distinguish between citizens and migrants when establishing social safety net programs.

As migration increased in the 1990s, policymakers began to roll back the socioeconomic rights of migrants in an effort to stem the influx of new residents. For example, many European governments, including Germany, had written liberal asylum provisions into their post–World War II constitutions so as to avoid repeating the situation in which refugees perished because other countries returned them to Nazi Germany. As a result, in the early 1990s, over 1,000 foreigners a day were applying for asylum in Germany, many from Turkey and other former guest-worker countries of origin. The German government distributed asylum seekers throughout the country and required local communities to provide them with housing and food. Over 90 percent of the foreigners applying for asylum were determined not to be refugees, and false asylum claims contributed to a backlash that included "skinhead" attacks on foreigners.

The German and other European governments responded to this "asylum crisis" in three major ways.[17] First, nationals of the asylum seekers' major countries of origin (such as Turkey) had to obtain visas, which allowed the receiving governments to prescreen prospective foreign visitors and not issue visas to those who might request asylum. Second, airlines were fined heavily for transporting foreigners to France or Germany without visas and other documents, enlisting them in the quest to reduce the number of applicants. Third, European Union member countries agreed to make it difficult for foreigners from "safe" countries, and those who transited through safe countries, to apply for asylum in the EU—so that an Iraqi who traveled through Poland en route to Germany would be returned to Poland to apply for asylum. In this way, richer European countries maintained the constitutional protection of asylum while reducing the number of asylum applicants.

In the mid-1990s, the United States pursued a similar strategy of trying to manage migration by restricting the access of migrants to welfare assistance. When President Clinton pledged to "end welfare as we know it," migrants collecting welfare benefits became a target for those seeking to reduce the costs of the national welfare program. Illegal migration also influenced the debate, especially after the passage of the North American Free Trade Agreement (NAFTA), which was expected to reduce unauthorized Mexico–U.S. migration but instead increased it during the worst recession in California in a half century.

In November 1994, a grassroots effort in California led voters to approve Proposition 187—which would have withheld social services, health care, and public education from illegal immigrants—despite the objections of almost all statewide political and opinion leaders.[18] In the ensuing national debate over immigrant numbers and rights, President Clinton argued that the number of needy migrants admitted to the United States should be reduced in order to maintain the access of legal immigrants (future Americans) to welfare benefits, while employers argued that the better solution was to allow the number of poor migrants arriving to remain at high levels and to cut welfare costs by reducing immigrant access to social assistance.[19] Employers won the debate in Congress, and immigration was allowed to remain high, but those arriving after August 22, 1996, saw their access to means-tested benefits reduced.

Balancing migrant numbers and migrant rights is a major challenge.[20] Countries with the highest shares of migrants in their labor forces, such as the oil exporters of the Persian Gulf, extend few rights to migrants. There are no minimum wages in oil-exporting countries such as Saudi Arabia or the United Arab Emirates, which depend on millions of guest workers to build new cities and serve residents as domestic workers. Countries with fewer guest workers, such as Sweden and other Scandinavian countries, tend to grant them more rights, including equal wages and equal treatment under labor laws. Such policies make migrants as expensive to employ as local workers and lead to the hiring of relatively few.

SHOULD COUNTRIES LIBERALIZE?

The numbers versus rights trade-off reflects the fact that the demand for labor is downward-sloping. As wages rise, economies adjust in ways that encourage the substitution of capital for labor, as when farmers use machines rather than workers to harvest crops. In some cases, rising wages prompt factories in the United States to close, and the production of toys and garments shifts to China and other lower-wage countries. There may be other adjustments to higher wages, such as self-service at gas stations. In industrial countries, wages and employment can rise together as the productivity of each employee increases.

There are millions of workers in developing countries who would like to move to industrial countries to earn in one hour what they earn in a day or a week at home. Should industrial countries open their doors wider to such low-wage workers? The World Bank and most international organizations promoting economic development say yes, pointing to the remittances that migrants send to their countries of origin to argue that migration can reduce poverty and speed development.[21] For example, one World Bank model estimated that increasing the number of migrants from developing countries in industrial countries by 50 percent would lift global economic output more than reducing trade barriers.[22] However, such models are based on many assumptions, including full employment, which assumes that all migrants find jobs and also that any local workers displaced by migrants find new jobs.

In the boom years before the 2008–2009 global recession, unemployment fell in industrial countries, despite high levels of migration. Economic studies that examined the impacts of immigrants on native-born workers found little evidence of lower wages that could be attributed to migration. However, these studies of migrant effects were not always convincing, because they were based on assumptions, such as the idea that if the presence of immigrants depresses wages, cities with a higher share of immigrants in their labor forces should offer lower wages to U.S. workers with qualifications similar to those of the immigrants, such as high school dropouts. Skeptics noted that, if natives move away from "migrant cities" or do not move to them, analysts can wrongly draw the conclusion that there is no migrant impact on wages.

Countries do not grow rich or poor because of immigration. An exhaustive study of the impact of immigrants on the U.S. economy by the National Research Council concluded that the United States obtained net economic benefits of $1 billion to $10 billion in the mid-1990s due to immigration.[23] Proponents of immigration stressed that the sign of the immigrant effect was positive; opponents argued that the impact of immigration was negligible because the then-$8 trillion U.S. economy was expanding by 3 percent, growing by $240 billion a year—or $10 billion in two weeks.[24]

The United States is a nation of immigrants that first welcomed virtually all newcomers, later excluded certain types of foreigners, and, since the 1920s, has limited the number of immigrants by means of quotas. Immigrants and refugees arrive through America's front door, which was opened wider in 1990 to accommodate more relatives of U.S. residents and more workers desired by U.S. employers. But the fastest growth in migrant ingress has been through the side and back doors, as nonimmigrant tourists, foreign workers, and students—as well as unauthorized foreigners—arrive in ever-larger numbers.

Research on the economic, social, and political effects of immigration does not provide clear guidelines for policy. Overall, immigrants have minor effects—for better or worse—on the huge U.S. economy and labor market. Most immigrants are better off financially in the United States than they were at home, even though many arrive with little education and find it hard to climb the American job ladder.

Given the eagerness of migrants to cross borders and of employers to hire them, should industrial countries open their doors wider? There are no easy answers. Despite the World Bank's promotion of liberalization, more open borders do not necessarily mean less poverty. Since the effects of liberalization on each country are not uniform; the question of whether to liberalize is one that each country will have to consider and answer on its own. Immigration means change, much of which is hard to predict. Despite intentions to return, many migrants settle, and they and their children eventually gain a voice in the society and economy in which they live. Some residents welcome the changes that newcomers bring while others fear them, which is why opening doors to newcomers has been and will continue to be controversial.

NOTES

1. United Nations, "Report of the Secretary-General on International Migration" (A/60/871), May 2006, www.unmigration.org. Table available at www.un.org/esa/population/publications/2006Migration_Chart/2006IttMig_chart.htm
2. The world's population was about 6.6 billion in 2007, including 4.8 billion of workforce age, defined as persons fifteen and older (http://laborsta.ilo.org). The world's workforce was 3.1 billion, including 2.9 billion employed and 200 million unemployed—an unemployment rate of 6.2 percent.
3. See Chapter 5 of Philip Martin, *Importing Poverty? Immigration and the Changing Face of Rural America* (New Haven: Yale University Press, 2009).
4. John Torpey. *The Invention of the Passport: Surveillance, Citizenship and the State* (Cambridge: Cambridge University Press, 1999).
5. Charles C. Lemert, *Social Things: An Introduction to the Sociological Life* (Boulder: Rowman & Littlefield, 2005), 176, says there were fewer than fifty nation states in 1900.
6. An editorial on July 3, 1986, first made this proposal, which was repeated in an editorial on July 3, 1990.
7. The National Front candidate, Jean Marie Le Pen, received 15 percent of the vote in the first round of presidential voting in 1995; www.irr.org.uk/europebulletin/france/extreme_right_politics/1995/ak000006.html.
8. Quoted in Michael S. Teitelbaum, "Right versus Right: Immigration and Refugee Policy in the United States," *Foreign Affairs* 59, no. 1 (Fall 1980): 45–46.
9. The average woman in developing countries (excluding China) has 3.5 children versus 1.5 children per woman in developed countries. According to the Population Reference Bureau (www.prb.org), the world's fastest-growing population is in Gaza, where the growth rate is 4.5 percent a year, and the fastest-shrinking population is in Russia, where the population is declining by 0.5 percent a year.
10. Young people are most likely to move over borders, because they have the least invested in jobs and careers at home and the most time to recoup their "investment

in migration" abroad. See also http://data.worldbank.org/indicator/NY
.GDP.PCAP.CD

11. Average per capita was $9,100 per person in 2010, according to the World Bank's
World Development Report 2011 Selected Economic Indicators, http://go
.worldbank.org/LOTTGBE9I0. At purchasing power parity, which takes into
account national differences in the cost of living, the world's gross national
income was $75 trillion or $11,000 per capita in 2010—$37,200 per capita in the
high-income countries and $6,000 in low and middle-income countries.

12. Taxes are extracted from agriculture via monopoly input suppliers who sell seeds
or fertilizers at high prices or via monopoly purchasers of farm commodities who
buy from farmers at less-than-world prices and pocket the difference when the coffee or cocoa is exported. In the high-income countries, farmers' incomes are generally higher than those of non-farmers, in part because high-income countries
transfer funds to producers of food and fiber.

13. United Nations Population Fund (UNFPA), *State of the World's Population, 2007*,
www.unfpa.org/swp/2007/english/introduction.html.

14. This situation is evident in Chinese coastal cities, where internal rural-urban
migrants fill 3-D jobs, and abroad, where Chinese migrants are employed in industries that range from services to sweatshops.

15. These farm-worker recruitment networks are examined in *Rural Migration News*,
http://migration.ucdavis.edu/rmn/index.php.

16. Even if migrants know that movies and TV shows portray exaggerated lifestyles,
those who find themselves in slave-like conditions abroad sometimes say that they
did not believe that things in rich countries could be "that bad."

17. Philip Martin, "Germany: Managing Migration in the 21st Century," in *Controlling
Immigration. A Global Perspective*, ed. Wayne A. Cornelius, Takeyuki Tsuda, Philip
L. Martin, and James F. Hollifield (Stanford: Stanford University Press, 2004),
221–252.

18. Proposition 187, approved by a 59–41 percent margin in November 1994, would
have created a state-funded screening mechanism to ensure that unauthorized
foreigners did not obtain state-funded services, including public school education.
Its implementation was stopped by a federal judge, but some of its provisions were
included in 1996 federal immigration reforms. See http://migration.ucdavis.edu/
mn/more.php?id=492_0_2_0.

19. Details of the three U.S. laws enacted in 1996 are at *Migration News*, 1996, http://
migration.ucdavis.edu/. One provision that was eventually dropped from the
final bill would have made legal immigrants deportable if they received more than
12 months of welfare benefits. In the late 1990s, the access of some legal immigrant
adults and children to some welfare benefits was restored.

20. Martin Ruhs and Philip Martin. "Numbers vs. Rights: Trade offs and Guest Worker
Programs," *International Migration Review* 42, no. 1 (2008): 249–265.

21. World Bank, *Global Economic Prospects: The Economic Implications of Remittances
and Migration*, 2005, www.worldbank.org/prospects/gep2006.

22. *Global Economic Prospects: The Economic Implication of Remittances and Migration,* Chapter 2 uses a computable general equilibrium (CGE) model to estimate the impacts of increasing by 14 million the number of developing-country migrant workers in industrial countries. The increased economic output was $356 billion (0.6 percent of global gross domestic product [GDP]) or more than the estimated gains from reducing trade restrictions.

23. James P. Smith and Barry Edmonston, eds., *The New Americans: Economic, Demographic, and Fiscal Effects of Immigration* (Washington, DC: National Academy Press, 1997).

24. The U.S. GDP was $15 trillion in 2010. If immigration added 1/10 of one percent to US GDP, the net economic benefits would be up to $15 billion in this larger 2010 economy. The U.S. economy is expanding slowly. If GDP grows by 2.5 percent a year, GDP rises by $375 billion a year or almost a billion a week.

culture and diversity

Should Development Efforts Seek to Preserve Local Culture?

YES: Elsa Stamatopoulou, *Secretariat of the United Nations Permanent Forum on Indigenous Issues*

NO: Kwame Anthony Appiah, *Princeton University*

Culture is a difficult concept to pin down. It is the composite of language, food, history, and social relationships that help to define a national, subnational, or cross-national identity. Without cultures, individuals would lose the social contexts on which they rely to define their identities. Without varying cultures, the world would be a far less innovative, resilient, and interesting place.

Still, many traditional cultures are at risk. Small tribes in the tropics are dwindling because of low reproduction rates and emigration to the cities, where their people are rapidly assimilated or tempted to adopt more modern habits and attitudes. Many traditional languages are at risk of extinction as a result of globalization, as more people feel the need to speak the major languages of international commerce: Mandarin Chinese, Spanish, English, and Arabic. The Worldwatch Institute reports that over 50 percent of the 6,800 languages spoken worldwide are likely to become extinct by the end of this century. Some 4,000 to 9,000 languages have disappeared over the past 500 years due to wars, genocide, legal restrictions, and the cultural assimilation of ethnic minorities. Table 1 (p. 432) shows just how tenuous the existence of a number of languages is, amid the dwindling numbers of their speakers. Table 2 (p. 432) shows that most of the world's population now only speaks a handful of languages.

Efforts are under way to preserve some cultures. Western anthropologists try to collect as much information as possible, and they even engage in educating younger generations in the traditions of their elders in hopes of restoring some cultures. Also, the **United Nations Educational, Scientific, and**

Table 1

The Status of the World's Languages (by Region)

Region	Number of Languages*	Languages at Risk of Extinction**
Africa	2,110	33
The Americas	993	191
Asia	2,322	53
Europe	234	30
Pacific	1,250	93
Totals	6,909	400

Sources: *M. Paul Lewis, ed. Ethnologue: Languages of the World. 16th ed. (Dallas: SIL International, 2009). Online version available at http://www.ethnologue.com/ethno_docs/distribution.asp?by=area **Payal Sampat, "World's Many Languages Disappearing," in Vital Signs, 2001: The Trends That Are Shaping Our Future, The Worldwatch Institute (New York: W. W. Norton & Company, 2001).
Note: Numbers represent languages with fewer than 10,000 speakers.

Table 2

Frequency of Language Worldwide, Present Day

Number of Languages	Spoken by Percentage of World's Population
Top 15	50%
Top 100	90%
Bottom 6,800	10%

Source: Payal Sampat, "Last Words: The Dying of Languages," Worldwatch Institute Magazine 14, no. 3 (May/June 2001). http://www.worldwatch.org/node/500.

Cultural Organization (UNESCO) adopted a declaration in 2001 protecting national cultures and linguistic diversity. But there remain strong outside pressures operating on national cultures that bend them toward adjustment to external norms.

Preserving traditional cultures, or cultures of any sort, can be difficult. They are often social constructs, invoked to create a national identity for political purposes. Thus the articulation of culture can be politically molded and used for nationalistic and xenophobic ends. France argues that the French movie industry and French food are national cultural icons and thus should be subsidized and protected from foreign competition, although these policies have been challenged by the World Trade Organization. Similarly, Japan has claimed that traditional modes of rice production are culturally grounded because of the distinctive type of rice that is grown locally and that Japanese consumers prefer. Thus the Japanese government uses a cultural argument to justify protection of a small, high-cost—but politically powerful—industry from foreign competition by means of import barriers that are counter to international trade law.

Japan also argues that whaling is a Japanese cultural activity, and it is willing to face the wrath of international environmental groups to protect its small whaling industry.

Views on the acceptability of particular cultural expressions vary widely. Indeed, in one extreme example from the human rights domain, what is denounced as female genital mutilation in the West is regarded as a cultural tradition in some African societies. And Turkey is embroiled in a national debate about whether women should be allowed to wear the traditional Islamic headscarf (as a legitimate cultural artifact of the country's Ottoman and Muslim past) or whether its prohibition should be upheld as an articulation of the more secular culture imposed by Kemal Ataturk in 1924 (along with abolishing the fez for men) and perpetuated by the military and secular leaders since then.

Another question has to do with how static cultures actually are. Most current cultures are, in fact, robust, and most have adopted elements from other cultures. Globalization acts as a giant hothouse in which cultures selectively interact and borrow from one another. Traditionalists may find this give-and-take offensive either because of beliefs about cultural purity or because their social status and influence thus become subject to question. The true policy challenge, however, is ensuring that traditional attitudes are not swamped by alien foreign views but rather are able to meld the foreign ones into a comfortable blend that is amenable to local customs and beliefs.

The articles that follow offer different views as to whether preserving local culture should have a place in development efforts. Elsa Stamatopoulou believes that cultures, particularly traditional cultures, should be actively protected from globalization. Kwame Anthony Appiah is much more skeptical, believing that cultures follow their own organic evolution and should be allowed to develop independently of state protection.

Discussion Questions

1. Is it possible to preserve a local culture in the age of globalization— against influences such as the Internet, more global trade, and easier means of travel? How? Is it important to preserve local cultures? Why?
2. What is culture? How does it relate to identity?
3. In what ways can development efforts impact local cultures? Is this effect avoidable?

4. In the face of issues such as extreme poverty and poor health, should trying to preserve local culture be a priority in development efforts? Why or why not?

5. What does Elsa Stamatopoulou think are the merits of the UN Declaration on the Rights of Indigenous Peoples? What issues does this declaration address that past declarations have neglected? What does Stamatopoulou propose as a strategy for continued improvements in development and preserving culture?

6. Are all cultures worth protecting?

7. Why is Kwame Anthony Appiah opposed to adopting formal efforts to protect cultures? How does he think cultures develop and evolve? Should any cultures be preserved, according to him?

YES: Elsa Stamatopoulou, *Secretariat of the United Nations Permanent Forum on Indigenous Issues*[1]

In 1923 Cayuga Chief Deskaheh, as the representative of the Six Nations of the Iroquois, traveled to Geneva to plead the cause of his people before the League of Nations. Despite one year of working for recognition by the League, he was not received, and so he returned to the United States. A few months before his death in 1925, Chief Deskaheh made a speech by radio from Rochester, New York. Here is an excerpt:

> This is the story of the Mohawks, the story of the Oneidas, of the Cayugas—I am a Cayuga—of the Onondagas, the Senecas, and the Tuscaroras. They are the Iroquois. Tell it to those who have not been listening. Maybe I will be stopped from telling it. But if I am prevented from telling it over, as I hope I do, the story will not be lost. . . . I am the speaker of the Six Nations, the oldest League of Nations now existing. . . . It is a League which is still alive and intends, as best it can, to defend the rights of the Iroquois to live under their own laws in their own little countries now left to them, to worship their Great Spirit in their own way, and to enjoy the rights which are as surely theirs as the white man's rights are his own.[2]

In 1925 Deskaheh did not mention "development" in conveying his vision of the future of his people, but today he might have done so. The verbs *to develop* and *to underdevelop* have sometimes been used to indicate top-down approaches to economic and social development, which sometimes lead to negative results. Indigenous leaders of today have also spoken of "development aggression" to indicate the imposition of the mainstream development paradigm on indigenous peoples—a paradigm that may be largely viewed as the promotion of industrialized societies and markets based on a continuously growing consumption of goods. Imposition of this paradigm has, more often than not, led to loss of indigenous peoples' lands, natural resources, and livelihoods; theft and patenting of their traditional knowledge; forced displacement of communities, often due to conflict; negation of benefit-sharing; forced assimilation, including loss of language and other aspects of culture; discrimination; marginalization; and extreme poverty.[3]

Often underlying the discussion about globalization and the expansion of free markets is a fear of the impact on local or national cultures. Some discussion—although not enough—has focused on this troubling issue at the intergovernmental level, where a few voices can be heard calling for more culturally sensitive development policies. The UN Scientific, Educational, and Cultural Organization (UNESCO), the UN Population Fund (UNFPA), and, especially, the UN Permanent Forum on Indigenous Issues (UNPFII) have been the most vocal actors, pointing out that culture is both the context for development as well as the missing factor in policies for development.[4]

Despite some progress at the international policy level, these steps are only initial moves at the normative level, while programs and other practices at the operational, country level demonstrate that there is still a lot to be done before the international community can justly claim that it supports cultural diversity in its development efforts. The parameters of this essay do not allow a full discussion of international practice, but research has demonstrated the inadequacy of current international practices.[5]

Any discussion in the public policy domain about globalization and local cultures begs a number of definitional clarifications, including the concept of development. This essay will thus start with conceptual issues. Given the existence of an organized indigenous movement and considerable international attention to indigenous peoples and their issues in the past thirty years, it will then bring into relief the subject of development and culture, using indigenous peoples' issues as a major focus. This approach will shed light on the overall challenges and opportunities of development with culture, an idea that is gaining increased visibility.

THE CONCEPT OF DEVELOPMENT WITHIN THE INTERNATIONAL NORMATIVE FRAMEWORK

Globalization is most often viewed as economic globalization of goods, services, and labor in accordance with the dominant development paradigm. In terms of international policy instruments and institutions, this paradigm is perceived as mostly expressed by international financial institutions such as the International Monetary Fund and the World Bank, as well as the World Trade Organization and relevant international agreements. However, these institutions and their policy instruments have not enjoyed the broad and democratic participation of governments and civil society, unlike the United Nations' global conferences of the 1990s, which have been reshaping the concept of development with the broad participation of the international community, both governments and civil society.[6]

What is still often forgotten in globalization debates is that, in addition to trade and other international financial agreements, international human rights treaties (which have received nearly universal acceptance by states) have for decades provided a comprehensive international legal framework of obligations by which states have voluntarily agreed to be bound and which provides the parameters of what governments may or may not do in the name of development. These human rights instruments, elaborated by the United Nations in the past five decades, include but are not limited to the following: the Convention on the Elimination of All Forms of Racial Discrimination; the International Covenant on Economic, Social and Cultural Rights; the International Covenant on Civil and Political Rights; the Convention on the Elimination of All Forms of Discrimination against Women; and the Convention on the Rights of the Child.[7] These treaties—and the international human rights treaty bodies[8] that monitor their implementation—have opened up considerable conceptual space in which to bring together human rights and development, creating what is now known as the human rights-based approach to development (HRBA), accepted since 2003 by the whole United Nations system in its development operations.

It is no exaggeration to say that the adoption of the HRBA as an international policy guideline put into sharper focus the increasing efforts to offset the macroeconomic approach to development, which has led to many failures around the world, and to redefine development as human development—combining social and economic development, placing the human being in the center, stressing participation, and requiring interventions targeted toward the most vulnerable. The HRBA was adopted by the **UN Development Group (UNDG),** which brings together all the UN development entities.

By stressing participation, the HRBA already prioritizes democratic principles and culture: if development is not a top-down but a bottom-up process, then peoples' wishes and expressions of their cultural particularities should find resonance in the development policies, programs, and budgets of their governments and those of international development actors. The common article 1 of both International Human Rights Covenants mentioned above recognizes that peoples have the right to self-determination and that, by virtue of this right, they freely pursue their economic, social, and cultural development.

Therefore, according to the international normative human rights framework, development is far from a single-model concept. If we accept peoples' human right to determine their fates, development should not be viewed as a linear concept, a mandatory recipe that will eventually turn all societies and economies into one homogeneous whole. Furthermore, the measure of democratic maturity of a state will be judged by how it treats its minorities, including how it factors in various visions of development.

Of course, the common perception of economic globalization would seem to counter such an understanding of democracy and human rights, including cultural rights. What we have noted in recent decades is that international trade negotiations have at times been conducted without attention to the already existing international human rights framework—sometimes forcing states, especially poor and powerless states, to accept trade agreements that would essentially weaken the human rights obligations they have undertaken toward their own populations under the human rights treaties. This contradiction has not escaped the attention of such human rights bodies as the Committee on Economic, Social, and Cultural Rights.

THE CONCEPTS OF CULTURE AND OF PRESERVING CULTURES

There are numerous definitions of "culture." A definition or, more precisely, an understanding of culture that derives from the examination of literature and the work of the UN bodies and that is useful for examining development and cultural rights operates at three levels:

1. in its material sense, as product, *as the accumulated material heritage of mankind*, either as a whole or a part of particular human groups, including but not limited to monuments and artifacts;

2. *as a process of artistic or scientific creation*—the emphasis being placed on the process and on the creator(s) of culture; and

3. in its anthropological sense—that is, culture *as a way of life*, or, in UNESCO's words, the "set of distinctive spiritual, material, intellectual and emotional features of society or a social group"—which encompasses, "in addition to art and literature, lifestyles, ways of living together, value systems, traditions and beliefs."[9]

Culture is dynamic, ever-changing as it enters into contact with other cultures, especially in the increasingly interconnected world of today, where the "information society" spins the globe faster, bringing people into contact at an unprecedented pace.

Societies today are more and more culturally diverse. Minorities, indigenous peoples, and migrants, as well as other non-ethnically identifiable groups—such as persons with disabilities, gay people, and others—coexist and interface. How will a state formulate its development policies? Which voices will it listen to from within its own populations? What if different groups of the population advocate different types of development for themselves—indigenous peoples, for example? How will the state conform to its human rights obligations? How will it deal with its international trade engagements? What if human rights obligations and trade agreements lead to different responses?

Other questions that arise concern the very concept of preserving culture. Given the dynamic nature of culture and the context of globalization, what does it mean to preserve culture? Does it require protective measures on the part of the state that will "freeze" a culture at a specific moment in time? Can government action shield a culture from outside influences? Who should decide which influences are positive or negative, and how should such protections be achieved? To what extent are protection measures even possible in the current context of globalization and trade liberalization?

THE CONCEPT OF LOCAL CULTURE

The "local" is often juxtaposed to the global. But if we talk about human development and a human rights approach to development, local culture is about people and their ways of life. "Local" can mean national or subnational. In fact, we know that in today's world—even more than before—a state is composed of various cultures, given the diversity of its population. There is hardly a single culture that we can speak about in an absolute way in any given state. Indigenous peoples and minorities are realities in most states of the world.

It is significant that the 2004 Human Development Report of the UN Development Programme (UNDP) was devoted to "Cultural Liberty in Today's Diverse World."[10] The report gave figures that show the richness of the human tapestry—the human mobility but also the destructive trends around it. There are about 175 million migrants in the world, of which asylum seekers represent only 9 percent (16 million). The world's nearly 200 countries are home to some 5,000 ethnic groups. More than 150 countries have significant religious or ethnic minorities. Some 370 million indigenous peoples live in more than 90 countries, representing more than 4,000 languages. Of the estimated 6,000+ languages spoken today, 90 percent may have become extinct or face extinction in the next 100 years. (It is important to recognize what a great percentage of indigenous languages, and therefore of cultures, this loss may represent.) About 518 million people face restrictions on religion, language, ceremonies, and appearance. An example of the inadequate attention given to preserving this diversity is that in sub-Saharan Africa, only 13 percent of children in primary school receive instruction in their mother tongue.

It is known that linguistic diversity coincides with biodiversity on the world's map, and that most of the world's still-unexplored natural resources lie on indigenous peoples' traditional territories. We also know that the driving forces of the dominant development paradigm—states, a number of intergovernmental organizations, and private corporations—are actively and, at times, aggressively seeking those remaining unexplored resources.

Where is the voice of the local people in the state of the world as revealed by the statistics cited here? Any public policy debate, national or international, ought to be concrete in terms of putting a human face in its goals, targets, and indicators. To know, therefore, what the "local" is about, the state—which is the main responsible actor for the respect, protection, promotion, and fulfillment of human rights—has to create a public space for democratic dialogue—for full and effective participation of the people in the definition of what development should consist of—and to pursue a culturally sensitive program of development. The local, in other words, is given meaning through the democratic participation of people, as agents of development and not as passive recipients.[11]

INDIGENOUS PEOPLES AND INTERNATIONAL STANDARDS

The history of indigenous peoples knocking at the door of the institutions of the international community of "nations" is old. Indigenous peoples' sense of themselves as sovereign nations, in parity with the other nations of the world, has always been very strong. The fact that states, the colonizing powers, concluded treaties with many indigenous peoples is a testimony that indigenous peoples were viewed as sovereign by those who invented international law. There has been a vigorous and dynamic interface between indigenous peoples and the international community, especially through the United Nations—an interface that, difficult as it is, has produced at least three results: (1) a new awareness of indigenous concerns and indigenous rights; (2) recognition of indigenous peoples' invaluable contribution to humanity's cultural diversity and heritage, not least through their traditional knowledge; and (3) awareness of the need to address the problems of indigenous peoples through policies, laws, and budgets. Along with the decolonization, human rights, and the women's movements, the indigenous movement has been one of the four strongest civil-society interlocutors of the United Nations since 1945.

Human rights and dignity have a very concrete meaning when we speak of indigenous peoples. The ways in which our legal and economic systems manage to deal with bio-prospecting, the use of "killer-seeds," and other kinds of exploitation of indigenous traditional knowledge will reflect how we are able to protect together or ignore together a whole slew of issues involving justice, health, culture, or economic and social development. Whether we teach the mother tongue at school will show not whether we are ready to provide some luxury but whether or not we care about pushing kids out of school, whether or not we discriminate against indigenous peoples and their cultural rights.

Indigenous peoples make up about 5 percent of the world's population but 15 percent of the world's poor, according to the World Bank. In face of that disparity, what constitutes development? What is "human development" for indigenous peoples? What do they think? On the basis of what norms should we, the inhabitants of a globalized world, accept the definition of human happiness as a linear mono-model based on the overconsumption and overharvesting of natural resources that the globe cannot sustain? Must happiness be understood as a process that takes people from hunting and gathering, say, to having a plasma TV in every room of their house? These are some of the questions that indigenous peoples are raising and that have to do with everybody's survival and development. Perhaps not surprisingly, there are today indigenous peoples who live in voluntary isolation, because they wish to follow their own mode of development without being contacted by outsiders.[12]

The UN Permanent Forum on Indigenous Issues, the highest international body in this field, has in fact expressed concern that, unless indigenous peoples' visions of development are taken into account, the implementation of the Millennium Development Goals entails risks to indigenous peoples that include accelerated loss of lands and natural resources, displacement, forced assimilation, and further impoverishment, discrimination, and marginalization.[13] The challenges are enormous, although there are some promising examples of local and international campaigns that have brought the rights of indigenous peoples to the forefront.[14]

Contradictory visions of development that differ from the dominant development paradigm are not easy for the national policymaker to resolve, even in the case of a well-meaning state that wants to achieve equality and nondiscrimination, including cultural sensitivity. There are enormous international pressures on the state to conform to specific economic paths, which in turn impact both the human rights of the population and the local culture.

At the same time that economic globalization may have a negative impact on culture, it is certainly not oblivious to it. One example is traditional knowledge—in particular, indigenous peoples' traditional knowledge (ITK). The economic stakes of this phenomenon are enormous, and so some fifteen intergovernmental entities are dealing with the subject, including the World Intellectual Property Organization (WIPO), the World Bank, the Inter-American Development Bank, UNESCO, and others.

ITK, which is the creation of indigenous cultures over millennia, can yield important financial gains at a global level. The questions that arise are multiple: What is the concept and full spectrum of ITK? What are the appropriate protection and promotion measures to take vis-à-vis traditional knowledge? How do intellectual property regimes impact on ITK? What should be the role of traditional knowledge-holders? How should benefits be shared in case ITK-holders wish to commercialize their ITK heritage? How should indigenous customary law on ITK interface with national and international law on the matter? What kind of international *sui generis* regime should be put in place to protect ITK? The UN Permanent Forum on Indigenous Issues has been making efforts to map and coordinate the international policy scene on this complex matter.[15]

Should respect for culture in the context of development lead to protectionism, censorship of foreign cultural products, or limitation of international cooperation in the cultural domain? Obviously, part of the answer lies in governments' providing unhindered participation in cultural life nationally, including the freedom to create cultural products. A free and robust cultural life at the national level will be better equipped to engage in dialogue with other cultures, including the forces of the market, than a stifled cultural life. In the case of developing countries, governments may consider seeking international development assistance in order to better promote national culture—including, for example, the teaching of indigenous or minority languages.

The Vision of the Declaration on the Rights of Indigenous Peoples

After more than twenty years of negotiations, the United Nations General Assembly adopted the UN Declaration on the Rights of Indigenous Peoples in September 2007. The text has extraordinary resonance and already constitutes a body of customary law, not least because of the time devoted to its negotiation and the unprecedented and democratic participation of indigenous peoples together with states. The participation of indigenous peoples was direct and exemplary, and it not only led to the creation of a real charter of indigenous peoples' human rights, but also, in the process, crystallized an international indigenous peoples' movement, created dialogue and partnerships with states, forged cooperation with the UN system, and—last but not least—launched a global solidarity movement among indigenous peoples.

The Declaration on the Rights of Indigenous Peoples[16] emphasizes the rights of such peoples to maintain and strengthen their own institutions, cultures, and traditions and to pursue their development in keeping with their own needs and aspirations. The declaration addresses both individual and collective human rights, including cultural rights and identity, rights to education, health, employment, and so on. The text states that indigenous peoples and individuals are free and equal to all other peoples and individuals, and that they have the right to be free from any kind of discrimination in the exercise of their rights, in particular, those rights based on their indigenous origin and identity.

Nine preambular and fifteen operative paragraphs deal with consultation, partnership, and participation of indigenous peoples in a democratic polity. Thus the text recognizes that indigenous peoples have the right to self-determination. By that right, they can freely determine their political status and pursue their economic, cultural, and social development. They have the right to maintain and strengthen their distinct political, legal, economic, social, and cultural institutions, while retaining their rights to participate fully, if they so choose, in the political, economic, social, and cultural life of the state.

Seventeen of the declaration's forty-six articles deal with indigenous cultures and how to protect and promote them by respecting indigenous peoples' direct inputs in decision making and providing resources for education in indigenous languages and other areas.

The declaration recognizes subsistence rights and rights to land, territories, and resources, proclaiming that peoples deprived of their means of subsistence and development are entitled to just and fair redress.

Essentially, the declaration outlaws discrimination against indigenous peoples and promotes their full and effective participation in all matters that concern them, including the right to remain distinct and to pursue their own visions of economic and social development. The adoption of the declaration requires new approaches to global issues—such as development, diversity, pluricultural democracy, and peace—and encourages the building of genuine partnerships with indigenous peoples.

Although the declaration is not legally binding, it represents a dynamic development of legal norms and reflects the commitment of states to move in a pluralistic direction, abiding by principles that respect the human rights of indigenous peoples.

The Linkage of Indigenous Peoples' Cultural Rights to Development

The cultural rights of indigenous peoples in the context of development are protected and promoted by international legal standards that are found in international human rights instruments and further developed via the interpretation of international law by international courts and the international human rights bodies.[17] Those standards enforce the following precepts:

- The cultural rights of minorities and indigenous peoples consist of the right to education; the right to use their language in private life and various aspects of public life, such as before judicial authorities and to identify themselves as well as place names; the right to establish their own schools; access to mother tongue education to every extent feasible; access to the means of dissemination of culture, such as the media, museums, theatres, and so on, on the basis of nondiscrimination; the right to practice their religion; the freedom to maintain relations with their kin beyond national borders and the right to participate in decisions affecting them through their own institutions; and the preservation of sacred sites, works of art, scientific knowledge (especially knowledge about nature), oral tradition, and human remains, that is, both the tangible and the intangible objects that comprise indigenous cultural heritage. In the case of indigenous peoples, special cultural rights also include the right to continue certain economic activities linked to the traditional use of land and natural resources.

- The state and its agents have an obligation to respect the freedom of persons belonging to minorities and minority groups to freely participate in cultural life, to assert their cultural identity, and to express themselves culturally in the ways that they choose, unless those ways involve human rights violations. The state, as part of the regular discharge of its police and justice functions, must also protect minorities' right to participate in cultural life from infringement by third parties, whether they are individuals, groups, or corporations, domestic or foreign.

- International norms prohibit cultural practices that contravene internationally recognized human rights. Minority and indigenous rights are part of the human rights regime. States should thus adopt preventive and corrective policies and promote awareness of such problems so that such practices stop.

- Individuals living within groups are free to participate or not to participate in the cultural practices of the group, and no negative consequences may ensue because of their choice. In other words, the cultural autonomy of the individual is guaranteed.

- Minorities and indigenous peoples have the right to pursue their cultural development through their own institutions and, through those institutions, they have the right to participate fully and effectively in the definition, preparation, and implementation of cultural policies that concern them and development policies that affect their cultures. The state must consult the groups concerned via democratic and transparent processes.

CONCLUSION: DEVELOPMENT WITH CULTURE

The concept of development with culture is enshrined in international human rights standards that have been elaborated in the past five decades. Despite the pressures that globalization poses on governments to conform to the dominant development paradigm, it is important to recognize that the laws and ethics of development that the international community has passed on as part of our modern heritage are also part of the globalized world. They require that states respect their international human rights obligations, including the full and effective participation of people and groups in setting development policies and programs, even when those voices reflect alternative visions and cultural perspectives of human development.

One could summarize the way forward in this area as follows:

1. Governments must now translate the international normative framework into *concrete policies* for, by, and with local communities, especially indigenous peoples and minorities—that is, with their genuine participation in decision-making processes; with respect for their identities as groups, as communities with their histories, cultures, and aspirations; and with respect for their human dignity and for their human rights. Welfare approaches to development have failed, to a large extent because of the indigenous communities' poor or nonexistent participation. Thus the human-rights approach to development is particularly relevant because it places major emphasis on genuine participation, empowerment of those addressed by development programs, and respect for international human rights standards.

2. Policies must be matched by *national legislation and institutions* that will deal with major concerns, such as systemic discrimination, whether in the justice system, in health and education systems, or in the political system. Such legislation and institutions must also aim to correct these long-term injustices through positive measures.

3. Governments need to achieve *an equitable shift of resources* by designing targeted programs that will address discrimination and make a real difference to the disadvantaged members of local communities, including indigenous peoples.

4. International solidarity *needs to be mobilized at various levels*—economic, social, cultural, and political—for those who have been marginalized or excluded by globalization, so that they too may benefit from the implementation of human rights, democracy, and cultural pluralism.

NOTES

1. The views expressed in this article do not necessarily represent those of the United Nations.
2. See the Web site of the Secretariat of the UN Permanent Forum on Indigenous Issues, www.un.org/esa/socdev/unpfii.
3. The term "development aggression" is used frequently by Victoria Tauli-Corpuz, an Igorot indigenous leader from the Philippines and chair of the UN Permanent Forum on Indigenous Issues (2005). See her excellent piece, "Our Right to Remain Separate and Distinct," in *Paradigm Wars: Indigenous Peoples' Resistance to Economic Globalization*, A Special Report of the International Forum on Globalization Committee on Indigenous Peoples, ed. Jerry Mander and Victoria Tauli-Corpuz (San Francisco: International Forum on Globalization, 2005), 9–16.
4. See, for example, the report of the Fourth Session of the UNPFII, E/2005/23, wherein the Forum made comprehensive recommendations in the context of indigenous peoples and the Millennium Development Goal 1, which calls for the eradication of extreme poverty by the year 2015. See also UNESCO's Universal Declaration on Cultural Diversity, adopted at the 31st General Conference of UNESCO in October 2001, www.unesco.org.
5. For a comprehensive discussion, see Elsa Stamatopoulou, *Cultural Rights in International Law: Article 27 of the Universal Declaration of Human Rights and Beyond* (Leiden/Boston: Martinus Nijhoff, 2007), 83–96.
6. These global conferences include the Rio Conference on Environment and Development, the Copenhagen Social Summit, the Vienna World Conference on Human Rights, the Beijing Conference on Women, and the Cairo Conference on Population and Development.
7. The text of these human rights treaties may be found in *Human Rights: A Compilation of International Instruments*, vol. I (Pt. I and Pt. II) and vol. II, Sales No. E.97.XIV.1 and E.02.XIV.4.
8. Of special importance is the work of the Committee on Economic, Social, and Cultural Rights, which monitors the implementation of the International Covenant on Economic, Social, and Cultural Rights. For its documentation, see the Web site of the Office of the UN High Commissioner for Human Rights, www.ohchr.ch.
9. Stamatopoulou, *Cultural Rights in International Law*, 108–109.
10. UNDP, *Human Development Report 2004: Cultural Liberty in Today's Diverse World*, http://hdr.undp.org/en/reports/global/hdr2004/.
11. In international forums, such as the World Intellectual Property Organization (WIPO) and the International Fund for Agricultural Development (IFAD), the term "local communities" almost always refers to indigenous peoples.
12. The UN Permanent Forum on Indigenous Issues and the Special Rapporteur on the human rights and fundamental freedoms of indigenous people of the UN Human Rights Council have expressed their concern about the situation of these peoples who are at times attacked by outsiders, including those prompted by mining or logging interests. An international UN expert workshop was organized in

2006 by the Office of the High Commissioner for Human Rights; for the comprehensive recommendations adopted at that workshop, see the report of the OHCHR
to the Sixth (2007) Session of the UNPFII, www.un.org/esa/socdev/unpfii.

13. E/2005/23, also available at www.un.org/esa/socdev/unpfii.

14. It was, for example, reported in October 2006 in the *New York Times* that a Chinese
oil company, SAPET, refused to drill on isolated indigenous peoples' land in the
Peruvian Amazon. In November 2005 SAPET had been awarded a concession
(known as Lot 113) that was superimposed over an existing reserve for indigenous
peoples who are not in contact with the non-indigenous society. Responding to the
advocacy of local indigenous organizations, SAPET asked for the boundary of Lot
113 to be modified to exclude the uncontacted indigenous peoples' reserve, and the
Peruvian government has agreed to this request. This kind of action by an oil company, while still rare, would have been unthinkable even ten years ago; it shows how
local and international campaigns have brought the rights of indigenous peoples to
the forefront of multinational firms' thinking.

15. At the request of the UNPFII, an interagency workshop took place in 2005 to dis-
cuss the issue; for the report, see www.un.org/esa/socdev/unpfii. For a discussion of
ITK within the context of cultural rights, see Stamatopoulou, *Cultural Rights in
International Law*, 207–225.

16. For the text of the Declaration on the Rights of Indigenous Peoples, see www
.un.org/csa/socdev/unpfii.

17. Ibid.; Stamatopoulou, *Cultural Rights in International Law*, 171–173.

NO: Kwame Anthony Appiah,
Princeton University

I'm seated on a palace veranda, cooled by a breeze from the royal garden.
Before us, on a dais, is an empty throne, its arms and legs embossed with
polished brass, the back and seat covered in black-and-gold silk. In front of
the steps to the dais, there are two columns of people, mostly men, facing one
another, seated on carved wooden stools, the cloths they wear wrapped around
their chests, leaving their shoulders bare. There is a quiet buzz of conversation.
Outside in the garden, peacocks screech. At last, the blowing of a ram's horn
announces the arrival of the king of Asante, its tones sounding his honorific,

---

kotokohene, "porcupine chief." (Each quill of the porcupine, according to custom, signifies a warrior ready to kill and to die for the kingdom.) Everyone stands until the king has settled on the throne. Then, when we sit, a chorus sings songs in praise of him, which are interspersed with the playing of a flute. It is a Wednesday festival day in Kumasi, the town in Ghana where I grew up.

Unless you're one of a few million Ghanaians, this will probably seem a relatively unfamiliar world, perhaps even an exotic one. You might suppose that this Wednesday festival belongs quaintly to an African past. But before the king arrived, people were taking calls on cell phones, and among those passing the time in quiet conversation were a dozen men in suits, representatives of an insurance company. And the meetings in the office next to the veranda are about contemporary issues: HIV/AIDS, the educational needs of twenty-first-century children, the teaching of science and technology at the local university. When my turn comes to be formally presented, the king asks me about Princeton, where I teach. I ask him when he'll next be in the States. In a few weeks, he says cheerfully. He's got a meeting with the head of the World Bank.

Anywhere you travel in the world today, you can find ceremonies like this one, many of them rooted in centuries-old traditions. But you will also find everywhere—and this is something new—many intimate connections with places far away: Washington, Moscow, Mexico City, Beijing. Across the street from us, when we were growing up, there was a large house occupied by a number of families, among them a vast family of boys; one, about my age, was a good friend. Today, he lives in London. His brother lives in Japan, where his wife is from. They have another brother who has been in Spain for a while and a couple more brothers who, last I heard, were in the United States. Some of them still live in Kumasi, one or two in Accra, Ghana's capital.

When I was a child, we used to visit the previous king, my great-uncle by marriage, in a small building that the British had allowed his predecessor to build when he returned from exile in the Seychelles to a restored but diminished Asante kingship. That building is now a museum, dwarfed by the enormous house next door, where the current king lives. Next to it is the suite of offices abutting the veranda where we were sitting, recently finished by the present king. The British, my mother's people, conquered Asante at the turn of the twentieth century; now, at the turn of the twenty-first, the palace feels as it must have felt in the nineteenth century: a center of power. The president of Ghana comes from this world, too. He was born across the street from the palace to a member of the royal Oyoko clan. But he belongs to other worlds as well: he went to Oxford University; he's a member of one of the Inns of Court in London; he's a Catholic, with a picture of himself greeting the pope in his sitting room.

What are we to make of this? On Kumasi's Wednesday festival day, I've seen visitors from England and the United States wince at what they regard as the intrusion of modernity on timeless, traditional rituals—more evidence, they think, of a pressure in the modern world toward uniformity. They react like the assistant on the film set who's supposed to check that the extras in a sword-and-sandals movie aren't wearing wristwatches. And such purists are not alone. In the past couple of years, the UN Scientific, Educational, and Cultural Organization's (UNESCO) members have spent a great deal of time trying to hammer out a convention on the "protection and promotion" of cultural diversity. (It was finally approved at the UNESCO General Conference in October 2005.) The drafters worried that "the processes of globalization . . . represent a challenge for cultural diversity, namely in view of risks of imbalances between rich and poor countries." The fear is that the values and images of Western mass culture, like some invasive weed, are threatening to choke out the world's native flora.

The contradictions in this argument aren't hard to find. This same UNESCO document is careful to affirm the importance of the free flow of ideas, the freedom of thought and expression and human rights—values that, we know, will become universal only if we make them so. What's really important, then—cultures or people? In a world where Kumasi and New York—and Cairo and Leeds and Istanbul—are being drawn ever closer together, an ethics of globalization has proved elusive.

The right approach, I think, starts by taking individuals—not nations, tribes, or "peoples"—as the proper object of moral concern. It doesn't much matter what we call such a creed, but in homage to Diogenes, the fourth-century Greek Cynic and the first philosopher to call himself a "citizen of the world," we could call it *cosmopolitanism*. Cosmopolitans take cultural difference seriously, because they take the choices individual people make seriously. But because cultural difference is not the only thing that concerns them, they suspect that many of globalization's cultural critics are aiming at the wrong targets.

COSMOPOLITANISM COMBATS HOMOGENEITY

Yes, globalization can produce homogeneity. But globalization is also a threat to homogeneity. You can see this as clearly in Kumasi as anywhere. One thing Kumasi isn't is homogeneous. English, German, Chinese, Syrian, Lebanese, Burkinabe, Ivorian, Nigerian, Indian: I can find you families of each description. I can find you Asante people, whose ancestors have lived in this town for centuries, but also Hausa households that have been around for centuries, too. There are people from every region of the country as well, speaking scores of languages.

But if you travel just a little way outside Kumasi, you won't have difficulty finding villages that are fairly monocultural. The people have mostly been to Kumasi and seen the big, polyglot, diverse world of the city. Where they live, though, there is one everyday language and an agrarian way of life based on some old crops, such as yams, and some newer ones, such as cocoa, which arrived in the late nineteenth century as a product for export. They may or may not have electricity. When people talk of the homogeneity produced by globalization, what they are talking about is this: Even here, the villagers will have radios; you will be able to get a discussion going about Ronaldo, Mike Tyson, or Tupac; and you will probably be able to find a bottle of Guinness or Coca-Cola. But has access to these things made the place more homogeneous or less? And what can you tell about people's souls from the fact that they drink Coca-Cola?

It's true that the enclaves of homogeneity you find these days—in Asante as in Pennsylvania—are less distinctive than they were a century ago, but mostly in good ways. More of them have access to effective medicines. More of them have access to clean drinking water, and more of them have schools. Where, as is still too common, they don't have these things, it's something not to celebrate but to deplore. And whatever loss of difference there has been, they are constantly inventing new forms of difference: new hairstyles, new slang, even, from time to time, new religions. No one could say that the world's villages are becoming anything like the same.

So why do people in these places sometimes feel that their identities are threatened? Because the world, their world, is changing, and some of them don't like it. The pull of the global economy—witness those cocoa trees, whose chocolate is eaten all around the world—created some of the life they now live. If chocolate prices were to collapse again, as they did in the early 1990s, Asante farmers might have to find new crops or new forms of livelihood. That prospect is unsettling for some people. Missionaries came a while ago, so many of these villagers will be Christian, even if they have also kept some of the rites from earlier days. But new Pentecostal messengers are challenging the churches they know and condemning the old rites as idolatrous.

Above all, relationships are changing. When my father was young, a man in a village would farm some land that a chief had granted him, and his maternal clan (including his younger brothers) would work it with him. When a new house needed building, he would organize it. He would also make sure his dependents were fed and clothed, the children educated, marriages and funerals arranged and paid for. He could expect to pass the farm and the responsibilities along to the next generation.

Nowadays, everything is different. Cocoa prices have not kept pace with the cost of living. Gas prices have made the transportation of the crop more expensive. And there are new possibilities for the young in the towns, in other parts of the country, and in other parts of the world. Once, perhaps, you could have commanded the young ones to stay. Now they have the right to leave—perhaps to seek work at one of the new data-processing centers down south in the nation's capital—and, anyway, you may not make enough to feed and clothe and educate them all. So the time of the successful farming family is passing, and those who were settled in that way of life are as sad to see it go as are American family farmers whose lands are accumulated by giant agribusinesses. We can sympathize with them. But we cannot force their children to stay in the name of protecting their authentic culture, and we cannot afford to subsidize indefinitely thousands of distinct islands of homogeneity that no longer make economic sense.

Nor should we want to. Human variety matters, cosmopolitans think, because people are entitled to options. What John Stuart Mill said more than a century ago in *On Liberty* about diversity within a society serves just as well as an argument for variety across the globe:

> If it were only that people have diversities of taste, that is reason enough for not attempting to shape them all after one model. But different persons also require different conditions for their spiritual development; and can no more exist healthily in the same moral, than all the variety of plants can exist in the same physical atmosphere and climate. The same things which are helps to one person towards the cultivation of his higher nature, are hindrances to another. . . . Unless there is a corresponding diversity in their modes of life, they neither obtain their fair share of happiness, nor grow up to the mental, moral, and aesthetic stature of which their nature is capable.

If we want to preserve a wide range of human conditions because it allows free people the best chance to make their own lives, we can't enforce diversity by trapping people within differences they long to escape.

THE AMBIGUITY OF AUTHENTICITY

Even if you grant that people shouldn't be compelled to sustain the older cultural practices, you might suppose that cosmopolitans should side with those who are busy around the world "preserving culture" and resisting "cultural imperialism." Yet behind these slogans you often find some curious assumptions. Take "preserving culture." It's one thing to help people sustain arts they want to sustain. I am all for festivals of Welsh bards in Llandudno financed by the Welsh arts council. Long live the Ghana National Cultural Center in Kumasi, where you can go and learn traditional Akan dancing and drumming. Restore the deteriorating film stock of early Hollywood movies; continue the preservation of Old Norse and early Chinese and Ethiopian manuscripts; record, transcribe, and analyze the oral narratives of Malay and Masai and Maori. All these are undeniably valuable.

But preserving culture—in the sense of such cultural artifacts—is different from preserving cultures. And the cultural preservationists often pursue the latter, trying to ensure that the Huli of Papua New Guinea maintain their "authentic" ways. What makes a cultural expression authentic, though? Are we to stop the importation of baseball caps into Vietnam so that the Zao will continue to wear their colorful red headdresses? Why not ask the Zao? Shouldn't the choice be theirs?

"They have no real choice," the cultural preservationists say. "We've dumped cheap Western clothes into their markets, and they can no longer afford the silk they used to wear. If they had what they really wanted, they'd still be dressed traditionally." But this is no longer an argument about authenticity. The claim is that they can't afford to do something that they'd really like to do, something that is expressive of an identity they care about and want to sustain. This is a genuine problem, one that afflicts people in many communities: they're too poor to live the life they want to lead. But if they do get richer, and they still run around in T-shirts, that's their choice. Talk of authenticity now just amounts to telling other people what they ought to value in their own traditions.

Besides, trying to find some primordially authentic culture can be like peeling an onion. The textiles most people think of as traditional West African cloths are known as Java prints; they arrived in the nineteenth century with the Javanese batiks sold, and often milled, by the Dutch. The traditional garb of Herero women in Namibia derives from the attire of nineteenth-century German missionaries, though it is still unmistakably Herero, not least because the fabrics used have a distinctly un-Lutheran range of colors. And so with our kente cloth: the silk was always imported, traded by Europeans, produced in Asia. This tradition was once an innovation. Should we reject it for that reason as untraditional? How far back must one go? Should we condemn the young men and women of the University of Science and Technology, a few miles outside Kumasi, who wear European-style gowns for graduation, lined with kente strips (as they do now at Howard and Morehouse, too)? Cultures are made of continuities and changes, and the identity of a society can survive through these changes. Societies without change aren't authentic; they're just dead.

ADAPTING AND INTERPRETING CULTURAL INFLUENCES

The preservationists often make their case by invoking the evil of "cultural imperialism." Their underlying picture, in broad strokes, is this: There is a world system of capitalism. It has a center and a periphery. At the center—in Europe and the United States—is a set of multinational corporations. Some of them are in the media business. The products they sell around the world promote the creation of desires that can be fulfilled only by the purchase and use of their products. They do so explicitly through advertising, but more insidiously, they also do so through the messages implicit in movies and in television drama.

That's the theory, anyway. But the evidence doesn't bear it out. Researchers have actually gone out into the world and explored the responses to the hit television series *Dallas* in Holland and among Israeli Arabs, Moroccan Jewish immigrants, kibbutzniks, and new Russian immigrants to Israel. They have examined the actual content of the television media in Australia, Brazil, Canada, India, and Mexico. They have looked at how American popular culture was taken up by the artists of Sophiatown, in South Africa. They have discussed *Days of Our Lives* and *The Bold and the Beautiful* with Zulu college students from traditional backgrounds.

And one thing they've found is that how people respond to these cultural imports depends on their existing cultural context. When the media scholar Larry Strelitz spoke to students from KwaZulu-Natal, he found that they were anything but passive vessels. One of them, Sipho—a self-described "very, very strong Zulu man"—reported that he had drawn lessons from watching the American soap opera *Days of Our Lives*, "especially relationship-wise." It fortified his view that "if a guy can tell a woman that he loves her, she should be able to do the same." What's more, after watching the show, Sipho "realized that I should be allowed to speak to my father. He should be my friend rather than just my father." It seems doubtful that that was the intended message of multinational capitalism's ruling sector.

But Sipho's response also confirmed that cultural consumers are not dupes. They can adapt products to suit their own needs, and they can decide for themselves what they do and do not approve of. Here's Sipho again:

> In terms of our culture, a girl is expected to enter into relationships when she is about 20. In the Western culture, a girl can be exposed to a relationship as early as 15 or 16. That one we shouldn't adopt in our culture. Another thing we shouldn't adopt from the Western culture has to do with the way they treat elderly people. I wouldn't like my family to be sent into an old-age home.

Dutch viewers of *Dallas* saw not the pleasures of conspicuous consumption among the superrich—the message that theorists of "cultural imperialism" find in every episode—but a reminder that money and power don't protect you from tragedy. Israeli Arabs saw a program that confirmed that women abused by their husbands should return to their fathers. Mexican telenovelas remind Ghanaian women that, where sex is at issue, men are not to be trusted.

Talk of cultural imperialism "structuring the consciousnesses" of those in the periphery treats people like Sipho as blank slates on which global capitalism's moving finger writes its message, leaving behind another cultural automaton as it moves on. It is deeply condescending. And it isn't true.

COSMOPOLITANISM VERSUS NEOFUNDAMENTALISM: TENSION BETWEEN LIBERTY AND DIVERSITY

Sometimes, though, people react to the incursions of the modern world not by appropriating the values espoused by the liberal democracies but by inverting them. One recent result has been a new worldwide fraternity that presents cosmopolitanism with something of a sinister mirror image. Indeed, you could think of its members as counter-cosmopolitans. They believe in human dignity across the nations, and they live their creed. They share these ideals with people in many countries, speaking many languages. As thoroughgoing globalists, they make full use of the World Wide Web. They resist the crass consumerism of modern Western society and deplore its influence in the rest of the world.

But they also resist the temptations of the narrow nationalisms of the countries where they were born, along with the humble allegiances of kith and kin. They resist such humdrum loyalties because they get in the way of the one thing that matters: building a community of enlightened men and women across the world. That is one reason they reject traditional religious authorities. Sometimes they agonize in their discussions about whether they can reverse the world's evils or whether their struggle is hopeless. But mostly they soldier on in their efforts to make the world a better place.

These are not the heirs of Diogenes the Cynic. The community these comrades are building is not a polis; it's what they call the *ummah*, the global community of Muslims, and it is open to all who share their faith. They are young, global Muslim fundamentalists. The ummah's new globalists consider that they have returned to the fundamentals of Islam; much of what passes for Islam in the world, much of what has passed as Islam for centuries, they think a sham. As the French scholar Olivier Roy has observed, these religionists—his term for them is "neofundamentalists"—wish to cleanse from Islam's pristine and universal message the contingencies of mere history, of local cultures. For them, Roy notes, "globalization is a good opportunity to dissociate Islam from any given culture and to provide a model that could work beyond any culture."

They have taken a set of doctrines that once came with a form of life, in other words, and thrown away that form of life.

Now, the vast majority of these fundamentalists are not going to blow anybody up. So they should not be confused with those other Muslims— the "radical neofundamentalists," Roy calls them—who want to turn jihad, interpreted as literal warfare against the West, into the sixth pillar of Islam. Nonetheless, the neofundamentalists present a classic challenge to cosmopolitanism, because they, too, offer a moral and, in its way, inclusive universalism.

Unlike cosmopolitanism, of course, it is universalist without being tolerant, and such intolerant universalism has often led to murder. It underlaid the French Wars of Religion that bloodied the four decades before the Edict of Nantes of 1598, in which Henri IV of France finally granted to the Protestants in his realm the right to practice their faith. In the Thirty Years' War, which ravaged central Europe until the Peace of Westphalia in 1648, Protestant and Catholic princes from Austria to Sweden struggled with one another, and hundreds of thousands of Germans died in battle. Millions starved or died of disease as roaming armies pillaged the countryside. The period of religious conflict in the British Isles, from the first Bishops' War of 1639 to the end of the English Civil War in 1651, which pitted Protestant armies against the forces of a Catholic king, resulted in the deaths of perhaps 10 percent of the population. All these conflicts involved issues beyond sectarian doctrine, of course. Still, many Enlightenment liberals drew the conclusion that enforcing one vision of universal truth could only lead the world back to the bloodbaths.

Yet tolerance by itself is not what distinguishes the cosmopolitan from the neofundamentalist. There are plenty of things that the heroes of radical Islam are happy to tolerate. They don't care if you eat kebabs or meatballs or kung pao chicken, as long as the meat is halal; your hijab can be silk or linen or viscose. At the same time, there are plenty of things that cosmopolitans will not tolerate. We sometimes want to intervene in other places because what is going on there violates our principles so deeply. We, too, can see moral error. And when it is serious enough, we will not stop with conversation. Toleration has its limits.

Nor can you tell us apart by saying that the neofundamentalists believe in universal truth. Cosmopolitans believe in universal truth, too, though we are less certain that we already have all of it. One tenet we hold to, however, is that every human being has obligations to every other. Everybody matters: that is our central idea. And again, it sharply limits the scope of our tolerance.

To say what, in principle, distinguishes the cosmopolitan from competing universalisms, we plainly need to go beyond talk of truth and tolerance. One distinctively cosmopolitan commitment is to pluralism. Cosmopolitans think that there are many values worth living by and that you cannot live by all of them. So we hope and expect that different people and different societies will embody different values. Another aspect of cosmopolitanism is what philosophers call fallibilism—the sense that our knowledge is imperfect, provisional, [and] subject to revision in the face of new evidence.

The neofundamentalist conception of a global ummah, by contrast, admits of local variations—but only in matters that don't matter. These counter-cosmopolitans, like many Christian fundamentalists, do think that there is one right way for all human beings to live; that all the differences must be in the details. If what concerns you is global homogeneity, then this utopia, not the world that capitalism is producing, is the one you should worry about. Still, the universalisms in the name of religion are hardly the only ones that invert the cosmopolitan creed. In the name of universal humanity, you can be the kind of Marxist, such as Mao or Pol Pot, who wants to eradicate all religion, just as easily as you can be the Grand Inquisitor supervising an auto-da-fé. All of these men want everyone on their side, so we can share with them the vision in their mirror. Join us, the counter-cosmopolitans say, and we will all be sisters and brothers. But each of them plans to trample on our differences—to trample us to death, if necessary—if we will not join them.

That liberal pluralists are hostile to certain authoritarian ways of life—that they're intolerant of radical intolerance is sometimes seen as a kind of self-refutation. That's a mistake: you can care about individual freedom and still understand that the contours of that freedom will vary considerably from place to place. But we might as well admit that a concern for individual freedom isn't something that will appeal to every individual. In politics, including cultural politics, there are winners and losers—which is worth remembering when we think about international human rights treaties. When we seek to embody our concern for strangers in human rights law, and when we urge our governments to enforce it, we are seeking to change the world of law in every nation on the planet. We have declared slavery a violation of international law. And, in so doing, we have committed ourselves, at a minimum, to the desirability of its eradication everywhere. This is no longer controversial in the capitals of the world. No one defends enslavement. But international treaties define slavery in ways that arguably include debt bondage, and debt bondage is a significant economic institution in parts of South Asia. I hold no brief for debt bondage. Still, we shouldn't be surprised if people whose incomes and style of life depend upon it are angry.

It's the same with the international movements to promote women's equality. We know that many Islamists are deeply disturbed by the way Western men and women behave. We permit women to swim almost naked with strange men, which is our business, but it is hard to keep the news of these acts of immodesty from Muslim women and children or to protect Muslim men from the temptations they inevitably create. As the Internet extends its reach, it will get even harder, and their children, especially their girls, will be tempted to ask for these freedoms, too. Worse, they say, we are now trying to force our conception of how women and men should behave upon them. We speak of women's rights. We make treaties enshrining these rights. And then we want their governments to enforce them.

Like many people in every nation, I support those treaties; I believe that women, like men, should have the vote, should be entitled to work outside their homes, should be protected from the physical abuse of men, including their fathers, brothers, and husbands. But I also know that the changes these freedoms would bring will change the balance of power between men and women in everyday life. How do I know this? Because I have lived most of my adult life in the West as it has gone through just such a transition, and I know that the process is not yet complete.

So liberty and diversity may well be at odds, and the tensions between them aren't always easily resolved. But the rhetoric of cultural preservation isn't any help. Again, the contradictions are near to hand. Take another look at that UNESCO Convention. It affirms the "principle of equal dignity of and respect for all cultures." (What, all cultures—including those of the KKK and the Taliban?) It also affirms "the importance of culture for social cohesion in general, and in particular its potential for the enhancement of the status and role of women in society." (But doesn't "cohesion" argue for uniformity? And wouldn't enhancing the status and role of women involve changing, rather than preserving, cultures?) In Saudi Arabia, people can watch *Will and Grace* on satellite TV—officially proscribed, but available all the same—knowing that, under Saudi law, Will could be beheaded in a public square. In northern Nigeria, mullahs inveigh against polio vaccination while sentencing adulteresses to death by stoning. In India, thousands of wives are burned to death each year for failing to make their dowry payments. Vive la différence? Please.

UNDERSTANDING, AND POSSIBLY (BUT NOT NECESSARILY) AGREEING

Living cultures do not, in any case, evolve from purity into contamination; change is more a gradual transformation from one mixture to a new mixture—a process that usually takes place at some distance from rules and rulers, in the conversations that occur across cultural boundaries. Such conversations are not so much about arguments and values as about the exchange of perspectives. I don't say that we can't change minds, but the reasons we offer in our conversation will seldom do much to persuade others who do not share our fundamental evaluative judgments already. When we make judgments, after all, it's rarely because we have applied well-thought-out principles to a set of facts and deduced an answer. Our efforts to justify what we have done are typically made up after the event, rationalizations of what we have decided intuitively to do. And a good deal of what we intuitively take to be right, we take to be right just because it is what we are used to. That does not mean, however, that we cannot become accustomed to doing things differently.

Consider the practice of foot binding in China, which persisted for a thousand years—and was largely eradicated within a generation. The anti-foot-binding campaign, in the first two decades of the twentieth century, did circulate facts about the disadvantages of bound feet, but those facts couldn't have come as news to most people. Perhaps more effective was the campaign's emphasis that no other country went in for the practice; in the world at large, then, China was "losing face" because of it. (To China's cultural preservationists, of course, the fact that the practice was peculiar to the region was entirely a mark in its favor.) Natural-foot societies were formed, their members forswearing the practice and further pledging that their sons would not marry women with bound feet. As the movement took hold, scorn was heaped on older women with bound feet, and they were forced to endure the agonies of unbinding. What had been beautiful became ugly; ornamentation became disfigurement. The appeal to reason can explain neither the custom nor its abolition.

So, too, with other social trends. Just a couple of generations ago, most people in most of the industrialized world thought that middle-class women would ideally be housewives and mothers. If they had time on their hands, they could engage in charitable work or entertain one another; a few of them might engage in the arts—writing novels, painting, or performing in music, theater, and dance. But there was little place for them in the "learned professions"—as lawyers or doctors, priests or rabbis; and if they were to be academics, they would teach young women and probably remain unmarried. They were not likely to make their way in politics, except perhaps at the local level. And they were not made welcome in science.

How much of the shift away from these assumptions is a result of arguments? Isn't a significant part of it just the consequence of our getting used to new ways of doing things? The arguments that kept the old pattern in place were not—to put it mildly—terribly good. If the reasons for the old sexist way of doing things had been the problem, the women's movement could have been done in a couple of weeks.

Consider another example: In much of Europe and North America, in places where a generation ago homosexuals were social outcasts and homosexual acts were illegal, lesbian and gay couples are increasingly being recognized by their families, by society, and by the law. This is true despite the continued opposition of major religious groups and a significant and persisting undercurrent of social disapproval. Both sides make arguments, some good, most bad. But if you ask the social scientists what has produced this change, they will rightly not start with a story about reasons. They will give you a historical account that concludes with a sort of perspectival shift. The increasing presence of "openly gay" people in social life and in the media has changed our habits. And over the past thirty years or so, instead of thinking about the private activity of gay sex, many Americans and Europeans started thinking about the public category of gay people.

One of the great savants of the postwar era, John von Neumann, liked to say, mischievously, that "in mathematics you don't understand things, you just get used to them." As in mathematical arguments, so in moral ones. Now, I don't deny that all the time, at every stage, people were talking, giving one another reasons to do things: accept their gay children, stop treating homosexuality as a medical disorder, disagree with their churches, come out. Still, the short version of the story is basically this: People got used to lesbians and gay men.

I am urging that we should learn about people in other places, take an interest in their civilizations, their arguments, their errors, their achievements, not because that will bring us to agreement but because it will help us get used to one another—something we have a powerful need to do in this globalized era. If that is the aim, then the fact that we have all these opportunities for disagreement about values need not put us off. Understanding one another may be hard; it can certainly be interesting. But it doesn't require that we come to agreement.

THE CASE FOR CONTAMINATION

The ideals of purity and preservation have licensed a great deal of mischief in the past century, but they have never had much to do with lived culture. Ours may be an era of mass migration, but the global spread and hybridization of culture—through travel, trade, or conquest—is hardly a recent development. Alexander's empire molded both the states and the sculpture of Egypt and North India; the Mongols and then the Mughals shaped great swaths of Asia; the Bantu migrations populated half the African continent. Islamic states stretch from Morocco to Indonesia; Christianity reached Africa, Europe, and Asia within a few centuries of the death of Jesus of Nazareth; Buddhism long ago migrated from India into much of East and Southeast Asia. Jews and people whose ancestors came from many parts of China have long lived in vast diasporas. The traders of the Silk Road changed the style of elite dress in Italy; someone buried Chinese pottery in fifteenth-century Swahili graves. I have heard it said that the bagpipes started out in Egypt and came to Scotland with the Roman infantry. None of this is modern.

Our guide to what is going on here might as well be a former African slave named Publius Terentius Afer, whom we know as Terence. Born in Carthage, Terence was taken to Rome in the early second century B.C., and his plays were widely admired among the city's literary elite. Terence's own mode of writing— which involved freely incorporating any number of earlier Greek plays into a single Latin one—was known to Roman littérateurs as "contamination."

It's an evocative term. When people speak for an ideal of cultural purity, sustaining the authentic culture of the Asante or the American family farm, I find myself drawn to contamination as the name for a counter-ideal. Terence had a notably firm grasp on the range of human variety: "So many men, so many opinions" was a line of his. And it's in his comedy, *The Self-Tormentor*, that you'll find what may be the golden rule of cosmopolitanism—*Homo sum: humani nil a me alienum puto*: "I am human: nothing human is alien to me." The context is illuminating. A busybody farmer named Chremes is told by his neighbor to mind his own affairs; the *homo sum* credo is Chremes's breezy rejoinder. It isn't meant to be an ordinance from on high; it's just the case for gossip.

The ideal of contamination has few exponents more eloquent than Salman Rushdie, who has insisted that the novel that occasioned his *fatwa* "celebrates hybridity, impurity, intermingling, the transformation that comes of new and unexpected combinations of human beings, cultures, ideas, politics, movies, songs. It rejoices in mongrelisation and fears the absolutism of the Pure. Mélange, hotch-potch, a bit of this and a bit of that is how newness enters the world." No doubt there can be an easy and spurious utopianism of "mixture," as there is of "purity," or "authenticity." And yet the larger human truth is on the side of contamination—that endless process of imitation and revision.

A tenable global ethics has to temper a respect for difference with a respect for the freedom of actual human beings to make their own choices. That's why cosmopolitans don't insist that everyone become cosmopolitan. They know they don't have all the answers. They're humble enough to think that they might learn from strangers; not too humble to think that strangers can't learn from them. Few remember what Chremes says after his "I am human" line, but it is equally suggestive: "If you're right, I'll do what you do. If you're wrong, I'll set you straight."

16

civil society

Do Nongovernmental Organizations Wield Too Much Power?

YES: Kenneth Anderson, *Washington College of Law, American University*

NO: Marlies Glasius, *University of Amsterdam*

Civil society is an all-encompassing title for a host of nonstate, noncorporate actors that participate in various ways in global governance. This category includes individual nongovernmental organizations (NGOs), **transnational action networks** (collections of NGOs in different countries with a shared vision and tactics), and social movements. The presence of these representatives of civil society at international negotiations and conferences has become a common feature of international politics. Environmental NGOs were identified as important actors at the 1992 Earth Summit, where they were recognized as a major group in the conference documents. Starting with protests at the 1999 Seattle World Trade Organization (WTO) meeting, large-scale public demonstrations against globalization have been widespread, and they commonly accompany meetings of major international organizations.

Given the large number of individual NGOs and the various types of actors, it is difficult to offer simple statements about civil society. It is equally unclear if any unifying political visions or beliefs exist within civil society. Many claim to act on behalf of the public good, although there are often variations between different actors' views of what constitutes the public good and how it is to be provided; some may have positive effects as a consequence of their global involvement by improving governments' accountability to their citizens and by directly delivering services to local communities.

A minimal definition of an NGO can be found in the list of required features that is used by the United Nations in granting recognition to these organizations: an established headquarters, an administration, authorized representatives, a policymaking body, and a presence in at least two countries. By conservative estimate, there were 37,281 international NGOs in 2000, which is 19 percent higher than the number from 1990. The growth in the number of NGOs registered with the UN Economic and Social Council (ECOSOC) demonstrates their increasing prevalence in world affairs (see Figure 1, this page).

NGOs engage in activities targeted at a wide range of issues. The largest numbers of NGOs are involved in matters of economic development, policy research, and social service provision.

NGOs also perform a wide array of functions. Activist NGOs contribute to international agenda setting by publicizing new issues. Many engage in public education and consciousness raising on the specific issues of importance to them. At international negotiations, NGOs lead lobbying efforts and provide valuable policy information to smaller delegations. NGOs contribute to the enforcement of international commitments by identifying state and corporate violators and shaming them through public campaigns. Many NGOs

Figure 1

NGOs with Consultative Status with the UN Economic and Social Council (ECOSOC), 1948–2008

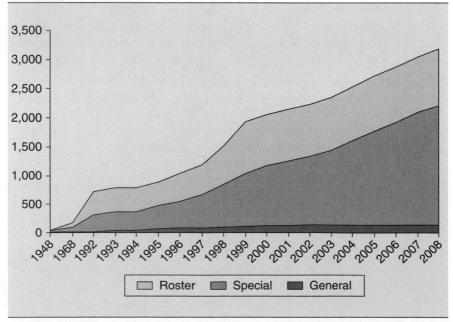

Source: United Nations Department of Economic and Social Affairs (http://esa.un.org/coordination/ngo/new/index
.asp?page-chart2007).

conduct human rights verification studies as well as monitoring compliance with various international agreements. For example, organized transnational NGO campaigns have led to the elimination of landmines and overturned an international treaty aimed at liberalizing international investment (the Multilateral Agreement on Investment).

Many NGOs also play key roles in delivering development services such as education, food and medicine, and job training in developing countries as well as in administering governmental foreign aid. Governments channel assistance through NGOs, which conduct the training activities on the ground. The share of governmental aid actually flowing through NGOs varied from 4 to 9 percent between 1994 and 2010. Figure 2 (this page) shows Organization of Economic Cooperation and Development (OECD) development assistance as actually disbursed through NGOs from 1994 to 2010. Many NGOs based in developing countries engage in public education, research, lobbying, and the local delivery of services.

Civil society's ability to effectively perform this array of governance functions has been subject to much debate in part because of the relative novelty

Figure 2

Trend in Net OECD Development Assistance Committee Grants Disbursed through NGOs, 1994–2010

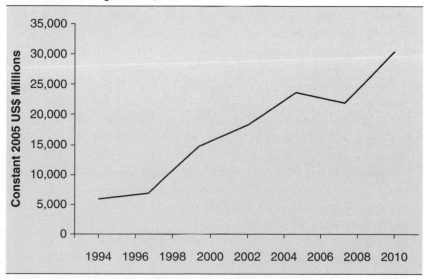

Source: Organization of Economic Cooperation and Development, *Statistics on Resource Flows to Developing Countries, Table 2: Total Net Flows from DAC Countries by Type of Flow*, http://www.oecd.org/document/9/0,3343, en_2649_34447_1893129_1_1_1,00.html (accessed December 23, 2011)[1].

of widespread involvement by nonstate networks at the international level. Civil society can be uncivil and unruly: the large public **antiglobalization demonstrations** since 1999 have often been disruptive of the routines of the host nations. In order to attract publicity for their activities, a small number of high-profile antiglobalization actors have engaged in property damage and **ecoterrorism**, such as the Sea Shepherd Society's ongoing antiwhaling campaigns and the French farmer José Bové's 1999 assault on a French McDonald's.

Some observers have suggested that NGO campaigns may be shaped by their need to attract publicity and funding. Consequently, they may choose topics by their potential to outrage rather than by a calculation of needs; and they may abandon campaigns before having fully achieved their goals.

Unchecked NGO activism may have detrimental effects on local communities. Journalist Sebastian Mallaby found that a Ugandan dam project that was intended to cut by 40 percent the number of people living below the absolute poverty line was opposed by international NGOs because of their general antipathy to dams, regardless of the specific benefits of individual projects. Mallaby suggests that NGOs may disregard such mitigating factors in their determination to elevate their own political standing or to promote their universal mission.[2]

The operation of Western NGOs in the global South may also be seen by host governments as an infringement on their sovereignty. Vladimir Putin tried to limit their civil rights within Russia. Prominent U.S. political scientist Robert Keohane cautiously notes that these agents of civil society may be internationally destabilizing, because they undercut the principle of national sovereignty on which international relations are grounded.[3] Thus states may be reluctant to actively involve civil society in global governance. Conversely, global governance catalyzed by civil society may lack legitimacy in the eyes of states.

Policy questions revolve around civil society's relationship with traditional authoritative actors. It is unclear to what extent NGOs are potentially coopted or diffused by having to deal with the extensive detailed procedural red tape that is associated with regular involvement with governments and international organizations or to what extent NGOs may be subversive by means of their ability to educate governments and other major actors as well as their impact in galvanizing local communities.

Many analysts and policymakers find civil society to be both analytically and normatively attractive as a liberal or cosmopolitan approach to world politics. Unlike international politics, which are usually understood as a hierarchical set of political relationships in which a few powerful states run things, NGOs operate more horizontally and in networks. Thus they provide a more attractive model of politics, which is potentially more egalitarian and efficient at diffusing information than the traditional hierarchical approach.

The following articles address the legitimacy of NGOs operating in the developing world and their accountability. Kenneth Anderson questions the authority of NGOs, asking whose interests they, in fact, represent and to whom they are accountable. Thus he challenges the legitimacy of the political and policy agenda that NGOs advance. Marlies Glasius argues that NGOs contribute to transparency and thus make governments more accountable to their citizens as well as to the international community.

Discussion Questions

1. What is civil society? Who are its members? Where does their power derive from? Who are they accountable to?
2. In what way does civil society's involvement in governance benefit society? Who does it benefit most? Are there drawbacks to its involvement?
3. Some claim that NGOs help to make international governance and decision making more democratic. Others contend that NGOs only add to the democratic deficit in international bodies. Which position do you agree with? Why?
4. Kenneth Anderson says that NGOs seek too much influence, depending on where they derive their power from and to what extent they seek to use their power. What does he mean? What examples does he give to make his argument? Do you agree with him?
5. What is the ethical contribution of NGOs as described by Marlies Glasius? What impact does she think this ethical contribution has on governments? Do you agree with her conclusion?

NOTES

1. *OECD Total Net Official Flows from DAC Member Countries and Multilateral Agencies by Type of Flow*, OECD Publishing, 2010, Table 6.
2. Sebastian Mallaby, "NGOs: Fighting Poverty, Hurting the Poor," *Foreign Policy* 144 (2004): 50–59.
3. Robert O. Keohane, "Global Governance and Democratic Accountability," in *Taming Globalization*, eds. David Held and Mathias Koenig-Archibui (Oxford: Polity, 2003).

YES: Kenneth Anderson, *Washington College of Law, American University*

N GOs [nongovernmental organizations] can claim excessive power depending on *where* the power they exercise, or hope to exercise, is supposed to come from and in what *capacity* they seek to use their power.

The Nobel Peace Prize Committee, in awarding the 1997 prize to Jody Williams and the International Committee to Ban Landmines, put forth the proposition that NGOs are full-fledged members of the global society, alongside states and public organizations:

> Public opinion must be formed and directed by the active involvement of individual members . . . in society's manifold organizations or associations. These are the fundamental institutional elements of what we have learned to know as a civil society. . . . [I]n the extensive cooperation . . . between . . . non-governmental organizations, . . . national governments, and the international political system . . . we may be seeing the outline of . . . a global civil society.[1]

When international NGOs assume power and authority to join with international organizations such as the United Nations on the grounds that they represent what the UN Charter calls the "peoples of the world" and claim authority to act on their behalf, then indeed they have too much power—or, at least, they claim power on the basis of a false premise.

If, on the other hand, they simply seek to lobby international organizations and governments by speaking for themselves and not claiming to speak for anyone else, and if they make their advocacy claims based on accurate and demonstrated evidence of expertise and competence at what they do, then they merit close attention by actual decision makers in governments and international organizations. Their legitimate power depends on what NGOs claim as the reason why anyone should listen to them, and on whether they claim that their point of view should prevail simply because they are NGOs and somehow "represent" the peoples of the world—whether the peoples of the world know it or not.

NGOs that are competent, expert, and knowledgeable in the way that good advocates should be merit the not-insubstantial power that goes along with powerful advocacy—not as a matter of right, but as a matter of persuasiveness.

FROM "INTERNATIONAL NGOS" TO "GLOBAL CIVIL SOCIETY"

With the end of the Cold War and the fall of the Soviet empire in 1989, the weight of bipolar superpower struggle ended. A broad but loose U.S. hegemony guaranteed the security of the world's industrialized democracies. The expanding NATO alliance and the demise of the Soviet Union and the Warsaw Pact meant that the United States had no external state enemies to speak of. Saddam Hussein's 1990 invasion and annexation of Kuwait, leading to the First Gulf War, raised hopes among many "liberal internationalists" that a new era could be ushered in—an era in which international law and institutions such as the UN could create "global governance" that would overcome the anarchy of states and their power struggles and establish some form, however loose, of binding law over states.

What did these geopolitical shifts among nation-states have to do with international NGOs? The end of the Cold War persuaded many NGOs, particularly in those focusing in the areas of human rights, the environment, and the women's movement, that the moment had come to claim their rightful part in globalization—and go global themselves. This prospect meant, first, expanding their activities, membership, and organizational structures across borders, so as to be genuinely cross-border organizations. But also, Western and northern-based NGOs that had not seen much point in engaging with the UN during the frozen decades of bipolar superpower struggle now came to see the UN as a fruitful—indeed, a *rightful*—place to lobby, advocate, and organize.

Throughout the decade that followed, international NGOs were taking part in, or else learning lessons from, the transformative experience of NGOs of the early 1990s. The most significant of these examples was the international campaign to ban antipersonnel landmines, begun in the 1980s initially as a grave concern of the International Committee of the Red Cross (ICRC), which saw firsthand the humanitarian damage of landmines, mostly in civil wars. This campaign took shape in the early 1990s as a loose coalition of leading international NGOs that crossed disciplinary lines—human rights, humanitarianism, medical relief, development, and others—and came together as the network of the International Campaign to Ban Landmines (ICBL). Along with its director, Jody Williams, the ICBL won the 1997 Nobel Peace Prize for the achievement of a comprehensive ban treaty, the Ottawa Convention, which has attained ratification by states worldwide.

The landmines ban campaign contains many lessons for international NGOs, but the one that concerns us here is perhaps the most abstract and most politically ambitious. It is the idea that international NGOs can be understood as more than simply skillful lobbyists and advocates for causes that concern their organizations and memberships. Instead, they can be perceived as advocating on behalf of the citizens of the world. Moreover, this lesson demonstrates that international NGOs should be regarded in the international community as a force for "democratizing" international politics by breaking down the state-centric nature of the international system and its core assumption that states deal only with one another or with the international organizations that states themselves create, such as the UN, and not with individuals or NGOs or citizens groups.

The landmines ban campaign, among its many other dimensions, challenged that state-centric model, asserting that the international system would henceforth have to deal, if not precisely with individuals, then with organizations that would advocate their interests before international bodies. International NGOs were to be understood as advocating on behalf of individuals and populations directly, as opposed to states advocating on behalf of their citizens. Hence, in virtue of this direct representation function, international NGOs must be accorded parallel status to states and international organizations in making decisions, creating treaties, and setting standards on issues ranging from human rights to international development to the content of international law. The landmines ban campaign had secured a place for NGOs alongside states in negotiating the Ottawa Convention; since the ICBL had been responsible for bringing the treaty about, it would have been unseemly, churlish even, for the negotiating states to exclude from their meetings its main promoter—and this recognition established a new precedent of international NGO participation as speaking on behalf of the world's peoples. No longer claiming merely to advise or advocate or lobby on the basis of their expertise and competence in a particular area, international NGOs now asserted a breathtakingly sweeping claim to a seat at the table of global governance on the basis of *speaking for* the "peoples of the world." Representation, in a word: international NGOs, rather than governments, would represent people.

The final version of the idea that emerged during the 1980s and 1990s was that civil society consisted of social and political activity that was neither part of the state, nor part of the market. Its locus was the space of social life, sometimes political and sometimes not, where human beings pursued interests that were ordered—and ordered about—by neither the state nor the market. Such social spaces made possible organized, civilized politics in a liberal sense because they allowed for organizing, for discussion, for mediation of social and political claims, outside the impositions of state authority but also outside the economic inequalities and hierarchies imposed by the market.

However, critical concerns were raised about the role of civil society in relation to domestic societies. The proposition that international NGOs should be conceived as a kind of global civil society was, in fact, a double assertion. First, the claim that this global civil society, analogous to domestic civil society, served as the organized response of citizens across the globe, as intermediaries on behalf of the world's peoples, and as representatives for their sakes, then, naturally, posed several questions: the organized response to whom, as intermediaries before whom, and representatives to whom?

Second, global civil society was claimed to act in those roles both "in front of" and "in partnership with" international organizations such as the UN. Regarding states, on the other hand, the relationship was always one of equality—as equal pretenders in addressing issues, on the one hand, and in addressing international organizations of global governance, on the other. Global civil society might work with states in "partnership," as representatives of the people of the world, or it might work against them, insofar as global civil society believed that states, or particular states, were not representing the interests of the world's peoples.

Theorists of global civil society took various positions on the exact relationships among global civil society, states, international organizations, and the "international community" generally. But the core point was that global civil society saw itself as at least as legitimate, if not more so, in proclaiming, advocating, and insisting that it was right in its representation and intermediation on behalf of the peoples of the world, as the states that otherwise purported to represent them. And if international organizations—such as the UN—wanted to have the legitimacy of a genuinely global constituency, they too would have to accept partnership with global civil society.

WHAT'S WRONG WITH THE CONVENTIONAL ACCOUNT OF GLOBAL CIVIL SOCIETY?

Given the undeniable attractions of greater transparency and visibility in the making of global policy—whether by states together or through the UN—what could possibly be wrong with this intellectual and ideological ratcheting up, in effect, of international NGOs from mere observers, advocates, and advisers to the status of representatives? What's not to like?

The most obvious problems are with the claims, made with greater and greater extravagance throughout the later 1990s, of the special status of global civil society as representatives and intermediaries. Policy analyst David Rieff put the matter bluntly in a sharp intellectual challenge in 1999, asking, "So who elected the NGOs?"[2] It was a question that increasing numbers of previously sympathetic observers began to ask following the antiglobalization riots in Seattle in December 1999, when violent protests succeeded in shutting down meetings of the World Trade Organization (WTO). Those disturbances were largely forgotten as the terrorist attacks of September 11, 2001, and the Iraq and Afghanistan wars took over the central attention of global elites, but they inaugurated a wave of skepticism about the inflation of ideological claims by international NGOs that still echoes today.

The Seattle riots, and the fact that so many supposedly "respectable" NGOs that had been considered to be desirable interlocutors of institutions such as the World Bank and the UN stood aside from criticizing the violence in the streets, caused what might be called the "responsible global business community" to question their support and to wonder aloud just who and, indeed, how many, these organizations actually represented. Influential global establishment voices such as *The Economist* magazine and the *Financial Times* had been favorable throughout the 1990s to the landmines ban campaign. Indeed, they had generally favored the role played by NGOs and had, in effect, endorsed the idea that a maturing global capital system would have a global civil society—which is to say, they had accepted uncritically the idea that global civil society really was the analogue of civil society in a domestic democratic society. Following Seattle, however, they began to sharply question the issue of representativeness.

For instance, when Fareed Zakaria, then managing editor of *Foreign Affairs*, contacted ten NGOs after the Seattle riots, he found that "most consisted of 'three people and a fax.'" He expressed the concern, which was widely echoed among global elites outside the NGOs and the antiglobalization community, that the "rich world will listen too much to the loud minority" of First World activists and "neglect the fears of the silent majority" in the developing world who would benefit from activities not considered virtuous by the elites of the developed world.[3] *The Economist* ran a series of articles with titles such as "NGOs: Sins of the Secular Missionaries" and "Citizens Groups: The non-governmental order: Will NGOs democratize, or merely disrupt, global governance?"[4]

These observers were not opposed ideologically to the idea of either international NGOs or global governance, but in their eyes, the claims of representativeness suddenly, after Seattle, appeared to be as dangerous as they were unfounded. Journalist Sebastian Mallaby, in a famous—or infamous—article in *Foreign Policy* and, later, in a section of his book on the World Bank, recounted his visit to an NGO in Uganda that had been widely touted by the International Rivers Network (an American NGO based in Berkeley, California), as representing local opposition to a dam project that promised to bring electricity to a vast number of people: he went to the Uganda offices and discovered, looking at the inscription record, that the NGO had a total of twenty-five members.[5]

Do NGOs wield too much power when they inflate themselves into global civil society, representing supposedly vast populations with which, in fact, they have no real contact at all? Yes. The claim of representation amounts to a claim of being the legitimate intermediaries for all these people, which in turn really amounts to a claim of knowing what they want and what is best for them. One is entitled to be skeptical of the power that NGOs claim. Can the world's peoples really set aside their governments so easily, and dismiss the complex trade-offs that governments—even ones that are not especially transparent or democratic—have to make in governing? It is one thing to criticize these governments for not representing their citizens democratically—and fair enough. But there is an immense gap between making that criticism and saying that international NGOs and their judgments should substitute for those governments and *their* judgments. Whatever one might (correctly) think about those governments, assessing the legitimacy of NGOs is another matter entirely.

These nonstate actors' claims to representativeness and intermediation are thus gravely suspect, and to the extent that international NGOs rely upon such claims—rely upon them and so characterize themselves as global civil society— they exercise, or seek to exercise, too much power. Or, more precisely, they seek to exercise power from a source to which they are not legitimately entitled. And the path of NGOs today has been one of carefully hedged retreat, at least in public, from these claims of representativeness. Thus, for example, the head of Greenpeace UK, Peter Melchett, stated in an interview not long after the Seattle riots what might seem to be the obvious view:

> Democratic governments are elected and have democratic legitimacy. Other organizations, such as Greenpeace, *The Spectator* and the *Guardian*, do not. We have the legitimacy of our market of who buys us or supports us. I don't claim any greater legitimacy than that, nor do I want it.[6]

The self-abnegation and self-effacement of this statement are admirable—if only one could quite believe it. However, the general experience of negotiations, discussions, and drafting sessions at international organizations such as the UN, the World Bank, the International Monetary Fund, the WTO, and so on, is that global civil society does indeed expect to be invited in and have a seat at the table. It really does believe that it is in partnership with democratic governments, or at least ought to be. This is what it learned from the landmines campaign, after all.

The UN Charter recognizes a certain advisory and expert role for NGOs, but what is sought and claimed here goes far beyond that status. To claim a role not merely as an advocate representing one's own organizational point of view, buttressed by expertise that is respected by others (or perhaps not), is really only possible if NGOs believe, and expect others to believe, that they cannot be kept out of the decision-making processes because they really *are*, even after all the skepticism, truly "representative" of the peoples of the world in a way that no one and nothing else is: not international organizations, and certainly not states, not even democratic ones.

Moreover—and this is a point not sufficiently acknowledged in the debate— to the extent that an NGO is granted access and status and legitimacy by virtue of being "representative" of someone or something, its actual expertise, competence, and accomplishment become correspondingly less relevant. The right of access is granted on account of the claim of representation, not on the claim of relevant expertise. Such access dangerously undercuts the idea that NGOs ought to know whereof they speak—and, because it empowers the incompetent equally as the competent, makes it more difficult for the objectively and genuinely competent NGOs to make their voices heard.

YES, TOO POWERFUL IF . . .

Expertise and competence are not everything. In democratic societies, we elect people who may indeed lack expertise and competence; the consent of the governed, including faith in those who rule them, wisely or unwisely, belongs to those same governed. Nor, for that matter, would most of us want to be governed by technical experts alone; too many of the questions that make up a politics cannot be settled on technical grounds alone, but inevitably involve questions of values.

The problem is that even if governments lack all the legitimacy one might want—even if they lack democratic legitimacy—that is very, very far from justifying the argument that therefore global civil society can take over for them. And the case is the same for international organizations that lack any real basis in democratic legitimacy. Expertise and competence are not enough to give international NGOs the kind of authority within the international system that they plainly believe—still believe—they merit.

In that sense—the sense of their self-proclaimed role as global civil society— NGOs will wield too much power if given the opportunity, because that is the power they believe they merit. Eventually, the role of faux-representativeness undermines such competence and expertise as the NGOs have, because over the long term their incentives are changed. Yet this change cannot be good for them or for those whom, without claiming to represent them in the world, at their best they can and should serve. The unpleasant burden upon states and international organizations, therefore, is to tell the international NGOs "no" when they overreach from claims of expertise to claims—however covert, however much at odds with their public proclamations of modesty—of representation of the peoples of the world. NGOs do not represent the people; they represent themselves, and their power ought to be tied strictly to that condition.

NOTES

1. Francis Sejersted, Nobel Prize Committee Chairman, Presentation Speech for Nobel Laureates ICBL and Jody Williams, December 10, 1997; this quotation borrows Roger Alford's useful interpolation in his "The Nobel Effect: Nobel Peace Prize Laureates as International Norm Entrepreneurs," *Virginia Journal of International Law* 49, no. 1 (2008): 61, 147.
2. David Rieff, "The False Dawn of Civil Society," *The Nation*, February 22, 1999.
3. Justin Marozzi, "Whose World Is It Anyway?" *The Spectator* (London), August 5, 2000.
4. *The Economist*, January 29, 2000; and December 11, 1999, respectively.
5. See Sebastian Mallaby, *The World's Banker: A Story of Failed States, Financial Crises, and the Wealth and Poverty of Nations* (New York: Penguin, 2004), 7–8. This incident has generated practically a whole industry in NGO responses, none of which I myself find very convincing. However, perhaps the best and most representative is that of the former director of International Rivers, Juliette Majot, "On Trying To Do Well: Practicing Participatory Democracy through International Advocacy Campaigns," in Lisa Jordan and Peter Van Tuijl, eds., *NGO Accountability: Politics, Principles, and Innovations* (London: Earthscan, 2006); and see my review of that book and article in Kenneth Anderson, "What NGO Accountability Does and Does Not Mean," *American Journal of International Law* (January 2009).
6. Marozzi, "Whose World Is It, Anyway?"

NO: Marlies Glasius, *University of Amsterdam*

Over the past fifteen years, diplomats and officials of international organizations have been celebrating the advent of newcomers in their midst. In 1994 Boutros Boutros-Ghali addressed a gathering of NGO [nongovernmental organization] representatives as follows: "I want you to consider this your home. Until recently, these words might have caused astonishment. The United Nations was considered to be a forum for sovereign states alone. . . . [NGOs] are now considered full participants in international life" (Boutros-Ghali 1994). According to Dutch diplomat Adriaan Bos, chair of the negotiations on the International Criminal Court, the presence of international NGOs "fills in gaps arising from a democratic deficit in the international decision-making process" (Bos 1999, 44–45). Why are these officials so pleased to be sharing the stage with new actors whose mandate to be part of the negotiations is much less obvious than their own? Should we share their enthusiasm?

International decision making has not traditionally been a democratic process. Yet there is an increasing sense among national and international diplomats that, as more decisions have moved up to the international level, international decision making, and international lawmaking in particular, ought to be (more) democratic. This idea is related to a more general recognition by political thinkers that, while more states have been converted to parliamentary democracy, the onset of globalization has eroded the substance of democratic participation and choice (see, for instance, Held 1995; McGrew 1997; Scholte 2001). The enthusiasm for NGOs, and the claim that they make international decision making "more democratic" should be seen in this context.

Assessing this claim requires, first of all, a brief enquiry into the meaning of *democracy*. Its Greek root means simply "rule by the people," but in its modern use, the term usually implies a system of governance whereby "the people" periodically elect representatives, while key civil and political rights are observed. It is difficult to make a direct link between either of these meanings and the contribution of NGOs to international decision-making processes. In fact, Kenneth Anderson's strong objection to the idea of a global civil society— echoed in his essay in this book—is based precisely on what he believes to be a conflation of the roles of elected representatives at the national level and of NGOs at the global level. "But who elected the international NGOs?" he asks, then going on to observe that most NGOs are "not very often connected, in any direct way, to masses of 'people'" (Anderson 2000, 112–118).

This is true. But neither, many democratic theorists would point out, are political parties. Since the 1970s, there has been a severe drop in the number of party members, in the attendance at party conferences, and in voter turnout in most established democracies. Like the electorate at large, democratic theorists have become increasingly disillusioned with representative democracy, calling it "thin" or "procedural" democracy. While by and large continuing to advocate representation and civil and political rights as minimum conditions for democracy, they have explored forms that would make citizens participate more actively in politics, referring to such forms as "strong" (Barber 1984), "participatory" (Pateman 1970), and, especially, "deliberative" (Bessette 1980; Cohen and Rogers 1983; Gutmann and Thompson 1996) democracy.

It is on such notions of democracy, rather than on classic representation, that the argument is built that NGOs democratize international decision making—or "global governance," as its proponents tend to call it. They agree that such processes are not democratic in their present form, but contend that NGO participation makes them more so than they would otherwise be (Scholte 2001; Van Rooy 2004). NGOs, grandly renamed "global civil society actors," have been conceptualized as a "functional equivalent" (Rosenau, 1998, 40–41) or "alternative mechanism" (Scholte 2001, 15) to the multiparty representational system for democratizing global governance.

Here I will first examine some of these supposed democratic functions of NGOs by considering their contribution to five generally accepted characteristics of democracy: transparency, equality, deliberation, representation, and participation. Subsequently, I will suggest that the tortured democracy question is not the only justification for NGO involvement in international politics. I will discuss the much-overlooked and by no means unproblematic "ethical contribution" of NGOs and then offer a qualified defense of more international law, with more NGO participation, on this basis.

TRANSPARENCY

Transparency or openness is a necessary condition of all forms of democracy. Whether in direct or in representative democracy, the process of deliberation and the eventual vote must take place openly. Even in experimental forms of democratic procedure that eschew the vote, public discussion is highly valued. Karl Popper (1952), the philosopher who profoundly influenced financier George Soros, considered "openness" the prime instrument to keep any form of government from usurping too much power. More recently, democratic theorists Amy Gutmann and Dennis Thompson have drawn on such different philosophers as Jeremy Bentham and **Immanuel Kant** to construct publicity as a necessary condition for deliberative democracy, while also insisting (in line with human rights law) that certain forms of regulated secrecy are necessary in a democratic society (Gutmann and Thompson 1996, 95–127).

Yet in international negotiations, secrecy has traditionally been the norm. All that became available to the public was the final product. This situation changed somewhat after the Second World War, with the advent of superpower summits and international UN conferences. Now, citizens would be informed via the media that negotiations were proceeding, politicians might make statements, and journalists would speculate about the outcome. Nonetheless, the substance of the negotiations would still take place behind closed doors.

NGO coalitions have really challenged this convention of secrecy, and the Coalition for an International Criminal Court (CICC) is a prime example. It tracked the state negotiations on the establishment of the International Criminal Court between 1995 and 1998, bringing 236 NGOs to the final leg of the negotiations in Rome. Its working methods included forming twelve shadow teams to monitor negotiations on different parts of the draft text, debriefing friendly state delegates after closed meetings, and keeping "virtual vote" tallies on crucial issues. These mechanisms made the official decision-making process more transparent: for its members, for journalists, and, through them, for a wider audience of interested parties and even for state delegates. The entire texts of interim proposals, with an analysis, were reprinted in special conference newspapers. Information was also sent to thousands of national activists and observers, by the Coalition itself, by some of its member NGOs, and by the press teams of two special news bulletins devoted to the conference's proceedings (Glasius 2005, 38–43).

More importantly perhaps, many state representatives found these channels of publicity useful, either to state their positions or to vent their frustrations with other states or with the process of negotiation, particularly when they believed that public opinion might be on their side. As the conference wore on, state delegates even began to complain in these media about a lack of transparency in the process itself ("Chairman Struggles" 1998; "Where Are Decisions Being Made?" 1998). This was a significant development, because state delegates thus addressed the interested wider public by making an appeal to a norm of transparency that has no tradition in international negotiations.

Beyond direct coverage of international negotiations, NGOs play an important role in public education on global issues: with respect to rather esoteric topics such as global warming, Third World debt, or intellectual property rights, they open up more general debates, in which active citizens can inform themselves and take part. As in national democracies, certain discussions and negotiations will continue to take place behind closed doors, but NGOs have shifted the balance much further toward openness as the default setting in international negotiations.

EQUALITY

Another key condition of democracy, representative or deliberative, is equality. According to political theorist David Beetham, "a system of collective decision-making can be said to be democratic to the extent that it is subject to control by all members of the relevant association, or all those under its authority, considered as equals" (Beetham 1999, 5). Formally, there is such equality between the members of the association called the United Nations, at least in its General Assembly and its Economic and Social Council, if not in the Security Council. Formal equality is also much bruited about as one of the characteristics of the World Trade Organization (WTO).

However, in practice, some states are more equal than others. This inequality is not just a question of perceived power, but also of capacity to be involved in multiple complex negotiations. Regardless of whether or not one believes that citizens should somehow be able to have a direct involvement in global processes that affect them, leveling the playing field between the formally equal players—the states—would contribute to democratizing international decision making. And NGOs do, at times, play such a role. Most eye-catching has probably been the expert advice, and publicity, given to developing countries in the negotiations of the WTO in recent years (Said and Desai 2003, 80–82). The documents produced by NGOs helped to educate those countries' representatives with respect to the issues involved. The provision of interns and legal experts swelled their delegations in quality and quantity. The NGOs' monitoring of both public and, as far as possible, secret negotiations, has made the process more transparent and easier to follow for such states.

The NGO Coalition for an International Criminal Court made another interesting contribution to formal equality: it periodically recorded a "virtual vote" (discussed extensively in Glasius 2005) on different aspects of the negotiations. This tally of the preferences of each state, gleaned from their official statements, focused attention on absolute numbers of states supporting particular positions. Without this effort, the fact that, for instance, more than 80 percent of the states favored an independent prosecutor would simply have gone unrecorded. Through the virtual vote count, this democratic preference became a topic of debate and a counterweight to the inevitable spotlight on the position of "important" states such as the five permanent members of the Security Council. Thus, the formal equality of states was given a little more substance by at least polling and publicizing each state's views, although actual voting was avoided until the very end.

DELIBERATION

The idea of deliberative democracy is that proposals can be debated on their merits through rational arguments rather than solely on the basis of representation of interests. (This aspect of democracy is therefore related to the ethical contribution discussed later in this essay.) Deliberative democracy entails giving and demanding reasons for each position—reasons that would at least theoretically be capable of swaying other participants in the debate. It also means participants should be prepared to be swayed to some extent by arguments that appear "reasonable." States' disposition to engage in such deliberations is fostered by their constant discussions with NGO representatives, who demand explanations for state policies, scrutinize them, and relay them to a wider audience.

The Bush administration's belated U-turn on climate change, while perhaps owing something to Al Gore's documentary, *An Inconvenient Truth*, might also be attributed to the drip-drip effect of years of NGO advocacy and ensuing public debate (Newell 2005).

On the matter of deliberation between NGOs, there is rather more doubt. NGOs are notoriously fractious. One of the most obvious differences between the functioning of NGOs at the international level and political parties at the national level is that one can have an infinite number of NGOs, each devoted to a single issue or representing a slightly different viewpoint on various issues, and so there is little incentive for either deliberation or compromise. On the contrary, NGOs depend on and compete for funding, and since funding is at least partly related to publicity, there is an incentive to shout each other down. However, Alison Van Rooy, who has written extensively on the role of NGOs in development, suggests that the lack of a united front detracts from the moral authority of NGOs: "The rule here suggests that if activists cannot agree on a united position, there are fewer reasons to listen to what they have to say" (Van Rooy 2004, 99).

Coalitions are sometimes held up as the solution. In its report, the Panel of Eminent Persons appointed by then UN Secretary-General Kofi Annan to make recommendations on United Nations–Civil Society Relations, expressed a desire for amalgamation of NGO views through "disciplined networking and peer review processes of the constituencies" ("We the Peoples," para. 26). But is such unity really the most desirable in terms of fostering deliberation? As the late political theorist Iris Marion Young put it, deliberative democracy should not be "a comfortable place of conversation among those who share language, assumptions, and ways of looking at issues" (Young 1997, 401). On the contrary, "confrontation with different perspectives, interests, and cultural meanings teaches individuals the partiality of their own, and reveals to them their own experience as perspectival" (403).

While precisely playing the role of bringing the experience of "others" to the attention of state representatives, NGO coalitions do often too much resemble a "comfortable place of conversation," and fall into the trap of providing a convenient single "NGO perspective" to the UN and state officials, instead of reflecting a sometimes confusing, sometimes confrontational plurality of voices.

On the other hand, global confrontations like that between women's groups and pro-family groups (Glasius 2004), or between anti-weapons activists and the fast globalizing pro-gun lobby (Bob 2007) do not meet the requirements of "deliberative democracy" either, for listening to one another and engaging in a rational set of arguments and counterarguments are also characteristics of the idea of deliberation, and there is certainly no such process of engagement between such opposing groups. Nonetheless, one could argue that the presence of both perspectives contributes to the deliberative process of the negotiations as a whole, even if the exchanges between NGOs are vitriolic.

If the UN is serious about the role of NGOs as fostering real deliberative processes, it should actively look for a *plurality* of views, including starkly opposing ones, instead of trying to weed out such controversy before allowing NGOs entry into its chambers. Networks are a powerful tool in strengthening the potential influence of NGOs on state negotiations, but they also tend to homogenize diverse views, to neglect minority views, and, of course, to exclude views that oppose their founding mission. Therefore, a heavy focus on networks is not conducive to the role of NGOs as fostering reasoned debate between different views.

REPRESENTATION

Representative democracy was invented because the decision-making constituencies, the *demos*, of nation states were too large and too dispersed to allow every individual to take part in debates and voting. It is therefore natural that, when thinking about the possibility of a global democracy or of democratizing existing global institutions, representative mechanisms of democracy spring to mind. Some would assert that the UN General Assembly already functions as such: now that three-quarters of the world's states are at least formally democratic, one could argue that citizens elect their governments, which then represent them in the United Nations.

However, there are various problems with this line of thinking. For one, governments, unlike parliaments, are formed only out of the winning party or parties. The General Assembly is therefore not comparable to national parliaments, because only the national "winners" (the governments) are represented. Moreover, complex international issues are not usually an important element in election campaigns. We still elect national governments primarily to govern us, not to represent us at the international level. So, as is often remarked, the United Nations do not, in fact, represent "We the peoples," but "We the governments."

So, can NGOs represent "We the peoples" instead? The Panel on UN–Civil Society Relations certainly seems to suggest that such popular representation is possible, by calling its 2004 report "We the Peoples: the United Nations, Civil Society and Global Governance." But how does this representation work? Some organizations have a mass membership. **Amnesty International** is considered a very large NGO, with more than 2.2 million members from 150 countries (amnesty.org), but this is nothing compared to the 168 million combined membership of the International Trade Union Confederation (ituc-csi.org). Other influential organizations, such as Greenpeace, **Oxfam**, and the **World Wide Fund for Nature,** do not have members, but instead rely on financial "supporters"—although Greenpeace does claim to speak for its 2.8 million supporters (greenpeace.org). As Van Rooy (2004, 62–76) has pointed out, the geographical spread and depth of members' commitment differ vastly between organizations, as do procedures for internal democracy. There are also very small organizations, and, in fact, many NGOs do not claim to represent anyone but themselves.

It becomes obvious very quickly that conceptualizing NGOs as a global equivalent of political parties, organizing the global electorate into voting blocs whom they represent in international negotiations, is inaccurate and misleading. Having a large membership base may be a source of legitimacy and influence to particular organizations, but democratic representation in the traditional sense cannot be considered a functioning attribute of NGOs as a group.

But are there other forms of representation? And who or what ought to be represented? David Held (1995, 136) uses the phrase "overlapping communities of fate" to express the fact that those who are affected by certain decisions are, due to globalization, no longer always found neatly in a single political entity, controlled by a democratic process. NGOs can sometimes be a solution to such situations where the decision-making power is not located where the voting is, through an informal form of representation. One could argue, for instance, that NGOs represented people living with HIV/AIDS in developing countries by means of their advocacy for the production of generic drugs during the WTO negotiations on intellectual property. In the absence of any other form of representation, such non-state-based advocacy may be helpful to those affected—as it certainly was in this case.

But the fact that there is no agreed form for consulting those who are supposedly represented remains problematic. The resistance against the Narmada dam in India, which if built would displace thousands of villagers, is an oft-cited example of a civil society success: the villagers' international advocates succeeded in dissuading the World Bank from funding the project, and their influence has even been institutionalized in the form of a World Commission on Dams, which advises the World Bank on similar projects. But only those who stood to lose their homes and livelihood from the building of the dam were represented at the international level. The arguably much larger number of people who might have benefited from its hydroelectric power did not have such advocates.

And who would constitute the "community of fate" for climate change? It may affect all our futures, but it is impossible to pinpoint in advance exactly who will be most affected, and in what ways. Representation should therefore be conceptualized in a very different way in these situations. NGOs can still make claims "on behalf of," but those made on behalf of the environment, on behalf of future victims of human rights violations, or on behalf of the unborn child, have little or nothing to do with a parliamentarian's work on behalf of his constituency. On the one hand, consultation mechanisms are not a necessary part of such claims. On the other hand, no formal voting rights can or should be based on it. NGOs are not, and should not be, seen as a kind of global parliament. Indeed, as the eminent "reflective practitioner" Mike Edwards (2003) put it, civil society is "a voice not a vote."

PARTICIPATION

Another way of conceptualizing this democratic characteristic is to say that participation, not representation, is the point of NGOs. As the Panel on UN–Civil Society Relations puts it: "Citizens increasingly act politically by participating directly, through civil society mechanisms, in policy debates that particularly interest them. This constitutes a broadening from representative to participatory democracy" ("We the Peoples," Executive Summary, x). But whose voices are, and should be, heard under the banner of global civil society? Who gets to participate?

Some actors, it should be said, do not wish to participate, or at least not on the invitation and according to the rules of the decision makers. As Iris Marion Young puts it, they typically "make public noise outside while deliberation is supposedly taking place on the inside," although sometimes they "invade the houses of deliberation and disrupt their business" (Young 2001, 673).

The Madres (mothers) de la Plaza de Mayo and the Abuelas (grandmothers) de la Plaza de Mayo typify the differences between "outsider" and "insider" activism. Both groups emerged during the Argentinian military regime (1976–1983) when thousands of political opponents were "disappeared" by government forces—kidnapped, held in secret detention, and mostly killed—and, after the advent of democracy, both have continued to look for their lost family members. The Abuelas focus on finding their grandchildren born in custody, who were given up for adoption. They go through the courts in their efforts to find the children of their disappeared children and to see the perpetrators punished; as a result of their efforts, Argentinian junta leader Jorge Videla was reimprisoned in 1997. The Madres, on the other hand, "think that accepting financial compensation and exhumation of bodies are a 'betrayal' for their children—because this, in a legal sense, stops what had been an ongoing crime" (Kirk 1998). As Young (2001, 676) points out, such outsiders do in fact "aim to communicate specific ideas to a wide public," so they do participate in politics even though they reject formal participation.

But what of those who cannot participate? Deliberate efforts to block the activities of NGOs, which were particularly evident at the 1995 Beijing Conference on Women, have become rarer, as the furor they cause tends to result in negative publicity for the state and more publicity for the NGO and its cause than those activities might otherwise have received. Nonetheless, states still have the power to block accreditation of NGOs to the United Nations. During the Cold War, states would routinely deny accreditation to organizations they labeled either "communist" or "imperialist." While such practices receded in the 1990s, today they have found a new label: "terrorist."

Beyond deliberate obstruction by states, there is a wider problem with participation. The UN Panel describes participatory democracy as a process in which "anyone can enter the debates that most interest them, through advocacy, protest, and in other ways" ("We the Peoples," para. 13). But, a few pages later, it acknowledges that there are practical constraints: "if the United Nations brought everyone relevant into each debate, it would have endless meetings without conclusion" (para. 23).

Not only is participation limited—it is typically limited in ways that confirm existing power imbalances. As Young (2001, 680) puts it: "Under conditions of structural inequality, normal processes of deliberation often in practice restrict access to agents with greater resources, knowledge, or connections to those with greater control over the forum." Even at the very local level, Young sums up a number of barriers to participation by "anyone with an interest." These constraints are, of course, multiplied at the global level. Although they are meant to be conduits for the marginalized, NGOs thus can also become mechanisms of exclusion.

Discussions of these inequalities often focus rather crudely on geographical representation, but the imbalance is not simply a matter of North versus South. Almost without exception, the international NGO staff represented at an international forum belong to an English-speaking, university-educated, computer-literate middle class. Perhaps such elitism is inevitable, but it does not reflect the diversity of the world population, nor does it necessarily mirror the profile of future victims of poverty, violence, or environmental disaster.

If participation in global processes is necessarily selective on practical grounds, then a particular effort should be made, particularly by NGOs but also by global institutions, to include the voices of "experiential experts"—on human rights violations, on HIV/AIDS, on child soldiers—and not just technical ones. In some forums, NGOs and networks have engaged in "accompaniment": people who are affected by the issues discussed, but who would normally have neither the means nor the political consciousness to get involved are taken to the negotiations under the tutelage of seasoned activists. Some small farmers have, for instance, been present at WTO negotiations under such constructions (Edelman 2003, 210–211). Such practices can lead to the inclusion of "experiential experts," provided that they offer real participation, and not a symbolic trotting out of "the victim" to support the NGO's already formed position. Unfortunately, given the very small number of people who can be offered "accompaniment" in relation to the numbers affected by global negotiations, it seems doubtful that such inclusion can ever be much more than symbolic.

THE ETHICAL CONTRIBUTION

NGOs have greatly contributed to strengthening certain features that are commonly associated with democratic procedure—in particular, transparency, equality, and deliberation. They should not be seen as offering a form of representation of the global *demos*, however, or at least not representation in its traditional form. Their activism could be conceptualized as a form of participation, but in practice this participation is so limited and so uneven that international NGOs cannot entirely be considered an adequate "functional equivalent" or "alternative mechanism" to parliamentary democracy, operating at the global level. NGOs do contribute to making international decision-making processes more democratic than they might otherwise be, but a democratic deficit remains. Another contribution made by NGOs, however, has received much less attention than the democratizing aspect: that of moral values.

The hundreds of groups and individuals who engaged in the International Criminal Court negotiations—whether they were criminal law experts, pro-family groups, or world federalists—all became involved because of their belief in, or concerns about, a particular kind of Court. For some, such as the European Law Students Association, career considerations may have played something of a role. For some NGO professionals, it was "their job" to be there. But even the involvement of these professionals went far beyond that of an ordinary job. Often, they had had to convince their own organizations of the importance of being there. The overriding motivation for being involved was that of ethical conviction.

But what of the states' representatives—do they have ethical convictions? In international relations, there are two classic theories on foreign policy and ethics. The first, and certainly the most influential until the 1990s, is realism. Based on a particular reading of Machiavelli or, alternatively, on a transposition of Hobbes's "war of every man against every man" theory to the international

plane (Walker 1993), realism teaches that international relations are an anarchi-
cal sphere, where each state pursues its national interest, and there is no place
for ethics. Liberal or idealist theory, in contrast, teaches that there is a "society
of states," where rules in the common interest of mankind are constructed, and
for the most part, obeyed. According to the latter theory, there is a space for
"ethics," or enlightened self-interest, in foreign policy. This theoretical bent also
gives more space to the conceptualization of intergovernmental organizations,
and sometimes even NGOs, as independent actors. But neither theory really
understands the diplomats themselves as social actors who are subject to environmental influences (as the social constructivist school does; see, for instance,
Onuf 1989; Walker 1993). Whether based on "national interest" or conceived
on a more cooperative plane, the policies of states are conceptualized as holy
writ, handed down from black-box foreign ministries. According to traditional
IR [international relations] theory, therefore, state representatives are not to
have convictions, ethical or otherwise.

In reality, state representatives do, of course, have value dispositions of their
own. Nor are state positions on issues such as the ICC [International Code
Council], intellectual property rights, or climate change arrived at in isolation from those who negotiate on them. In fact, they are gradually formulated,
informed by inside expertise and outside information, and constantly re-adjusted;
even the atmosphere of the negotiations can influence the substance of the
positions. As discussed earlier, NGOs have transformed that atmosphere in
terms of transparency and deliberation. But another aspect of the sustained
presence of NGOs is that they constantly invoke ethical considerations—claims
about the needs of humankind.

International relations theories such as realism and idealism do not seek
merely to explain state behavior—or as I would rather put it, the behavior of
state representatives—they also end up informing such behavior. In domestic
politics, it is not ethically acceptable for politicians to defend policies simply as
being in the self-interest of a particular group: "This policy is good for the small
businessmen, or for the Catholic minority, who vote for me." Instead, they need
to present such policies as being for the common good: "Small businesses will
kick-start the national economy," "Catholic emancipation will make our society
more equitable." The dominance of realist theory made any such arguments for
the general interest unnecessary in the international sphere—it even characterized them as foolish—by legitimizing the invocation of a (flexibly definable)
"national interest" by diplomats as the sole motivation for this or that position.

International NGOs present themselves precisely as the champions of values
beyond such state interests, working toward a global common good. But having
a majority of such actors around is like being accompanied to a brothel by a

delegation of priests—even without any formal status, they constrain behavior and change the terms of debate. Nowadays, forthright statements that "this is not in our nation's interest" can still be heard in international negotiations, but they jar in an environment where appeals to reason and to universal justice are increasingly common currency. States are thus more motivated to frame their proposals in terms of appropriateness and justice in the presence of NGOs.

If it is accepted that NGOs move states toward appreciating, or at least appearing to appreciate, "ethical" or "common good" arguments over national-interest arguments in international negotiations, the question remains which ethical projects make it to those forums and get taken up. Those who do not agree on the dominant projects will point to the democratic deficit—the lack of representation and limits to participation—and they are likely to point back to national democracy as the solution.

The existence of a democratic deficit at the global level, and the fact that NGOs cannot entirely fill it, should not be denied. But the number of victims created by states violating human rights over the past century is staggering. Some of these governments were flawed democracies, too. This is why it is worth giving up some national democratic supremacy in exchange for international law—first, to frame norms on human rights, disarmament, and the environment; and second, to actually enforce them. And NGOs should be there to help make these laws and get them enforced; to strengthen transparency, equality, and deliberation in international decision-making processes; and to help inch states from narrow interests toward global common interests. Those who think that this wider participatory process is not, in fact, in the interest of humanity, should come and join the debate with their own ethical projects— and, perhaps, found their own NGOs.

democracy

Should All Nations Be Encouraged to Promote Democratization?

YES: Francis Fukuyama, *The Center on Democracy, Development, and the Rule of Law at Stanford University,* and Michael McFaul, *U.S. Ambassador to Russia*

NO: Edward D. Mansfield, *University of Pennsylvania,* and Jack Snyder, *Columbia University*

Since Woodrow Wilson's presidency (1913–1921), the United States has promoted democratization as a foreign policy goal. Democracy promotion or *democratization* has been particularly salient on the international agenda since the 1990s, when it informed the design of UN post-conflict peacemaking missions. Since the 1960s, the United States had replaced its historical penchant for armed intervention in Latin America with foreign aid as an instrument of building democracy.

In general, Western governments promote democratization for both principled and instrumental reasons. These countries value individual rights, including numerous social and political freedoms and liberties, and share a set of liberal political values and experiences dating back to the Enlightenment. Instrumentally, democratization has been put forward most forcefully in the *Democratic Peace* hypothesis, which posits that democracies are more peaceful—at least in their relations to other democracies—than are other political systems, because it is harder to mobilize a society to fight when citizens have a direct say over government policy. In particular, citizens in a democracy are believed to have an affinity for their counterparts in other democracies. Democracies may also be capable of more robust and sustainable economic development, because democratic institutions tend to reward technological innovation.

Since 1972, democratization has been spreading worldwide, and when the Cold War ended, the transition from authoritarian political structures to more democratic ones accelerated.

Figure 1 (this page) presents these trends, showing that the number of countries ranked as "free" grew from forty-four in 1972 (forty-three is South Africa under apartheid and is regarded as only partly free)—or 29 percent of all the independent countries in the world—to eighty-seven (45 percent) by 2010. Meanwhile, the number of partly free countries also increased slightly, from thirty-eight (25 percent of independent countries) in 1972 to sixty (31 percent) in 2010, and the number of not-free countries fell from sixty-nine (46 percent) to forty-seven (24 percent) over the same period.

However, democratization is not a geographically universal trend. It has occurred primarily in Southern and Eastern Europe and Latin America. Following the collapse of the Soviet Union, many countries in Eastern Europe tried to emulate the West. In Latin America, democratization has occurred as a combination of blossoming organic processes, supported by initiatives from the United States and other Western nations.

Figure 1

Freedom in the World (Country Rankings), 1972–2010

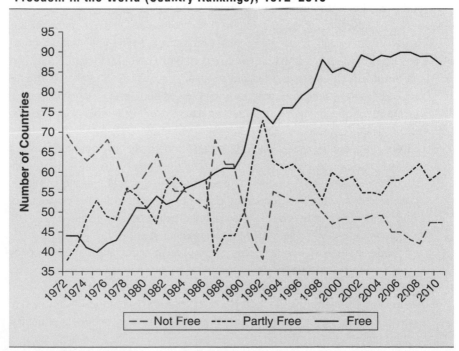

Source: Freedom House, Freedom in the World Comparative and Historical Data. http://www.freedomhouse.org/template .cfm?page=439 (accessed January 7, 2011).

Definitions of democracy vary, and the spread of democratization does not make for a standard that is universally understood. A minimalist sense of democracy is limited to holding multiparty elections in which the losing party voluntarily transfers power. A much more demanding vision of a fully democratic society is articulated by prominent Yale political scientist Robert Dahl, whose list of requirements entails inclusive participation; a one-vote, one-person equality; and informed consent by citizens about the agenda and platforms of candidates. Many of these more demanding definitional elements overlap with the human rights protected by the UN. Achieving such a vision in practice calls for literacy, a free press, a multiparty political system, judicial independence, a trustworthy police force, and respect for individual rights.

Democracy creation is a long and difficult process. Even attempting to meet the weak definition requires assuring citizens that they will not be punished by other ethnic or political groups when power shifts. Consequently, provisions for dealing with prior human rights abuses, an independent judiciary and police force, and impartial elections are necessary. More demanding approaches to democratization may necessitate extensive social engineering in order to promote increased gender equality, respect for democratic values and institutions, literacy, and an independent media.

Not all countries or peoples share a commitment to the Western political values of open participation in political processes. Prime Ministers Mahathir Mohamed of Malaysia and Lee Kwan Yew of Singapore, for instance, claimed that Asian countries share a distinct political culture of Asian values that prefers autocratic systems because of habits of social deference and obligation. An important question is whether these systems are sustainable over time and across different rulers.

Democratization is beset with challenges, and it may not occur smoothly or easily. Transitional democracies are in a particularly delicate stage, for democratic openings offer opportunities for authoritarian and nationalistic groups to gain political power. If the economy does not flourish under the new democratic institutions, groups will fight to control the distribution of state resources, and the populace will lose confidence in democracy.

In addition, the ideal of democracy promotion may conflict with other policy goals. During transitional periods, trade-offs must often be made, as scarce state resources have to be allocated either to democracy-building or to economic development. Also, democratization often involves the redistribution of economic control away from a plutocracy or small number of firms that control domestic markets.

Trade-offs may also be needed between democratization and domestic political stability. This potential exchange of values is of particular concern in the Middle East, where, for security purposes, the United States supports many governments that are not democratic. In countries such as Pakistan, Kazakhstan, Saudi Arabia, Egypt, China, Armenia, Azerbaijan, and maybe even Russia, democracy promotion would undermine the government's domestic political support by creating the potential for alternative governing elites or coalitions. Promoting democracy forcefully in such situations could weaken potential allies during a period when the United States needs the full cooperation of states sympathetic to U.S. interests.

The writers in this chapter look at the ease with which democratization can be achieved, the attendant risks associated with promoting democracies, and the question of whether democratization should be promoted in all countries. They engage such issues as the background conditions for democratization, the relationship between foreign and domestic pressures for democratization, and the timing of the democratization process.

Discussion Questions

1. Can democracy be imposed on a country or encouraged from the outside? Or can it only develop within a country on its own? Explain.
2. Are democracy promotion and advocacy for human rights inextricably linked? Can you promote one and not the other?
3. What three reasons do Francis Fukuyama and Michael McFaul give to explain why the United States should promote democracy abroad? What new strategies or foreign policy approaches do they suggest as a way for U.S. policymakers to effectively promote democracy? Do you agree with their proposals?
4. What risks of indiscriminate democracy promotion do Edward D. Mansfield and Jack Snyder highlight? What are the steps in the sequencing strategy they propose for promoting democracy? Do you agree with their proposal?

YES: Francis Fukuyama, *The Center on Democracy, Development, and the Rule of Law at Stanford University,* and Michael McFaul, *U.S. Ambassador to Russia*

In his second inaugural address on January 20, 2005, President George W. Bush used the word *freedom* twenty-five times, *liberty* twelve times, and *democracy* or *democratic* three times. Bush did not enter the White House with a mission to promote freedom around the world. Instead, as a presidential candidate, he had put forward a modest foreign policy agenda that eschewed nation-building. The events of September 11, 2001, however, radically jarred his thinking on the nature of international threats and triggered a fundamental reevaluation of his administration's national security policy that elevated democracy promotion as a central objective of his foreign policy agenda.

In the years since that September 11, though, the rhetorical attention devoted to the advance of freedom, liberty, and democracy has greatly outpaced any actual progress in expanding democracy. To date, democracy has failed to take hold in the two countries where Bush ordered the forcible ousting of autocratic regimes: Afghanistan and Iraq. Nor did the toppling of these dictatorships send liberty rippling through the greater Middle East, as some Bush officials and supporters had hoped. Instead, autocratic regimes in the region have used the excuse of terrorism (Egypt, Pakistan) or the alleged threat of U.S. invasion (Iran) to tighten their grip on power. Outside this region, some countries have made some progress toward developing democracy (Georgia, Ukraine), but just as many have moved toward greater autocracy. Freedom House concluded, "The year of 2006 saw the emergence of a series of worrisome trends that together present potentially serious threats to the stability of new democracies as well as obstacles to political reform in societies under authoritarian rule . . . the percentage of countries designated Free has failed to increase for nearly a decade. . . ."[1]

Not surprisingly, many in Washington are pressing for a change in U.S. foreign policy objectives. Only those at the extremes on both ends of the political

Source: Revised from Francis Fukuyama and Michael McFaul, "Should Democracy Be Promoted or Demoted?" in *Bridging the Foreign Policy Divide: A Project of the Stanley Foundation,* ed. Derek Chollet, Tod Lindberg, and David Shorr. Copyright 2007. Reproduced with permission of Taylor & Francis Group LLC – Books in the format Textbook via Copyright Clearance Center.

spectrum advocate the complete abandonment of democracy promotion as a U.S. foreign policy objective. Instead, skepticism is largely couched as "realism" and a "return" to a greater focus on "traditional" U.S. national security objectives. From this perspective, democracy promotion should take a back seat to strategic aims such as securing U.S. access to energy resources, building military alliances to fight terrorist organizations, and fostering "stability" within states.

We do not reject the importance of focusing on more traditional goals of national security. However, we do reject the simple assumption that there is a zero-sum trade-off between these traditional security objectives and democracy promotion. We also share the negative assessments of the Bush administration's efforts to promote democracy. However, our response to this mixed record of achievement is not to downgrade or remove democracy promotion from U.S. foreign policy priorities. Instead, we analyze why the United States *should* promote democracy. First, we present the positive case for including democracy promotion as an important component of U.S. foreign policy. Then we present the counterarguments and our reasons for viewing these counterarguments as unpersuasive. Finally, we suggest new strategies and better modalities for promoting democracy.

THE CASE FOR DEMOCRACY PROMOTION

While we believe that the spread of democracy is a good thing in itself, no administration can sell democracy promotion to Congress or the American people unless it is linked to American interests. Fortunately, there are a number of ways in which democracy serves U.S. interests.

U.S. Interests

No country in the world has benefited more from the worldwide advance of democracy than the United States. Not all autocracies are or have been enemies of the United States, but every U.S. enemy has been an autocracy. The transformation of powerful autocracies into democracies has served U.S. national security interests. Most obviously, the end of dictatorship and the consolidation of democracy in Germany, Italy, and Japan after World War II made the United States safer.

During the Cold War, some viewed the Soviet threat as so paramount that all enemies of communism, including dictators, had to be embraced. They predicted that any political change to the status quo in autocratic societies would produce not democratic regimes and U.S. allies but communist regimes and U.S. enemies. There were enough examples of this trajectory—Cuba, Angola, and Nicaragua—to warrant worry. But these were failed cases of democratic transition. In contrast, successful democratic transitions did not undermine U.S. security interests. Transitions in Portugal, Spain, Taiwan, the Philippines, South Korea, Chile, and South Africa helped to deepen American ties with these countries.[2]

The parallels to today's situation are obvious. Once again facing a new worldwide ideological threat in the form of radical Islamism, strategic thinkers both inside and outside the U.S. government worry that political change in autocratic U.S. allies will produce theocratic regimes hostile to U.S. interests. The concern is valid, but is often overplayed by the very same autocrats as they seek to retain power. So far, successful democratization has never brought to power a government that then directly threatened the national security interests of the United States or its allies.

The advance of democracy in Europe and Asia over the past century made the United States safer—giving reason to hope that democracy's advance in other regions of the world will also strengthen U.S. national security. In the long run, we expect that consolidation of democratic regimes in the greater Middle East would increase the legitimacy of those governments and thereby reduce the appeal of anti-systemic movements such as al-Qaeda. In the shorter term, democratic government throughout the region would increase internal stability within states, since democracies have longer life spans than autocracies. If democratic regimes ruled all countries in the region, conflicts between states would be less likely, and, consequently, demand for weapons—including weapons of mass destruction—would decrease. Finally, a more secure and stable region would reduce the need for a U.S. military presence.

In the short run, however, there are potential risks for U.S. security associated with democratic development in the greater Middle East. Without question, the toppling of the Taliban regime in Afghanistan deprived al-Qaeda of a base of operations that offered more assets than its current base in Pakistan. Yet this advantage for U.S. strategic interests was not a result of democratization. In fact, the difficult process of developing democratic institutions in Afghanistan has so far failed to produce stable government or a growing economy—a situation that has created an opening for the Taliban's resurgence. In Iraq, neither democratic government nor an effective state has taken root. To date, the American people are not safer as a result of regime change in Iraq. In both countries, U.S.-led invasions brought about regime change. But because these operations were neither launched to bring democracy nor followed through toward that end, the resulting new or resurgent threats to U.S. national security emanating from Afghanistan and Iraq cannot be blamed on democratization or U.S. democracy promotion.

We admit that we do not know whether the analogy between democratization in the wider Middle East and democratization in other regions will hold and yield the same benefits. The destruction of fascist and communist regimes and the emergence of more democratic regimes—first in Europe and Asia after World War II and more recently in Eastern Europe and the former Soviet Union—significantly enhanced U.S. national security. It is reasonable to expect a similar outcome in the wider Middle East; that is, the emergence of more democratic regimes in the most autocratic region of the world should also make the United States more secure.

American Values

Debates about democracy promotion cannot be couched solely as a balance sheet of material benefits and liabilities for the United States. American values must also enter the discussion. Since the beginning of the Republic, U.S. presidents have to varying degrees invoked America's unique, moral role in international affairs. Apart from serving U.S. strategic interests, democracy promotion is also the right thing to do.

First and foremost, democracy is the best system of government. It provides the best institutional form for holding rulers accountable to their people. If leaders must compete for popular support to obtain and retain power, they will be more responsive to the preferences of the people. The institutions of democracy also prevent abusive rule, constrain bad rule, and provide a mechanism for removing corrupt or ineffective rule. Furthermore, democracy provides the setting for political competition, which in turn is a driver of better governance. Like markets, political competition between contending leaders, ideas, and organizations produces better leaders, ideas, and organizations. The absence of political competition in autocracies produces complacency and corruption, and it offers no mechanism for producing new leaders.

Second, democracies provide more, or more stable, welfare for their people than do autocracies. Democracies avoid the worst threats to personal well-being, such as genocide and famine. Over the past several decades, democracies around the world have not produced higher economic growth rates than autocracies: "The net effect of more political freedom on growth is theoretically ambiguous."[3] Instead, autocracies produce both much higher and much lower rates of growth than democracies: for every China there is a Burma. Democracies tend to produce slower rates of growth than the best autocratic performers, but also steadier rates of economic development. The old conventional wisdom that dictators are better at economic modernization than their democratic counterparts is not supported by data.

Third, the demand for and appeal of democracy as a system of government are widespread, if not universal. Public opinion surveys conducted throughout the world show that majorities of people in most countries support democracy.[4] Ideological challengers remain, but compared to earlier historical periods, these opponents of democracy have never been weaker.

The United States, therefore, has a moral interest in promoting democracy. If democracy is the best system of government, demanded by the majority of people around the world, then the United States should help to promote its advance. Conversely, any U.S. involvement in sustaining autocracy is immoral. Obviously, American leaders constantly face situations in which immediate security interests require cooperation with autocratic regimes. But such policies should not be defended on moral or ethical grounds.

ENGAGING THE CASE AGAINST DEMOCRACY PROMOTION

Three arguments are generally offered for why the United States should not pursue democracy promotion. The first argument—that democracy is not a universally valid or desirable goal—has a number of proponents. Postmodernism and other relativist philosophies argue that there are no universally valid political or institutional orders because it is impossible to arrive at philosophical certainty per se. A more common assertion is that democracy is culturally rooted, and that societies with other cultural backgrounds may choose other forms of government as they wish. The late political scientist Samuel Huntington makes this kind of case.[5] According to him, liberal democracy is rooted in Western Christianity, which proclaimed the universal dignity of man made in God's image; thinkers from Tocqueville to Nietzsche have argued that modern democracy is simply a secularization of Western values. There is no particular reason why other civilizations based on other cultural preferences should prefer democratic governments. Former Singaporean prime minister Lee Kwan Yew and other proponents of "Asian values" have argued that, given the poor performance of many democratic regimes in non-Western settings, this form of government is distinctly less desirable than a growth-orientated authoritarian regime.

There are certainly serious philosophical and political cases to be made against a universality of liberal democratic values on a number of grounds. While acceptance of democratic norms and basic human rights has spread far and wide since the onset of the Third Wave democratization that began in the mid-1970s, there are still parts of the world where they are openly rejected on cultural grounds. The Chinese government, various East Asian leaders and thinkers, Islamists of assorted stripes, and many Russian nationalists are among those arguing that their cultures are inherently inimical to one or another aspect of liberal democracy.

We offer the following observations in contention. First, democracy promotion never implied *imposition* of either liberalism or democracy on a society that did not want it. By definition, this is impossible: democracy requires popular consensus, and it works only if the vast majority of a society's citizens believe it is legitimate. Democracy promotion is intended only to help to reveal public preferences in the society itself. Dictatorships often resort to violence, coercion, or fraud to prevent those preferences from carrying political weight; democracy promoters simply try to level the playing field by eliminating the authoritarians' unfair advantages.

A second counterargument that is somewhat more difficult to make is that human rights and the democratic institutions that spring from them are immanently universal. In keeping with the case made by Tocqueville in *Democracy in America*, the historical arc toward universal human equality has been spreading for the past 800 years. Not only has it now encompassed the Western, culturally Christian world, but it has spread and taken root in many other parts of the world as well. This wide-ranging acceptance suggests that democracy has spread not as a manifestation of a particular civilization's cultural preferences, but because it serves universal needs or performs functions that are universally necessary. One can argue that the procedural rule of liberal democracy guarantees that governments behave in a transparent, law-governed way and remain accountable to the people they serve. Even if a culture does not put a value on individual rights per se, liberal democracy is ultimately required for good governance and economic growth.

A second argument against democracy promotion is made by international relations "realists"—namely, that world order depends on states accepting the Westphalian consensus to respect each other's sovereignty and mutual agreement not to meddle in the internal character of each other's regimes. There are countless variants of realist theory today, united primarily in their opposition to democracy promotion as a component of foreign policy. Some argue not from a world-order point of view, but from the perspective of narrower American interests: the United States needs oil, security, trade, and other goods whose availability is compromised by an emphasis on human rights or democracy. These views have acquired particular resonance since the Iraq war, which was seen as being driven by a neoconservative agenda of democracy promotion and political transformation in the Middle East. These critics would argue that U.S. pressure for liberalization of political space and calls for elections have brought to power groups such as Hamas in Palestine, Hezbollah in Lebanon, and the Muslim Brotherhood in Egypt—all of which are illiberal and hostile to

U.S. interests. There has been criticism, especially, of the Bush administration's use of coercive regime change as a means to spur the political transformation of the Middle East.

We make several arguments in response to the realists. The first has to do with prudence in means. To say that the United States should promote democracy in its foreign policy does not mean that it should put idealistic goals ahead of other types of national interests at all times and places—or that it should use military force in pursuit of these goals. Indeed, the United States has never made democracy promotion the overriding goal of its foreign policy. The Bush administration invaded Iraq primarily out of concern over weapons of mass destruction and terrorism; democracy promotion was a tertiary goal that received heavier emphasis only when the other justifications of the war proved hollow. The United States has promoted democracy in such places as Germany and Japan after World War II, but only in concert with its security goals. In these cases, transformation of two former enemies into democratic countries did indeed align with U.S. strategic interests, and few realists would argue that the United States would have been better served by an alternative policy.

The Bush administration made the general argument that the deep root cause of terrorism and Islamist radicalism is the Middle East's lack of democracy, and that promoting democracy is therefore one route to eradicating the terrorist threat. It is quite clear in retrospect that this reading of the sources of Arab radicalism was too simplistic. The deep sources of terrorism are much more complex than just the Middle East's democratic deficit. Many of the Iraqis who went to the polls in the various elections in 2005 were Shi'ites who wanted not liberal democracy but Shi'ite power, and who have subsequently worked to establish an Iranian-style Islamic republic in areas under their control. The winners of democratic elections elsewhere in the region tend to be profoundly illiberal Islamist groups, who are also more hostile to America's ally Israel than to the authoritarian governments they would like to displace. The political tide in the Middle East is not running in favor of pro-Western liberal opposition groups. The assertion in President Bush's second inaugural address that there is no necessary trade-off between U.S. security interests and its idealist goals would thus seem to be false.

In our view, the appropriate policy in response to this political landscape needs to be a calibrated one that takes account of particular circumstances. There are some countries, such as Saudi Arabia, where there is no realistic democratic alternative to the current authoritarian leadership, or where likely alternatives would clearly be worse from a strategic perspective. In these cases, authoritarian allies indeed represent the lesser of two evils. On the other hand, there are some countries, such as Pakistan, where there is hope for a democratic alternative.

The final argument against the current agenda of democracy promotion concerns the sequencing of democratic reforms. State-building, creation of a liberal rule of law, and democracy are conceptually different phases of political development, which in most European countries occurred in a sequence that was separated by decades, if not centuries. State-building and creation of a rule of law are more critical for economic development than democracy is. Political scientists Jack Snyder and Edward Mansfield have argued that democratization's early phases pose special dangers of promoting nationalism and illiberal politics.[6] Authors from Samuel Huntington to journalist Fareed Zakaria have consequently argued that U.S. policy ought to focus on a broad governance agenda and delay pushing for democracy until a higher level of economic development has been achieved.[7] This so-called "authoritarian transition" has been followed by a number of countries, such as South Korea, Taiwan, and Chile, and is often recommended as a model for U.S. policy in regions such as the Middle East.

There is no question that such liberal authoritarianism has worked quite successfully in places such as Singapore, and even less liberal variants, as in China, can boast impressive economic growth rates. If these countries eventually follow the Korean and Taiwanese paths toward a broadening of political participation, it is not obvious that an accelerated democratic transition would bring about a better long-term result. In addition, there are specific instances where outside pressure for early elections arguably resulted not in the emergence of democratic political parties but in the locking in place of the same groups responsible for the original conflict.

As the analyst of democracy promotion Thomas Carothers has pointed out, however, there are a number of problems with the sequencing strategy.[8] First, in most parts of the world it is very difficult to find liberal, developmentally minded authoritarians on whom such a strategy can be built. The more typical cases in Africa, the Middle East, and Latin America have been characterized by authoritarian governments that are corrupt, incompetent, or self-serving.

A further problem with the sequencing strategy is that it presumes that the United States and other foreign powers can somehow control democratic transitions, holding back pressure for democratic elections while pushing for rule of law and good governance. This assumption vastly overestimates the degree of control that outsiders have over democratic transitions. The toolbox for democracy promotion is more modest, a subject that we will consider next.

MODALITIES OF DEMOCRACY PROMOTION

To argue that the United States has strategic and moral interests in the spread of democracy does not mean that the United States *can* spread democracy. Domestic factors, not external forces, have driven the process of democratization in most countries. Consequently, and especially in light of the tragedy in Iraq, some have argued that the United States can best promote democracy abroad by simply watching it develop "naturally."

We disagree. While we recognize the limits of America's ability to promote democracy abroad, we also know that U.S. policies can be very important in helping to nurture democratic development. The war in Iraq has fostered the false impression that military force is the only instrument of regime change in the U.S. arsenal, when in fact it is the most rarely used and least effective way to promote democratic change abroad. A wiser, more effective, and more sustainable strategy must emphasize nonmilitary tools aimed at changing the balance of power between democratic forces and autocratic rulers and, only after there has been progress toward democracy, building liberal institutions.

Restoring the American Example

Inspiration for democrats struggling against autocracy and a model for leaders in new democracies are two U.S. exports that are now in short supply. Since the beginning of the Republic, the American experiment with democracy has provided hope, ideas, and technologies for others working to build democratic institutions. In the second half of the twentieth century, when the United States developed more intentional means for promoting democracy abroad, the preservation and advertisement of the American democratic model remained a core instrument.

Today, this instrument needs repair. The American model has been severely undermined by the methods that the Bush administration used to fight the so-called global war on terrorism. Irrespective of the legal particulars that may or may not justify the indefinite detention of combatants/terrorists at Guantánamo Bay in Cuba, opinion polls demonstrate overwhelmingly that most of the world views U.S. detention policies as illegitimate and undemocratic. Furthermore, the debate surrounding the unauthorized wiretappings of U.S. citizens helped to create an impression abroad that the U.S. government will sacrifice the civil liberties of individuals in the name of fighting terrorism—the very argument that autocrats across the world use to justify their repressive policies. Finally, the Bush administration's propensity for unilateralism, most centrally in its decision to invade Iraq, coupled with its general suspicion of international law and international institutions, has encouraged the perception that Americans do not believe in the rule of law. The merits of these claims about U.S. behavior are debatable. But it is indisputable that America's image abroad as a model for democracy has been tarnished.

Therefore, the first step toward becoming a more effective promoter of democracy abroad is to get our own house in order. To begin with, the political costs to America's credibility as a champion of democratic values and human rights outweigh the value of holding prisoners at Guantanamo indefinitely. The facility should be closed, and, in place of legalistic attempts to pretend that the United States does not engage in torture, a broader range of prohibited techniques should be explicitly defined and ruled out. More generally, the president of the United States must demonstrate a clear commitment to restoring and perfecting the U.S. democratic system of government.

In parallel, our efforts at public diplomacy have to improve.

The United States cannot hope to recruit people to the side of democratic values if it does not pay attention to what non-Americans say they want, rather than what we think they should want. In the Middle East, many Arabs have argued that the United States is disliked not for its basic values, but for its one-sidedness in the Palestinian–Israeli conflict. In Latin America, populist leaders such as Hugo Chavez and Evo Morales have gained enormous support by promoting social policies aimed at the poor—an issue that America's democratic friends in the region have largely ignored. The starting point for a better public diplomacy, therefore, is to stop talking so much about ourselves and start listening to other people.

Indeed, it may be better for the United States to dramatically tone down its public rhetoric about democracy promotion. The loudly proclaimed instrumentalization of democracy promotion in pursuit of U.S. national interests (such as the war on terrorism) taints democracy promotion and makes the United States seem hypocritical when security, economic, or other concerns trump our interests in democracy (as they inevitably will). Acting in concrete ways to support human rights and democratic groups around the world, while speaking more modestly about American goals, might serve both our interests and our ideals better.

The idealistic component of U.S. foreign policy has always been critical to maintaining a domestic American consensus in favor of a strongly internationalist stance, so we do not recommend permanently abandoning this rhetorical stance. We have to recognize, however, that the Iraq war and other events related to the war on terrorism have for the moment tainted such valid and important concepts as democracy promotion and democratic regime change.

Revitalizing Dual Track Diplomacy

It is naïve to believe that the United States should deal only with other democracies. After all, in our own history, the creation of the United States as an independent country required military assistance from France's absolute monarchy. The alliance with Stalin's Soviet Union was necessary for victory in World War II. Today, the wide range of U.S. security, economic, and environmental interests around the world necessitates diplomatic engagement with autocracies.

Nonetheless, American policymakers can conduct relations with their counterparts in autocratic regimes while simultaneously pursuing policies that may facilitate democratic development in these same countries. When it comes to autocratic regimes with which the United States is friendly, American leaders have real leverage to press for evolutionary change, especially over countries that are dependent on U.S. military protection or economic assistance. Rather than coercing them, U.S. officials must first try persuading our autocratic friends that they can ultimately best protect their material and security interests by proactively leading rather than reactively resisting a process of evolutionary change. American officials did exactly this when they helped to coax allies in South Korea, Chile, and South Africa toward embracing democratic change.

Paradoxically, the same logic of engagement applies when considering the promotion of democracy in dictatorships that are hostile to the United States. Attempts to isolate or sanction these regimes have rarely worked. Sanctions against the apartheid regime in South Africa succeeded only because the United States, Great Britain, and other European countries had developed deep economic ties beforehand. Because the United States does not have significant trade with or investments in Iran, Cuba, or Burma, sanctions against these autocracies do little to help the pro-democracy forces inside these countries. However, diplomatic relations with such regimes create a more hospitable environment for internal democratic development.[9] In the USSR, for instance, democratic forces gained strength in the late 1980s when U.S.–Soviet relations were improving, not earlier in the decade when tensions were high. With rare exception, policies that open societies and economies up to international influence have helped to spur democratic change, while policies that isolate societies impede such progress.

Reorganizing Democracy Assistance

For most of American history, U.S. foreign assistance did not explicitly aim to promote democracy. President Kennedy created the United States Agency for International Development (USAID) in 1961 to counter communism, but the agency's focus was economic development. Over time, however, the U.S. government has increasingly become a direct provider of democracy assistance. Ronald Reagan made democracy promotion a central objective when he worked with Democrats in Congress to create the National Endowment for Democracy (NED) in 1983. With the announcement of its "Democracy Initiative" in December 1990, USAID made democracy promotion a core focus and soon became the main source of funding for many nongovernmental organizations (NGOs) in the democracy promotion business.

After September 11, 2001, President Bush increased general foreign assistance funding, including support for democracy promotion. Within the State Department, the Bush administration established the Middle East Partnership Initiative, which became a new funding source for democracy assistance programs, among others. At State, the Bureau for Democracy, Human Rights, and Labor Affairs received major increases in its democracy assistance budget. To better coordinate civilian, military, and intelligence operations in post-conflict settings, the Bush administration established the Coordinator for Reconstruction and Stabilization, a new office within the State Department. Most dramatically, under Secretary of State Condoleezza Rice's transformational diplomacy initiative, the department tried to reform the way in which foreign assistance is funded and delivered.

This focus on how the government is organized to provide democracy assistance is badly needed. The reform ideas to date, however, have not been ambitious enough. Any strategy for more effective democracy promotion must include significantly greater resources as well as reorganization of all U.S. government bureaus and agencies that are tasked with providing democracy assistance.

Democracy promotion should also be placed in a broader context of promoting economic development, reducing poverty, and furthering good governance. The four objectives are interlinked in multiple ways: good governance is widely accepted as a requisite for economic growth; widespread poverty undermines democracy legitimacy; growth reduces poverty; democratic accountability is often required to combat corruption and poor governance; and growth creates a favorable climate for democracy consolidation. Good governance in recipient countries is also critical to maintaining congressional and popular support for assistance programs. Nothing undermines support as much as the perception that U.S. taxpayers' dollars are going into a proverbial Swiss bank account. The United States cannot limit itself to the promotion of democracy—it must also use its leverage to promote development and good governance. These connections need to be reflected in how policy is articulated as well. Senior foreign policy officials in the Bush administration rarely invoked values such as equality and justice; yet historically, American leaders have considered these ideas fundamental to shaping our own government.

Enhancing and Creating International Institutions for Democracy Promotion

After World War II, American internationalists spearheaded the creation of a military alliance—the North Atlantic Treaty Organization (NATO)—to contain the Soviet threat in Europe, and crafted bilateral security pacts with Japan and South Korea to thwart the communist menace in Asia. American leaders also launched the Bretton Woods system and its institutions, the International Monetary Fund (IMF) and the World Bank, as a strategy for maintaining an open, liberal capitalist order and avoiding a repeat of the protectionist-driven meltdown of the 1930s. Democracy promotion was not an explicit objective of either NATO or the IMF; member states in these institutions did not even have to be democracies. Nonetheless, NATO's security umbrella did help to prevent communist coups in Western Europe, to keep the peace between formerly hostile countries within the alliance, and to contain Soviet military expansion in Europe—all of which surely would have undermined democratic institutions.

The stable security environment was conducive to the deepening of democracy within member states and to increasing economic and political cooperation among those states, later culminating in the creation of the European Union. NATO expansion after the collapse of the Warsaw Pact offered Western multilateral connectivity to the new democracies in East Central Europe and served as a bridge as they prepared bids to join the European Union. The gravitational pull of the European Union may be the most powerful tool of democratic consolidation in the world today. The U.S. security umbrella in Asia provided a similar facilitating condition for democratic development first in Japan, then in South Korea, and eventually in Taiwan.

Given the success of these multilateral institutions in promoting democracy, it is striking how little effort President Bush devoted to creating new multilateral institutions or reforming existing ones to advance freedom. After September 11, 2001, not one new major international organization was formed to promote democratic reform. Nor did the Bush administration devote serious effort toward boosting existing international organizations' focus on democracy promotion. This neglect of multilateral institutions must end.

More than any other region in the world, the greater Middle East is devoid of multilateral security institutions. The United States, Canada, the European Union, and other consolidated democracies should partner with their Middle East counterparts to establish regional norms, confidence-building measures, and other forms of dialogue and political reassurance. The goal should be to establish a regional architecture that will affirm human rights and promote regional security.

The impetus for creating regional structures must come from within the region, but the initiative should also be supported from the outside. Such efforts can draw inspiration and lessons from past experiences in Europe, such as the Helsinki process in Eastern Europe, and elsewhere. At the heart of the Helsinki process was the recognition that true security depended not only on relations among states but also on the relationship between rulers and the ruled. Many Middle Eastern governments have signed statements committing themselves to democratic reform, yet the Middle East lacks a regime that can empower citizens to hold their rulers accountable to such pledges at home and in their relations with their neighbors.

The idea of a new multilateral organization committed to advancing democratic practices—be it a revamped Community of Democracies (the international grouping formed during the Clinton administration) or a new League of Democracies—is needed.[10] More boldly, American leaders must embrace new modalities of strengthening ties within the community of democratic states, whether through a new treaty or an alliance.[11]

Even the World Trade Organization (WTO) and other trade agreements must be viewed as levers that help to open up economies, which in turn fosters democratic development. Excluding countries such as Iran from the WTO only hurts the democratic forces inside Iran who favor more, not less, integration of their country into the world system. In some rare circumstances such as South Africa under apartheid, economic sanctions have effectively pressured autocratic regimes to liberalize. The list of failures—including decades-long sanctions against Cuba and Iran—is equally striking. As a rule of thumb, the world democratic community should take its cues about sanctions from the democratic opposition in the target country.

Strengthening International Norms

The collapse of communism ushered in a giddy era for democracy promotion. Because so many autocratic regimes disappeared at the same time, new postcommunist regimes welcomed Western democracy promoters into their countries with few restrictions. Today, however, the atmosphere for democracy promotion is markedly different. The allegedly easy cases for democratic transition in East Central Europe have consolidated and require no further assistance from democracy promoters. Autocratic regimes, at first weak after communism's collapse, have themselves consolidated and now have the means to push back.

Finally, the war in Iraq has greatly tainted the idea of external regime change and put under suspicion all foreigners working to promote democratic change.

The new context requires a new strategy for bolstering the legitimacy of democracy promotion and the defense of human rights. Governments must come together to draft a code of conduct for democratic interventions in the same way that governments and the international human rights community have specified conditions in which external actors have the "responsibility to protect" threatened populations. A "right to help" doctrine is needed. A starting point for this new normative regime would be the "right" to free and fair elections, which in turn would legitimize international election monitors and international assistance targeted at electoral transparency. Once these rules of the road are codified, signatories to such a covenant would be obligated to respect them. And if they did not, the violation would serve as a license for further intrusive behavior from external actors.

The United States and other democracies will be effective in promoting freedom abroad only if we develop international institutions that enhance mutually beneficial cooperation, and then abide by the rule of these institutions in the conduct of our foreign policy.

In highlighting the moral and strategic imperatives for promoting democracy abroad, President Bush continued a long-standing tradition in U.S. foreign policy. Declaration of any important objective, however, must be accompanied by a realistic and comprehensive strategy for achieving it. Simply trumpeting the importance of the objective over and over again is not a substitute for a strategy. The tragic result of the gap between objectives and strategies is that many Americans are starting to view this goal as no longer desirable or attainable. A more effective strategy for promoting democracy and human rights is both needed and available.

NOTES

1. *Freedom in the World 2007: Selected Data from the Freedom House Annual Global Survey of Political Rights and Civil Liberties* (Washington, D.C.: Freedom House, 2007), 1.
2. David Adesnik and Michael McFaul, "Engaging Autocratic Allies to Promote Democracy," *Washington Quarterly* 29, no. 2 (Spring 2006): 7–26.
3. Robert Barro, *Determinants of Economic Growth: A Cross Country Empirical Study* (Cambridge, Mass.: MIT Press, 1997), 58.
4. Ronald Inglehart, "The Worldviews of Islamic Publics in Global Perspective," in *Worldviews of Islamic Publics*, ed. Mansour Moaddell (New York: Palgrave, 2005), 16; James Zogby, *What Arabs Think; Values, Beliefs and Concerns* (Washington, D.C.: Zogby International, 2002); Mark Tessler, "Do Islamic Orientations Influence

Attitudes toward Democracy in the Arab World? Evidence from Egypt, Jordan, Morocco, and Algeria," *International Journal of Comparative Sociology* 43, nos. 3–5 (June 2002): 229–249; and the cluster of articles under the rubric "How People View Democracy" in *Journal of Democracy* 12, no. 1 (January 2001): 93–145.

5. Samuel Huntington, *The Clash of Civilizations and the Remaking of World Order* (New York: Simon and Schuster, 1996).

6. Jack Snyder, *From Voting to Violence: Democratization and Nationalist Conflict* (New York: Norton, 2000); and Jack Snyder and Edward D. Mansfield, *Electing to Fight: Why Emerging Democracies Go to War* (Cambridge, Mass.: MIT Press, 2007).

7. Samuel P. Huntington, *Political Order in Changing Societies* (New Haven, Conn.: Yale University Press, 1968); Fareed Zakaria, *The Future of Freedom: Illiberal Democracy at Home and Abroad* (New York: Norton, 2003).

8. Thomas Carothers, "The 'Sequencing' Fallacy," *Journal of Democracy* 18, no.1 (2007): 12–27.

9. Michael McFaul, Abbas Milani, and Larry Diamond, "A Win-Win U.S. Strategy for Dealing with Iran," *Washington Quarterly*, Winter 2006–2007.

10. Senator John McCain proposed the idea of a new league of democracies in a speech at the Hoover Institution on May 2, 2007.

11. On these other modalities, see Tod Lindberg, "The Treaty of the Democratic Peace," *Weekly Standard*, February 12, 2007, 19–24; and Ivo Daalder and James Lindsey, "Democracies of the World Unite," *The American Interest* 2, no. 3 (January–February 2007): 5–19.

NO: Edward D. Mansfield, *University of Pennsylvania*, and Jack Snyder, *Columbia University*

The Bush administration argued that promoting democracy in the Islamic world, rogue states, and China would enhance America's security, because tyranny breeds violence while democracies coexist in peace. But recent experience in Iraq and elsewhere shows that the early stages of transitions to electoral politics have often been rife with violence.[1]

Such episodes are not just a speed bump on the road to the Democratic Peace. Instead, they reflect a fundamental problem with the strategy of forced-pace democratization in countries that lack the political institutions to support this process.

It is true that mature, stable democracies do not fight each other and rarely become embroiled in civil and ethnic warfare. However, countries that are just starting down the path toward democracy are at high risk for war, especially if they are ill prepared for the journey. Pushing countries too soon into competitive electoral politics not only risks stoking war, sectarianism, and terrorism, but it also makes the future consolidation of democracy more difficult. Pressure to democratize, applied under the wrong conditions, is likely to be counterproductive and dangerous.

President Bush claimed that it is the practice of democracy that makes a nation ready for democracy, and every nation can start on this path.[2] Perhaps, but for ill-prepared countries, this initial practice means starting to build the governmental institutions that underpin democracy, not holding immediate elections. Without a coherent state grounded in a consensus on which people constitute the nation that will exercise self-determination, unfettered electoral politics often gives rise to nationalism and violence at home and abroad. Absent these preconditions, democracy is impossible, and such ill-founded transitions toward democracy usually revert to autocracy or to chaos.

THE DEMOCRATIC PEACE

One of the best-known findings in the field of international relations is that democracies rarely go to war with each other.[3] This finding has stimulated much of the recent interest in democracy promotion. Two principal reasons have been advanced for what is known as *the Democratic Peace.* The first explanation is that effective democratic institutions and elections render the government accountable to the people, who bear the costs and risks of war. The philosopher Immanuel Kant, who is often considered the intellectual architect of arguments about the Democratic Peace, grounded his claims in this institutional explanation. Monarchs could shift the costs of war to their subjects without fearing the loss of power, he argued, whereas elected heads of state would suffer at that ballot box if they become embroiled in bloody and expensive overseas conflicts. The electoral consequences of war, Kant predicted, would make democratic governments more prudent when deciding whether to resort to the sword. As a result of this prudence, democracies do not fight each other and are generally better than other regimes at avoiding unsuccessful, costly wars.

A second explanation for the Democratic Peace is that mature democracies do not fight each other, because they share a liberal democratic identity and common norms governing appropriate political behavior. Advocates of this explanation hold that democracies have deeply ingrained civic norms, such as rule by consent of the governed, the right to free speech, due process of law, fair electoral competition, and the settlement of political disputes by peaceful procedures. A society that has internalized these norms will consider it illegitimate to use military force against another democratic country and will expect such a country to behave in an equally nonthreatening way. Consequently, relations between mature democracies are not characterized by security fears that can otherwise trigger conflict in the anarchic international system.

Although debates over which of these two explanations truly accounts for the Democratic Peace have yet to be resolved, it is widely acknowledged that mature democracies rarely come to blows with one another. Frequently, however, the process of becoming a democracy is anything but peaceful. The early stages of democratic transitions are often quite violent if the necessary institutional infrastructure to help manage regime change is lacking.

The Democratic Peace rests on the presence of coherent domestic institutions that regulate mass political participation, including the rule of law, civil rights, a free and effective press, and representative government. These institutions render foreign-policymakers accountable to society at large. Even those observers who argue that liberal norms underpin the Democratic Peace realize that these norms only operate in conjunction with coherent democratic institutions.[4]

In certain cases, demands for broader political participation that arise as an autocratic regime breaks down can be managed through institutions that either already exist or can be rapidly established. When this kind of managed transition occurs, democracy is usually consolidated relatively smoothly and peacefully. More commonly, however, demands for broader participation are voiced in countries where authoritarian rule has broken down but the institutional preconditions needed for democracy to function effectively are missing. The rule of law is poorly established, state officials are corrupt, elections can be rigged, militaries or warlords threaten to overturn electoral outcomes, and journalistic media are unprofessional and dependent on the state or economic elites. As political scientist Samuel Huntington has argued, when demands for greater mass political participation are made in the face of domestic institutions that are too weak to manage such political activity, the result is likely to be a chaotic situation in which key groups in society threaten to take unilateral actions to protect their parochial interests.[5] Governing in this setting requires an ideological basis for popular political support, since ideology can help to fill the gap between high levels of participation and weak political institutions. This ideology may appear in several forms, but it usually takes the form of some variety of nationalism.[6]

TRANSITIONS TO NATIONALISM AND WAR

From the French Revolution to contemporary Iraq, the beginning phase of democratization in unsettled circumstances has often spurred a rise in militant nationalism. Democracy means rule by the people, but when territorial control and popular loyalties are in flux, a prior question has to be settled: which people will form the nation? Nationalist politicians vie for popular support to answer that question in a way that suits their purposes. When groups are at loggerheads and the rules of the game remain uncertain, the answer is more often based on a test of force and political manipulation than on democratic procedures.[7]

When authoritarian regimes collapse and countries begin the process of democratization, politicians of all stripes have an incentive to play the nationalist card. Holdovers from the old regime know that they need to recruit mass support if they are to survive in the new, more open political setting. For them, nationalism is attractive as a populist doctrine, promising rule for the people but not necessarily rule by the people. Slobodan Milosevic, for example, opportunistically misled Serbs about threats from ethnic Albanians in order to win votes in the elections after Josip Broz Tito's death. This hollow populist appeal is a tried-and-true strategy with a long, bloody pedigree. German Chancellor **Otto von Bismarck** and his successors between 1870 and 1914 used belligerent, divisive nationalism to maintain the authority of the monarchy and the aristocracy in the face of universal suffrage. Exaggerating foreign threats rallied middle-class and rural Germans to the regime, but it contributed to the onset of World War I as well.

Rising political figures also have incentives to tout nationalism in the early stages of a democratic transition. Nationalist rhetoric often involves criticism of monarchs, colonial overlords, dictators, and communist apparatchiks for ruling in their own interest rather than in the interest of the people. Where ethnic or religious groups were oppressed under the old regime, the emergence of a new regime often emboldens them to demand a state of their own. This solution strikes these groups as safer than counting on the hypothetical success of ethnicity-blind liberal democracy.

Elections in many newly democratizing states have been an ethnic census, not a deliberation about public issues. Ethnic leaders can quickly mobilize nationalist mass movements based on crony and clan ties, common language, and cultural practices. It is harder for secular or catch-all leaders to forge new ties across groups. When Saddam Hussein's regime collapsed in Iraq, for example, Shi'a groups readily formed political parties and militias based on existing social networks and religious authority figures; Kurds did the same from their regional base; and Baathist remnants were able to mount a fierce insurgency among some elements of the divided but resentful Sunni. In contrast, secular leaders worked futilely against the grain of the existing social timber to construct an army and credible political parties.

The earlier the elections come during the process of democratization in deeply divided societies with weak political institutions, the worse this problem is. In Bosnia, after the 1995 Dayton peace accord, early elections were won by nationalist parties representing the three major ethnic groups, because the power of ethnic factions was not yet broken. Ten years later, they remain locked into this pattern. Early elections likewise reinforced the divisions in Iraqi society, reflecting the party organizations that could be fashioned quickly rather than ones that might have fostered more effective governance but would have taken longer to forge. Even worse, the Iraqi electoral law, which was based on countrywide proportional representation rather than local districts, magnified the exclusion of the Sunni from the political process, since the insurgency kept a disproportional number of Sunni voters away from the polls.

The nationalist and ethnic politics that prevail in many newly democratizing states load the dice in favor of international and civil war. The decade following the end of the Cold War witnessed some peaceful transitions to democracy in parts of Eastern Europe and other countries where the preconditions for democracy were in place. Elsewhere, however, turbulent experiments with democratic politics led to bloody conflicts. In 1991, Yugoslavia broke up into separate warring nations within six months of elections, in which ethnic nationalism was a powerful factor.[8] In the wake of the Soviet collapse, popular sentiment expressed in the streets and at the ballot box fueled warfare between Armenia and Azerbaijan over the disputed enclave of Nagorno-Karabakh.[9] As Peru and Ecuador democratized fitfully during the 1980s and 1990s, troubled elected governments gained popularity by provoking a series of armed clashes that culminated in a war in the upper Amazon in 1995.[10] Several years after the collapse of Ethiopia's Dergue dictatorship, the country's elected government fought a bloody border war from 1998 to 2000 with Eritrea, which had just adopted (though not yet implemented) a democratic constitution.[11]

In an especially worrisome case, the nuclear-armed, elected regimes of India and Pakistan fought the Kargil War in 1999. After the 1988 death of Pakistani military dictator Zia ul-Haq, a series of revolving-door elected civilian governments had presided over a rise in militant Islamic efforts to liberate majority-Muslim Kashmir from Indian control. In Kashmir itself, the restoration of elections after Indira Gandhi's period of emergency authoritarian rule (1975–1977) had polarized politics and led to violent conflict between Muslims and the state. These turbulent processes culminated in the 1999 war, when Pakistani forces infiltrated across the mountainous frontier in northern Kashmir. The war broke out as Pakistan was taking steps toward greater democratization, including constitutional changes in 1997 that were intended to strengthen the powers of elected civilian rulers.[12]

Democratization also played a catalytic role in the horrible slaughters that engulfed central Africa. The 1993 elections in Burundi—even though they were internationally mandated, free, and fair—intensified ethnic polarization between the Hutu and Tutsi ethnic groups, resulting in some 200,000 deaths. In neighboring Rwanda, an internationally orchestrated power-sharing accord intended to usher in more pluralistic and open politics instead created the conditions for the 1994 genocide that killed nearly a million Tutsi as well as some moderate Hutu.[13]

In East Timor, a favorable vote on independence from Indonesia in an internationally mandated 1999 referendum prompted a violent response by Indonesian-backed Timorese militias, creating an international refugee crisis. Newly democratizing Russia fought two wars against its breakaway province of Chechnya. Vladimir Putin won election in 2000 as Russia's president mainly on the popularity of his plan to invade Chechnya in order to clean out what was characterized as a lair of terrorists and brigands. In each of these varied settings, the turbulent beginning phase of democratization contributed to violence in states with weak political institutions.

War-prone transitions to democracy were not just an aberration of the 1990s. Since the origins of modern mass politics around the time of the French Revolution, virtually all of the great powers turned belligerent and fought popular wars during the early phases of their experiments with democracy. Indeed, democratizing countries of any size have been war prone. Throughout the nineteenth and twentieth centuries, incomplete democratic transitions—those that get stalled between the breakdown of an autocratic regime and the emergence of full-fledged democracy—increased the likelihood of involvement in external war for countries that had weak governmental institutions at the outset of the transition. In such states, war was four to fifteen times more likely than in other countries, based on various measures of regime type.[14] In these wars, the democratizing country was usually the attacker. Seven percent of all international and colonial wars since 1816 are associated with incomplete democratic transitions. The pattern holds for civil wars in more recent decades, too. Statistical studies show that a country undergoing an incomplete democratic transition is more likely to experience civil war than either a pure autocracy or a fully consolidated democracy.[15] Democratic transition is only one of many causes of war, but it can be a potent one.

THE DAUNTING "TO DO" LIST OF DEMOCRATIZATION

There is little reason to believe that the long-standing link between democratization and nationalist war is weakening. Many of the countries that remained on the Bush administration's "to do" list of democracy promotion lack the institutional infrastructure needed to manage the early stages of a democratic transition. The third wave of democratization in the 1980s and 1990s consolidated democratic regimes mainly in the richer countries of Eastern Europe, Latin America, Southern Africa, and East Asia.[16] A fourth wave would involve more challenging cases: countries that are poorer, more ethnically divided, and ideologically more resistant to democracy, with more entrenched authoritarian elites and a much frailer base of governmental institutions and citizen skills.[17]

Many Islamic countries that figured prominently in the Bush administration's efforts to promote democracy are particularly hard cases. Since the end of 2010, various Middle Eastern countries have experienced tremendous domestic political change. The Arab Spring has spurred democratic transitions in Egypt and Tunisia. Compared to some of the other Arab states undergoing political turmoil, both of these countries are characterized by relatively stable administrative institutions, which have helped to manage the democratization process. Likewise, both countries face more limited ethnic, tribal, or sectarian divisions than states with more turbulent politics, so illiberal factions' efforts to exploit splits between Egyptian Muslims and Coptic Christians, for example, have gained only limited traction. If the military in Egypt and Tunisia chooses to remain outside of civilian affairs and submits to civilian control, the presence of relatively robust administrative institutions and the absence of extreme divisions within society are likely to mute the dangers of democratization. That said, a full year after the toppling of Mubarak, the Egyptian military was still glacially slow in granting meaningful political authority to elected representatives.

Various other countries in the region that are experiencing significant political change as a result of the Arab Spring are not so fortunate. Libya, Syria, and Yemen, for example, are vested with relatively weak domestic institutions. They are also ethnically and geographically very splintered. For each of these countries, the Arab Spring has proven to be a chaotic and violent episode. Pressing these states to hold elections before they start developing the institutional infrastructure to manage democratic politics risks promoting additional civil and international violence.

Indeed, there is reason to proceed with substantial caution in efforts to promote democracy in most of the Islamic world. Although democratization in the Islamic world might contribute to peace in the very long run, Islamic public opinion in the short run is generally hostile to the United States, ambivalent about terrorism, and unwilling to renounce the use of force to regain disputed territories. Although the belligerence of the Islamic public is partly fueled by resentment of the U.S.-backed authoritarian regimes under which many of them live or have lived, renouncing these authoritarians and pressing for a quick democratic opening is unlikely to lead to peaceful democratic consolidations.[18]

On the contrary, unleashing Islamic mass opinion through sudden democratization might well raise the likelihood of war. All of the risk factors are there: the media and civil society groups are inflammatory, as old elites and rising oppositions try to outbid each other for the mantle of Islamic or nationalist militancy.[19] The rule of law is weak, and existing corrupt bureaucracies cannot serve a democratic administration properly. The boundaries of states are mismatched with those of nations, making any push for national self-determination fraught with peril. Per-capita incomes, literacy rates, and citizen skills in most Muslim Middle Eastern states are below the levels normally needed to sustain democracy.[20] The richer states' economies are based on oil exports, which exacerbate corruption and insulate regimes from accountability to citizens.

Our argument is not that Islam is culturally unsuited for democracy. Public attitude surveys in Islamic states typically record large majorities that favor democracy of some kind, including a certain segment of society that favors secular democracy and another segment that prefers religious varieties of democracy. In several non-Arab, Muslim-majority states—most notably Turkey and Indonesia—moderate Muslim parties that seem committed to democratic processes vastly outpoll antidemocratic Islamicist parties.[21] The problem is not religion and culture per se but rather the fact that the institutional preconditions needed for democracy to function effectively have not been met in most Islamic states. Consequently, sudden increases in mass political participation are likely to be dangerous.

The theocratic, illiberal semidemocracy established by the popular **Iranian Revolution**, for example, relentlessly pressed the offensive in a bloody war of attrition with Iraq and supported violent movements abroad. A quarter of a century later, Iranian electoral politics still bear the imprint of incomplete democratization. Because liberal democratic reformers were barred from running for office, Iranian voters looking for a more responsive government turned in the June 2005 presidential election to the religious fundamentalist, populist mayor of Tehran, Mahmud Ahmadinejad, a staunch proponent of the Iranian nuclear program. Appeals to popular nationalism thus remain common in electoral systems that rule out liberal alternatives.

Islamic democratization is hardly the only such danger on the horizon. A future democratic opening in China, though much hoped for by advocates of human rights and democratization, could produce a sobering outcome.[22] China's Communist rulers have presided over a commercial expansion that has generated wealth and a potentially powerful constituency for broader political participation. However, given the huge socioeconomic divide between the prosperous coastal areas and the vast, impoverished hinterlands, it seems unlikely that economic development will lead as smoothly to democratic consolidation in China as it has in Taiwan. China's leadership cracked down on student pressures for democratic liberalization at Tiananmen Square in 1989, but party elites know that they will need a stronger basis of popular legitimacy to survive the social and ideological changes that economic change has unleashed.

Nationalism is a key element in their strategy. China's demand to incorporate Taiwan in the People's Republic of China, its animosity toward Japan, and its public displays of resentment at U.S. slights are themes that resonate with the Chinese public and can be used to rally national solidarity behind the regime. At the same time, newly rising social forces see that China's leaders permit more latitude to expressions of nationalism than to liberalism. Thus, some of the same intellectuals who played a role in the Tiananmen prodemocracy protests turned up a few years later as authors of a nationalist text, *The China That Can Say No.*[23]

Like many other established elites who have made use of popular nationalist rhetoric, China's party leadership has walked a fine line, allowing only limited expressions of popular nationalist outrage after such perceived provocations as the U.S. bombing of the Chinese embassy in Belgrade in 1999, anti-Chinese pogroms in Jakarta in 1998, the U.S. spy plane incident of 2001, and the Japanese bid for a permanent seat on the UN Security Council in 2005. These leaders realize that criticism of external enemies can be quickly transformed into popular criticism of the government for not being sufficiently diligent in defense of Chinese national interests. It is doubtful that they could maintain such fine-tuned control over an aroused nationalist public opinion if an incompletely democratizing China should become embroiled in a future crisis with Taiwan.

THE OXYMORON OF IMPOSED DEMOCRACY

If a country lacks the preconditions for democracy, can this infrastructure be forcefully supplied by an external source? Few would argue in favor of conquering countries simply to make them democratic, but democratic great powers—particularly Great Britain and the United States—have sometimes conquered countries for other reasons and then struggled to remake them as friendly democracies before withdrawing. Those who are nostalgic for empire view this secondary democratization as a policy with a future. Indeed, if it were not for the establishment of courts, free press, and rational public administration in British colonies, democracy would probably be scarcer in the developing world today. Most of the postcolonial states that have remained almost continuously democratic since independence—such as India and some West

Indian island states—are former British possessions. Still, many former British colonies have failed to achieve democratic stability: Pakistan and Nigeria oscillate between chaotic elected regimes and military dictatorships; Sri Lanka has held elections that stoked the fires of ethnic conflict; Malaysia has averted ethnic conflict only by limiting democracy. The list continues with even more parlous cases, from Burma to Zimbabwe.

In part, this mixed result reflects the difficulty of establishing democracy anywhere the preconditions are initially lacking. However, it also reflects the counterproductive expedients of imperial rule while the institutions of democracy are being built. Until that task is completed, the empire must often govern through local elites whose legitimacy or political support is based on traditional authority or ethnic sectarianism. To retain power without devoting massive resources to the military occupation of the country, the empire plays the game of divide-and-rule, favoring some groups who help it stay in power at a manageable cost. Such short-run expedients hinder the long-run transition to stable democracy by increasing ethnic polarization. Even if the empire does not take active steps to politicize ethnicity, the act of unleashing demands for mass political participation that nascent democratic institutions are not strong enough to manage is likely to increase the risk of a polarized, violent, unsuccessful transition. British imperialists repeatedly fell prey to these dilemmas between the 1920s and 1960s, even when their intentions were benign.[24]

The United States fell into the same trap as it tried to promote democracy in the wake of military interventions. In Iraq, the United States found that it had to rely on Shi'a clerics and Kurdish ethnic nationalists in trying to create political order. In Afghanistan, as a second cousin of President Hamid Karzai put it on the eve of the violence-marred September 2005 election, the newly elected Parliament "will have tribal leaders, warlords, drug lords, but also democratic new faces and policies."[25] And this is the view of an optimist.

When outside powers have succeeded in establishing democracy by military intervention, it has usually been in countries where favorable preconditions existed and, indeed, where the countries had had a history of democracy.[26] Germany and Japan enjoyed many such preconditions before U.S. troops set foot on their soil: wealth, literacy, an effective state bureaucracy, and a historical legacy of well-developed political parties. Panama was a harder case, but it nonetheless had a democratic legacy to build on. Where those conditions do not exist, the occupying power usually must resort to heavy-handed methods or rule through ethnic elites in the short run, making it difficult to peacefully navigate the initial stages of democratization. Even in the tiny countries of Bosnia and Kosovo, peace through imposed democracy seems likely to last only as long as the presence of international military forces.

BEING PATIENT AND GETTING THE SEQUENCE RIGHT

Military occupation is a costly and risky method for promoting democratization, but other kinds of inducements and pressures can be helpful. The lure of potential membership in the European Union (EU), conditioned on democratic reform and respect for minority rights, has helped to realign incentives for several multiethnic states—such as Slovakia, Croatia, Romania, and some smaller Baltic countries—that might otherwise have turned down the path toward nationalism and violence. These same incentives helped to consolidate Turkey's democracy and improve the position of its ethnic Kurds, notwithstanding the rise to power of an Islamic party. These achievements may or may not endure if the likelihood of EU membership fades.[27] Likewise, the U.S. military umbrella and its leadership in constructing an open, stable trading system permitted states such as West Germany, Taiwan, and South Korea to create the preconditions for stable democracy, although their nations were divided by the Cold War.

International democracy promoters can also take some active steps to help put in place the preconditions of democracy, but these actions need to be undertaken in the right sequence. Generally, the starting point should consist of economic reform and the development of impartial state administration.[28]

Taking these steps strengthens the rule of law and provides the state with effective administrative arms that will be capable of carrying out the edicts of a democratically elected government and independent courts when these institutions come to fruition. For the most part, this was the path followed by the former British colonies that democratized successfully; by Taiwan and South Korea; and by Chile, the Latin American country that had the most successful experience with democratization.

But even if an authoritarian regime undertakes these reforms to improve its own economic and administrative performance, why would it take the next step and allow broad political competition? Normally, this next step is prompted by more than international cajoling—there also needs to be a strong domestic constituency that favors taking it. A labor movement, civil society groups, or internationally oriented business groups typically need to organize to reinforce the pressure to liberalize.[29] Professionalized, objective journalists need the freedom to evaluate the regime's policies and rhetoric.

However, this phase of open contestation should come after institutional reform has been completed, especially in multiethnic societies. Otherwise,

political rivalry is likely to degenerate into ethnicity baiting, patronage grab-
bing, and election fixing. Sometimes these outcomes are unavoidable, but
democracy promotion strategies should be sequenced to try to prevent them.
The danger is not just that the transition will be messier and more violent but
also that antidemocratic groups and ideas will be mobilized and will become
a long-lasting fixture on the political scene. Out-of-sequence, incomplete
democratization often creates an enduring template for illiberal, populist politics, such as the cycling between military dictatorship and illiberal democracy
in Pakistan, the theocratic populism of Iran, and ethnic tyrannies of the majority in many transitional states. These political habits, once rooted in ideologies
and institutions, are hard to break. It is preferable to wait and get the process
right the first time.

IN THE MEANTIME, NORMAL DIPLOMACY

While conducting a patient strategy to promote a longer-term global
Democratic Peace, the United States can use the tools of diplomacy to protect its security interests in a world where nondemocracies persist. President
Bush had high praise for Natan Sharansky's book *The Case for Democracy*,
which argues that the Israelis should not negotiate with the Palestinians
until they are a full democracy of Sweden-like perfection.[30] This is
poor advice.

Diplomacy works better between democracies, but it often works well
enough between democracies and nondemocracies to head off tensions and
forge peace. Israel's security was immeasurably enhanced by the Camp David
Accord, concluded with the undemocratic Egyptian president Anwar Sadat.
Normal diplomacy can often be effective in maintaining peace between democracies and nondemocratic states (not to mention gradually reforming states).
More recently, diplomacy worked without regime change to neutralize the
threats from undemocratic Libya.

Rarely are matters so desperate that there is no alternative to forced-
pace democracy promotion at gunpoint. It is better to be patient and get the
sequence right.

NOTES

1. This chapter is a revised version of Edward D. Mansfield and Jack Snyder, "Prone
   to Violence: The Paradox of the Democratic Peace," *The National Interest* 82
   (Winter 2005–2006): 39–47.
2. George W. Bush, Remarks by the President, November 6, 2003.

3. See Michael Doyle, "Liberalism and World Politics," *American Political Science Review* 80, no. 4 (1986): 1151–1169; and Bruce Russett, *Grasping the Democratic Peace: Principles for a Post-Cold War World* (Princeton: Princeton University Press, 1993).

4. See, for example, John M. Owen, "Perceptions and the Limits of Liberal Peace: The Mexican–American and Spanish American Wars," in *Paths to Peace: Is Democracy the Answer?* ed. Miriam Fendius Elman (Cambridge: MIT Press, 1997).

5. Samuel P. Huntington, *Political Order in Changing Societies* (New Haven: Yale University Press, 1968).

6. Jack Snyder, *From Voting to Violence: Democratization and Nationalist Conflict* (New York: Norton, 2000).

7. This section is based on Edward D. Mansfield and Jack Snyder, *Electing to Fight: Why Emerging Democracies Go to War* (Cambridge: MIT Press, 2005).

8. Susan Woodward, *Balkan Tragedy* (Washington, DC: Brookings Institution, 1995), 17.

9. Stuart Kaufman, *Modern Hatreds: The Symbolic Politics of Ethnic War* (Ithaca: Cornell University Press, 2001), chap. 3.

10. David R. Mares, *Violent Peace: Militarized Interstate Bargaining in Latin America* (New York: Columbia University Press, 2001), chap. 7.

11. Franklin Steves, "Regime Change and War: Domestic Politics and the Escalation of the Ethiopia–Eritrea Conflict," *Cambridge Review of International Affairs* 16, no.1 (2003): 119–133.

12. On India, see Ian Talbot, *India and Pakistan* (London: Arnold, 2000), 275; on Pakistan, see Hasan-Askari Rizvi, *Military, State and Society in Pakistan* (New York: St. Martin's, 2000), chap. 10. Bruce Russett and John Oneal, in *Triangulating Peace: Democracy, Interdependence, and International Organizations* (New York: Norton, 2001), 48, discuss whether the Kargil War should be counted as a war between democracies.

13. Gérard Prunier, *The Rwanda Crisis: History of a Genocide* (New York: Columbia University Press, 1995), chaps. 3 and 5.

14. See Mansfield and Snyder, *Electing to Fight*, chaps. 5 and 6.

15. James Fearon and David Laitin, "Ethnicity, Insurgency, and Civil War," *American Political Science Review* 97, no. 1 (2003): 91–106.

16. Larry Diamond, "Is the Third Wave Over?" *Journal of Democracy* 7, no. 3 (July 1996): 20–37.

17. Adrian Karatnycky, ed., *Freedom in the World: The Annual Survey of Political Rights and Civil Liberties, 2001–2002* (New York: Freedom House, 2002), 11–15, 20–34.

18. F. Gregory Gause, "Can Democracy Stop Terrorism?" *Foreign Affairs* 84, no. 5 (September–October 2005): 62.

19. Sheri Berman, in "Islamism, Revolution, and Civil Society," *Perspectives on Politics* 1, no. 2 (June 2003): 257–272, esp. 265, draws parallels to belligerent civil society in the flawed democracy of Weimar Germany and stresses the "Huntingtonian gap" between high demand for political participation and ineffective state institutions. See Huntington, *Political Order in Changing Societies*.

20. United Nations Development Programme, *Human Development Report 2004* (New York: Oxford University Press, 2004); Adam Przeworski et al., *Democracy and Development* (Cambridge: Cambridge University Press, 2000), 101; Council on Foreign Relations, *In Support of Arab Democracy: Why and How*, task force report 54 (New York: Council on Foreign Relations, 2005), 61–62; and Daniela Donno and Bruce Russett, "Islam, Authoritarianism, and Female Empowerment: What Are the Linkages?" *World Politics* 56, no. 4 (July 2004): 582–607.

21. Vali Nasr, "The Rise of Muslim Democracy," *Journal of Democracy* 16, no. 2 (April 2005): 13–27.

22. For a balanced view that discusses many of the following points, see David Bachman, "China's Democratization: What Difference Would It Make for U.S.– China Relations," in *What If China Doesn't Democratize?* ed. Edward Friedman and Barrett McCormick (Armonk: M.E. Sharpe, 2000).

23. The authors are Song Qiang, Zhang Zangzang, and Qiao Bian.

24. Jack Snyder, "Empire: A Blunt Tool for Democratization," *Daedalus* 134, no. 2 (Spring 2005): 58–71.

25. Carlotta Gall, "New Generation of Afghan Voters Is Finding Its Voice," *New York Times*, September 15, 2005, A3.

26. Mark Peceny, "Forcing Them to Be Free," *Political Science Quarterly* 52, no. 3 (September 1999): 549–582, esp. table 1, p. 564.

27. On the links between membership in regional organizations and democratization, see Jon Pevehouse, *Democracy from Above* (New York: Cambridge University Press, 2005).

28. For a balanced discussion, see "Is Gradualism Possible? Choosing a Strategy for Promoting Democracy in the Middle East," in *Critical Mission: Essays on Democracy Promotion*, ed. Thomas Carothers (Washington, DC: Carnegie Endowment for International Peace, 2004), chap. 18.

29. Adrian Karatnycky and Peter Ackerman, *How Freedom Is Won: From Civic Resistance to Durable Democracy* (New York: Freedom House, 2005).

30. Natan Sharansky and Ron Dermer, *The Case for Democracy: The Power of Freedom to Overcome Tyranny and Terror* (New York: Public Affairs, 2004), 173.

GLOSSARY

Amnesty International A nongovernmental organization aimed at protecting human rights by raising awareness of human rights abuses.

Antiglobalization movement A radical protest movement—which started with the 1999 anti-WTO demonstrations in Seattle—that is generally opposed to globalization. Antiglobalization activists argue that globalization tends to disproportionately benefit multinational corporations and international financial institutions and even may be promoted by them. While many different philosophies are associated with antiglobalization, supporters of the movement generally believe that governments are working to further the interests of corporations at the expense of citizens.

Asian Development Bank A regional development bank focused on Asia and the Pacific, with aims and methods that are similar to those of the World Bank. Its goals are reducing poverty and promoting development through loans and other assistance.

Autarky An autocratic government or a state where the government retains absolute sovereignty.

Balance of payments An economic measure of the total capital of a country's international economic transactions. This measurement includes trade and monetary transfers to both nonresidents within the country and residents abroad.

Barriers to trade Government policies that restrict international trade, such as the establishment of import or export quotas or tariffs.

Bilateral aid Assistance that is given directly by one country to another.

Brain drain The migration of trained professionals from poor to rich countries, leading to a shortage of skilled technical workers or adept bureaucrats in the sending countries.

Cairo Declaration A nonbinding declaration signed in 1943 by the victorious Allies, returning territories taken by the Japanese—including Taiwan—to China. It has become a point of contention in debates over Taiwan's independent status.

Camp David Accords Agreements signed in 1978 by the leaders of Israel and Egypt, facilitated by President Jimmy Carter at Camp David. The Accords led to the Israel–Egypt Peace Treaty in 1979.

Cap-and-trade system A pollution control technique used by governments to reduce emissions by placing a cap on overall emissions and then granting to each company that produces pollutants an allowance or credit to emit that amount. Companies can then trade credits in order to keep the aggregate emissions level at the cap.

Carbon Capture and Storage (CCS) A technique that involves capturing and storing carbon emissions before they are released into the atmosphere. While it is projected that this technology could significantly reduce emissions, there is still a debate surrounding the viability of long-term carbon storage.

Center for Disease Control and Prevention (CDC) An agency of the U.S. government that is tasked with developing methods to combat disease and promote health. Its research is used by the United States and by other entities in setting policy and in evaluating threats to both national and global health.

Clean Air Act Legislation passed by Congress in 1967 (and most recently amended in 1990) that aimed to reduce air pollution by setting limits on auto and other emissions. The most recent amendments included provisions for dealing with acid rain and proposed emissions-trading programs.

Clean Development Mechanism (CDM) A provision of the Kyoto Protocol that allows industrialized countries to fund emissions reductions in developing countries rather than in their own countries, where it would be more expensive. In order to qualify under this provision, the emissions-reduction project must be unachievable without the aid or funding of the industrialized country.

Cold War The period between the end of World War II and the collapse of the Soviet Union (1991), characterized by extreme political cleavages between the U.S. and the USSR.

Comparative advantage An economic theory holding that countries should devote their resources to only the outputs that they produce most efficiently and should gain all other products through trade. The theory states that if every country specializes, all countries will gain through trade.

Credit default swap A financial instrument where the seller guarantees the buyer compensation if there is a default, and the buyer pays the seller for the duration of the contract. It is, in effect, insurance against an asset default or nonpayment.

Crimes against humanity Crimes committed systematically against a civilian population—including, but not limited to, murder, enslavement, and apartheid.

Cultural Revolution A period of power struggles within China from 1966 to the mid-1970s, during which a campaign to eliminate the "four olds"—old customs, old culture, old habits, and old ideas—led to gross violations of human rights, the death of many Chinese citizens (particularly intellectuals), and the destruction of many important artifacts of Chinese culture and history. The activity of the Revolution was mainly carried out by the Red Guards, groups of young Chinese who were told that it was their duty to combat the "four olds" but who ultimately ended up beyond of the control of the Communist Party.

Cyberterrorism An attack against a computer or network with the intent to cause harm in order to achieve political or ideological ends.

Democratic Peace The view that democracies are more peaceful than non-democracies, especially toward other democracies.

Deterrence The strategic practice of inhibiting countries from doing things they would otherwise have done, such as threatening with nuclear annihilation.

Direct Foreign Investment (DFI) Investment in one country's industries by a company that is based in another country.

Dirigisme An economy directed by the government or with heavy government participation. Such economies can be capitalist or socialist, and most modern economies contain some level of dirigisme.

Ecoterrorism The use of or threat of violence (such as sinking whaling ships) to advance
an environmental agenda. As with more general types of terrorism, the exact
definition of this phenomenon remains highly debated.

Emissions trading (see *cap-and-trade system*)

Enlightenment, the A new political ideology that emerged in Europe in the eighteenth
century, based on the belief that human progress was possible through the systematic application of reason. Gaining credence during a time of optimism and
concern for the rights of the individual, its principles heavily influenced the
drafting of both the U.S. Constitution and the French Declaration of the Rights
of Man and of the Citizen.

Environmental Protection Agency (EPA) A U.S. federal government agency that is
charged with the protection of the environment and the nation's health. The EPA
sets and enforces national environmental standards.

European Union A formal political institution of 27 European states. Major bodies of
the EU include the European Commission, the Council of the European Union,
the European Council, the Court of Justice of the European Union, and the
European Central Bank.

Failed state A state where the central government no longer has effective control over
the territory within its borders. The degree of control that must be retained by
the government to avoid this status is highly debated.

Fossil fuels Fuels derived from hydrocarbons, often petroleum, coal, or natural gases.
These fuels are a nonrenewable resource, and their use produces greenhouse
gases.

Free trade A system of trade that is free from government-imposed barriers (see *barriers to trade*).

Gender Empowerment Measure (GEM) A scale for determining the level of inequality
between men and women using both economic and political factors.

General Agreement on Trade and Tariffs (GATT) The international organization for the
regulation of trade policy from 1948 until 1995, when it was replaced by the
WTO.

Geneva Conventions A group of treaties drawn up in Geneva, Switzerland, all four of
which address the rights of prisoners of war and noncombatants. The Conventions
have been ratified by almost every nation.

Genocide Acts committed to intentionally eliminate an ethnic, religious, national,
or racial group. This phenomenon was recognized internationally as a crime
in 1948.

Gini coefficient A ratio used to measure inequality of income distribution between 0
and 1, where 0 is perfect equality and 1 is perfect inequality.

Glass-Steagall Act Named after the bill's sponsors (Representatives Carter Glass of
Virginia and Henry Steagall of Alabama), the Banking Act of 1933 established the

Federal Deposit Insurance Corporation and instituted other reforms to limit banking speculation on the heels of the banking crash of 1929. Much of Glass-Steagall was repealed in 1999 by the Gramm-Leach-Bliley Act.

Great Powers Nations with preponderant military, economic, diplomatic, and cultural power, capable of exercising influence over other countries.

Greenhouse gases (GHG) Gases in the earth's atmosphere that cause the greenhouse effect, warming the earth's temperatures. Some of these gases—such as carbon dioxide—are naturally present in the atmosphere, but emissions from the use of fossil fuels have drastically increased their concentrations, causing global warming.

Greenpeace International A nongovernmental organization aimed at preventing environmental harm and promoting behaviors and technology to protect the Earth.

Green revolution The spread of advanced agricultural technologies from developed to developing countries, allowing many of those countries to become major agricultural exporters and increasing food security.

Gross Domestic Product (GDP) A measure of a country's output—or goods and services produced—within any given year. It is derived by adding the following components: consumption, investment, government spending, and the balance of trade. GDP is an important gauge of a country's standard of living and economic health.

Gross Fixed Capital Formation (GFC) A measure of a country's spending on physical infrastructure.

Gross National Product (GNP) A measure that includes the same components as GDP but also adds income from citizens abroad and subtracts income from foreigners working within the country. GNP is also an indicator of economic health.

Group of 77 (G77) A group of developing nations formed in 1964 to advocate for the collective economic interests of its members. The group now includes 130 nations.

Group of 8 (G8) A group of eight states (Canada, France, Germany, Italy, Japan, Russia, the United Kingdom, and the United States) and the EU, whose annual summit is meant to serve as a forum for issues of global or mutual concern and as a way for its member countries to pool resources and share information.

Hegemony The domination or heavy influence of one country over others.

Housing bubble A rapid increase in real estate prices that outstrips actual real estate values, driven by sometimes-irrational beliefs that real estate prices will always continue to rise, resulting in a precipitous burst where real estate prices decline rapidly.

Humanitarian intervention The interference, usually militarily, by one or more states in another state, with the express purpose of ending a humanitarian crisis and aiding the civilian population of that state.

Import substitution A technique for reducing dependency on foreign goods whereby the government promotes internal production of important goods rather than relying on imports.

Intergovernmental Panel on Climate Change (IPCC) A panel established by the World Meteorological Organization and the United Nations Environmental Programme in order to provide policy-neutral scientific reports to aid governments in addressing climate change and to provide information for the United Nations Framework Convention on Climate Change.

Internally displaced person (IDP) An individual who has been forced from his/her home but has remained within his/her country's borders and therefore is not classified as a refugee.

International Atomic Energy Agency (IAEA) An independent international organization established in 1957 to promote the peaceful use of nuclear technology and end its use as a weapon. Though independent, the IAEA reports to both the United Nations General Assembly and the United Nations Security Council.

International Criminal Court (ICC) A tribunal established in 2002 as a forum to prosecute perpetrators of genocide and other crimes against humanity. A total of 108 countries have signed on to the Rome Statute establishing the ICC, though China, the United States, and India are among the prominent nations that have not signed.

International Criminal Police Organization (INTERPOL) An international agency founded to facilitate cooperation among national police agencies to combat international crime. INTERPOL remains politically neutral, only involving itself in crimes that concern two or more of its member countries and that do not have a political, military, religious, or racial nature.

International Monetary Fund (IMF) An international financial institution that, like the World Bank, offers loans and technical assistance. The IMF, however, focuses not only on development but also on stable exchange markets and international monetary cooperation.

Iranian Revolution The 1979 revolution that deposed the shah of Iran and instated Ayatollah Ruhollah Khomeini as the leader of Iran as an Islamic republic.

Joint Chiefs of Staff A group of the chiefs of each branch of the U.S. military—the army, navy, Marine Corps, and air force—that is tasked with unifying strategy and ensuring integration of the branches as well as advising the president in his role as commander-in-chief.

Joint United Nations Programme on HIV/AIDS A program started by the United Nations Economic and Social Council in 1996 to facilitate collaboration between governments and private entities in combating the AIDS epidemic.

Kant, Immanuel An 18th-century philosopher, born in Germany, who tried to balance empiricism and rationalism in his work. He believed that constitutional republics were necessary to bring about world peace (see *Democratic Peace*).

Khmer Rouge The political party, led by Pol Pot, that ruled Cambodia from 1975 to 1979 and derived its philosophy from a number of nations' communist parties. It was responsible for the deaths of 1.5 million of its citizens.

Kyoto Protocol An agreement reached under the United Nations Framework Convention on Climate Change in which the signatories agreed to either reduce greenhouse-gas emissions or to practice emissions trading if they found themselves unable to do so on their own. The only industrialized country that did not ratify the protocol is the United States.

League of Nations An international organization replaced by the United Nations in 1946. As a significant component of U.S. President Woodrow Wilson's Fourteen Points for Peace, it was intended to prevent and resolve conflict by providing a forum for international negotiation.

Maastricht Treaty The treaty, signed in 1992, that created the European Union and laid the groundwork for the adoption of the euro.

Marshall Plan A plan created by the United States to provide financial aid to rebuild Europe following World War II.

Millennium Development Goals (MDGs) Eight objectives—covering issues such as eradicating poverty and promoting development, protecting the environment, promoting human rights and democracy, meeting the special needs of Africa, and strengthening the United Nations—that were developed at the Millennium Summit in 2000. The United Nations member nations have pledged to try to achieve these goals by 2015.

Monterrey Consensus An agreement signed by numerous countries as well as the heads of the United Nations, International Monetary Fund, World Bank, and the World Trade Organization concerning international cooperation to promote development.

Montreal Protocol An international treaty, established in 1989, aimed at protecting the ozone layer by limiting the use and production of harmful substances such as chlorofluorocarbons (CFCs).

Multilateral aid Relief assistance from many countries or sources, usually distributed through an organization such as the World Bank or the International Monetary Fund.

Multinational corporation A corporation that operates in numerous countries and often has significant economic influence.

Multipolar global structure A distribution of worldwide power among several great powers.

Neoclassical economic thinking A school of thought—focused on supply and demand as they affect prices and outputs—that influences most mainstream economics. Rational choice theory forms the basis of many of its models.

New Economic Partnership for African Development (NEPAD) An African Union program that is aimed at facilitating economic cooperation between African countries and promoting African development.

Nongovernmental organization (NGO) An organization that is legally independent from any government, although it can be a recipient of government funds. No government representative may be a member of an NGO.

Non-refoulement A principle of international law that protects refugees from being returned to a country where their lives would be in danger or their rights would be violated.

Norms Universal principles guiding behavior, often expressed through international law.

North American Free Trade Agreement (NAFTA) A trade bloc formed by Canada, Mexico, and the United States, allowing free trade between the three countries. It has been debated whether NAFTA has had an overall positive effect or if it has harmed the countries involved, particularly Mexico.

North Atlantic Treaty Organization (NATO) A military alliance formed in 1949 between Belgium, Canada, Denmark, France, Iceland, Italy, Luxembourg, the Netherlands, Norway, Portugal, the United Kingdom, and the United States in order to check the Soviet Union.

Nuclear Nonproliferation Treaty (NPT) A treaty signed in 1968 to limit the proliferation of nuclear weapons. It is considered to have three principles: nonproliferation, disarmament, and the right to peaceful use of nuclear technology.

Official Development Assistance (ODA) A type of development aid that is given to developing countries by Organization for Economic Cooperation and Development member states.

Organization for Economic Cooperation and Development (OECD) An international organization composed of the world's principal industrialized countries. It serves primarily as a policy think tank for these governments.

Outsourcing The practice of hiring an outside company to perform a function (such as manufacturing) that is traditionally performed by the original company. The second company is frequently based in another country and can perform the same tasks either more cheaply or more efficiently. Labor in the original country fears job loss from outsourcing.

Oxfam A nongovernmental organization aimed at combating poverty and injustice. Originally, Oxfam was solely concerned with famine relief, but the organization has developed a much broader focus in order to deal with the root causes of famine.

Permanent Five (P5) The five permanent members of the United Nations Security Council—China, France, Russia, the United Kingdom, and the United States—which are the only members to have veto powers.

Planned Parenthood A nongovernmental organization, originally based in the United States, that has created an international network of nongovernmental organizations tasked with providing reproductive health services and promoting reproductive rights.

President's Emergency Plan For AIDS Relief (PEPFAR) A U.S. federal government program initiated in 2003 to provide antiretroviral drugs to those infected with HIV/AIDS in fifteen countries with high rates of infection and limited resources. The program was designed to promote the ABC ideology (Abstain, Be faithful, and use Condoms) and to fund AIDS research. The focus on abstinence-only programs has been criticized as a moral choice rather than one that is crafted in the interests of public health.

Prima facie A term usually used in legal proceedings to refer to evidence that is sufficient to prove the fact or argument in question, barring rebuttal.

Protectionism A government policy aimed at protecting domestic industry by restricting imports by means of barriers such as tariffs or quotas or by providing subsidies.

Purchasing power parity A measure of how much can be bought with a particular currency.

Rotary International The umbrella organization for various chapters (known as Rotary Clubs) aimed at promoting humanitarianism and ethics among business and professional leaders.

Sovereignty The right, in international law, of a country's government to control its own domestic affairs without intervention or direct interference from other countries. This right, which is considered integral to many of the principles of international law, can also complicate international intervention in cases of failed states and/or humanitarian crisis.

Terrorism A concept whose definition is a controversial issue in international law. Generally, it is agreed that terrorism involves criminal acts intended to provoke fear and intimidate a population or government in order to achieve political ends. Whether a state can commit an act of terrorism is highly debated.

Trade deficit A negative balance of trade, produced when the net value of imports exceeds the net value of exports—the deficit country then owes the difference to the surplus country. A positive balance of trade is known as a trade surplus.

Trade liberalization The removal of trade barriers in order to move closer to free trade.

Tragedy of the commons A classic problem in game theory that is often used as a metaphor for the overexploitation of resources whose use is not regulated. The inherent conflict is between the common good and the motivation for each individual entity to take or use as much of the resource as possible without regard for the needs of others or the long-term sustainability of that resource.

Transnational Action Networks An international organization or coalition of independent nongovernmental organizations that share a similar vision or goals.

UNAIDS (see *Joint United Nations Programme on HIV/AIDS*)

United Nations (UN) The international organization with universal state membership, created in 1946 and responsible for providing a venue for international discussions about common issues and developing common rules and norms governing global issues.

United Nations Charter The 1945 treaty that established the United Nations and outlined the principles of the organization and powers given to it.

United Nations Children's Fund (UNICEF) An organization that provides assistance to children and mothers in developing countries. It is entirely funded by voluntary contributions from United Nations member nations and private donors.

United Nations Development Fund for Women (UNIFEM) A United Nations fund created to promote the human rights of women and gender equality.

United Nations Development Group (UNDG) A division of the United Nations created in 1997 to reform and improve the effectiveness of United Nations development programs. The United Nation's other development funds are members of the group.

United Nations Development Programme (UNDP) A United Nations organization that provides development assistance to developing nations in the form of grants, advice, and other assistance. The UNDP focuses on factors such as democratic governance and poverty reduction in promoting development.

United Nations Educational, Scientific, and Cultural Organization (UNESCO) An agency of the United Nations that is aimed at promoting international cooperation in areas of education, science, and culture—reflecting a core belief that world peace can be fostered through education and cultural familiarity. UNESCO contributes to achieving the Millennium Development Goals.

United Nations Framework Convention on Climate Change (UNFCCC) An international treaty, which contains the provisions for the Kyoto Protocol, aimed at reducing emissions to stabilize greenhouse-gas levels.

United Nations High Commissioner for Refugees (UNHCR) A United Nations agency tasked with coordinating international efforts to protect refugees and ensuring that their rights are protected.

United Nations Population Fund (UNFPA) An international organization that provides funding for population and reproductive health programs and is particularly concerned with ending unwanted pregnancy, unsafe birth, and the spread of HIV/AIDS as well as promoting the equality of and respect for women.

Universal Declaration of Human Rights (UDHR) A declaration passed by the United Nations General Assembly in 1948, detailing the human rights recognized in international law. Articles include the right to life, the right to be presumed innocent until proven guilty, and the right to freedom of movement within a nation's borders.

Veto powers The ability—given only to the five permanent members of the Security Council (see *Permanent Five*)—to prevent, by a single negative vote, the passage of a nonprocedural decision of the Security Council.

Von Bismarck, Otto The first chancellor of the second German Empire. Also known as the *Iron Chancellor*, he was largely responsible for the unification of Germany. Both his domestic and his foreign policy strategies have continued to inform international politics and theory since his death in 1898.

Warlordism A situation occurring in failed states where rival warlords, rather than the central government, have de facto control over various parts of the country.

Westphalian state A nation that retains its sovereignty based on the principles of territoriality and the governance of domestic affairs free from external actors. This concept of sovereignty is traced back to the Peace of Westphalia in 1648, but the term is currently used to describe the modern nation state.

World Bank The International Bank for Reconstruction and Development and the International Development Association, created after World War II to provide financial and development assistance to developing countries.

World Health Organization (WHO) An agency of the United Nations that combats disease and promotes international health.

World Trade Organization (WTO) An international organization that succeeded the General Agreement on Tariffs and Trade (GATT) as the international body responsible for supervising and liberalizing international trade between its member nations.

World Wide Fund for Nature (WWF) A nongovernmental organization aimed at promoting conservation and protecting the environment. It mostly focuses on three types of habitats: forest, freshwater ecosystems, and oceans and coastal ecosystems.

Xenophobia The fear or distrust of that which is foreign. It is often coupled with a belief in the superiority of one's homeland over other cultures or countries.

REFERENCES

Introduction: Understanding Globalization

Beck, U. *Risk Society: Towards a New Modernity*. Newbury Park: Sage, 1992.

Bello, Walden. *DeGlobalization: Ideas for a New World Economy*. London: Zed Books, 2004.

Bhagwati, J. "Globalization with a Human Face." In *The Future of Globalization*, edited by E. Zedillo. New York: Routledge, 2008.

Biersteker, T. "Globalization as a Mode of Thinking in Major Institutional Actors." In *The Political Economy of Globalization*, edited by N. Woods. New York: St. Martin's, 2000.

Blanning, Tim. *The Pursuit of Glory*. London: Penguin, 2008.

Brzezinski, Z. *Second Chance*. New York: Basic Books, 2007.

Burman, Stephen. *The State of the American Empire: How the USA Shapes the World*. London: Earthscan, 2007.

Castells, Manuel. "Global Governance and Global Politics." *PS*, January 2005, 9–16.

Cavanagh, J., ed. *South-North: Citizen Strategies to Transform a Divided World*. San Francisco: International Forum on Globalization, 1995.

Chasek, Pam. "Environmental Organizations and Multilateral Diplomacy." In *Multilateral Diplomacy and the United Nations Today*, edited by James P. Muldoon Jr., 156–157. Boulder: Westview, 1995.

Clark, W. C., and R. E. Munn, eds. *Sustainable Development of the Biosphere*. Cambridge: Cambridge University Press, 1986.

Cohen, Benjamin. *The Geography of Money*. Ithaca: Cornell University Press, 1998.

Cooper, Richard. "Economic Interdependence and Foreign Policy in the Seventies" *World Politics* 24, no. 2 (January 1972).

Crutzen, P. J. "Geology of Mankind—The Anthropocene." *Nature* 415 (2002): 23.

Fishman, C. *The Wal-Mart Effect*. New York: Penguin, 2006.

Frieden, Jeffry A. *Global Capitalism*. New York: Norton, 2006.

Friedman, Thomas L. *The Lexus and the Olive Tree*. New York: Anchor Books, 2000.

Garrett, Geoffrey. *Partisan Politics in the Global Economy*. Cambridge: Cambridge University Press, 1998.

Giddens, Anthony. *Runaway World*. New York: Routledge, 2003.

Gilani, Ijaz, S. *Uncovering the Ethical: Recovering Meaning in International Relations Scholarship*. Conference Honoring the Memory of Hayward R. Alker, Watson Institute, Brown University, 2008.

Haq, M. ul. *Reflections on Human Development*. New York: Oxford University Press, 1995.

Held, D., and A. McGrew. "Globalization." *Global Governance* 5, no. 4 (1999):483–496.

———. *Globalization/Anti-Globalization*. 2nd ed. Cambridge: Polity, 2007.

Huntington, Samuel P. *The Third Wave: Democratization in the Late Twentieth Century*. Norman: University of Oklahoma Press, 1991.

Jervis, R. *System Effects: Complexity in Political and Social Life*. Princeton: Princeton University Press, 1997.

Kates, R., B. L. Turner II, and William C. Clark. "The Great Transformation." In *The Earth as Transformed by Human Action*, edited by B. L. Turner II, R. Kates, J. Richards, J. Mathews, and W. Meyer, 1–17. Cambridge: Cambridge University Press, 1990.

Katzenstein, Peter J. *Small States in World Markets*. Ithaca: Cornell University Press, 1985.

Keck, Margaret E., and Kathryn Sikkink. *Activists beyond Borders*. Ithica: Cornell University Press, 1998.

Khagram, Sanjeev, James V. Riker, and Kathryn Sikkink, eds. *Restructuring World Politics*. Minneapolis: University of Minnesota Press, 2002.

Khor, Martin. "Effects of Globalisation on Sustainable Development after UNCED," http://www.twnside.rog/sg/title/rio-cn.htm.

Kissinger, Henry. *Does America Need a Foreign Policy?* New York: Simon & Schuster, 2001.

Klein, Naomi. *No Logo*. New York: Picador, 2002.

Knowlton, Brian. "Globalization, According to the World, Is a Good Thing. Sort Of." *New York Times*, October 5, 2007.

Krugman, Paul. *Peddling Prosperity*. New York: Norton, 1994.

La Porte, T. R., ed. *Organized Social Complexity: Challenge to Politics and Policy*. Princeton: Princeton University Press, 1975.

Ling, C. Y., and M. Khor. *International Environmental Governance: Some Issues from a Developing Country Perspective*. Penang, Malaysia: Third World Network, 2001.

Maddison, A. *Contours of the World Economy, 1–2030 AD*. Oxford: Oxford University Press, 2007.

Nye, Joseph S. *The Paradox of American Power*. Oxford: Oxford University Press, 2002.

Perrow, C. *Normal Accidents: Living with High-Risk Technologies*. Princeton: Princeton University Press, 1999.

Ponting, C. *A Green History of the World: The Environment and the Collapse of Great Civilizations*. New York: Penguin Books, 1993.

Rice, Condoleeza. "Promoting the National Interest." *Foreign Affairs*, February 2000.

Rodrik, Dani. *The Global Governance of Trade as if Development Really Mattered*. New York: United Nations Development Program, 2001.

Rosenau, J. N. *Distant Proximities*. Princeton: Princeton University Press, 2003.

Roy, Arundhati. *Power Politics*. Boston: South End Press, 2001.

Ruggie, John Gerard. *Constructing the World Polity*. London: Routledge, 1998.

Schellnhuber, H. J., P. J. Crutzen et al., eds. *Earth System Analysis for Sustainability*. Cambridge: MIT Press, 2004.

Scott, James. *Seeing Like a State*. New Haven: Yale University Press, 1998.

Scholte, J. A. *Globalization: A Critical Introduction*. New York: St. Martin's, 2000.

Shiva, Vandana. *Earth Democracy*. London: Zed Books, 2005.

Simmons, Beth A., Frank Dobbin, and Geoffrey Garrett. "Introduction: The International Diffusion of Liberalism." *International Organization* 60, no. 4 (2006): 781–810.

Simon, H. A. "The Architecture of Complexity." *The Sciences of the Artificial*. Cambridge: MIT Press, 1981.

Slaughter, Anne-Marie. *A New World Order.* Princeton: Princeton University Press, 2004.

Speth, J. G. *The Bridge at the Edge of the World.* New Haven: Yale University Press, 2008.

Stiglitz, Joesph E., and Andrew Charlton. *Fair Trade for All.* Oxford: Oxford University Press, 2005.

World Bank. *Mini Atlas of Global Development.* Washington, DC: The World Bank, 2004.

Zedillo, E., ed. *The Future of Globalization.* New York: Routledge, 2008.

Chapter 1: Trade Liberalization and Economic Growth

YES

Bhagwati, J. 1992. *India's Economy: The Shackled Giant.* Oxford: Clarendon Press.

Bourguignon, F., and C. Morrison. 2002. "Inequality among World Citizens: 1820–1992." *American Economic Review.*

Chen, S., and M. Ravallion. 2004. "How Did the World's Poorest Fare Since the Early 1980s?" World Bank mimeo.

Collier, P., and Reinikka. 2001. "Reconstruction and Liberalization: An Overview." In *Uganda's Recovery: The Role of Farms, Firms, and Government,* edited by R. Reinikka and P. Collier. Washington, D.C.: World Bank, Regional and Sectoral Studies.

Dollar, David, and Aart Kraay. 2002. "Institutions, Trade, and Growth." *Journal of Monetary Economics.*

Dollar, David, and Borje Ljunggren. 1997. "Going Global, Vietnam." In *Going Global: Transition from Plan to Market in the World Economy,* edited by Padma Desai, 439–471. Cambridge, Mass.: MIT Press.

Eckaus, R. 1997. "Going Global: China." In *Going Global: Transition from Plan to Market in the World Economy,* edited by Padma Desai, 415–437. Cambridge, Mass.: MIT Press.

Lindert, P., and J. Williamson. 2001. "Does Globalization Make the World More Unequal?" National Bureau of Economic Research Working Paper No. 8228. Cambridge, Mass.: National Bureau of Economic Research.

Romer, P. 1986. "Idea Gaps and Object Gaps in Economic Development." *Journal of Monetary Economics* 32.

Chapter 2: Trade and Equality

YES

Atkinson, A. B., and A. Brandolini. 2001. "Promise and Pitfalls in the Use of 'Secondary' Data-Sets: Income Inequality in OECD Countries as a Case Study." *Journal of Economic Literature* 39, no. 3: 771–800.

Bhalla, S. 2005. *Imagine There's No Country: Poverty, Inequality, and Growth in the Era of Globalization.* Washington, DC: Institute for International Economics.

Chang, R., L. Kaltani, and N. Loayze. 2005. "Openness Can Be Good for Growth: The Role of Policy Complementarities." World Bank Policy Research, Working Paper no. 3763.

Dollar, D., and A. Kraay. 2002. "Growth is Good for the Poor." *Journal of Economic Growth* 7, no. 3: 195–225.

Fields, G. S. 1989. "Changes in Poverty and Inequality in Developing Countries." *World Bank Research Observer* 4, no. 2: 167–185.

Kraay, A. 2006. "When Is Growth Pro-Poor? Evidence from a Panel of Countries." *Journal of Development Economics* 80, no. 1: 198–227.

McCulloch, N., L. A. Winters, and X. Cirera. 2001. *Trade Liberalization and Poverty: A Handbook.* London: Center for Economic Policy Research.

Milanovic, B. 2005a. *Worlds Apart: Measuring International and Global Inequality.* Princeton, N.J.: Princeton University Press.

———. 2005b. "Can We Discern the Effects of Globalisation on Income Distribution?" *World Bank Economic Review* 19, no. 1: 21–44.

Noguer, M. and M. Siscart. 2005. "Trade Raises Income: A Precise and Robust Result." *Journal of International Economics* 65, no. 2: 447–460.

Ravallion, M. 2001. "Growth, Inequality and Poverty: Looking Beyond Averages." *World Development* 29, no. 11: 1803–1815.

———. 2005. "Globalization and Poor People: The Debate and Evidence." Max Corden Lecture, University of Melbourne.

Reinikka, R., and P. Collier, eds. 2001. *Uganda's Recovery—The Role of Farms, Firms, and Government.* Washington, DC: World Bank.

Rodriguez, F., and D. Rodrik. 2001. "Trade Policy and Economic Growth: A Skeptic's Guide to the Cross-National Evidence." *NBER Macroeconomics Annual 2000* 15: 261–325. Cambridge, Mass.: MIT Press.

Wacziarg, R. T., and N. H. Welch. 2005. "Trade Liberalization and Growth: New Evidence." NBER, Working Paper no. 10152.

Winters, L.A. 2002. "Trade Liberalisation and Poverty: What Are the Links?" *The World Economy* 25, no. 9: 1339–1367.

———. 2004. "Trade Liberalisation and Economic Performance: An Overview." *Economic Journal* 114, no. 493: F4–21.

———. 2006. "International Trade and Poverty: Cause or Cure?" *Australian Economic Review* 39, no. 4: 347–358.

———. 2008. "North-South Trade," in *Princeton Encyclopedia of the World Economy.* Princeton, N.J.: Princeton University Press.

Winters, L. A., ed. 2007. *Critical Perspectives on the World Trading System: The WTO and Poverty and Inequality.* Cheltenham, U.K.: Edward Elgar. 2 vol.

Winters, L. A., N. McCulloch, and A. McKay. 2004. "Trade Liberalization and Poverty: The Evidence So Far." *Journal of Economic Literature* 42 (March): 72–115.

NO

Atkinson, A. B., ed. 2004. *New Sources of Development Finance*. WIDER Studies in Development Economics. Oxford: Oxford University Press.

Bannister, Geoffrey, and Kamau Thugge. 2001. "International Trade and Poverty Alleviation." Washington, DC: International Monetary Fund. Working Paper 01/54.

Bardhan, P. 2004. "The Impact of Globalization on the Poor," in *Globalization, Poverty, and Inequality*, edited by S. M. Collins and C. Graham. Brookings Trade Forum 2004. Washington, DC: Brooking Institution Press.

Barro, Robert. 2000. "Inequality and Growth in a Panel of Countries." *Journal of Economic Growth* 5, no. 1.

Birdsall, Nancy. 2005. "The World Is Not Flat: Inequality and Injustice in Our Global Economy." WIDER Annual Lecture 9, UNU-WIDER, Helsinki.

———. 2007a. "Stormy Days on an Open Field: Asymmetries in the Global Economy." Working Paper 81. Washington, DC: Center for Global Development.

———. 2007b. "Income Distribution: Effects on Growth and Development." Working Paper 188. Washington, DC: Center for Global Development.

———. 2008. "Reflections on the Macro-Foundations of the Middle Class." Policy Brief. Washington, DC: Center for Global Development and International Food Policy Research Institution.

Birdsall, Nancy, Augusto de la Torre, and Rachel Menezes. 2007. *Fair Growth: Economic Policies for the Poor and Middle-Income Majority*. Washington, DC: Center for Global Development.

Cline, William. 2007. "Global Warming and Agriculture: Impact Estimates by Country." Washington, DC: Center for Global Development.

Corden, W. M. 1974. *Trade Policy and Economic Welfare*. Oxford: Oxford University Press.

Cornia, Giovanni Andrea, Tony Addison, and Sampsa Kiiski. 2004. "Income Distribution Changes and Their Impact in the Post-Second World War Period" in *Inequality, Growth, and Poverty in an Era of Liberalization and Globalization*, edited by Giovanni Andrea Cornia. Oxford: Oxford University Press.

Dixit, Avinash, and Victor Norman. 1980. *Theory of International Trade*. Cambridge: Cambridge University Press.

Diwan, I. 2001. "Debt as Sweat: Labor, Financial Crisis, and the Globalization of Capital." Washington, DC: World Bank Mimeo.

Duryea, S., and M. Székely. 1998. "Labor Markets in Latin America: A Supply-Side Story." IDB OCE. Working Paper 374. Washington, DC: Inter-American Development Bank.

Easterlin, Richard A. 1995. "Will Raising the Incomes of All Increase the Happiness of All?" *Journal of Economic Behavior and Organization* 27, no. 1: 35–47.

Easterly, William. 2004. "Channels from Globalization to Inequality: Productivity World versus Factor World," in *Brookings Trade Forum 2004: Globalization, Poverty, and Inequality*, edited by S. M. Collins and C. Graham. Washington, DC: Brookings Institution Press.

Edwards, Sebastian. 1993. "Openness, Trade Liberalization, and Growth in Developing Countries." *Journal of Economic Literature* 31: 3.

Elliott, Kimberly. 2005. "Big Sugar and the Political Economy of U. S. Agricultural Policy." Washington, DC: Center for Global Development.

Fernandez de Cordoba, Santiago, Sam Laird, and Jose Maria Serena. Nd. "Trade Liberalization and Adjustment Costs." United Nations Conference on Trade and Development.   http://r0.unctad.org/ditc/tab/events/nama/docs/Adjustment-_Cost17Jan_v1.pdf.

Government Accountability Office. 2007. "Industry Certification Would Likely Make More Workers Eligible, but Design and Implementation Challenges Exist." Washington, DC: GAO Report 07–919.

Higgins, Matthew, and Jeffrey Williamson. 1999. "Explaining Inequality the World Round: Cohort Size, Kuznets Curves, and Openness." Boston: National Bureau of Economic Research. Working Paper 7224.

Hirschman, Albert O. 1973. "*The Changing Tolerance for Income Inequality in the Course of Economic Development, with a Mathematical Appendix* by Michael Rothschild." *Quarterly Journal of Economics* 87: 544–566.

Hoekman, Bernard, and Susan Prowse. 2005. "Economic Policy Responses to Preference Erosion: From Trade as Aid to Aid for Trade." Washington, DC: World Bank Policy Research. Working Paper No. 3721.

Krugman, Paul, and Maurice Obstfeld. 1999. *International Economics: Theory and Policy*. Reading, Mass.: Addison Wesley.

Lawrence, Robert, and M. Slaughter. 1993. "International Trade and American Wages in the 1980s: Giant Sucking Sound or Small Hiccup?" Brookings Papers on Economic Activity. Washington, DC: Brookings Institution Press.

Levy, F. 1999. *The New Dollars and Dreams: American Incomes and Economic Change.* New York: Russell Sage Foundation.

Lindert, Peter, and Jeffrey Williamson. 2001. "Does Globalization Make the World More Unequal?" Boston: NBER. Working Paper 8228.

Milanovic, Branko. 2005. *Worlds Apart: Measuring International and Global Inequality.* Princeton, N.J.: Princeton University Press.

Milanovic, Branko, and Lyn Squire. 2005. "Does Tariff Liberalization Increase Wage Inequality? Some Empirical Evidence." Boston: NBER. Working Paper 11046.

Ravallion, Martin. 1999. *Protecting the Poor in Crisis.* PREM Note No. 12. Washington, DC: The World Bank.

Ravallion, Martin, and Michael Lokshin. 2005. "Who Cares about Relative Deprivation?" World Bank Policy Research. Working Paper 3782. Washington, DC: The World Bank.

Sachs, Jeffrey D., and Andrew Warner. 1995. "Economic Reform and the Process of Global Integration." *Brooking Papers on Economic Activity* 1: 1–118.

Sachs, Jeffrey, and H. J. Shatz. 1994. "Trade and Jobs in U.S. Manufacturing." *Brookings Papers on Economic Activity* 1: 1–84.

Saggi, Kamal. 2002. "Trade, Foreign Direct Investment, and International Technology Transfer: A Survey." *World Bank Research Observer* 17, no. 2: 191–235.

Stiglitz, J. 2002. *Globalization and Its Discontents.* New York: Norton.

Székely, M. 1999. "Volatility: Children Pay the Price." *Latin American Economic Policies* 8 (Third quarter): 3–4.

Terrell, K. 2000. "Worker Mobility and Transition to a Market Economy: Winners and Losers," in *New Markets, New Ideas: Economic and Social Mobility in a Changing World,* edited by N. Birdsall and C. Graham. Washington, DC: Brookings Institution and Carnegie Endowment for International Peace.

UN World Institute for Development Economics Research. 2008. World Income Inequality Database.

UNCTAD. 2001. *World Investment Report 2001: Promoting Linkages.* New York: United Nations Conference on Trade and Development.

Vyborny, Katherine. 2005. "What Could the Doha Round Mean for Africa?"

Wade, Robert. 2004. "Is Globalization Reducing Poverty and Inequality?" *World Development* 32, no. 4: 567–589.

Winters, Alan. 2000. "Trade Liberalization and Poverty." Poverty Research Unit at Sussex. Working Paper 7. University of Sussex.

Wood, Adrian. 1995. "How Trade Hurt Unskilled Workers." *Journal of Economic Perspectives* 9: 3.

———. 1994. *North-South Trade, Employment and Inequality.* Oxford: Clarendon Press.

Chapter 6: Nuclear Weapons

NO

Blair, Bruce G. 1994. *The Logic of Accidental Nuclear War.* Washington, DC: Brookings Institution.

Feaver, Peter D. 1997. "Neooptimists and the Enduring Problem of Nuclear Proliferation." *Security Studies* 6, no. 4: 93–125.

Lewis, Jeffrey G. 2007. *The Minimum Means of Reprisal: China's Search for Security in the Nuclear Age.* Cambridge: MIT Press.

Sagan, Scott D. 1993. *The Limits of Safety: Organizations, Accidents, and Nuclear Weapons.* Princeton: Princeton University Press.

Sagan, Scott D., and Kenneth N. Waltz. 2003. *The Spread of Nuclear Weapons: A Debate Renewed.* New York: Norton.

Sanger, David E., and William J. Broad. 2007. "U.S. Secretly Aids Pakistan in Guarding Nuclear Arms." *New York Times,* November 17.

Sechser, Todd S. 1998. "How to Live with the Bomb." *Wall Street Journal,* September 1, A18.

Chapter 7: Military Intervention and Human Rights

YES

Donnelly, Jack. *International Human Rights*. 4th ed. Boulder: Westview Press, 2013.

Forsythe, David P. *Human Rights in International Relations*. 3rd ed. Cambridge: Cambridge University Press, 2012.

Hehir, Aidan. *Humanitarian Intervention: An Introduction*. London: Palgrave Macmillan, 2010.

Walzer, Michael. *Just and Unjust Wars: A Moral Argument with Historical Illustrations*. New York: Basic Books, 1977.

Weiss, Thomas G. *Humanitarian Intervention*. 2nd ed. Oxford: Polity, 2012.

Chapter 9: International Conflict

NO

Angell, Norman. *The Great Illusion: A Study in the Relation of Military Power in Nations to Their Economic and Social Advantage*. New York: Knickerbocker Press, 1910.

Crawford, Neta C. *Argument and Change in World Politics: Ethics, Decolonization, and Humanitarian Intervention*. Cambridge: Cambridge University Press, 2002.

Engels, Friedrich. *The Origin of the Family, Private Property, and the State*. 1884. Translated by Ernest Untermann. Chicago: Charles H. Kerr, 1902.

Fortna, Virginia Page. *Does Peacekeeping Work? Shaping Belligerents' Choices after Civil War*. Princeton: Princeton University Press, 2008.

Goldstein, Joshua S. *Winning the War on War: The Decline of Armed Conflict Worldwide*. Boston: Dutton, 2011.

Goldstein, Joshua S., and Jon C. Pevehouse. *International Relations*, 10th ed. New York: Pearson, 2012.

Hellman, Martin E. "How Risky Is Nuclear Optimism?" *Bulletin of the Atomic Scientists* 67, no. 2 (2011): 47–56.

Hobbes, Thomas. *Leviathan*. 1651. Edited by Richard Tucker. Cambridge: Cambridge University Press, 1991/1996.

Kahneman, Daniel, and Amos Tversky. "Prospect Theory: An Analysis of Decision under Risk." *Econometrica* 47, no. 2 (1979): 263–91.

Kaplan, Robert D. "The Coming Anarchy: How Scarcity, Crime, Overpopulation, Tribalism, and Disease Are Rapidly Destroying the Social Fabric of Our Planet." *Atlantic Monthly* 273, no. 2 (1994): 44–76.

Levy, Jack S. *War in the Modern Great Power System 1495–1975*. Lexington: University Press of Kentucky, 1983.

Mearsheimer, John J. "Back to the Future: Instability in Europe after the Cold War." *International Security* 15, no. 1 (1990): 5–56.

Mearsheimer, John J. "The Gathering Storm: China's Challenge to US Power in Asia." *Chinese Journal of International Politics* 3 (2010): 381–96.

Pinker, Steven. *The Better Angels of Our Nature: Why Violence Has Declined*. New York: Viking, 2011.

Ruggie, John Gerard. *Winning the Peace: America and World Order in the New Era*. New York: Columbia University Press, 1996.

Shanker, Thom. "Warning Against Wars Like Iraq and Afghanistan," *The New York Times*, February 25, 2011.

Smillie, Ian, and Larry Minear. *The Charity of Nations: Humanitarian Action in a Calculating World*. Bloomfield: Kumarian, 2004.

Stiglitz, Joseph E., and Linda J. Bilmes. *The Three Trillion Dollar War: The True Cost of the Iraq Conflict*. New York: Norton, 2008.

Chapter 11: The Future of Energy

NO

Lynch, Michael C. 2003. "The New Pessimism about Petroleum Resources: Debunking the Hubbert Model (and Hubbert Modelers)." *Minerals and Energy* 18, no. 1.

Rifkin, Jeremy. 2003. *The Hydrogen Economy*. New York: Penguin.

Chapter 14: Immigration

YES

Alba, Richard, and Victor Nee. *Remaking the American Mainstream: Assimilation and Contemporary Immigration*. Cambridge: Harvard University Press, 2003.

Bhagwati, Jagdish. *A Stream of Windows: Unsettling Reflections on Trade, Immigration, and Democracy*. Cambridge: MIT Press, 1998.

Brimelow, Peter. *Alien Nation: Common Sense about America's Immigration Disaster*. New York: Random House, 1995.

Brochmann, Grete, and Tomas Hammar, eds. *Mechanisms of Immigration Control: A Comparative Analysis of European Regulation Policies*. Oxford: Berg, 1999.

Brubaker, Rogers, ed. *Immigration and the Politics of Citizenship in Europe and North America*. Lanham: University Press of America, 1989.

———. *Citizenship and Nationhood in France and Germany*. Cambridge: Harvard University Press, 1992.

Calavita, Kitty. *Inside the State: The Bracero Program, Immigration and the INS*. New York: Routledge, 1992.

Castles, Stephen, and Mark Miller. *The Age of Migration: International Population Movements in the Modern World*. New York: Guilford, 1998.

Cornelius, Wayne A., Takeyuki Tsuda, Philip L. Martin, and James F. Hollifield, eds. *Controlling Immigration: A Global Perspective, 2nd Edition.* Stanford: Stanford University Press, 2004.

Freeman, Gary. "Migration and the Political Economy of the Welfare State," *The Annals* 485 (May 1986): 51–63.

Geddes, Andrew. *The Politics of Migration and Immigration in Europe.* London: Sage Publications, 2003.

Ghosh, Bimal. *Gains from Global Linkages: Trade in Services and Movement of Persons.* London: Macmillan, 1997.

Gibney, Matthew J. *The Ethics and Politics of Asylum: Liberal Democracy and the Response to Refugees.* Cambridge: Cambridge University Press, 2004.

Givens, Terri E. *Voting Radical Right in Western Europe.* Cambridge: Cambridge University Press, 2005.

Hatton, Timothy J., and Jeffrey G. Williamson. *The Age of Mass Migration: Causes and Economic Impact.* New York: Oxford University Press, 1998.

Hollifield, James F. "The Politics of International Migration: How Can We 'Bring the State Back In?'" in *Migration Theory: Talking Across Disciplines*, eds. Caroline B. Brettell and James F. Hollifield (New York: Routledge, 2008).

_____. "The Emerging Migration State," *International Migration Review* 38 (2004): 885–912.

_____. "Migration and the 'New' International Order: The Missing Regime," in *Managing Migration: Time for a New International Regime*, ed. B. Ghosh. Oxford: Oxford University Press, 2000.

_____. "Immigration and Integration in Western Europe: A Comparative Analysis," in *Immigration Into Western Societies: Problems and Policies*, ed. Uçarer, E. and D. Puchala. London: Pinter, 1997.

_____. *Immigrants, Markets and States: The Political Economy of Postwar Europe.* Cambridge: Harvard University Press, 1992.

Hollifield, James F., and Thomas Osang. "Trade and Migration in North America: The Role of NAFTA," *Law and Business Review of the Americas* 11, no. 3–4 (2005): 327–360.

Hollifield, James F., Pia Orrenius, and Thomas Osang, eds. *Trade, Migration and Development.* Dallas: Federal Reserve Bank of Dallas, 2007.

Hollifield, James F., Valerie F. Hunt, and Daniel J. Tichenor. "The Liberal Paradox: Immigrants, Markets and Rights in the United States." *SMU Law Review* 16, no. 1 (2008): 67–98.

Huntington, Samuel P. "The West: Unique, Not Universal," *Foreign Affairs* 75, no. 6 (1996): 28–46.

———. *Who Are We? The Challenges to America's Identity.* New York: Simon & Schuster, 2004.

Ireland, Patrick. *Becoming Europe: Immigration, Integration and the Welfare State.* Pittsburgh, PA: University of Pittsburgh Press, 2004.

Jacobson, David. *Rights across Borders: Immigration and the Decline of Citizenship.* Baltimore: Johns Hopkins University Press, 1996.

Joppke, Christian, ed. *Challenge to the Nation-State: Immigration in Western Europe and the United States.* Oxford: Oxford University Press, 1998.

Keohane, Robert O., and Joseph S. Nye. *Power and Interdependence: World Politics in Transition.* Boston: Little, Brown, 1977.

Kettner, James H. 1978. *The Development of American Citizenship, 1608–1870.* Chapel Hill: University of North Carolina Press, 1978.

King, Desmond. *Making Americans: Immigration, Race and the Diverse Democracy.* Cambridge: Harvard University Press, 2000.

Klausen, Jytte. *The Islamic Challenge: Politics and Religion in Western Europe.* New York: Oxford University Press, 2005.

Koslowski, Rey. *Migrants and Citizens: Demographic Change in the European System.* Ithaca: Cornell University Press, 2000.

Kyle, David and Rey Koslowski. *Global Human Smuggling: Comparative Perspectives.* Baltimore: Johns Hopkins University Press, 2001.

Lahav, Gallya. *Immigration and Politics in the New Europe.* Cambridge: Cambridge University Press, 2004.

Martin, Philip L. *Trade and Migration: NAFTA and Agriculture.* Washington, DC: Institute for International Economics, 1993.

Massey, Douglas et al. 2002. *Beyond Smoke and Mirrors: Mexican Immigration in an Era of Economic Integration.* New York: Russell Sage Foundation.

Messina, Anthony. *The Logics and Politics of Post-WWII Migration to Western Europe.* New York: Cambridge University Press, 2007.

Nugent, W. *Crossings: The Great Transatlantic Migrations, 1870–1914.* Bloomington: Indiana University Press, 1992.

Portes, Alejandro, and Ruben Rumbaut. *Immigrant America: A Portrait.* Berkeley and Los Angeles: University of California Press, 1996.

Rosecrance, Richard. *The Rise of the Trading State.* New York: Basic Books, 1986.

Rudolph, Christopher. *National Security and Immigration: Policy Development in the United States and Western Europe since 1945.* Stanford: Stanford University Press, 2006.

Sassen, Saskia. *Losing Control? Sovereignty in an Age of Globalization.* New York: Columbia University Press, 1996.

Schlesinger, Arthur Jr. *The Disuniting of America.* New York: W. W. Norton, 1992.

Schuck, Peter H. *Citizens, Strangers and In-Betweens: Essays on Immigration and Citizenship.* Boulder: Westview, 1998.

Smith, Rogers. *Civic Ideals: Conflicting Visions of Citizenship in U.S. History.* New Haven: Yale University Press, 1997.

Soysal, Yasemin N. *Limits of Citizenship: Migrants and Postnational Membership in Europe.* Chicago: University of Chicago Press, 1994.

Straubhaar, Thomas. *On the Economics of International Labor Migration.* Bern: Haupt, 1988.

Teitelbaum, Michael S. "Right versus Right: Immigration and Refugee Policy in the United States," *Foreign Affairs* 59, no. 1 (1980): 2–59.

Tichenor, Daniel J. *The Politics of Immigration Control in America.* Princeton: Princeton University Press, 2002.

Torpey, John. 1998. "Coming and Going: On the State's Monopolization of the Legitimate 'Means of Movement,'" *Sociological Theory* 16, no. 3: 239–59.

Waltz, Kenneth N. *Theory of International Politics.* Reading: Addison-Wesley, 1979.

Weiner, Myron. *The Global Migration Crisis: Challenge to States and to Human Rights.* New York: HarperCollins, 1995.

Zolberg, Aristide R., Astri Suhrke, and Sergio Aguayo. *Escape from Violence: Conflict and the Refugee Crisis in the Developing World.* New York: Oxford University Press, 1989.

Chapter 16: Civil Society

NO

Anderson, Kenneth. 2000. "The Ottawa Convention Banning Landmines, the Role of International Non-governmental Organizations and the Idea of International Civil Society." *European Journal of International Law* 11, no. 1: 91–120.

Barber, Benjamin. 1984. *Strong Democracy: Participatory Politics for a New Age.* Berkeley: University of California Press.

Beetham, David. 1999. *Democracy and Human Rights.* Cambridge: Polity Press.

Bessette, Joseph. 1980. "Deliberative Democracy: The Majority Principle in Republican Government." In *How Democratic is the Constitution?* edited by Robert A. Goldwin and William A. Schambra. Washington, D.C.: American Enterprise Institute.

Bob, Clifford. 2007. "Conservative Forces, Communications, and Global Civil Society: Toward Conflictive Democracy." In *Global Civil Society 2007/8,* edited by Martin Albrow, Helmut Anheier, Marlies Glasius, and Mary Kaldor, 198–201. London: Sage.

Bos, Adriaan. 1999. "The International Criminal Court: Recent Developments." In *Reflections on the International Criminal Court: Essays in Honour of Adriaan Bos,* ed. Herman A. M. von Hebel, Johan G. Lammers, and Jolien Schukking. The Hague: T.M.C. Asser Press.

Boutros-Ghali, Boutros. 1994. Speech to the 1994 DPI Annual Conference, United Nations, New York, September.

"Chairman Struggles to Define Compromise Package." 1998. *On the Record* 1, no. 14 (July 7).

Cohen, Joshua, and Joel Rogers. 1983. *On Democracy: Toward a Transformation of American Society.* Harmondsworth, U.K.: Penguin.

Edelman, Marc. 2003. "Transnational Peasant and Farmer Movements." In *Global Civil Society 2003,* edited by Mary Kaldor, Helmut Anheier, and Marlies Glasius. Oxford: Oxford University Press.

Edwards, Michael. 2003. "NGO Legitimacy: Voice or Vote?" *BOND Networker.* February.

Glasius, Marlies. 2004. "Who is the Real Civil Society? Women's Groups versus Pro-Family Groups at the International Criminal Court Negotiations." In *Gender and Civil Society*, edited by Jude Howell and Diane Mulligan. London: Routledge.

————. 2005. *The International Criminal Court: A Global Civil Society Achievement.* London: Routledge.

Gutmann, Amy, and Dennis Thompson. 1996. *Democracy and Disagreement.* Cambridge, Mass: Belknap Press.

Held, David. 1995. *Democracy and the Global Order: From the Modern State to Cosmopolitan Governance.* Cambridge: Polity Press.

Kirk, Alejandro. 1998. "Desaparecidos: A Festering Wound." *Terra Viva.* June 24.

McGrew, Anthony. 1997. *The Transformation of Democracy? Globalization and Territorial Democracy.* Cambridge: Polity Press.

Newell, Peter. 2005. "Climate for Change? Civil Society and the Politics of Global Warming." In *Global Civil Society 2005/6*, edited by Marlies Glasius, Mary Kaldor, and Helmut Anheier. London: Sage.

Onuf, Nicholas Greenwood. 1989. *World of Our Making: Rules and Rule in Social Theory and International Relations.* Columbia: University of South Carolina Press.

Pateman, Carole. 1970. *Participation and Democratic Theory.* London: Cambridge University Press.

Popper, Karl R. 1952. *The Open Society and Its Enemies.* 2nd ed. (revised). 2 vols. London: Routledge and Kegan Paul.

Rosenau, James. 1998. "Governance and Democracy in a Globalizing World." In *Re-Imagining Political Community: Studies in Cosmopolitan Democracy*, edited by Daniele Archibugi, David Held, and Martin Köhler. Stanford, Calif.: Stanford University Press.

Said, Yahia, and Meghnad Desai. 2003. "Trade and Global Civil Society: The Anti-Capitalist Movement Revisited." In *Global Civil Society 2003*, edited by Mary Kaldor, Helmut Anheier, and Marlies Glasius. Oxford: Oxford University Press.

Scholte, Jan Aart. 2001. *Civil Society and Democracy in Global Governance.* CSGR Working Paper No. 65/01, Centre for the Study of Globalisation and Regionalisation, Warwick University, U.K.

Van Rooy, Alison. 2004. *The Global Legitimacy Game: Civil Society, Globalization, and Protest.* Basingstroke, U.K.: Palgrave Macmillan.

Walker, Rob. 1993. *Inside/Outside: International Relations as Political Theory.* Cambridge: Cambridge University Press.

"We the Peoples: Civil Society, the United Nations and Global Governance." 2004. Report of the Panel of Eminent Persons on United Nations–Civil Society Relations. UN Doc. A/58/817, http://www.un-ngls.org/Final%20report%20-%HLP.doc.

"Where Are Decisions Being Made?" 1998. *Terra Viva*, July 15.

Young, Iris Marion. 1997. "Difference as a Resource for Democratic Communication." In *Deliberative Democracy: Essays on Reason and Politics,* edited by James Bohman and William Rehg. Cambridge, Mass.: MIT Press.

————. 2001. "Activist Challenges to Democracy." *Political Theory* 29, no. 5 (October).

INDEX

Note: Page numbers in **bold** indicate glossary definitions.

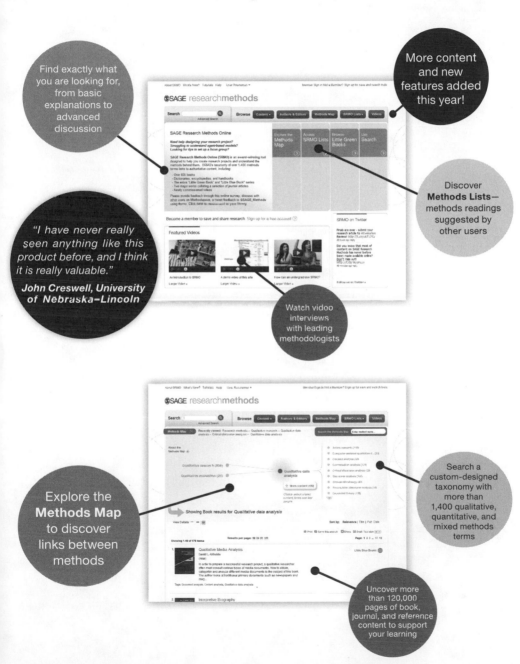

⑤SAGE research**methods**

The essential online tool for researchers from the world's leading methods publisher

Find exactly what you are looking for, from basic explanations to advanced discussion

More content and new features added this year!

"I have never really seen anything like this product before, and I think it is really valuable."
John Creswell, University of Nebraska–Lincoln

Discover **Methods Lists**— methods readings suggested by other users

Watch video interviews with leading methodologists

Explore the **Methods Map** to discover links between methods

Search a custom-designed taxonomy with more than 1,400 qualitative, quantitative, and mixed methods terms

Uncover more than 120,000 pages of book, journal, and reference content to support your learning

Find out more at
www.sageresearchmethods.com